S FROM
TALINGRAD TO BERLIN

THE ILLUSTRATED EDITION

EARL ZEIMKE

EDITED AND INTRODUCED BY
BOB CARRUTHERS

Pen & Sword
MILITARY

This edition published in 2014 by

Pen & Sword Military
An imprint of
Pen & Sword Books Ltd
47 Church Street
Barnsley
South Yorkshire
S70 2AS

First published in Great Britain in 2013 by Coda Books Ltd.

ISBN: 9781783462476

A CIP catalogue record for this book is available from the British Library

Printed and bound in England
By CPI Group (UK) Ltd, Croydon, CR0 4YY

Pen & Sword Books Ltd incorporates the imprints of Pen & Sword Aviation, Pen & Sword
Family History, Pen & Sword Maritime, Pen & Sword Military, Pen & Sword Discovery, Pen
& Sword Politics, Pen & Sword Atlas, Pen & Sword Archaeology, Wharncliffe Local History,
Wharncliffe True Crime, Wharncliffe Transport, Pen & Sword Select, Pen & Sword Military
Classics, Leo Cooper, The Praetorian Press, Claymore Press, Remember When, Seaforth
Publishing and Frontline Publishing

For a complete list of Pen & Sword titles please contact
PEN & SWORD BOOKS LIMITED
47 Church Street, Barnsley, South Yorkshire, S70 2AS, England
E-mail: enquiries@pen-and-sword.co.uk
Website: www.pen-and-sword.co.uk

Contents

Introduction 5

The Author 7

Preface 8

CHAPTER I Invasion! 10

CHAPTER II Retreat 36

CHAPTER III Stalingrad, the Encirclement 54

CHAPTER IV Stalingrad, the Turning Point 88

CHAPTER V The Countermarch 106

CHAPTER VI The Center and the North 127

CHAPTER VII Operation ZITADELLE 150

CHAPTER VIII The First Soviet Summer Offensive 181

CHAPTER IX The Battle for the Dnepr Line 220

CHAPTER X The Rising Tide 247

CHAPTER XI Offensives on Both Flanks—the South Flank 273

CHAPTER XII Offensives on Both Flanks—the North Flank ... 310

CHAPTER XIII Paying the Piper 340

CHAPTER XIV Prelude to Disaster 370

CHAPTER XV The Collapse of the Center 392

CHAPTER XVI The South Flank.. 433

CHAPTER XVII Retreat and Encirclement 457

CHAPTER XVIII Defeat in the North.. 485

CHAPTER XIX The January Offensive....................................... 512

CHAPTER XX The Defense of the Reich................................... 547

CHAPTER XXI Berlin 582

CHAPTER XXII Conclusion 625

Appendices 633

Appendix A 633

Appendix B..633

Note on Sources..634

Glossary...645

Code Names 648

Introduction

This excellent and much sought after publication was originally published by the Centre Of Military History of the United States Army.

Based in Washington, DC, it now forms part of the developing series entitled 'The Eastern Front from Original Sources.' The aim is to provide the reader with a varied range of materials drawn from original writings covering the strategic, operational and tactical aspects of the weapons and battles of Hitler's war. The concept behind

One of the last defenders of Berlin lies lifeless before the Brandenberg gates.

the series is to provide the well-read and knowledgeable reader with access to long out of print sources to build a picture of a particular aspect of that titanic struggle.

I am pleased to report that the series has been well received and it is a pleasure to be able to bring these original sources back to new life and to the attention of an interested readership. I particularly enjoy re-discovering good sources like these , and I am pleased to be able to present them unadorned and unvarnished to a sophisticated audience. The readership I strive to serve is the increasingly well informed community of reader/historians which needs no editorial lead and can draw its own conclusions. I am well aware that our community is constantly striving to discover new nuggets of information, and I trust that with this volume I have managed to stimulate fresh enthusiasm and that at least some of these facts will be new to you and will provoke readers to research further down these lines of investigation, and perhaps cause established views to be challenged once more. I am aware at all times in compiling these materials that our relentless pursuit of more and better historical information is at the core our common passion. I trust that this selection will contribute to that search and will help all of us to better comprehend and understand the bewildering events of the last century.

In order to produce an interesting compilation giving a flavour of events at the strategic and operational level I have returned once more to the Centre Of Military History series, which contain an intriguing series of near contemporary reviews. I find this series particularly fascinating as they provide us with a sense of what was happening at the face of battle almost as the events unfolded.

Thank you for buying this volume in the series we hope you will enjoy discovering some new insights you will go on to try the others in the series.

Bob Carruthers
Edinburgh 2013

The Author

Earl F. Ziemke is a graduate of the University of Wisconsin, where he received a Ph. D. degree in history. In World War II he served with the U.S. Marine Corps in the Pacific theater. In 1951 he joined the staff of the Bureau of Applied Social Research, Columbia University, and in 1955 he moved to the Office of the Chief of Military History. Since 1967 he has been a member of the history faculty at the University of Georgia.

Dr. Ziemke is author of *The German Northern Theater of Operations, 1940-1945* (Washington, 1959), and of chapters in *Command Decisions* (New York: Harcourt, Brace and Company, 1959), *A Concise History of World War II* (New York: Frederick A. Praeger, Inc., 1964), and *Soviet Partisans in World War II* (Madison: University of Wisconsin Press, 1965). His other publications include *The Battle for Berlin: End of the Third Reich* (New York: Ballantine, 1968), *The U.S. Army in the Occupation of Germany* (Washington, D.C.: Government Printing Office, 1975), and *The Soviet Juggernaut* (Alexandria, Va.: Time-Life Books, 1981).

Preface

Save for the introduction of nuclear weapons, the Soviet victory over Germany was the most fateful development of World War II. Both wrought changes and raised problems that have constantly preoccupied the world in the more than twenty years since the war ended. The purpose of this volume is to investigate one aspect of the Soviet victory—how the war was won on the battlefield. The author sought, in following the march of the Soviet and German armies from Stalingrad to Berlin, to depict the war as it was and to describe the manner in which the Soviet Union emerged as the predominant military power in Europe.

The author is grateful to Mr. Hanson W. Baldwin, military editor of the New York *Times,* and to Dr. Stetson Conn, Col. Albert W. Jones, and Mr. Charles B. MacDonald of the Office of the Chief of Military History, for reading the manuscript and for their many valuable suggestions, to which he hopes he has done justice in the final version. He is indebted

Keitel (centre) signs the official surrender of Berlin. With the Nazi-Soviet pact to dismember Poland conveniently overlooked, he was later to hang at Nuremberg for his part in bringing about World War II.

to Generaloberst a. D. Franz Halder for assistance in securing source materials and for encouragement in the early stages of the writing. In his struggles with the vast German documents collections and the numerous details of German tactics and organization, the author received valuable advice from his colleagues in the former Foreign Branch, OCMH, Mrs. Magna E. Bauer, Mr. Detmar H. Finke, and Mr. Charles V. P. von Luttichau. The writing of the volume would not have been possible without the help of Mr. Sherrod East and the other members of the World War II Reference Branch, National Archives and Records Service. They granted the author unrestricted access to their German collections and gave generously of their own time and effort.

Most of the burden of converting the manuscript into a book was borne by other members of the OCMH staff. Mr. David Jaffé, editor, accomplished a thoroughgoing job, aided by Mrs. Marion P. Grimes, assistant editor, and saw the book through to publication. Mr. Elliot Dunay compiled and supervised production of the maps. Miss Ruth A. Phillips selected the photographs. The index was prepared by Mrs. Gay Morenus Hammerman.

Possible errors and omissions can only be attributed to the author's failure to profit from the assistance available to him.

Earl F. Ziemke
Washington, D.C.
15 December 1983

CHAPTER I

Invasion!

As the war passed into its fourth year in early September 1942, Adolf Hitler, the German Fuehrer, Commander in Chief of the German Armed Forces and Commander in Chief of the German Army, was totally absorbed in his second summer campaign against the Soviet Union. [1]For the last month and a half he had directed operations on the southern flank of the German Eastern Front from a Fuehrer headquarters, the WERWOLF, set up in a small forest half a dozen miles northeast of Vinnitsa in the Ukraine. With him, in the closely guarded headquarters community he rarely left, one of pleasantly laid out prefabs and concrete structures, he had his personal staff, through which he exercised the political executive authority in Germany and the occupied territories; the chief of the Armed Forces High Command (Oberkommando der Wehrmacht (OKW)), Generalfeldmarschall Wilhelm Keitel; and a field detachment of the Armed Forces Operations Staff (Wehrmachtfuehrungsstab (WFSt)) under its chief, Generaloberst Alfred Jodl. In Vinnitsa, a hot, dusty provincial town, the Army High Command (Oberkommando des Heeres (OKH)), had established its headquarters under the Chief of Staff, OKH, Generaloberst Franz Halder. Through it Hitler commanded the army groups and armies in the Soviet Union.

During the summer German Army groups A and B had made spectacular advances to the Volga at Stalingrad and into the western Caucasus. In August mountain troops had planted the German flag at the top of Mount Elbrus, the highest peak in the Caucasus. But before the month ended, the offensive had begun to show signs of becoming engulfed in the vast, arid expanses of southern USSR

---

1. As the Fuehrer, Hitler exercised the combined functions of President, Chancellor, and head of the National Socialist Party.

without attaining any of its strategic objectives; namely, the final Soviet defeat, the capture of the Caucasus and Caspian oil fields, and the opening of a route of debouchment across the Caucasus into the Middle East. Hitler had become peevish and depressed. At the situation conferences his specific objections to how the offensive was being conducted almost invariably led on to angry questioning of the ability of the generals and their understanding of the fundamentals of military operations.

On the afternoon of 9 September, after a particularly vituperative outburst the day before against Generalfeldmarschall Wilhelm List, whom he had repeatedly accused over the past weeks of not following orders and of not properly deploying his troops, Hitler sent Keitel to Vinnitsa to tell Halder that List should submit his resignation as Commanding General, Army Group A. Hitler intended to take command of the Army group in person. To Halder, Keitel "hinted" that changes in other high posts were in the offing, including Halder's own. In fact, Hitler had already decided to dismiss Halder, who, he claimed, was "no longer equal to the psychic demands of his position." He also considered getting rid of his closest military adviser, Jodl, who had made the mistake of supporting List.

Germany in August 1942 was at the peak of its World War II military expansion. It held Europe from the Pyrenees to the Caucasus, from Crete to the North Cape, and Panzer Army Africa had pushed into Egypt. During the summer's fighting in southern USSR mistakes— for which Hitler was trying to give the generals all the blame—had been made, but these mistakes alone were not enough to account for the massive frustration that was being felt. It was rooted in a more fundamental miscalculation.

In the directive for the 1942 offensive Hitler had established as the paramount objective, "… the final destruction of the Soviet Union's remaining human defensive strength." He had assumed that the Soviet Union would sacrifice its last manpower reserves to defend the oil fields and, losing both, would be brought to its knees. That had not happened. In late August the Eastern Intelligence Branch, OKH, had undertaken to assess the Soviet situation as it would exist at the close of the German offensive. It had concluded that the Soviet objectives were

A Russian Highway.

to limit the loss of territory as much as possible during the summer, at the same time preserving enough manpower and matériel to stage a second winter offensive. It had assumed that the Soviet command had resigned itself before the start of the German offensive to losing the North Caucasus and Stalingrad, possibly also Leningrad and Moscow and that consequently the territorial losses sustained, though severe, had not been unexpectedly so. Moreover, the Soviet casualties had fallen considerably below what might have been anticipated on the basis of the German 1941 offensive. In sum, the Eastern Intelligence Branch had judged that the Soviet losses were "on an order leaving combat worthy forces available for the future" and that the German losses were "not insignificant."

THE GERMAN COMMAND

On 24 September 1942 General der Infanterie Kurt Zeitzler replaced Halder as Chief of Staff, OKH. In his farewell remarks to Halder, delivered in private after that day's situation conference, Hitler said that Halder's nerves were worn out and that his own were no longer fresh; therefore, they ought to part. He added that it was now necessary to educate the General Staff in "fanatical faith in the Idea" and that he was determined to enforce his will "also" on the Army, implying thereby—and by his lights no doubt with some justification—that under Halder's stewardship the Army had clung too stubbornly to the shreds of its independence from politics and to its traditional command principles.

Zeitzler's appointment surprised everyone, including himself. He was a competent, but not supremely outstanding, staff officer. As Chief of Staff, Army Group D, defending the Low Countries and the Channel coast, his energy and his rotund figure had earned him the nickname "General Fireball." In one of the long evening monologues that have been recorded as table talk, Hitler, in June 1942, had remarked that Holland would be a "tough nut" for the enemy because Zeitzler "buzzes back and forth there like a hornet and so prevents the troops from falling asleep from lack of contact with the enemy." Apparently, Hitler had decided that he preferred a high level of physical activity in the Chief of Staff to the, as he saw it, barren intellectualism of Halder and his like among the generals.

THE EVOLUTION OF THE COMMAND

The dismissal of Halder and Zeitzler's appointment as Chief of Staff, OKH, marked another stage in an enforced evolution that Hitler had imposed on the German command structure since early 1938. At that time, also to an accompaniment of dismissals in the highest ranks, he had abolished the War Ministry and personally assumed the title and functions of Commander in Chief of the German Armed Forces. To take care of routine affairs and to provide himself with a personal staff as Commander in Chief, he had created the Armed Forces High Command and placed Keitel at its head with the title Chief, OKW. As the country moved toward and into the war, the Armed Forces Operations Staff, one of the sections within the OKW, under its capable chief, Jodl, would assume staff and planning functions paralleling and often competing with those of the service staffs. Seeking a more pliant top leadership in the Army High Command, Hitler had at the same time appointed Generaloberst (later Generalfeldmarschall) Walter von Brauchitsch, Commander in Chief, Army, and Halder,

Chief of Staff, OKH. As Chief of Staff, OKH, Halder also headed the most exclusive and influential group within the Army, the Army General Staff.

Very early in the war Hitler had revealed that he was going to take an active part in directing military operations. His formal instrument for exercising control was the Fuehrer directive, which laid down the strategy and set objectives for a given operation or a major part of a continuing operation. At least in the early years, it usually embodied the thinking of the staffs as approved or amended by Hitler. The Fuehrer directives were issued through the Operations Staff, OKW, which gave that organization a voice in all crucial, high-level decisions even though it did not bear direct command responsibility.

The invasion of Norway and Denmark in April 1940 had introduced new planning and command procedures and had set precedents that were to be followed on a larger scale in the future. The Operations Staff, OKW, under Hitler, had then assumed direct planning and operational control, and the service commands had only supplied troops, equipment, and support. That change in the long run affected the Army most because land operations could be more easily parceled out among the commands and because neither Hitler nor Jodl and the Operations Staff, OKW, were competent to handle the technical aspects of air or naval operations and were therefore inclined to leave them to the appropriate service staffs. By the summer of 1941 the OKW commanded—usually through theater commanders—in Norway, the West (France and the Low Countries), the Balkans, and North Africa. The OKH bore command responsibility for the Eastern Front (USSR) only and not for the forces in northern Finland or for liaison with the Finnish Army, both of the latter being included within the OKW's Northern Theater.

THE PLAN FOR INVASION

By the time the campaign against the Soviet Union came under consideration in the late summer of 1940, Hitler and the German Army had three brilliant victories behind them—Poland, Norway and Denmark, and France. The German Army appeared invincible, and even to the skeptics Hitler had begun to look like an authentic military genius. In that atmosphere there probably was more fundamental unanimity in the upper reaches of the German command than at any other time, either before or later.

The main problems associated with an operation in the Soviet Union appeared to be geographical, and they were obvious, if not necessarily simple, of solution. One such was the climate, which was markedly continental with short, hot summers, long, extremely cold winters, and an astonishing uniformity from north to south, considering the country's great expanse. The climate, unless the Germans wanted to risk a long, drawn-out war or a winter campaign for which the Wehrmacht was not trained or equipped, imposed on them a requirement for finishing off the Soviet Union in a single summer offensive of not more than five months' duration. Consequently, in the very earliest planning stage, at the end of July 1940, Hitler had put off the invasion until the following summer. The rasputitsy (literally, traffic stoppages) brought on by the spring thaw and the fall rains, which turned the Soviet roads into impassable quagmires for periods of several weeks, imposed additional limitations on the timing.

The paramount problem was the one which had also confronted earlier invaders, how to accomplish a military victory in the vastness of the Russian space. Apart from the Pripyat Marshes and several of the large rivers, the terrain in European USSR did not offer notable impediments to the movement of modern military forces. But maintaining concentration of forces and supplying armies in the depths of the country presented staggering, potentially even crippling, difficulties. The whole of the Soviet Union had only 51,000 miles of railroads, all broader gauged than those in Germany and eastern Europe. Of a theoretical 850,000 miles of roads, 700,000 were no more than cart tracks; 150,000 miles were allegedly all-weather roads, but only 40,000 miles of those were hard surfaced.

Hitler and the generals agreed that the solution was to trap and destroy the main Soviet forces near the frontier. In December 1940, however, when the strategic plan was being cast into the form of a Fuehrer directive, the generals disagreed with Hitler on how to go from that to the next stage, the final Soviet defeat. Halder and Brauchitsch proposed to concentrate on the advance toward Moscow.

In that direction the roads were the best, and they believed the Soviet Union could be forced to commit its last strength to defend the capital, which was also the most important industrial complex and hub of the country's road and railroad networks. Hitler, however, was not convinced that the war could be decided at Moscow, and he had his way. Fuehrer Directive 21 for Operation BARBAROSSA, the invasion of the Soviet Union, when it was issued on 18 December 1940, provided for simultaneous advances toward Leningrad, Moscow, and Kiev and for a possible halt and diversion of forces from the Moscow thrust to aid the advance toward Leningrad. For the moment, the difference of opinion on strategy cast only the slightest shadow on the prevailing mood of optimism. Staff studies showed that the Soviet Union would be defeated in eight weeks, ten weeks at most.

The Army operation order for BARBAROSSA was issued in early February 1941, and the build-up on the eastern frontier began shortly thereafter, gradually at first. (Map 1) The OKH assigned 149 divisions, including 19 panzer (armored) divisions, to the operation. The total strength was 3,050,000 men. Army of Norway was to deploy another 4 divisions, 67,000 troops, in northern Finland. The Finnish Army eventually added another 500,000 men in 14 divisions and 3 brigades, and Rumania furnished 14 infantry divisions and 3 brigades, all of them understrength, about 150,000 men. The BARBAROSSA force initially had 3,350 tanks, 7,184 artillery pieces, 600,000 motor vehicles, and 625,000 horses.[2]

The most significant assets of the German Army on the eve of the Russian campaign were its skill and experience in conducting mobile warfare. The panzer corps, employed with great success in the French campaign of 1940, had been succeeded by a larger mobile unit, the panzer group. Four of these were to spearhead the advance into the Soviet Union. The panzer groups were in fact powerful armored armies, but until late 1941, conservatism among some senior generals prevented them from getting the status of full-fledged armies.

---

2. Throughout the war, the German and Soviet forces used horses extensively for moving supplies and artillery and, on the Soviet side, in cavalry units. The horses were a means of conserving gasoline and rubber, did not require complicated and expensive maintenance, and under the Soviet road conditions were frequently more reliable than motor vehicles.

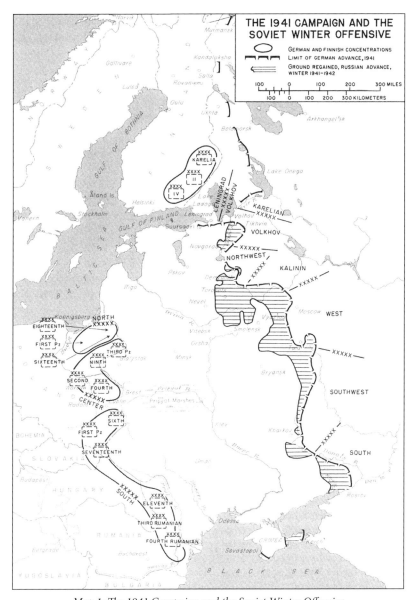

Map 1: The 1941 Campaign and the Soviet Winter Offensive

Seven conventional armies and four panzer groups were assigned to three army groups, each responsible for operations in one of the main strategic directions. Army Group North, commanded by Generalfeldmarschall Wilhelm von Leeb, was to attack out of East Prussia, through the Baltic States toward Leningrad. Army Group

Center, under Generalfeldmarschall Fedor von Bock, assembled on the frontier east of Warsaw for a thrust via Minsk and Smolensk toward Moscow. Army Group South, Generalfeldmarschall Gerd von Rundstedt commanding, was responsible for the sector between the Pripyat Marshes and the Black Sea and was to attack toward Kiev and the line of the Dnepr River. The Finnish Army, operating independently under its own Commander in Chief, Marshal Carl Mannerheim, was to attack south on both sides of Lake Ladoga to increase the pressure on the Soviet forces defending Leningrad and so facilitate Army Group North's advance. An Army of Norway force of two German and one Finnish corps, under OKW control, was given the mission of attacking out of northern Finland toward Murmansk and the Murmansk (Kirov) Railroad. The Rumanian forces, Third and Fourth Armies, attached to Army Group South, had the very limited initial mission of assisting in the conquest of Bessarabia.

The German Air Force High Command (Oberkommando der Luftwaffe (OKL)), assigned to BARBAROSSA some 2,770 aircraft out of a total Air Force first-line strength of 4,300. Planes for the invasion of the Soviet Union were nearly 700 fewer than the number used in the much smaller French campaign; and the Air Force was, in the first five months of 1941, almost totally committed against Great Britain and would have to continue so on a reduced scale after BARBAROSSA began. Because of the strain the fighting in two widely separated theaters would impose on his resources and organization, the Commander in Chief, Air Force, Reichsmarschall Herman Goering, had strongly opposed the operation against the Soviet Union. The campaign in the Balkans in the spring of 1941, added a further complication, as it also did for some of the ground forces.

Because of the danger of giving the operation away by a sudden drop in the intensity of the attacks against Great Britain, the flying units could not be shifted east until the latest possible moment and then only after an elaborate radio deception had been arranged to give the impression that they were being redeployed for an invasion of England. In spite of that and the other problems, however, the German Air Force looked forward to the campaign with confidence. It had the advantage of first-rate equipment, combat experience, and surprise.

The air units deployed on the eastern frontier, between the Baltic and the Black Sea, were organized as First Air Force, supporting Army Group North; Second Air Force, supporting Army Group Center; and Fourth Air Force, supporting Army Group South. Fifth Air Force, its main mission the air defense of Norway, was to give modest support to the Army of Norway and Finnish Army forces operating out of Finland. In accordance with standard German practice, the relationship between the air forces and the army groups was strictly limited to co-operation and co-ordination.

The German Navy's first concern in BARBAROSSA was to be maintaining control of the Baltic Sea. It had additional limited missions in the Arctic Ocean and the Black Sea, both of which the Navy High Command, (Oberkommando der Kriegsmarine (OKM)), believed could not be executed until after the air and land operations had eliminated the Soviet naval superiority. The Navy was also heavily engaged in operations against Great Britain, and the Commander in Chief Navy, Grossadmiral Erich Raeder, like Goering, would rather have avoided further commitments.

BARBAROSSA

When Operation BARBAROSSA began on 22 June 1941, the military and political centers of gravity in Germany moved from Berlin to the forests of East Prussia. There, beside the railroad running east from Rastenburg, an elaborate Fuehrer headquarters, the WOLFSSCHANZE (Wolf's Lair), of painstakingly camouflaged concrete bunkers protected by rings of steel fences, palisades, and earthworks, had been constructed. In one closely guarded compound Hitler lived and worked with his intimate military and political advisers; another a short distance away housed the Operations Staff, OKW, and the communications center. The OKH was located just outside Rastenburg, a half hour away by rail. The railroad was closed to all traffic east of Rastenburg except that between the OKH headquarters and the WOLFSSCHANZE and the courier trains that shuttled back and forth to Berlin.

From the outset Hitler demonstrated that he did not mean to let the conduct of operations rest entirely in the hands of the professionals.

Hitler conferring with Keitel and von Brauchitsch near Fuehrer Headquarters.

During the first weeks his interference took the form mostly of nervous meddling and random attempts to impose on the battlefield tactical conceptions that occurred to him in his remote position. Halder, possibly with more trenchant insight than he realized, characterized Hitler's behavior as symptomatic of a lack of confidence in the executive commands and a failure to grasp the essential feature of the German command system—its reliance on training in a common body of doctrine to make each command level capable of performing its functions with a minimum of interference from above. Unfortunately for the German Army, Brauchitsch was no longer, if indeed he ever had been, the man to defend this principle. Conscious that he was both used and despised by Hitler, he vacillated futilely between complete subservience to the Fuehrer and the urgings of his professional conscience and most often ended by trying to suppress the latter with the excuse that he could not oppose his commander in chief.

In the field the invasion forged ahead more rapidly even than the staff and command post exercises had forecast. Before the end of the second week it appeared that the first-phase objective, destruction of the Soviet Army main force close to the western frontier, had been accomplished. In twin pockets at Bialystok and Minsk, Army Group Center estimated that it had taken over 300,000 prisoners. After a comparatively slow start by Army Group South, all three German army groups were advancing at high speed. By mid-July, Army Groups North and Center reached and crossed the Dvina and Dnepr Rivers, the easternmost lines on which, according to German calculations, the Russians could defend their chief industrial areas. Army Group Center was completing another vast encirclement near Smolensk, and Army Group South had begun a gigantic enveloping operation in the Ukraine west of the Dnepr.

Halder even looked forward hopefully to the time when the front would become so fluid that the battles would outrun Hitler's capability as a tactician. That was not going to happen. In fact, Hitler had arrived at the stage where he was prepared to free himself entirely from professional tutelage. On 19 July 1941 he completed a directive about which the OKH had not been consulted at all and which, although it was initialed by Jodl and Keitel, apparently did not reflect any significant consultation with the Operations Staff, OKW. In it Hitler reaffirmed his conviction that Moscow was not the primary strategic objective. He directed that in the next phase Army Group Center, the strongest of the three army groups in the Soviet Union, was to continue toward Moscow with its infantry alone and was to divert its armor to help Army Group North toward Leningrad and Army Group South in the conquest of the Ukraine. In effect the advance on Moscow was to be stopped. He had revealed that intention in the original BARBAROSSA directive, but the generals had assumed that the logic of events, particularly—after the invasion began—the indications that the Russians were massing their main forces in front of Moscow, would force him to change his mind.

In the ensuing month Halder and Brauchitsch marshaled all the arguments they could and enlisted backing from Jodl and two of the army group commanders to help oppose the strategic change. Hitler from time to time showed signs of attempting to form a decision based on the realities of the situation and at one point revised his directive. But in the directive as issued on 21 August, he stated, "The proposals of the OKH for the continuance of the operation in the East do not conform with my intentions," and ordered that Moscow was not to be considered the principal objective but was to be ranked after the

Crimea and the Ukrainian coal fields in the south and Leningrad in the north.

Two small incidents revealed how far the OKH had lost ground. Hitler, also on 21 August, accused Brauchitsch of having failed all along to conduct the offensive on the lines he, the Fuehrer, desired. Three days later Generaloberst Heinz Guderian, who would have to execute the maneuver and who claimed that turning the armor south from Army Group Center was impossible, was called in to make a last-ditch attempt to dissuade Hitler. In the Fuehrer's presence he reversed himself completely, later lamely explained that confronted with the Fuehrer's resolve he had had "to make the impossible possible."

By 6 September Hitler, concluding that the army groups on the flanks had been helped enough, decided to renew the Army Group Center advance toward Moscow. Army Group North in the meantime had closed up to Leningrad on the south but had yet to complete the encirclement on the east by joining hands with the Finns. Hitler had decided literally to starve the city out of existence. Army Group South, reinforced by Guderian's tanks, was completing an enormous encirclement east of Kiev but still had long distances to go to take the Donets Basin and the Crimea. Hitler ordered both army groups to complete the operations with their own resources and return the units they had received from Army Group Center.

Army Group Center jumped off on 2 October and within a week had broken open the Soviet front west of Moscow and formed two massive encirclements. The victory then appeared so near that the OKW canceled the expeditions out of northern Finland aimed at cutting the Murmansk Railroad, the supply line for outside aid to the Soviet Union. Then, at the end of the first week in October, in the Army Group Center and Army Group North areas, it began to rain. Relentlessly, through the rest of the month and into early November, rain, snow, and alternate freezing and thawing turned the roads into oozing ribbons of mud. Between 2 and 10 October Army Group Center's armies gained 30 miles a day. In the next twenty days their advance fell off to 2 to 5 miles a day; in the first two weeks of November they remained practically at a standstill on the line Kalinin-Tula, 54 miles west of Moscow.

In mid-November, after several cold, bright days, Army Group Center began to roll again. From the first it was apparent that the army group was not the fighting machine it had been. After five months' combat the troops were tired, and, if not discouraged, the troops and command both were becoming uneasy over the offensive that dragged on without a satisfactory end in sight. The equipment was showing wear and supplies and parts now had to come over long and unreliable lines. Losses in the campaign were approaching three-quarters of a million, no more than half of them replaced. Infantry companies were down to 25 and 30 percent of authorized strengths; first lieutenants were commanding battalions.

At the beginning of the fourth week of the month Army Group Center had put its every man and weapon into the attack. The best hope was that the Russians had done the same. That they had not, began to become apparent at the end of the month when Soviet forces launched heavy counterattacks against Army Group South that forced the Germans to give up Rostov, the gateway to the Caucasus.

On 5 December Army Group Center, which had a spearhead on the north within sight of Moscow, reported that it was at the end of its strength; it could go no farther. The next morning, in snow and fog and forty below zero temperature, the Russians counterattacked.

HITLER IN COMMAND

The month of December 1941 ended the three-and-one-quarter years' string of German victories with a jolt that shook the German Army to its boot soles. Hardest hit in the long run was the Army command. Brauchitsch, who had had a heart attack in November, decided in early December to ask for retirement. By then he had been reduced to nothing more than a "messenger boy"; on important matters Hitler communicated directly with the army groups. On 19 December Hitler assumed the post of Commander in Chief, OKH, himself, and thereby wiped out the Army's last vestige of service independence.

Ignoring his advisers, Hitler ordered the field commands to stand fast and called for fanatical resistance by the troops. In fact, they had no other choice. No positions existed in the rear, and none could be built in ground frozen so hard that impacting heavy artillery shells chipped out craters only inches deep. No one had given thought to fighting in the Russian winter. Weapons not conditioned for severe cold jammed; and lack of winter clothing, antifreeze, and low-temperature lubricants immobilized both men and vehicles. Commanders who lacked the stamina or the stomach for fanatical resistance as Hitler conceived it were removed. Von Rundstedt, the senior field marshal, had been dismissed as Commanding General, Army Group South, in Hitler's first pique over the retreat from Rostov. In mid-December, von Bock relinquished command of Army Group Center, pleading illness. Later, von Leeb, whose Army Group North had been stopped and turned back at Tikhvin in an attempt to join hands with the Finns and then was caught up in the Soviet counteroffensive, asked to be relieved. Making examples of generals who ordered retreats, Hitler dismissed Guderian and Generaloberst Erich Hoeppner and deprived the latter of his rank and privileges, including the right to wear the uniform.

Hitler's determination and repeated appeals to the troops for fanatical resistance were not enough to prevent the expanding Soviet offensive from chopping deep into the front at numerous places in the Army Group Center and Army Group North sectors. At the turn of the year a breakthrough on the Army Group Center north flank and a deepening dent on its south flank brought the Germans to the astonished, horrified realization that the Russians were trying nothing less than to encircle the whole Army Group Center. On 15 January 1942, Hitler for the first time in the war ordered a major withdrawal. He authorized Army Group Center to take its front opposite Moscow back to a north-south line eighty-five miles west of the capital. That was not enough to escape the threatening encirclement; it only shortened the Army Group Center front somewhat and thus freed some troops for the flanks. The orders to stand and fight remained in full effect.

From mid-January until well into February the crisis at the front deepened. Although Army Group Center regained some control on its south flank, it was for weeks nearly helpless against the thrust on the north and barely managed to keep open its lifeline, the road and railroad running east from Smolensk. Astride the Army Group North-Army Group Center boundary the front was torn open on a 160-mile stretch between Rzhev and Lake Ilmen. At Demyansk, south of the lake, two German corps, 100,000 men, were completely encircled and had to be supplied by air.

After mid-February the Soviet offensive began to lose momentum and appeared no longer to have any other objective than to gain some additional ground and inflict random damage on the Germans. In the first week of the month Army Group Center had managed to anchor its north flank around Rzhev, and in the second and third weeks fresh divisions from Germany began moving in from the west to narrow the gap to Army Group North. In March the gradual German recovery continued until the spring mud and floods brought operations on both sides to a temporary halt.

The winter crisis of 1941-42 gave Hitler a personal triumph: he had ordered his armies to stand, and they had stood. His decision not to permit a general retreat, some suggest, was made less on military grounds than out of a desperate necessity to protect his image as an infallible leader; nevertheless, even his harshest critics later had to concede that the German armies, caught as they were without prepared positions to fall back on or even adequate winter equipment and clothing, might well have disintegrated if the command had conceded a necessity to retreat. Hitler not only did not lose but probably gained stature in the eyes of, at least, the rank and file. His confidence in his own military judgment was strengthened—this at a time when the terms on which the war was being fought were undergoing a drastic alteration. As a consequence, the German conduct of the rest of the war was dominated by a conflict between the military professionals' principles, flexibility and mobility, and Hitler's rigidity—between command initiative and blind execution of the Fuehrer's will.

OPERATION BLAU

A PROMISE, DOUBTS, AND A PLAN

On 15 March 1942 Hitler delivered a Memorial Day (Heldengedenktag) address in Berlin. He promised that "Bolshevism" would be destroyed in the coming summer and that "the Bolshevik Colossus" would not thereafter "again touch the sacred soil of Europe." Privately he and his confidants did not look to the future with assurance quite that strong. The Propaganda Minister, Joseph Goebbels, and Goering had nagging qualms, chiefly on the score of Soviet capabilities. Hitler talked to Goebbels about the coming campaign and declared that he intended only to take the Caucasus, Leningrad, and Moscow—one after the other and not simultaneously. He was determined whatever the circumstances, he said, to go into winter quarters in time. He blamed Brauchitsch, whom he described as "a nincompoop and a coward," for overextending in 1941.

On 26 April Hitler undertook to present an accounting to the Reichstag. Grandly, he claimed that in the days of crisis during the winter he had felt compelled to place his "own person at the forefront in meeting whatever Fate had in store." He thanked the soldiers, noncommissioned officers, and officers "up to those generals who, recognizing the danger, risked their own lives to urge the soldiers onward." The only other reference to the generals was that "in a few individual cases, where nerves gave way, discipline broke down or insufficient sense of duty was displayed" he had found it necessary to intervene severely. He asked and was automatically granted sweeping authority to dismiss or demote any civil servant or officer as it suited him. That in effect swept away the remnants of administrative independence in the German Government and the armed forces. Ominous as this strengthening of the dictatorship was, however, it attracted less attention than the almost offhand remark: "Next winter, no matter where it finds us, will find us better prepared."

The directive for the 1942 summer campaign, Operation BLAU, provided for a full scale offensive only on the south flank of the Eastern Front, toward the Don River, Stalingrad, and the Caucasus oil fields. (Map 2) Hitler was in complete command. Halder and his staff assistants had drafted the directive in accordance with Hitler's detailed instructions, and Hitler had then dictated the final version, revising and expanding as he went along.

The advance into the Caucasus had the characteristics of an expedition, albeit a massive one. In fact it had been regarded as such when it was first considered in the late fall of 1941. In the directive for BLAU Hitler elevated it to the level of a strategic, decision-seeking,

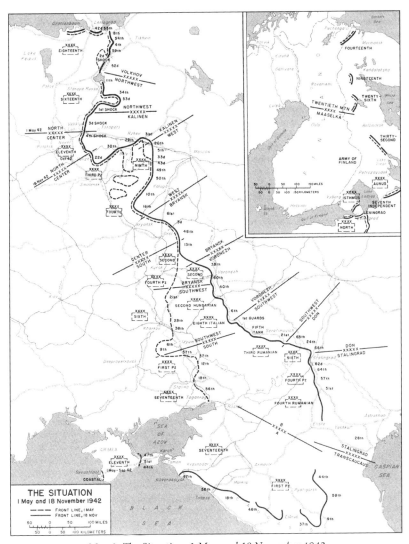

Map 2: The Situation, 1 May and 18 November 1942

offensive. It was to be executed in two stages. First, several successive
enveloping thrusts, beginning on the north along the Kursk-Voronezh
axis, were to smash the Soviet south flank and carry the front out to
the Don River. After that the advance would proceed to Stalingrad
and across the lower Don into the Caucasus. For the operation, Army
Group South was to be split to form two army groups designated
as A and B. Army Group B, to be under von Bock, who now found

himself well enough to command, would open the attack on the north. Army Group A, under List, would start somewhat later and be primarily responsible for the thrust across the lower Don and into the Caucasus.

In the regroupment Army Group B took command of Second, Fourth Panzer, and Sixth Armies, the first two detached from Army Group Center. Army Group A was assigned First Panzer, Eleventh, and Seventeenth Armies. For the first time in the East, the German allies, Italy, Hungary, and Rumania, took to the field in earnest, each providing an army. All three of the allied armies were deficient in equipment and training; and the Rumanians and Hungarians would much rather have fought each other than the Russians. But then, the allied armies were expected only to lend substance to Hitler's claim that he was conducting a selfless "crusade against Bolshevism" and occasionally to provide cover on the German flanks.

Hitler's decision to limit the 1942 campaign was not a free choice. After the strains and drains of the 1941 offensive and the winter battles just ended, even Operation BLAU as planned bore discernible marks of austerity. Of the 65 to 67 divisions that were to participate in the offensive, fully two-thirds had to be rebuilt and rehabilitated while committed at the front and only one-third were new or rebuilt behind the front. As of 1 May 1942 the infantry divisions were at 50 percent of their authorized strengths. They were brought up to 100 percent by the time the offensive started, but, as a consequence, the divisions of Army Groups Center and North would not attain more than 55 percent of authorized strengths before August 1942. The panzer divisions in the offensive would have three tank battalions apiece, but those of the other army groups only one. The spearhead divisions in BLAU would have 85 percent of their organic motor vehicle allowances, but the other divisions would have far less. Artillery, antitank, and antiaircraft weapons could be brought to authorized levels for the units in the offensive—in some instances only by reaching into stocks of captured equipment—but an ammunition drought had set in during the winter and was expected to continue through the autumn of 1942.

Only in the air did the German strength fully equal that of the 1941 campaign. During the winter, the transfer of Second Air Force to the

Mediterranean to participate in the attempted reduction of Malta and to support operations in North Africa had reduced air strength on the Eastern Front to 1,700 planes. The necessity for flying supply missions to numerous cut-off and encircled forces had further reduced the flying units' combat effectiveness. In the spring, in anticipation of the summer offensive, the air strength in the East had been raised to a total of 2,750 aircraft. Fourth Air Force on the southern sector of the front received by far the largest share—1,500 planes.

THE CAMPAIGN, 1942

At dawn on 28 June Second Army and Fourth Panzer Army opened the offensive. They smashed through the Soviet front east of Kursk and pushed east toward Voronezh, reaching the outskirts of the city in four days and taking it on 6 July. Fourth Panzer Army then turned southeast along the Don to meet Sixth Army, which had moved out east of Kharkov on 30 June. The German armies again held the upper hand; but the first two thrusts, to Voronezh and east of Kharkov, which had been planned as great encirclements on the 1941 pattern, brought in less than 100,000 prisoners. Disappointed, Hitler on 13 July replaced von Bock as Commanding General, Army Group B, with Generalfeldmarschall Maximilian von Weichs.

Hitler had originally intended to execute a third encirclement inside the Don bend that would have cleared the entire line of the Don before the offensive was carried toward Stalingrad and the Caucasus. On 13 July he changed his mind and ordered Army Group A, to which he attached Fourth Panzer Army, to turn south, cross the lower Don, and force the Russians into a pocket around Rostov. Rostov fell on 23 July, without bringing in the expected large bag of prisoners.

On that day Hitler issued the order that set the final stamp of failure on the summer offensive. He put the two army groups on courses that took them away from each other at a right angle, Army Group B going east toward Stalingrad, Army Group A going south past Rostov to the Caucasus. At the same time, he ordered Army Group A to give up the headquarters, all of the artillery, and about half the divisions of Eleventh Army, which was then getting ready to join the army group main force after taking Sevastopol. Eleventh Army was to go

Street scene in Voronezh.

north for an attempt to take Leningrad and thereby pave the way for a later German-Finnish thrust to cut the Murmansk Railroad. As he had at the same stage of the 1941 offensive, Hitler was dispersing the German effort.

Army Group A was on the threshold of the Caucasus, but the distances were tremendous, 200 miles to the Maikop oil fields, nearly 400 to those at Grozny. To reach Baku and Tiflis the mountains themselves had to be crossed. On 29 July the army group cut the last Soviet rail line into the Caucasus. Two days later Hitler issued another directive. The Russians, he reasoned, could do nothing more about defending the Caucasus, but they could be forced to expend their last reserves defending Stalingrad and their lifeline, the Volga. He ordered Fourth Panzer Army to make a 180° turn and advance on the city from the south.

Through August and September the offensive continued—without attaining any of the major objectives. Army Group A took Maikop but found the oil fields destroyed. Two panzer corps headed for Grozny but were slowed and finally stopped for several weeks by gasoline shortages. The trucks making the long trip from Rostov were burning nearly as much gasoline as they could haul. Spearheads pushed into the Caucasus, but the Russians continued to hold all the passes. Sixth Army and Fourth Panzer Army closed in on Stalingrad from the west and south but had to spread their forces thin to cover their flanks and so lost momentum.

THE MANPOWER SQUEEZE

On 8 September 1942 the Organizational Branch, OKH, reported, "All planning must take into account the unalterable fact that the predicted strength of the Army field forces as of 1 November 1942 will be 800,000, or 18 percent, below established strength [approximately 3,200,000] and that it is no longer possible to reduce those numbers."[3]

It had already predicted that the best to be expected was that the available manpower reserves would cover the next winter's losses and prevent a further decline before the spring of 1943. "False impressions will result," the report continued, "if units continue to be carried as before with this great loss of strength." The Organizational Branch proposed reducing better than half the divisions on the Eastern Front from three regiments to two.

The larger and far more difficult problem was finding actual relief from the manpower squeeze. Since May 1942, General der Infanterie Walter von Unruh, armed with the authority to order irrevocable transfers to the Eastern Front, had been combing the rear areas as Hitler's personal representative. Unruh, whose visits generally met with dismay if not terror and who earned the nickname "General Heldenklau" (hero snatcher), had succeeded in paring down some of the rear echelon staffs; but after three or four months it had become apparent that the results, though worthwhile, would not be decisive. The Organizational Branch, OKH, in the fall of 1942 proposed to release some 180,000 men from the rear echelons by using Hilfswillige (army auxiliaries) recruited among the Russian prisoners of war to take over service and supply jobs behind the lines

---

3. As of the first week in September 1942 the German strength on the Eastern Front totaled 2,490,000 men in 163 divisions, not including the Twentieth Mountain Army in northern Finland which had 6 divisions. The attached forces of Germany's allies, Italy, Rumania, and Hungary, totaled 48 divisions (including one Spanish and one Slovakian division) and 648,000 men. The Finnish Army, which operated independently, had some 17 divisions and brigades, slightly less than 400,000 men.

and thought it might gain another 80,000-90,000 by tightening the tables of organization.

A potential source of relief for the Army's manpower problem was the Air Force, which had a sizable surplus. In September 1942 Hitler agreed to tap that surplus, but at Goering's insistence decided not to use the men as Army replacements but to form Air Force field divisions manned and officered exclusively by Air Force personnel. In September and October Hitler ordered twenty such divisions created with a combined strength of about 200,000 men. From the Army point of view a more unsatisfactory arrangement would have been difficult to devise. The Air Force troops had no training in land warfare and, because Goering restricted the Army's influence on them to the absolute minimum on the ground that the "reactionary" attitudes of the Army would impair his troops' National Socialist indoctrination, were not likely to be given enough to make them anywhere near suitable for employment on the Eastern Front. Worse yet, the Army had to scrape together enough new equipment to outfit the twenty divisions, and the diversion of vehicles alone forced postponement of plans to bring four or five panzer divisions up to strength.

One other promising palliative was the employment of larger numbers of heavy and automatic weapons. The Operations Branch, OKH, proposed to supply the front-line units with new and more efficient weapons as they became available without withdrawing the older weapons and so wind up with both more and better firepower. Germany's newest and most promising weapon, however, the Tiger tank, was slow getting into production. Tests of two prototypes in July 1942 had revealed that the tanks would not be battleworthy before the end of the year.

A COMMAND SHAKE-UP

Hitler could hardly have expected to solve or greatly mitigate any of his immediate problems by changing chiefs of staff in September 1942. The tighter personal hold he got on the command apparatus of the Army by the shift from Halder to Zeitzler was also not very significant and took the form mainly of a symbolic downgrading of a very senior post by the appointment to it of a very junior general.

Nevertheless, by the change, Hitler proposed more than merely to give vent to his personal animosity against Halder. What he had in view—probably motivated by even deeper seated animosities—was nothing less than a recasting—to his mind rejuvenation—of the whole German officer corps, the General Staff and general officer ranks in particular. To enable himself to do this—and to get close control of all officer appointments as well—he assumed personal supervision of the Heerespersonalamt, Army officer personnel office, and placed it under his Chief Adjutant, Generalmajor Rudolf Schmundt. To Schmundt he outlined a policy of rapid promotion, particularly of younger, battle-tested officers, to the highest ranks. Zeitzler, forty-seven years old and a general officer less than a year at the time of his appointment, was an example. He also proposed to break the General Staff's hold on the higher appointments by training good line officers to qualify for advancement to the top positions and by requiring General Staff officers to acquire experience as troop commanders. He talked about eventually abolishing the General Staff's distinctive red trouser stripes and silver collar tabs.

As Chief of Staff, OKH, Zeitzler quickly demonstrated that he did not intend to be merely a yes-man, and during his first days in the post he secured a major victory in the intramural cold war that was a part of the functioning of the German command. The Army had long regarded as unfortunate, if not baneful, the influence of the Operations Staff, OKW—Jodl—on the drafting of Fuehrer directives, many of which although ostensibly strategic were primarily concerned with tactical operations on the Eastern Front. The irritation had increased after Hitler became Commander in Chief, Army, and thereby converted the Army staff into a second personal staff. It had been sharpened by the freewheeling criticism Keitel and Jodl had indulged in from their technically loftier positions on the command chain. Taking advantage of Jodl's having fallen into disfavor, Zeitzler, immediately upon his appointment, demanded and secured the OKW's exclusion from the drafting of Fuehrer directives applying solely to the Eastern Front. Henceforth such directives were to be issued as "operations orders" through the OKH. He also succeeded in having the reporting procedure at the daily situation conferences changed. Instead of Jodl's reporting on all theaters, the Chief of Staff, OKH, opened the conference with a report on the East and then Jodl followed with a report on the other theaters.Subsequently, on the ground that the "need to know" no longer existed, Zeitzler managed, further, to cut off the OKW Operations Staff's access to detailed information concerning Eastern Front operations. In the long run, he achieved another effect in no way less important for its being inadvertent, namely, the hardening of the concept of OKH and OKW theaters that made the Eastern Front the OKH's exclusive and only operational concern and bred competition and rivalry with the OKW theaters, the West, the Balkans, Italy, and northern Europe, where earnest co-ordination would doubtless have served the German cause better.

OPERATIONS ORDER I

On 14 October 1942 Hitler issued Operations Order I in which he announced, "This year's summer and fall campaign, excepting the operations under way and several local offensives still contemplated, has been concluded." The order was purportedly aimed at initiating a shift to the defensive before winter set in; its effect was the opposite. Hitler ordered Army Group North, Army Group Center, and Army Group B to get ready for winter in the lines they held; but Sixth Army was to continue the attack at Stalingrad and Army Group A was to stand by for further orders, which meant that in the two sectors where German forces were still in motion he was going to continue the offensive.

In Operations Order I and a supplement issued some days later, Hitler elevated to the level of doctrine the fanatical resistance formula he had employed during the Soviet 1941-42 winter offensive. He ordered that: the winter positions were to be held under all circumstances; there would be no evasive maneuvers or withdrawals; breakthroughs were to be localized and any intact part of the front was "absolutely" to be held; cut-off and encircled elements were to defend themselves where they stood until relieved. He made every commander responsible to him personally for the "unconditional execution" of those orders. In the supplement he extended the orders down to the lowest leadership level. "Every leader," the supplement read, "down to squad leader must be convinced of his sacred duty, to stand fast come what may even if the enemy outflanks him on the right and left, even if his part of the line is cut off, encircled, overrun by tanks, enveloped in smoke or gassed." That order was to be repeatedly "hammered into all officers and noncommissioned officers."

CHAPTER II

Retreat

If tension ran high in the German headquarters at the end of summer 1942, it was scarcely less in the Soviet command. On 30 August the Germans broke through the intermediate Stalingrad defense ring forcing the defenders back toward the inner ring on the outskirts of the city itself. Two days later, General Polkovnik Andrei I. Yeremenko, commanding at Stalingrad, and his commissar, General Leytenant Nikita S. Khrushchev, appealed to the troops to stand and defend the city. On 3 September the Soviet Supreme Commander, Joseph V. Stalin, declared that Stalingrad "could be taken today or tomorrow" if the forces between the Don and the Volga north of the city did not counterattack immediately. In haste the Soviet command committed three reserve armies of untrained replacements in a counterattack on 5 September. Halder observed several days later that the German Sixth Army, attacking toward Stalingrad, was making good progress and had had a "defensive success" on its north flank.

The Russians did not know what sacrifices the current campaign might yet entail, and the cost of war was already truly colossal. To certainly 6,000,000, possibly as many as 8,000,000, military losses in killed and captured were added millions of civilian casualties, a million or more dead of starvation alone in Leningrad during the winter of 1941-42. The Soviet Union had lost 47 percent of its inhabited places, territory in which 80,000,000 persons had resided. That territory had produced 71 percent of the Soviet pig iron, 58 percent of its steel, 63 percent of its mined coal, and 42 percent of its electricity. By the end of their 1941 offensive the Germans had occupied areas that had produced 38 percent of the grain and cattle and 84 percent of the Soviet sugar.

THE SOVIET COMMAND

The price was not more than the Soviet regime was willing to pay.

Stalin was in a duel to the death and knew it, and he had never counted the cost of sacrifices that furthered the ends of the Communist system or sustained his power. The capacity to sacrifice lives and territory was in fact the historic Russian strategic asset. But the issue of survival in a war with a technically and militarily proficient enemy ultimately had to be decided on other terms. That these would be far more stringent than anyone had supposed had been fully brought home only under the shock of invasion. Since then the Soviet leadership had worked feverishly to make good the deficiencies. In the waning days of summer 1942, when it again appeared that the German armies could march wherever they pleased in the heart of the Communist homeland, the burning question was whether those labors would become engulfed in a general collapse of the national will to resist. Morale of the troops and the people showed signs of breaking. The burden of suffering, of defeats, and of mistakes weighed more heavily than at any time in the war. The confidence and hope the winter's successes had raised were dissipated. The Soviet command, it appeared, might have taken its people close to the edge of disaster too many times.

ON THE EVE OF WAR

From the outbreak of World War II in September 1939 until mid-1941 Soviet policy was compounded of a nice mixture of ambition and apprehension. Alternately aggressive and timorous, the Soviet Union cultivated an offensive military posture but at the same time sedulously maneuvered to avoid a genuine military confrontation. The Nazi-Soviet pact signed in August 1939 and the secret protocols added in September of that year gave the Soviet Union substantial new territory in the west, a free hand in the adjacent areas of eastern Europe and, on paper, immunity from direct German aggression. The 1939-40 Winter War with Finland brought a victory of sorts, some territorial gains, an unwholesome international reputation, and a loss of military prestige. The German victories of 1940 in France and the Low Countries raised doubts on both sides concerning the profitability of the pact. Joseph Stalin almost certainly was not pleased suddenly to find himself alone on the Continent with Hitler. To the Germans, the Soviet moves into the Baltic States and Bessarabia and the renewed threats against

Finland appeared as blackmail, which in fact they were. After mid-1940 both parties felt increasingly restive in the partnership, but only one, Germany, was ready to do something about it. In November, Soviet Foreign Minister Vyacheslav M. Molotov went to Berlin to negotiate an increase in his country's share and received a barely veiled warning that Germany would not tolerate any further Soviet expansion on its western borders—the warning was heeded. In April 1941 the Soviet Union stood by while Germany pocketed the Balkans, the traditional Russian sphere of interest. Throughout, and up to the day before the invasion, the Soviet Union adhered scrupulously to the schedule of economic exchange on which Germany by then had fallen substantially behind.

In late April 1941, at the end of the Balkan campaign, the German Ambassador to the Soviet Union told Hitler that Stalin was "prepared to make even further concessions to us." On 6 May, Stalin, who until then had preferred to exercise power from behind the scenes, for the first time assumed an executive post in the government, becoming, as Chairman of the Council of People's Commissars, the official chief of the Soviet state. The move, prompted by awareness of a growing danger, was, as the German Ambassador interpreted it, primarily designed to give Stalin a stronger and more open position from which to direct his efforts at staying on good terms with Germany.

On the eve of the war both dictators plunged determinedly onward toward disaster. Hitler, who had not yet completely overawed his advisers, brushed aside all arguments against his impending Russian adventure. Stalin's men were hardly likely to tell him things he did not wish to hear; nevertheless, for him too, holding the course he had set required a deliberate exercise of will. The German deployment to the east, which went into full swing in early 1941, could be ignored or misinterpreted, but it could not have escaped the notice of an intelligence apparatus as highly developed as that of the Soviet Union. That it had not, could be inferred from the 10 April alert, which ordered an increased state of readiness for the military districts on the western frontier. The German Ambassador, however, told Hitler that the Soviet activity on the frontier was nothing more than an automatic reaction prompted by the "well-known Russian urge for 300 percent security." That same urge for security, had the German deployment been properly interpreted at the highest level, would beyond doubt have set in motion mobilization measures on an altogether different order of magnitude from those which were actually undertaken. But Stalin held the lid on tight, coldly ignoring official warnings from Britain and the United States and apparently oblivious to the impending military showdown between Germany and the Soviet Union, rumors of which, the German Ambassador observed, were being brought along with facts to confirm them by "every traveler" from Germany to Moscow. On 14 June 1941, Tass, the official Soviet news agency, published a communiqué which stated that according to Soviet Government information, Germany was observing the nonaggression pact as strictly as the Soviet Union was and no grounds existed for thinking that Germany meant to break the pact.

PREPAREDNESS AND DOCTRINE

The Soviet Union was neither devoted to peace—in the last half of the decade of the 1930's it had fought in Spain, in the Far East, and against Finland—nor was it unprepared for war in the same sense that Great Britain and the United States, for instance, were not ready. It was badly prepared owing chiefly to administrative malfunctions that, despite substantial effort and some remarkable achievements, prevented attainment of readiness for war on the plane to which the Germans had by the early 1940's raised the military art.

The great and persistent Soviet weakness was lack of initiative at all levels, which resulted in dogmatism, slavish dependence on orders from the top, and preference for the fixed and approved formula even when it was contradicted by reason or experience. That weakness had been made much worse by the great purges of the 1930's, which had removed the most experienced and independent commanders and had made conformity a near-absolute prerequisite for survival. The immediate and aggravating influence was the so-called personality cult associated with Stalin, but it may be doubted whether under the Soviet system, in any case, a complete cure would have been possible or desired.

Soviet T34 tank in Stalingrad.

Although the Soviet command had direct combat experience and the examples of the early World War II campaigns in western Europe to learn from, the most important lessons had in some instances been misinterpreted and in others unsuccessfully applied. From the Spanish Civil War it had drawn the conclusions that large armored units were not worthwhile and that aircraft would only be useful for operations over the battlefield. Consequently, the mechanized corps in the Army had been abolished, and aircraft production had concentrated on fighter and close ground support types. From 1939 until shortly before the invasion, the largest Soviet armored unit was the tank brigade. Soviet doctrine in that period regarded the tank as primarily an infantry support weapon. After mid-1940, apparently under the influence of the German example in France, the mechanized corps and tank divisions were reinstituted, but then in the haste to get a large number fast few were fully equipped.

For the Soviet command the war with Finland had been a traumatic experience. It had disclosed deep-seated weaknesses in the military structure. Finnish Marshal Carl Mannerheim aptly compared the Soviet performance to one by a badly conducted orchestra in which the players could not keep time. By the Russians' own later admission, many of the officers "had no clear conception of modern war" and could not plan or command a co-ordinated operation. The damage to the Soviet military reputation abroad was enormous, greater, perhaps, than it should have been in the light of the recent and successful Soviet actions against the Japanese at Khassan Lake and on the Khalkhin Gol in the Far East.

The experience in Finland may have been in considerable part responsible for Stalin's determination to avoid a clash with Germany at any cost. Quickly thereafter the Soviet Union had displayed an intense desire to avoid becoming militarily embroiled with either side in the big war. When the Germans invaded Norway in April 1940, allegedly to forestall the British and French who had talked about sending troops through Norway to aid the Finns, they thought they would have to make explanations to the Soviet Union and were surprised when the invasion elicited a figurative "big sigh of relief" even though the Soviet-Finnish war was by then over.

How fundamental were the defects which the Finnish war had revealed was demonstrated by the reforms undertaken in the Soviet military system. In April 1940, as soon as the war had ended, the Army abolished the old, formula-ridden, oversimplified training instructions and undertook to establish combat-oriented officer training courses. In May general and admiral ranks were reinstituted in the armed forces and other egalitarian holdovers from the Revolution were abandoned. In August the commissar system was abolished. A conference held in December 1940, however, revealed that most officers were still receiving stereotyped training and that only small progress was being made toward achieving individual initiative and flexibility.

In weapons the Soviet Union had made some remarkable advances. It had developed multiple rocket projectors, the famous Katyushas; the T34 medium tank, which was diesel-propelled, faster, and more heavily armed and armored than any of the German tanks; and the— for that time—superheavy KV (Klimenti Voroshilov) models of tanks that ranged in weight to upwards of sixty tons. But the tanks and rocket projectors as well as new aircraft types had not been put into full-scale production by the time of the invasion. Armament production had been high and steadily increasing throughout the period of the Five

Year Plans but without emphasis on or appreciation of new weapons. The Commisariat of Defense had, for instance, classified submachine guns as police weapons and therefore had not included them in the military production plans.

From the German victories in western Europe the Soviet command had apparently also failed to draw pertinent conclusions. It saw as the chief causes for the Polish and French defeats the lack of will to resist and the fifth column. That reasoning, projected into the Soviet period of great defeats, was to occasion vast, pointless, and at times paralyzing suspicion and terror. The Soviet command, moreover, had no clear conception of what would happen when war began. It assumed that initially both sides would be engaged in mobilization and strategic deployment and therefore not ready to launch major operations for several weeks. Hence, it assumed further that the frontier military districts would be capable of holding the enemy until mobilization was completed and the Soviet forces could take the offensive.

In June 1941 the defense of the Soviet western frontier was assigned to the Leningrad, Baltic Special, Western Special, Kievan Special, and Odessa Military Districts.[4] If war broke out they were to become front (army group) headquarters commanding initially twelve armies, three on the Finnish border and nine on the frontier between the Baltic and Black Seas. While it is difficult to accept that the western frontier military districts were in as austere a condition as the Soviet post-Stalin accounts would have them appear, they were undoubtedly not prepared for the test to which they were about to be subjected. They were established along a line that had over nearly all of its length less than two years before, in places less than a year before, been deep in foreign territory. The border defenses and the communications lines were still mostly under construction. The much more highly developed Stalin Line behind the old border had lately been neglected and, in any event, was not included in the war plan.

---

4. The sector boundaries were as follows: Leningrad Military District—the Finnish border from the Arctic coast to the Isthmus of Karelia; Baltic Special Military District—the East Prussian border; Western Special Military District—from the southern border of the Lithuanian SSR to the northern border of the Ukrainian SSR, Kievan Special Military District—from the northern border of the Ukrainian SSR to the Rumanian border; Odessa Military District—the Rumanian border to the mouth of the Danube.

Most serious, the Soviet Army was then a rigid instrument, uncertain in its responses under the best conditions, with a very low probability of successful reaction to surprise. It was to face as near total surprise as any army has encountered in modern times. The directive placing the frontier military districts on a war footing was issued from Moscow at 0030 on 22 June. Three hours later, before any warning had reached the forward units, the Germans crossed the border.

Because of the Soviet reluctance to release hard statistics, nearly all Soviet strength figures must remain estimates (as must to a much greater degree all Soviet casualty figures). The best available Soviet figure on troop strength gives a total of 4,207,000 men in the Soviet armed forces "by 1941." If the German estimate which places roughly 70 percent of the Soviet strength in divisions on the western frontier is accepted, and if allowances are made for naval and air force personnel and a possible strength increase during 1941, the actual combat-ready Soviet strength in the western military districts amounted to about 3,000,000 men. Undoubtedly, the war plan envisaged a very rapid increase in the days immediately after the outbreak of hostilities, and very likely such an increase was partially accomplished even under the conditions that accompanied the German attack.

In military equipment and weapons the Soviet forces had some striking numerical superiorities and qualitative deficiencies. Of 6,000 combat aircraft at stations in Europe (8,000 planes estimated in the whole Soviet Air Force), for example, only 1,100 were recent models. According to German intelligence estimates the Soviet Army had 10,000 tanks (out of a total of 15,000) in armored units on or near the western frontier. The far greater part of those were older types but the western military districts had 1,475 KV and T34 tanks, both of which were superior to any of the German tanks. Production of the newest models of weapons and tanks was rising rapidly. In the first five and one-half months of 1941, 1,500 KV and T34 tanks had been built against less than 400 in the previous year.

On balance, the Soviet Union was not at a positive disadvantage initially except in the air, and, even in the short term, it had the potential to achieve superiority in troops and possibly also in war production.

INVASION AND RETREAT

Under the shock of invasion the Soviet Government responded predictably with a series of decisions aimed at centralizing military and political controls and strengthening the influence of the Communist Party. On 23 June it created the Stavka (Staff) of the High Command of the Soviet Armed Forces under the Commissar of Defense Marshal Sovetskogo Soyuza Semen K. Timoshenko. That same day the military commissars were reinstituted in the armed forces and given equal command responsibility with the military commanders. A week later all the powers of government, including the ultimate authority over the armed forces, were concentrated in a 5-man State Defense Committee under Stalin. An important member of the State Defense Committee was Lavrenti P. Beria, the police chief, whose NKVD (secret police) units were setting up blocking detachments behind the front to catch stragglers and prevent unauthorized retreats. On the first day of the war the five military districts on the western frontier became Leningrad, Northwest, West, Southwest, and South Fronts.

On the frontier, surprise soon turned to confusion and in not a few instances panic. To hold with the first echelon until a counterattack could be prepared, although now clearly an impossibility, remained the whole basis of Soviet strategy. A reserve front of four armies created on the third day in the most endangered sector due west of Moscow was first ordered to be ready to counterattack and then, on 1 July, combined with the shattered West Front. Still trying to halt the retreat, Stalin had the Commanding General, West Front, and his staff shot and some days later applied the same Draconian remedy to the Northwest Front. Henceforth an officer who permitted a retreat forfeited his life. The pistol shot in the back of the neck became a very common occupational hazard for all ranks in the Soviet Army.

In the first two weeks of July the Soviet Command, stripped by the force of events of its earlier illusions, set about organizing for a desperate, bitter, and costly struggle. On the 3d, Stalin, who had not made any public statement until then, in a nationwide radio address called for a "patriotic," nationalistic effort against the foreign invader, for a scorched-earth policy in the threatened areas, and for partisan warfare in the occupied territory. The creation of the Stavka of the

Supreme Command (supplanting the High Command Stavka) with Stalin at its head continued the centralization that had been begun at the start of the war and that was completed when Stalin assumed the posts of Defense Commissar (19 July 1941) and Commander in Chief of the Soviet Armed Forces (7 August 1941).

The Stavka of the Supreme Command remained the highest Soviet military planning and executive group throughout the war. The Stavka was, under the State Defense Committee, a strategic planning council rather than a general staff, but it could issue orders through the Army General Staff, the administrations and commands of the service arms, or directly to the field commands. Its dozen or so members included the Army Chief of Staff, the Chief of the Naval Staff, high-ranking representatives of the combat arms, and top experts from the technical services.

More genuinely urgent than the reorganization of the top level command, which after all served mainly to strengthen Stalin's position, was the necessity for devising a workable system of command in the field. Three of the five original front commands had proved unequal to their missions. The degree of incompetence in the lesser commands was as high or higher. The purges had removed too many experienced officers and had brought many others too rapid advancement, especially in the higher ranks. The only solution was to bring the unit organizations more nearly within the range of command capabilities. In mid-July the rifle corps and mechanized corps were abolished and the armies were reduced to at most five or six divisions. The rifle divisions, which had had actual peacetime strengths of about 12,000 men, were for the most part already being reduced by attrition and drastic organizational shortcuts to 6,000 to 9,000 men. The tank divisions were broken up into smaller independent units which were assigned directly to the armies. In essence, the armor was again reduced to an infantry support role.

The one shift away both from the trend toward centralization and from the reduction in the sizes of commands was the creation on 10 July of three high commands for the so-called strategic directions, Northwest, West, and Southwest. They were expected to co-ordinate the operations on broad sectors comparable to those of the German army groups and eliminate the time lag in the transmission of orders and decisions from Moscow. They were turned over to Marshals Klimenti I. Voroshilov (Northwest), Timoshenko (West), and Semen M. Budenny (Southwest), men whose military experience had been acquired in the civil war and whose exalted ranks reflected political rather than professional competence. The commands for the strategic directions, as far as can be determined, never assumed their full functions and were, except for the Southwest Command, which survived into early 1942, soon quietly abolished.

In mid-July, when German Army Group Center pushed into the gap between the Dvina and Dnepr Rivers, the strategic gateway to Moscow, and formed several large encirclements north and south of Smolensk, the Stavka deployed a second reserve front of six armies east of Smolensk. The Soviet command was doing exactly what the Germans had hoped it would; it was standing and fighting and not voluntarily retreating into the interior. It had, moreover, made the decision that Halder and Brauchitsch had predicted, namely, to put its main effort in the center, in front of Moscow.

While Army Group Center stood by in August and September awaiting the return of its big armored formations, the Soviet build-up continued. At the end of September, two days before Army Group Center went back into motion, the fronts on the Moscow approaches had more than 40 percent of the Soviet Army personnel and artillery and 35 percent of the aircraft and tanks. The strategy was still the same: meet the enemy head-on, wear him down, stop him, and then counterattack. Again it failed. In a week the Germans trapped the greater part of six armies in pockets at Bryansk and Vyaz'ma. On 10 October the Army Chief of Staff, General Armii Georgi K. Zhukov, took command of the West Front into which the reserve front had been merged and therewith assumed responsibility for the defense of Moscow.

October was a black month for the Soviet Union, the darkest of the entire war. Leningrad was under tight siege; Moscow was threatened; Kharkov fell; and German armies closed in on the Donets Basin industrial area. The human cost was appalling. The Germans claimed 3,000,000 prisoners alone.

On the other hand, the Germans, in action continuously for four months, had to contend with the added strains that the fall rains and mud inflicted on men and equipment. The margin of German superiority was narrowing. In the second half of October the Soviet command created three new reserve armies. In the first two weeks of November, it deployed six additional reserve armies to backstop the whole front on the line Lake Onega-Gorki-Stalingrad-Astrakhan. By the end of November five reserve armies, two of them new, were deployed in and around Moscow.

THE FIRST WINTER OFFENSIVE

The German weakness showed first on the flanks. In November Army Group North was stopped at Tikhvin; Army Group South was stopped at Rostov and then, before the end of the month, had to fall back to the Mius River. At the end of November the Stavka released three reserve armies plus better than a dozen divisions to the West Front. On the morning 6 December Zhukov counterattacked. It was in fact the moment the Russians had been waiting for since June, but the Stavka moved cautiously, giving the West Front and the Kalinin Front (created on 17 October) on its right only enough strength from the reserves initially to achieve a 1.5:1 superiority in troops, tanks, and artillery and 2:1 in aircraft. In December, while West, Kalinin, and Southwest Fronts fought to eliminate the German threat to Moscow, the Stavka extended the counteroffensive north and south along the length of the front from Tikhvin to the Kerch' Peninsula. By the turn of the year it had worked out plans and deployed the reserves for a general offensive that would have as its objectives the destruction of Army Group Center, the liberation of Leningrad, and the reconquest of the Donets Basin and the Crimea. On 7 January 1942 the Stavka gave Kalinin and West Fronts, assisted by the fronts on their flanks, the mission of "not only encircling, but also splitting and destroying piecemeal," the main force of Army Group Center.

In deciding to go to the general offensive the Stavka overreached itself. On 10 January it called attention to serious and elementary tactical errors that had been made during the period of the December counteroffensive, among them failure to concentrate at the points of main effort, dispersal of armor and artillery, and poor co-ordination of the combat arms. For the Stavka to recognize the weaknesses was one thing; for the field commands to correct them was quite another. In the general offensive the fronts and armies frittered away the reserves and, despite frequent admonitions, failed to observe the principles of concentration and mass in employing their troops, artillery, and tanks. On 1 February, trying to save part of the offensive, the Stavka gave Zhukov full command of the operation against Army Group Center, but it was too late. By then the reserves were all committed. After midmonth the power of the offensive began to decline everywhere.

Although the 1941-42 winter offensive failed to accomplish a clear-cut victory, it dealt the enemy a damaging blow. Most important, it destroyed the myth of German invincibility and raised immeasurably Soviet military prestige abroad and political prestige at home. It imbued the Russian people with confidence and gave the regime a renewed hold on the population on both sides of the front. It gave the Army a fund of experience to exploit in developing viable offensive doctrine. The opportunity was not wasted. Special detachments in the General Staff, the staffs of the service arms, staff and command schools, fronts, and armies set about collecting and evaluating information and producing instructional materials.

1942, RETREAT AND RECOVERY

Encouraged by the winter's successes, the Stavka planned to keep the initiative and, after the spring thaw, attack at Leningrad, Demyansk, Orel, Kharkov, in the Donets Basin, and on the Crimea, to forestall the Germans and create conditions for another Soviet general offensive. Defensively it built up the central sector of the front, expecting the German main effort again to be directed toward Moscow. The German attack on the south flank was considered a likely possibility, but it was expected to bear north toward Moscow, not south toward the Caucasus and Stalingrad. Consequently, instead of going to Southwest and South Fronts, the greater part of the Soviet reinforcements went to the central sector, and to Bryansk Front, which was expected to cover Moscow and Tula from the south. By those false estimates the Stavka placed itself in an only slightly less dangerous strategic position than that of the previous year.

On 12 May 1942, at Kharkov, the Southwest Front opened the first of the projected preliminary offensives. The plan was to envelop the city from the north and south, the main thrust being made from the south out of a bridgehead that had been created on the Donets around Izyum during the winter fighting. The operation had been conceived with total disregard for the condition of the enemy and for the complications that could result from an attempt to execute an unsupported thrust out of an unstable bridgehead position. Perhaps for those two reasons more than any others, the attack out of the western end of the bridgehead achieved some surprise and gained ground in the first four days; but the Izyum bridgehead had been on Army Group South's own schedule of preliminaries to the summer offensive. On the 17th a German armored force cut into the bridgehead from the south and in a week converted it into a pocket and a trap for 240,000 Soviet troops. The Soviet summer offensive evaporated in the Kharkov debacle, and the Southwest Front was weakened beyond repair in the time that was left before the German offensive began.

The Soviet command at least did not enter the second summer campaign with all the self-imposed handicaps of the first. In July the Stavka gave the orders in time to save Southwest Front and South Front from encirclements. Between 28 June and 24 July, Bryansk, Southwest, and South Fronts fell back 80 to 120 miles and gave up the important Donets Basin. The retreat severely damaged morale throughout the country, and the forces it saved were seriously weakened, but it did deny the Germans a victory of the kind they wanted and needed.

In the continuing absence of a clear Soviet explanation, the strategy of the 1942 summer campaign seems to have been rooted in a misreading of the German intentions which, costly as the consequences were, may inadvertently have forestalled greater disasters. With the same stubborn consistency it had displayed the year before, the Soviet Command kept its main forces in the center. At the end of June 1942 it had 28 armies between Leningrad and Tula and 18 armies between Tula and the Caucasus, the latter including Bryansk Front's 5 armies which had as their main mission the defense of Moscow on the south. Southwest Front and South Front had between them 10 armies, 3 of them not much more than cadres left from the Kharkov battle. Kalinin

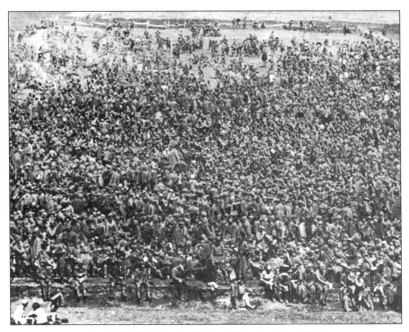

Soviet POW's after the Battle of Kharkov, May 1942.

Front and West Front, on the direct approaches to Moscow, had a total of 15 armies. That deployment prevailed through the summer. The reinforcement of the south flank, when it took place, came out of newly formed reserves, not, as the Germans had expected, out of the substance of the forces at the front.

The essential aspect of the 1942 summer campaign was that, while both sides fought it on false premises, the permanently damaging consequences fell entirely on the Germans. In August and September the Soviet armies on the south flank retreated another 80 to 360 miles, but the German armies became overextended and began to outrun their supplies. In the meantime, Soviet reserves had begun to move in along the lower Volga and in the Caucasus. By the fall of 1942 the combination of sheer space, Soviet resistance, and the German failure to attain a balance between means and objectives had brought the German armies for a second time to a state of dangerous overextension. Russia was engulfing the German forces as it had those of Napoleon and Charles XII; but to smother an invasion by exploiting space had not, in fact, been a deliberate element in Soviet strategy. In the late prewar period Soviet strategic doctrine, as far as it was formulated, had emphasized the attack and the destruction of the enemy "on his own territory." Although, in the post-war Stalinist era, the so-called strategic retreat was elevated after the fact to the status of doctrine, it was not a consciously applied doctrine in either of the first two summer campaigns. Nevertheless, both in 1941 and in 1942 it served better than any other strategy the Soviet command was able to devise.

During the summer, in the midst of the second great retreat, the Soviet Union finally passed its crisis as a military power. In spite of a decline in basic industrial capacity occasioned by the loss of the Donets Basin and the disruption of oil production, direct output of military items rose. Aircraft production increased 60 percent above that of 1941, to 25,000 planes by the end of the year, according to Soviet figures—which appear high. Tank output nearly quadrupled. The Russians officially claimed a total production of better than 24,000 tanks in 1942, 66 percent of them T34's. Over 3,000 multiple rocket projectors were produced in 1942 as against a few hundred the year before. In the Army, tank corps were reintroduced, and, following the German example, tank armies were created. In troop strength the Soviet Union held a clear superiority. As of 20 September, according to German estimates, the Soviet forces opposing the German armies numbered 4,255,840 men, 3,013,370 of them at the front and 1,242,470 in reserve. German Army Groups North and Center were outnumbered at the front and, with the Soviet reserves counted in, all of the army groups faced potentially superior forces.[5]

---

5. The Eastern Intelligence Branch, OKH, comparative force estimates were as follows:

German and Allied Forces
Total: 3,388,700*
Army Group North: 708,400 Army Group Center: 1,011,500
Army Group B: 1,234,000 Army Group A: 434,800

Soviet Forces Opposite the German Army Groups			
	In the Front	Reserves	Total
Total	3,013,370	1,242,470	4,255,840
Army Group North	916,700	84,910	1,001,610
Army Group Center	1,012,070	344,270	1,356,340
Army Group B	818,250	561,050	1,379,300
Army Group A	266,350	252,240	518,590

* The German figures are ration strengths which in this instance were some 250,000 men higher than the actual combat strengths.

For the future a further shift was in prospect: the Soviet recruit class of 1925 numbered 1,400,000 men while that of the Germans would yield only slightly more than one-third as many.

In the midst of the second German offensive, the Soviet military reforms begun in 1940-41 and reversed after the invasion were finally carried through. In the late summer, at the height of the retreat, officers and commissars were authorized, in fact encouraged, to carry out summary executions of "cowards and traitors." This gesture of desperation soon had to be modified. Equally desperate, from the doctrinaire Party point of view, but more to the point, was the simultaneous realization that the traditional military principles, feudal and reactionary as they might be considered, gave armies staying power in the field. Suddenly the Soviet Army began to assume all the old, long-despised trappings of military authority: sharp and rigid rank differentiation as the basis for discipline, strict observance of military etiquette, class status for officers, including special privileges and distinctive uniforms and insignia, the recognition of a Russian, as opposed to the revolutionary, military tradition, and the awarding of medals and decorations. At the same time, such men as Voroshilov and Budenny, who had achieved high ranks chiefly through political channels, were quietly moved into the background. A most important step toward the professionalization of the Army was the reintroduction on 9 October 1942 of the principle of the single commander. The commissars, who until then had been at least the co-equals of the military commanders, were reduced to deputies responsible primarily for political indoctrination and morale.

In the higher reaches of the Soviet command the war experience was being rapidly assimilated. In the 1942 retreats the Soviet front and army commands showed some of the flexibility that had been completely absent before. A year of war had produced a core of seasoned, capable officers in the higher commands. Two of the best, Zhukov and General Polkovnik Aleksander M. Vasilevskiy, were with the fronts on the south flank during the summer campaign as representatives of the Stavka. The practice of assigning representatives, begun during the summer of 1941 and further developed throughout the war, gave the Stavka a means of exercising effective control in crucial areas and provided an echelon of command capable of translating strategic guidance from the Stavka into operations. At the end of August 1942 German intelligence concluded that the Soviet higher commands had mastered the tactical principles of modern warfare and would be capable of applying them fully as ably as the Germans themselves were it not for the continuing inferiority of the lower and intermediate staffs.

CHAPTER III

Stalingrad, the Encirclement

Stalingrad—Tsaritsyn before the Revolution, Volgograd after the de-Stalinization of the mid-1950's—stands on the high west bank of the Volga 560 miles from Moscow, 1,400 miles from Berlin. Around the city the flat, treeless steppe stretches away in all directions, hot, dry, and dusty in summer, cold, sometimes bitterly cold in winter. For half a year, under the burning August sun and in the frigid January calm, armies of a million and a half or more men fought in the city and around it. On the 60,000-square-mile battlefield the two sides committed, according to Soviet estimates, 2,000 tanks, 25,000 artillery pieces, and 2,300 aircraft.

Possessing some strategic attributes in its own right, Stalingrad became, in part by accident in part by design, the focal point of one of the decisive battles of World War II. The city's half-million population, large tractor plants converted to tank production, a gun factory, metallurgical and chemical works, railroads, and oil tank farms made it an important war asset. Equally important was Stalingrad's commanding position on the lower Volga River, the Soviet Union's chief waterway and the main route for shipment of oil from the Caucasus. By the late summer of 1942 the Germans had accomplished successes more sweeping than capture of Stalingrad could be—without putting victory within their grasp.

Strategically Stalingrad was no Moscow; nevertheless, as a symbol it acquired commanding proportions. The name alone implied a personal contest between the Soviet dictator and his German counterpart. Hitler had made Stalingrad the end objective of the summer offensive and could not claim a full success without it. Conversely, holding the city gave the Soviet command its last chance to demonstrate to the world that the Germans had not completely regained the upper hand.

What was to happen at Stalingrad had occurred at Moscow the year before. In the midst of the engagement the relative strengths of the offense and the defense began to shift and the result of the battle came to hinge on how far that shift went and how fast.

THE ADVANCE ON STALINGRAD

Soviet historians set the starting date of the Stalingrad battle (the battle on the Volga in post-Stalin Soviet usage) as 17 July 1942, the day on which Stalingrad Front, which had replaced Southwest Front (disbanded on 12 July), committed two newly created armies, the Sixty-second and Sixty-fourth Armies, in the Don bend, their forward elements on the Chir and Tsimla Rivers 100 miles west of Stalingrad. (Map 3) The date corresponds closely with the recasting of the German offensive which, together with the appearance of the fresh Soviet armies, set the stage for the coming battle. Four days before, Hitler had ordered the attack toward Rostov and had turned Fourth Panzer Army south, leaving Sixth Army to carry the advance toward Stalingrad alone.

Map 3: The Advance to Stalingrad, 17 July-18 November 1942

For the next several weeks Hitler tinkered with the machinery, trying to find the precise minimum of power that would bring Stalingrad into his hands. To meet the Soviet forces behind the Chir and Tsimla, General der Panzertruppen Friedrich Paulus, commanding Sixth Army, initially had one infantry corps approaching the Chir, two others farther back and coming up slowly. On the 18th Hitler took an infantry corps and XIV Panzer Corps out of the concentration north of Rostov, where units were beginning to pile up anyway, gave them to Paulus, and ordered him to strike fast for Stalingrad before the Soviet resistance had a chance to harden. In two days XIV Panzer Corps reached the Chir, and on the 21st took a bridgehead, but then it ran out of gasoline and had to stop. On 23 July, in the directive that sent Army Group A south into the Caucasus, Hitler gave Paulus another corps, XXIV Panzer Corps, from Fourth Panzer Army and, for the first time, a definite order to take Stalingrad.

By the 25th, Sixth Army had cleared the Don bend except for two strongly held Soviet bridgeheads flanking the direct approach route to Stalingrad and a third, smaller bridgehead upstream around

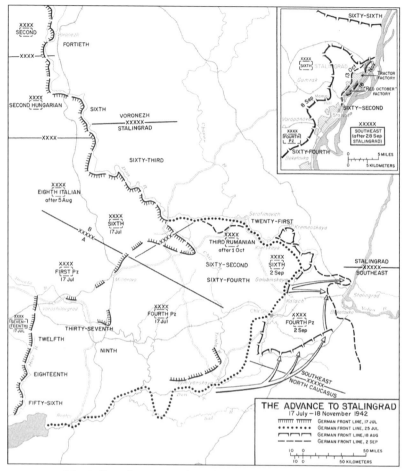

Map 3: The Advance to Stalingrad, 17 July-18 November 1942

Serafimovich. Then the army stopped, having run low on gasoline and nearly out of ammunition. Hitler desired that the "emphasis" be put on the Army Group A operations. Consequently, the OKH quartermaster had to divert half of Army Group B's motor transport to Army Group A, leaving less than enough to sustain Sixth Army as it moved farther into the steppe away from the railheads. Lack of gasoline also slowed the redeployment for the attack toward Stalingrad. The Hungarian Second Army had taken over a sector on the Don below Voronezh, but Paulus still had strung out along the middle Don the better part of two corps that he could not bring east until the Italian Eighth Army arrived to replace them.

On the last day of the month Hitler, still tinkering, ordered Generaloberst Hermann Hoth's Fourth Panzer Army to do an aboutface at Tsymlyanskaya and strike toward Stalingrad from the south along the east bank of the Don. For his mission, Hoth was to have only XXXXVIII Panzer Corps, which had already covered 400 miles in the summer campaign, an infantry corps, and a Rumanian corps. The distance from Tsymlyanskaya to Stalingrad was 120 miles.

In the meantime the *Stavka* had committed the newly formed *First* and *Fourth Tank Armies* against Sixth Army. The Italian Eighth Army was beginning to relieve the Sixth Army divisions upstream on the Don, but Paulus reported that at the rate he was getting gasoline and ammunition, 200 tons a day, he would not have enough to start operations against the two large Soviet bridgeheads until 8 August. Hitler demanded that he start a day earlier to prevent the Russians from escaping across the river.

Sixth Army attacked the strongest of the bridgeheads, the one west of Kalach, on 7 August, and before the day ended had encircled the forward elements of *Sixty-second Army* and *First Tank Army.* In the next four days it mopped up the pocket, taking 50,000 prisoners, and then turned against the less strongly held bridgehead north of Kalach, where the Russians fought stubbornly but did not repeat the mistake of standing and letting themselves be encircled.

The defeats on the west bank of the Don sent a nervous tremor through the Soviet command. On 5 August, to reduce the span of control, the *Stavka* had created the *Southeast Front* out of the southern half of *Stalingrad Front.* On the 10th it reversed itself and made *Headquarters, Stalingrad Front* subordinate to *Headquarters, Southeast Front.* Two days later it sent Vasilevskiy to co-ordinate, and on the 13th it put Yeremenko in command of both *fronts,* with Khrushchev as member of the Military Council (political commissar) and the *front* commanders as deputies.

By 18 August Sixth Army had bridgeheads across the Don, but the fighting in the river bend had been exhausting and costly, and the army, particularly the infantry, was not in condition to make the 35-mile thrust to Stalingrad. On the 21st, XIV Panzer Corps broke out and in three days drove a slender spearhead through to the Volga north of

Stalingrad. To keep its toehold on the river, from which it brought the shipping under artillery fire, the corps had to break contact with the army and form a hedgehog.

On the 24th the Soviet *Twenty-first, Sixty-third,* and *First Guards Armies* attacked Sixth Army's deep left flank out of the small bridgeheads they held at Serafimovich and Kremenskaya. Paulus reluctantly decided that he could not spare enough infantry to open a corridor to XIV Panzer Corps, at least not until Fourth Panzer Army freed his right flank. At the moment that prospect did not look good. Like Paulus, Hoth was having to hold his attack to a narrow front. He was making his thrust along the chain of salt lakes due south of Stalingrad. This drive threatened the Soviet *Sixty-second* and *Sixty-fourth Armies* with an encirclement west of Stalingrad but left a 40-mile gap between his and Paulus' flanks.

After fighting off a strong, well co-ordinated counterattack on 26 August, XIV Panzer Corps reported that it probably could not resist a second such attempt, but during the following two days the crisis suddenly evaporated. The counterattacks against XIV Panzer Corps weakened, and Russian morale appeared to be breaking. Sixth Army reported a marked increase in Russian deserters, including—and this was unusual—tank crews with their tanks. Fourth Panzer Army, which had regrouped and shifted its panzer corps west to make contact with Sixth Army sooner, experienced a similar slackening in the Soviet resistance.

When Hoth observed that the Russians were falling back toward Stalingrad, he turned east on the 30th, and in three days pushed his armored points through to Pitomnik and nearly to Voroponovo Station due west of Stalingrad. On 2 September at noon Sixth Army attacked toward Stalingrad, opening a secure corridor to XIV Panzer Corps that day and making contact with Fourth Panzer Army near Pitomnik the next.

THE SIEGE

The *Stavka* had declared a stage of siege in Stalingrad on 25 August and had begun a total civilian evacuation. A few of the shops and plants were kept running to repair military equipment. The city, a typically unprepossessing Russian mixture of stone and concrete government buildings, sprawling factories, and drab, unpainted wooden dwellings lying in a tight 2½-mile by 12-mile band along the cliffs of the river's edge, was about to enter history.

During the night of 2 September the Soviet *Sixty-second* and *Sixty-fourth Armies* withdrew to the inner Stalingrad defense ring. Sixth Army's lead corps aimed toward the 300-foot-high Mamai Hill, the city's central and dominant topographical feature. Fourth Panzer Army closed in on the southern outskirts.

Responding to Stalin's 3 September call for a counterattack, *Stalingrad Front,* which as the battle developed had been pushed away from the city to Sixth Army's north flank, hastily deployed the *First Guards, Twenty-fourth,* and *Sixty-sixth Armies* on a short front due west of the Volga and on the 5th attacked south. The counterattack, although it was conducted by incompletely trained armies and practically without preparation, carried enough weight to keep Sixth Army preoccupied for several days. In three days, 8 to 10 September, Fourth Panzer Army, spearheaded by a motorized battalion, drove a wedge through to the Volga on the southern edge of the city. Although the battalion was forced to fall back a half mile or so and took another five days to fasten its hold on the river, *Sixty-second Army,* General Leytenant Vasili I. Chuikov commanding, was then in effect isolated in the Stalingrad bridgehead.

On 13 September Sixth Army attacked into the center of the city past Mamai Hill and to Railroad Station I, a third of a mile from the river. From then on the battle assumed the character it was to retain for the next two months: a bloody, relentless struggle in which single blocks and buildings became major military objectives and in which the opponents often occupied parts of the same building, sometimes different floors. In the succeeding days the fighting at Mamai Hill and the railroad station became so heavy that it was all but impossible to tell who was attacking and who defending, and the Sixth Army troops needed a week to push from the station through to the river. In the meantime the OKH had given Paulus command of XXXXVIII Panzer Corps to help in cleaning out the southern half of the city. After the breakthrough to the river was made, that mission was accomplished in

Germans advancing over the Steppe toward Stalingrad.

another five days; and on the 26th Paulus reported that the army had raised the Swastika over the government building in the Red Square.

By the turn of the month the Stalingrad bridgehead had been reduced to a breadth of six miles and a depth of nine. Neither side had space to maneuver. The situation favored the defender, as long as he was willing to pay the price in blood, and this the *Stavka* was obviously willing to do. Between mid-September and the first days of October *Sixty-second Army* received reinforcements amounting to nine rifle divisions, two tank brigades, and a rifle brigade. The command was reorganized and tightened. General Leytenant Konstantin K. Rokossovskiy assumed command of *Stalingrad Front,* which was renamed *Don Front.* Yeremenko took command of *Southeast Front,* renamed *Stalingrad Front.*

Toward the end of September, Paulus began shifting his full weight east when the Rumanian Third Army moved up to take over Sixth Army's front west of the Don. The Rumanians were neither trained nor equipped for fighting on the Eastern Front. In the last three days of the month, in the Fourth Panzer Army zone, the Germans were given a demonstration of their capabilities that was a dark omen of events to come. On the 28th the Rumanian divisions on the army's right flank along the range of hills south of Stalingrad gave way before a halfhearted Soviet attack and fell into a retreat that could not be stopped until two days later, after a German panzer division had been committed. Hoth reported, "German commands which have Rumanian troops serving under them must reconcile themselves to the fact that moderately heavy fire, even without an enemy attack, will be enough to cause these troops to fall back and that the reports they submit concerning their own situation are worthless since they never know where their own units are and their estimates of enemy strength are vastly exaggerated." He recommended that the Rumanians be assigned very narrow sectors and that every four Rumanian divisions be backstopped by one German division as a "corset stay."

The Germans still had the initiative, but to exercise it they were forced to accept battle on the enemy's terms in the bloody house-to-house fighting inside Stalingrad. There, nothing could prevail but elemental force capable of mastering men, concrete, stone, and steel. Four times between 20 September and 4 October Paulus reported that his infantry strength in the city was fading more rapidly than he could find troops to replenish it. He predicted that unless the decline was reversed the battle would stretch out indefinitely.

Strategically Sixth Army had accomplished its mission by the end of September. The Volga was closed. Half of Stalingrad was in German hands and all the rest could be brought under fire. Prudence would have recommended that Sixth Army stop, consolidate its front, and wear down the Russians gradually. Hitler himself had always been against wasting troops in street fighting. Paulus may have been about to make such a recommendation. On 4 October he warned that he had no reserves and the Russians, if they counterattacked, might break through. But Hitler's frustration at that stage of the campaign had overcome reason. On 28 September he opened the drive for the Winter Relief at the *Sportpalast* in Berlin with a speech in which he ridiculed the publicity he had lately been receiving in the world news media. Pinpricks like the Dieppe raid of mid-August, he complained, were touted as brilliant Allied victories while his own march from the Donets to the Volga and the Caucasus was "nothing." To carry his point home he added, "When we take Stalingrad—and you can depend on that—that is nothing." As a clincher, he vowed a second time to take Stalingrad and assured the audience, "You can be certain no one will get us away from there."

On 6 October Paulus temporarily stopped the attack in Stalingrad. His infantry strength was too low. In one division the infantry battalions were down to average strengths of 3 officers, 11 noncommissioned officers, and 62 men. Ammunition also was beginning to run short. In September alone the army had fired 25 million rounds of small arms ammunition, better than half a million antitank rounds, and three-quarters of a million artillery rounds. The army's losses since crossing the Don in August numbered 7,700 killed, 30,200 wounded, and 1,100 missing.

After receiving five special pioneer battalions from the OKH, taking an infantry division from his flank, and getting a panzer division from Fourth Panzer Army, Paulus renewed the attack in Stalingrad on 14 October. Soviet historians have described the next two weeks as the period of the bitterest fighting of the whole battle. The second day, the Germans took the tractor factory in the northern quarter and reached the Volga, splitting the bridgehead in two. From the left bank of the Volga massed Soviet artillery laid down fire on the German lines now everywhere within reach.

With characteristic suddenness, the season was changing. Several days of cold were followed on the 18th by heavy rain that next day turned to wet snow. On the steppe, mud engulfed the German supply convoys. Nevertheless, in the city, without managing to repeat their first two days' success, the Germans for a while maintained more momentum than in their earlier attempts. On an especially successful day, 23 October, they took half the "Red October" metallurgical works, several blocks of houses, and the greater part of the ruin that formerly had housed the municipal bakery. A week later, however, the army had to report that its ammunition was running short and it, therefore, could not sustain the attack at its former intensity.

In early November a hard freeze set in, creating a condition that complicated the Soviet defense in Stalingrad. Most Russian rivers freeze solid from bank to bank in a few days. The lower Volga does not. It first forms slush, then ice floes, which combine into large masses of ice that drift downstream with the current. In the latter stage crossing the river becomes slow and hazardous for even the strongest boats. At the latitude of Stalingrad the river takes weeks, sometimes months, to freeze over, and *Sixty-second Army* depended entirely on supplies and replacements coming across from the other side.

By the time the freeze began Chuikov's hold at Stalingrad was reduced to two bridgeheads, one six miles wide and at most a mile and a half deep in the city, the other in the northern suburbs less than half that size. On 11 November the Germans broke through to the river near the northern end of the larger bridgehead and cut off one division. On 17 November, in an order to Sixth Army, Hitler stated, "The difficulties of the battle around Stalingrad and the decline in combat strength are known to me. But for the present the Russians' difficulties occasioned by the drift ice on the Volga are even greater. If we exploit this time interval we will save ourselves much blood later." He called for "one more all out attempt."

GERMAN EXPECTATIONS

When the Eastern Intelligence Branch, OKH, concluded at the end of August 1942 that in the coming fall and winter the Russians would retain a considerable offensive potential, it undertook also to predict where they would attack. The Army Group B and Army Group Center zones seemed, from the Soviet point of view, to offer the best prospects. In the Army Group B area the relatively weak German front and easy terrain favored a Soviet bid to recapture Stalingrad and raised the prospect of a thrust across the Don west of Stalingrad to Rostov, which, if successful, would collapse the greater part of the Army Group B front and the entire Army Group A front. But the Eastern Intelligence Branch believed that the Russians would be more eager to remove the threat to Moscow posed by the forward elements of Army Group Center and would therefore most likely exploit the salients at Toropets and Sukhinichi for converging attacks on Smolensk, with the objective of destroying the Ninth, Third Panzer, and Fourth Armies. It assumed that the Russians were not yet capable of directing and sustaining offensives toward remote objectives, for instance Rostov or the Baltic coast, and so would attack where the configuration of the front offered greatest prospects of success without overtaxing their tactical capabilities.

CROSSCURRENTS

The trend of the following two months appeared to the Eastern Intelligence Branch to confirm its August forecast. Having maintained through the summer a relatively stronger deployment against Army Group Center than against the two southern German army groups, the Russians in September began, on Army Group Center's north flank around Toropets, an offensive buildup that had progressed so far by the second week of October that Hitler wanted to attempt a spoiling attack. The Germans believed the offensive would start immediately after the fall rains, which began on 16 October and were expected to last two to three weeks. Shortly before the middle of that month the beginnings of a build-up were also detected opposite Army Group B, but they did not appear to be on a scale that would indicate an offensive in the near future. On 15 October the Eastern Intelligence Branch concluded that the Russians would eventually attempt an offensive in the Army Group B zone, but the main significance of the deployment there for the present was that to make the necessary forces available they would have to give up whatever thoughts they might have had of enlarging the forthcoming operation against Army Group Center.

In the last two weeks of the month intelligence reports indicated that the build-up opposite Army Group B was limited to the Serafimovich bridgehead opposite Rumanian Third Army. On 31 October the Eastern Intelligence Branch reported that the level of activity in the bridgehead did not presage a major attack but rather appeared more and more to indicate that only local attacks were to be expected. At the same time, in the Army Group Center zone, Ninth Army recorded that the offensive against it could begin any day, and as of 30 October the army anticipated at best no more than a week's respite in which to complete its regrouping.

Hitler's interpretation of the enemy activity in Army Group B's zone was less sanguine than that of the Eastern Intelligence Branch. As early as mid-August he had begun to worry that Stalin might attempt,

Bridging an arm of the Don.

as he put it, the Russian "standard attack"—a thrust toward Rostov directed across the Don in the vicinity of Serafimovich—which the Bolsheviks had executed with devastating success in 1920 against the White Russian army of General Peter Nikolayevich Wrangel. On 26 October he reiterated his anxiety over a major offensive against the allied armies ranged along the Don and ordered Air Force field divisions moved in to stiffen the Italian, Hungarian, and Rumanian fronts on the Don.

On 2 November, when aerial photographs revealed that the Russians had thrown several new bridges across the Don to the Serafimovich bridgehead, Hitler once more predicted a major offensive toward Rostov. Realizing the Air Force field divisions would be small help in a real crisis, he canceled the order concerning them and on 4 November had the 6th Panzer Division and two infantry divisions transferred from the English Channel coast to Army Group B, where they were to be employed as a ready reserve behind the Italian Eighth and Rumanian Third Armies. Since those divisions required a certain amount of refitting and could not have reached the Eastern Front in less than four to five weeks, it appears that Hitler did not expect the offensive to begin before December.

During the first two weeks of November new clues came in almost daily. By the 4th it was clear that a build-up was also under way south of Stalingrad for an attack on Fourth Panzer Army, and on the 8th a division of the Soviet *Fifth Tank Army,* still believed to be in the Orel-Sukhinichi area, was identified opposite Rumanian Third Army. Two days later another division of *Fifth Tank Army* was identified and the appearance of a new headquarters, *Southwest Front,* was detected—an important sign, since it could be assumed that as long as only one *front* headquarters, *Don Front,* commanded all the Soviet forces against Army Group B north of Stalingrad, the span of control there would be too great for the Russians to attempt a major offensive. Despite these ominous portents the Eastern Intelligence Branch, as late as 6 November, was certain that the main effort would be against Army Group Center and that the offensive on the Don would come later. On 12 November it described the picture as too obscure to warrant a definitive prediction but hedged only to the extent of stating, "However, an attack in the near future against Rumanian Third Army with the objective of cutting the railroad to Stalingrad and thereby threatening the German forces farther east and forcing a withdrawal from Stalingrad must be taken into consideration."

ARMY GROUP B'S DISPOSITIONS

Although the Eastern Intelligence Branch possibly was right in assuming that the Russians intended to direct a heavy blow, possibly even the winter's main effort, against Army Group Center, it was clear to Army Group B by the second week of November that there would be an offensive against Rumanian Third Army and probably also Fourth Panzer Army; and against the Rumanian troops even a secondary offensive was cause for utmost concern. On 9 November Weichs, commanding Army Group B, considered taking the 29th Motorized Infantry Division from Fourth Panzer Army and stationing it behind Rumanian Third Army but dropped the idea because Fourth Panzer Army was also expecting an attack. Instead, on 16 November, he decided to shift the 22d Panzer Division from Italian Eighth Army to Rumanian Third Army where, together with the Rumanian 1st Armored Division, it would become part of a reserve corps under the command of Headquarters, XXXXVIII Panzer Corps, transferred from Fourth Panzer Army.

On paper XXXXVIII Panzer Corps constituted a fairly strong reserve; in fact it was nothing of the sort. The 22d Panzer Division, hardly more than a regiment, had 46 tanks, 38 of them in working order, on 19 November; and Rumanian 1st Armored Division, which had not yet seen action, had 122 tanks, 21 of them old German Panzer III's armed with 50-mm. guns, the rest captured Czech tanks mounting 37-mm. guns.

SOVIET INTENTIONS

THE BUILD-UP

On 4 October Zhukov and Vasilevskiy, representing the Stavka, headed a conference that initiated planning for a Soviet counteroffensive at Stalingrad. (Map 4) During the remainder of October and the first two weeks of November, while German Sixth Army strained to end the battle in the city, the Russians carried through a build-up on the army's flanks. On 28 October, Headquarters, Southwest Front, under General Leytenant N. F. Vatutin, moved in to take command of Sixth, First Guards, Sixty-third, Fifth Tank, and Twenty-first Armies on the Don upstream from Kletskaya. Don Front, its sector reduced by better than half, kept Sixty-fifth, Twenty-fourth, and Sixty-sixth Armies on the front between Kletskaya and the Volga; and Headquarters, Stalingrad Front, remained in command of Sixty-second, Sixty-fourth, Fifty-seventh, and Fifty-first Armies in Stalingrad and opposite Fourth Panzer Army. The strongest of the reinforcements, Fifth Tank Army, consisting of six rifle divisions, two tank corps, a guards tank brigade, a cavalry corps, artillery, antiaircraft, and mortar regiments, began moving into the line opposite Rumanian Third Army in the latter half of October, completing the redeployment on about 6 November.[6] Except for Fifth Tank Army the reinforcement was accomplished with units of less than army size. The infantry

---

6. Soviet rifle divisions were authorized about 10,000 men each; tank corps (comparable to U.S. Army armored divisions), 10,500 men and 189 medium and heavy tanks; cavalry corps, 19,000 men and approximately 100 armored vehicles.

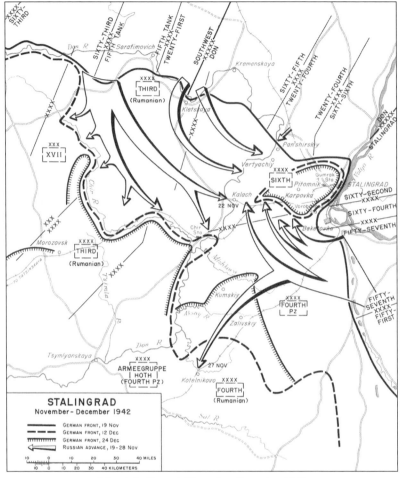

Map 4: Stalingrad, November-December 1942

strengths were increased, and the armies in the main attack were given mobile forces in the form of tank, mechanized, and cavalry corps.[7]

By the time the deployment was completed Soviet armored strength around Stalingrad stood at 4 tank and 3 mechanized corps,

---

7. Soviet mechanized corps were authorized strengths of 16,000 men and 186 tanks. Some of the tank and mechanized corps could have come from the *First* and *Fourth Tank Armies. Fourth Tank Army* no longer appeared in the order of battle in the Stalingrad area after September. *First Tank Army* disappeared after the encirclement west of Kalach where it was badly mauled if not, as the Germans claimed, destroyed.

14 independent tank brigades, and 3 tank regiments—all together 900 tanks, 60 percent of all the Soviet tanks at the front. The *Stavka* had also moved in one-third of the Soviet Army's rocket launchers, 115 battalions, and had significantly reinforced the other types of artillery and the air forces. The number of Soviet troops in the offensive zone was slightly over one million.

Soviet estimates make the two sides about equal in numbers of troops and the Soviet advantages in tanks, artillery, and aircraft slight—about 1.3:1, 1.3:1, and 1.1:1 respectively. The actual ratios could not have been anywhere near that close. The Soviet 1,000,000-man strength approximates the total strength of Army Group B, of which not much more than half was deployed around Stalingrad. Assuming the figure for the Soviet strength to be accurate, the Soviet over-all superiority was probably in the neighborhood of 2:1, much higher in the crucial sectors and, considering the quality of the troops the Germans had committed on Sixth Army's flanks, relatively overwhelming. The same was, no doubt, also true of the other ratios. The armored strength of Army Group B, all told, could not have amounted to more than 500 tanks, at least a third of them outmoded Czech models and Panzer II's and III's. The aircraft ratio appears to have been secured by figuring in the entire German air strength on the Eastern Front.

THE PLAN AND TACTICS

The Soviet plan was to tie down Sixth Army on the front between the Don and the Volga and in Stalingrad, smash the Rumanians on its left, and thrust behind the army to cut its lines of communications across the Don. The main effort was to be in the *Fifth Tank Army* sector where, after 6 rifle divisions, 4 in the first wave and 2 in the second, opened a gap in the Rumanian Third Army's front, 2 tank corps would break through aiming for Kalach on the Don due west of Stalingrad. Following behind the tank corps, the cavalry corps and 3 rifle divisions of *Sixty-third Army* would fan out to the right to cover the outer flank by establishing a line on the Chir River. Inside the arc of the tank corps, advance elements of *Twenty-first Army* and *Sixty-fifth Army* were to break through on either side of Kletskaya and encircle the four Sixth Army divisions west of the Don. They would get help from *Twenty-fourth Army,* which was to prevent the divisions from joining the Sixth Army main force by taking the Don crossings at Pan'shirskiy and Vertyachiy. To complete the encirclement, *Fifty-seventh* and *Fifty-first Armies* were to cut through Fourth Panzer Army south of Stalingrad and strike northwestward to meet *Fifth Tank Army* at Kalach.

The Stalingrad offensive ushered in a new stage in the Soviet conduct of operations, a stage in which the Russians demonstrated a command of offensive tactics equal to that of the Germans in conception and sufficiently effective in execution to prevail against an opponent who had passed the peak of his strength. Most significant was the use of infantry massed on a narrow front to open a gap that was then exploited by strong, independent armored forces for a breakthrough deep into the enemy rear. Formerly the Russians had almost always employed mixed armor and infantry in frontal attacks, which, though less effective and more costly, were easier to command. The new tactics showed that the Soviet higher commands had achieved a level of competence that enabled them to take the risks and reach for the greater rewards of mobile warfare. An increased sophistication was evident in all phases of operations. The deployment for the Stalingrad offensive, for instance, was executed rapidly, smoothly, and unobtrusively without the heavy-handed probing for weak spots and lengthy artillery duels with which the Soviet commanders in their earlier offensives had often frittered away the element of surprise.

SIXTH ARMY ENCIRCLED

BREAKTHROUGH

After waiting for the Allied landings in North Africa to tie down the Germans in the West—and for the ground to freeze hard enough to carry tanks—the Russians opened the offensive at Stalingrad on 19 November 1942. At midnight it had begun to snow, so heavily that visibility was reduced to zero. The temperature was 20° F. At 0850, in the wake of an artillery barrage that lasted about an hour and a half, *Fifth Tank Army* and the *Twenty-first Army* launched their infantry against Rumanian Third Army.

By early afternoon the Rumanian line was breached, and at 1400 the two tank corps and one cavalry corps of *Fifth Tank Army* began to move through. An hour later a tank corps and a cavalry corps were committed to exploit the breakthrough in the *Twenty-first Army* sector. Rumanian Third Army had collapsed under the first assault, and the Soviet tanks, against which the Rumanians had no antitank weapons heavier than 4.7-mm., completed their demoralization. *Sixty-fifth Army* also began its attack on the morning of the 19th, but it faced the German divisions on the left flank of Sixth Army and made practically no progress except against the Rumanian cavalry division on its right flank and there advanced only about 3 miles as opposed to 13-14 miles gained by the other two armies.

The next day *Fifty-seventh* and *Fifty-first Armies* broke through the front of Rumanian VI Corps south of the Beketovka bridgehead. Fourth Panzer Army recorded that the Rumanian corps disintegrated so rapidly that all measures to stop the fleeing troops became useless before they could be put into execution. At nightfall the army concluded that by morning Rumanian VI Corps would have no combat value worth mentioning. Hoth reported that what had taken weeks to achieve had been ruined in a day; in many places the Rumanians had offered no resistance—they had fallen victim to an "indescribable tank panic." He wanted to pull back Rumanian VII Corps, which was holding the army right flank south of VI Corps; but Army Group B refused permission on the grounds that once the Rumanians began to retreat they would not stop.

Shortly before midnight on 19 November Army Group B ordered Paulus to stop operations against the Soviet bridgeheads in Stalingrad and take three panzer divisions and an infantry division out of the city to meet the attack on his left flank. The next day the divisions, under the command of Headquarters, XIV Panzer Corps, shifted to the west bank of the Don where, together with the three divisions already there, they prevented the *Twenty-first* and *Sixty-fifth Armies* from forming a secondary pocket west of the river; but confronted by superior forces and unable to achieve full mobility because of gasoline shortages, they were not able to operate against the more important outer arm of the envelopment. The only obstacles in the path of the

Fifth Tank Army advance were the XXXXVIII Panzer Corps and remnants of Rumanian Third Army. The Rumanians hardly counted any longer, although some, notably elements of one division under the Rumanian General Mihail Lascar, fought valiantly. XXXXVIII Panzer Corps, on which Hitler at first pinned all his hopes, could not establish contact between its two divisions and in the end barely managed to escape to the west bank of the Chir River.[8] At most, all the German and Rumanian troops accomplished was to set the *Fifth Tank Army* timetable back about twenty-four hours—and this was less their doing than a consequence of the tank army's allowing itself to be drawn into local engagements contrary to its original orders. Subsequently, the army's two tank corps continued on toward Kalach and Chir Station while the cavalry corps, aided by several infantry divisions, cleared the line of the Chir River, east of which the Germans and Rumanians had no hope of holding out in any case.

On the south flank Fourth Panzer Army was no better off. The offensive had split the army in two, trapping IV Corps and the 29th Motorized Infantry Division inside the pocket forming around Stalingrad and leaving Hoth the Headquarters, Rumanian Fourth Army, Rumanian VI and VII Corps, and the 16th Motorized Infantry Division as all that remained of his army.[9] The 16th Motorized Infantry Division, protecting the Army's outer flank, was cut off at Khalkuta on the first day of the offensive and had to fight its way west to Jashkul. In that condition, Fourth Panzer Army not only could not stem the advance of the Russian units encircling Stalingrad from the south, but it had no real hope of preventing the Russians from also advancing southwest along the left bank of the Don.

In fact, though it was not known at the time, the army was saved more by the Russians' tactical shortcomings than by any efforts of its

8. On 26 November XXXXVIII Panzer Corps crossed to the west bank of the Chir with 6,000 of General Lascar's troops which it had rescued from an encirclement. Hitler, who persisted in believing that the corps was strong enough to have stopped *Fifth Tank Army*, ordered the commanding general, Generalleutnant Ferdinand Heim, back to Germany, where he was stripped of his rank and jailed without trial. Released in August 1943, still without having been tried, he was restored to rank a year later and appointed to command the Boulogne Fortress.

9. In late October, Headquarters, Rumanian Fourth Army, bringing with it the VII Corps and three divisions, had arrived to take command on the Fourth Panzer right flank.

Stalingrad in flames.

own. After the breakthrough *Fifty-seventh Army* had the relatively limited mission of turning in on the flank of Sixth Army while *Fifty-first Army* had the dual mission of sending its strongest force, a paired tank corps and cavalry corps, in a wide sweep northwestward to complete the encirclement in the vicinity of Kalach and simultaneously directing its infantry divisions southwestward toward Kotelnikovo to cover the flank. Considering the shattered state of Fourth Panzer Army, this splitting of forces should not have caused trouble; but the *Headquarters, Fifty-first Army,* was not equal to the task of controlling forces moving in divergent directions; and, as a result, the advance toward Kalach and that toward Kotelnikovo were both conducted more slowly and hesitantly than was necessary. Toward Kotelnikovo, in particular, the Russians, after their initial success, advanced cautiously. Even so, Fourth Panzer Army was in near mortal danger. On 22 November Hoth described Rumanian VI Corps as presenting "a fantastic picture of fleeing remnants."

MANSTEIN, PAULUS, HITLER

A sudden encirclement of a modern army is a cataclysmic event, comparable in its way to an earthquake or other natural disaster.

On the map it often takes on a surgically precise appearance. On the battlefield it is a rending, tearing operation that leaves the victim to struggle in a state of shock with the least favorable military situation: his lines of communications cut, headquarters separated from troops, support elements shattered, and front open to attack from all directions. The moment the ring closes every single individual in the pocket is a prisoner. Death is in front of him and behind him; home is a distant dream. Fear and panic hang in the air. Escape is the first thought in the minds of commanders and men alike, but escape is no simple matter. With the enemy on all sides, with rivers to cross, turning around an army that numbers in the hundreds of thousands with all its men, weapons, vehicles, supplies, and equipment and marching it 10, 20, 30, or more miles is a cumbersome and perilous undertaking.

The first effect of the impending encirclement is vastly to intensify the normal confusion of battle because the attack is carried into the areas most difficult to defend and because as the advance continues the victim progressively loses the points of reference, the means, and the ability to orient himself for a coherent response. That was what was happening to Sixth Army in the first days of the offensive. It was 70 miles from the Serafimovich bridgehead to the bridge at Kalach, a few miles farther to the Sixth Army's railhead at Chir Station. In between, in the angle of the Chir and the Don, lay army and corps staffs, ammunition and supply dumps, motor pools, hospitals, workshops—in short, the nerve center and practically the entire inner workings of the army. All of these merged into one southward rolling wave of men, horses, and trucks trying to escape the Soviet tanks. The Don was frozen and probably could have been crossed even by trucks, but those who would retreat east as long as they had any other choice were few. Not many had ever seen a Soviet tank or wanted to and, in fact, not many would, but rumor had the Russians everywhere. Disbelief added to the confusion; the Russians had never yet executed a completely successful breakthrough in depth.

In the Fuehrer headquarters the events were not clear, but their probable consequences were obvious. Short of a miracle, Sixth Army would either have to be permitted to withdraw from Stalingrad—which from Hitler's point of view was unthinkable—or a relief would have to be organized. On 20 November Hitler created a new army group, Army Group Don, which would be composed of Sixth Army, Rumanian Third Army, Fourth Panzer Army, and Rumanian Fourth Army, and gave Generalfeldmarschall Fritz Erich von Manstein command. Manstein was commanding Eleventh Army on the left flank of Army Group Center and would need about a week to transfer his headquarters.

Manstein's appointment completed the Stalingrad triumvirate, Hitler, Manstein, Paulus—a fateful combination of personalities.

Hitler could not stand to see an animal injured or to view the human consequences of battles, but in his headquarters remote from the battlefield, where he and his staffs dealt with unit symbols on maps and those mostly in the abstract as "blocks," he could coldbloodedly give orders that were certain to cost thousands of men their lives. Governed by emotions and inclined to rely on intuition rather than reason, he was incapable of objective or dispassionate thought on any matter that affected his own image of himself and he could, therefore, not tolerate defeat. At Stalingrad he had publicly staked his personal prestige. In the previous winter he had discovered—and successfully employed—the one reaction to military adversity that suited his personality, the rigid defense.

Manstein in his professional sphere, and without Hitler's irrationality, was nearly as much of an egoist as Hitler. In the 1930's he had held the two top posts under the Chief of Staff, OKH, in the Army General Staff and had, before the 1938 shake-up brought in Brauchitsch and Halder, been the leading candidate for the next appointment as Chief of Staff, OKH. Relegated to an assignment as army group chief of staff, he had proposed changes in the plan for the French campaign of 1940 that were received without enthusiasm in the OKH but which caught Hitler's imagination and ultimately contributed to the swift German victory. No favorite in the OKH—Brauchitsch described him as too ambitious and too conscious of his own achievements—he was first given a panzer corps to command in the Russian campaign. But Hitler held him in high regard, gave him command of Eleventh Army in September 1941, and in July 1942, after the conquest of the Crimea that culminated in the brilliantly executed capture of Sevastopol, promoted him to field marshal. Manstein, when he took command of

The Swastika over Red Square, Stalingrad.

Army Group Don, had a reputation to uphold, and possibly enlarge, as an engineer of victories and as an inspired, even daring, commander and tactician. He had Hitler's confidence. Had the Fuehrer decided to appoint another Commander in Chief, Army, he would have been one of the likeliest candidates. In his own mind Manstein seems to have begun to envision at least an appointment as Chief of Staff, OKH, with enough added authority to make him Hitler's Ludendorff.

Paulus was the ideal staff officer, thoroughly trained, conscientious, capable, hard-working, and reserved. Nearly all of his military career had been spent as a staff officer, culminating in an appointment in 1940 as *Oberquartiermeister I,* the plans chief in the OKH. Sixth Army was his first combat command and the 1942 summer offensive his first campaign in the field. He lacked the ability to inspire the personal loyalty enjoyed by some of the other army commanders, but he had fought the campaign well by professional standards. Like Manstein's his career was also on the rise. Reportedly, Hitler planned to bring him back to Fuehrer headquarters after Stalingrad to replace Jodl, who was in lingering disfavor.

On 21 November Hitler ordered Sixth Army to stand where it was "regardless of the danger of a temporary encirclement." At the same time, he promised Manstein reinforcements totaling 6 infantry divisions, 4 panzer divisions, an Air Force field division, and an antiaircraft artillery division, but of those only 2 infantry divisions were available immediately, the others not to be expected until the first week of December.

The order reached Paulus at Nizhne Chirskaya behind the Chir River and outside the developing encirclement, where the Sixth Army's winter headquarters had been built. He had stayed at his forward command post at Golubinskaya, on the bank of the Don ten miles north of Kalach, until nearly noon, when Soviet tanks headed toward Kalach came into sight on the steppe to the west. The XIV Panzer Corps staff moved into the headquarters at Golubinskaya and from there, with parts of the 14th and 16th Panzer Divisions, tried to lure the Russian spearhead into a stationary battle. Wherever they could, the Russian tanks ignored the Germans and roared on past. *IV Tank Corps* lost a little speed. Its neighbor on the west, *XXVI Tank Corps,* was not affected at all. In a daring raid before dawn on the morning of 22 November, a battalion from *XXVI Tank Corps* captured the Don bridge at Kalach and formed a hedgehog around it.

That morning, Paulus flew into the pocket. From the Gumrak airfield, he informed Hitler by radio that the Russians had taken Kalach and that Sixth Army was encircled. In the strictest sense, the report was not correct. The Germans in Kalach held out until the next day; it was late on that day, the 23rd, that, after an exchange of green recognition flares, *IV Tank Corps,* which had crossed the Don and covered the intervening ten miles, met *IV Cavalry Corps* at Sovetskiy, and closed the ring.

In the message to Hitler on 22 November, Paulus also stated that he did not have any kind of a front on the south rim of the pocket, between Kalach and Karpovka; therefore, he would have to call XIV Panzer Corps back and use its divisions to close the gap. If enough supplies could be flown in and the gap could be closed—the latter doubtful because of shortages of motor fuel—he intended to form a perimeter around Stalingrad. If a front could not be established in the south, the only solution, as he saw it, was to evacuate Stalingrad, give up the north front, pull the army together, and break out to the southwest toward Fourth Panzer Army. He requested discretionary authority to give such orders if they became necessary.

Having waited in vain throughout the day on the 23rd for a decision from Hitler and by then aware that the Russians had plugged the last gap, completing the cordon, Paulus that night radioed a second appeal to the OKH in which he stated that the German front still open in the south would expose the army to destruction "in the very shortest time" if the breakout were not attempted. As the first step he would have to strip the northern front and deploy the troops south for the escape effort. He again asked for freedom of decision, buttressing his request with the statement that his five corps commanders concurred in his estimate. In a separate message Weichs seconded Paulus' request; and during the night General der Artillerie Walter von Seydlitz-Kurzbach, Commanding General, LI Corps, concluding that a breakout was inevitable and that Hitler would have to be presented with a *fait accompli,* began pulling back several of his divisions on the northeastern tip of the pocket—which brought a prompt and angry protest from Hitler.[10] Seydlitz, for whom destiny was preparing

---

10. On 24 November Hitler demanded a report on the LI Corps' withdrawal and forbade any further measures contrary to Operations Order 1. Weichs attempted to gloss over the matter by explaining that the troops had been taken back to prepared positions in order to gain a division for other employment; but Hitler was not convinced and, suspicious of Paulus, gave Seydlitz, of whose action he apparently was not aware, command of the entire north front, making him personally responsible for holding that side of the pocket.

a unique place among the Stalingrad generals, was in personality the antithesis of Paulus, impulsive, temperamental, and enterprising.

Manstein, who also submitted an estimate to the OKH, was less positive than Paulus and Weichs. He agreed that the breakout was the safest course and that an attempt to hold out was extremely dangerous; but he did not support an immediate attempt. He believed a relief operation could start in early December if the promised reinforcements were made available. At the same time, he warned that the breakout could still become necessary if the relief forces could not be assembled.

That Hitler was not being influenced by any of these communications soon became clear. On 24 November he ordered Sixth Army to draw the northwest and southwest fronts inward slightly and then hold the pocket. He promised to supply the army by air.[11] Over Zeitzler's strenuously expressed doubts, Goering had assured him that the Air Force would be able to transport 600 tons of supplies per day into the pocket. Hitler also ordered Fourth Panzer Army to stop the Russians north of Kotelnikovo and get ready to counterattack north to re-establish contact with the Sixth Army.

Two days later Hitler set out the details of his intentions in a message to Manstein. To evacuate Stalingrad would mean giving up the "most substantial achievement" of the 1942 summer campaign; therefore, the city would have to be held regardless of the cost, especially since to retake it in 1943 would require even greater sacrifices. Fourth Panzer Army was to "extend a hand" to Sixth Army from the Kotelnikovo area and hold a bridgehead around the confluence of the Don and Chir Rivers to facilitate a secondary advance to Stalingrad from the west. When contact with Sixth Army was re-established supplies would be moved in, the city would be held, and Army Group Don could begin to prepare for a northward advance to clear out the area of the breakthrough between the Don and the Chir.

After he had made his decision Hitler was confident. That feeling was not shared at the front. On receiving the Hitler order of 24 November,

---

11. At the same time Hitler declared Stalingrad a fortress, a designation of no particular military significance under the circumstances other than as emphasizing his determination to stay there at all costs.

Seydlitz told Paulus there could be no question of holding; the army had either to break out or succumb within a short time. He believed supplies, which had already been running short before the Russian offensive began, would decide the issue; and to base any hopes on air supply was to grasp at a straw since only thirty JU-52's were at hand (on 23 November), and even if hundreds more could be assembled, a feat which was doubtful, the army's full requirements would still not be met. Paulus commented sharply that Seydlitz was interfering in affairs which were no concern of his but nonetheless agreed in substance and on 26 November in a personal letter to Manstein again asked permission to act at his own discretion if necessary, pointing out that the first three days of air supply had brought only a fraction of the promised 600 tons and 300 JU-52's per day. Manstein, who assumed command of Army Group Don on 27 November, knew Hitler's plans and did not reply.

THE RUSSIANS NEGLECT THE FLANKS

As bad as the situation at Stalingrad was, it could have been far worse. Once the Russians had completed the encirclement, they devoted their main strength to fastening the hold on Sixth Army and virtually discontinued the offensive in the Chir River and Fourth Panzer Army sectors. By 28 November they had concentrated 94 brigades and divisions against Sixth Army and about 49 opposing the remnants of Rumanian Third Army and Fourth Panzer Army, no more than 20 of those in the line.

On the German side, the line of the Chir was held in the north by XVII Corps and, south to the confluence of the Chir and Don, by Rumanian Third Army. XVII Corps had two German divisions and most of the remaining Rumanian troops. Rumanian Third Army existed in name only; its headquarters was manned by German staff officers and its front held by a scratch force of smaller German units.[12] In the

---

12. In the German Army among all ranks disgust at the conduct of the Rumanian units was widespread; and until well into 1943 Hitler and the Army Group commands had to intervene periodically with orders forbidding open expressions of contempt. Observers who retained some objectivity concluded that the individual Rumanian was not a bad soldier, but that he was poorly trained, badly led, and miserably equipped. The Rumanians argued that they had made no secret of their capabilities. One point on which most Germans and, at least, the rank and file

Germans amid the ruins of Stalingrad.

Fourth Panzer Army sector the remnants of Fourth Panzer Army and Rumanian VI and VII Corps were redesignated Armeegruppe Hoth.[13] Under Hoth, Headquarters, Rumanian Fourth Army, took command of the two Rumanian corps. With the Rumanians and a scattering of German rear area troops, Hoth attempted to stop the Russians north of Kotelnikovo; but, he reported on 24 November, if they made anything approaching a serious effort they could not help but have the "greatest" success. By 27 November Kotelnikovo was within Russian artillery range, but *Stalingrad Front* and *Fifty-first Army* were moving cautiously; and in the last four days of the month the first transports of German troops for the counterattack began to arrive.

WINTERGEWITTER

Hitler's decision to hold Sixth Army at Stalingrad had embodied two assumptions: sufficient forces to conduct a successful relief operation could be assembled; and Sixth Army could be maintained as a viable

---

of the Rumanians agreed was that the Rumanian officer corps, with very few exceptions, was thoroughly incompetent, corrupt, and divided by political quarrels. Army Group B reported that in the early stages of the offensive, division and corps staffs took to their heels without bothering about their troops.

13. The change had been planned before the Russian attack as a means of keeping closer control of the Rumanian units after Headquarters, Rumanian Fourth Army, assumed command.

fighting force by air supply until that was accomplished. The air supply problem appeared to be one of simple arithmetic, of matching the number of planes to tonnages. Such was not the case, but even if it had been, the problem would still have been beyond solution. In late November 1942, the German Air Force was undergoing its greatest strain since the start of the war. At Stalingrad and in North Africa, it was fighting a two-front war in earnest. By the end of November 400 combat aircraft had gone out of the USSR to North Africa, reducing the total strength by one-sixth and the effective strength by nearly one-third. Of 2,000 planes left in the east, the OKW estimated 1,120 were operational on 29 November.

Generaloberst Wolfram von Richthofen, commanding Fourth Air Force, reported on 25 November that he had 298 trimotor JU-52 transports; to supply Stalingrad he needed 500. He recommended that Sixth Army be allowed to break out, a suggestion which Hitler "rejected out of hand." The subsequent employment of HE-111 twin-engine bombers as transports further reduced the number of aircraft available for combat missions without decisively improving the air supply. As it was, even the number of aircraft at hand could not be organized into an effective airlift across enemy-held territory, through contested air space, in uncertain weather, and without adequate ground support. On 29 November, 38 JU-52's (load 1 ton per plane) and 21 HE-111's (maximum load 1,000 pounds) took off. Of those, 12 JU-52's and 13 HE-111's landed inside the pocket. The following day 30 JU-52's and 36 HE-111's landed out of 39 and 38 committed. If Sixth Army was to be saved, it would have to be done soon.

On 1 December Army Group Don began preparations for Operation WINTERGEWITTER, the relief of Sixth Army, assigning the main effort to Fourth Panzer Army's LVII Panzer Corps which with two fresh panzer divisions (6th and 23d) then on the way would advance northeastward from the vicinity of Kotelnikovo toward Stalingrad. Rumanian VI and VII Corps were to protect the flanks. For the secondary effort Fourth Panzer Army was given XXXXVIII Panzer Corps to strike toward Kalach out of the small German bridgehead astride the confluence of the Don and Chir Rivers. Headquarters, XXXXVIII Panzer Corps, left its two original divisions, the 22d Panzer

Division and the 1st Rumanian Armored Division, on the Chir front and assumed command in the bridgehead of three divisions then arriving, the 11th Panzer Division, 336th Infantry Division, and 7th Air Force Field Division. Paulus was to concentrate all of his armor on the southwest rim of the pocket and be ready to strike toward LVII Panzer Corps if ordered. He was also to be prepared to break out toward Kalach, but was at the same time to hold the fronts on the north and in Stalingrad. Manstein wanted to be ready to start any time after daybreak on 8 December.

DOUBTS AND DELAYS

The outlook for WINTERGEWITTER was not auspicious from the first and grew less promising with each passing day. Sixth Army moved two motorized divisions and one panzer division with 80 tanks to its southwest front for the breakthrough, but beginning on 2 December the *Don* and *Stalingrad Fronts* for a week staged a full-fledged effort to liquidate the pocket and tied down the three divisions in defensive fighting. On 3 December the Russians also became active along the Chir in the Rumanian Third Army sector, forcing Manstein to commit there the divisions for XXXXVIII Panzer Corps and making it extremely unlikely that the corps would be able to participate in the advance toward Stalingrad. Further, the divisions for LVII Panzer Corps were slow in arriving, and the OKH instructed the army group to use the Air Force field divisions, one with XXXXVIII Panzer Corps and one with Fourth Panzer Army, for defensive missions only.

By 9 December WINTERGEWITTER had dwindled to a two-division operation. Nevertheless, the next day Manstein decided to go ahead, and he set the time for the morning of 12 December, having to delay that much because freezing weather had just begun to set in after several days' rain and thaw had made the roads impassable. A further postponement, he believed, could not be tolerated because supplies were running short in the pocket and because Soviet armor had been detected moving in opposite Fourth Panzer Army. Sixth Army reported that an average of only 70 tons of supplies per day had been flown in and that ammunition stocks were declining dangerously and rations, except for odds and ends, would run out by 19 December.

Weichs, Paulus and Seydlitz at LI Army Corps Headquarters.

Hitler was optimistic. On 3 December, answering a gloomy Army Group Don report, he cautioned Manstein to bear in mind that the Soviet divisions were always smaller and weaker than they first appeared to be and that the Soviet Command was probably thrown off balance by its own success. A week later his confidence had grown, and, concluding that the first phase of the Soviet winter offensive could be considered ended without having achieved a decisive success, he returned to the idea of retaking the line on the Don. By 10 December his thinking had progressed to the point where he planned to move the 7th and 17th Panzer Divisions to the Army Group Don left flank and use them to spearhead an advance from the Chir to the Don. The next day he ordered Manstein to station the 17th Panzer Division in the XVII Corps sector, thereby, for the time being, ending the possibility of its being used to support Fourth Panzer Army's attack toward Stalingrad.

WINTERGEWITTER BEGINS

Jumping off on time on the morning of 12 December—the German forces being probably about equal to those opposing them—LVII Panzer Corps made good, though not spectacular, progress. During the afternoon situation conference at Fuehrer headquarters, Zeitzler tried to persuade Hitler to release the 17th Panzer Division for WINTERGEWITTER; but Hitler refused because a Russian threat appeared to be building up on the Army Group Don left flank where it joined the right flank of the Italian Eighth Army. In the conference he restated his position on Stalingrad, saying, "I have reached one conclusion, Zeitzler. We cannot under any circumstances give that [pointing to Stalingrad] up. We will not retake it. We know what that means… if we give up that we sacrifice the whole sense of this campaign. To imagine that I will get there again next time is insanity."

On the second day Of WINTERGEWITTER, LVII Panzer Corps reached the Aksay River and captured the bridge at Zalivskiy; but, on the Chir and at the Don-Chir bridgehead XXXXVIII Panzer Corps barely held its own against the *Fifth Tank* and *Fifth Shock Armies,* which were attempting to fasten the Soviet hold on Sixth Army by enlarging the buffer zone on the west. Before noon Manstein reported to Hitler that the trouble on the Chir had eliminated any chance of XXXXVIII Panzer Corps' releasing forces for a thrust out of the bridgehead and that without such help LVII Panzer Corps, east of the Don, could not restore contact with Sixth Army. He wanted the 17th Panzer Division to take over the attack from the bridgehead and the 16th Motorized Infantry Division—then stationed between the Army Group Don and Army Group A flanks—to support the LVII Panzer Corps offensive. Concerning Hitler's plan for an advance to the Don north of Stalingrad, he stated that it could not start before 10 January 1943 if at all, and, in the meantime, the success of WINTERGEWITTER had to be assured by all possible means. Hitler released the 17th Panzer Division but not the 16th Motorized Infantry Division. The decision regarding the 17th Panzer was made somewhat easier by a growing impression that the Russians were merely simulating the offensive build-up opposite the Army Group Don left flank.

THE OUTCOME

During the next four days WINTERGEWITTER went ahead but without gaining enough momentum to ensure an early success. On 14 December that part of the Don-Chir bridgehead east of the Don had to be evacuated. The attack out of the bridgehead would have been abandoned in any case since the one-division reinforcement Hitler had approved was by then needed in the LVII Panzer Corps sector. On the 17th and 18th, LVII Panzer Corps, increased to three divisions by the arrival of the 17th Panzer Division, became tied down in fighting around Kumsky, half way between the Aksav and Mishkova Rivers.

On the 19th LVII Panzer Corps suddenly shook itself loose and pushed to the Mishkova, thirty-five miles from the pocket. Manstein, however, informed Hitler that LVII Panzer Corps probably could not achieve contact with Sixth Army and certainly could not open a permanent corridor into the pocket. He believed the only answer was to order the army to break out, gradually pulling back its fronts on the north and in Stalingrad as it moved toward LVII Panzer Corps. That, he maintained, would, at least, save most of the troops and whatever equipment could still be moved. To Sixth Army he sent advance notice of the breakout order. The army's mission, he stated, would have to include an initial breakout to the Mishkova where, after contact with LVII Panzer Corps was established, truck convoys which were moving up 3,000 tons of supplies behind the corps would be sluiced through to the pocket. Subsequently Sixth Army, taking along what equipment it could, would evacuate the pocket and withdraw southwestward. The army was to get ready but not start until ordered.

Hitler, encouraged by LVII Panzer Corps' recent success, refused to approve. Instead, he ordered the SS Panzer Grenadier Division Wiking transferred from Army Group A to Fourth Panzer Army. Sixth Army, he insisted, was to hold out until a firm contact was established and a complete, orderly withdrawal could be accomplished. In the meantime, enough supplies were to be flown in, particularly gasoline, to give the army thirty miles' mobility; Hitler had heard that the army's vehicles had fuel for no more than eighteen miles.

On 21 December, after LVII Panzer Corps had failed to get beyond the Mishkova in two days' fighting, Generalmajor Friedrich Schulz, Chief of Staff, Army Group Don, conferred with Generalmajor Arthur Schmidt, Chief of Staff, Sixth Army, over a newly installed decimeter wave telecommunications system. After Schmidt, replying to a question forwarded from OKH, declared that the army's fuel on hand was only enough for twelve miles, Schulz turned to the question of a breakout. Permission for the breakout and evacuation, he stated, had not been received; but because of the unlikelihood of LVII Panzer Corps' getting any farther north, Manstein wanted to go ahead as soon as possible. Schmidt replied that the breakout could begin on 24 December, but he did not believe the army could continue to hold the pocket thereafter if heavy losses were incurred; if Stalingrad was to be held it would be better to fly in supplies and replacements, in which case the army could hold out indefinitely. He and Paulus thought the chances for success would be better if the evacuation followed immediately upon the breakout, but they regarded the evacuation as an act of desperation to be avoided until it became absolutely necessary. The conference ended on that indeterminate note.

Manstein transmitted the results of the conference to OKH. He could give no assurance, he added, that if the army were to hold out contact could be re-established. Further substantial gains by LVII Panzer Corps were not to be expected. In effect, WINTERGEWITTER had failed. Later that day Hitler conferred at length with the Chiefs of Staff, OKH and OKL, but to those present "the Fuehrer seemed no longer capable of making a decision."

CHAPTER IV

Stalingrad, the Turning Point

SIXTH ARMY ISOLATED

By the end of the 1942 summer campaign the southern flank of the Eastern Front was split in two. Army Groups A and B stood almost back to back nearly four hundred miles apart, the one facing south along the high ridge of the Caucasus, the other northeast along the west bank of the Don. The whole Army Group B front on the Don had one function—to protect the forces to the south, at first Sixth Army and Army Group A, later also Army Group Don. That mission, not crucial as long as the offensive kept rolling, had fallen chiefly to the allied armies. In mid-December Hungarian Second Army and Italian Eighth Army still held the 200-mile front on the Don south of Voronezh. Their future performance was predictable: of the three allied armies the Rumanians had been considered the best.

A glance at the map reveals how vulnerable Army Groups Don and A were; they dangled like puppets on strings at the ends of the few railroads that reached into the steppe east of the Don and Donets. (Map 5) The critical points on those lines were the river crossings. Everything east of the Dnepr Bend depended on the bridges at Dnepropetrovsk and Zaporozhye. The distance from Dnepropetrovsk to the Russian line at Novaya Kalitva in the center of the Italian Eighth Army sector was 250 miles, while from Dnepropetrovsk to the Army Group Don front on the Chir River the distance was 330 miles and to the left flank of Army Group A, 580 miles. But the Russians did not need to strike that far west. On the left flank of Army Group Don they were within 80 miles of the three Donets crossings: Voroshilovgrad, Kamensk, and Belokalitvenskaya. A 150-mile march from the left flank of Army Group Don would take them to Rostov. Both Army Group A and Fourth Panzer Army were entirely dependent on the railroad through Rostov. The Army Group A left flank was 350 miles

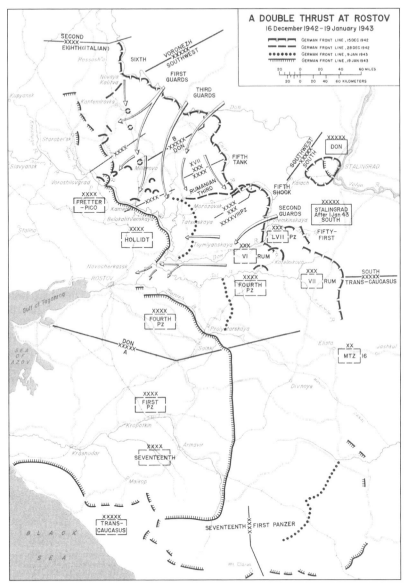

Map 5: A Double Thrust at Rostov, 16 December 1942-19 January 1943

and the Fourth Panzer Army right flank 220 miles from Rostov.
Although the Stavka was not yet so self-confident as to set about
trying to bag two army groups in a single sweep, geography, the state
of the German forces, and Hitler's generalship were encouraging such
an attempt.

SOUTHWEST FRONT RENEWS THE OFFENSIVE

In late November, when it could be seen that the Germans would attempt to relieve Stalingrad, the Stavka gave Southwest Front the mission of creating a massive diversion by attacking southwest and west against the Italian Eighth and Rumanian Third Army fronts from Novaya Kalitva south to the mouth of the Chir. Zhukov planned and co-ordinated the operation as representative of the Stavka, leaving Stalingrad to Vasilevskiy.[14] The offensive was to go deep—to the lower Kalitva, the Donets, and the Derkul. When the planning began Southwest Front had the First Guards and Fifth Tank Armies. Subsequently First Guards Army was enlarged, then split—its right flank becoming Third Guards Army—and Voronezh Front's Sixth Army was attached.

In December, when the front around the Stalingrad pocket had stabilized, the Russians began to get nervous. The almost simultaneous failure of the Fifth Tank Army—Fifth Shock Army offensive on the lower Chir and the beginning of WINTERGEWITTER south of Stalingrad increased the nervousness, briefly at least, to a near case of jitters. Southwest Front's offensive, conceived as an embellishment, began to look like a salvage operation. Under orders, Vatutin changed the main direction from southwest to southeast and reduced the projected depth of the advance by half.

On 16 December the Russians began to move again. Soviet Sixth Army broke through the Italian line east of Novaya Kalitva, sweeping an Italian corps out of its path. In the succeeding days Vatutin committed the First and Third Guards Armies to extend the breakthrough downstream along the Don. On the 10th the Celere and Sforzesca Divisions on the Italian Eighth Army right flank collapsed, carrying with them two Rumanian divisions on the left flank of Army Group Don. In four days the Russians had ripped open a 100-mile hole

---

14. The Soviet official history, which plays down Zhukov's role throughout but makes a particular effort to do so in connection with Stalingrad, states that Stalin on 27 November instructed Vasilevskiy to devote his full attention to Stalingrad and, as to the Southwest Front's offensive, said, "Let Vatutin and Kuznetsov [General Leytenant V. I. Kuznetsov, Commanding General, First Guards Army] handle it alone." (IVOV (R), III, 43.) It is inconceivable that Stalin at this stage would have casually entrusted so important an operation to a front and an army commander.

and were driving south behind Army Group Don toward Millerovo and the Donets crossings.

For the Germans, the first problem was somehow to screen the deep northern flank of Army Group Don. The OKH transferred a corps headquarters, commanded by General der Artillerie Maximilian Fretter-Pico, from Army Group North to take over the right flank of Army Group B as the Armeeabteilung Fretter-Pico. It gave the Armeeabteilung one fresh infantry division, the headquarters and elements of the 3d Mountain Division, and remnants of a weak German corps that had attempted to backstop the Italians. Fretter-Pico's mission was to protect the Donets bridges east of Voroshilovgrad and at Kamensk, establish a line away from the river, and tie in with Army Group Don.

On 23 December Manstein informed Hitler that the breakthrough on the army group left flank required an immediate shift of at least one division, perhaps two, from LVII Panzer Corps. That would mean relinquishing the idea of relieving Sixth Army soon and necessitate long-term air supply for the army. The army needed 550 tons of supplies a day; but von Richthofen, commanding Fourth Air Force, believed 200 tons a day was the most that could be delivered. If, as it appeared, air supply could not be guaranteed, Manstein saw a breakout as the only solution despite the risk. He pointed out that the appearance of Soviet reinforcements along the Mishkova meant the Russians would soon also be able to go over to the offensive there, a situation which was extremely dangerous since Fourth Panzer Army was relying on Rumanian troops to cover its flanks.

Hitler's decision, in fact no decision at all, came in the early hours of the following morning. He authorized the transfer of "elements" of LVII Panzer Corps to the army group left flank to protect at Morozovsk and Tatsinskaya the air bases which were essential for Sixth Army's air supply. But the LVII Panzer Corps main force was to stay on the Mishkova until the advance toward Stalingrad could be resumed. As if it would make all the difference, he informed Manstein that one battalion of Tiger tanks being sent by railroad to the army group would that day cross into Russia near Brest-Litovsk.

THE LAST CHANCE FOR SIXTH ARMY

A month is a long time to an encircled army. Its moral and physical sustenance reduced to the thinnest streams, it begins to wither. The entire organism is affected, most dramatically and dismayingly the men themselves. In 1941 the Germans had noticed and then forgotten that large numbers of Russians captured in the great encirclements died suddenly without detectable symptoms. In December, the same sort of deaths began to be reported in the Stalingrad pocket. A pathologist flown in to perform autopsies in secret discovered that undernourishment, exhaustion, and exposure had caused the complete loss of fatty tissue, changes in the internal organs and the bone marrow and, as the apparent cause of death, a shrinking of the heart except for the right ventricle, which was greatly enlarged. Such heart damage, in normal medical practice, had been regarded as a condition that chiefly affected the aged; among the soldiers of Sixth Army at Stalingrad, as the days passed, it was observed to be common in both the dead and the living. In the Stalingrad pocket death was no novelty. Sixth Army lost 28,000 men between 22 November and 23 December.

On 18 December the army reported a ration strength of 246,000, including 13,000 Rumanians, 19,300 Russian auxiliaries, and 6,000 wounded; but that was far from representing its effective combat strength. Already in mid-October the army had reported that it was reduced to a front-line infantry strength of 56,500. Service troops were converted to infantry, but experience showed that even under the exceptional conditions of an encirclement, such conversions were neither easy to accomplish nor especially worthwhile in terms of combat effectiveness.

At the end of the first month, the hard winter had not yet set in. The temperature lingered close to freezing—some days above, some below. Cold days were apt to be clear and only occasionally snowy or windy. Warmer days brought clouds, fog, light rain, snow, and, always when there were two or three such days in succession, mud. Not as extreme as it might have been, the weather, nevertheless, was not easily borne by soldiers who were inadequately sheltered and clothed and were living on slender rations of bread, soup, and occasional horse meat.

The instability of the weather also seriously affected the air supply. In the early winter, particularly, continental and maritime air masses met over the region of the lower Don and Volga, producing not only frequent and rapid changes in the weather but great variations within relatively short distances. Consequently, when the skies over the air bases at Tatsinskaya and Morozovsk were clear the Stalingrad pocket was sometimes buried in fog.

The relief attempt had failed. That another could be made or that the army could survive until then were both daily becoming more doubtful. On the afternoon of 23 December, Manstein called for a teletype conference with Paulus. He asked Paulus to consider whether, if no other course remained open, the breakout (which by then was assumed automatically to include the evacuation) could be executed provided limited quantities of motor fuel and rations were flown in during the next few days. Paulus replied that the breakout had become more difficult because the Russians had strengthened their line, but if it had to be, it was better done right away than later. Then he asked, "Do you empower me to begin the preparations? Once begun they cannot be reversed."

Manstein replied, "That authority I cannot give today. I am hoping for a decision tomorrow. The essential point is do you consider the army capable of forcing its way through to Hoth if supplies for a longer period cannot be assured?" Paulus answered, "In that case, there is nothing else to be done." He thought the army would need six days to get ready and an added 300,000 gallons of motor fuel plus 500 tons of rations.

Within the hour Manstein dispatched a situation estimate to Hitler in which he outlined three possibilities: (1) leave the army where it was and assure a daily air supply of at least 500 tons; (2) order Paulus to break out, taking the risk that the army might not get through; (3) transfer immediately the 16th Motorized Infantry Division and two panzer divisions from First Panzer Army (Army Group A) to enable Fourth Panzer Army to resume the advance toward Stalingrad. Again Hitler could not make up his mind and, in lieu of a decision, the next day countered with a series of questions. Was a breakout actually possible, and would it succeed? When could it start? How long could

Devastation along the railroad southeast of Stalingrad.

Paulus stay in the pocket, given the current level of supplies or, perhaps "somewhat" increased air supply? When could the relief operation be resumed if Manstein were given both the SS Panzer Grenadier Division Wiking and the 7th Panzer Division? Did Manstein think the Russians would soon be stopped by supply and fuel shortages? Would Manstein "welcome" being given command of Army Group A as well as Don in light of the fact "that the further developments could lead to momentous decisions?" (Hitler had relinquished personal command of Army Group A on 22 November and turned over command to Generalfeldmarschall Ewald von Kleist.)

Mainstein answered that the breakout could begin, as reported, in six days. As to success, nobody could predict that with certainty; and, if even a moderate degree of assurance were desired, it would be necessary to transfer two more divisions from First Panzer Army. The SS Wiking Division and the 7th Panzer Division would be needed on the army group left flank when they arrived. There were no reasons for thinking the Russians would run out of supplies. As far as his also taking command of Army Group A was concerned, nobody would "welcome" it in the existing circumstances, but it was unavoidable. Even so, it appeared that for Sixth Army, and Army Groups Don and

A as well, the announced "momentous decisions" would come too late. Manstein concluded, "I ask that it be considered how the battle would develop if we commanded on the other side."

OPERATIONS ORDER 2

On 24 December Vatutin pushed a spearhead through to Tatsinskaya and came within artillery range of Morozovsk. That same day Second Guards Army, rushed to the Mishkova by Stalingrad Front, threw LVII Panzer Corps back to the Aksay River. To hold the air supply base for Sixth Army at Morozovsk and recapture the one at Tatsinskaya, Manstein had to take the 11th Panzer Division from the hard-pressed Fourth Panzer Army. He created the Headquarters, Armeeabteilung Hollidt, under General der Infanterie Karl Hollidt, and gave it command of the north flank. The Headquarters, Rumanian Third Army, he sent behind the Donets to reorganize the Rumanian stragglers and start building defenses downstream from Kamensk.

To gain a respite north of Tatsinskaya-Morozovsk, Manstein had been forced to reduce Fourth Panzer Army's effective strength by a third; nevertheless, Hitler still hoped to bring up the 7th Panzer Division and the SS Panzer Grenadier Division Wiking in time to renew the advance toward Stalingrad. Manstein's situation report of 25 December demonstrated how slight that hope was. In a day or two, he said, the Fifty-first and the Second Guards Armies would attempt to encircle Fourth Panzer Army on the Aksay River. Nothing could be expected of Rumanian VI and VII Corps, and the two divisions of LVII Panzer Corps could muster no more than nineteen tanks between them. If Sixth Army was not to be left entirely in the lurch at Stalingrad, a panzer corps (two divisions) and an infantry division would have to be shifted from Army Group A to Fourth Panzer Army and at least one infantry division to the Army Group Don left flank.

The next two days proved that Manstein was by no means painting too dark a picture. On the 26th Paulus reported that casualties, cold—the temperature that day was -15° F.—and hunger had so sapped his army's strength that it could not execute the breakout and evacuation unless a supply corridor into the pocket was opened first. The next day Rumanian VII Corps, holding the LVII Panzer Corps flank on the east, collapsed and fell into a disorganized retreat, leaving the German corps stranded. Hoth hoped to get the panzer corps back to Kotelnikovo where it might make another temporary stand.

On the 27th Hitler, looking for a cheap way out, ordered Army Groups Don and A to hold where they were while Army Group B, to protect the rear of Don, retook the line of the Rossosh'-Millerovo railroad. Army Group A, he told Manstein, could not spare any divisions, and Army Group Don would have to make do with the SS Wiking, the 7th Panzer Division, and the battalion of Tiger tanks. The only hint of flexibility was an order to Army Group A to begin evacuating its wounded and scout a bridgehead on the Taman Peninsula. Manstein protested that Fourth Panzer Army's 2 panzer divisions and the 16th Motorized Infantry Division faced a total of 43 enemy units (brigades and divisions, tank, cavalry, and mechanized corps) while First Panzer Army in a well-constructed line was opposed only by an equal number, and Seventeenth Army had to deal with no more than 24 Soviet units. He was convinced, he wrote, that events would compel a shift of forces from A to Don. The sooner the decision to do so was made the cheaper it would be in the long run.

Hitler countered with Operations Order 2. Army Group A, holding its line on the Black Sea coast and in the Caucasus, would swing its right flank back by stages to Salsk, where it would be able to take over its own flank defense. Fourth Panzer Army, if forced to, could fall back to the line Tsymlyanskaya-Salsk. To co-ordinate those movements Manstein would assume command of Army Group A at a time to be decided by Manstein himself. Hitler passed over in silence Manstein's earlier contention that his taking command of both army groups would be worthwhile only if it included full operational freedom.

The last days of the year brought another crisis. On the afternoon of 28 December Fourth Panzer Army had to rescue LVII Panzer Corps by permitting it to withdraw from Kotelnikovo to the Sal River. That opened up the south bank of the Don to Rostov and exposed the deep right flank of Armeeabteilung Hollidt. The next day the Russians pushed out of a small bridgehead they held around Potemkinskaya, and Hollidt had to shift the 11th Panzer Division to Tsymlyanskaya, seventy miles downstream, to brake their advance. Because of the growing danger, Hitler ordered the 7th Panzer Division held at Rostov for a possible last-ditch defense of the city.

On the 28th Manstein reported to Hitler that Fourth Panzer Army was no longer capable of holding a broad front south of the Don and that the Armeeabteilung Hollidt line could be penetrated from the north or south at any time. He intended to turn Fourth Panzer Army east south of the Sal River to protect the rear of Army Group A, taking the chance that the Russians might cut through to Rostov between the Sal and the Don. Armeeabteilung Hollidt would have to be pulled back, possibly, to a line slightly forward of the Donets, more likely to the river itself.

On New Year's Eve Manstein told Paulus that the army group's first objective was to liberate Sixth Army, but the army would have to hold out in the pocket a while longer. Hitler, he said, had ordered Goering to increase the air supply to at least 300 tons a day. Whether he knew it or not, Manstein had said farewell to Sixth Army. Army Group Don would henceforth be fighting for its own life. Southwest Front's armies, having reached their original end objectives, were surging past Millerovo on the east and west toward the Donets between Voroshilovgrad and Belokalitvenskaya. Stalingrad Front, after transfer of its three armies on the south face of the Stalingrad pocket to Don Front, was renamed South Front on 1 January and given the mission of attacking toward Rostov on both sides of the Don with the Fifth Shock, Second Guards, and Fifty-first Armies.

Ignoring Manstein's report of the 28th, Hitler, on New Year's Day, announced in a supplement to Operations Order 2 that he was going to send the Grossdeutschland Division and the SS Divisions Adolf Hitler, Das Reich, and 7th SS to relieve Stalingrad. Army Groups B and Don were to hold the most favorable positions for the jump-off. All the provisions of Operations Order No. 2 remained in effect. In it he had given permission for Hollidt to withdraw no farther than the line Morozovsk-Tsymlyanskaya.

Even Hitler did not expect the divisions for the relief to be deployed before mid-February. To imagine that Fate and the Russians would allow that much time was the merest self-deception.

At the turn of the year, very little had been accomplished. The withdrawals Hitler approved were piecemeal; he still talked in terms of "definitive" lines and was beginning to lose himself in nebulous plans for a counteroffensive. The decision to bend back the left flank of Army Group A was a significant step, but after he had issued the order he showed no desire to see it executed quickly and, on the contrary, seemed to welcome delays.

On 2 January, in a dispatch to Zeitzler, Manstein no longer attempted to conceal his irritation. He pointed out angrily that although it could have been seen as soon as Sixth Army was encircled that the Russians were developing a major offensive on the southern flank of the Eastern Front and might strike into the rear of Army Group A, nothing had been done until the last few days about evacuating the wounded and the heavy equipment from the Caucasus. The consequences of that neglect would be either to slow the movements of Army Group A or to force a sacrifice of large quantities of equipment. Because the OKH (Hitler) was controlling all the substantial shifts of Army Group A forces no purpose would be served by Army Group Don's taking over A. Since the OKH had ordered the divisions intended for Fourth Panzer Army, the 7th and 11th Panzer Divisions, sent elsewhere, all Army Group Don could do was to instruct Hoth to hold as long as he could keep his flanks free. Army Group A would have to speed up its withdrawal and transfer a corps to Salsk. Unlike some that had gone before, this communication had at least one effect: Hitler did not again mention Manstein's taking command of Army Group A.

RETREAT TO THE MANICH AND THE DONETS

In the first week of the new year Armeeabteilung Hollidt began a hectic 90-mile retreat to the Donets. On 3 January Armeeabteilung Fretter-Pico reported that the 304th Infantry Division, which had been assigned the mission of keeping touch with Hollidt's left flank, could not be depended on. It lacked training and combat experience; panic was breaking out in the ranks. East of the Fretter-Pico—Hollidt boundary the Russians had massed two tank corps for an attack toward the Donets crossing at Belokalitvenskaya, and Hitler, on 4 January, had to release the 4th Panzer Division to prevent a breakthrough.

On the 5th, having retreated forty miles in six days, Hollidt gave up Morozovsk, the air base closest to Stalingrad. The next day Hitler tried to call a halt "for the sake of morale and to conserve the strength of the troops"; but with the Russians probing across the Don in the south and threatening to advance down the Donets from the north Hollidt had not a chance of holding any line east of the Donets more than a few days.

On the other side of the Don, Fourth Panzer Army ranged its two panzer divisions and the Wiking Division along the Kuberle River, which flowed into the Sal from the south. In the gap between the Don and the Sal the III Guards Tank Corps pushed downstream along the south bank of the Don and at the end of the first week of January sent reconnaissance patrols to within twenty miles of Rostov. Hitler urged Manstein to commit the Tiger tanks, which he predicted would be able to destroy a Soviet tank corps; but when the Tigers went into action for the first time they failed to live up to that expectation. They claimed to have destroyed eighteen enemy tanks, but of the twenty Tigers half were damaged. Hoth reported that the tank crews needed more training and experience.

When a motorized corps and guards rifle corps began making their way around Fourth Panzer Army's north flank, Hitler, on 6 January, had to permit Manstein to withdraw the 16th Motorized Infantry Division from Elista. Manstein warned that the division could do no more than stabilize the Fourth Panzer Army line temporarily. He again asked for a panzer corps from Army Group A and complained bitterly that everything was expected of Don while nothing was possible for A.

In the second week of January, even though the crisis deepened, the fronts of the two southern army groups began to assume some coherence. Armeeabteilung Hollidt, shifting its panzer divisions back and forth to counter threats from the north and south, continued its march to the Donets. Hitler permitted Fourth Panzer Army to swing back to a line facing north along the Manich Canal. First Panzer Army, though slowed by its heavy equipment and by what Manstein, at least, considered exaggerated worries about what the Russians might do, gradually narrowed the gap between the army groups.

Wrecked German equipment on the outskirts of Stalingrad.

Between 15 and 19 January the stage was set for new decisions which, in fact, were already overdue. Armeeabteilung Fretter-Pico, after successfully extricating some 14,000 troops from an encirclement at Millerovo, went into a line behind the Donets. Hollidt's units likewise gained the slight protection of the frozen river. On the Manich Canal between the Don and Prolyetarskaya Fourth Panzer Army set up a strongpoint defense, and First Panzer Army extended its left flank north to tie in east of Salsk.

SIXTH ARMY DESTROYED

By the beginning of the year Sixth Army was dying a lingering death from starvation and exhaustion. The supplies trickling in were sufficient to prolong but not to mitigate the agony. Between 1 and 23 December the amounts airlifted into the pocket had averaged 90 tons a day. In the first three weeks of January they came to 120 tons a day; but on only one day, 7 December, had the air supply reached 300 tons, the daily tonnage promised and about half the army's daily requirement.

Nevertheless, the army was not yet completely at the Russians' mercy. The original success at Stalingrad had been the work of the Soviet armor, not the infantry; and when Fifth Tank Army and other armored elements had pulled out after the pocket was formed, the infantry had showed itself to be distinctly inferior. By January the weather, hunger, and fatigue had also taken their toll of the Russians. In fact, Sixth Army possessed some small advantages. The chief one was that the pocket enclosed nearly all of the built-up areas in and around Stalingrad; consequently, the German troops had some shelter and could obtain wood for fuel from the demolished buildings, while the Russians had none. Secondly, the terrain, flat and treeless, but cut by deep balkas (gullies), somewhat favored the defense. Lastly, the Germans had field fortifications of their own and some the Russians had built to defend the city.

After the Russians resumed the offensive west of Stalingrad the task of reducing the pocket was left to Don Front. General Polkovnik Nikolai N. Voronov was assigned as Stavka representative. Don Front in early January had a strength, according to Soviet figures, of 281,000 men and 250 tanks.[15] The final push, originally scheduled to begin on 6 January and take seven days, started on 10 January after Sixth Army had rejected surrender ultimatums on the two preceding days.

The attack, it appeared, could hardly fail, since it was directed mainly against the pocket's west and south fronts, which were weak, having been improvised after the encirclement. Late on 10 January Paulus reported that after that day's fighting there was no longer any prospect of holding out until mid-February; relief would have to come much earlier; the promised quantity of supplies would have to be delivered; and replacement battalions would have to be flown in immediately.

On 12 January the army lost Pitomnik, the better of its two airstrips. Six of the fourteen fighters based there took off under fire. Five attempted to land on the strip at Gumrak and crashed. The pilot of the sixth flew out to the west, thus ending the fighter defense over the pocket. In the northwest and south fronts the Russians had torn

---

15. *Sbornik Nomer 6* states that in January 1943 Sixth Army had a numerical superiority in artillery (6,200 guns to 3,770), machine guns (13,700 to 7,300), tanks (1,800 to 250), and motor vehicles (18,000 to 9,400). It admits that these figures include pieces of equipment possibly knocked out long before the final battles and some the Germans might not have been able to use far lack of fuel or ammunition. Sixth Army in early December reported a strength of about 100 tanks; probably by January many, if not most of these, were damaged, destroyed, or unserviceable for lack of parts and fuel.

gaps which could not be closed because the army did not have enough troops or the gasoline to move them. Paulus reported on the 13th that there the artillery ammunition would run out by the end of the day and the guns were being abandoned where they stood.

Nevertheless, from the Soviet point of view, the first phase of the final attack was a disappointment. It did not have the crushing effect initially expected, and after the first few days it lost momentum. The Soviet account blames an intelligence error which led to too low an estimate of the German strength. Most likely, Don Front was in almost the condition Sixth Army had been in during the previous September and October. Five of Rokossovskiy's seven armies had been in combat since midsummer. If the Soviet strength figures are accurate, the armies were at least 150,000 men understrength. Stalingrad was not coming cheap to the Russians either.

On 15 January Hitler, after repeated pleas from Paulus, appointed Generalfeldmarschall Erhard Milch to direct the air supply for Sixth Army, giving him authority to issue orders to all branches of the Wehrmacht. Hitler's order for the first time established a command powerful enough to override all other claims on planes, fuel, and ground crews and organize the air supply on the scale which had been promised for Stalingrad; but it was too late. Daylight landings in the pocket were becoming too dangerous. On the 17th, after a pilot reported German troops falling back toward Stalingrad on either side of the airstrip, Fourth Air Force for a time suspended landings at Gumrak. Two days later the Russians took Tatsinskaya, forcing the planes to shift to bases at Rostov and Novocherkassk, over 200 miles from the pocket.

As the Russians moved in for the kill, Paulus reported on 20 January that the "fortress" could not hold out more than a few days longer. In some sectors the defenders had all been wiped out and the Russians could march through the front at will. During the next night Gumrak was lost, leaving airdrops the army's only means of supply.

The day of 22 January marked the beginning of Sixth Army's death agony. The Russians, pressing in from the southwest on a 3-mile-wide front along the railroad, broke through the outer ring of the Stalingrad city defenses at Voroponovo Station and marched east into the city with battle flags unfurled. To close the gap was impossible. Ammunition had run out on that stretch of the front and neither troops nor ammunition could be brought in from other sectors.

That night Paulus radioed Hitler via the OKH:

Rations exhausted. Over 12,000 unattended wounded in the pocket. What orders should I give to troops, who have no more ammunition and are subjected to mass attacks supported by heavy artillery fire? The quickest decision is necessary since disintegration is already starting in some places. Confidence in the leadership still exists, however.

Hitler answered:

Surrender is out of the question.

The troops will defend themselves to the last. If possible the size of the fortress is to be reduced so that it can be held by the troops still capable of fighting.

The courage and endurance of the fortress have made it possible to establish a new front and begin preparing a counteroperation. Thereby Sixth Army has made an historic contribution to Germany's greatest struggle.

As the front fell back from the west, the inner city, which after months of bombardment had the appearance of a landscape in Hell, became a scene of fantastic horror. Sixth Army reported 20,000 uncared-for wounded and an equal number of starving, freezing, unarmed stragglers. As many as could took shelter in the basements of the ruins where the tons of rubble overhead provided protection against the constant rain of artillery shells. There, in darkness and cold, the sick, the mad, the dead, and the dying crowded together, those who could move not daring to for fear of losing their places. Over the tallest of the ruins in the center of the city Sixth Army ran out the Reich battle flag "in order to fight the last battle under this symbol."

On 26 January Sixty-second Army captured Mamai Hill, and tanks of Twenty-first Army linked up from the west to split the pocket in two. XI Corps formed a perimeter anchored on the tractor works on the northern edge of Stalingrad while Sixth Army headquarters, and LI, VIII, and XIV Panzer Corps dug in around and northwest of Railroad Station I. IV Panzer Corps, which had been holding the south front, was destroyed on that day by a Russian push across the Zaritsa River from the south. A day earlier Sixth Army had asked the Air Force to drop only food, ammunition was not needed—there were too few guns.

The end was clearly at hand. On 28 January Sixth Army stopped issuing rations to the wounded in order to preserve the strength of the fighting troops. That day the main theme of the midnight situation conference at the Fuehrer headquarters was Hitler's desire to have Sixth Army reconstituted quickly, using as many survivors of the original army as could be found.

By 29 January the south pocket was split, leaving army headquarters in a small enclave in the south and the remnants of LI and VIII Corps in the north. XIV Panzer Corps ceased to exist on that day. During the night ten small groups departed in a forlorn attempt to make their way west across almost 200 miles of enemy territory. By the following night, LI and VII Corps had been pushed into a small area around the engineer barracks, where they surrendered the following morning. The headquarters staff, Sixth Army, and survivors of the 194th Grenadier Regiment still held a 300-yard perimeter around the Red Square.

At 0615 on the morning of 31 January the radio operator at army headquarters in the basement of the Univermag on Red Square sent the following message: "Russians are at the door. We are preparing to destroy [the radio equipment]." An hour later the last transmission from Sixth Army came through: "We are destroying [the equipment]."56 Paulus, failing to appreciate all the implications of his promotion to generalfeldmarschall the day before, became the first German officer of that rank ever to be taken prisoner. Hitler's comment: "Paulus did an aboutface on the threshold of immortality."

In the north pocket around the tractor works, the 33,000 men of XI Corps, under General der Infanterie Karl Strecker, held out another forty-eight hours. On 1 February Hitler called on the corps to fight to the last man, saying "Every day, every hour that is won benefits the rest of the front decisively." At 0840 the next day Army Group Don received the last message from the north pocket:

XI Corps, with its six divisions, has done its duty to the last.

Long live the Fuehrer!

Long live Germany!

-Strecker

In the Stalingrad pocket the Germans lost somewhat over 200,000 men. The exact total was apparently never determined. During the fighting 30,000 wounded were flown out. The latest Soviet figures, which are substantially lower than those originally given but still apparently high, set the German casualties at 147,200 killed and wounded and over 91,000 captured, the latter including 24 generals and 2,500 officers of lesser rank. The Soviet Union has not made public its own losses. If the casualties of the VIII Cavalry Corps and III Cavalry Corps, 36 percent and 45 percent in the period 19 November to 2 December 1942, are representative, the Soviet losses must also have been substantial. An impression of what the final conquest of the pocket cost can be deduced from Don Front's ammunition expenditure between 10 January and 2 February 1943: 911,000 artillery rounds of all calibers up to 152-mm., 990,000 mortar shells, and 24,000,000 machine gun and rifle rounds.

As Hitler frequently stated, Sixth Army performed a valuable service by tying down several hundred thousand Russian troops; on the other hand, it is possible to imagine a much less catastrophic development of the 1942-43 winter battles on the German southern flank in Russia had the army been permitted to withdraw its twenty divisions from Stalingrad in time. Nor was the magnitude of the defeat in any way lessened by the fact that it resulted more from Hitler's errors than from Soviet military skill. Historically, Stalingrad, along with Guadalcanal and the North African invasion, marks the start of the Axis' recession on all fronts in World War II.

CHAPTER V

The Countermarch

THE FIGHT FOR SURVIVAL

At Stalingrad Germany lost both an army and a campaign. What Hitler had sacrificed Sixth Army to keep—the fruits of the summer's victories—slipped from his grasp along with the dying army. The banks of the Don as well as the Volga became a graveyard of German ambitions.

Since mid-December Weichs, the Army Group B commander, had helplessly watched the Russians massing against his two left flank armies on the Don, north of the bend at Novaya Kalitva. In early January his worst fears had been confirmed when Third Tank Army, formerly in the Bryansk area, appeared south of Novaya Kalitva. On the morning of 13 January the Russians reached up the Don a third time—to hit Hungarian Second Army. The first assault, by Fortieth Army of the Voronezh Front, carried away the left flank of Hungarian Second Army. To the north, the German Second Army hastily screened its flank to protect Voronezh. On the south between Liski and Novaya Kalitva Hungarian VII Corps and Italian Alpini Corps, backstopped by a German provisional corps, were not touched for a day or two; but as Third Tank Army pushed behind their line from the south, their front disintegrated.

By the end of the third week in January, Army Group B front was torn open on a 200-mile stretch between Voronezh and Voroshilovgrad. Weichs reported to Hitler that he saw no way of stopping the Russians and was worried about the German Second Army which, with an open flank in the south and a front that bent back sharply in the north, was exposed to a double envelopment. Second Army would have its turn before the month was out.

THE SOUTH FLANK THREATENED

While the Russians were opening the way for a cut deep to the southwest, Army Group Don stayed tied down on the Donets and east of Rostov protecting the rear of Army Group A. (Map 6) Although Hitler had indicated at the end of December that he intended to withdraw Army Group A to a bridgehead on the Taman Peninsula, he had only allowed the army group to bend back its left flank to tie in with Don. On 13 January Kleist asked for a decision on what to do next. He wanted to evacuate most of his troops through Rostov and hold a small Taman bridgehead. Zeitzler replied that despite all efforts, it was very difficult "at the present time" to get decisions from Hitler, who claimed to be occupied with other problems and considered that decisions such as that pertaining to Army Group A still had time. Zeitzler added that he believed it was too late for the army group to escape through Rostov, and on his own responsibility admonished Kleist to get into the GOTENKOPF, the Taman bridgehead, fast.

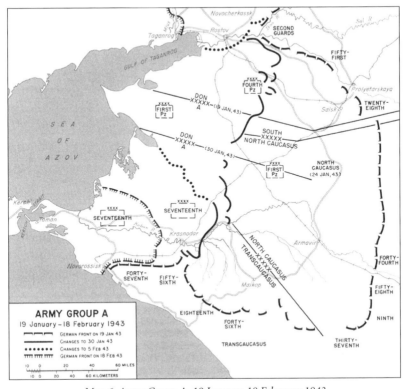

Map 6: Army Group A, 19 January-18 February 1943

Without expressly confirming it, Hitler let Zeitzler's instruction stand, except for an attempt on 21 January to get the GOTENKOPF extended to include the Maikop oil fields.

Manstein, having just rescued his army group from one threatened envelopment, found himself about to be caught in another. (Map 7) On 19 January his left flank north of the Donets was still protected by a thin line of Army Group B and Armeeabteilung

Fretter-Pico troops on the Derkul River, but Fretter-Pico was being forced back to the Donets north and west of Voroshilovgrad, and the Army Group B remnants were beginning to fall back to the Aydar River, forty miles to the west. Manstein gave Hitler two choices: either stop the Soviet advance in the gap between Voronezh and Voroshilovgrad far enough east to prevent Second Army at Voronezh and Army Group Don on the Donets from being completely outflanked, or assemble a strong offensive force north of the gap and another on the south to strike the enemy flanks. For the first, the SS divisions coming in might be used provided they arrived in time. Were the second course to be chosen, Army Group Don would have to pull back to avoid being cut off before the offensive forces were assembled. Two days later Manstein warned that in another four or five days he would have to take two divisions away from Fourth Panzer Army (which Hitler had ordered to hold open the railroad south of Rostov until supplies for the GOTENKOPF were hauled through) and shift them to his north flank to keep the Russians from crossing the Donets west of Voroshilovgrad.

While Manstein showered the Fuehrer headquarters with situation reports, most of which went unanswered, the Russians stayed on the move. South of the Don they forced their way across the Manich, threatening Rostov and the rear of Fourth Panzer Army. The 11th Panzer Division had to be transferred from the Armeeabteilung Hollidt to push the line back to the Manich. Off the left flank of Army Group Don on 23 January, First Guards Army spearheads drove across the Aydar River, crossed the Donets west of Voroshilovgrad, and headed toward Lisichansk farther upstream. East of Voroshilovgrad three Soviet armies, throwing in all the manpower they could scrape together, including supply troops and armed civilians, launched

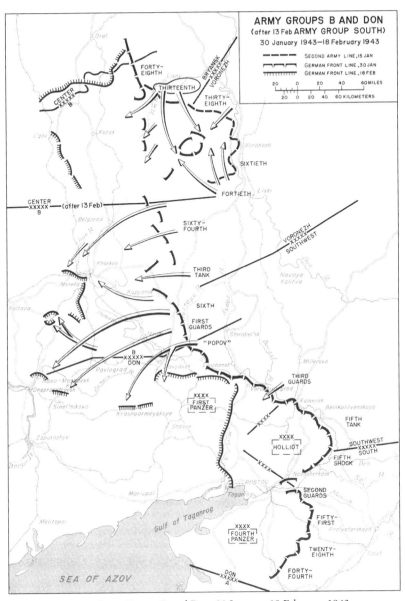

Map 7: Army Groups B and Don. 30 January-18 February 1943

strong probing attacks across the Donets, some of which were beaten off only in the nick of time.

As the winter deepened, the rivers lost their defensive value and the vagaries of the Russian weather added to the Germans' troubles.

On 24 January the temperature rose above freezing, and puddles of water lay on the roads. That night it sank to below zero. The next day the roads were sheeted with slick ice. On the 27th a snow storm blew down from the north and in three days blanketed the land in deep drifts.

On 25 January the Russians extended their offensive north to the left flank of Army Group B, where the Second Army front was precariously anchored on the Don west of Voronezh. Hitler had authorized the army to withdraw to the line of the Tim River, but he had insisted that it be done by stages, without sacrificing any supplies or equipment. On the 25th, having just taken the last troops out of the Voronezh bridgehead, the Second Army was beginning to take the first step back from the Don when Fortieth Army attacked and broke through the lightly screened south flank. The next morning Bryansk Front struck in the north due south of Livny. Vasilevskiy was co-ordinating the operation for the Stavka. With the snow drifted too deep for trucks, the Russians brought gasoline to their leading tanks by air, using single-engine U-2 biplanes that landed on the snow at night in the light of bonfires. In a couple of days two of Second Army's three corps were encircled. The third, tying in with Army Group Center on the north, was badly shaken. While the trapped corps struggled to break out, the army had only one weak panzer division with which to block the Soviet westward advance.

THE MAIN EFFORT AGAINST ARMY GROUP DON

As the month drew to a close, the Soviet winter offensive was in full swing. The main effort was against Army Group Don. Vatutin's Southwest Front struck for the crossings in the middle reaches of the Donets, and South Front, under General Armii Rodion I. Malinovskiy, applied pressure from the east. Zhukov co-ordinated operations of these two fronts. Against Army Group B, Bryansk Front, under General Leytenant M. A. Reuter, and Voronezh Front, under General Leytenant F. I. Golikov, bore west and southwest toward Kursk and Kharkov.

Unpleasant decisions were again being forced on Hitler. Once more, he tried to make half measures do. On 27 January, at the last minute, he ordered Headquarters, First Panzer Army, two corps headquarters, one panzer division, one infantry division, and two security divisions transferred via Rostov to Army Group Don.[16] Kleist, worried about getting his supplies across Kerch' Strait, asked that the entire army group be taken out through Rostov; but it was too late for that. Badly as troops were needed in the north, Kleist had to take 400,000 men into the GOTENKOPF, where the most they could accomplish would be to maintain the fiction of a threat to the Caucasus.

That the German Command could still make relatively deliberate decisions respecting Army Group A resulted mainly from the Soviet failure to mount more than a token offensive against the army group itself. The Stavka plan apparently envisioned a gigantic encirclement of Army Group A that would be completed from the south and east by Transcaucasus Front; but organizational and transportation troubles and the cautious leadership of General Armii I. V. Tiulenev had prevented the front from taking the initiative anywhere on a scale sufficient to cause the Germans genuine trouble.

Several days earlier Manstein had asked what was going to be done to relieve the pressure on his left flank, since the units he might have used there had been ordered to stay south of the Don to hold open Rostov. Hitler, on 27 January, promised an offensive from the vicinity of Kharkov by the SS Divisions Das Reich and Adolf Hitler, to begin on 12 February. Manstein replied that he doubted whether the offensive would do any good because the two divisions would probably be forced to the defensive and, in any case, would be too far away and not strong enough to affect his flank.

At the end of the month Manstein's northern front reached the breaking point as he was forced almost daily to stretch it westward to keep up with the Russians. Southwest Front had bridgeheads on the south bank of the Donets west of Voroshilovgrad and between Voroshilovgrad and Kamensk. On the Krasnaya River one Army Group B division still attempted to shield the left flank of Army Group Don north of Lisichansk. On 1 February that division's line collapsed

---

16. The German security divisions were not intended for front-line combat. They were composed mostly of older men and usually lacked the artillery and heavy weapons of the regular infantry divisions.

Khrushchev (left) and Malinovskiy

and the newly created Popov Group (under General Leytenant Markian M. Popov), with four tank corps and a rifle corps, moved into the 40-mile gap, crossed the Donets near Lisichansk, and headed west toward Slavyansk. Between Voroshilovgrad and Kamensk the Soviet bridgehead expanded like a giant inverted balloon, which might burst any time.

General der Kavallerie Eberhard von Mackensen was bringing his first Panzer Army headquarters up from the south to take over the old Armeeabteilung Fretter-Pico zone and the new front to the west, but his main reinforcements, the 3d and 11th Panzer Divisions, were stalled north of Rostov by snowdrifts. North of the Donets Army Group B turned over the scattered units on the southern half of its front to the Headquarters, Armeeabteilung Lanz, under General der Gebirgstruppe Hubert Lanz, giving it the all but impossible mission of protecting Kharkov and the northern flank of Army Group Don.

Hitler was intent on a counteroffensive. On 3 February he issued Operations Order 3. A recently activated headquarters, the SS Panzer Corps, would advance with the SS Division Das Reich and elements of Division Adolf Hitler out of the area south of Kharkov to Kupyansk and then strike south in the rear of the Russians crossing the Donets behind Army Group Don. Over-all control would be assigned to Army Group Don.

Manstein, who placed no confidence in a counteroffensive by one division, dismissed the order with a reply that Army Group Don could not take control until after the enemy west of Kupyansk was wiped out. Turning to more immediate problems, he stated that Southwest Front had strong forces ready to attack on the middle Donets east of Voroshilovgrad and between Slavyansk and Lisichansk; therefore, he would have to transfer Fourth Panzer Army's last panzer and motorized divisions north, leaving Hoth without enough strength to hold his line on the lower Don. He asked permission to pull the Armeeabteilung Hollidt front back to the line Kamensk-Novocherkassk and, if necessary, to take the entire eastern front of the army group back forty-five miles to the Mius River.

On 5 February the Russians took Izyum, the last German strongpoint off the deep left flank of Army Group Don. Manstein reported that he was being outflanked to the west, and neither he nor Weichs had the means to prevent it. By advancing about seventy miles more Vatutin's forces could cut both railroads into the Army Group Don sector. Manstein called for emergency measures: transfer of the 7th Air Division to Stalino to protect the Dnepropetrovsk-Stalino rail line; a large-scale air supply capability for Army Group Don; an increase of rail traffic through Kharkov to Army Group Don at the expense of Army Group B (the Italians and Hungarians, he thought, could be left to live off the land); and two divisions to be transported by air from Army Group A to Dnepropetrovsk.

RETREAT TO THE MIUS

With the surrender at Stalingrad still painfully alive in his memory, the prospect of another encirclement was too much for Hitler. On 6 February he sent a fast Condor transport to fly Manstein to the Fuehrer headquarters at Rastenburg. When the two met, Hitler, with no preliminaries, declared that he accepted sole responsibility for the debacle at Stalingrad. Manstein had come intending to propose that Hitler lay down the active command and appoint a qualified professional (Manstein?). He was so taken aback by Hitler's assumption of responsibility for Stalingrad, his professed refusal to find fault with any of the others who had participated, and by the general amiability of the reception, that he only suggested that Hitler consider appointing a military deputy with somewhat more authority than the Chief of Staff, OKH, then had. Hitler led the conversation away into a discussion of the "disillusionment" he had experienced with von Brauchitsch and others and then to the situation at the front.

When the discussion turned to the front Hitler again became evasive. After Manstein demonstrated in detail that it was necessary to get behind the Mius River without losing another day, Hitler took refuge in a variety of tangential arguments: shortening the front released as many Russian as German troops; if the Russians were forced to fight for every foot of ground they would soon be worn out; Germany could not afford to lose the Donets coal (Manstein had learned before going to the Fuehrer headquarters that the coal mined east of the Mius could not be used either for coking or as locomotive fuel). After a 4-hour debate, Hitler reluctantly gave Manstein permission to withdraw to the Mius, and then asked him to consider whether it could not, at least, be postponed for a while.

On 8 February Armeeabteilung Hollidt took the first backward step to the Mius. Thereafter, together with Fourth Panzer Army, it covered the 100-mile distance in nine days. Demolition crews gave the retreat a thunderous accompaniment as they dynamited the mines and factories. Malinovskiy kept his armies close on the German's heels all the way. In the coal fields the Russians sent detachments down into the pits, probing for footholds behind the German front. Behind the German line several hundred thousand civilians migrated west: refugees from the Caucasus, specialists and men fit for military service whom the Germans evacuated from the cities, and personnel of the German economic offices. On 18 February Armeeabteilung Hollidt and Fourth Panzer Army crossed the Mius and occupied the positions which had been built by Army Group South the year before. Whether the line would hold or not was in doubt for several days. On the night of the 18th, III Guards Mechanized Corps crossed the Mius and rolled 18 miles west. Only a sudden thaw gave the Germans time to push the corps out and close the line before the Russians could bring in reinforcements.

KHARKOV FALLS

Off the north flank of Army Group Don Armeeabteilung Lanz struggled to stem the Soviet thrust toward Kharkov. Early in February Hitler had declared Kharkov a fortress, to which Lanz had objected on the grounds that the city was not fortified and that he had no troops with which to hold it. On 6 February Hitler called Lanz to Fuehrer headquarters where he personally gave the general two missions: to hold Kharkov; and to counterattack with two divisions of SS Panzer Corps to the southwest toward Manstein's north flank.

By then SS Panzer Corps, under unrelenting enemy pressure, had for several days been trying in vain to muster enough strength for a counterattack. On 7 February the army group warned that no more excuses would be accepted; Weichs had given his word to Hitler; but the next day SS Panzer Corps had to evacuate Belgorod, northeast of Kharkov, and go behind the Donets along the rest of the line. On the 10th Lanz ordered the counterattack to begin the following day, but he told Weichs that he had only three divisions—Adolf Hitler, Das Reich, and Grossdeutschland—fit for combat and so could not be expected to hold off four Soviet armies, defend Kharkov, and counterattack. If the attack were started, he warned, the risk of losing Kharkov would have to be accepted.

As was soon to be shown, Lanz also had other troubles. Headquarters, SS Panzer Corps, was new and afflicted with both inexperience and overconfidence. The SS-men often regarded their subordination to the Army as an unnecessary formality and used their

Mounted Soviet troops pass wrecked German aircraft.

private channels to Fuehrer headquarters for optimistic reporting on their own capabilities and to make certain that their setbacks were blamed on the Army.

On 11 February, starting from Merefa, SS Panzer Corps attacked south. In three days it gained about thirty miles, but without really managing to come to grips with the enemy. Snow forced the German tanks to stay on the roads. The Russians, mostly cavalry with sleds, took to the woods.

On the 13th the north flank of SS Panzer Corps was forced back to the outskirts of Kharkov. Hitler next morning ordered the front around Kharkov absolutely to be held, even if the counterattack in the south had to be stopped temporarily.

That day Headquarters, Army Group Don, assumed command of Armeeabteilung Lanz. Hitler took Headquarters, Army Group B, out of the front, giving its northern force, Second Army, to Army Group Center. Army Group Don he then renamed Army Group South. Manstein's first step was to order the SS Panzer Corps' correspondence with "higher" headquarters stopped. He suspected the SS-men had been responsible in the first place for giving Hitler the idea that Kharkov could be held.

In Kharkov, on 14 February, an uprising broke out, and in the night, disregarding a direct order from Lanz, the Commanding General, SS Panzer Corps, Obergruppenfuehrer (Lt. Gen.) Paul Hausser, decided to evacuate Kharkov. Before midnight, reminded of Hitler's order, Hausser changed his mind and reported that he was determined "to hold Kharkov to the last man." The next morning Hitler set holding Kharkov as Lanz's sole mission, but it was too late. By afternoon the corridor out of the city to the southwest had shrunk to a width of a little more than a mile, and elements of the SS Division Das Reich, against orders, had pulled out of the northern suburbs. Lanz found himself forced to approve an SS Panzer Corps' decision to withdraw to the Uda River. In another twenty-four hours the SS troops were pushed entirely out of the city toward the southwest and south. Losing Kharkov which, like Stalingrad, had become a symbol was a blow to Hitler's prestige and a scapegoat had to be found. On 20 February he relieved Lanz and replaced him with General der Panzertruppen Werner Kempf.

THE LAST GERMAN VICTORY

Of the successive Russian right hooks against the southern flank of the German Eastern Front, the last was potentially the most dangerous. By the time First Panzer Army, Armeeabteilung Hollidt, and Fourth Panzer Army had drawn their front back into the angle of the Donets and Mius Rivers, strong Soviet tank and cavalry forces had moved in across their rearward lines of communications. On 13 February the Popov Group took Krasnoarmeyskoye and cut the Dnepropetrovsk-Stalino railroad. By the 19th tanks of First Guards Army, after crossing the Samara River and taking Novo-Moskovsk and Pavlograd, were converging on Sinel'nikovo, the railroad junction twenty miles east of Dnepropetrovsk.

MANSTEIN CASTLES TO THE LEFT

The Soviet tide was at the flood. But, though momentum might still carry it far, new influences were coming into play. Army Group Don, now South, had conducted its retreat without excessive loss of strength or decline in morale. It had shortened its line and had freed itself of the responsibility for defending Army Group A's northern flank. In SS Panzer Corps it had a fresh, powerful—though somewhat erratic—striking force. The Russians, on the other hand, although they had carved out vast stretches of territory, had still not attained their primary objective, the destruction of the German armies in the south. In recent weeks, as glowing opportunities for cheap successes beckoned them at every turn, they had shown an increasing tendency to follow the line of least resistance.

In Operations Order 4 of 12 February 1943, Hitler had taken another step toward stopping the offensive. He had told Army Group South to establish a firm front on the Mius-Donets line and close the gap between Armeeabteilung Lanz and First Panzer Army. Harking back to one of the proposals Manstein made in January, he talked about creating two new "attack armies," one behind the Army Group South in the vicinity of Pavlograd and the other on the Army Group Center south flank. The plan was, to say the least, Utopian. It ignored the fact that the Russians were still rolling at full tilt and that the question was not simply one of closing gaps in the front and then going over to the offensive with two widely spaced armies.

But, in ordering seven fresh divisions from the West transferred to Army Group South by the end of the first week in March, Hitler did provide Manstein with the means to brake the Soviet advance and possibly, given a little luck and a great deal of skill, to seize the initiative.

On the afternoon of 17 February, Hitler, with Jodl, Zeitzler, and a retinue that included the Fuehrer's personal cook, arrived at Army Group South headquarters in Zaporozhye. Hitler's visits to the front, even as distant as an army group headquarters, were rare. In this instance the reasons that brought him there were also unusual. On the one hand, he longed to put an end to the winter's string of defeats; on the other, he had learned the full import of Manstein's 6 February proposal concerning the supreme command and he had all but made up his mind to hand Manstein his dismissal.

If he had any doubts, Hitler discovered that the situation of Army Group South was truly, as one general described it, "hair raising." On 18 February Soviet tanks were thirty-six miles east of Zaporozhye, and

Germans attacking south near the Mius Line.

there were no German troops in between. From the Armeeabteilung Kempf right flank to the left flank of First Panzer Army a 110-mile gap afforded the First Guards Army and Sixth Army open roads to the south and west. They had cut the railroad east of Dnepropetrovsk, and First Guards Army's tanks, those east of Zaporozhye, were, for a day or so, in a position to bag the top German command. On the east, Soviet Third Tank Army and Fifth Shock Army had broken through the Mius line at separate places.

The time was obviously not appropriate for getting rid of a field marshal, and Hitler quickly became absorbed in planning. Moreover, he wanted and needed a big success that would attract worldwide attention and no doubt sensed that Manstein was the man who could get it for him. Manstein, however, insisted on first closing the gap between Armeeabteilung Kempf and First Panzer Army. Kharkov, he argued, could wait but the army group could not survive if the gap remained, particularly since the spring thaw, which might start any time, would for several weeks rule out any attempt to close it. Hitler refused to give in, and in the end an accident decided the argument. On 18 February the SS Totenkopf Division reported that its vehicles were stuck in mud east of Kiev, and Manstein persuaded Hitler that

Manstein (center) and Hitler plan the defense of Zaoprozhye.

if SS Panzer Corps had not been able to hold Kharkov with two of its divisions, it would certainly not be able to retake it without the third.

During the night of 18 February the train carrying Headquarters, Fourth Panzer Army, arrived in Zaporozhye. Hoth had turned his front on the Mius over to Armeeabteilung Hollidt the day before, after being ordered to transfer to Dnepropetrovsk. At the Army Group South headquarters Manstein outlined the army's mission orally to Hoth. He told him he intended to create a new Fourth Panzer Army in the gap between Armeeabteilung Kempf and First Panzer Army. Hoth's first assignment would be to stop the First Guards and Sixth Armies east of Dnepropetrovsk and throw them back across the Samara River. Von Mackensen would stretch his left flank west and northwest to narrow the gap. Fourth Panzer Army would be given two panzer corps headquarters, two panzer divisions, and two infantry divisions from Armeeabteilung Hollidt and First Panzer Army; and it would take over from Armeeabteilung Kempf the Headquarters, SS Panzer Corps, with the SS Divisions Das Reich and Totenkopf. Manstein intended to provide three or four more infantry divisions later.

Before he left Zaporozhye, Hitler, on 19 February, called in Kleist and directed him to evacuate as many Army Group A troops as possible from the Taman bridgehead and transfer them to Army Group South. In the next eight days 50,000 men were airlifted out of the bridgehead, and by 6 March the number had risen to 100,000. But the gain for Army Group South was less than it appeared because the planes could carry only troops, not weapons and equipment.

Even though Hitler's decision to rectify the mistake of sending nearly a half million men into isolation on the Taman Peninsula came too late, Army Group South was able to extract at least one important dividend from the disasters of the previous months. Since December 1942 the OKL had supplied reinforcements to Richtofen's Fourth Air Force, in the Army Group South (Don) zone. By early February Fourth Air Force controlled 950 planes, 53 percent of the 1,800 first-line aircraft then on the Eastern Front. The percentage was even more impressive if reckoned in terms of the best and most efficient aircraft types. During the first months of the Soviet winter offensive the performance of Fourth Air Force had not been commensurate with its strength for a variety of reasons: bad weather, dispersion of effort, and loss of its forward bases. By mid-February Richthofen had reorganized and regrouped. Keeping most of the long-range bombers under the control of his own headquarters at Zaporozhye, he had divided his close-support elements into three main forces, stationing one west of Poltava behind Armeeabteilung Kempf, another at Dnepropetrovsk in back of Fourth Panzer Army, and the third at Stalino in the First Panzer Army sector. In the period 20 February to 15 March, he maintained a daily average of 1,000 sorties, a tremendous improvement over the January average of 350 sorties per day. For the last time in Russia the German Air Force managed to provide offensive support in the style of the old blitzkrieg days of 1940 and 1941.

THE PANZER ARMIES ATTACK

By the time Fourth Panzer Army established its headquarters at Dnepropetrovsk the counteroffensive had begun. After assembling at Krasnograd, on the right flank of Armeeabteilung Kempf, SS Division Das Reich had started a rapid march due south behind the points of

Sixth and First Guards Armies east of Dnepropetrovsk. (Map 8) On 20 February the division took Novo-Moskovsk, and the next day, turning east, it pushed into Pavlograd. By those swift blows it eliminated the threat to the Dnepr crossings and trapped a sizable force south of the Samara, where the Soviet commands had spread out their advance units, and in the next two days the division easily destroyed some of them and drove the rest north across the Samara River.

On 23 February elements of SS Totenkopf Division began advancing east north of the Samara on a line extending to the Orel River. East of Pavlograd the 6th and 17th Panzer Divisions moved in to form the right flank of Fourth Panzer Army and began to push north. Manstein then ordered the First and Fourth Panzer Armies to smash the Popov Group south of the line Pavlograd-Lozovaya-Barvenkovo. Hoth, in his orders to Fourth Panzer Army, emphasized that for the time being the main objective was not to gain ground but to destroy the estimated six tank corps and one guards rifle brigade of Popov Group and so open the way to the north.

On the eastern edge of the gap von Mackensen had thrown First Panzer Army into the offensive with speed and vigor that took the Russians completely by surprise. After evacuating Slavyansk to free a panzer division, von Mackensen committed SS Wiking Division against the Russians on the railroad at Krasnoarmeyskoye and dispatched two panzer divisions in wide sweeps from the east and west to create a large pocket north of the town. For several days, Popov's staff misjudged its situation. On 22 February it reported, in a radio message which the Germans intercepted, that it intended to block the German "retreat." To von Mackensen no decision could have been more welcome. His greatest worry had been that the Soviet mobile units would slip out of the encirclement. By the next day Popov Group realized that it was in trouble. It reported that most of its communications were cut and that in one unit panic was having to be suppressed "by the harshest measures." On the 24th, as the Russians maneuvered desperately to escape, the pocket disintegrated into several small encirclements. Popov Group had taken a severe beating, but succeeded in extricating enough of its tanks and troops to make another stand farther north in the vicinity of Barvenkovo.

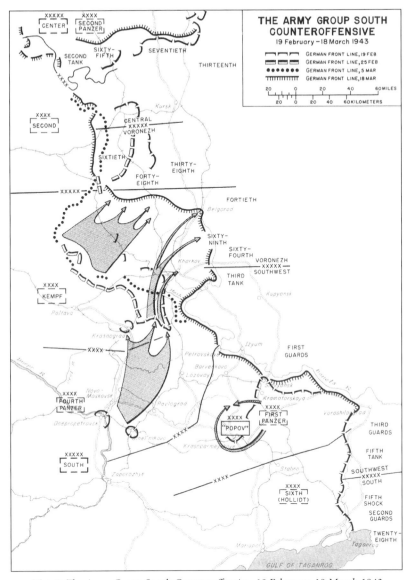

Map 8: The Army Group South Counteroffensive, 19 February-18 March 1943

KHARKOV RETAKEN

The opening phase of the counteroffensive had succeeded beyond all expectations.

The two panzer armies had scored shattering successes against Southwest Front. West of Kharkov Armeeabteilung Kempf was still retreating, but nothing could be done about that for the present and it might in the further course of events even prove an advantage. On 25 February Manstein issued orders to clear the way for a thrust into the south flank of the Voronezh Front west of Kharkov. First Panzer Army was to take Petrovskoye and Izyum to close the Donets crossings. Fourth Panzer Army was to go northeast until it had passed Lozovaya and then be ready to swing its main force north for a thrust along the railroad toward Kharkov.

On 26 February the point of Fourth Panzer Army reached Lozovaya. To the east the First Panzer Army's left flank drew abreast. In two more days Hoth took Petrovskoye on the Donets, and von Mackensen began swinging north on the line Lozovaya-Petrovskoye. Around Barvenkovo, in the First Panzer Army sector, the Russians still resisted desperately; the Popov Group had run out of gas and had no choice but to fight to the end where it was. Farther east, First Panzer Army spearheads were rapidly approaching Slavyansk from the south and east.

On 28 February Manstein ordered Hoth to begin the attack toward Kharkov and von Mackensen to push to the Donets in the area east of Petrovskoye. Time was running short. For several days the daytime temperatures had risen above freezing. Forced to slog through mud and standing water, the troops were beginning to tire. Soon the roads would become completely impassable.

In spite of the thaw, both armies made astonishingly rapid progress. Fourth Panzer Army, starting on 1 March, covered 50 miles in five days, reaching the Mosh River, 10 miles south of Kharkov, on the 5th. Off the front of Armeeabteilung Kempf east of Krasnograd it trapped and destroyed three rifle divisions and three tank brigades of Third Tank Army. Over most of the distance it was opposed only by First Guards Army elements, which had been badly mauled and cut off from their rearward communications in the fighting for Lozovaya and Petrovskoye. First Panzer Army, by 5 March, had reached the line of the Donets in all of its corps sectors. In some of the sharp bends of the river, such as that south of Izyum, the Russians still held bridgeheads, but because of the thaw, the army decided to call a halt and leave the bridgeheads to be eliminated when better weather set in.

For Fourth Panzer Army the question was whether or not to continue toward Kharkov at the risk of being stopped any day by the thaw. The prospect was tempting, particularly since it appeared that the Russians were not prepared to put up a fight north of the Mosh River and, after 7 March, the weather turned colder again. Manstein and Hoth decided to go ahead, but, in order not to risk losing contact with Armeeabteilung Kempf, to strike west of the city instead of sweeping to the east. They planned to cut the Russians' lines through Kharkov on the west and then encircle the city by dropping down on it from the north.

Again the advance went amazingly well. SS Panzer Corps broke away from the Mosh River on a broad front. On 9 March, as the corps right flank drew level with the western outskirts of Kharkov, the SS general, Hausser, reported that he had decided to take the city the next day in a surprise raid; but Hoth warned against tying down troops in street fighting and ordered him to stick to the plan. On the 11th, against a direct order to stay out of the city, Hausser, impatient for victory, sent one division into Kharkov from the west and another from the north. In three days of heavy fighting the SS divisions retook the city. Meanwhile, they also opened a road around the northern suburbs, which enabled them to execute the envelopment in the east about as quickly as had been planned—at least, so Hoth said when he declined to bring charges against Hausser.

After Kharkov fell, the resistance west of the Donets collapsed. Voronezh Front, obviously afraid the Germans might attack across the river, began hastily building defenses on the east bank.

The Soviet winter offensive was over. It had made massive gains, but the Stavka had meant to reach for a great deal more. In the latter half of February it had deployed Central Front (the former Don Front) northwest of Kursk for an attack toward Bryansk. Voronezh Front had been given orders to go past Kharkov to Poltava and the Dnepr between Kiev and Kremenchug. Southwest Front's final mission had been to strike for Melitopol and Mariupol and clear the Donets Basin.

On the morning of 18 March SS Panzer Corps, advancing along the railroad running north out of Kharkov, covered the thirty miles to Belgorod and captured the city in four hours. On the 21st Manstein proposed crossing the Donets to get a line that did not have to follow the zigzag bends of the river south of Kharkov, but Hoth refused on the grounds that the troops were worn out and that the defensive advantages of the river outweighed those of a shorter line in the open steppe.

Manstein declared the operation completed as of 17 March. South of Belgorod, Army Group South stood along approximately the same line the German armies had held before the 1942 summer offensive began. North of the city the Russians occupied a large bulge west of Kursk, but there, too, the front was being stabilized. After its long retreat, Second Army, once the Army Group South counteroffensive had begun taking effect, had been able to slow the Soviet advance, and in the first weeks of March had even regained some ground on its flanks.

CHAPTER VI

The Center and the North

AT THE END OF SUMMER 1942

ARMY GROUP CENTER

Army Group Center had borne the main weight of the Soviet 1941-42 winter offensive. On both sides of the Army Group North-Army Group Center boundary the Russians had broken through to depths of 150 miles and more and for a time had nearly encircled Ninth and Third Panzer Armies. In fighting that lasted well into the summer, the army group, Generalfeldmarschall Guenther von Kluge commanding, had destroyed or pushed back the most advanced Russian elements and had set up a front anchored on Velikiye Luki, Velizh, Bely, and Rzhev. That left the Russians in possession of a gigantic bulge around Toropets, about one-third (Demyansk-Kholm) in the Army Group North zone and two-thirds in the Army Group Center zone. (Map 9)

The western rim of the bulge from the army group boundary to a point several miles east of Demidov was held by LIX Corps, renamed in October 1912 Gruppe (Group) von der Chevallerie (Generalleutnant Kurt von der Chevallerie). With five divisions and more than 100 miles of front it could not establish a continuous line and, instead, had to depend on a strongpoint system that thinned out dangerously on the left flank. During the summer the swampy, wooded terrain and poor roads made a Soviet breakthrough attempt unlikely, but in the winter conditions would favor another thrust deep between the two army groups.

On the eastern rim of the bulge, Ninth Army held the Rzhev salient. On Ninth Army's right, Third Panzer Army, in a narrow sector, straddled the Warsaw-Moscow highway eighty miles west of Moscow. On Third Panzer Army's right the Fourth Army-Second Panzer Army line extended south to the army group boundary below

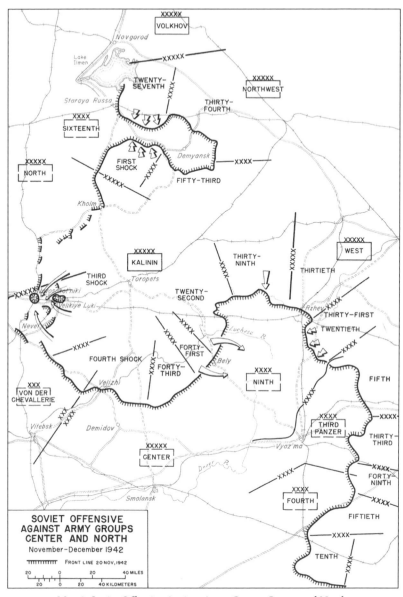

Map 9: Soviet Offensive Against Army Groups Center and North,
November-December 1942

Orel. On the boundary between the latter two armies the Russians held a deep salient east of Sukhinichi, not as large as the bulge in the north, but enough to pose an obvious threat of thrusts from the north and southeast to cut off the Ninth, Third Panzer, and Fourth Armies east of Smolensk. In the summer the Russians had launched strong attacks against Ninth Army, Third Panzer Army, and Second Panzer Army. When those failed to gain ground they were broken off in the Third Panzer and Second Panzer Army zones early in September but continued with unabated violence against the Ninth Army line at and south of Rzhev until 7 October.

By the time the Rzhev fighting had ended it was apparent that the Russians were getting ready for a new offensive after the fall rains. One strong force was assembling in the area west of Sukhinichi and a second in the Toropets bulge on the north flank. The concentration around Toropets was obviously the more dangerous. On 5 October Kluge promised von der Chevallerie a panzer division from Army Group North and three Air Force field divisions, which would have to be provided with training cadres since they were newly formed and had no training in ground warfare. On 14 October Hitler ordered von der Chevallerie to begin planning for a pre-emptive attack east from Velikiye Luki to Toropets. At the end of the month three additional divisions were moved into the Gruppe von der Chevallerie zone and the Headquarters, Eleventh Army, was transferred from the sector around Leningrad to plan and command the operation.

ARMY GROUP NORTH

The Army Group North front was a not very satisfactory legacy of the unfinished 1941 operations and the subsequent Soviet winter offensive. On the left flank the Eighteenth Army front formed an arc around Oranienbaum on the Gulf of Finland and bent eastward south of Leningrad, anchoring on Lake Ladoga at Schluesselburg. East of Schluesselburg the army held six miles of the Ladoga shore; then its line dropped off sharply southeastward to the Volkhov River and followed the river south to the northern tip of Lake Ilmen. South of Lake Ilmen, Sixteenth Army held a scalloped line; its main feature, projecting from the front like a misplaced thumb, was the Demyansk pocket. South of Demyansk the line curved west anchoring on Kholm. From Kholm to the army group boundary, north of Velikiye Luki, the front was a loose chain of strongpoints.

In July 1942 Hitler ordered Generalfeldmarschall Georg von

Soviet gun emplacement near Rzhev.

Kuechler, commanding Army Group North, to prepare an operation against Leningrad. He wanted the city taken by early fall in order to free Finnish forces for an operation against the Murmansk Railroad. In August Hitler took the Leningrad operation out of Kuechler's hands and gave it to Manstein, who had conducted a similar operation against Sevastopol. Manstein, bringing with him the Headquarters, Eleventh Army, two corps headquarters, and four infantry divisions, assumed command of the front facing Leningrad and was made directly subordinate to OKH. Before the preparations could be completed, the Russians opened an offensive on the line facing east just south of Lake Ladoga and quickly scored a breakthrough that threatened the German hold on Leningrad. On 4 September Manstein took command in the breakthrough area, and thereafter his first concern was to restore the front, which, in the face of stubborn Russian resistance, was not accomplished until 15 October. By that time all hope that the Finns would execute their projected operation that year had vanished, and it had been decided that the attack on Leningrad could not begin before freezing weather set in. On 20 October the OKH announced that the Leningrad offensive was postponed indefinitely. In the meantime, the heavy siege artillery, which had also been brought up from Sevastopol, was to be used to smash the city's defenses and inch the line forward gradually. Postponement of the offensive freed Headquarters, Eleventh Army, for the shift to the Velikiye Luki area.

In the Sixteenth Army zone the Demyansk pocket was a source of constant concern. On 14 September Kuechler in a personal letter attempted to persuade the OKH that to continue to hold the pocket was useless. II Corps, in the pocket, he wrote, had been fighting under adverse conditions since the last winter, and with the known superiority of the Russians in winter warfare serious developments could be expected in the coming months. Operationally, the pocket performed two services: it kept Russian troops tied down; and it might be used as one arm of an encircling operation against the Toropets bulge, but the question was whether anything of the sort was intended or could be executed. If not, Kuechler maintained, the pocket's value was practically nil.

A week later Halder answered that he was not convinced that the reported endurance of the Russians in winter was as great as had been claimed, and, in any case, the II Corps would not be the only unit having to endure hardships. To pull the corps back would gain Army Group North 12 divisions but would also free 26 divisions and 7 tank brigades for the Russians; anyway, Hitler completely rejected the idea of withdrawing the corps. Subsequently, in October and early November, Army Group North executed two small operations, which were only moderately successful, to widen the corridor leading into the pocket and braced itself for the expected Soviet winter offensive.

FINLAND—TWENTIETH MOUNTAIN ARMY

On the extreme left flank of the Eastern Front, Twentieth Mountain Army and the Finnish Army held the line they had occupied at the end of the 1941 campaign. In the Far North, forty-two miles northwest of Murmansk, XIX Mountain Corps faced the Soviet Fourteenth Army across the Litsa River. The corps' primary mission was to protect the Kolosyoki nickel mines. The idea of an overland advance to Murmansk had not been revived during the year; and while a thrust into the Rybatchiy Peninsula remained vaguely under consideration, the likelihood of its being attempted was slight because of the difficulty of assembling and maintaining sufficient forces.

In the roadless Arctic forests between the Litsa River and the Salla-Kandalaksha rail line no front existed—neither side bothered with more than scattered patrols. Astride the railroad XXXVI Mountain Corps held a line it had taken a year earlier a few miles east of the 1939 Finnish border and forty-five miles west of Kandalaksha. On the Twentieth Mountain Army right flank XVIII Mountain Corps occupied a short front straddling the Kesten'ga-Loukhi spur line about twenty miles west of the Murmansk railroad.

The Finnish Army, which had assumed responsibility for all operations out of Finland south of the line Oulu-Belomorsk, held three fronts: one (the Maaselkä Front) running north from the northern tip of Lake Onega; the second (the Aunus Front) between Lake Onega and Lake Ladoga along the general line of the Svir River; and the third (the Isthmus Front) across the Isthmus of Karelia north of Leningrad, approximately following the 1939 Finnish border.

In the Finnish Army and Twentieth Mountain Army zones there had been no combat activity worthy of note since the spring; and although the German and Finnish forces enjoyed an almost 2:1 superiority over their Soviet opponents, the chances of resuming the offensive in the foreseeable future were slim. For nearly a year the Finns had displayed extreme reluctance to assume any new military commitments and had insisted on the capture of Leningrad as an absolute prerequisite to new offensive operations. In August 1942 the Finns had agreed to take part in a two-pronged attack to the Murmansk railroad by Finnish forces (to Belomorsk) and XXXVI Mountain Corps (to Kandalaksha), but in October the OKW was forced to cancel the plans when the preliminary Army Group North operation to capture Leningrad was abandoned.

PARTISAN WARFARE

Communist tradition and the experiences of the civil war made it a foregone conclusion that the Soviet Union would attempt to exploit to the utmost all forms of irregular and clandestine warfare for both military and political reasons. However, although the Russians had created partisan units in large numbers immediately after the war started, the partisan movement in 1941 had remained ineffectual and by the late fall of that year was, if anything, on the downgrade. The

Partisans in the Bryansk forest.

impact of the rapid German advance and the apparent helplessness of the Soviet regime had made it difficult to kindle, even artificially, a spirit of resistance. Those partisan units that did appear were small, ineffective, usually isolated, and in constant danger of disintegrating. Communist Party and NKVD (secret police) attempts to leave behind a network of Party and partisan groups had failed because of lack of time and because the local Party authorities, on whom the burden of the work fell, either had no clear conception of what was required or lacked enthusiasm for underground activity. It was clear that, contrary to propaganda claims, neither the masses nor the Party elite would voluntarily spring to the defense of the Soviet system in a time of crisis.

THE RISE OF THE SOVIET PARTISAN MOVEMENT

The Soviet 1941-42 winter offensive prepared the ground for a new, more purposeful approach to partisan warfare. In a few weeks victories restored the prestige of the Soviet Government. In the occupied territories the heightened awareness that the former regime was still to be reckoned with, aroused a nice mixture of fear and patriotism. Moreover, the population by then had been exposed to German rule

Soviet tanks approach Velikiye Luki.

long enough to know that it had nothing to look forward to from that quarter. While this psychological shift was not sufficient in itself to bring about active resistance, it could be exploited by the Soviet regime which, in any event, no longer toyed with the illusion of a spontaneous partisan movement.

Taking advantage of the great gaps torn in the German line, particularly in the zones of the Army Groups North and Center, and the virtual disappearance of security forces in the enemy rear, the Russians set about systematically organizing partisan forces. Soviet-trained organizers and cadres roamed the countryside recruiting men by the authority of the Soviet draft law. Air supply was stepped up; military organization was introduced in the partisan detachments; and regular army officers appeared as instructors, advisers, and members of the partisan command staffs. The surviving 1941 units and the new units were brought under direct Soviet control by radio and air and by the creation of army and front partisan control staffs. Partisan detachments that had averaged less than 100 men in November 1941 more than doubled in strength by February 1942, and in the spring and summer of that year the "brigade" of 1,000 men or more, became the standard unit. By the late summer of 1942 the partisan movement was solidly established. The organizational work had been completed, and the lines of control were firmly in Soviet hands. The total partisan forces numbered between 150,000 and 200,000 men. The partisan movement had become a major prop of home front morale, and in August 1942 its more prominent leaders were called to Moscow, many of them flown in from behind the German lines, in order to be shown off at a conference.

Attempts by Soviet authorities to stir up partisan activity in all German-occupied areas, brought mixed success. Nearly nine-tenths of the partisan forces were located in the rear areas of Army Groups North and Center with the greatest concentrations behind Army Group Center, particularly in the Bryansk Forest north and south of Bryansk and behind the great Soviet salient west of Toropets. There vast stretches of forest and swamp provided cover for the partisan units. In the Ukraine and southern Russian the movement hardly gained a foothold before the late summer of 1943.

FUEHRER DIRECTIVE 46

On 18 August 1942, Hitler, confirming that the partisan movement had become much more than a local nuisance, issued a drastic order, Fuehrer Directive No. 46. The directive opened with the statement "The bandit monstrosity in the East has assumed a no longer tolerable scope and threatens to become a serious danger to front supply and exploitation of the land." Hitler wanted the partisans rooted out before winter "to avoid important disadvantages in the Wehrmacht's conduct of winter operations." He made the Reichsfuehrer-SS, Heinrich Himmler, responsible for collecting and evaluating information on antipartisan warfare and gave him sole responsibility for antipartisan operations in the territories under civil administration. He charged the Chief of Staff, OKH, with the conduct of antipartisan warfare in the zone of operations and ordered elements of the Replacement Army transferred east to be used as antipartisan forces while completing their training.

Conceding that the partisan movement could not be mastered by military means alone, Hitler recognized for the first time that a successful antipartisan campaign would have to take into account the attitude of the population in the affected areas. It would, on the one hand, have to offer them at least a subsistence standard of living to prevent their going over to the partisans and, on the other, make active collaboration against the partisans attractive by the promise of substantial rewards. Also for the first time, he approved recruitment of indigenous military units from among prisoners of war for employment against the partisans.

The Army regarded the directive as a significant advance in Hitler's concept of antipartisan warfare, particularly because it permitted efforts to win over the population and the use of indigenous troops. The Organizational Branch, OKH, had long maintained that Germany did not have the manpower to stage an effective antipartisan campaign with its own forces. But, regardless of the directive, Hitler did not abandon his plans to reduce the Russians to servitude and subject them to the most ruthless exploitation; consequently, he refused to offer sufficient inducements to stimulate genuine popular support for the German cause. Furthermore, as the year drew to a close, the Russian people grew increasingly aware that the chances of a German victory were fading.

A COMPANION PIECE TO STALINGRAD

Up to 19 November the Eastern Intelligence Branch, OKH, had predicted that the main Soviet winter offensive would be directed against Army Group Center. Later it defended the prediction by pointing out that the great success at Stalingrad obviously came as a surprise to the Russians and that they were at first clearly not prepared to exploit it by continuing the advance west of Stalingrad, where the road to even greater victories lay open. The Eastern Intelligence Branch was, perhaps, not as far wrong as might appear. Certainly, the Stavka could not have fully anticipated the speed of the Rumanian collapse nor could it have counted in advance on Hitler's offering up a whole German army.

On the other hand, an element of self-deception in the German thinking was to have baneful and lingering effects. The conviction that the moment when the Soviet Union would have dredged up its last reserves must soon be reached was slow in melting away and kept alive

Mannerheim (right) with Generalleutnant Erwin Engelbrecht, during the German occupation of Finland.

the notion that the Soviet capability to stage a second winter offensive would have to fall within predictable limits. After Stalingrad the idea took hold that, because the Russians had attacked in the south, they could not do the same in the center. On 21 November, Ninth Army recorded, "Numerous signs indicate that major Soviet offensives in two separate sectors of the front are no longer possible." Actually, the Stavka was able to launch, almost simultaneously, two offensives of approximately equal scope, and later greatly expand one of them.

THE RZHEV SALIENT

In the Army Group Center sector, as at Stalingrad, the front's configuration presented a ready-made opportunity for a large encirclement, yet one which would not require too high a level of tactical proficiency. On a 20-mile front due south of Rzhev the West Front deployed the heavily reinforced Thirty-first and Twentieth Armies—some 45 divisions and brigades, 2 tank corps, and 2 guards corps. On the eastern face of the Rzhev salient, Kalinin Front stationed Forty-first and Twenty-second Army—about 25 divisions and brigades plus 2 motorized-mechanized corps and the elite VI

Stalin Corps, for attacks on either side of Bely. On the north, at the apex of the salient, Thirty-ninth Army concentrated a half dozen or so divisions for a thrust due south.

The offensive began on the morning of 25 November, repeating the pattern of Stalingrad in its initial phase. But the German position there was different than it had been on the Don. Ninth Army was a first-class force which, having weathered the summer battles successfully, was not to be overawed by numerical and matériel superiority. After a month's respite and with three panzer divisions in reserve, the army faced the attack with confidence, particularly since the Soviet main effort came exactly where it had been expected, south of Rzhev. After Twentieth Army, conducting the main effort, made the mistake of committing its armor in piecemeal breakthrough attempts that cost the Soviet units better than half their tanks, one panzer corps handled the defense with ease.

On the west the defense was, at first, less successful; the Russians broke through on both sides of Bely, penetrating to within twenty miles of the town on the south and about ten miles along the valley of the Luchesa River in the north. But in ten days of fighting they failed to exploit their initial success, and on 7 December the Germans executed a surprise counterattack that turned the breakthrough south of Bely into a pocket. In another ten days the Germans cleaned out the pocket and regained their original front at a cost to Kalinin Front of 15,000 men killed and 5,000 captured.

On 11 December West Front launched a final attempt south of Rzhev which, in terms of sheer weight, surpassed anything Ninth Army had yet encountered. In the first two days of what the army described as the greatest defensive victory of the war thus far, the Russians lost 295 tanks without making any notable gains. During the next two days the offensive slackened rapidly, ending on 16 December, the day on which Ninth Army also finished mopping up the pocket south of Bely. Thereafter the last tangible remnant of the offensive was the penetration in the Luchesa River valley, where later, in fighting extending into the new year, Ninth Army also regained its original front. "General Winter" had for once failed the Russians: the Germans were better equipped than at the same time a year earlier, and the weather was milder—the lowest temperature reached by mid-December being about 15° F.

VELIKIYE LUKI

On the Ninth Army left flank, beginning on 25 November, Gruppe von der Chevallerie, holding the strongpoint line along the western rim of the Toropets bulge, also came under attack by Kalinin Front. In that area of forests, lakes, and swamps Velikive Luki constituted a kind of island base for the Germans. It anchored the center of the front in that sector; it was an important junction on the lateral railroad line closest to the front; and it straddled several east-west roads. In the two weeks before 25 November Kalinin Front had built up Third Shock Army to an absolute superiority in armor and better than 5:1 superiority in infantry and artillery. Bothered most by the forests and the swamps, which had not yet frozen solid, Third Shock Army in two days pushed through, encircled Velikiye Luki, and trapped 7,000 German troops in the town.

On the 27th, with Novosokol'niki, fifteen miles west, similarly threatened, von der Chevallerie reported that if the troops in Velikiye Luki were to be saved they would have to break out immediately. Three days later Hitler countered with an order stating that to evacuate Velikiye Luki was out of the question. The garrison would have to hold out until contact was restored and the former front line retaken.

In the third week of December, when the pressure abated slightly, von der Chevallerie began a relief operation; but his troops were worn out, and the attempt had to be abandoned after the second day. On 4 January 1943 a second attempt began. In the interval the garrison in Velikiye Luki had been split in two: a small group held out in the old kremlin (citadel) on the western edge of the town; the main body had been driven back to the eastern suburbs. The relief column, it was clear, could hope to do no more than rescue the garrison. To open a permanent corridor into the town was impossible.

For ten days the relief force inched its way eastward, being halted, finally, within a few hundred yards of the kremlin. On 15 January, when troops in the kremlin and east pocket were ordered to break out, the garrison commander, who was in the east pocket, radioed that this

German communications men checking a telephone line, Northern Front.

was not possible, and thereafter all contact was lost. The next morning 176 survivors broke through from the kremlin, and the relief column began to fall back.

THE QUIET FRONT

In the northern reaches of the Soviet Union, the Twentieth Mountain Army zone stayed quiet throughout the winter. In the Arctic Ocean, British and American convoys shuttled back and forth to Murmansk during the dark months carrying supplies to support the Soviet winter offensive. The Allied landing in North Africa in November 1942 had drawn off nearly all of the torpedo planes formerly employed against the convoys, and, in December, an unsuccessful sortie by the cruisers Hipper and Luetzow brought Hitler's wrath down on the Navy. As a consequence Raeder resigned and was replaced as Commander in Chief, Navy, by Grossadmiral Karl Doenitz, the submarine specialist. Hitler threatened to scrap all German heavy ships.

In southern Finland the Finnish Army fronts were also quiet. The Finns were less interested in their own than in the main sectors of the Eastern Front, and they watched the Soviet progress with mounting dismay. In January 1943, as Army Group North's hold on Leningrad began to slip, the Finnish Commander in Chief, Mannerheim, asked Twentieth Mountain Army to give back all Finnish troops still under its command. On 3 February, the day after the last German units surrendered at Stalingrad, Mannerheim, the Finnish President, Risto Ryti, and members of the Cabinet met and decided that the war had reached a decisive turning point and that it would be necessary for Finland to get out at the first opportunity. Six days later they informed a secret session of the Parliament that Germany could not win and Finland would have to accustom itself to thinking in terms of another Treaty of Mocow, the treaty which ended the Winter War of 1939-40. A month later a new Foreign Minister, Dr. Henrik Ramsay, appointed because he was reputed to have contacts in Great Britain and the United States, made the first move toward negotiating a separate peace.

To the Germans it was obvious that, for the time being, only fear of the Russians would keep Finland in the war. Fresh German victories in the coming summer might yet restore the Finns' morale, but the war had changed since 1941. It required resources, training, and masses of men which the Finns did not have. By the early months of 1943, the Twentieth Mountain Army staff had concluded that future offensive support was hardly to be expected of the Finnish Army and that the Finns probably could not withstand a full-scale Soviet attack.

ON THE DEFENSIVE

LENINGRAD AND THE DEMYANSK POCKET

In Leningrad the second winter of the siege was not as bad as the first. While Lake Ladoga was open, boats had brought in supplies for the troops and civilians and had evacuated close to half a million persons. A German attempt to use the Siebel ferries—catamarans driven by airplane engines and mounting a light antiaircraft gun—to interdict the lake traffic had failed. In the fall of 1942 the Russians had laid an electric cable and a gasoline pipeline in the lake. When the lake froze, they built an ice road and set up high tension lines. In the city the people had enough food at least to survive and sufficient electricity to operate some industrial plants. But the five or six thousand tons of supplies trucks could haul across the ice per day could barely sustain the city and the front; and Leningrad, normally the second largest industrial center in the country, was capable of a far greater contribution to the Soviet war effort than it was now making—by operating plants within sight of the front for propaganda as much as for production. Consequently, after their first attempt to overcome the siege failed in October 1942, the Leningrad and Volkhov Fronts had promptly begun the build-up for another try. When the winter darkness set in, reinforcements from the east crossed the lake and moved into the line.

Army Group North watched anxiously. Occupying a relatively inactive front, it had been neglected during most of 1942, had not fully replaced its losses of the previous winter, and was committed to a static defense that might be attacked at any of a number of critical points. Around Leningrad, particularly at the "bottleneck"—the narrow tie-in to Lake Ladoga—Army Group North functioned as the main support of German strategy in northern Europe. (Map 10) If the hold on Leningrad were broken, Germany would, in the long run, lose control of the Baltic Sea. Finland would then be isolated; the iron ore shipping from Sweden would be in danger; and the all-important submarine training program would be seriously handicapped.

In the 16 months they had held the "bottleneck" the Germans had built a tight network of defenses in the swampy terrain and had converted Schluesselburg, several small settlements, and scattered patches of woods into fortified strongpoints. But, with only six to eight miles between fronts, one facing west and the other east, the defenders had little room to maneuver. The Russians had found highly instructive their experience in the summer, and in the intervening months had rehearsed every tactic and maneuver for taking each individual German position. This method the Germans themselves had used in 1940 to train for the assaults on the Belgian forts.

The attack on the "bottleneck" began on 12 January. Sixty-seventh Army, its troops wearing spiked shoes to help them climb the frozen river bank, struck across the ice on the Neva River while Second Shock Army, on the east, threw five divisions against a 4-mile stretch of the German line. Methodically, the Russians chopped their way through, and by the end of the first week had taken Schluesselburg and opened a corridor to Leningrad along the lake shore. Thereafter, in fighting

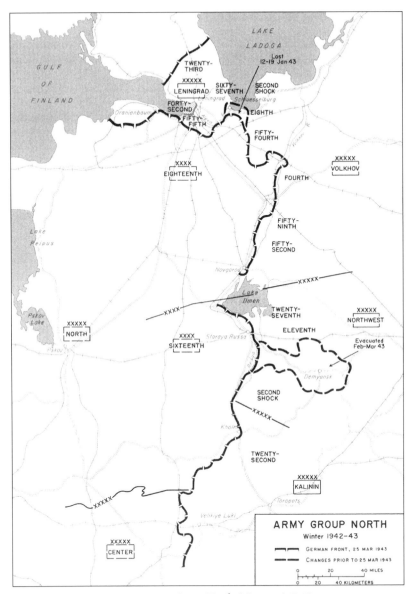

Map 10: Army Group North, Winter, 1942-43

that lasted until the first week of April, the two Soviet fronts made little headway. When the fighting ended, they held a strip 6 miles wide, all of it within range of German artillery. When the battle ended, Army Group North claimed a defensive victory, but its hold on the second city of the Soviet Union was not as tight as before.

On the Army Group North right flank the Demyansk pocket had been under continuous attack since the end of November 1942. By mid-January the fighting in the pocket had drained off the last army group reserves. On 19 January, Zeitzler told Kuechler that he intended to take up with Hitler the question of evacuating the Demyansk pocket. He and Kuechler agreed that the principal reason for the setback the army group had just suffered south of Lake Ladoga was the shortage of troops and that the only way to avoid similar mishaps was to create reserves by giving up the pocket. That Hitler would bitterly resist any such proposal went without saying; and Kuechler, who had been sharply rebuffed in the fall of 1942 when he suggested abandonment, refused to take the initiative in reopening the question.

On the night of 31 January, after a week-long debate, Hitler finally gave way to Zeitzler's arguments. The Operations Section, OKH, informed Kuechler that the struggle to get the decision had been unprecedentedly difficult and asked him to get the troops out fast in order not to give Hitler a chance to change his mind. Kuechler, however, refused to risk losing the vast quantity of equipment and supplies poured into the pocket during the past thirteen months. He began pulling back the line on 20 February, after three weeks preparation, and then collapsed the pocket by stages, completing the last on 18 March.

ARMY GROUP CENTER—ANTIPARTISAN WARFARE
Through the winter Army Group Center stood as the bulwark of the Eastern Front, but its underpinnings were weak. Its front, projecting eastward—once a giant spearhead aimed at Moscow—was, under the influence of the second Soviet winter offensive, becoming badly eroded and an invitation to disaster. (Map 11) On the north flank, around the bulge west of Toropets, the army group had not had a secure line since December 1941. After mid-January 1943, the Soviet armies gouged deeply into the south flank, forcing it back west of Kursk.

On 20 January, to shore up what was then the weakest spot in his front, Kluge moved Headquarters, Third Panzer Army, into the sector on the western rim of the Toropets bulge. The attempt to relieve Velikiye Luki had failed five days earlier. After his first look at the

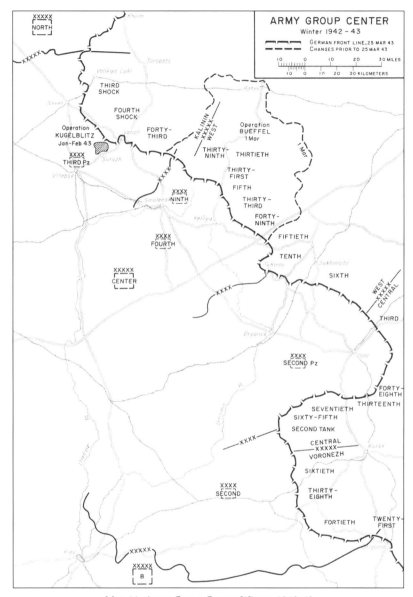

Map 11: Army Group Center, Winter, 1942-43

front, the Commanding General, Third Panzer Army, Generaloberst Hans Reinhardt, reported that the sector was in "appalling condition." Gruppe von der Chevallerie had thrown every unit it could lay hands on into the thrust toward Velikiye Luki. In the army rear area an estimated 20,000 partisans roamed the countryside at will. The army's first task would be to gain enough troops to establish some sort of defensible line by pulling back and sorting out the jumbled units west of Velikiye Luki.

In the first week of February, having set up a line of strongpoints, Third Panzer Army turned to the partisan menace. Throughout the zones of Army Groups North and Center, partisan activity had flared up dangerously since the beginning of winter. As in the previous year, the Soviet commands employed the partisans as an adjunct to the winter offensive. Again the conditions were favorable. Hard-pressed to man the front, the Germans could only commit second- and third-rate troops in the rear areas. The Soviet victories raised the partisans' morale and made the civilians in the occupied territory amenable to Soviet and partisan influences.

Hitler, as he had since the start of the war, called for the utmost severity. In January 1943 he decreed that soldiers could not be brought to trial for atrocities committed while fighting partisans. The Geneva Convention and the rules of chivalry, he declared, had no place in antipartisan warfare. The generals, on the other hand, were fully aware that they lacked the strength to master the partisan movement by Draconian methods and would, if they tried, only succeed in totally alienating the civilian population. Consequently, most of them attempted, for humanitarian and practical reasons, to avoid interpreting Hitler's decree literally. The Commanding General, Second Panzer Army, General der Panzertruppen Rudolf Schmidt, for instance, directed that it would apply only to acts committed in the heat of battle and would, under no circumstances, be considered a license to kill and plunder wantonly.

In late February Third Panzer Army conducted an operation (KUGELBLITZ) against the partisan center in the Surazh Rayon northeast of Vitebsk. Although it had little effect on the course of the war, the operation is worth examining for two reasons: it is representative of dozens of similar antipartisan operations the Germans conducted in the years 1942-44, and it gives an unusually clear-cut picture of partisan and antipartisan warfare. The area concerned, the Surazh Rayon, lay directly behind the Third Panzer Army front. It had been partisan-infested for more than a year and had won acclaim on the

Russian evacuees on the road, 1943.

Soviet side for the so-called Vitebsk Corridor, where in the late winter of 1941-42 the partisans and the Red Army had maintained truck and horse-drawn supply traffic through the large gaps in the German line. By February 1943 the front had not greatly changed. The sector north of Surazh, a thin line of strongpoints spaced two to three miles apart, was held by German Air Force field divisions. In the gaps and in the extensive forests and swamps behind the front the Germans had been forced by lack of troops to permit the partisans virtually free rein. The partisans, numbering an estimated four to five thousand, were organized into brigades. They had built permanent, fortified encampments, and operated their own airfields.

To execute the antipartisan operation, Reinhardt detailed two security divisions. The first step, completed on 21 February, was to draw a skirmish line around the partisan area, which encompassed most of the Surazh Rayon. When that had been done, the troops began to advance inward, drawing the ring tighter and driving the partisans ahead of them toward the center. Contact was difficult to maintain, and the troops, pushing across rough terrain and through forests deep in snow, soon tired. The partisans, for their part, evaded pitched battles and, whenever they could, hid or slipped through the encirclement. When the operation ended, on 8 March, the army claimed 3,700 partisans killed, but it had no way of telling with certainty how many of the casualties were actually partisans and how many noncombatant civilians. As soon as the German units withdrew, the partisans reorganized and within a few months they had nearly regained their former strength.

OPERATION BUEFFEL

Although the Army Group Center zone was quiet in the early winter of 1942-43 except for partisan activity, its front in the long run, clearly was untenable. The army group had no reserves. Its left flank was weak and, after the collapse of Second Army, its right flank was left dangling in a void. When Army Group North secured permission to evacuate the Demyansk pocket, the great eastward projection of Army Group Center ceased to serve any, even remotely, useful purpose. To pinch off the Toropets salient was no longer possible, and no one was thinking seriously any more of an advance to Moscow. On 26 January Kluge recommended to Hitler a large-scale withdrawal that would shorten the front and eliminate the danger of the Ninth and Fourth Armies' being encircled. As was to be expected, Hitler resisted bitterly, but finally, on 6 February, he yielded to Zeitzler's and Kluge's arguments.

During the rest of the month the army group readied itself for the withdrawal, which was given the code name BUEFFEL. The chief task was to build a fortified line in the rear between Velizh and Kirov. At midmonth the armies began combing the towns and the countryside for able-bodied men and others who might be useful to the Russians if left behind. Long columns of evacuees, whom one army commander described as presenting pictures of absolute misery, were marched off to the west through the dead, late winter cold. Fourth Army alone reported evacuating 45,000 persons.

On 1 March Ninth Army began drawing back its front north and west of Rzhev. In twenty-three days Operation BUEFFEL was completed. The units that originally stood farthest east had covered a distance of 90 miles. The length of the front in the BUEFFEL area was reduced from 340 miles to 110 miles.

On his south flank, after 14 February, Kluge faced the problem of finding enough troops to halt Second Army's retreat and to man the lengthening line of Second Panzer Army, its neighbor on the north. As the Russians advanced west past Kursk, the army group front began to bulge dangerously east of Orel. On 20 February Kluge proposed pulling back the Panzer and Second Armies to the line of the Desna River, but Hitler was through retreating. He was already at work on other plans, and before many months had passed, the names of two provincial Russian towns, Kursk and Orel, would gain renown on the Eastern Front.

CHAPTER VII

Operation ZITADELLE

THE LULL IN THE STORM

In the years past, the arrival of spring had always heralded new German triumphs. Even the black winter of 1941-42 had been followed by a surge of fresh strength and confidence. But 1943 was different. The day of the whirlwind offensive was gone and with it the grandiose plans that less than a year earlier had included a gigantic pincers movement through the Caucasus and Egypt into the Middle East. During the winter Hitler had been forced to use the slogan "defense of the Homeland" in rallying the armies on the southern flanks of the Eastern Front. Although the front was still deep in the Soviet Union, several hundred miles from the German border, that appeal was beginning to have a literal significance that was not lost on the troops. The victory on the Donets, which ended the long winter retreat of Army Group South, and the successful withdrawals by the other army groups, restored morale at the front, but no one deluded himself into believing the next summer would see the swastika replanted on Mt. Elbrus or German outposts again looking east into Asia from the high bank of the Volga. Henceforth the war would be fought on other terms. The crucial question was to what extent, if at all, Germany would still be able to set those terms. For a time, the front settled down to an ominous quiet, waiting.

A DARK SPRING

After the first week of April, when the Russians gave up their second attempt to liberate Leningrad, both sides paused to rest and regroup. The Russian spring with its mud and swollen rivers could be depended on to enforce at least a few weeks' truce. Only Army Group A had a tactical mission still to be executed. Hitler had ordered it to eliminate a beachhead the Russians had established early in February south of

Novorossisk in the Kuban. He wanted to anchor the GOTENKOPF firmly at Novorossisk so as to deny the enemy the port that had formerly been an important base for the Soviet Black Sea Fleet.

After several false starts and delays caused by bad weather, the attack began on 18 April. When five days of fighting, which Seventeenth Army described as the heaviest it had experienced since the battle for Sevastopol in 1942, failed to dent the Soviet line, the attack had to be given up as too costly in men and matériel. Seventeenth Army charged much of the blame for its failure to a condition then widespread among the armies in the east: its divisions, after nearly a year of uninterrupted combat, were simply not as effective as they once had been. The divisions needed rest and time to train their replacements, who in the past months had been thrown directly into combat from the basic training camps in Germany.

Since June 1941 German attention had centered on the Eastern Front. Now, quite suddenly, the situation changed. Dangers that might have been disposed of handily had the campaign against the Soviet Union gone according to schedule loomed ominously all around. In January U.S. Army Air Forces flying fortresses staged the first daylight bombing attack on Germany, a massive strike at Wilhelmshaven. Two months later the British Royal Air Force (RAF) resumed night bombing, using 4-engine bombers instead of the 2-engine planes that had carried out most of the earlier raids. In the cities, particularly in the Ruhr, bomb damage increased alarmingly; and in one of the ironic twists of the war the army groups in the East began keeping tabs on home front morale.

As their air forces struck at the center of the so-called Fortress Europe, the British and American ground forces deployed to storm the outer defenses. A second Stalingrad had long been in the making in North Africa. After British Eighth Army broke the Mareth Line in the last week of March defeat became inevitable, and on 12 and 13 May the last elements of Fifth Panzer Army and Italian First Army surrendered in Tunisia. That the Western Allies would follow up their victory in North Africa with an invasion of southern Europe, either in Italy or in the Balkans, seemed certain. If they were committed, as it appeared, to Winston S. Churchill's strategy of attacking on the periphery, landings in Norway were also possible. There, growing hostility in Sweden added to the danger. In the west the Channel coast would probably not be threatened in 1943, but it would be foolhardy to count on more than a year's respite before the decisive battle that was to be expected there. In short, the keystone of Hitler's strategy was crumbling; he had failed to make good the boast that he would deal with his enemies one by one; Germany was confronted with a 2-front war, that old specter that had haunted the General Staff since the latter years of the nineteenth century.

Since 1939 Hitler had been fighting the "poor man's war," trying to compensate for inferior resources of manpower and personnel by relying on surprise, relentless exercise of the initiative, and his opponents' lack of preparedness. Now his enemies were on the ascendant, and the indications were that he would be hard put to meet them on their terms.

Paradoxically, of the major belligerents, Germany had been the slowest in fully mobilizing its national resources. Dazzled by cheap successes and confident that victory was just around the corner, Hitler had for the first two and a half years of the war been content to live off the lead he had gained before 1939. Early in 1942, in one of his most fortunate choices, he had appointed Dr. Albert Speer Minister for Armament and Munitions. Under Speer German war production rose sharply and continued to rise until 1945, but the production gap remained.

In the early months of 1943, influenced by a second disastrous winter, Hitler again undertook to intensify the German war effort. In January he appointed the Committee of Three, composed of the Chief, OKW, Keitel, the Chief of the Party Chancellory, Martin Bormann, and the Chief of the Reichs Chancellory, Hans Lammers. The committee was to procure 800,000 men for the armed forces, and it was given broad powers to make the men available by eliminating nonessential industries and occupations. They expected to fill the 800,000-man draft by placing the civilian economy on what was called a "total war" footing. Consequently, subsequent drafts would bring the armed forces and the war industries into direct competition for men, and the OKW estimated that between October 1943 and April 1944 the armed services would need another 973,000 men. Since the new class of eighteen-year-olds would number no more than 460,000, most of the remainder would have to come from the deferred groups, a move which would cut deep into the labor force of the armament industry.

Among the service arms, the German armored forces had long shown serious symptoms of neglect. In the winter battles of 1942-43 in the USSR the German tanks were outnumbered and, to a large extent, outclassed. The most powerful tank in quantity production, the Panzer IV, was a prewar model known since 1941 to be no match for the Soviet T34. The winter disasters forced Hitler to call back the Army's outstanding tank expert, Guderian, whom he had summarily dismissed in December 1941. He appointed Guderian Inspector General for Armor, gave him control of tank development and allocation and authorized him to devise improvements in tank tactics and the employment of panzer units.

New tank models were on the way. The Tiger, which so far had fallen somewhat short of expectations, was in full production. The Panther, lighter and more mobile than the Tiger, was scheduled to start coming off the assembly lines in the late spring. Through the combined efforts of Speer and Guderian German tank output rose rapidly in the early months of 1943, reaching 621 units in April and 988, including 300 of the new Panthers, in May. In June and July it fell off slightly to 775 and 811, largely because of production difficulties with the Panthers. Impressive as they were, the figures probably fell well below the current monthly output of the Soviet Union alone and certainly far less than the combined American, British, and Soviet production. Furthermore, the gain in strength was less than appeared at first glance because the new models were being rushed to the front before they had been thoroughly tested and without fully trained crews.

In at least one phase of weapons development, however, the Germans were still far ahead of their enemies. In April 1943 they completed firing the first test series of seventeen A-4 (V-2) rockets. By July they had fired another thirteen missiles in guidance and accuracy tests, and in August they put in production the first series of missiles. In February 1943 component development was begun for the C-2,

Wasserfall, a large antiaircraft rocket. It was expected to reach the testing stage by the end of the year.

GERMANY'S ALLIES

The strongest reaction to the Germans' waning fortunes came from their allies. Late in March the recently appointed Finnish Foreign Minister, Ramsay, flew to Berlin for a conference with Reichsminister Joachim von Ribbentrop. On 20 March the U.S. State Department had offered its good offices in establishing contact between Finland and the Soviet Union for the purpose of bringing an end to hostilities between the two. Ramsay, new to diplomacy and apparently not well acquainted with the character of the German Foreign Minister, informed Ribbentrop of the American note and, while denying that Finland intended to make peace behind the Germans' back, indicated that Finnish "private circles" were coming to favor a change on the part of Finland to something like armed neutrality. Ribbentrop promptly undertook to dispel Ramsay's illusion of opening the way out of the war by a friendly agreement with Germany. The German people, he said, who were also fighting the war for Finland, would not appreciate having the Finns "cast come-hither looks" at the Russians. To drive the point home, he presented two demands: the United States' offer must be promptly and firmly rejected; and the Finnish Government must declare its intention not to conclude a separate peace without German consent. The second came as a considerable blow to the Finns, since to meet it meant giving up the independent status Finland claimed as a cobelligerent, not a formal ally, of Germany. Actually, the problem of Finland was not yet acute. Even if the Finns evaded a binding declaration of loyalty to Germany, it could be safely assumed that for the present they had no place to go. They were completely dependent on German economic and military assistance, and eager as they might be to leave the war, they were undoubtedly not ready to trust themselves to Soviet mercy.

For the near future Italy was a more pressing problem. That Mussolini's regime, shaken by the defeat in North Africa, would survive an invasion of the Italian mainland was highly doubtful, and to imagine that in such a case the Axis could be preserved was completely fatuous. Mussolini was worried. In December 1942 and again in March 1943 he proposed negotiating a peace with the Russians to avoid the trap of a 2-front war. "On the day the Russian campaign is liquidated," he wrote, "we can hoist the flag. Victory is ours!" As an alternative, he thought of creating an "East Wall," a permanent, fortified front in the East that would free enough troops to meet the expected British-American offensives in western and southern Europe.

In the second week of April Hitler and Ribbentrop received Mussolini and his acting foreign minister at Schloss Klessheim near Berchtesgaden. Hitler had already rejected the idea of negotiating with the Russians on the ground that Stalin could not be trusted and "if given a half-year's peace" would use it to prepare his revenge, but it was necessary to try to revive the Italians' confidence and set at least some of their fears to rest. Ribbentrop told the Duce that in a war of ideologies such as that between Germany and the Soviet Union compromise was out of the question; the Soviet Union was three-fourths defeated; and the German armies would take the offensive again in the coming summer. At the same time, he indicated that Germany would not stage another all-out offensive in the style of the previous two years. Instead, the strategy would be to wear down the Soviet Union gradually.

The idea of an "East Wall," as proposed by Mussolini, had also begun to appeal to some of the German generals. After the winter battles ended, Zeitzler suggested building a fortified line to backstop the Eastern Front, but Hitler would have none of it. He claimed it would undermine the troops' will to fight. He still envisioned an eventual decline in Soviet strength to the point where the German armies could advance eastward again, perhaps to the line of the Don River, and then establish a sort of Limes Germanicus beyond which the Russians, reduced to military impotence, could be left to their own devices.

After Mussolini came a procession of leaders of the lesser allies, first Marshal Antonescu, the Rumanian head of state, then Admiral Miklos Horthy, Regent of Hungary, and later Msgr. Joseph Tiso, the Slovakian head of state, and Ante Pavelic, the Poglavnik of Croatia. Antonescu, like Mussolini, worried about the consequences of a 2-front war, but he recommended making peace with the Western Allies in order to gain a free hand against the Soviet Union. The Rumanians, with a long frontier bordering on the Soviet Union, had no choice but stay in the war. The Hungarians, all along more interested in their quarrels with their immediate neighbors than in the campaign against the Soviet Union, henceforth kept their Army, except for a few token divisions, at home.

VLASOV

One potential ally many Germans thought might still be able to turn the tide against the Soviet Union was the Russian people. The population of the German-occupied territories in the Soviet Union plus the millions of Russian prisoners of war constituted a potential reservoir of economic and military power second only to that of Germany itself. Given some independence and a reasonably attractive government, it appeared those people might yet prove willing to forget the years of hardship and oppression under the Germans and turn against their former masters in the Kremlin, from whose return they expected to profit little. Although the chances were not as good as in former years, it also appeared possible that the example of a non-Communist Russian state would seriously undermine Stalin's authority in the rest of the Soviet Union.

Late in 1942 the sentiment in German military circles for an alliance with the Russian people produced the first tentative step toward a positive program. The propaganda section of the OKW and the Eastern Intelligence Branch, OKH, tried to set up the captured Soviet general, Andrei I. Vlasov, as the leader of an anti-Communist Russian national movement. He was named head of a shadow government, the Russian National Committee, and given nominal command of the Russian Army of Liberation, a miscellaneous collection of collaborator units recruited by the Germans. The Wehrmacht propaganda officers prepared a 13-point program promising the Russians private property, peasant ownership of the land, and—vaguely—national independence. When that program, published over Vlasov's signature as the so-called Smolensk Manifesto, was given limited publicity during the winter of 1942-43, the popular response appeared encouraging but also quickly revealed that, to have any lasting effect, it would have to be implemented by concrete measures, and Hitler refused to go that far. He held to the dictum he had established when he began the campaign in the USSR—that he was not fighting the war and sacrificing German men for the sake of the Russians.

Early in 1943, when it became clear that anything that promised to contribute toward restoring the German fortunes was worth a try, Hitler's stubborn hard line on the Soviet Union aroused dismay even among some who rarely allowed themselves to doubt the Fuehrer's judgment. Propaganda Minister Goebbels tried to persuade him at least to offer the Russian peasants land and freedom of worship, but without success. In May, Kluge, Commanding General, Army Group Center, having failed a month earlier to persuade Goebbels to approach Hitler again concerning a more liberal policy for the east, forwarded a long memorandum to the Chief of Staff, OKH, in which he set down his and his army commanders' beliefs regarding the future of German relations with the Russian people. In blunt language, Kluge, who, when it came to expressing opinions that might come to Hitler's notice was not the most outspoken of the generals, outlined the following reasons for a change in policy:

The development of the total situation is forcing, with growing insistence, the establishment of clear objectives with respect to the Russian people whose collaboration including military collaboration must be won because it will have a decisive influence on the war. The methods employed so far have failed: force is not enough. The Russian people must be won by other means and be persuaded to fight for our cause because they also see it as theirs.

Economic concessions—which would have the most reliable effect—are not at our disposal. The only possibility is to grant the Russian people a share in the administration of their country immediately in order to demonstrate that the German war aims are not limited to the worn out slogan "the crusade against Bolshevism."

Kluge added that the Smolensk Manifesto and a recent Vlasov visit in the army group zone had aroused a favorable popular response, but he warned that it was high time to follow this up with deeds, otherwise the propaganda itself would become dangerous and have to be abandoned. He recommended creating a Russian national committee in the Army Group Center zone that would be given a gradually increasing role in the civil administration of the occupied territory. "We will have to accept the fact," Kluge concluded, "that the last stage will be full self-government under the occupying power."

That Kluge's memorandum had no chance of influencing Hitler was a foregone conclusion. To have accepted it would, as far as Hitler was concerned, have made nonsense out of the whole war in the Soviet Union. A month earlier, at a conference of the economic administrators for the occupied territories, Goering had laid down the policy to be followed. Maximum exploitation of the Eastern territories to meet German needs was to be the watchword. Even the subsistence requirements of the people were to be disregarded "because the Russian people cannot be won over to the German cause in any case."

A LIMITED OFFENSIVE

By early March 1943 it was evident that Germany would be able to salvage two significant assets from the wreckage of the winter. Manstein's advance to the Donets would throw the Russians temporarily off balance in the zone of their main effort, and as a dividend of Operation BUEFFEL and the retreat in southern USSR, a fairly strong operational reserve would be created. These were enough to afford Hitler, at least to a limited degree, a free hand in planning.

STRATEGIC PLANS—OPERATIONS ORDER 5

On 13 March the plan was ready, embodied in Operations Order 5. After the end of the winter and the spring muddy season, it stated, the Russians would return to the offensive. The German armies would have to strike first in several places and, as Army Group South was currently doing, definitely seize the initiative in at least one. The spot Hitler chose was the Kursk bulge. By mid-April Army Group South was to assemble a strong panzer army for an attack north toward Kursk from the Kharkov area. (Map 12) On the northern rim of the bulge Army Group Center was to create an offensive force in the Second Panzer Army zone, using divisions released by BUEFFEL. The offensive would begin as soon as the muddy season ended and before

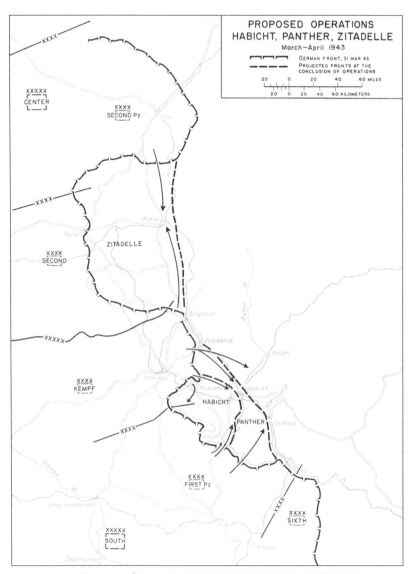

Map 12: Proposed Operations HABICHT, PANTHER, ZITADELLE,
March-April 1943

the Russians had a chance to launch an attack of their own. Army
Group A would reduce the size of the GOTENKOPF, and its primary
mission would be to release troops for transfer to Army Group South.

Although the Kursk offensive, given the code name ZITADELLE,
subsequently acquired the character of a desperate and tragic gamble,

it was conceived as part of a coherent and not unpromising strategy that envisioned a series of limited offensives to consolidate the German defenses. A victory in the Kursk bulge would straighten the German front and could be expected to keep the Russians off balance a while longer. In his order Hitler instructed Army Group North to be ready to follow up ZITADELLE with an operation against Leningrad. By taking Leningrad he intended to tighten his hold on the Baltic Sea and northern Europe, where growing hostility on the part of Sweden and war weariness in Finland were adding to his long-standing concern over the vulnerable Norwegian coast.

During the winter he had several times talked about strengthening the forces in Norway, and in February the Army of Norway had begun work on a defense plan which included the occupation of Sweden. On 13 March, the day Operations Order 5 was issued, he told Jodl that he intended to shift a mountain division plus six battalions to Norway and planned to equip the panzer division then forming in Norway "with the heaviest assault weapons, ones against which Sweden possesses no means of defense."

The timing was crucial. If ZITADELLE succeeded in the spring, the operation against Leningrad, using troops from ZITADELLE, could start in early summer; and once Leningrad was safely in hand, Finnish interest in the war could be expected to revive, Sweden could be dealt with at will, and Norway would become a much less attractive target for the Western Allies. If ZITADELLE were completed promptly, there would also be time and troops enough to strengthen the Mediterranean front. On the other hand, the cost of failure would run high. The two armies intended for ZITADELLE comprised the entire German strategic reserve. They were working capital which, lost or tied down in a fruitless enterprise, could not be quickly replaced.

At the time Hitler issued Operations Order 5, the front in the Army Group Center and South zones was still fluid. As so often happened, Hitler's planning was based in important particulars on conditions which did not yet exist and which might not come into being exactly as he anticipated. Army Group Center was in the midst of Operation BUEFFEL. Second Army and Second Panzer Army were struggling to stop the Russians in the bulge west and northwest of Kursk. The striking force of Army Group South, Fourth Panzer Army, was adding the finishing touches to its victory at Kharkov, but it had been on the move without pause for nearly a month, and its troops were nearly exhausted. Both army groups needed time to rest and refit before embarking on an offensive. Army Group South was already feeling the effects of the spring thaw. Farther north, in the Army Group Center zone, the thaw would set in during the next few weeks and last through April. To get ready for ZITADELLE by mid-April would be difficult, maybe impossible.

HABICHT AND PANTHER

After Fourth Panzer Army, in the third week of March, cleared the right bank of the Donets north to Belgorod, Hitler temporarily left ZITADELLE in abeyance and turned his attention to the Donets line southeast of Kharkov. There, it appeared, the opportunity for a quick, relatively easy victory was beckoning. Frantic enemy activity east of the river showed the Russians were worried. From the German point of view a thrust across the Donets had tactical advantages. It would straighten and shorten the front southeast of Kharkov and, by pushing it farther east, might discourage the Russians from again attempting to cut off the Army Group South right flank by striking at Dnepropetrovsk and Zaporozhye. It would also facilitate the execution of ZITADELLE by eliminating the danger of a counterthrust from the south into the rear of the ZITADELLE advance.

On 22 March Hitler issued an order for Operation HABICHT, an offensive thrust across the Donets, to be undertaken as soon as the river receded enough to permit a crossing. He assigned responsibility for HABICHT to First Panzer Army and Armeeabteilung Kempf. Armeeabteilung Kempf was to put one assault force across the Donets in the vicinity of Chuguyev and strike southward behind the Russian line on the river. A second force was to cross farther north and advance east to Kupyansk. First Panzer Army was to tie down the Russians around Izyum and send a force north along the west bank of the Oskol River to Kupyansk.

Two days later Hitler directed Army Group South also to begin planning a more ambitious operation, code-named PANTHER, to be executed by the First and Fourth Panzer Armies, which would force the Russians away from the Donets and back to the line Volchansk-Kupyansk-Svatovo-Krasnaya River. Neither of the new operations aroused enthusiasm at the headquarters of the armies concerned. The First Panzer Army and Armeeabteilung Kempf chiefs of staff worried that Hitler would fall into his old habit of driving the armies on from victory to victory without rest until, as in previous years, they again became hopelessly overextended.

At the end of the month, with three operations in planning, Hitler faced the problem—which to execute and when. HABICHT was comparatively minor and would hardly be worthwhile unless it could be a prelude to ZITADELLE. PANTHER, larger and tactically more profitable, would require much more time and would necessitate an indefinite postponement of ZITADELLE. One thing was certain, every week's delay reduced the chances of success no matter what the choice. The advantages on the German side were slight enough as it was. On the Armeeabteilung Kempf front alone the Russians had an estimated 1,000-1,500 tanks, more than twice the number Army Group South could muster in its entire zone. To achieve genuine surprise with any of the three proposed operations was already out of the question. Everything hinged on being ready to exploit the first onset of good weather in the hope of catching the enemy momentarily off guard and not solidly dug in.

On 2 April Hitler issued his "decision." HABICHT would be made ready so that it could begin on four days' notice any time after 13 April. By placing HABICHT first on the list he had virtually eliminated it. The Donets was expected to reach the flood stage in the second half of April, and Manstein had said that Army Group South could not be ready to resume the offensive by mid-April because the panzer units would have to be allowed to complete their rest and refitting "at least to a certain degree." Aware of those difficulties, Hitler ordered that if HABICHT could not start by 17 April, it would be superseded by PANTHER, which would then have to be ready by 1 May; if neither HABICHT nor PANTHER could be executed, he added, Army Groups Center and South would go over to ZITADELLE. Three days later

Manstein told his subordinate commanders the final choice would probably be ZITADELLE.

OPERATIONS ORDER 6—ZITADELLE POSTPONED

On 15 April, Hitler announced his "definitive decision." ZITADELLE, he directed in Operations Order 6, would be ready to start on six days' notice after 28 April. PANTHER would follow, taking advantage of the confusion ZITADELLE was expected to create on the Soviet side. The special instructions for ZITADELLE reveal why Hitler had taken so long making up his mind. He was fully aware that the operation was an extremely touchy undertaking. He warned, first, that it would have to be done fast because troops were needed for other missions. Secondly, he ordered Army Groups Center and South to be on guard against Soviet attacks in the exposed sectors on either side of the Kursk bulge. Operation ZITADELLE, as he was painfully aware, would be launched not out of a solid front but rather out of the tips of two far from stable salients, the outer faces of which invited Soviet attention as much as the Kursk bulge did German. The danger was greater northwest of Orel but not much less south of Kharkov, where the Soviet line projected westward into the bend of the Donets below the city.

ZITADELLE could become a case of a herring intent on gulping a sardine swimming into the jaws of a shark. That had raised the question whether ZITADELLE could not more safely be conducted as a "backhand stroke" (aus der Nachhand schlagen) that would leave the first move to the Russians. Nevertheless, Hitler had suppressed his doubts and had decided to go ahead with ZITADELLE as he originally conceived it. The reason why is also to be found in Operations Order 6. "The victory at Kursk," he stated, "must have the effect of a beacon seen around the world."29 He needed a victory in the old style, a gigantic encirclement to bring in hundreds of thousands of prisoners and thousands of tons of booty. Only ZITADELLE could provide those.

No sooner did Operations Order 6 reach the front commands, than new obstacles appeared. Ninth Army, which was to command the offensive in the Army Group Center zone, protested that its

Soviet anti-aircraft gun firing near Orel.

deployment could not be completed by 3 May. The OKH proposed granting postponements on a day-to-day basis, but Ninth Army insisted that either its mission be reduced or ZITADELLE be put off at least to 15 May.

On 18 April air reconnaissance reported long truck columns moving out of Moscow

toward Kursk and out of Stalingrad toward Valuyki, due east of Kharkov. This sign that the Russians were on the alert was scarcely needed: Army Group South estimated that from reserves already at hand the Russians could throw 8 tank, 5 mechanized, and 5 cavalry corps against its main force, Fourth Panzer Army, in the first six days of the offensive.

On the morning of 30 April, having agreed four days earlier to postpone ZITADELLE for two days, the OKH granted four more days' delay because of heavy rains. That afternoon it ordered all directives setting a time for ZITADELLE canceled and destroyed. A new date would not be set until after Hitler had conferred with the commanding generals.

On 3 May Hitler called Manstein, Kluge, and the Commanding General, Ninth Army, Generaloberst Walter Model, to a conference to be held the next day in Munich. The others to be present were Zeitzler, Guderian, Speer, and the Chief of Staff, OKL, Generaloberst Hans Jeschonneck.

The discussion centered on Model's report describing the problems he expected Ninth Army to encounter in breaking through the well-fortified Russian front. In particular, Model believed the Mark IV tanks, the heaviest he had except for a few Tigers, would not be able to stand up to the new Soviet antitank weapons. Hitler, who apparently had begun to have qualms on his own account, was impressed. He proposed letting ZITADELLE wait until June; by then he expected to have the newer model tanks available in quantity. Manstein, Kluge, and Zeitzler objected, maintaining that the delay would benefit the Russians more than the Germans by giving them time to recover from the winter battles and that their tank output, which was known to be higher than that of the Germans, would cancel any gains anticipated from waiting for the new tanks.

Manstein said he believed ZITADELLE could succeed if it were executed in May. He considered a longer wait dangerous for the reasons he, Kluge, and Zeitzler had given and because the collapse of German and Italian resistance in Tunisia, expected any day, would probably be followed within a matter of weeks by a British-American landing in the Mediterranean, which would create more complications. Kluge, perhaps chiefly out of annoyance at seeing one of his subordinates given direct access to Hitler, declared that Ninth Army was not as badly off as Model thought. Jeschonnek added that a delay would not benefit the Air Force. The others present, Guderian and Speer, objected to ZITADELLE's being executed at all, because, successful or not, it would occasion heavy tank losses and thus upset their plans for increasing German armored strength. Hitler closed the conference without giving a decision, but he indicated privately to Model that there would be a postponement.

On 6 May the OKH announced that ZITADELLE was postponed to 12 June. The next day in a telephone conference with Zeitzler, Kempf protested that the delay was "undesirable" from both the psychological and operational points of view. He believed it would benefit the defender more than the attacker. Zeitzler agreed and said he was glad to have such an "observation from the front" to lay before Hitler at the next opportunity. But further argument proved useless; Hitler was determined to wait for the new tanks, especially the Ferdinands, ninety of which he would have in June. He expected them to increase the penetrating power of the attack. The Ferdinand mounted a long-barreled 88-mm. gun on a Tiger chassis. Guderian considered it a mediocre weapon because of its low speed, fixed turret, and lack of machine guns for use in close combat; but its heavy armor and powerful gun had impressed Hitler. He succumbed once more to his weakness for new weapons and the visions of easy victories they aroused in his imagination.

May was a troubled month. A week after the Munich conference Guderian asked Hitler why he wanted to start an offensive in the East at all in 1943. Hitler replied that he had doubts himselfthe very thought of the offensive gave him "butterflies in his stomach." On the 13th the last German and Italian units in Tunisia surrendered. The defeat had been inevitable for two months or more, but, as in the case of Stalingrad, Hitler, to the last, had only half-believed it could actually happen. Confronted in earnest with the necessity for strengthening Italy and the Balkans, his doubts about ZITADELLE grew. On the 14th Kluge told one of his army commanders that it was completely uncertain when ZITADELLE would begin. Ten days later Goebbels believed that Hitler had adopted an "After you, my dear Alphonse," attitude and intended to let the Russians make the first move.

Probably the most illuminating insight into Hitler's state of mind occurred early in May at a meeting of high Nazi Party officials. He drew a detailed comparison between the year 1932, when the party—after victories at the polls—appeared to be going down to defeat at the hands of Papen and Hindenburg, and the current situation. "In 1932," he said, "we attained victory only by stubbornness that sometimes looked like madness, so too shall we achieve it today." This was a theme which, over the years, he had come to regard as the first principle of his military and political leadership. It expressed his deep-seated belief, shared by many Germans, that his primary claim to greatness was his ability to achieve victory against impossible odds, sometimes almost by will power alone. As had happened several times in the past, the apparent doubts and uncertainty were a phase in the period of incubation from which he invariably emerged determined to follow the most radical course.

SILBERSTREIF

As Operation ZITADELLE receded farther into the future, an unnatural quiet settled over the Eastern Front. The Russians, who for two months had appeared to be racing desperately to get in the first blow, seemed to have decided instead on a courteous "After you, my dear Gaston." During the pause Army Group Center diverted a number of line divisions, rarely available for such tasks, to antipartisan operations. Front activity, except for random local skirmishing, was restricted to Operation SILBERSTREIF, the most ambitious German propaganda campaign of the war.

SILBERSTREIF was a byproduct of the Army's desire to draw the Russian people into an alliance against the Soviet regime. In April the OKH had established in Basic Order No. 13, a policy of preferred treatment for Russian deserters. They were to be segregated from the other prisoners of war and housed in better quarters. When they crossed into the German line they were to be given a "generous" issue of rations and transported to the rear aboard trucks, not marched back on foot. Officers were to be assigned orderlies. Prisoners of war who had volunteered for German service were to be formed into units, one officer and twenty-four men for each German division. These units would conduct loudspeaker propaganda at the front and act as welcoming committees for the incoming deserters.

SILBERSTREIF, conducted in May, June, and July, was an attempt to advertise Basic Order No. 13 to the Russian soldier. Its results were disappointing. Army Group North reported distributing forty-nine million propaganda leaflets in May and June. During the same period a total of 622 deserters came in, less than half of them directly attributable to SILBERSTREIF. The propaganda officers believed that SILBERSTREIF would have been more successful had it been conducted in conjunction with ZITADELLE, as was originally intended, rather than at a time when the front was stable and desertion, consequently, more difficult.

HITLER DECIDES FOR ZITADELLE

As summer approached, tension increased on both sides of the front. Late in May Ninth Army reported that the Russians had strong reserves echeloned in depth behind the front, ready to meet any threat. In the first weeks of June the forces for ZITADELLE reached their peak strength. The troops were rested, and they had received 900 tanks and over 300 self-propelled assault guns since March. Still, as far as anyone knew, ZITADELLE was no nearer execution. A conference at the OKH on 10 June again considered the tactic of the "backhand stroke."

On 18 June the Operations Staff, OKW, entered the picture and recommended to Hitler that ZITADELLE be abandoned. They characterized the coming summer as a period of uncertainty and proposed pulling together all the troops that could be spared into two strong strategic reserves, one in Germany and the other, comprising the two armies for ZITADELLE, behind the Eastern Front but close to railroads so that it could be moved to Italy or the Balkans in case of need. On the same day, Hitler replied that although he fully appreciated the Operations Staff's point of view, he had definitely decided to go ahead with ZITADELLE. Two days later he announced his decision to the army groups and armies, but another five days passed before he set the time—5 July.

In the three months after Operations Order No. 5 appeared the situation at the front had so changed that ZITADELLE would have to be fought under conditions exactly opposite those originally anticipated. The time for exploiting the enemy's temporary weakness was long past. The chances of a quick thrust were slight; the armies would have to grind through a fortified front miles deep and backed by waves of reserves. A Ninth Army report described the coming offensive as "a collision between armies at the peak of readiness on both sides" in which the skill of the German soldiers and the superiority of their leaders would have to be enough to tip the balance. On 26 June Fourth Panzer Army warned that the prospects of success were declining daily. On the other hand, from the OKH point of view, to cancel the offensive could prove worse than to go ahead and risk a setback. If ZITADELLE were given up, Hitler was certain to accept the OKW proposal concerning reserves, with the result that the OKH would lose control of Ninth Army and Fourth Panzer Army, which would probably be taken away from the Eastern Front altogether and shifted to the OKW theaters in Italy and the Balkans.

As if the picture was not gloomy enough, ZITADELLE, coming when it did, automatically invited comparison with the German summer offensives of 1941 and 1942. In order to disguise the fact that this time Germany could only mount a limited offensive and as a hedge against the possibility that even this might miscarry, Jodl instructed Wehrmacht Propaganda to depict ZITADELLE as a counteroffensive, thereby creating the impression of a strong defensive capability and establishing an alibi in advance in case ZITADELLE failed.

On 1 July, in a special order for the German officers down to the rank of battalion commander, Hitler summarized the reasons for ZITADELLE. It would not only strengthen the morale of the German people and make the rest of the world "take notice," it would also instill new confidence in the German soldiers. Germany's allies would gain faith in the final victory, and the neutrals would be admonished to behave with caution and restraint. The victory would snatch the initiative away from the Soviet Union for the foreseeable future and could have extensive, "if not decisive," effects on the morale of the Soviet soldiers.

ZITADELLE

TACTICS AND FORCES

The tactical plan for ZITADELLE had remained the same throughout the months of delay: Ninth Army was to strike due south along the line Orel-Kursk, while Fourth Panzer Army, its flank on the east screened offensively by Armeeabteilung Kempf, advanced north from Belgorod to Kursk. (Map 13) The plan was logical to a fault; it had not the slightest chance of achieving surprise.

Recognizing that weakness, Hitler in April had thought of combining the offensive forces of Army Groups Center and South in a single thrust east from the vicinity of Rylsk to Kursk, but he had

Map 13: Operation ZITADELLE and the Withdrawal to the HAGEN Position,
5 July-18 August 1943

quickly given up the idea because of the tremendous difficulties involved in transferring and regrouping the units. Toward the end of June, Manstein had considered shifting the line of advance east toward Staraya Oskol to bypass the heavy Soviet fortifications astride the direct route to Kursk, but the drawbacks—greater distances and the need to reshuffle the forces at the last minute—outweighed the probable advantages of the change. In the end, the best hope was that, having expected a German offensive against Kursk for months, the Russians might have become distracted and so might yet be caught slightly off guard.

Although the risks were obvious, ZITADELLE was not absolutely foredoomed to failure. The strengths of the three assault armies could be considered about adequate for the missions. Their divisions were in excellent shape, and they had received large numbers of new tanks, including the latest models. The Air Force, owing largely to the production genius of Armaments Minister Speer, had about 2,500 first-line combat planes on the Eastern Front, only a few hundred less than the peak strengths of previous years. Of those it was prepared to commit about half in direct support of ZITADELLE. During the last two weeks of June long-range bombers had struck nightly at the most important Soviet industrial centers within their reach, the Gor'kiy tank works, the rubber plants at Yaroslavl' and the oil refineries at Saratov and Astrakhan. Simultaneously, low-level bombers had attacked the railroads and airfields in the Kursk area.

The Soviet commands in the Kursk bulge were, on the north, Central Front under Rokossovskiy and, in the south, Voronezh Front under Vatutin. Both fronts had concentrated about two-thirds of their artillery and tanks in the sectors where the German attacks were expected. In the main line of resistance, 2 to 3 miles deep, the armies had dug three to five trench lines and built weapons emplacements and dugouts. At depths of 6 and 18 miles, they had constructed similar secondary lines. Behind those, the first about 25 miles back, lay another three lines that constituted the front defense zone. The Central Front alone, using troops and local civilians, had dug over 3,000 miles of trenches. Every village and every hill in the steppe had been fortified, and in the fields, that summer mostly overgrown with grass and thistles, the engineers had set 400,000 mines. Across the open eastern end of the bulge, General Armii Ivan S. Konev's Steppe Front had established three armies in a screening line to prevent the Germans from carrying the offensive east if the Soviet defense in the bulge failed. As additional insurance, an army and two tank armies were held in reserve northeast of Orel and an army and a tank army stood by east of Kharkov-Belgorod. The representatives of the Supreme Command were Vasilevskiy and Zhukov, the proved Stalingrad offensive-defensive team.

THE OFFENSIVE BEGINS

On the morning of 5 July, with Fourth and Sixth Air Forces' Stukas blasting paths through the enemy line, Army Groups Center and South launched ZITADELLE. Ninth Army, its main force the heavily armored XXXVII Panzer Corps in the center, XXXI and XXXXVI Panzer Corps on the flanks, and XXIII Corps in reserve, attacked south on a 35-mile front. By the end of the first day it had broken Rokossovskiy's first line and had penetrated the second in the zone of the main effort immediately west of the Orel-Kursk railroad. In the Fourth Panzer Army zone, XXXXVIII Panzer Corps and II SS Panzer Corps (so designated after the SS began organizing another panzer corps in the spring of 1943) struck northward out of a 30-mile front anchored on the right at Belgorod. The two corps got off to a flying start, cutting through Vatutin's first line in two hours.

But the day brought several unpleasant surprises. No sooner had II SS Panzer Corps passed through the first line than the Russians brought it under heavy artillery fire that forced the tanks to take cover. At the same time a sudden, brief but violent thunderstorm swept the Fourth Panzer Army zone, flooding the numerous, normally dry, gullies that cut the landscape. One of these stopped XXXXVIII Panzer Corps dead, and it was near nightfall before the last tanks were gotten across. At midmorning, after Stukas had silenced the artillery, II SS Panzer Corps moved out again, expecting to reach the second line before the end of the day; but in a few hours it was stopped, this time by a mine field cleverly laid in tall grass. Meanwhile Vatutin had pulled his divisions back into the second line without heavy losses.

South of Belgorod III Panzer Corps and Provisional Corps Raus of Armeeabteilung Kempf, after crossing the Donets, ran into a 3-mile-deep belt of fortifications between the river and the railroad. Without air support of their own and harried incessantly by Soviet planes, they inched along while their casualties mounted alarmingly.

The faltering start of the Armeeabteilung Kempf pointed up a troublesome weakness which was to continue to plague ZITADELLE. Although the Luftwaffe maintained a rate

of 3,000 sorties per day during the offensive, it did not have air superiority over the battlefield. Because of the more pressing need for close ground support of the front-line units, it could not seriously challenge the Russians in the air. Even so, it was unable to provide simultaneous support for all of the ground units. Those slighted were usually slowed down and often had to stop. To maintain the advance at a fairly uniform pace, the air units had to shift their points of main effort from day to day.

On the second and third days the battle appeared to be developing well enough. By nightfall on 6 July Ninth Army had gained about thirteen miles except on its right flank, where XXXVI Panzer Corps was hanging back. In the south the lead elements of II SS Panzer Corps had advanced nearly twenty-five miles. On the 7th the rate of gain declined somewhat; fierce tank battles erupted on both sides of the bulge. The Russians were committing their reserves. Rokossovskiy had put in two reserve tank corps and a guards rifle corps. Vatutin was getting two tank corps from the Stavka's reserves to beef up First Tank Army with which he was trying to hold the second line.

The Germans were mildly surprised to find the Russians reacting so fast; on the other hand, in terms of strength and performance, they were pleased to discover that the reserves appearing thus far were about what their intelligence had led them to expect. The two most troublesome developments were Armeeabteilung Kempf's failure to keep pace with Fourth Panzer Army, which forced the latter to divert an SS division to screen its flank on the east, and the rapid decline of tank strength in some of the divisions. The Grossdeutschland Division, for instance, had only 80 of its 300 tanks still fit for combat. Most of the disabled tanks were new models laid up in the shops by mechanical troubles.

THRUST AND COUNTERTHRUST

On 8 July the first clear-cut crisis developed. The center corps of Ninth Army, straining to shake off Rokossovskiy's tank reserves and strike out into the open, ran into a heavily fortified ridge southwest of Ol'khovatka. Denied air support because of bad weather, the corps was forced to stop, and that night Model reluctantly decided to wait a day and regroup for an assault on the ridge. Dismayed at finding so strong an obstacle far behind the original front, Model predicted that even after the ridge was taken there would be no quick breakthrough to Kursk. He characterized the probable future course of the offensive as a "rolling battle of attrition." After two well-prepared attempts, on 10 and 11 July, failed to carry across the ridge, Headquarters, Army Group Center, promised an additional infantry division and a panzer division to help break the deadlock.

On the morning of the 12 July, by then confident that the German reserves were tied down in the Kursk battle, Bryansk Front, under Popov, and the left flank armies of General Polkovnik Vasili D. Sokolovskiy's West Front opened a three-pronged offensive against the north face of the Orel salient. Second Panzer Army, holding a 170-mile front with 14 divisions, could not prevent quick, deep penetrations. Before noon Kluge was forced to divert the 2 divisions intended for Ninth Army to Second Panzer Army, and in the afternoon and evening he had to call on Ninth Army to give up 2 panzer divisions, half of its Ferdinand tanks, and substantial quantities of artillery and rocket projectors.

Meanwhile, Army Group South's fortunes were improving. By 11 July II SS Panzer Corps had a bridgehead north of the Psel River. Although the Russians were still hanging on obstinately south of the Psel in the XXXXVIII Panzer Corps sector, Fourth Panzer Army considered the enemy situation there hopeless. Hoth reported that he expected the going to be easier north of the river.

Vatutin, it appeared, had about reached the end of his ready reserves. Manstein, on the other hand, had a trump left. He had begun moving XXIV Panzer Corps (23d Panzer Division and the SS Wiking Division) out of reserve behind First Panzer Army and into the Belgorod area, where it would be at hand when the time came to give weight to the final drive to Kursk.

East of the Donets Armeeabteilung Kempf had made painfully slow progress in the first six days, but on 11 July in an almost desperate effort III Panzer Corps broke out to the north. The next day Vatutin threw Fifth Guards and Fifth Guards Tank Armies, the latter from the reserve, the former from Steppe Front, into a counterattack; but III Panzer Corps stayed on the move and by nightfall on the 13th had trapped a sizable Soviet force between its flank and the right flank of II SS Panzer Corps.

HITLER CANCELS ZITADELLE

On 13 July Hitler called Manstein and Kluge to Fuehrer headquarters. He had decided to Stop ZITADELLE. The Orel salient was in danger, and Soviet buildups opposite First Panzer Army and Sixth Army (formerly Armeeabteilung Hollidt, renamed in March 1943) had aroused his concern for defense of the Donets basin. But his greatest worry was Sicily, where the Americans and British had landed on 10 July. The Italians, he said, were not fighting, and it was becoming necessary to create new armies to defend Italy and the Balkans. Troops would have to be taken from the Eastern Front.

Manstein protested that ZITADELLE was just reaching its turning point. In the Army Group South zone, he insisted, the Russians could be considered defeated, and if Ninth Army resumed its offensive within the next few weeks, victory might yet be secured. But he was alone; Kluge declared that Ninth Army could not advance again and in a few days would have to withdraw to its line of departure. At the close of the conference Hitler reaffirmed his decision to stop ZITADELLE, but agreed to give Army Group South enough time to deal the Russians at least a partial defeat and so cut down the chances of their staging a counteroffensive soon.

To Fourth Panzer Army and Armeeabteilung Kempf, convinced that victory lay in their grasp, the order to stop ZITADELLE came as a shock. Manstein and the commanding generals of the armies at first still hoped to be able to mop up south of the Psel River, but even that satisfaction was denied them. On 17 July Hitler ordered II SS Panzer Corps out of the front. He planned to transfer the corps to Italy as soon as the threats to First Panzer and Sixth Armies were eliminated.

On the morning of 17 July the Southwest and South Fronts opened the offensive Hitler expected on the Army Group South right flank. The Germans had for nearly a week been watching feverish activity on the other side; and on the 14th, in what at the time seemed to the army command an excess of caution, Hitler had ordered XXIV Panzer Corps shifted back behind First Panzer Army. In the first twenty-four hours' fighting two points of main effort emerged, one in the First Panzer Army zone near Izyum and the other north of Golodayevka on Sixth Army's Mius River line.

The Russians quickly scored sizable breakthroughs which they fought stubbornly to expand, and the Germans concluded with some astonishment that the offensive was actually intended to recapture the Donets basin, not merely to draw off reserves from ZITADELLE, as had been expected. During the next two weeks, although the Russians never came close to making good their bid for a decisive penetration, the battle seesawed violently and at times dangerously.

By the end of the month the offensive had lost its momentum, and the Germans moved in quickly to restore their front. Those were small battles, like so many others quickly lost in the rush of greater events, but, nevertheless, enormously costly for both sides. Sixth Army, for instance, between 17 July and 6 August captured 17,000 Russians. Its own casualties totaled 23,855.

In the Army Group Center zone the ZITADELLE offensive, already stalled, ended on 12 July. The next day, after the conference at Fuehrer headquarters, Hitler gave Model command of both Ninth Army and Second Panzer Army, ordering him to close the breakthroughs and retake the original front. Model's appointment signalized the emergence of a new type of German higher commander—the specialist in stubborn defense. Hitler had once called on men like Manstein to engineer victories. After the summer of 1943 he came more and more to rely on Model and a few others because they seldom disputed his orders and because they appeared to have a knack for staving off catastrophe. Model was the best and most successful of the type. Aside from being a convinced Nazi whose faith in Hitler outlasted that of most other officers of his rank, he was a first-rate tactician. In combat he spared neither himself nor his subordinates.

By the time Model took command in the Orel salient the Second Panzer Army front had been punctured in three places. Two of the penetrations, one due east of Orel and another south of Sukhinichi,

Model and Hollidt.

were growing wider and deeper by the hour. On 15 July the offensive expanded into the Ninth Army sector.

A day later, as a precaution, the army group and the armies began work on the HAGEN position, a line of field fortifications across the base of the Orel salient, For once, Hitler, distracted by events in the Mediterranean and in the Army Group South zone, did not insist on a rigid linear defense. He had quickly amended his original order to call only for a continuous front, and on 22 July he agreed to let Model conduct an "elastic defense."

In the meantime, on the 18th and 19th, relieved of the threat of ZITADELLE, the Stavka had committed powerful forces from its reserves. Popov received Third Guards Tank Army to lend weight to the thrust toward Orel, and Sokolovskiy was given the Fourth Tank and Eleventh Armies to widen the gap on the north face of the salient. However, heavy rains, which set in at the beginning of the third week in July, and superior German tactics, which if they could not stop the Soviet onslaughts managed most of the time to rob them of their full effects, began to take some of the power out of the offensive.

In the last week of the month Hitler's fears concerning Italy were confirmed. On the 25th the King dismissed Mussolini, who was placed under arrest as he left the palace. The Badoglio government said it intended to continue the war, but no one at Fuehrer headquarters, least of all Hitler, believed that. Hitler set off an avalanche of planning to rescue Mussolini and to strengthen the German hold on Italy.

From the Eastern Front he called in the Commanding General, Army Group Center. When Kluge arrived at noon on 26 July Hitler explained that he was going to transfer II SS Panzer Corps from Army Group South to Italy. The politically trained SS divisions, he thought, would form a nucleus around which the fascist elements in the Italian Army could rally. The SS Adolf Hitler Division already had orders to entrain at Stalino. Army Group Center would have to provide replacements for the SS divisions and would in the near future be expected to release other divisions, approximately two dozen in all, for transfer to Italy and the West. The only way they could be obtained was by giving up the Orel salient. The Second Panzer and Ninth Armies would have to begin moving into the HAGEN position at once. To Kluge's protests that he could not take the armies back into a line which was far from finished, Hitler replied that there was nothing else to be done. Army Group Center would have to start releasing divisions, and soon. Above all, he had to have II SS Panzer Corps, which he described as the equivalent of twenty Italian divisions.

In three days Model had his armies ready to move, but he had to postpone their start until 1 August because of the poor state of the roads. A week and a half of heavy rains had turned even the main roads into quagmires. In some places they had become broad bands of ruts, as much as a hundred yards wide, where the vehicles had wandered off to the sides searching for firm ground. Overhead the Soviet Air Force had practically undisputed command of the sky.

Throughout it all, the armies had to move their heavy equipment and supplies. Ninth Army had hundreds of tons of supplies and ammunition originally earmarked for ZITADELLE stored in dumps around Kromy, south of Orel. The rear area commands set about destroying the rye harvest, which was just ready to be brought in, and began herding some 250,000 civilians and their cattle, carts, and personal possessions down the side roads. In Orel demolition crews set charges in all buildings and installations which might be of use to the Russians.

The withdrawal began on time on the night of 1 August. By then the Russians were fully aware of what was going on, and unlike the BUEFFEL operation earlier, being already geared for an offensive, they could react quickly. On the nights of 3 and 4 August partisan activity flared up in the entire Army Group Center rear area. On the 4th the army group rear area command counted a total of 4,110 partisan-laid demolitions on the railroads. A day later waves of Soviet fighters and bombers swept over the front and across the clogged roads in the rear. All over the salient telephones were out for hours at a time.

On 6 August, certain the Second Panzer and Ninth Armies were on the run, the Stavka extended the offensive north into the Fourth Army zone. Voronov, co-ordinating for the Stavka, put seven armies on West Front's left flank into an attack toward Spas-Demensk and Yel'nya. Its end objective was to take Roslavl and lift the HAGEN position off its hinges. During the following days the air and partisan raids multiplied, blacking out telephone communications over much of the Army Group Center zone and tying up the rail lines.

As the second week of the withdrawal began, the battle reached its climax. Model predicted that the Russians would try to overrun the HAGEN position—if they did not succeed in pushing through on its flanks before then. The Fourth Army front was strained to the breaking point. The quality of the Soviet troops was low but they came on in massive, seemingly endless, waves of infantry and tanks. One of the Fourth Army corps commanders reported that the enemy losses were five times his own but that the Russians still had the advantage because they had begun the battle with a 10:1 superiority. On 13 August West Front's armies took Spas-Demensk, and Voronov put two armies of Kalinin Front into an attack at the Third Panzer-Fourth Army boundary. That day Ninth Army took over the Second Panzer Army sector and began throwing up a switch position behind the HAGEN position.

On the 14th the first units moved into the HAGEN position. For three days the army kept as many of the divisions as it could east of the line, while the engineers, using Russian civilian laborers of both sexes, rushed ahead with the work on the still far from finished line. On the night of the 17th the last troops moved into the HAGEN position. The withdrawal was a major tactical achievement, but how long the line would hold was anybody's guess.

Model's retreat to the HAGEN position brought to an end the chain of events directly associated with ZITADELLE. Hitler had intended once more to make the world sit up and take notice. Instead, he had touched off a gigantic convulsion of the Eastern Front that weakened the armies in the East and left the Soviet Union in full possession of the initiative. By the time the divisions of Army Group Center moved into the HAGEN position, the Soviet armies in the south were on the march again. The summer campaign was far from over.

CHAPTER VIII

The First Soviet Summer Offensive

TROOPS AND TACTICS

As the war in the Soviet Union entered its third year the world watched, expecting summer to bring answers to two crucial questions. Could the German armies again shake off the effects of the winter battles and make a strong bid for victory? If not, could the Soviet Army prove itself master of the field without its old ally, "General Winter?" ZITADELLE provided an explicit answer to the first question. After ZITADELLE, in two and one-half months the Soviet Army erased the last lingering doubt inherent in the second.

THE MAIN EFFORT IN THE SOUTH

In the spring of 1943 Soviet planning for the coming summer no doubt concentrated on two possibilities: a German offensive in the style of the previous two summers and, if that failed to materialize or could be stopped, a Soviet offensive similar in scale and conception to that of the last winter. Although they would have been the last to admit it, the Russians were already benefiting mightily from the Allied operations in the Mediterranean and the threats of invasions there and on the Atlantic coast. Had Hitler been able to count on another year's respite in the south and west he might have made far more ambitious plans for the coming summer in the USSR. As it was, the chances were that the Germans would not be able again to seize the complete initiative and prevent the Soviet forces from getting in substantial blows of their own before the summer ended.

The most vulnerable sector of the German front was still the southern flank. Below Kharkov the Army Group South front stretched east 150 miles along the Donets and then dropped off south along the

Mius River to the Gulf of Taganrog. Soviet troops held several small bridgeheads on the south bank of the Donets, the most significant one in the sharp bend of the river south of Izyum. To defend more than 250 miles of front, Army Group South had two armies, First Panzer Army on the Donets and, in the Mius line, Sixth Army—the upgraded Armeeabteilung Hollidt, which resembled its powerful predecessor in name only. A Soviet advance of a little more than 100 miles along the line Kharkov-Dnepropetrovsk could cut off both armies, break open the southern flank of the German front, and isolate Army Group A in the Kuban and the Crimea. The past winter's experience had shown that German skill and Soviet lack of finesse often combined to prevent such maneuvers from achieving their full effect, but it had also demonstrated that even so the dividends could be substantial for the Russians. Knowing that those considerations could not have escaped the Soviet Command, the Eastern Intelligence Branch, OKH, predicted in May 1943 that the main effort of the Soviet summer offensive would be on the southern flank, either at Kharkov or against Sixth Army, and that it would be preceded or accompanied by a secondary attack in the Army Group Center zone to tie down troops and eliminate the Orel salient as a threat to the flank of the offensive in the south.

Even if the tactical advantages had been less obvious, the Stavka would still probably have given first priority to the southern flank in the summer of 1943. Of the shortages created by the German invasion, those still being most acutely felt were in coal, ferrous metals, and foodstuffs, particularly grain and animal products. All could be most quickly alleviated by recapturing the Ukraine. Between Stalino and the Mius lay the better half of the Donets Basin coal fields. Inside the great bend of the Dnepr were the Krivoi Rog iron mines, which before the war had supplied 40 percent of Soviet iron ore. And, in spite of efforts in the past two years to open up new lands east of the Urals, the black-earth region of the Ukraine was needed if the food shortage was to be overcome any time soon.

COMPARATIVE STRENGTHS

By the summer of 1943 the Germans had succeeded, for the time being at least, in stopping the Eastern Front's decline in strength which had aroused so much concern during the previous fall and winter. On 20 July the total troop strength in the East exclusive of the allies and the Twentieth Mountain Army stood at 3,064,000 men. This was only about a quarter-million men less than the peak strength of 1941 and 574,000 more than that of 1 September 1942. Italian Eighth Army had been recalled in the spring, but Rumania and Hungary still had between 150,000 and 200,000 men in the East. South of Leningrad the Spanish 250th "Blue" Division held a sector of the Army Group North front.

In considerable part the restoration of strength on the Eastern Front had been accomplished by shifting troops from the Air Force, the Waffen-SS, and the OKW theaters. Also, the three months' quiet at the front had meant that for the first time in more than a year the number of men returning to duty from the hospitals exceeded the casualty rate. The 1943 class of eighteen-year-olds and the screening of deferred workers had produced enough men to cover the winter's losses and leave a few hundred thousand to spare.

On 20 July 1943 the Soviet strength, according to German estimates, had reached 5,755,000 men, a gain of a million and a half over September 1942 and about three times the German increase in the same period. The Russians had at the front an estimated 7,855 tanks and 21,050 antitank guns, the Germans 2,088 tanks and 8,063 antitank guns.[17] Ordinarily, superiorities of 2:1 in troops, nearly 4:1 in tanks, and better than 2:1 in antitank guns could in themselves be regarded as enough to justify an offensive. On the German-Soviet front that was not necessarily the case. The Germans had been operating against preponderant Soviet forces since the start of the war. It would take something more than weight of numbers and equipment if the Russians were to beat the Germans at their own game, the summer offensive.

THE STATE OF SOVIET MILITARY ART

O ne consideration which must have weighed heavily in the Stavka's decision to undertake a summer offensive was the knowledge that the

17. The German estimates could have been somewhat low. According to Soviet postwar figures, the Soviet tank strength at the front, for instance, was 8,500 tanks, and the *Stavka* was holding another 400 in reserve.

Soviet Army had passed beyond its apprenticeship. In two years Stalin's generals had learned much and, not content to be blind imitators, had adapted the German methods to suit their own capabilities and limitations. While they had not attained the facility of the Germans, they had, at least at the upper command levels, acquired the flexibility so conspicuously lacking earlier and had improved their large-scale offensive tactics. The latter they had successfully tested and refined during the 1942-43 winter offensive.

The German technique of blitzkrieg had been to deliver the decisive stroke with precision, speed, and economy of effort. Its distinguishing characteristics had been penetration and avoidance of broad frontal engagements. To the German staffs Schwerpunktbildung, concentration of force at the most advantageous point, was the very core of military art. The Russians, on the other hand, favored a broader lateral scope and more conservative execution. They adopted the breakthrough and penetration as basic tactical maneuvers but preferred to achieve the decisive effect by a few deep thrusts. They also accepted the breadth of the front rather than by one or a few deep thrusts. They also accepted the principle of the Schwerpunkt, but usually their concentration in the zone of the main effort was less pronounced than in the German practice, and almost always the main effort was built up gradually by successive thrusts.

Accordingly, although the Russians claimed that Stalingrad had supplanted Cannae as the classic encirclement battle, they did not employ the double envelopment as frequently as did the Germans. More often they were content with a single thrust or multiple thrusts, the objective being not so much to achieve a deep penetration along one line of advance as to force the opponent back on a broad front. Those tactics were particularly suited to southern USSR where the successive, roughly parrallel rivers afforded natural defense lines. Thrusts from one river line to the next could be depended on to bring back long stretches of the German front with them.

The first objective of German offensives, in theory at least, had been to annihilate the enemy main force quickly. The purpose was not to gain ground or merely alter the respective positions of the opposing forces but to produce a decision. The Russians, for their part, cared

Soviet troops nearing Orel.

less for speed or the fatal stroke; they were content to wear the enemy down blow by blow. Contrary to the general conception that the Russians were relatively indifferent to geographical space, they were inclined to reckon their victories as much in terms of ground regained as in terms of damage to the enemy or other tactical advantage. Their ultimate objective was to annihilate the enemy, but by the cumulative effect of repeated offensives, not by the single battle—by weight rather than by the skillful blow.

Probably no better historical example exists of offensive tactics successfully tailored to the shortcomings of an army than that afforded by the Soviet Army in World War II. Despite the smoke screen of high-flown theorizing which the Russians have thrown around the two basic elements, the single, or "salient," thrust and the broad front offensive, both can be most simply and, it appears, most logically explained in terms of Soviet shortcomings. As the most cursory reading of Stalin's speeches and orders of the day will show, the Russians regarded the encirclement as the most expeditious means of destroying large enemy forces; on the other hand, as a practical matter, they apparently regarded the double envelopment as an unreliable maneuver and adjusted their planning to the concept of the single thrust. To complete a double envelopment required co-ordination and a high degree of skill at all levels in the leadership. It required, in particular, troop commanders at the middle and lower levels who possessed the initiative and ability to meet and master unforeseen developments without disrupting the over-all plan. Those the Russians did not have, at least not in sufficient numbers. Further, the double envelopment required troops of a uniform high quality. Those they did not have either.

On the basis of conclusions drawn from the 1941 disasters, the Soviet Army had concentrated on developing its artillery and armor. In both arms the emphasis was on increased output of weapons and machines and on their organization for mass employment.

By mid-1943 the Soviet artillery was vastly expanded, equipped with reliable weapons, and, while not always accurate against pinpoint targets, was capable of laying down preparatory fires of an intensity comparable to those fired in the great battles of World War I. Eleventh Guards Army in the Orel offensive of July 1943, for example, had 3,000 guns and heavy mortars, almost double the standard issue to the armies in the Stalingrad operation and three times the complement of the armies in the 1941 counteroffensive at Moscow. At the end of 1942 the Soviet Army had 17 rocket launcher brigades and had begun organizing an initial increment of 30 self-propelled artillery regiments. In the spring of 1943 it began forming artillery brigades and antitank artillery regiments and in the second half of the year created 26 artillery divisions.

The armored forces were well trained and to a large extent equipped with the Soviet-designed-and-built T34 tank. American and British lend-lease models were still used but were regarded as too light. The earlier practice of scattering the armor piecemeal among the infantry had been abandoned, and the brigades and corps had become the standard armored unit organizations. The tank armies, of which there were five by the end of summer 1943, each had two tank and one mechanized corps and were fully capable of executing independent tactical missions.

By early summer 1943 the Russians had at least a 2.5:1 advantage over the Germans in the air. The Soviet air arm remained subordinate to the Army and concentrated almost exclusively on close ground support, air defense, and tactical bombing. At the end of 1942 each front had been assigned an air army for support.

In 1943 the infantry, particularly the guards units, received increased numbers of antitank weapons and began getting the Sudayev submachine gun and the new Goryunov machine gun to replace the 1910 Maxim. But the massive effort to develop the technical arms had resulted in persistent neglect of the infantry, which received the lowest grade recruits, least competent officers, and very little training. In 1943 the Germans observed that the quality of the Soviet infantry was lower than in 1941 and that the decline was continuing. In mass attacks the infantry could be crushingly effective, but it was not an instrument that could be maneuvered with tactical precision. On its own the infantry lacked staying power; without heavy tank and artillery support it lost momentum and its progress was often erratic.

The deficiencies which made the double envelopment unreliable also limited the effect of the single thrust. Aware of their own weaknesses and those of their troops, the Soviet commanders almost always displayed an excessive flank sensitivity. After the breakthrough—which could be guaranteed by the artillery and tanks—they were reluctant to concentrate on the forward advance and often began to strike out on all sides in an attempt to keep their flanks open, with the result that forward momentum dropped off. Even when the tanks were able to keep up a rapid pace, the infantry frequently fell behind; consequently, the deep thrusts took the form of tank raids which often ended in near disaster, as in the case of the Popov Group in February 1943.

The depth of the single thrust was further limited by considerations of control and supply. Since the offensive by nature made it difficult to plan for in detail beyond the first few days of fighting, more and more unforeseeable factors came into play as the advance proceeded, with the result that the burdens on the initiative and judgment of the field commander, and on the troops themselves, increased. Therefore, given the weaknesses of the Soviet Army, the chances of a single thrust's succeeding declined as the distance from the point of breakthrough to the objective increased.

Finally, the Soviet supply system, while it could on occasion perform near miracles of improvisation, was not equipped or organized to handle in a routine fashion the logistics of rapid advances over long distances. The Soviet soldier, who subsisted almost exclusively on what he could carry in the sack he customarily slung over his shoulder or tied to his belt, who preferred German boots, hand weapons, and other items of equipment to his own, and who was—out of necessity as much as by inclination—an expert scrounger, was one of the least demanding in the world. The armies were expected to forage and collect booty with utmost diligence. An example of what could be achieved along those lines was that of an army which in the winter of 1942, passing through an area the Germans had subjected to scorched-earth treatment, collected the following percentages of its monthly requirements of staples: flour, 54 percent; vegetables, 97 percent; meat, 108 percent; hay, 140 percent; and oats, 68 percent. But modern armies could not live entirely off the land and rely exclusively on booty; Soviet armies were therefore generally—but not invariably—adequately provisioned and supplied with ammunition and motor fuel in advance of offensives, the rule of thumb being that each army should have stocks on hand for a 10-day operation and an advance of up to sixty or seventy miles. Beyond this range, and not too infrequently even short of it, inadequacies of transport and a lingering cavalier attitude toward the problems of supply in general placed checks on Soviet mobile operations. Before the July 1943 offensive in the Orel bulge, for instance, the infantry had been neglected in the supply build-up, and later, infantry ammunition had had to be flown in to keep the offensive going. That led to the following admonition— apparently not considered axiomatic—to the Soviet commands, "Experience… shows that it is necessary to arrange for supplies and ammunition for the infantry as well as for the artillery." Often enough, mobile forces also had supply troubles, as is evinced by the following warning, "Disregard of the necessary supply planning for the mobile group may lead to its extinction or, in the most favorable case, failure to achieve success."

As the single thrust afforded an escape from the more onerous requirements of the double envelopment, so the concept of multiple thrusts on a broad front avoided the ultimate problems of the single thrust. The broad front possessed the great advantage of extending the offensive laterally, which enabled the Stavka to bring strength to bear on a number of points and eliminate the risks inherent in attempting to pursue one clearly defined line of advance. The offensive was relatively easy to control since success did not depend on maneuvering one or a few bodies of troops in motion but could be attained instead by a series of thrusts launched more or less at will from convenient lines of departure. The supply problems, if not eliminated, were significantly eased: the assembly could be carried out over a number of rail lines, and none of the thrusts needed to go so deep as to outrun its supplies. Of course, Soviet protests to the contrary notwithstanding, the broad front offensive was at best a modified linear method of warfare. It required massed troops, repeated frontal encounters, and an enemy willing—as Hitler was—to respond with a linear defense.

THE PSYCHOLOGICAL WARFARE VICTORY

In one sphere, psychological warfare, Operation ZITADELLE brought the Soviet Union a clear-cut and final victory. German psychological warfare and propaganda, always hobbled by Hitler's racial theories and his extreme war aims, had declined steadily in effectiveness since the winter of 1941-42, but as late as the spring of 1943 the Smolensk Manifesto had given the Soviet authorities some cause for worry and the SILBERSTREIF propaganda had shown latent promise even though it failed to achieve much in the way of practical results. After ZITADELLE German psychological warfare was completely on the defensive. The Soviet propagandists held the initiative. They could exploit two years of accumulated German injustices and atrocities and an almost painful desire on the part of the Russian people to believe that things would be better once the Soviet Army returned. Above all, they could promise an early end to the war.

ZITADELLE and its aftermath also placed the Soviet propaganda directed to the Germans on a new and more substantial footing. In the late summer the Russians created the National Free Germany Committee and its subsidiary, the League of German Officers. The Free Germany Committee was composed mostly of emigrè Communists, but the League of German Officers was allegedly voluntary, noncommunist, and devoted exclusively to overthrowing Hitler and restoring the traditional social order in Germany. The league, headed by General Seydlitz, had an original membership of three other Stalingrad generals and 100 officers of lower ranks. It issued a newspaper which was dropped behind the German line, and Seydlitz from time to time addressed personal letters to army and army group commanders calling on them to join the Free Germany Movement.

THE FOURTH BATTLE OF KHARKOV

Northwest of Belgorod on the right flank of Fourth Panzer Army, its own right tying in with the left flank of Armeeabteilung Kempf, stood the 167th Infantry Division. It was a good division, "good" meaning it was not greatly understrength and was battleworthy by the then current standards on the Eastern Front. On the morning of 3 August 1943 the massed artillery of Sixth Guards Army laid down a several hours' barrage on the division sector. When the artillery lifted its fire, 200 tanks roared into the German line, followed by waves of closely packed infantry. Before nightfall, the 167th Division had shrunk to a scattering of odds and ends. Its infantry regiments were completely smashed, and the survivors were dazed and shaken.

Near the center of the Fourth Panzer Army front a secondary attack hit the 332d Infantry Division, and by the end of the day its front too had begun to crumble. On the 4th two Soviet tank corps pushed south, elbowing aside the shattered 167th Infantry Division and the 6th Panzer Division, which had moved up in a vain attempt to close the breach. During the day the tanks opened a 7-mile gap between Fourth Panzer Army and Armeeabteilung Kempf and dragged the German line on the east back to the outskirts of Belgorod.

TACTICAL SURPRISE

An attack on the north flank of Army Group South aimed at recapturing Kharkov and breaking through to the Dnepr had been considered one of the most likely possibilities in all of the German forecasts for the summer of 1943. (Map 14) On 21 July Manstein had asked the OKH for a decision either to hold the Donets line, which

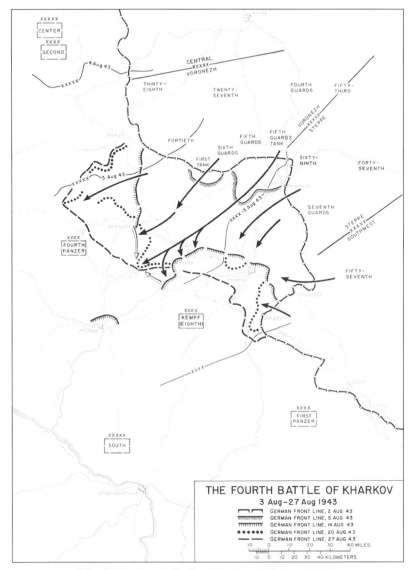

Map 14: *The Fourth Battle of Kharkov, 3-27 August 1943.*

would require more troops, or to prepare for a gradual withdrawal to the Dnepr in order to gain enough troops to prevent a breakthrough on his north flank. None was made. At the end of the month Army Group South had a total of 822,000 troops opposing an estimated 1,713,000 Russians. The army group had 1,161 tanks, about half of them operational, and the Russians had 2,872 tanks.

Against Fourth Panzer Army and Armeeabteilung Kempf, the Stavka had committed Voronezh Front and Steppe Front, both reinforced with armies held in reserve during ZITADELLE. In the last two weeks of July, Konev's Steppe Front had taken over Vatutin's left flank east and south of Belgorod, assuming command of the two armies there and bringing with it two armies from the reserve. The plan envisioned a kind of flying wedge of four armies—Fifth and Sixth Guards, Fifth Guards Tank and First Tank Armies—aimed southwest between Akhtyrka and Kharkov toward Poltava. While Vatutin thus split apart Fourth Panzer Army and Armeeabteilung Kempf, forcing Fourth Panzer Army away toward Akhtyrka, Konev was to bear down on Kharkov from the north. Fifty-seventh Army, Southwest Front's right flank army, was to close in on Kharkov from the east.

On 1 August Manstein informed the OKH that he was expecting an attack on Kharkov as the inevitable next item on the Soviet agenda; nevertheless, when two days later an attack did come it achieved a degree of surprise and caught Fourth Panzer Army and Armeabteilung Kempf standing forward of their pre-ZITADELLE front. After ZITADELLE Manstein had concluded that the Army Group South offensive had upset the Soviet dispositions enough to force a several week's delay in their plans for a counteroffensive; and on 2 August, believing there was still time, he had decided "to wait for more definite signs of an impending offensive" before pulling back to the original line.

BREAKTHROUGH

On 5 August the Russians marched into Belgorod. That same day, in the Army Group Center zone, Bryansk Front captured Orel. To celebrate the twin victories Stalin ordered an artillery salute of twelve volleys from 120 guns. It was the first time in the war that such a salute had been fired, and in Moscow some of the citizens, thinking it was an air raid, took to their cellars. In the coming months the booming of victory cannon would become commonplace in the Soviet capital. As an added honor, the first divisions into Belgorod and Orel were authorized to include the names of the cities in their unit designations. In his order of the day Stalin stated, "In this way the legend of the Germans that Soviet troops are allegedly unable to wage a successful offensive in the summer has been dispelled."19 In that cry of relief and jubilation Stalin revealed that the Soviet Government had reached an optimistic assessment of its military prospects and had decided to commit itself publicly to a full-scale summer offensive.

With a total of fifteen divisions between them, only three of them panzer divisions, the Fourth Panzer Army and Armeeabteilung Kempf faced two Soviet fronts and part of a third. Together, the three fronts brought eleven armies to bear against the two German armies. Even taking into account that Soviet units were generally smaller than German units of the same type, these were tremendous odds.

One of Hitler's first moves after the offensive began had been to order the Grossdeutschland Division back from Army Group Center and to return the 7th Panzer Division which was being held as the OKH reserve. On the second day he also decided to leave the SS Das Reich and Totenkopf Divisions in the Army Group South zone. Since the Headquarters, II SS Panzer Corps, and the Adolf Hitler Division had already been transferred to Italy, Manstein placed the two SS panzer divisions under the Headquarters, III Corps, together with the 3d Panzer Division. These and the SS Wiking Division he ordered into the Armeeabteilung Kempf zone.

In the first six days of the fighting Army Group A sent one and Army Group Center three infantry divisions, but on 7 August Kluge reported to OKH that the battle of the Orel bulge was clearly approaching its climax and insisted that no more divisions could be withdrawn from Army Group Center without impairing the defense of the HAGEN position. Several days later Model submitted a similar report. The result was that in the critical early days of the battle Army Group South received only driblets of assistance from Army Group Center while the combined Second Panzer and Ninth Armies, the one great potential reservoir of reserves on the Eastern Front, fought a secondary battle in the Orel bulge with forty-five divisions.

In the breakthrough area the most Army Group South could do during the first days was to throw some obstacles in the way of the Soviet flood. To gain room to maneuver, Fourth Panzer Army stretched its boundary north, taking 40 miles of front and four weak divisions from Second Army. While three divisions, cut off in the first onslaught, fought their way out to the west, Hoth moved the newly arrived Grossdeutschland Division into a bridgehead east of Akhtyrka as an anchor for his right flank and to prevent the Russians' rolling up his line farther to the north and west. But he could do nothing about the gap to the Armeeabteilung Kempf flank, which by 8 August had opened to a width of 35 miles and, except for one infantry division ranged northwest of Poltava, gave the Russians a clear road to the Dnepr 100 miles to the southwest.

On the right side of the gap Kempf struggled to avoid being encircled as Steppe Front forced his northern front down on Kharkov and, on the west, Voronezh Front's First Tank Army attempted to push south past the city. The SS divisions coming from the Army Group South right flank had to be thrown in to screen the Armeeabteilung rear west of Kharkov. Manstein had intended using them in a counterattack to close the gap, but they were tied down singly as soon as they reached the front. The most they could do was carry the line out parallel to the Merlya River on either side of Merefa, which only narrowed the gap slightly but did deflect the Russian advance southwestward and away from Kharkov.

On 12 August Kempf, worried by his declining infantry strength, proposed to evacuate Kharkov the next day and retreat to a shorter line south of the city. Manstein did not object, but Hitler promptly countered with an order that Kharkov be held under all circumstances, and demanded "the most severe measures" against any units that failed to execute their assigned missions. Kempf, who expected a breakthrough on the east at any moment (Fifty-seventh Army had already crossed the river and taken Chuguyev), predicted that the order to hold Kharkov would produce another Stalingrad. On the 14th Manstein relieved Kempf and appointed General der Infanterie Otto Woehler in his place. A few days later the Armeeabteilung was redesignated Eighth Army.

Meanwhile, Manstein and the Chief of Staff, OKH, had tried again to persuade Hitler to adopt a coherent plan. On 8 August Zeitzler visited the Headquarters, Army Group South, where Manstein told him that the existence of the entire army group was at stake. The alternatives, he said, were either to give up the Donets front immediately, and so gain troops for the north flank, or provide twenty fresh divisions for the army group, ten for Fourth Army and the others to backstop the rest of the army group front.

HITLER DECIDES TO BUILD AN EAST WALL

As he had on other occasions when confronted with unpleasant choices, Hitler avoided the decision by taking an altogether different tack. He suddenly resurrected the idea of an East Wall which he had categorically rejected earlier in the year. On 12 August he ordered work started at once on the wall which was to begin in the south on the Kerch' Peninsula, continue on the mainland at Melitopol, run in an almost straight line to the Dnepr near Zaporozhye, swing eastward around Zaporozhye in a large bridgehead and follow the Dnepr northwest to Kiev with bridgeheads east of the major cities. North of Kiev it was to follow the Desna River to Chernigov and then run almost due north along a line somewhat east of the cities of Gomel, Orsha, Vitebsk, Nevel, and Pskov to the southern tip of Pskov Lake. From there it would continue north along the western shore of the lake and the Narva River to the Gulf of Finland. Since the term "East Wall," applied to a line which in its southern half might have to be occupied even before work on it could be begun, could prove psychologically dangerous, the OKH later in the month adopted two more innocuous code names: WOTAN position in the Army Groups South and A zones and PANTHER position in the Army Groups North and Center zones.

While, at first glance, it would appear that in the East Wall order Hitler accepted a general retreat on the Eastern Front as inevitable, the decisions which followed indicate that he actually wanted to establish an absolute barrier beyond which the armies could not retreat and, since no work of any kind had yet been done on the so-called East Wall, give himself an excuse for not retreating in the meantime. The one major withdrawal he tentatively approved after issuing the East Wall order, evacuation of the GOTENKOPF, he postponed on 14

August, claiming it would have unfavorable repercussions among Germany's allies and in neutral Turkey.

KHARKOV EVACUATED

While Hitler was attempting a diversion in the running dispute with his generals, the battle on the north flank of Army Group South raged on, acquiring toward the end of the second week of August a somewhat amorphous character, largely as a result of the Russians' indecisive operating methods. (Map 15) The way to Poltava remained open, but Vatutin hesitated to push through while the Germans flanking the gap held firm. Instead, he turned his left flank armies, the Fifth Guards and Fifth Guards Tank Armies, against the west front of Eighth Army (formerly Armeeabteilung Kempf) where the SS divisions fought to keep the front angled southwestward away from Kharkov. On the weaker Eighth Army east front Fifty-seventh Army cleared the right bank of the Donets between Chuguyev and Zmiyev, but the army command somehow could not quite bring itself to try for a full-scale breakthrough.

Manstein, although forced by Hitler's order to undertake the dangerous and, in the long run, futile exercise of holding Kharkov, concentrated his effort on the tactically decisive point, the gap between Fourth Panzer Army and Eighth Army. After the SS divisions became tied down on the Eighth Army west front, Manstein transferred responsibility for the counterattack to Fourth Panzer Army. On 18 August the Grossdeutschland Division and the 7th Panzer Division broke out of the Akhtyrka bridgehead. In two days they sliced across the gap and established contact with the SS Totenkopf Division, which succeeded in extending its left flank across the Merlya River. The counterattack eliminated the direct threat to Poltava, but, in the meantime, the Fourth Panzer Army front had broken open farther north.

On 18 August Vatutin, repeating the tactics he had employed in opening the offensive, brought the 57th Infantry Division, holding a sector midway between Akhtyrka and Sumy, under concentrated artillery, mortar, and tank fire. By midafternoon the division had lost all its lieutenants and most of its senior NCO's. It reported that the

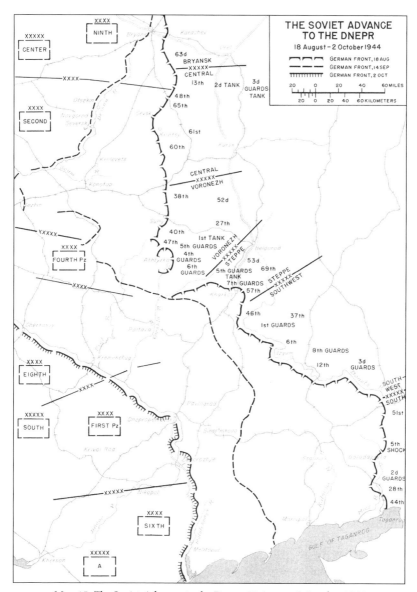

THE SOVIET ADVANCE
TO THE DNEPR
18 August – 2 October 1944

GERMAN FRONT, 18 AUG
GERMAN FRONT, 14 SEP
GERMAN FRONT, 2 OCT

20   0   20   40   60 MILES
20   0   20   40   60 KILOMETERS

Map 15: The Soviet Advance to the Dnepr, 18 August-2 October 1944

battalion commanders had yelled themselves hoarse but could not keep the troops from retreating. In the next two days the Russians tore open ten miles of the front, shouldering aside what was left of the 57th Division, which was redesignated a kampfgruppe, a term then beginning to be applied to units so drastically reduced in strength that to continue carrying them as divisions would be misleading if not downright ridiculous.

On 20 August, the day the Grossdeutschland and Totenkopf Divisions joined hands to close the gap west of Kharkov, the Commanding General, Eighth Army, Woehler, asked permission to evacuate the city that night. After the first few days in his new command, Woehler was no more optimistic than Kempf had been. XI Corps, holding the front on the northern outskirts of Kharkov, had a strength of 4,000 infantrymen, one man for each ten yards of front. The artillery, which, as the infantry strength ebbed away, had been forced to carry the main burden of the fighting, was running out of ammunition. The army's supply depots in Kharkov had five trainloads of spare tank tracks left over from ZITADELLE but very little else. The high consumption of ammunition in the last month and a half had cut into supplies put aside for the last half of August and the first two weeks of September; until the turn of the month the army would have to get along with 50 percent of its average daily requirements in artillery and tank ammunition.

Grudgingly, Hitler gave Manstein permission to evacuate Kharkov but asked that the city be held if at all possible. He claimed the loss would damage German prestige, particularly in Turkey. In the spring the Turkish commander in chief had inspected the "impregnable" defenses of the city as a guest of Armeeabteilung Kempf.

On the 20th Manstein still thought he might be able to hold Kharkov and ordered the SS Das Reich Division shifted north to support XI Corps. The next day he changed his mind and gave Woehler permission to pull back "if necessary." The following morning the SS Das Reich Division launched a counterattack in the XI Corps zone, but Woehler informed Manstein that he intended to give up the city anyway. His artillery situation was catastrophic. The artillerymen, after firing their last rounds, were abandoning their guns to fight as infantry. Manstein replied that twenty-four trainloads of ammunition were on the way from Germany but had to agree that they would hardly come in time. In the afternoon Hitler, characteristically, requested that if the counterattack by the Das Reich Division improved things "somewhat" Kharkov not be given up. Woehler and Manstein agreed that this was no longer possible. During the night the city changed hands for the fourth and final time.

While Eighth Army withdrew south of Kharkov, massive Soviet efforts to expand the breakthrough in the Fourth Panzer Army zone and reopen the route to Poltava forced Hoth to fall back south of Akhtyrka on either side of the Vorskla River. By 25 August he had regained sufficient equilibrium to be able to spare two divisions for a counterattack into the gap. It was successful, and by the 27th the Fourth Panzer and Eighth Armies held a continuous line on a rough arc bending southwestward between Sumy and Zmiyev.

THE FRONT IN FLAMES

By re-establishing a continuous front on the Army Group South left flank the Fourth Panzer and Eighth Armies had for the moment blunted a deadly thrust, but to the north and south fresh blows had already been dealt or were in the making. Employing the peculiar rippling effect that marked their offensives, the Russians, thwarted in one place, had shifted to others, adding weight to the offensive laterally. For the first time in the war they had the full strategic initiative, and they grasped it jealously without regard for economy of effort, tactical sophistication, or the danger of overreaching themselves. The Stavka, apparently worried that the Germans would try for a stalemate, aimed at keeping the enemy off balance and not letting him establish a stable front anywhere in the Army Group Center and Army Group South sectors. Vasilevskiy co-ordinated the fronts on the south flank and Zhukov those opposite the Army Group Center right flank and the left flank of Army Group South.

Only the outer flanks of the Eastern Front remained quiet. In the zone of Army Group North, on 23 August, the Leningrad and Volkhov Fronts finally abandoned a costly and unpromising drive they had begun four weeks earlier against the Mga bottleneck south of Lake Ladoga. The Germans never were much worried since the offensive was a fairly ramshackle affair from the start. They guessed that its main purpose was to prevent the shifting of reserves to the south. In the last two weeks it had degenerated into a series of random assaults by units of divisional size or smaller. In the south, the greatest concern of Army Group A was to secure a decision to get out of the GOTENKOPF before the fall rains set in. Hitler insisted on first talking it over with Antonescu. At the end of August Zeitzler on his own responsibility told Army Group A to go ahead and get ready to evacuate, since such a decision was inevitable.

ARMY GROUP CENTER

Beginning on 20 August, the pressure on Army Group Center subsided for a week. The Bryansk and Central Fronts closed to the HAGEN position, and the Stavka had directed Voronov to abandon the Roslavl thrust and regroup for an attack via Yel'nya toward Smolensk. The OKH took advantage of the pause to transfer five more divisions from Ninth Army to Army Group South.

When the last of those divisions left on 23 August, Kluge informed the OKH that he could no longer guarantee prevention of a breakthrough on his front. He offered as alternatives either giving the army group a large contingent of replacements and quantities of new matériel or allowing it to draw back forty-five miles to the SDB position, a recently surveyed but not yet constructed line roughly following the courses of the Seym, Desna, and Bolva Rivers. He had reason for concern. All the signs indicated that the Russians would shift the weight of their effort away from Ninth Army to the armies on its flanks. Fourth Army, on the left, had just barely been able to hold its line earlier in the month, and Second Army, on the right, although its front had been quiet thus far, was the victim of considerable neglect. It had been thoroughly mauled during the winter battles and later slighted because its front on the western rim of the Kursk bulge was expected to be eliminated by ZITADELLE. Second Army's strength was 7 divisions and 2 kampfgruppen, that of Fourth Army, 11 divisions and 7 kampfgruppen. Ninth Army still had some 26 divisions, 6 kampfgruppen, and miscellaneous smaller units, but Kluge could not count on drawing on them to bolster the other two armies. As one of Hitler's favorites, Model could operate with much more independence than the average army commander, and he was known to be something less than generous in weakening his own front for the sake of other sectors. That tendency, it may be said, had not disturbed Kluge earlier when the question was one of giving up divisions to Army Group South.

On 26 August Central Front resumed the offensive against Army Group Center, striking at the Ninth Army right flank east of Karachev and near Second Army's center at Sevsk and east of Klintsy. During the day it took Sevsk and scored a deep penetration east of Klintsy. Army Group Center and Second Army, assuming that Rokossovskiy was going to turn north and strike in the rear of Ninth Army, decided to deal first with the threat at Sevsk. That decision was no doubt correct, even though it helped raise an equal danger elsewhere. At that time Rokossovskiy had two tank armies standing in reserve behind his right flank, and he probably intended to commit them at Sevsk. Kluge had shifted one panzer and two infantry divisions south from Ninth Army several days earlier. Those he put into a counterattack northwest of Sevsk on 29 August.

Although only a moderate success, the counterattack, together with a sudden jump Sixtieth Army made that day to Yesman' on his left flank, was enough to persuade Rokossovskiy to change his plan. He began regrouping Second Tank and Thirteenth Armies from the right to the left flank. No matter which direction the Russians took, Second Army was in trouble. At Yesman' Sixtieth Army was twenty-five miles behind Second Army's south flank, and there a counterattack was out of the question.

Kluge allowed the army to bend XIII Corps back southwest of Yesman' and warned the OKH that Second Army would soon have to retreat farther and thereby also affect the north flank of Army Group South. Enough reinforcements to regain control were not to be had. The most Kluge could do was transfer two more divisions from Ninth Army, which was having troubles of its own. On 28 August two of West Front's armies, West Front's Tenth Guards and Twenty-first, had attacked at the Ninth Army-Fourth Army boundary. In two days they drove a 20-mile-deep wedge through to Yel'nya, forcing the German armies to bend their flanks back to keep contact.

On 29 August Kluge asked to take the Ninth and Second Armies into the SDB position. Second Army was split in two, and it seemed at the moment that with a little determination West Front would quickly push past Yel'nya to Smolensk, the eastern gateway to the Dvina-Dnepr gap. Kalinin Front had failed to break open the Third Panzer and Fourth Armies' flanks, but it was building up to another attempt. Hitler countered by asking for an opinion on another stand-and-fight order similar to the one which had been issued in the winter of 1941-42. Kluge replied that such an order would be futile: the troops would not carry it out, and the Soviet capabilities were much greater than they had been then. Finally, Hitler agreed to a half measure allowing Army Groups Center and South to swing their adjacent flanks back as far west as Krolevets.

Two days later, on 2 September, after Model had reported that Ninth Army could not establish a permanent front east of the Desna, Kluge issued preliminary instructions for a general withdrawal to the SDB position. In the Second Army zone it was already too late. XIII Corps, told to fall back to the west and maintain contact with Army Group South, allowed itself instead to be pushed south across the Seym River into the Fourth Panzer Army sector, thereby opening a 20-mile gap between the flanks of the army groups. Ignoring this fresh crisis, Hitler canceled the Army Group Center withdrawal orders. On 3 September, in a mood of near desperation, Kluge and Manstein went to Fuehrer headquarters to argue with Hitler in person.

FIRST PANZER ARMY AND SIXTH ARMY

During the last week of August, in spite of a momentary improvement on the north flank, the situation of Army Group South had also taken an alarming turn. On 13 and 18 August Southwest and South Fronts extended the offensive into the zones of the First Panzer and Sixth Armies and struck south of Izyum and east of Golodayevka, exactly the same spots where their breakthrough attempts had failed in July.

For the second time, the First Panzer Army line held, even though the artillery and mortar fire, described as the heaviest yet seen in the war, produced so many casualties that the army was forced to call for replacements after the first forty-eight hours. Sixth Army had worse luck. Instead of following the usual Soviet practice of bringing up fresh divisions before an offensive General Polkovnik F. I. Tolbukhin, commanding South Front, had fleshed out the units in the line;

Soviet troops storm a burning town.

consequently, the German intelligence officers, watching for what they regarded as an infallible sign of coming trouble, were misled by the absence of changes in the Second Guards and Fifth Shock Armies' orders of battle. When the attack came on 18 August it repeated the pattern of overwhelming concentration, particularly of artillery, on a narrow front. Before the end of the day Fifth Shock Army spearheads had penetrated three and a half miles behind the front through a mile-and a-half-wide gap. During the night, in the light of a full moon, they spread out north and south behind the German front.

Hollidt, commanding Sixth Army, decided against attempting to seal off the breakthrough and to try instead to close the gap in the front. That was the sort of bold decision which formerly had brought handsome rewards for comparatively little effort, but under present circumstances it had more the character of an all-or-nothing gamble. The army could spare very little infantry, and it had not a single tank. On 20 August the attack began from both sides of the gap. It made fair progress and by nightfall the two forces had almost joined hands, but during the night the IV Guards Mechanized Corps realized what was happening and, turning around, attacked from the west the next morning. The Soviet superiority was too great. By nightfall the gap had reopened to a width of nearly five miles.

By 20 August, Manstein had secured the 13th Panzer Division from Army Group A, but when it arrived at Sixth Army it was found to consist of only one regiment plus three companies. Moreover, Soviet espionage was working so well that the Russians knew about the division almost as soon as Sixth Army did. On 23 August, 13th Panzer Division attacked from the north side of the gap, which by then had widened to seven miles. For it to have closed the gap would have been a miracle. As it was, the three miles the division gained before being stopped by two mechanized corps constituted a startling success. Meanwhile, Tolbukhin, even though he operated cautiously, worried by the threat in his rear, had expanded the breakthrough to the point where Sixth Army could no longer muster the resources for an attempt to contain it.

By 23 August First Panzer Army was also in trouble. It reported that the corps south of Izyum was reduced to a combat strength of 5,800 men, not enough to maintain a continuous line. All Manstein could do was issue an unconvincing prediction that the battle was approaching its climax, and the victory would go to him whose strength lasts "one minute longer than his opponent's."

On 25 August the operations officers of First Panzer Army and Sixth Army flew to army group headquarters with a joint proposal for a withdrawal. There they learned that Manstein had told Hitler that if five fresh divisions, at least two of them panzer, could not be supplied, a retreat and, eventually, evacuation of the Donets Basin would be necessary. Manstein did not believe Hitler would accept that estimate, but gave the armies permission to start getting ready to go back to the general line of the Kalmius River, just east of Stalino.

Two days later, at Hitler's headquarters near Vinnitsa, Manstein presented the alternatives again, this time asking for twelve divisions. Hitler promised "all the divisions that could possibly be spared" by Army Groups North and Center. Both army groups promptly protested that they could not give up as much as a single division.

While Hitler was at Vinnitsa on 27 August more trouble developed for Sixth Army. II Guards Mechanized Corps turned south out of the breakthrough area and began a dash to the coast behind the XXIX Corps on the army right flank. Sixth Army was virtually helpless. It had 35,000 front-line troops and 7 tanks against 130,000 Russians with 160 to 170 tanks. Reluctantly, Manstein gave Hollidt two weak divisions, one infantry and one panzer, recently arrived from Army Group Center, and a panzer division, also weak, from First Panzer Army. Those, organized into a corps, Hollidt used to draw some of the pressure off XXIX Corps. On 29 August the Russians reached the coast west of Taganrog, driving XXIX Corps back into a pocket at the mouth of the Mius River.

The next day, coming from the west, 13th Panzer Division opened a narrow gap in the Russian line while XXIX Corps assembled its 9,000 troops in three columns headed by its few undamaged self-propelled assault guns. The Russians were misled by the heavy cloud of dust the German assembly raised. Believing that a strong tank attack was in the making, they gave way after the assault guns fired their first rounds, and, during the night, the German columns marched out to the west with hardly any losses.

On 31 August Manstein authorized Sixth Army, and First Panzer Army to fall back to the Kalmius River. That night Hitler approved "if the withdrawal was absolutely necessary and no other course was open."

MANSTEIN AND KLUGE CONFRONT HITLER

When Manstein and Kluge presented themselves at Fuehrer headquarters on 3 September they believed the time had come for radical measures. They wanted to convince Hitler that the situation demanded nothing less than a major overhaul of German strategy and a unified, militarily competent, command at the top level. During August, Manstein had several times called for the creation of a strategic main effort. He had proposed stripping the OKW theaters—the West, Italy, and the Balkans—and throwing the full weight of the German Army against the Russians.

The OKW had given some thousands of men to the Eastern Front in the form of replacement battalions, but it resisted giving up whole divisions, insisting that its theaters were underdefended as it was. In late August, perhaps influenced by Stalin's incessant demands for a second front, the Operations Branch, OKW, professed to see a danger of an Allied invasion on the Atlantic coast in the coming fall. On 2 September the Deputy Chief, Operations Branch, OKW, prepared a memorandum in which he maintained that attacks were to be expected on the Atlantic coast, in Italy, and in the Balkans. In contrast to the East, he pointed out, where there was still ample room for maneuver, these attacks would directly threaten the borders of the Reich. He concluded, therefore, that the OKW theaters could not spare any more troops for the East. The Chief, Operations Branch, OKW, Jodl, at first did not concur entirely, but in the next few days he worked out estimates of his own in which he reached essentially the same conclusion.

In the conference on 3 September, Manstein and Kluge asked Hitler to abolish the dualism between the OKH and OKW theaters and make the Chief of Staff, OKH, responsible for all theaters. Kluge had reported to Hitler several days before that he saw as the main source of the present troubles the lack of a single military adviser responsible to the supreme commander (Hitler) for all theaters.

The idea of a single chief of staff was militarily unexceptionable. Unfortunately, as the two field marshals must have known, it could not be presented in any form Hitler would accept. In the first place, conducting operations in all theaters through the OKH would automatically enhance the power of the Chief of Staff, OKH. At the same time, it would weaken Hitler's personal control by nullifying the claim that he alone could form a complete strategic picture and by depriving him of the device, which he had used often, of playing the OKW and OKH off against each other. Finally, it could result in his losing his grip on the Eastern Front. A more powerful Chief of Staff, OKH, might bring actual over-all control in the East into the hands of the Army General Staff and end the compartmentalization Hitler used to maintain himself as supreme arbiter over the four army groups and the OKH. That Hitler would reject any such abridgments of his personal authority was a foregone conclusion. In the end, he chose to consider the problem a purely technical one of co-ordinating troop transfers between the OKH and OKW theaters and ordered that henceforth all decisions by the OKH or the OKW affecting each other's strengths would be communicated to him personally in the presence of both the Chief, OKW, and the Chief of Staff, OKH.

Having demonstrated that, whatever the state of the war, he was and would remain the master in Germany, Hitler turned to the situation at the front. To Manstein he conceded nothing, rejecting his pleas for large-scale reinforcement of Army Group South from other theaters. He gave Kluge permission to take Second Army and the right flank of Ninth Army behind the Desna River. On the afternoon of 3 September, after conferring with Antonescu, he ordered Army Group A to start evacuating the GOTENKOPF. All civilians were to be evacuated to the Crimea, and the Russians were to be left "an uninhabitable desert."

HITLER APPROVES A WITHDRAWAL "IN PRINCIPLE"

After 3 September the offensive against Army Group Center subsided briefly. West of Yel'nya the Ninth and Fourth Armies re-established a continuous front. On the southern flank, Rokossovskiy shifted his attack to the left flank of Fourth Panzer Army, and, as a consequence, Second Army's withdrawal to the Desna proved fairly easy. Fourth Panzer Army took over XIII Corps and, after replacing the commanding general, used it to screen its lengthening north flank.

The drive against Army Group Center had obviously gone somewhat awry, although it had perhaps accomplished as much as was needed for the time being. The Stavka had probably realized that though substantial, its superiority was not enough equally to sustain simultaneous advances into Belorussia and the Ukraine. On 4 September it committed itself definitely to a main effort in the Ukraine against the Army Group South left flank. On that day Voronezh Front, reinforced by Third Guards Tank Army (transferred from the Central Front), Fifty-second Army, and several tank and mechanized corps, launched a powerful attack on a broad front between the Psel and Vorskla Rivers that threatened to break open the Fourth Panzer Army right flank and leave the army with both flanks hanging in the air.

On the night of 4 September Sixth Army and First Panzer Army went into the Kalmius line, and the Sixth Army commander, Hollidt, declared there would be no more withdrawals, the front would absolutely be held. He could not have been more wrong. As long as

German self-propelled assault gun.

it had the protection of the Donets River along nearly all of its front, First Panzer Army presented at least an appearance of strength, but after it had bent its right corps back from the river even that was lost. The army, severely strained by battles of attrition since July, had asked for nine or ten days to move into its new line but was given only three. Southwest Front, after following close on its heels all the way, opened a slashing attack on the morning of 6 September. In a few hours I Guards Mechanized Corps and nine rifle divisions rammed through north of the First Panzer Army-Sixth Army boundary. That night von Mackensen told the army group chief of staff that all that was left to do was to retreat to the Dnepr, since neither his army nor Sixth Army had strength enough to restore the front. The next day XXIII Tank Corps slipped through the gap and joined I Guards Mechanized Corps. Leaving the infantry behind, the two armored corps broke away to the west. By 8 September their reconnaissance detachments were approaching Pavlograd and Sinel'nikovo, a hundred miles behind the front and about thirty miles east of the Dnepr.

Early on the morning of the 8th Hitler's plane carrying him and Zeitzler landed at Zaporozhye, Manstein's headquarters. Some sort of reasonably thoroughgoing decision could no longer be avoided. During the day's conferences Manstein argued that Army Group Center should be pulled back to the PANTHER position to shorten its front by about one-third and free a commensurate number of divisions for Army Group South. Hitler objected that such a withdrawal would take too long. Instead, he ordered Kleist, who was present, to speed up evacuation of the GOTENKOPF, a move expected to yield three divisions.

As far as the right flank of Army Group South was concerned, to patch the line on the Kalmius River was clearly out of the question; therefore, Hitler approved "in principle" the withdrawal of First Panzer and Sixth Armies to the WOTAN position between Melitopol and the Dnepr north of Zaporozhye. For the north flank of the army group he promised reinforcements, four infantry divisions for the Dnepr crossings and a corps headquarters with two infantry and two panzer divisions from Army Group Center to close the gap between the Second Army and Fourth Panzer Army flanks. Manstein immediately told the First Panzer and Sixth Armies to go over to "a mobile defense." With that the retreat to the Dnepr was on.

TO THE DNEPR

As usual, Hitler's main concern in the conferences on 8 September had been to avoid any decision that was not already inevitable. Finding himself forced to give up the Donets Basin, he was doubly reluctant to concede the necessity for a similar decision with respect to the Fourth Panzer and Eighth Armies. Instead, he took refuge in dubious promises, one of which evaporated the next day when he learned that of the four divisions designated for the Dnepr crossings only one would be available and it would have to come all the way from Army Group North. The other he gave somewhat more substance before leaving Zaporozhye by issuing specific orders to Army Group Center concerning transfer of the corps headquarters and four divisions that were to come under Army Group South control as soon as they crossed the Desna. But three of the divisions were to come from Second Army, which in its weakened state could hardly spare the divisions on 8 September, and on the 9th, after Rokossovskiy's troops crossed the

Desna south of Novgorod-Severskiy and at Otsekin, could not spare them at all. The 8th Panzer Division, the one division Second Army did release, it used to protect its own flank south of the Desna.

FIRST PANZER ARMY AND SIXTH ARMY RETREAT

In the south the First Panzer and Sixth Armies lost no time starting their march to the Dnepr. In two days their inner flanks covered seventy miles, about half the distance, and on 12 September panzer units of First Panzer Army pushing south re-established contact with the left flank of Sixth Army. As the gap between the armies narrowed, I Guards Mechanized Corps and XXIII Tank Corps, operating toward Pavlograd and Sinel'nikovo, slowed down. On the night of the 12th the Headquarters, Southwest Front, ordered the two corps to turn back and escape to the east. During the next two days First Panzer Army beat off several breakout attempts. On the night of 14 September remnants of the corps slipped through an accidental gap in the Sixth Army line.

The experience of I Guards Mechanized Corps demonstrated once more the Russians' difficulties in fully exploiting their armor. After the breakthrough at Golodayevka, Tolbukhin had been criticized for using his tank units too cautiously and dissipating their strength in numerous small skirmishes. Malinovskiy, apparently determined not to make the same mistake, had unleashed I Guards Mechanized Corps and XXIII Tank Corps. Their dash toward the Dnepr, though spectacular, had been tactically unproductive. It had pointed up the already obvious weakness of the two German armies, but this could probably have been done with greater effect by keeping the corps in contact with the front. As soon as their supply lines were cut, the corps had lost momentum, and when the front closed behind them they had had to fall back precipitously, taking a thorough drubbing on the way.

After 12 September First Panzer Army and Sixth Army set a more deliberate pace. Behind Sixth Army, which, to protect the land routes into the Crimea, would have to hold a line whose only natural advantage was the small Molochnaya River, Army Group A began moving in troops and artillery. Worried that Manstein might later be tempted to siphon these off to other sectors of Army Group South,

Kleist asked for command of Sixth Army when it reached the WOTAN position. At midmonth Hitler agreed that Army Group A would take over Headquarters, Sixth Army, and its two southern corps, the third corps going to First Panzer Army.

FOURTH PANZER ARMY AND EIGHTH ARMY WEAKEN

On its north flank the Army Group South front was becoming tauter and more brittle by the hour. Eighth Army reported shortly after the turn of the month that it could no longer hold a continuous line. It had established a system of strongpoints with connecting trenches for patrols. Its rear echelon troops consisted exclusively of "sole surviving sons" and "fathers of large families," two categories that were still, by Hitler's order, exempt from front-line duty, all the rest having been sent to the front. Even so, one infantry division was reduced to a strength of six officers and 300 men. Exhaustion and apathy had set in, and the "most severe measures" no longer helped to stiffen the troops' resistance.

Fourth Panzer Army was in worse straits. On the 30-mile stretch of front between the Vorskla and the Psel, its front sagged under the weight of six tank and mechanized corps and an estimated nineteen rifle divisions. In the gap off its left flank the most it could do was to try to create an island of resistance around Nezhin, the last obstacle in Central Front's way on the road to Kiev. There the slow arrival of the promised divisions from Army Group Center so exasperated Hoth that, finally, on 12 September, he claimed command of all units south of the Desna, in accordance with Hitler's order, and took the 8th Panzer Division off the Second Army flank.

KLUGE BEGINS THE RETREAT TO THE PANTHER POSITION

Kluge made a conscientious, though hardly heroic, effort to get the four divisions promised Army Group South. On 10 September, when he asked the Commanding General, Second Army, General der Infanterie Walter Weiss, to reconsider whether he could not somehow spare two more divisions, Weiss replied that his army was down to an average combat strength of 1,000 men per division. The next day, after Weiss reported that the Russians had increased the number of their bridgeheads across the Desna to six, Kluge decided to take the two divisions from Fourth Army instead. At the same time he told the OKH, "The door to Smolensk now stands open."

On the 12th he informed the OKH that the army group could not supply a fourth division. The pause in the offensive against Army Group Center had ended. The Russians were expanding their bridgeheads on the Desna; a cavalry corps, attacking south of Kirov, had sliced through behind the center of Ninth Army; and an offensive toward Smolensk was to be expected any day against Fourth Army.

By the 12th, Army Group Center, in fact, was in serious trouble; the Stavka was obviously determined not to let the army group come to rest. The cavalry corps that had penetrated the Ninth Army left flank, thrusting deep to the southwest, took Zhukovka on the Bryansk-Roslavl' railroad. Model set about closing his front, but the effort merely emphasized the futility of Ninth Army's continuing to hold a rigid line when it was obvious that the armies on its flanks would give way before the next onslaught. The build-up opposite Fourth Army had gone so far that the army would not dare meet the impending attack head on. Second Army's front on the Desna was riddled with bridgeheads, and to man its lengthening right flank it had committed two security divisions and a Hungarian division, none of them equipped or trained for front-line fighting.

On 13 September Kluge issued the warning order for a withdrawal to the PANTHER position. In a meeting at army group headquarters, the chief of staff gave the officers present an idea of the magnitude of such an operation. It would mean, he stated, relinquishing half, qualitatively the better half, of the territory the army group still held in the Soviet Union. Work on the PANTHER position would require 400,000 civilian laborers. Between 2.5 and 3 million persons would have to be evacuated to the west—this as compared to some 190,000 evacuated from the Orel bulge. Six hundred thousand cattle would have to be herded to the rear, and the army group would have to shift all of its rear area installations. For instance, new hospital facilities for 36,000 beds would have to be built.

The next morning West Front renewed the thrust toward Smolensk. In the afternoon the Chief of Operations, OKH, called the army

Soviet troops boarding a raft on a branch of the Dnepr.

group headquarters to inform Kluge that Manstein intended ordering Fourth Panzer Army to withdraw behind the Dnepr. The Chief of Operations believed the time had come for Army Group Center to start its pullback to the PANTHER position.

He wanted to know whether Kluge considered that he, Kluge, had the authority to issue such an order. Kluge replied that he did not: an order would have to come from Hitler through the OKH. Certain that the order would come within a matter of hours, Kluge that night directed Model to start taking the center of the Ninth Army line behind the Desna and gave Weiss permission to begin falling back west of the Desna.

HITLER AND KLUGE GO SLOW

In the Army Group South zone on 14 September, Fourth Panzer Army wavered on the brink of collapse. On its left Central Front troops were pushing into Nezhin, and in the center Voronezh Front had broken through, splitting the army into three parts. Hoth reported that the Russians could march to Kiev unhindered. The situation, he stated, was similar to that the army had faced south of Rostov during the winter, the difference being that then it had some battleworthy units with which to maneuver. The greatest danger was that the army would be pushed south parallel to the Dnepr and leave a long stretch of the river on either side of Kiev completely exposed.

Manstein instructed Hoth to break contact with Eighth Army and swing his right flank west, orienting his front on a north-south axis to cover Kiev. He ordered Woehler to take Eighth Army back as quickly as he could without impairing the troops' fitness for combat and so release enough troops to screen the gap that would open between the two armies. In his report to Hitler, Manstein stated that on 15 September he was going to order Fourth Panzer Army to retreat behind the Dnepr, otherwise the army would soon be destroyed. Since he would have to take divisions from the Eighth and First Panzer Armies for Fourth Panzer Army, he saw no chance of holding any ground forward of the river. On the night of the 14th Hitler told Manstein and Kluge to report in person the next day.

Meanwhile, the loss of Nezhin early on the 15th touched off a near panic at Fuehrer headquarters. The OKH urged Army Group Center to speed up the withdrawals already under way in order to free units for Army Group South. After Manstein and Kluge arrived, Hitler told Kluge to transfer four divisions to Army Group South and agreed to a general retreat to the WOTAN (Dnepr) and PANTHER positions. By the end of the day, however, he began to have second thoughts, and before Kluge left Fuehrer headquarters he instructed him to execute the Army Group Center withdrawal by phases, avoiding "excessive speed." He was not interested, he said, in executing the operation quickly. Every major step back would require his prior concurrence.

For Army Group South the decision to go behind the Dnepr, welcome though it was, posed problems that would test the skill and stamina of the leadership and troops as severely as anything they had yet undertaken. The first of these was to disengage the scattered pieces of Fourth Panzer Army, a move accomplished on the nights of 16 and 17 September in what Hoth described as "two great leaps backward"— through which the army regained some freedom of maneuver and restored contact between its units. Next came the more difficult and dangerous task of getting the Fourth Panzer, Eighth, and First Panzer Armies across the river. The three armies, occupying a front nearly

400 miles in breadth, had at their disposal only five crossings—Kiev, Kanev, Cherkassy, Kremenchug, and Dnepropetrovsk—which meant splitting their forces, establishing bridgeheads that could be held until the troops were funneled across, and then fanning out behind the river before the Russians could get bridgeheads of their own in the undefended areas on the west bank.

Very little had been done to improve the crossings. Regarding Cherkassy, swiftly being congested with evacuated cattle and piles of goods, Headquarters, Army Group South, and Eighth Army argued over who would furnish engineers and bridging equipment. At the last minute Hitler added another complication by insisting that First Panzer Army strengthen the bridgehead east of Zaporozhye to protect the nearby Nikopol manganese mines. Hitler's tendency to place economic objectives above tactics was once more to have baneful effects, for in following orders Manstein had to shift nearly all of the few units he could spare, and would otherwise have used to shore up the army group's weak left flank, to the tactically worthless Zaporozhye bridgehead.

At the 15 September conference, Manstein had insisted that Army Group Center transfer the newly promised four divisions to Army Group South at top speed. Before the end of the day marching orders came through for two of the divisions; but by the time Kluge left Fuehrer headquarters Hitler had given him two mutually contradictory missions: to release the divisions for Army Group South quickly—but to conduct the withdrawal to the PANTHER position at a deliberate pace. The latter coincided with Kluge's own thinking; consequently, he was in no hurry to get the general withdrawal under way and waited three days before issuing a basic order. In that order he emphasized that the armies would stay forward of the PANTHER position at least until 10 October. As a result, the army group remained tied down in heavy fighting at the front, and the transfer of two of the four divisions promised Army Group South was first postponed and finally canceled.

Tactically, Kluge's decision to go slow gave the Stavka an opportunity to continue developing its two currently most dangerous offensive thrusts, the one toward Smolensk and the other toward the Dnepr between the flanks of Army Groups Center and South. While West

UkrainIian evacuees at a river crossing.

Front forced the Fourth Army right flank back southeast of Smolensk, Kalinin Front, under Yeremenko, bore down north of the city on both sides of the Third Panzer-Fourth Army boundary. South of the Desna, off the Second Army right flank, on 16 and 18 September Central Front moved in a fresh guards mechanized corps; during the next two days, without slackening the advance toward the Dnepr, it aimed a two-pronged thrust northward across the Desna on either side of Chernigov. The Second Army flank collapsed under the first wave of the attack. The army group recorded that on 19 September the Hungarian division stationed east of Chernigov "dissolved completely."

Between 20 and 23 September disastrous developments on both flanks forced Kluge to abandon his plan for a leisurely withdrawal. North of Smolensk, Kalinin Front broke through the Third Panzer Army right flank, taking Demidov and threatening the PANTHER position. Southeast of Smolensk, the Fourth Army line was beginning to crack. In the Second Army zone, east of Chernigov, Central Front carried its advance north behind the army flank toward Gomel, the most important road and railroad junction on the southern half of the Army Group Center front.

ARMY GROUP SOUTH GOES BEHIND THE RIVER

During the last week of the month the Army Group South's retreat degenerated into a race with the Russians for possession of the right bank of the Dnepr. At the confluence of the Pripyat and the Dnepr some of Rokossovskiy's troops had crossed as early as 19 September, and before the end of the month they had a bridgehead reaching 15 miles west along both sides of the Pripyat to Chernobyl.

Anxious to keep the Germans from digging in on the Dnepr and thereby possibly effecting a stalemate, the Stavka had directed the fronts and armies to cross the river on the run. To the officers and soldiers who distinguished themselves in river crossings, it offered the highest Soviet military decoration, Hero of the Soviet Union, which meant a life pension and public recognition—a life-sized bust of the recipient was to be displayed in his home town. The technique of the crossings was the same everywhere, crude, but conducted on so large a scale and with such great persistence that it was overwhelmingly effective. For instance, near Bukrin, forty-eight miles southeast of Kiev, four soldiers of a guards submachine gun company crossed the Dnepr in a rowboat after dark on 22 September. They waded ashore, climbed the bank, at this point steep and several hundred feet high, and from the gullies near the top drew fire from the German outposts.

Other small parties followed. By daylight the whole company had crossed and taken a foothold at the top of the bank. Then, in an antlike procession, the whole Third Guards Tank Army began to cross, the infantry using anything that would float—timbers, gasoline drums, wooden doors, even straw wrapped in ponchos—while the engineers built causeways for the heavy equipment, and other troops set up artillery on the east bank to deliver covering fire. The four submachine gunners became Heroes of the Soviet Union. Up and down the river, the Stavka, to keep the armies moving and as if intent on paving the crossings with medals, awarded 2,000 Hero of the Soviet Union decorations and ten thousand lesser ones.

On the 26th, Voronezh Front took a bridgehead in the bend of the Dnepr below Pereyaslav, and Steppe Front made three smaller crossings between Kremenchug and Dnepropetrovsk. These it expanded in the next few days to form a single bridgehead thirty miles wide and at one point ten miles deep. Lying, as they did, almost exactly midway between the Germans' own crossing points, the bridgeheads were each established in places the Germans would have trouble reaching.

Hitler worried most about the bridgehead at the mouth of the Pripyat. On 25 September he ordered Army Groups Center and South to eliminate it immediately, but that was not easily done. While the two army groups sent the few, nearly exhausted, divisions they could spare probing into the swamps that fringed the rivers, the Russians, determined not to be dislodged, moved in fresh well-rested troops.

By the end of the month Army Group South had taken the last of its troops across the river and was struggling to establish a front. Sixth Army, having gone into the WOTAN position below Zaporozhye on 20 September, was already straining to beat off an armored offensive at the center of its front—a certain sign that the Stavka would not relax the pressure, at least as long as the good weather lasted. On 2 October the last units of Army Group Center moved into the PANTHER position, which followed the general line of the Sozh and Pronya Rivers about thirty miles east of the Dnepr. In the south Army Group A completed its withdrawal from the GOTENKOPF on 29 September. It still held a small bridgehead on the Taman Peninsula but evacuated it during the next ten days.

In two and one-half months Army Groups Center and South had been forced back an average distance of 150 miles on a front 650 miles long. Economically, the Germans lost the most valuable territory they had taken in the Soviet Union. In an effort at least to deny the Soviet Union the fruits of these rich areas Hitler had initiated a scorched-earth policy, but, in the end, even that satisfaction was denied him. At the end of September Army Group Center reported that it had succeeded in evacuating no more than 20 to 30 percent of the economic goods in its rear area.

In the Army Group South zone the failure was, if anything, greater. The economic staffs did not have the personnel to accomplish total destruction, and they lacked the equipment to remove more than a part of the useable goods. Large numbers of factories, power plants, railroads, and bridges were in fact destroyed, but many of them had never been fully restored after the Soviet retreat in 1941. The people, influenced by Soviet propaganda promising that there would be no reprisals, sabotaged the evacuation to save their own possessions and to establish alibis that would be useful after the Germans departed. The only willing evacuees were the outright collaborators, those from some of the districts along the Donets who had had a taste of a Soviet "liberation" during the last winter, and those who resided in the few areas completely laid waste. The armies and economic staffs organized caravans of civilians numbering all together about 600,000 persons, or one-tenth of the population. They estimated later that about 280,000 of these eventually reached and crossed the Dnepr. In addition to 268,000 tons of grain and 488,000 cattle and horses taken across the river, the Germans destroyed 941,000 tons of grain and 13,000 cattle; but they left behind 1,656,233 tons of grain, much of it standing in the fields ready to be harvested, and 2,987,699 cattle and horses.

The Russians lost no time in exploiting the fruits of victory. As they pursued the right flank of Army Group South across the southern Ukraine they drew on the local population for replacements. Sixth Army estimated that about 80,000 men were drafted in the reoccupied towns and cities, given a uniform jacket or pants and a rifle, and thrown into the front line.

On reaching the Dnepr River the Soviet Army attained the original objectives of its summer offensive. The shortening of the German front, the defensive advantages of the river, the lengthening Soviet lines of communications, and the attrition of Soviet forces should have brought the two sides into balance temporarily. In early October the Germans still believed they had a chance of achieving some sort of a balance, but their own mistakes and the Soviet numerical superiority were working against them. By trying to hold out east of the Dnepr, Hitler had sacrificed too much of the strength of Army Groups South and Center; consequently, the so-called East Wall could not be properly manned or fortified and in the end was breached in several places while the front was still in motion. The Russians' manpower advantage, on the other hand, had enabled them to rest and refit their units in shifts. As a result, they reached the Dnepr with their offensive capability largely intact, and before the last German troops crossed the river the battle for the Dnepr line had begun.

CHAPTER IX

The Battle for the Dnepr Line

ARMY GROUP SOUTH

The Dnepr, the second largest Russian river, affords the strongest natural defense line in western Russia, especially when the battle is moving from east to west. At the confluence of the Pripyat the Dnepr broadens to about a half mile, and downstream the meandering main channel varies in width from a third of a mile to more than a mile. Below Kiev the river valley is twenty to twenty-five miles wide and the east bank is swampy and laced with secondary channels. At Kiev the west bank rises nearly 300 feet to form a fringe of steep cliffs. Below the city the west bank continues high, averaging between 150 and 300 feet along most of the lower course. The east bank is flat and treeless, and the bare steppe stretches away beyond the far horizon.

Fortified and adequately manned, the Dnepr line would have been almost ideally defensible; but the condition of Army Group South in the fall of 1943 was such that the river provided at most a modest degree of natural protection and a tenuous handhold. (Map 16) The troops, influenced by talk of an "East Wall," were dismayed to find on crossing that nothing had been built and that much of the proposed front had not even been surveyed. Later, one of the army chiefs of staff was to warn that troop morale could not again withstand such a shock.

In the first week of October, Army Group South had 37 divisions with an average front-line infantry strength of 1,000 men each, or about 80 men per mile of front. This highly unfavorable ratio of troop strength to frontage was the price the army group had to pay for the protection of the river. Whether it was worth paying was doubtful from the first. Below Kiev the Dnepr angles southeastward for 250 miles; at Zaporozhye it doubles back to the southwest another 150 miles before reaching the Black Sea below Kherson. In making this great bend it

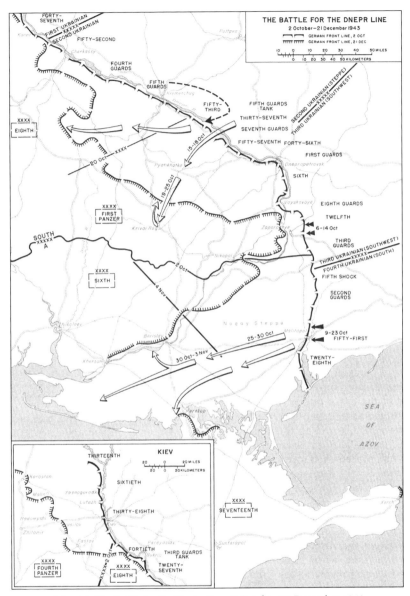

Map 16: The Battle for the Dnepr Line, 2 October-21 December 1943

travels nearly twice the straight-line distance between Kiev and the coast. The front of Army Group South and the Sixth Army, dropping off south of Zaporozhye to Melitopol, did not follow the lower angle of the river, but even so it was over a third longer than, for instance, a line Kiev-Nikolaev would have been. Tactically the Dnepr confronted

Army Group South with the problem that had dogged its steps since Stalingrad—defending a front angled away to the east.

THE ZAPOROZHYE BRIDGEHEAD LOST

On 1 October Southwest Front launched a strong attack against the Zaporozhye bridgehead, making a small penetration that First Panzer Army eliminated before the end of the day. But in reporting the success to the army group von Mackensen asked permission to give up the bridgehead anyway, stating that to attempt a stand there would consume too many troops.

The next day the Russians, realizing that they had reached the line the Germans meant to hold, broke off the offensive along the entire Eastern Front for a week while they regrouped and brought up fresh units. To underscore the victories so far, and to mark the entry into a new phase of the war, the Stavka began renaming the front commands. Opposite Army Group South and Sixth Army the Voronezh, Steppe, Southwest, and South Fronts became the First, Second, Third, and Fourth Ukrainian Fronts.

After a conference at the Fuehrer headquarters on 8 October the Chief of Staff, Army Group South, informed von Mackensen that Hitler had denied the request to evacuate the Zaporozhye bridgehead, because to do so would expose the left flank of Sixth Army. Hitler's thinking coincided exactly with that of the Stavka, which considered the bridgehead the key to cleaning out the east bank of the lower Dnepr and gave the mission of eliminating it to Third Ukranian Front.

On the morning of 10 October the Eighth Guards and Third Guards Armies renewed the offensive against the, by then, solidly dug-in Germans in the bridgehead. The attack began with an extraordinarily powerful artillery preparation. This and the other battles then developing along the front demonstrated that the Russians had reached a new stage in their employment of artillery. Artillery divisions made their first appearance, and the duration and weight of the barrages indicated that the Soviet Army now had enough guns and ammunition to employ them lavishly to level the defenses and make the way easier for tanks and infantry. The bridgehead line held, but on the second day von Mackensen indicated that his losses were so heavy that he could not hold out more than a few days longer. The next day he reported that gaps had appeared in the line and could not be closed and that by holding the bridgehead he was risking not having enough troops left to establish a front behind the river.

When Manstein informed the OKH that he intended to give up the bridgehead on 14 October, Hitler called in the Commanding General, Army Group A. Kleist was worried about his north flank, and both he and Hitler suspected that Manstein was merely trying to slough off a mission he had not wanted in the first place. Hitler ordered Kleist to investigate—without informing Manstein—whether Army Group A could take over the bridgehead. On the 13th Kleist reported that to hold the bridgehead he would need one or two more divisions. Since the fighting on the Sixth Army front was imposing a heavy drain on the army group's reserve strength, he would, if he had to supply the divisions from his own resources, have to evacuate the Crimea. That prospect was completely unpalatable to Hitler; he therefore reverted to his habitual device of simply refusing to approve a withdrawal.

XXIII Tank Corps and I Guards Mechanized Corps, rested and recovered from the beating they had taken in September, settled the issue. In a daring tank attack on the night of the 13th they cut through the northeast corner of the bridgehead, pushed to the outskirts of Zaporozhye, and forced First Panzer Army back into a shallow arc around the city. The next day the army rear guard crossed to the west bank after holding around the bridges and the dam south of the city long enough to assure their being blown up.

SIXTH ARMY—BREAKTHROUGH AND RETREAT

Kleist had cause for concern over his left flank. After the week's respite, which it had used to muster a lopsided superiority of troops and matériel, Fourth Ukrainian Front on 9 October had resumed the offensive against Sixth Army. Against 13 German divisions—the total Army Group A strength in German units, except for three divisions on the Crimea—and 2 Rumanian divisions, Tolbukhin massed 45 rifle divisions, 3 tank corps, 2 guards mechanized corps, 2 guards cavalry corps, and 400 batteries of artillery. He had 800 tanks against the Germans' 83 tanks and 98 self-propelled assault guns.

Soviet artillery near Kiev.

Tactically the Nogay Steppe, one of the least hospitable regions of southern USSR, presented all kinds of difficulties for the defense. The Sixth Army front spanned the open end of the V formed by the Dnepr River on the north and the Sea of Azov and the Black Sea on the south. The army's communications lines were three single-tracked railroads that crossed the Dnepr at Nikopol, Berislav, and Kherson. The barren steppe afforded neither cover nor natural defenses. On the roads, the deep dust slowed traffic and billowed above moving columns, choking men and horses and sifting into motors. Sixth Army's single advantage was a fairly well-fortified front; because the line above Melitopol was naturally weak more work had been put into it than on the rest of the WOTAN position.

The attack began on a 20-mile front straddling Melitopol. The artillery preparation was devastating. In an hour two German divisions each counted 15,000 shellbursts in their sectors. The German batteries replied in kind as far as they were able. On both sides the artillery wasted no time on counterbattery fires but brought down its full weight on the infantry.

Tolbukhin's objective, obviously, was to dislodge Sixth Army from Melitopol, the southern anchor of its front, and force it north away from the Isthmus of Perekop, the entrance to the Crimea. By 12 October Fifty-first Army had pushed into the city from the south, but it took another twelve days of bitter street fighting to break the German grip.

On 23 October Melitopol fell; this was the signal for the thrust by the main forces, which so far had been holding back. Two days later Twenty-eighth and Fifty-first Armies drove southwest and south of the city, splitting Sixth Army in two. South of the breakthrough the army had two German and two Rumanian divisions. Since these could hardly be expected to establish a line that would protect the Isthmus of Perekop—the Rumanians were already beginning to panic—the army decided to try closing the gap from the north. On the 27th the 13th Panzer Division struck south into the gap, but it did not have enough power to go all the way. Meanwhile, the army moved its heavy weapons into position for another attempt several days later. Before that attack could be launched Fifty-first and Twenty-eighth Armies, on the 30th, smashed the weak Sixth Army south flank and began swift thrusts to the Isthmus of Perekop and to Kherson at the mouth of the Dnepr. During the next two days the remnants of the south flank, abandoning all their heavy equipment and most of their vehicles, retreated behind the Dnepr. The stronger north flank fell back to a large bridgehead south of Nikopol, which Hitler then ordered held to protect the city and as a springboard for a counterattack to reopen the Crimea.

THE CRIMEA CUT OFF

After the middle of October Army Group A had grown increasingly concerned over the future of Seventeenth Army in the Crimea. On the 18th, when it appeared that the Russians might penetrate the Army Group South right flank and strike for the coast west of the Dnepr, Kleist had warned the OKH that the time had come to start evacuating the peninsula. The battle on the Sixth Army front, he reported, was siphoning off the strength of Seventeenth Army; sooner or later it would become too weak to defend itself.

The next day and again five days later Kleist asked the Chief of Staff, OKH, to get a decision. Zeitzler replied that Hitler would not allow the word Crimea to be mentioned in his presence. On 26 October, when the Sixth Army front broke in two, Kleist declared that he was having to transfer another division from Seventeenth Army to Sixth Army, and that with one German and seven unreliable Rumanian divisions Seventeenth Army could not defend the Crimea. He added that he therefore intended to begin the withdrawal by evacuating the Kerch' Peninsula that night. Hitler promptly forbade any withdrawals.

Two days later Antonescu, worried about the effect the loss of another seven divisions would have in his country, appealed to Hitler to give up the Crimea. In reply Hitler undertook to justify his decision. His most substantial arguments were that the Soviet Union could use the Crimea as an air base for attacks on the Rumanian oil fields and as a staging area for landings on the Rumanian and Bulgarian coasts and that it was too late to evacuate the peninsula anyway.

On the night of 28 October the Commanding General, Seventeenth Army, General der Pioniere Erwin Jaenecke, declaring that he refused to take the responsibility for another Stalingrad, informed Kleist that he proposed to execute the command to evacuate which the army group had issued on the 26th and Hitler had canceled. Kleist countered with an order to hold the Crimea no matter how the battle went. He offered the explanation that Hitler had said things would look better in two weeks and then the Crimea could be reopened with fresh forces. Jaenecke refused to accept that order. Kleist then put through a personal phone call to Jaenecke.

Since much has been written about the blind obedience of the German generals, it may be worthwhile to recount the ensuing conversation as an example of what an attempt to disobey an order involved. After stating that Jaenecke's intention had possibly been misinterpreted and receiving his assurance that it had not, Kleist went on:

Kleist: You are to defend the Crimea.

Jaenecke: I cannot execute that order. No one else will execute it either; the corps commanders believe the same as I do.

Kleist: So, collusion, conspiracy to disobey an order! If you cannot, someone else will command the army.

Jaenecke: I report again that in the light of my responsibility for the army I cannot execute the order.

Kleist: As a soldier I have often had to struggle with myself in similar situations. You will not save a single man. What is to come will come one way or another. This attitude only undermines the confidence of the troops. If I get one more division [for you] everything will be all right.

Jaenecke: That is building castles in the air. One must deal with realities here.

Kleist: To retreat under pressure of the enemy is well and good; to retreat this way is something else.

Jaenecke: I cannot wait until Army Group South has gone that far. [Jaenecke was referring here to the threatening breakthrough to the coast on the Army Group South right flank. See below.]

Kleist: The army has not yet been attacked. A little reinforcement on the isthmus and everything will be in order. The enemy will prefer to strike west and then north into the flank of First Panzer Army rather than into the Perekop narrows.

Jaenecke: The Crimea must be defended on its entire perimeter. If the Russians attack the catastrophe is at hand. I must recall once more the example of Generalfeldmarschall Paulus at Stalingrad.

Kleist: The details of events there are not known. The accounts of what happened vary. Do you believe that the Fuehrer will let himself be influenced by you? He has already said once that he will not allow any general to subject him to blackmail. If the Commanding General, Seventeenth Army, does not execute the order he will break every rule of soldierly deportment. Will you execute the order or not?

When Jaenecke asked for time to consult his chief of staff, the exchange broke off.

Afterward, the Chief of Staff, Army Group A, called the Chief of Staff and the Operations Officer, Seventeenth Army, and admonished them to give their commanding general "proper" advice. The question, he said, was purely one of obedience. If Jaenecke refused, a new commanding general would be sent who would be less well acquainted with local conditions and the consequences would fall entirely on the troops. An hour later Jaenecke capitulated and recalled his order. In relaying an account of the incident to Zeitzler, Kleist said that he did not want to court-martial Jaenecke but could not keep him as an army commander. Jaenecke stayed on, however, possibly because Zeitzler and Kleist, on second thought, decided it would be better not to bring a further example of a general's alleged unreliability to Hitler's attention.

Probably, no amount of argument would have persuaded Hitler to give up the Crimea. As always, he expected his luck to change and had vague plans to recoup his losses. On their side, the generals, optimism and determination being among the most highly regarded virtues of their profession, were for the most part unwilling to proclaim a cause lost as long as a glimmer of hope, no matter how remote, remained.

In this instance, Hitler at the end of the month found support in another quarter. Manstein, who was getting five fresh panzer divisions from Italy and the West to clean up the breakthrough in his own sector, proposed to attach them to First Panzer Army for a quick counterattack and then, as soon as the Russians were stopped, shift them south to the Dnepr Bend to attack into the flank of the thrust against Sixth Army. Manstein's plan was reminiscent of the Kharkov offensive earlier in the year, and Hitler, seeing in it not only a chance to keep the Crimea open but the prospect of a full-scale victory as well, approved immediately. For Manstein, too, the plan must have had an extraordinary attraction, as an exercise in virtuosity and as another opportunity to demonstrate the tactics he had long advocated of using the retreat to trap and waylay the enemy.

KONEV DRIVES TOWARD KRIVOI ROG

Before Manstein could execute his plan he first had to stop a thrust west of the Dnepr that was threatening to cut off the First Panzer Army and Army Group A as well. Second Ukrainian Front had massed four armies, including Fifth Guards Tank Army, behind its bridgeheads below Kremenchug and at midmonth was bringing Fifth Guards Army down from the bridgehead above the city. On the morning of 15 October a dozen rifle divisions attacked out of the larger of the bridgeheads, and that afternoon Konev committed Fifth Guards Tank Army. The next day he had three armies across the river. That night Manstein and von Mackensen agreed that the best decision would be to give up the Dnepr Bend and take First Panzer Army and Army

*Army commander reports to Konev and Zhukov on preparations for Dnepr crossing,
September 1943.*

Group A back to the Bug River above Nikolaev, but Manstein added
that such a decision was hardly to be expected.

During the next few days Konev poured divisions across the river
and tore open the First Panzer Army left flank. On 18 October his
troops took Pyatikhatka, thirty-five miles south of the Dnepr, and cut
the main railroads to Dnepropetrovsk and Krivoi Rog. For a time von
Mackensen thought the Russians had gone as far inland as they had
planned and would henceforth concentrate on rolling up the army's
front from the north. He decided to wait until he could assemble a
force—two panzer divisions the army group was transferring from
Eighth Army and two others (14th and 24th Panzer Divisions) coming
from the West and Italy—for a concerted counterattack. By the 20th
he had changed his mind: the Russians were obviously ready to go for
bigger prizes—Krivoi Rog, where they would cut the army's lines of
communications, or maybe even Kherson or Nikolaev. Krivoi Rog had
to be held. It controlled all the rail lines running east to the army front
and was the site of large ammunition and supply dumps which would
take weeks to evacuate. Von Mackensen decided to counterattack
with the divisions coming from the Eighth Army and not wait for the
others, which would be another eight to twelve days in transit.

For once, though somewhat belatedly, the OKH could offer effective help. Earlier in the month the Operations Branch, OKW, had decided that the danger of an invasion in the West had passed for the time being and that the Eastern Front had to be reinforced even if it meant taking risks in other heatres. Subsequently the OKW had released the 14th and 24th Panzer Divisions. On 20 October it also offered the 1st and 25th Panzer Divisions, the SS Leibstandarte Adolf Hitler, and the 384th Infantry Division. The five panzer divisions (the Adolf Hitler Division was the 1st SS Panzer Division) constituted a powerful mobile reserve, but the question was whether they would get to Russia in time.

On 21 October, as the Russians pushed toward Krivoi Rog, von Mackensen had to give up his plan to counterattack with the divisions from Eighth Army—the 11th Panzer and SS Totenkopf—and had to put them in the line separately to do what they could toward braking the Russian momentum. He informed Manstein that the Russians, if they wanted to, could also turn east into the Dnepr Bend and strike in the rear of the army's line on the river. He proposed giving up the eastern half of the river bend and drawing back to a line anchored on the river and the left flank of Army Group A near Nikopol. Manstein agreed, but, after relaying the proposal to the OKH, called at midnight and said that Hitler insisted on keeping the Dnepr front where it was.

Two days later Eighth Guards Army battered its way out of a small bridgehead around Voyskovoye in the Third Ukrainian Front sector halfway between Dnepropetrovsk and Zaporozhye. At the same time Forty-sixth Army bore down from the north. Von Mackensen then barely had time to get his troops out of Dnepropetrovsk and away from the river on what was left of his front upstream.

The alarm had finally gone through, but would the firemen come in time to save the building? On 24 October Manstein transferred XXXX Panzer Corps to Eighth Army on the northern flank of Konev's thrust toward Krivoi Rog. He ordered the corps to counterattack southeast across the Russian spearhead, using the 14th and 24th Panzer Divisions and the SS Totenkopf Division. The other three divisions being furnished by the OKW were still on the way. While XXXX Panzer Corps deployed, Konev's lead elements, on 25 October, entered the outskirts of Krivoi Rog. Starting a day early because of the threats to that city, XXXX Panzer Corps attacked on 27 October and in three days destroyed the better part of two mechanized corps and nine rifle divisions and forced Konev's armor out the city and back about twenty miles.

Having accomplished that much, Manstein wanted to shift XXXX Panzer Corps and two of its divisions to the Sixth Army bridgehead below Nikopol for the attack into the Nogay Steppe. On 2 November von Mackensen protested that he had thought the objectives were to hold Krivoi Rog and Nikopol. If XXXX Panzer Corps were transferred, he was convinced the Russians would start up again, take Krivoi Rog, and sooner or later take Nikopol as well. Manstein answered that if contact with the Crimea could not be reestablished the whole line of the lower Dnepr would have to be held and there were not enough troops for that.

Two days later Manstein changed his mind. He told the OKH that his plan had been based on an assumption that Sixth Army would keep strong forces forward of the Dnepr. As it was, he had no confidence in a XXXX Panzer Corps counterattack and proposed instead that two divisions of the corps be held as a ready reserve for the Nikopol bridgehead and the Krivoi Rog. Before another twenty-four hours passed, Manstein's attention was completely diverted to the army group left flank, where another storm was breaking.

KIEV AND THE CRIMEA

For a month Fourth Panzer Army had kept an uneasy balance along its front on both sides of Kiev. On its flanks the Russians held two large bridgeheads, around the mouth of the Pripyat and below Kiev at Bukrin. In the first week of October they had taken two smaller bridgeheads, one at Lutezh, twelve miles north of Kiev, and the other around Yasnogorodka, twenty-five miles north of the city.

The Stavka had first instructed Vatutin to take Kiev by a wide sweep west and north out of the Bukrin bridgehead. From 12 to 15 and from 21 to 23 October three armies had tried to break out of the bridgehead. Because the Russians lacked the bridging material to get the heavy artillery across, and because the fields of observation on that stretch of the river were too limited to permit accurate fire from the left bank, the attempts failed. In the meantime the two bridgeheads north of Kiev had been expanded, the one at Lutezh having been extended south to within easy artillery range of Kiev. After the second attempt to break out at Bukrin failed, the Stavka had ordered Vatutin to move Third Guards Tank Army and the artillery north to the Lutezh bridgehead and try from there.

On 3 November, after several days of intense activity behind the front, in the bridgehead, and east of the river, the Russians began to roll. In the wake of a massive artillery preparation, six rifle divisions and a tank corps, elements of Third Guards Tank Army and Thirty-eighth Army, hit the center of the German line around the Lutezh bridgehead and broke through. At the same time, Sixtieth Army broke out of the bridgehead at Yasnogorodka. In two days the Fourth Panzer Army front around Lutezh had collapsed. During the night of 5 November the battle swept through the streets of Kiev, and the next morning the last Germans retreated south.

Lacking reserves of any kind, Fourth Panzer Army was helpless. At first Hoth had thought Vatutin might content himself with Kiev, but by the 5th both he and Manstein concluded that the Russians would swing wide to the southwest and, if they could, outflank the entire Dnepr front. The first objective, then, would be Fastov, forty miles southwest of Kiev, the railroad junction which controlled the important double-track line feeding the center of the Army Group South front. On 6 November Manstein ordered the 25th Panzer Division, arriving from the west, to deploy to hold Fastov.

At Fuehrer headquarters the next day, Manstein learned how much of a mistake had been his plan for a counterattack in the Nogay Steppe. Manstein argued, as he had since the beginning of the year, that the Army Group South main effort had to be on the north flank; he wanted to shift 2 of XXXX Panzer Corps' divisions and the 3 panzer divisions, including the 25th, coming from the West, to the Kiev area. But Hitler would not be deprived of his dream—a big success south of the Dnepr Bend to generate fresh confidence in the troops and enable him to retain Nikopol and the Crimea. He agreed to let Manstein divert the 3 new panzer divisions to Fourth Panzer Army but insisted on leaving the XXXX Panzer Corps divisions with First Panzer Army.

To make up the difference, he promised the 2d Parachute Division, the SS Brigade Nordland, and the 4th Panzer Division—promised before from Army Group Center and never delivered. That Manstein accepted those terms aroused considerable irritation in the OKH. After the conference, in a telephone conversation with Kluge at Army Group Center, the OKH operations chief said that Manstein could have had the 5 panzer divisions he originally asked for if he had not, by prematurely agreeing to take less, undercut Zeitzler, who was ready to give him unqualified support.

For a time Manstein considered going ahead at once with the attack to reopen the Crimea since it appeared that Seventeenth Army could not hold out the three or four weeks he expected the battle around Kiev to last—the Russians had landed on both sides of Kerch' and on the south shore of the Sivash near the base of the Isthmus of Perekop. An encouraging sign was a small successful attack the 24th Panzer Division had made out of the Nikopol bridgehead several days before; but on 8 November Manstein decided that First Panzer Army did not have enough strength to handle the breakthrough in its own front and attack to the south. The next day he instructed von Mackensen to plan an attack that would be carried out when more units became available. In the succeeding weeks, when the Russians showed no haste in retaking the Crimea, Manstein, amply occupied on his own front, let the plan for an operation south of the Dnepr slip into abeyance.

A LESSON IN MANEUVER

In the second week of November, while the 1st and 25th Panzer Divisions and the Adolf Hitler Division struggled with the formidable task of assembling and reloading their elements that had already unloaded at First Panzer Army and of rerouting to Fourth Panzer Army troops still aboard trains coming from Germany, First Ukrainian Front continued its advance southwestward past Kiev against spotty German resistance. Fourth Panzer Army was split into three isolated parts that were moving away from each other as if along the spokes of a wheel. Its left flank corps, LIX Corps, was being pushed northwestward toward Korosten. The two corps in the center, VII and XIII Corps, fell back due westward toward Zhitomir. On the south XXIV Panzer

Corps, still holding part of the river line, had swung its left flank back to block the Russians due south of Kiev. On its left the Headquarters, XXXXVIII Panzer Corps, transferred from First Panzer Army, tried to bring the advance elements of the divisions coming from the south into position to establish a line flanking Fastov.

On the morning of 7 November, when the Commanding General, 25th Panzer Division, moved up with as much of his division as he could muster to execute his assigned mission of defending Fastov, he discovered that Third Guards Tank Army's mobile units had arrived there before him. For the next three days, in wet snow and rain, the division, not trained for fighting on the Eastern Front and lacking much of its equipment, tried futilely to retake the town.

In the meantime, the Russian advance past Fastov to the west gathered momentum. Manstein decided he had better leave Fastov alone and relieve the pressure on VII and XIII Corps. On 12 November XXXXVIII Panzer Corps committed its three divisions, all of them still lacking vital components, in an attack northwestward from the vicinity of Fastov into the rear of Thirty-eighth Army's spearhead, then pushing into Zhitomir ninety miles west of Kiev. The attack made little progress. In the north Sixtieth Army was forcing LIX Corps back rapidly toward Korosten and threatening to snap its contact with the Army Group Center right flank.

As had happened before, the Russians themselves afforded Fourth Panzer Army its best chance for recovery. Vatutin had split his effort and was attempting to go in two directions, southwest and west. Manstein decided to concentrate first on Zhitomir and then turn east behind Fastov.

Beginning on 14 November XXXXVIII Panzer Corps tried again, the veteran 7th Panzer Division from XXIV Panzer Corps taking the place of the 25th Panzer Division. This time it had better luck. After the first day the Russians, touchy about their flanks and rear, began to hesitate and slow down. Even so, it appeared that the counterattack had come too late to save LIX Corps. The corps, fighting alone, was nearly surrounded in Korosten and had to be supplied by airdrops. The commander wanted to pull back farther west while he still could, but on 16 November Hitler ordered Korosten held at all costs.

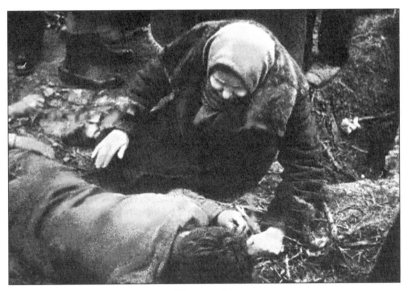

Kiev casualty.

On 19 November XIII Corps and XXXXVIII Panzer Corps recaptured Zhitomir, and the next day the Adolf Hitler Division turned east, reaching Brusilov, north and slightly west of Fastov, on the 23d, but by then several days of rain had turned the roads to mud. In the north LIX Corps, after being pushed out of Korosten in spite of Hitler's order, was able at the last minute to take advantage of the Russians' growing uncertainty and retake the town on the 24th. The next day Manstein called a temporary halt because of the weather.

"HE WHO HOLDS HIS POSITIONS A MINUTE LONGER…"

The last two weeks of November sealed the fate of the Dnepr line. What time was left could be credited partly to the lessons in concentration and maneuver Manstein had given Vatutin east of Zhitomir; however, the main reason was that Vatutin, waiting for more settled weather, held back a stronger punch. Had the two panzer divisions Hitler insisted on keeping on the army group right flank been at hand, Fourth Panzer Army might have been able to deal the three Soviet armies a full-fledged defeat. As it was, Hoth and Manstein decided late in the month that it was useless even to talk about getting back to the Dnepr at Kiev.

While Fourth Panzer Army was occupied west of Kiev the situation in the rest of the Army Group South zone had continued to deteriorate relentlessly. After gaining small bridgeheads on both sides of Cherkassy on 13 November, Second Ukrainian Front had quickly expanded the one on the north until it threatened to engulf the city and tear open the Eighth Army front. North and east of Krivoi Rog and against the Nikopol bridgehead, which First Panzer Army had taken over from Sixth Army, the Russians kept up constant pressure. On 20 November Generaloberst Hans Hube, who had replaced von Mackensen in command of First Panzer Army, reported to the army group that his infantry strength had sunk to the lowest tolerable level. The front could not be completely manned, and on days of heavy fighting casualties were running at the rate of one battalion per division under attack. Without an extraordinary supply of replacements by air he did not believe further defense of the Dnepr line was possible.

That same day, Manstein, looking ahead, advised the OKH that besides their reserves—an estimated 44 rifle divisions and an unknown but large number of tank brigades set up in 1943—the Russians had 33 rifle divisions and 11 tank and mechanized corps resting behind the front. With these they would be able to mount a full-scale winter offensive, and Army Group South, completely tied down at the front, would be tactically at their mercy. The army group, he wrote, needed "sufficient and powerful reserves" which, if they could not be sent from other theaters, would have to be acquired by shortening the southern flank of the Eastern Front and taking Seventeenth Army out of the Crimea.

Glum as Manstein's analysis was, it was more optimistic as far as the near future was concerned than those of his army commands. Eighth Army had gaps in its front around the Cherkassy bridgehead and north of Krivoi Rog. On 24 November the Chief of Staff, Eighth Army, asked whether "large operational decisions" (a general withdrawal) could be expected when freezing weather set in. Manstein could only reply with the lame aphorism: "He who holds his positions a minute longer will have won."34 Two days later Hube warned that the decision to give up the Nikopol bridgehead and the Dnepr Bend would have to come soon or the army would have to get substantial replacements.

The next day, the 27th, he told Manstein the army had exhausted all its means of self-help and needed to know how much longer it would have to hold the Nikopol bridgehead. The Russians were filling up their units with men from the recently reoccupied territory; as soldiers they did not amount to much, but their number alone was creating an ammunition shortage on the German side. Manstein replied that he agreed but could not get Hitler to change his earlier orders.

At the end of November Hitler wanted to take units away from Fourth Panzer Army and First Panzer Army to strengthen the front around Cherkassy, but Manstein insisted that if the Russians broke loose again on either the army group's north or its south flank, holding Cherkassy would be a waste of time anyway.

In the first week of December the weather turned cold, and in a few days the roads had frozen solid enough for the panzer divisions to move again. Manstein ordered XXXXVIII Panzer Corps to shift north of Zhitomir, push east to the line Radomyshl'-Malin, and then turn northeast into the flank of Sixtieth Army operating against LIX Corps at Korosten.

XXXXVIII Panzer Corps began attacking north of Zhitomir on 6 December. For two days the corps made good progress against gradually stiffening resistance; but by the 10th the resistance had become strong; and Hoth, taking no chances, told XXXXVIII Panzer Corps to restore contact between XIII Corps and LIX Corps as its first order of business after taking Radomyshl'. On the 19th XXXXVIII Panzer Corps was ready to execute the secand part of its original mission, the turn into the flank of Sixtieth Army. But in the next three days the panzer corps made almost no gain; it was meeting forces massed for another advance toward Zhitomir. On 21 December Fourth Panzer Army ordered it to go over to the defensive.

In the Eighth Army and First Panzer Army zones through November and during the first three weeks of December the Russians were content to fight a battle of attrition, which they could afford but the Germans could not. The two armies managed to keep their fronts fairly stable until the second week of the month, when the northwest side of the line around the bridgehead above Krivoi Rog gave way. Before a new front could be established Second Ukrainian Front had cleared the Dnepr north to Cherkassy. After mid-month all Army Group South held of the original WOTAN position was a 50-mile stretch of the Dnepr between Kiev and Cherkassy.

THE DNEPR BRIDGEHEAD, ARMY GROUP CENTER

In the Army Group Center zone the most prominent feature of the PANTHER position was the bridgehead located east of the Dnepr from Loyev on the south to east of Orsha and 190 miles long and 30 to 40 miles deep. (Map 17) The PANTHER protected a great switch position on the line Nevel-Vitebsk-Orsha-the Dnepr. At the end of September the army group began building up that line, which was potentially stronger than the PANTHER position itself but which was also the last natural defense line of any consequence forward of the Polish border.

Although Army Group Center had sharply declined in strength during the summer through transfers and losses, it was still stronger than either of its neighbors. Its total complement on 1 October was 42 infantry divisions, 8 panzer and panzer grenadier divisions, and 4 Air Force field divisions. Of those 12 infantry and 4 panzer divisions were kampfgruppen, actually no more than regiments. Opposite the army group stood four Soviet fronts, none of them showing any marked decline in offensive capability. Off the south flank of the army group the Stavka, in the first week of October, combined the zones of the Bryansk and Central Fronts under Rokossovskiy's headquarters, which was redesignated Belorussian Front.

ROKOSSOVSKIY HOLDS THE PRIPYAT BRIDGEHEAD

Even though it could be safely assumed that the Stavka would keep its main effort against Army Group South (best evidence was the combining of the Bryansk and Central Fronts under a single command, since the Russians never undertook anything really ambitious with one front in so broad a sector), Army Group Center was concerned over its south flank. Second Army was weak, it had its back to the Pripyat Marshes, and it was vulnerable on both flanks. In the north it had to hold a bridgehead east of the Sozh River to protect the valuable railhead at Gomel, and in the south the Russians had driven a wedge

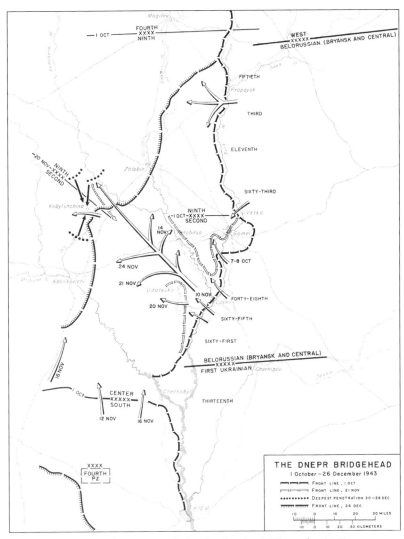

Map 17: *The Dnepr Bridgehead, 1 October-26 December 1943*

between it and the left flank of Army Group South along the lower reaches of the Pripyat River.

At the end of September Kluge had directed Weiss to shift three panzer divisions to his right flank and join Fourth Panzer Army in a counterattack to wipe out the bridgehead and restore contact between the two groups on the Dnepr. But the Russians brought reinforcements across the Dnepr from the east faster than the German panzer divisions could assemble and maneuver on the marshy west bank, and for the first few days the Germans were forced to the defensive and in some places lost ground. When Second Army finally got its tanks into motion on 3 October, the Russians countered with punishing air strikes. On 4 October units of Fourth Panzer Army took Chernobyl, but in two more days' fighting the Second Army force made no headway.

On the 6th Weiss reported that to go on was useless. He proposed to take his front back to a shorter line, use the troops gained thereby to throw a screening line around the western edge of the bridgehead, and so restore contact with Army Group South. Kluge approved, and on 11 October Second Army put a division across the Pripyat where it made contact with Fourth Panzer Army northwest of Chernobyl. First Ukrainian Front remained in undisputed control of a bridgehead fifteen miles deep and thirty miles wide.

GOMEL-RETCHITSA

On the Second Army left flank Belorussian Front held two bridgeheads west of the Sozh flanking Gomel, one ten miles north of the city across the river from Vetka on the boundary with Ninth Army, and the other fifteen miles south of the city. In the first week of October it expanded the one on the south, thereby threatening Gomel and Second Army's own bridgehead east of the river. On 9 October Kluge reported that an orderly evacuation of the Second Army bridgehead was already in doubt. Hitler agreed to give up the bridgehead "if there is a danger of the troops being destroyed." The next day, as the troops came out they were shifted south of the city where their presence was promptly effective, and the Russians advance slowed down.

By that time more trouble was brewing farther south. While Second Army was occupied on its flanks, Rokossovskiy had built a strong concentration south of Loyev, just below the confluence of the Dnepr and the Sozh. There a thrust across the Dnepr toward Rechitsa could outflank both the PANTHER position and the Dnepr switch position and confront Second Army with the unhappy task of trying to create a front in the partisan-infested woods and swamps west of the Dnepr.

On 15 October the attack began on 20-mile-wide front south of Loyev. It gained ground fast, partly because Kluge, still more worried about keeping contact with Army Group South, hesitated for two days before letting one of the panzer divisions be taken off the Second Army right flank. By the 10th the Russians had carved out a bridgehead sixty miles wide and ten miles deep on both sides of the Dnepr. Then, for two days, they attempted to thrust northeast toward Retchitsa on the railroad west of Gomel.

On 22 October Kluge called Zeitzler to ask for replacements. Second Army, he said, was exhausted and could not stand up against the continuing attack. The army group could give no guarantees with respect to future developments, and unless help were given it might become necessary to pull the whole front back. On the same day, having failed to achieve a breakout, Rokossovskiy stopped his offensive in the Loyev bridgehead.

In the last week of the month Rokossovskiy shifted his attack to the Ninth Army's flanks, denting the PANTHER position in several places and posing a threat of multiple breakthroughs. On 27 October Kluge and Model discussed taking Ninth Army and Second Army back to the Dnepr below Mogilev. The next day Rokossovskiy added to their concern by resuming the offensive in the Loyev bridgehead; but at the end of the month, satisfied for the time being with local gains, he called another halt.

The end of October saw a change of the Army Group Center command. On 28 October, Kluge, who had commanded the army group since December 1941, was severely injured in an automobile accident, and to replace him Hitler the next day appointed Generalfeldmarschall Ernst Busch. As Commanding General, Sixteenth Army, Busch had been on the Eastern Front since the start of the campaign. He was a highly regarded army commander, but most of his experience had been gained on a static front. He had not had a chance really to prove himself as a tactician; consequently, in his relations with Hitler he was more compliant than some of the other commanding generals and tended to welcome the Fuehrer's guidance.

In the first week of November Vatutin's offensive at Kiev renewed Army Group Center's concern for its south flank. When the offensive started, Busch told Weiss to use the two panzer divisions he still had in that area (two had been shifted to the Loyev bridgehead) to hold Chernobyl and, if necessary, stretch Second Army's flank south to keep contact with Fourth Panzer Army. By 7 November the Russians were moving so fast that Busch became alarmed and asked for permission to take his flank back from Chernobyl, but Hitler, who was never willing to give way on the flanks of a breakthrough, refused.

On the 10th Rokossovskiy tried for the third time to break out of the Loyev bridgehead. The German line held the first day but broke on the second. At the same time, the right flank army of First Ukrainian Front began pushing north forty miles west of Chernobyl into the undefended Second Army flank. On 12 November Weiss asked permission to take troops off his south flank to meet the greater danger in the center, but the OKH again ordered him to hold Chernobyl. The next day, when Belorussian Front's thrust carried to west of Retchitsa, he proposed giving up Gomel and taking the army north flank back to the Dnepr to gain troops. This Hitler forbade. By the 14th Rokossovskiy had spearheads turning east toward the Dnepr from northwest of Retchitsa.

After the gap in the Second Army center had opened to eight miles, Hitler told Model to supply one division and Weiss another for a counterattack to close it. Adding a third division, one of the two panzer divisions from his south flank, Weiss opened the counterattack on 18 November, but when the divisions failed to make headway in two days, the attack had to be canceled. Vatutin's forces in the meantime had taken Chernobyl and Rokossovskiy's had turned west behind Retchitsa toward Kalinkovichi, the railroad junction controlling all of the Second Army supply lines.

On 20 November Weiss shifted two of the divisions that had taken part in the counterattack west, to screen Kalinkovichi, and transferred control of his sector north of the Beresina and east of the Dnepr, including Gomel, to Ninth Army. Thereafter Second Army's paramount concern was to establish a defensible front forward of the Pripyat Marshes. As almost always happened in such situations, the first problem was to get an agreement on tactics. Weiss, Busch, and Zeitzler wanted to seek a balance by maneuver. Hitler, on the other

Panje wagon in the Pripyat marshes.

hand, stood by his old formula of holding the remnants of the original front as "corner posts" and counterattacking to patch the gaps. On the night of the 19th he commanded Weiss to keep the part of his front that had not been broken through where it was until further orders. That left the army in the peculiar, though by then no longer unusual, position of having its main force tied down forty miles forward of the crucial zone of the battle.

The next morning, with Busch's permission, Weiss called Zeitzler. Soviet tanks and cavalry with strong infantry support, he reported, were within nineteen miles of Kalinkovichi. If they took the town, the army would be out of motor fuel in two days and out of ammunition in four. Actually, he added, the same effect could be accomplished simply by cutting the two railroads. That could be done by the cavalry alone, which in the wooded and swampy terrain was far more maneuverable than the defending German armor. Even if the two panzer divisions managed to stop the advance on Kalinkovichi, it would only be a matter of time until the Russians, bypassing the town to the north, forced them to extend until the whole line was hopelessly weakened. Therefore, the entire front had to be taken back, and the decision had to come soon because if the withdrawal was executed in haste most of the heavy vehicles would be left stuck in the swamps. Zeitzler replied that he had tried the night before to talk Hitler into giving Second Army freedom of movement and failed. He would try again but at the moment could promise nothing. Shortly before midnight the OKH operations chief called the Army Group Center headquarters to report that Hitler had again refused to permit any withdrawal.

The next day the Russians tore through Second Army north of Udalevka and started a sweep to the southwest that threatened to envelop the army's right flank. On the afternoon of 22 November Hitler finally accepted the inevitable and allowed Weiss to take his front back—but no farther than a line he had plotted in detail, running east of Kalinkovichi and the railroad north of the town. The army diary noted that had the order been given a week earlier it could have been executed smoothly and would have prevented sizable losses. That night Weiss reported to army group that the line Hitler had laid out would be difficult "to reach, occupy, or hold." It traversed a swampy forest with thick undergrowth, an old and established partisan haunt. He asked for freedom within the limits of his mission—to establish a front east of the Pripyat Marshes—to operate without reference to a specific line.

In the meantime Rokossovskiy had readied an unpleasant surprise. Early on 22 November, after a quick regrouping undetected by the Germans, he launched a thrust into the Ninth Army center south of Propoysk. It dealt Ninth Army a sudden, staggering blow. The next day he pushed a strong spearhead into the gap between the Second and Ninth Armies south of the Beresina and cut the railroad that ran north from Kalinkovichi.

The Ninth Army front around Gomel had by then become a great, sagging, tactically useless bulge. As a railhead the city had lost its value ten days before when the Russians cut the railroad west of Retchitsa. On 23 November Hitler allowed Model to begin taking out troops, but he hesitated another twenty-four hours before signing the evacuation order because he was worried about the "echo" the loss of Gomel would create. Reluctant as he was to give ground under any circumstances, he had lately become even more reluctant when the loss of territory also involved the loss of a city large enough to be noticed in the world press and set off a celebration in Moscow.

NIKOLAUS

On 25 November Busch ordered Ninth Army to seal off the bridgehead at Propoysk and the Ninth and Second Armies to counterattack into the gap between their flanks, close it, and regain control of the railroad. The first order could not be executed for lack of troops. The Russians had already torn open a 50-mile stretch of the PANTHER position and gone twenty miles west. The most Ninth Army could do was try to exert a slight braking action. The armies intended to execute the second order on 30 November, but in the next few days the Russians advanced to the northwest so rapidly and in such strength that neither army could spare troops for the counterattack. The OKH promised the 16th Panzer Division from Italy, and, since that one division would not be enough, Busch proposed taking the Ninth Army center back to the Dnepr to gain two more divisions. Hitler resisted until the 30th. By then Rokossovskiy's troops were on the Dnepr west of Propoysk and had smashed the last remnants of the PANTHER position farther south.

At the end of the month Second Army had set up a new front east of Kalinkovichi, albeit some miles west of the line Hitler had demanded. During the night of 4 December Ninth Army completed its withdrawal. Having improved their positions somewhat, the armies could prepare the counterattack to close the gap. On 6 December they issued the orders for the counterattack, code-named NIKOLAUS, and, allowing time for the 16th Panzer Division to arrive, set 16 December as the starting date. After the 8th heavy attacks on the north flank of Second Army tied down all that army's reserves; and on the 14th a flareup in the angle of the Beresina and the Dnepr forced Ninth Army to ask for a delay to 20 December.

That the counterattack began on time on the 10th was itself something of a surprise; and its initial success surpassed all expectations. On the second day the Ninth Army and Second Army spearheads met at Kobyl'shchina. The army group ordered the divisions to regroup fast and turn east to clear the railroad. Until then neither the army group nor the army commands had expected to do more than close the gap, and they had not been very confident of accomplishing that.

On the 22d the attack continued, gaining ground to the east against stiffening resistance as the Russians poured in troops from the flanks. In three more days the Germans reached the railroad in the north, but in the south were stalled by a strong line on the Ipa River. On the 26th, Busch, worried about his north flank, took out the 16th Panzer Division for transfer to Third Panzer Army and told Model and Weiss to stop the counterattack and find a favorable defense line.

After nearly three months the Ninth and Second Armies once more held a continuous front. They had eluded a succession of dangerous thrusts, often just in the nick of time. The price was high. Half of the Dnepr bridgehead was lost and with it a 100-mile stretch of the river. In the south a 60-mile gap yawned between the flanks of Army Groups Center and South.

Nevertheless, the distinguishing aspect of the Belorussian Front's three-months' fall campaign was its drab pointlessness. It had operational, even strategic, possibilities, but the indications are that the Stavka could not have exploited these and, in fact, had not wanted to do so. The battles, expensive to both sides, were fought only because the Soviet Union, having the initiative, feared either to lose it or to be trapped into a stalemate.

CHAPTER X

The Rising Tide

BREAKTHROUGH AT NEVEL

ARMY GROUP NORTH

In the summer of 1943 the Army Group North zone, by comparison with the other army group zones, was quiet. In a battle that flared up toward the end of July around Mga, Leningrad Front's performance fell far below that of the commands operating against Army Groups Center and South. The front-line strengths of the opposing forces in the Army Group North zone were almost equal. The army group had 710,000 men. Leningrad, Volkhov, Northwest, and Kalinin Fronts, the latter straddling the Army Group North-Army Group Center boundary, had 734,000 men. For the future, however, Army Group North also had to reckon with some half a million reserves echeloned in depth behind the northern fronts. In artillery the two sides were about equal, but again the Russians were known to have substantial reserves. In mid-July Army Group North had 49 tanks, 40 fit for combat. The Russians had 209 tanks at the front and an estimated 843 in reserve. By 15 September Army Group North had 7 tanks still serviceable. In the last six months of 1943, First Air Force, which was responsible for air operations in the army group zone, flew just half as many sorties as its Russian opponents.

During August air reconnaissance detected increasing enemy activity off both Army Group North flanks. A rise in the number of boats making the short but extremely hazardous trip in the Gulf of Finland between Leningrad and the Oranienbaum pocket indicated that the Russians might soon attempt to break out and unite the pocket with the front around Leningrad. In the south Kalinin Front, under Yeremenko, began a build-up opposite the Army Group North-Army Group Center boundary. To meet those and other possible threats, the army group created a ready reserve by drawing five infantry divisions out of the front. In the first and second weeks of September the OKH ordered two of the reserve divisions transferred to Army Group South.

On 19 September, in conjunction with the Army Group Center withdrawal to the PANTHER position, Army Group North took over XXXXIII Corps, the northernmost corps of Army Group Center. That transfer brought the army group three divisions, forty-eight more miles of front, and responsibility for defending two important railroad and road centers, Nevel and Novosokol'niki. (Map 18) By late September no one doubted that the Russians were preparing for an offensive in the vicinity of the North-Center boundary. That area of forests, lakes, and swamps, and of poor roads even by Russian standards, heavily infested by strong partisan bands, had long been one of the weakest links in the Eastern Front. During the 1941 winter offensive the Russians had there carved out the giant Toropets salient, and in the 1942-43 winter campaign they had encircled and captured Velikiye Luki and nearly taken Novosokol'niki. Compared with the losses elsewhere, particularly after Stalingrad, these were mere pinpricks; but there always was a chance that the Stavka might one day try the big solution, a thrust between the flanks of the two army groups to the Gulf of Riga.

SURPRISE-REPERCUSSIONS-PARTISANS

At the end of September and during the first few days of October the Germans lost track of Kalinin Front's troop movements. Bad weather prevented aerial reconnaissance, and the Russians first changed their radio traffic patterns and then maintained radio silence.

Early on 6 October four rifle divisions and two tank brigades of Third Shock Army attacked the 2d Air Force Field Division, the left flank division of Third Panzer Army, and ripped through. Probably somewhat startled by their success, for the 2d Air Force Field Division had not merely given way but had fallen apart under the first assault, the Russians hastily loaded a guards infantry division on trucks and tanks and dispatched it northwestward behind the Army Group North flank toward Nevel. Before the Germans could form a clear picture

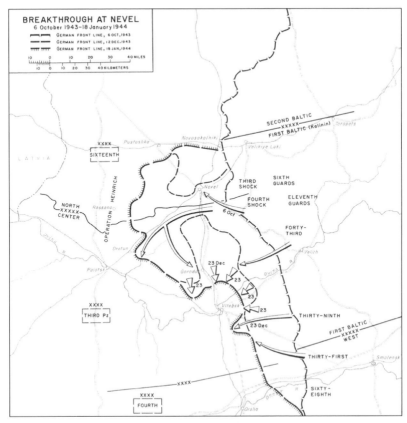

Map 18: Breakthrough at Nevel, 6 October 1943-18 January 1944

of what had happened at the front the Russians were in Nevel. The surprised garrison, after putting up scattered resistance, retreated out of the town early in the afternoon.

The Germans' first impression was that they had fumbled badly but not irrevocably. Kuechler ordered the three Army Group North reserve divisions into the breakthrough area; and Hitler, reverting to his sovereign remedy for such calamities, ordered the "corner posts" held at all costs. Late on the 6th a regiment of one of the reserve divisions arrived north of Nevel, and Kuechler told the whole division to counterattack the next day.

The next two days brought a rash of troubles. The division that was to counterattack could not bring its artillery up on time and had to wait another twenty-four hours. When it did get going on the 8th, it ran into a superior force attacking out of Nevel and was thrown back. At the end of the day the gap between the flanks of the army groups had opened to fifteen miles. Meanwhile, the partisans had so thoroughly disrupted the railroads that the other two reserve divisions had to be routed to Pskov, 130 miles north of Nevel, and there loaded in trucks, not enough of which were available. On 9 October Kuechler decided to wait until the reinforcements were assembled before trying again to close the gap.

Besides creating tactical difficulties, the loss of Nevel brought down on Army Groups North and Center verbal thunderbolts from Fuehrer headquarters. In Fuehrer Order 10 Hitler condescendingly pointed out that the Russians had a habit of trying to break through at the unit boundaries and that such breakthroughs always took excessively long to clean up because each of the affected units attempted to saddle the other with most of the responsibility. He "demanded" that the armies and army groups "consider it a point of honor" to maintain contact with each other.

Not satisfied with that indirect rebuke, he demanded explanations for the breakthrough and the loss of Nevel. Kluge replied that under heavy artillery and rocket fire for the first time, the 2d Air Force Field Division had lost its nerve, and the tank attack had thrown it into a panic. What was needed, in Kluge's opinion, was awareness that the armies in the USSR were increasingly being forced to operate with troops who could not or would not withstand a determined attack. Army Group Center, he added, had recently received replacement battalions, one-third composed of Volksdeutsche (racial Germans from outside the original territory of the Reich) who said openly that they did not intend to fight for Germany. The Chief of Staff, Sixteenth Army, when he was asked why a well-fortified town like Nevel was lost so quickly, replied, "What good are the best positions when you have no troops to hold them?"

On 10 October Hitler took another tack in giving vent to his annoyance. Army Group Center had asked to merge the remnants of the 2d Air Force Field Division with an Army division. Hitler refused, stating that he did not want to water down good Air Force troops with bad Army troops.

To the army group commands Fuehrer Order 10 was offensive, particularly because it implied that the generals had to be instructed on one of the oldest and by then best known Russians tactical tricks. During the past year, in nearly every instance, the initial blows of Soviet offensives had come at unit boundaries. Possessing a vast and active intelligence network of partisans and agents, the Russians never had trouble locating the boundaries. From the point of view of the German commands, that such a crude and unimaginative tactical device often proved frustratingly effective was irksome enough. Nor could they find comfort in the knowledge that the reason why was to be found in the condition of the German forces, not in the Russians' skill. With the front undermanned and stretched taut in all sectors, it was almost inevitable that when an attack hit a boundary the units involved would wait to see which way the main effort would go, with each perhaps hoping its sector would be the least affected. Even when both were willing to act they usually had trouble making forces available at the same time, and almost always the first concern of each was not to close up but to prevent further damage in its own sector. In short, much as they might resent Hitler's reminding them of "points of honor," the army groups, armies, and lesser commands, burdened by defeats, lack of reserves, and chronic shortages of equipment and personnel replacements, had in fact fallen prey to the philosophy of every man for himself.

But in warfare combatants can occasionally have more good luck than convenient to handle, and apparently something of that sort befell Kalinin Front in the attack on Nevel. For a highly skilled, flexible leadership such an occurrence could be a pleasant challenge; for a Soviet front command, even in late 1943, it raised many distressing uncertainties. On 9 October, the day Kuechler postponed his counterattack, Yeremenko suddenly reined in on the offensive. During the several days' pause that followed, Army Groups North and Center threw a line around the western limits of the breakthrough and each moved in a corps headquarters to command in the battle area. To take further advantage of the respite the two army groups planned a counterattack by three divisions, two from Army Group North and one from Center, timed for midmonth; but at the last minute, on 14 October, Hitler forbade it because he believed the force was not strong enough.

On the 15th the Russians became active again. However, their main effort was on the northeastern rim of the breakthrough—which indicated that Yeremenko, not yet ready to resume the offensive, was suffering a seizure of the old Russian malady, flank sensitivity. Army Group North had in the meantime become worried by the signs of a build-up east of Novosokol'niki and the possibility of another breakthrough there. When Army Group Center, on the 19th, proposed a joint effort to close the gap, Kuechler declared that he could not make troops available because of the danger at Novosokol'niki. Convinced that Yeremenko would soon be able to resume the offensive in earnest, Army Group Center wanted to go ahead alone, but, for the second time, Hitler intervened to cancel the army group plans. After 26 October, when Army Group Center was forced to transfer to Ninth Army the panzer division it had been holding in reserve for a counterattack, neither army group was able to mount an offensive around Nevel.

At the end of the month the Russians still had the initiative and showed they intended to exploit it soon. Since the middle of the month rail traffic through Toropets and Velikiye Luki from the east had been growing steadily. A sure sign of something big in the making was the appearance of the former Headquarters, Bryansk Front, which as Headquarters, Second Baltic Front, Popov commanding, took over the northern half of Kalinin Front (renamed First Baltic Front). In the Nevel bulge Fourth Shock Army moved in on the left of Third Shock Army.

In the light of those ominous portents, it was high time the Germans did something at least to reduce the partisan menace at their backs. The area due west of Nevel was probably the most thoroughly partisan infested on the whole Eastern Front. In a 2,000-square-mile rectangle of forests and swamps Army Group North had identified nineteen partisan brigades totaling some 25,000 men. At the approximate center of the rectangle, in the Rossono Rayon (fifty miles west of Nevel), the partisans had completely re-established Soviet rule, were operating collective farms, and even had occasional mail service to and from the unoccupied Soviet territory. To the north, west, and south partisans were scattered behind the fronts of Army Groups North and Center, some as roving bands and others in stationary concentrations like that around Rossono.

In the past neither army group had been able to mount a thoroughgoing antipartisan campaign; and by the fall of 1943 there was no chance at all of their being able to do so. In October the larger part of Army Group North's antipartisan force, twelve battalions of Osttruppen (former Russian prisoners of war, mostly Cossacks, who had volunteered to fight on the German side) were transferred to Germany and France at Kuechler's request. They had become unreliable, and whole units were deserting to the partisans with their weapons and equipment. On 14 October Hitler ordered SS-Obergruppenfuehrer (Lt. Gen.) Erich von dem Bach-Zelewski, who was responsible for antipartisan warfare in the area of Belorussia under civil administration, to stage an operation against the Rossono partisans. During the next two weeks von dem Bach moved in nineteen mixed battalions of police, Latvian volunteers, and security troops, and on 1 November he launched Operation HEINRICH, employing two approximately division-sized units in a converging attack toward Rossono from the north and south.

ATTACK AND COUNTERATTACK

In an early morning fog on 2 November the Third and Fourth Shock Armies penetrated the Third Panzer Army left flank southwest of Nevel. They had paved the way during the five previous days with heavy attacks that drove a deep dent in the Third Panzer Army line. After the breakthrough, which opened a 10-mile-wide gap, Third Shock Army turned north behind Sixteenth Army's flank, and Fourth Shock Army turned southwest behind Third Panzer Army.

Army Group Center shifted a panzer division north from Ninth Army. With that division it was able to strengthen the Third Panzer Army flank below the breakthrough and deflect Fourth Shock Army southwestward away from the panzer army's rear. Army Group North was less fortunate. Third Shock Army's more aggressive mode of operating indicated that it had been assigned the main effort in the renewed offensive. Kuechler transferred six infantry battalions from

Eighteenth Army, and with these Sixteenth Army managed to bend its right flank around to the northwest. Both the army group and army expected the Russians to continue pressing around that flank.

On 4 November Hitler called Kuechler and Busch to Fuehrer headquarters. After characterizing the October Nevel battle as a Schweinerei (filthy mess) and blaming the subsequent failure to recoup the loss on the chief of staff of Army Group North's right flank corps, an officer whom he described as a defeatist to whom everything was impossible, Hitler declared that he intended to eliminate the new gap at once. Busch, whose headquarters had already proposed a joint counterattack by the two army groups, agreed. Kuechler objected. He did not want to risk a counterattack while his flank was exposed, and, as he revealed indirectly, he did not fully share Hitler's and Busch's feeling of urgency about the army groups' flanks. He was more worried by the signs of a build-up for an attempt to liberate Leningrad, and he warned Hitler that since the temperature there had been well below freezing for the past several days, that offensive could come at any time. For those reasons Kuechler was reluctant to weaken the north by taking out troops for the flank. To try to gain troops by shortening the front, he maintained, would be particularly dangerous since it might set off a chain reaction. Brushing aside Kuechler's doubts, Hitler at the close of the conference ordered the two army groups to be ready on 8 November to counterattack from the north and south, close the gap, and cut off the two shock armies.

At the end of the first week in November the Germans were still holding fast on the flanks of the breakthrough, but Fourth Shock Army had sent parts of two divisions probing as far west as Dretun, thirty miles behind the Third Panzer Army flank. To place at least token limits on the Russians' westward advance, the Germans stopped Operation HEINRICH before it was completed and turned von dem Bach's antipartisan units east to form a screening line behind the army groups' flanks.

Kuechler ordered four infantry divisions, two from Eighteenth Army and two from Sixteenth Army, to his right flank, but they had to be taken out of static positions and, in some instances, moved several hundred miles by truck and rail, which took time. On 7 November

Third Shock Army gained more ground behind Army Group North. Yeremenko was pouring troops of the Sixth and Eleventh Guards Armies through the gap and by a process of rapid erosion carving out a pocket, elongated on its north-south axis, behind both army groups. He appeared still to be concentrating on the northern rim of the pocket. So far he had not shown much interest in directing his weight west, which was fortunate for the Germans since the army group commands had observed that the SS generals were conducting operations in their sector "in broad impressionistic strokes."

On 8 November two Third Panzer Army divisions, one infantry and one panzer, attacked north into the breakthrough area. Before the end of the day they gained nearly five miles. Army Group North was scheduled to attack from its side on the morning of the 9th, but Kuechler protested that all of his units were tied down. Army Group Center accused Army Group North of refusing to attack simply "because it did not want to." Hitler, apparently irked by Kuechler's lukewarmness at the conference four days earlier, refused to "accept any further excuses" and ordered Army Group North "as a matter of honor" to begin the counterattack in its sector no later than 10 November. The next day, while the Army Group Center force waited for Army Group North to make the next move, Kuechler hastily assembled a scratch force of seven battalions. When these units attacked as ordered on the 10th, they ran into heavy artillery fire and then were thrown back to their line of departure by a counterattack.

Meanwhile, the Russians had continued on the move behind the flanks of the army groups, extending the pocket to a length of fifty miles. In the south they were at the level of Polotsk and Gorodok, and in the north, south of Pustoshka, less than ten miles from the railroad running west out of Novosokol'niki. Once again, this time with greater strength than before, they began turning east behind the right flank corps of Army Group North.

For a week Hitler and Kuechler debated the next move. Hitler demanded a counterattack and instructed Kuechler to strip Eighteenth Army if he had to. Kuechler insisted on getting rid of the threat to his flank first. Finally, on 18 November, after a trip to Fuehrer headquarters, Kuechler secured an order giving the army group the missions of first eliminating the bulge behind its flank and then mounting an attack into the gap south of Nevel. The next day Kuechler transferred another division from Eighteenth Army. On 21 November, the weight of nearly the whole Eleventh Guards Army forced Army Group Center to take its two divisions which had advanced into the gap back to their line of departure. How greatly that reduced the chances of closing the front was demonstrated by the increase in the number of Soviet units moving into the pocket; but Hitler insisted that Army Group North go ahead with both of its assigned missions.

After mid-November, following several weeks of below-freezing weather, the temperature began to rise, an unusual phenomenon for that time of the year in northern Russia and a disastrous one for the German plans. Since the temperature hovered just above freezing, the ground began to thaw. At the beginning of the last week in the month the roads were stretches of mud two feet deep. Supplies could only be moved to the front on tracked vehicles, and in some places Army Group North had to resort to airdrops.

The counterattack, set for 24 November, could not begin until 1 December, and then in rain and mud. The weather ruled out air support entirely. On the first day the two divisions, attacking due west across the northern quarter of the pocket, gained less than three miles before they were stopped. The self-propelled assault guns coming up behind stalled on the bank of a small river and stayed bogged down there for the next five days. On the 6th Kuechler reported that he intended to go ahead. He had another division coming from Eighteenth Army, and he believed the weather was giving the Russians trouble with their supplies; but Hitler, who was intent on closing the Nevel gap, refused to allow any more divisions to be committed on the west. On 8 December he called Kuechler to Fuehrer headquarters and ordered him to launch an attack into the gap before the end of the month.

VITEBSK

The warm weather had also imposed a drag on the Russians' movements. In the third week of November Fourth Shock Army, which until then had been working its way south and west without giving any clear indication of its actual objective, had turned east behind Third Panzer

Army toward Gorodok and Vitebsk. By 23 November it had pushed to within three miles of Gorodok, the road and rail center controlling the communications lines to the Third Panzer Army north flank, and had tank and cavalry spearheads standing ten miles northwest of Vitebsk. That confronted Third Panzer Army with a choice of either pulling back its flank, in which case it would be able to defend Vitebsk handily, or running the risks of having the flank smashed and losing Vitebsk as well. The Commanding General, Third Panzer Army, Reinhardt, urged taking back the flank, but Busch refused, citing two of Hitler's favorite tactical principles which, valid as they were under the proper circumstances, had lately produced more than one disaster or near-disaster: shortening the front freed more Soviet than German troops, and flank insensitivity on the German side reduced the force of Soviet offensives. During the thaw Fourth Shock Army failed to carry its advance any farther toward Gorodok and was forced to draw back slightly northwest of Vitebsk.

After Army Group North's attempt to pinch off the north end of the bulge failed, the Russians had a free hand, in fact their opportunities exceeded their resources. They had paved the way for a deep, possibly even strategic, thrust to the west between Army Groups North and Center, but with its main forces committed in the south and a winter campaign in the offing the Stavka was not inclined to attempt anything of that magnitude. Large as they were, its reserves were not inexhaustible; during the fall the Stavka had frequently thrown green conscripts from the recently reoccupied territories into the assault waves to spare trained troops. On the south, Vitebsk afforded a lesser but tactically useful and propagandistically valuable prospect. Aside from being an important road and rail center, Vitebsk, together with Orsha, guarded the 50-mile-wide land bridge between the Dvina and the Dnepr, the historic gateway to the Russian heartland. Between October and the first week of December West Front had tried four times to take Orsha and had been beaten off in furious battles by Fourth Army.

On 13 December Eleventh Guards Army attacked the northern tip of the Third Panzer Army flank from the northeast, northwest, and southwest. In two days it cut in deeply and was clearly on the way

A mounted Cossack.

toward forming two encirclements and trapping a German division in each. A request to take his front back brought Reinhardt a blunt refusal from Busch and a further admonition from the OKH that Hitler wanted the flank held under all circumstances because he was determined to close the gap from the north. In another day Reinhardt's northernmost division was encircled and the division southwest of it cut off from the road and railroad. Reinhardt then had no choice but to order the encircled division to break out, which it did on 16 December at a cost of 2,000 of its 7,000 troops, and all of its artillery, heavy weapons, and vehicles.

On the 16th Hitler at last conceded that to close the Nevel gap was no longer possible. But, as always, reluctant to permit any changes in the front, he told the army groups to deny the enemy any further successes. Between 17 and 23 December Reinhardt, harassed all the way by reminders from Hitler that withdrawals were not permitted except under overwhelming pressure, took his army's flank back to an irregular arc twenty miles north of Vitebsk.

The still unanswered question was what the Russians would do next. On the chance that they might turn west, Reinhardt strengthened his line on the west, and the OKH transferred two divisions from Army

Group North to the Army Group Center left flank east of Polotsk. On 23 December Yeremenko gave the answer. Fourth Shock, Eleventh Guards, Thirty-ninth, and Forty-third Armies attacked around the Vitebsk perimeter. In the first two days they pushed the German line back several miles. Northwest and southeast of the city tanks and infantry drove deep wedges into the Third Panzer Army front, cutting the Vitebsk-Polotsk rail line and threatening the Vitebsk-Orsha line. To prevent an encirclement Army Group Center moved in the two divisions recently received from Army Group North and on the 28th transferred a division each from the Ninth and Second Armies. Thereafter the front held even though Yeremenko kept punching away with rigid determination for another six weeks.

After Third Panzer Army retreated to the Vitebsk perimeter, the flank of Army Group North projecting toward Nevel became a useless appendage. Late on the night of 27 December Hitler decided to let Kuechler straighten his line and so gain enough troops to strengthen the west face of the Nevel bulge, which was still manned only by miscellaneous SS and security troops. After 29 December Sixteenth Army in six days drew back to an almost straight line south of Novosokol'niki.

At the situation conference on the night of 27 December, Hitler blamed the Nevel breakthrough and the subsequent German setbacks entirely on the "petty egoism" of the two army group commanders. Although in so doing he conveniently overlooked occasions when he had intervened to stop projected counteroperations, his criticism had merit. Both army groups had been reluctant to do more than they conceived to be their fair share. Army Group North, in particular, had been unwilling to weaken its otherwise quiet front. Kuechler eventually did transfer six divisions to the breakthrough area—but too late for them to affect the outcome. On the other hand, as became fully evident later, Army Group North, weakened by the defensive battles around Leningrad and Nevel and by transfers to the other army groups, was in fact rapidly drifting into dangerous straits.

Looking at the Nevel battles in retrospect, Hitler was somewhat encouraged. He saw in the Stavka's failure to grasp the strategic opportunity a sign of weakness. It proved, he said, coining an inaccurate simile, that the Russians were not like "the giants of Antiquity who gained strength every time they fell down."14 Going on, he reiterated his old theory that the Soviet Union was approaching the limit of its strength and, therefore, a little more determination on the German side would be enough to turn the tables. The point he missed, of course, was that the Soviet weakness, as far as it existed, was psychological rather than actual, that the Stavka had not intended to reach for a strategic objective, but in the Nevel breakthrough and its companion piece, the fall offensive against the Army Group Center south flank, had adopted elaborate, strenuous, and probably in the long run superfluous, means of reassuring itself and preserving an initiative that it stood in no great danger of losing.

THE GERMAN ALLIES

The winter battles of 1942-43 had ended Germany's prospects—never very great—of profiting militarily from the coalition of small nations that had joined in the war against the Soviet Union. At the same time, the governments of those countries had discovered that they stood in grave danger of riding the German coattails straight into the jaws of disaster. In September 1943, when Italy dropped out of the war, Finland, Hungary, and Rumania would gladly have followed had they been able. Only Bulgaria, until then a noncombatant, was struck by a sudden, apparently irrational, fit of martial spirit and offered the Germans a corps for employment in the Southeastern Theater. The puppet government of Slovakia, on the other hand, had decided several months earlier that henceforth its two divisions were not to be employed by the Germans without approval of the Slovak Minister of War.

Generalissimo Francisco Franco of Spain, no ally but an old if unreliable friend, dealt a particularly rude blow, which was the more painful because it was militarily not very significant and so could be taken as a gratuitous commentary on the German condition. He recalled the 250th Blue Division, which, as Spain's one tangible contribution to the Axis cause, had fought well on the Eastern Front, mostly in the vicinity of Leningrad. Later, to soothe the German feelings, he relented to the extent of allowing a thousand-man replacement battalion recently sent to the division to stay as a "Spanish Legion."

HUNGARY—OPERATION MARGARETHE

In the fall the Operations Staff, OKW, worked on the problem of dealing with Hungary and Rumania if either or both should attempt to defect. Hungary, which in the past months had dissociated itself almost entirely from the Axis war effort, appeared the mostly likely candidate; and at the end of September the Operations Staff completed a preliminary plan for Operation MARGARETHE, the military occupation of Hungary. In November the transfer to the Eastern Front of the divisions allocated for MARGARETHE and intelligence reports that the Rumanians and Hungarians had secretly ironed out their differences and might try to desert the Axis in conjunction with an American-British invasion of the Balkans, complicated the problem. After reviewing its plans, the Operations Staff concluded that by mid-December it would again have enough forces to occupy Hungary but not Rumania as well.

FINLAND—FUEHRER DIRECTIVE 50

Most worrisome was the question of Finland. A resort to force there, as was contemplated in the cases of Hungary and Rumania, was impossible. On the other hand, although the Finns for a year and a half had limited themselves to a passive defense, they could not simply be written off as excess baggage. The Finnish Army tied down an estimated 180,000 Soviet troops and, more important, protected the southern flank of Twentieth Mountain Army and its rearward lines through the Finnish Baltic ports. Finland's quitting the war would deal a serious, if not fatal, blow to Twentieth Mountain Army and, possibly, to the entire German position in the Baltic and Scandinavian areas. The one potent trump left in the German hand was the Finns' longstanding fear of the Soviet Union.

During the spring and early summer of 1943 Hitler had taken some tentative steps toward shoring up the northern bastion of his Fortress Europe. On his orders Army Group North had drafted a plan for the capture of Leningrad, which would have established overland contact between Germany and Finland and would have given the Finns security in their most vulnerable area, the Isthmus of Karelia. Army of Norway at that time had devised a defense plan for Norway which envisioned a possible occupation of Sweden. Between March and mid-July the OKW, under Hitler's constant prodding, had moved the equivalent of three infantry divisions to Norway and had converted the 25th Panzer Division, which would have been the main striking force in an attack on Sweden, into a strong armored force—by Scandinavian standards though not, as was later demonstrated, by the standards of the Eastern Front.

Had ZITADELLE succeeded, Hitler would very likely have set about tightening his grip on northern Europe. When ZITADELLE failed, the reverberations spread north like a shock wave. The ambitious defense plan for Norway had to be dismantled and the reserves recalled to the Continent. Sweden, long leaning away from the benevolent neutrality forced on it early in the war, abrogated the transit agreements that had put the Swedish railroads at German disposal for movement of most kinds of supplies and military equipment to Norway.

In July Finland had "unofficially" received an oral offer to discuss peace through the Soviet legation in Stockholm. The next month three members of the Finnish Parliament had delivered to Ryti, the President, a petition signed by thirty-three prominent men and calling on him to take steps toward restoring good relations with the United States and toward getting Finland out of the war. When the contents of the petition were published in a Swedish newspaper they touched off a press and public discussion in Finland which heavily favored a separate peace.

In that disturbed atmosphere Army Group North, in August, began work on the PANTHER position along the Narva River-Lake Peipus line 125 miles southwest of Leningrad. When, after the end of the month, it appeared that the army group might have to be taken back to the PANTHER position to release troops for the south, Twentieth Mountain Army replied to an OKW request for an opinion that Army Group North should not be pulled back under any circumstances. The Finns, the army memorandum stated, already felt betrayed because the capture of Leningrad had been repeatedly promised and never carried out, even in times when, in their opinion, it had been possible. If Army Group North went back to the PANTHER position the Finnish Aunus and Maaselkä Fronts would project into Soviet territory like spearheads and would have to be pulled back under circumstances which made establishment of a tenable line to the rear highly doubtful. More than likely, the army predicted, a government oriented toward the Soviet Union would be brought to power. If the Soviet Union then offered anywhere near bearable peace terms Finland would leave the war, and Twentieth Mountain Army would have to leave Finland, an undertaking which in winter, over the roads of northern Finland and Norway, would be exceedingly hazardous. A week later the Finnish Government warned, both through the German Minister in Helsinki and its own Minister in Berlin, that a withdrawal south and west of Leningrad would have the most serious consequences for Finland.

On 28 September, in Fuehrer Directive 50, Hitler told Twentieth Mountain Army to prepare for the worst. The Army Group North front was "completely stabilized," he said, and the danger point on the Army North-Army Group Center boundary (Nevel) was being reinforced, but for insurance the army group was fortifying the Narva River-Lake Peipus line. If Army Group North was forced to retreat to the PANTHER position, and as a result, Finland left the war, Twentieth Mountain Army's mission would be to swing its two right flank corps back to a line across northern Finland south of Ivalo and defend the Pechenga nickel-mining region as long as might be necessary. When the time came, the army would be given two additional divisions from Army of Norway. Construction and supply stockpiling were to begin in secret immediately.

In the second week of October, after the breakthrough at Nevel, the Finnish commander in chief, Mannerheim, requested clearance to begin building a line behind Twentieth Mountain Army for the event of a German withdrawal. That signal mark of failing confidence led the German representative at Finnish Army headquarters to ask the OKW to send a top-level representative to Finland immediately. On 14 October Jodl flew to Helsinki and in two days of conferences with Mannerheim and the Finnish Minister of Defense gave them a picture of the war as the OKW professed to see it. The Italian surrender, he explained, was not important because Italy had never constituted an element of strength in the alliance. As far as an invasion of France was concerned, Germany would welcome it as an opportunity to deal Great Britain and the United States a resounding defeat, put an end to the second-front idea, and free troops for the Eastern Front. At Leningrad, he admitted, the balance was precarious, and a withdrawal on the northern flank had been considered; but, out of regard for Finland, Germany had abstained from taking that course. Germany, he let it be known, was aware of the Finnish efforts to get out of the war and took the attitude that no nation could ask another to risk destruction for its sake; but, he pointed out, Finland's future in the clutches of Stalin would not be bright.

To add bite to what Jodl had to say, Hitler sent along a letter to the Finnish President which was an indirect but pointed reminder that Finland was economically and militarily dependent on Germany. He also took Ryti to task over the lack of discipline in Finnish internal policy and for the Finnish press's hostility toward Germany. A week later the Finnish Minister of Defense, in an interview with Generaloberst Eduard Dietl, the Commanding General, Twentieth Mountain Army, promised the "truest brotherhood in arms" and declared that the newspaper talk of a separate peace was groundless. Jodl, he said, had explained everything "openly and completely."26 At the end of the month Ryti replied to Hitler in a letter which, while it contained no specific commitments, was taken to be positive in tone.

As the year drew to a close, a measure of stability appeared to have been restored between Germany and Finland, and Hitler ordered that Fuehrer Directive 50 be held in abeyance for the time being. The balance was delicate, however. In late October Mannerheim renewed his request to lay out a defense line behind the German front, and in November Finland resumed its contact with the Soviet Union. On 20 November Kuechler proposed taking Sixteenth Army to the PANTHER position and using the divisions released to clean up the Nevel breakthrough. Hitler thought then that work on the PANTHER position had not progressed far enough, but a month later, when he needed troops for Army Group South, he returned to the idea. At the turn of the year, the OKW had drafted a letter to Mannerheim telling him that Army Group North would have to go back, but Keitel then decided to hold the letter while Hitler mulled over the decision.

LEADERSHIP, MANPOWER, STRATEGY

COMMAND CHANGES

Since 1939 Hitler had been fighting the war with a body of higher officers whom he mistrusted collectively and, for the most part, disliked individually. As victory drifted beyond his grasp, he convinced himself that the generals and the General Staff corps were at the root of his trouble. More and more he longed to rid himself of those cold-eyed technicians and surround himself instead with men like his old party stalwarts who, uncontaminated by intellectual doubts and unhampered by scruples, got things done by hook or by crook.

In November 1943, after a disastrous year, he returned to the idea he had outlined to his Army personnel chief, Schmundt, in October 1942, of overhauling the higher command echelons of the Army. Declaring that many senior generals would soon have to be relieved "because of illness or for other reasons," he instructed Schmundt to work up a list of junior generals and staff officers who would form a reservoir of potential army commanders. The aim was for every commanding general of an army to have a successor ready and, as it were, waiting in the wings. The generals selected for advancement, Hitler specified, were to be those "who exude confidence" and who "have positive inner convictions favoring the National Socialist Weltanschauung."32 In the long run, that order would, in large part, be negated by the homogeneity of the German officer corps; however, it was useful to Hitler in that it lent an appearance of logic to his dismissal of officers in whom he had lost confidence but whom the Army and the public still held in high esteem.

The first of the generals to go was the Commanding General, Fourth Panzer Army, Hoth. In the past year Hoth's army had played a crucial part in most of Army Group South's battles. When given the chance, Hoth had proved his mastery of the mobile defense, but Hitler did not want mobility on the defensive, he wanted generals who would hold without giving an inch. In November Hoth was scheduled for a long leave "to unwind"; in December, after the Russian breakthrough at Kiev, Hitler ordered that he was not to return to his army or be given any other command. Speaking to Zeitzler and Jodl later in the month, Hitler described Hoth as "a bird of ill-omen" and "an instigator of defeatism of the worst sort."34

At the same time as Hoth, Model was also given an extended leave, with the expectation that when he returned it would be to replace Manstein in command of Army Group South. Of all the generals, Manstein, who in the past year had several times suggested that it was high time he be given a chance to try to extricate Germany from its military quagmire, was probably the one Hitler could stomach least. Only Manstein's tremendous reputation and undeniable skill as a tactician had saved him thus far.

The most important command shift in the second half of 1943 was the appointment in September of General der Flieger Guenther Korten as Chief of Staff, OKL. While the Air Force generals were somewhat farther removed from Hitler's scrutiny than their Army counterparts, when the time came to find a scapegoat the consequences were often more severe for the officer concerned because of Hitler's desire—not to mention Goering's—to protect Goering as Commander in Chief, OKL, and as Hitler's heir apparent.

From February 1939 to August 1943 Jeschonnek had been Chief of Staff, OKL. While Goering indulged his sybaritic inclinations and dabbled in a variety of interests outside the Air Force, Jeschonnek had developed the doctrine of close air support for the Army. Successful at first, that doctrine lost most of its effectiveness when the Army was forced to the defensive, and its last application, during ZITADELLE, was a complete failure. Concurrently, the fighter defense of Germany had been neglected; as a result, the Air Force's response to the big Allied bombing raids during the summer of 1943 was dismayingly feeble. The failure was in large measure Jeschonnek's responsibility, but Jeschonnek could, and in an August 1943 memorandum to Hitler did, cite numerous mistakes Goering had made. After that, in a stormy telephone conversation Hitler told Jeschonnek that he was being held completely responsible for the failure of the Air Force and concluded with, "You know what is left for you to do now." Jeschonnek shot himself.

Korten was a believer in strategic bombing. He was also associated with the body of opinion in the Air Force that favored fighter defense. For the armies in the East, Korten's appointment was no gain. In September he took six fighter squadrons off the Eastern Front to strengthen the Reich defenses; and in November, when bad weather began to hamper flying, he started withdrawing bombers and crews from close support for retraining in strategic bombing. He predicted that by careful target selection 50 to 80 percent of Soviet tank and aircraft production could be eliminated. He promised Hitler 400 bombers for long-range missions by mid-February 1944, but the demands for troop support and air supply delayed the start of retraining until late March. By then many of the targets were beyond the reach of most of the German bombers. The net impact on the Eastern Front was a loss of six fighter squadrons, which were never replaced, and a substantial weakening of the close support bomber strength.

MANPOWER

If Hitler's personnel troubles had been confined to the upper command echelons he could still have considered himself fortunate. By the fall of 1943 the manpower squeeze, which at midyear had been temporarily mitigated, was on again more strongly than ever. On 1 September, for the first time in the war, the Army strength on the Eastern Front (not including the Air Force field units and the Waffen-SS) fell below two and one-half million men. In the first three years of the war the total permanent losses on all fronts (dead, missing, and disabled) had been 922,000, or 14.3 percent of the total Army strength. In the thirteen months between 1 September 1942 and 20 November 1943 that number rose to 2,077,000, or 30 percent of the Army strength. Between 1 November 1942 and 1 December 1943, an OKH survey revealed, the number of German units on the Eastern Front stayed constant even though the actual strength declined—in short, the armies in the East were being gradually burned out.

Furthermore, the Army was confronted with an almost complete drying up of its sources of new recruits. The 800,000-man draft ordered in January 1943 brought in about 580,000 men by September, when it was stopped. In July Hitler added a requirement for another

700,000 men but it ran into heavy resistance from industry and the civilian bureaucracy. In September, after 120,000 draft notices had been issued, the Army recruitment chief reported that he would hardly get 50,000 men all together.

The Eastern Intelligence Branch, OKH, reckoned that between 1 September 1943 and 1 January 1944 the Soviet losses in killed, disabled, and prisoners of war amounted to 1,200,000 men. The German dead and missing for the same period were 243,743. The Germans estimated the front-line and front-line reserve strength of the Soviet forces in Europe on 1 January 1944 was 5.5 million men. (The estimate was apparently close: the Soviet official figures are 5,568,000 men in formations at the front and 419,000 in units in the Stavka reserves.)43 The encouragement to be found in the assumption that Soviet manpower was declining and Soviet losses were about five times their own was slight. The Eastern Intelligence Branch predicted that relatively the German strength would continue on the downgrade during the subsequent months for the following reasons:

 1. The Soviet numerical superiority was already great.

 2. The annual classes of recruits were about three times larger than those of the Germans.

 3. The Soviet Union was gaining and Germany losing manpower from the reoccupied territories (some 500,000 to 600,000 men between July and mid-October 1943).

 4. The Russians were more stringent and more successful in screening their deferred men.

The Eastern Intelligence Branch concluded that Germany was at a further disadvantage in that it had to divert at least 30 percent, and usually more, of its total strength to the OKW theaters while the Soviet Union diverted only 7 percent to its Far Eastern Theater.

In early November the OKW considered making women between the ages of eighteen and forty-five liable for military service and began contingency planning for a levy in mass (letztes Aufgebot). The idea of drafting women had to be dropped because it conflicted with Hitler's philosophy concerning the roles of the sexes, and on 8 November, with a disconcerting jolt, Hitler set the OKW planners off in another direction. Speaking to the Nazi Party leaders in Munich, he criticized the unfavorable ratio of front-line to rear area troops in terms which came close to implying that the German Armed Forces had become a refuge for slackers.

During the next few weeks the OKW hastily initiated studies that culminated in Basic Order 22 of 5 December 1943. The order set a requirement for one million combat troops to be wrung out of the rear echelons. Besides directing the services and their subordinate commands to reduce and simplify their staff and support overhead and to restrict the so-called "paper war," it laid down several specific regulations: No men under thirty years of age and no able-bodied men were to remain in rear area assignments. The standards of physical fitness were lowered, and men with chronic but not acute ear, stomach, and lung complaints were to be considered fit for front duty. All rear and command staffs were automatically to reduce their strengths by 10 to 25 percent. To make certain that the order was executed, the OKW created Feldjaeger (courier) battalions which were to comb the rear areas, conducting their visitations by surprise and dispatching the men they found to central collecting points without delay.

That more economical employment of the men already in the service could contribute toward alleviating the manpower squeeze was certain. The OKH estimated that its forces on the Eastern Front consisted of 47 percent combatants and 53 percent noncombatants. If individual armies, corps, and divisions were considered, the disproportion was often even greater. Frequently, for instance, divisions reduced to combat strengths of a thousand men or less had three or four times as many men in their rear echelons. But to convert this apparently superfluous manpower to combat effectives was no easy matter. The German Army was accustomed to operating with extensive supply and support services. It could not, as the Soviet Army frequently did, rely on poorly equipped and scantily provisioned masses of men; and one of its continuing advantages over the Russians was its superiority in logistics, communications, and transportation in the rear areas. For those reasons unit commanders, even when the men in the rear outnumbered the troops at the front, were unwilling to risk losing valuable equipment and trained specialists for the sake of a temporary gain in front strength. Added to the natural reluctance of commanders to dismantle their support elements was the resistance of the rear area bureaucracy, particularly its members who were themselves candidates for reassignment. By 1943 the bureaucracy was firmly entrenched behind ramparts of paper and entanglements of red tape, and rear area personnel were past masters at avoiding assignments which by even the remotest mischance might bring them to a hero's grave; hence the Feldjaeger battalions. But whether even they would be completely successful was doubtful since General Unruh, the dreaded "hero snatcher," had been operating along similar lines for nearly two years with only middling success.

Along with anxiety over dwindling numbers went growing concern in the higher German command circles over the multiplying signs of a deterioration in troop quality among the armies of the East. Kluge and others had reported that the German soldiers were no longer as reliable as they had been. In the late summer and fall of 1943 a new term, Krisenfestigkeit (ability to withstand crises), was brought into use in judging the caliber of individual divisions. The best divisions were described as Krisenfest (able to stand up under a crisis) and the others, on a descending scale, as either Krisenfest to a limited extent or unreliable in various degrees. Dismayingly few German divisions qualified as Krisenfest. The allied troops (excepting the Spanish and the Finns) and the Russian collaborators stood at the bottom of the scale. Before the end of the year all of the Russians organized into units were transferred away from the Eastern Front to prevent their defecting to the partisans.

Hitler saw the apparent drop in the quality of the German troops as entirely a problem of leadership. "The condition of the troops," he said, "is a reflection of the commander's disposition." Therefore, the solution, in his opinion, was simple—get better commanders. But he was forced to admit that at the battalion and regimental levels, where the officer losses ran high, that might not be easy.

Guderian, in his capacity as Inspector General for Armor, proposed a different approach. He believed the time had come to rationalize the German defensive tactics. The infantry, he reported to Hitler on 20 October 1943, had lately lost some of its ability to withstand crises; on the other hand, the new model German tanks had just about overcome their breaking-in troubles and could be considered the best weapons of their kind in the world. What was needed was to create mobile tank reserves to backstop the infantry. Panzer divisions would have to be taken out of the front, rested, re-equipped, and then held back to form a powerful striking force for emergencies. The result, besides providing stiffening for the infantry, would, Guderian contended, be to restore the panzer divisions to their proper role as mobile offensive units.

Guderian wanted to begin putting his proposal into effect with the five rebuilt panzer divisions he sent to Army Group South in October. The success at Krivoi Rog of the first two to arrive convinced him he was right. Subsequently he argued for employing all five of the divisions in the battle around Kiev, even if the Dnepr Bend and the Crimea were lost as a consequence. There his plan foundered, as others had before, when it encountered Hitler's unwillingness to sacrifice ground for the sake of creating a clear-cut main effort. The five divisions never did get into battle as a single force, and after the end of December, when the Soviet winter offensive started, all hope of reconstituting that strong a reserve vanished.

FUEHRER DIRECTIVE 51

Ultimately, the conduct of the war on the Eastern Front was to be most greatly affected by a decision which Hitler elevated to the level of national strategy in Fuehrer Directive 51, issued 3 November 1943. The two-and-one-half-year campaign against Bolshevism, he asserted, had required full commitment of the greater part of Germany's military strength and effort. That was consistent with the extent of the danger and the total situation, but, in the meantime, the latter had changed. The Soviet danger was still there, but a greater danger had arisen in the West—the Anglo-American invasion. "In the most extreme instance" Germany could still sacrifice fairly extensive areas in the East without being fatally injured. Not so in the West, There, a breakthrough on a broad front would have "unforeseeable consequences in a short time." "Therefore," Hitler concluded, "I can no longer take the responsibility for allowing the Western Front to be weakened for the benefit of other theaters of war."

In his directive Hitler completely took the side of the Operations Staff, OKW, which had all along contended that it was necessary to keep strong forces in France, Scandinavia, and the Balkans. In so doing he rejected the OKH argument that it was wrong to risk losing a battle already in progress by holding back troops to meet future threats. While it was probably too late for Manstein's radical strategy, namely, stripping the other fronts bare for an attempt to defeat the Soviet Union first, Hitler in the directive went almost to the other extreme, putting the Army on notice that for the near future at least the Eastern Front would have to get along on its own resources, come what might. He implied that he might consider trading space for time, but events were soon to prove he was constitutionally incapable of that exchange.

CHAPTER XI

Offensives on Both Flanks— the South Flank

THE BATTLE RESUMES WEST OF KIEV

Manstein had gone forward on 24 December to celebrate Christmas Eve with one of the reserve divisions. During the day he learned that First Ukrainian Front was attacking west on both sides of the Zhitomir-Kiev road. (Map 19) Whether a full-scale offensive was in the making could not be determined for certain. That the Soviet units could have recovered so soon from the beatings many of them had taken during the German counterattack appeared doubtful. Moreover, the weather had turned warm and rainy which, although the roads were still firm on the 24th, did not augur well for armored operations. But the Fourth Panzer Army evening report, which Manstein received after returning to his headquarters in Vinnitsa late that night, convinced him that a big offensive was imminent.

VATUTIN ATTACKS

The next day brought confirmation. First Guards and First Tank Armies with fourteen rifle divisions and four tank and mechanized corps in the front, veered southwestward below the Zhitomir-Kiev road toward Berdichev and Kazatin. During the day Vatutin extended his offensive north into the XIII Corps zone east of Zhitomir, and on the Fourth Panzer Army left flank LIX Corps east of Korosten expected an attack at any hour. In the afternoon Manstein ordered Fourth Panzer Army to prevent an irruption to Berdichev and Kazatin by taking XXXXVIII Panzer Corps out between LIX and XIII Corps and bringing it down for an attack into the Soviet flank.

Manstein was fully aware of the terms on which the winter battles would have to be fought. The long-standing strategic

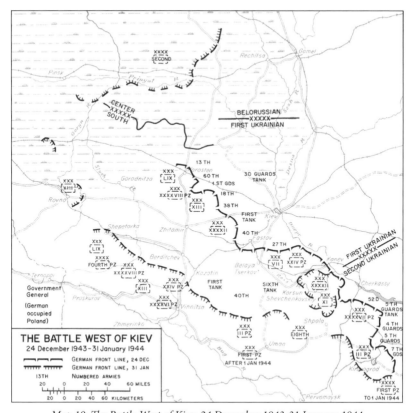

Map 19: The Battle West of Kiev, 24 December 1943-31 January 1944

threat to the Army Group South left flank was stronger than ever. It could take the form of a deep envelopment carried west to the Carpathians or a shorter southward thrust between the Dnepr and the Dnestr. In his order to Fourth Panzer Army Manstein chose to concentrate on defending against the southward thrust as the most immediately dangerous and the one on which Vatutin appeared to be concentrating.

Additionally, since the front had moved back to the Dnepr a new menace had come to the fore. It was the threat to the army group's lifelines, the railroads. They were two: on the north the line Lublin-Kovel'-Shepetovka-Berdichev-Kazatin and about fifty miles farther south the roughly parallel line L'vov-Ternopol-Proskurov-Zhmerinka. If they were cut, all of the Army Groups South and A supplies would have to be rerouted over the Rumanian railroads, which were in dismal condition and were certain to become worse as the front drew closer to the Rumanian border.

Turning to the OKH, Manstein, on 25 December, reported that Fourth Panzer Army was not equal to the approaching test. The army would have to be given five or six divisions. If Army Group South was to supply them it would need authority to shorten its right flank. Otherwise the OKH would have to provide the divisions. He requested a speedy decision. On 26 December the OKH instructed Army Group A to transfer one division to Army Group South, and Hitler authorized Manstein to take the easternmost projection of the First Panzer Army line back fifteen miles behind Zaporozhye to gain another division, but the OKH indicated that a fundamental decision of the sort Manstein had requested was not being made.

Meanwhile, Vatutin had expanded the offensive. Fortieth Army began pushing south below Fastov, and Third Guards Tank, First Guards, Thirteenth, and Sixtieth Armies advanced west and northwest toward Zhitomir and Korosten. On 26 December Manstein thought XXXXVIII Panzer Corps might still be able to attack into the flank of the thrust toward Berdichev and Kazatin, but the Commanding General, Fourth Panzer Army, General der Panzertruppen Erhard Raus, maintained that the assembly would take too long. The best the army could do, he argued, was to hem in the Russian spearheads, slow them down, and try to stop them forward of the two cities.

HITLER FENDS OFF A DECISION

On 27 December Manstein turned to Hitler and the OKH again. Half measures to gain a division or two, he said, would do no good. He would have to shift his main effort from the right to the left flank, and to do that First Panzer Army had to be taken back to the Kamenka River line in order to release at least five divisions. At the situation conference that night Hitler refused. Manstein, he asserted, could propose anything he liked; he did not bear the final responsibility. If First Panzer Army withdrew and so touched off trouble on the Crimea that gave the Russians and the Western Powers the argument they needed to bring Turkey into the war against Germany, Manstein would not take the blame. He would merely say it was a political problem.

Early on 28 December thirty Soviet tanks with infantry aboard burst into Kazatin where they destroyed some hundreds of German trucks. By late afternoon the Germans had retaken about half of the city but had no real prospect of maintaining their grip on it more than a few hours. Manstein reported to Hitler that the Russians had so far thrown a total of forty-seven rifle divisions and nine tank and mechanized corps against Fourth Panzer Army. Against that array the army would not be able to defend the railroads behind its front. As in his earlier dispatches, Manstein suggested that if he were allowed to shift the main effort to the left flank he could mount a strong counteroffensive. The day before, he had hinted that he might manage to repeat something like the March 1943 victory at Kharkov, which, he pointed out, had been possible because Rostov and the eastern half of the Donets Basin were given up in time. He again wanted to execute the "Rochade" (castling) that had been so successful there.

At the Fuehrer headquarters the Manstein telegram unleashed a storm. In a rage, Hitler declared that Manstein was only trying to make himself look good by his "pompous" talk of counteroperations. He should give what he was doing its real name, "running away." Manstein, Hitler went on, was losing his nerve, probably because his headquarters was too close to the front. He should get out of Vinnitsa. Then Hitler broke off his tirade to discuss possible new locations for Manstein's headquarters and to demand that the headquarters at Vinnitsa, the former Fuehrer headquarters for the southern flank of the Eastern Front, be completely destroyed so that the Russians would find nothing "to haul away and put on display in Moscow." After that Hitler shifted to the subject of retreats in general, shouting, "Everything back! Sometimes that becomes an outright mania." He could make himself sick with aggravation over "those retreats," he continued. He was sorry he ever gave permission for the first one; it could not have been worse if the armies had stayed where they were. The conference ended with nothing more than a decision to move Manstein's headquarters to Ternopol.

Behind the cloud of accusations and protests he had thrown up, Hitler had, nevertheless, grudgingly come to realize that thoroughgoing measures were necessary if the south flank of the Eastern Front was to be saved. On 27 December he had talked briefly of taking back Army Group North to the PANTHER position to gain a dozen divisions for the south. At the noon conference on the 29th he told Zietzler that after thinking it over during the night he had concluded that the southern flank had to be strengthened. In the north, as he saw it, the worst that could happen was that a greater burden would be thrown on the Finns, whereas in the south, Germany would lose the Crimea, Krivoi Rog, and Nikopol, which would be bad economically and could have dangerous political repercussions in Turkey and the Balkans. He indicated that he had decided to let Army Group North withdraw to the PANTHER position.

The next day, however, when Kuechler came to Fuehrer headquarters, Hitler changed his mind. Kuechler described the Eighteenth Army front around Oranienbaum, below Leningrad, and along the Volkhov as strongly fortified, and stated that the army commander thought the army stood a good chance of beating off the offensive expected during the winter. That was enough to arouse all of Hitler's old antipathy toward giving ground voluntarily. Later he apparently also had second thoughts regarding the Finns and the effect a withdrawal might have in the Baltic area.

FIRST PANZER ARMY REDEPLOYED

While Hitler procrastinated, the Fourth Panzer Army front was breaking apart. By 30 December LIX Corps on the army's north flank was in full retreat west of Korosten.

Between its right flank and the XIII Corps left north of Zhitomir, a 35-mile gap had opened. From Zhitomir to southwest of Kazatin the army main force, XIII Corps, XXXXVIII Panzer Corps, and XXXXII Corps, tried to keep a solid front against the main weight of the offensive. A 45-mile gap separated the XXXXII Corps right flank southwest of Kazatin and the left flank of VII Corps south of Belaya Tserkov'. On the army's right the VII Corps and XXIV Panzer Corps held a still stationary front running east to the Dnepr and tying in with Eighth Army at Kanev. The commanding general, Raus, told Manstein that the army could do nothing about the gaps and intended to concentrate on keeping the three "blocks" from disintegrating.

Soviet assault gun, 1943.

Manstein had decided the day before to stretch his authority to the utmost and assume that the logic of events would force Hitler to approve. He ordered the Headquarters, First Panzer Army, to move to Uman on 1 January and take command of Fourth Panzer Army's two right corps, VII Corps and XXXXII Corps (XXIV Panzer Corps and XXXXII Corps traded sectors on 1 January 1944). To give First Panzer Army a striking force he took the Headquarters, III Panzer Corps, and two panzer divisions from Eighth Army and added a panzer-grenadier division and a Jaeger (light infantry) division being transferred from Army Group A. III Panzer Corps was to assemble its four divisions east of Vinnitsa. To provide a similar force for Fourth Panzer Army, he gave it the Headquarters, XXXXVI Panzer Corps, and a panzer division coming from Army Group Center, an infantry division being transferred from Army Group North, and a mountain division coming from Army Group A. Whether those two corps would be sufficient to stop the Russians and close the gaps was still extremely doubtful.

On 31 December Hitler concurred but refused to approve the necessary next step, the withdrawal of the Army Group South right flank in the Dnepr Bend to the Kamenka position. All the signs indicated that the Russians were preparing an offensive in the Dnepr

Bend. Once it started, it would be too late to take out divisions for the left flank.

THE BATTLE EXPANDS

Until the end of December, Army Group South was fortunate in one respect, that Vatutin concentrated his forces against Fourth Panzer Army's three groups without attempting to exploit the gaps in the army front. After the turn of the year the battle began to develop much more dangerously. While maintaining strong frontal pressure that forced Fourth Panzer Army westward, the Russians began working their way around the flanks and threatened to encircle the army main force, the XIII, XXXXVIII Panzer, and XXIV Panzer Corps.

On the north LIX Corps, what was left of it, had by 3 January been pushed back to Gorodnitsa on the pre-1939 Polish border. East of Shepetovka the railroad to Berdichev was virtually undefended except for scattered XXXXVI Panzer Corps components trying to assemble there. From northwest of Berdichev to northeast of Vinnitsa the three corps of Fourth Panzer

Army's main force held a continuous but extremely fragile line. On 4 January XIII Corps, holding at and northwest of Berdichev, reported that it was falling apart. The troops were exhausted; the divisions had front-line strengths of 150 to 300 men; and the whole corps had the infantry strength of one regiment. The gap between the Fourth Panzer Army flank and what on 1 January became the First Panzer Army left had widened to nearly seventy miles. VII Corps on the east side of the gap had been pushed south and east of Belaya Tserkov' to where its front and that of XXXXII Corps on the Dnepr stood back to back and formed a pocket open on the south. III Panzer Corps was moving up from the south to plug the gap but a Soviet attack, which began on 3 January at Kirovograd in the Eighth Army zone, delayed the transfer of the two panzer divisions intended for III Panzer Corps.

On 4 January Manstein went to Fuehrer headquarters and tried again to talk Hitler into giving up the Dnepr Bend. By then Manstein believed that the Kamenka River would be only the first phase line in a retreat that would probably have to go all the way to the lower Bug River before the balance of the front could be restored, but he knew any discussion of a larger withdrawal would be completely futile. Hitler, for his part, refused even to consider letting Army Group South go to the Kamenka, and added that he could not supply reinforcements from outside the army group zone. Divisions could not be given from the West, he insisted, before the expected British-American invasion had been beaten off; until then the Eastern Front would have to fight for time.

During the coming months the invasion in the West was to be Hitler's standard excuse for avoiding decisions in the East. Characteristically, he ignored current crises and closed his mind to reality while he looked to the future for the opportunity that he imagined would restore his fortunes with one bold stroke. For the Eastern Front commands this meant a close approach to the ultimate in frustration by adding to the normal rigidity of Hitler's tactical concepts the drag of a massive indifference.

When Manstein went to Fuehrer headquarters he still thought he would be able to patch the gaps on both sides of the Fourth Panzer Army main force with the two panzer corps then forming, but the events of the succeeding days compelled him to change his plans. After 4 January LIX Corps on the north flank had to sideslip southwest to avoid being pushed into the Pripyat Marshes and to do what it could to cover Shepetovka and Rovno. That opened the breach between Army Groups Center and South to a width of 110 miles. Neither army group had the slightest prospect of doing anything to restore contact, and the gap came to be referred to as the Wehrmachtsloch (armed forces hole) which gave it virtually the status of a permanent feature of the Eastern Front. Manstein proposed moving in a whole new army, but neither he nor anyone else knew where such an army might come from. In the second week of the month the gap opened even wider when Belorussian Front pushed Second Army to the line of the Ipa River. Nevertheless, the army groups could count themselves fortunate in two respects: the abnormally warm weather had kept the marshes from freezing, and the three armies operating against LIX Corps had resumed the offensive without being rested and resupplied after the fall battles, so that by mid-January they had lost much of their momentum.

To narrow the open expanse off the right flank of the LIX Corps, Manstein on 3 January had ordered XXXXVIII Panzer Corps to shift west of Berdichev. Berdichev was lost before the end of the first week in January, but by extending its flank out to the Sluch River XXXXVIII Panzer Corps kept the Russians from getting behind the army. Between the inner flanks of the Fourth and First Panzer Armies, III Panzer Corps, still assembling, maneuvered elements of two divisions and attempted to establish a screening line. On 6 January Vatutin showed for the first time that he was fully aware of the opportunity there. The pressure against the Fourth Panzer Army main force declined sharply, and the First Tank and Fortieth Armies turned south into the gap.

MANSTEIN CONCENTRATES ON THE SOUTHWARD THRUST

On that day Manstein, in a directive to Fourth and First Panzer Armies, predicted that Vatutin would either try to encircle the Fourth Panzer Army main force or attempt to strike deep toward Shepetovka and Rovno in the north and toward Zhmerinka in the south. The latter appeared to him the more likely. Having already told the armies that it would not be possible to deal with both thrusts at the same time, he instructed them to concentrate on stopping the southward advance of First Tank and Fortieth Armies. In the first phase of the counterattack First Panzer Army would deploy III Panzer Corps against Fortieth Army operating on the east side of the gap. To gain additional divisions the army would collapse the pocket formed by the VII and XXXXII Corps fronts and take them south to the Ross River. In the second phase, beginning on approximately X plus eight days, III Panzer Corps would turn west into the left flank of First Tank Army while XXXXVI Panzer Corps, which Fourth Panzer Army would have shifted south by then, attacked the right.

The directive went out to the armies subject to Hitler's concurrence. On the afternoon of 7 January Hitler approved it in general but strictly prohibited the proposed withdrawal of the VII and XXXXII Corps to the Ross River, thus greatly diminishing the chances of the counterattack's achieving a complete success as well as perpetuating a danger which before the end of the month was to produce the Cherkassy pocket. First Panzer Army had warned two days earlier that to leave the two corps standing in a vulnerable open loop was to court disaster.

In the second week of January the two Soviet armies continued probing southward. By the 10th First Tank Army had opened a hole between the flanks of XXXXVI Panzer Corps and III Panzer Corps and had turned a guards tank and a guards mechanized corps due west toward Zhmerinka. It took the German armor two days' heavy fighting to eliminate the threat to Zhmerinka for the time being. On the east Fortieth Army opened a wider breach between the flanks of III Panzer Corps and VII Corps, and by the 10th its spearheads had pushed nearly to the outskirts of Uman. The two German corps struggled to prevent the Russians from breaking loose completely before the units for the counterattack, some of which were still in transit from the West, could be assembled. Manstein held to his original plan of dealing first with Fortieth Army and then turning against First Tank Army.

Between 10 and 15 January III Panzer Corps shifted the 17th Panzer Division from its left flank to the right flank north of Uman, leaving only the division's reconnaissance battalion to hold on the left. Behind the 17th Panzer Division the corps echeloned the main force of its other division, the 16th Panzer Division. (Two of the divisions intended for the corps were tied down in other sectors.) Minor elements of the 16th Panzer Division were left in the corps front facing north. In effect, what the corps had to accomplish was to close the front by starting from a weak handhold in the center of the gap and drawing the dangling ends of the front inward toward it. By the time the two panzer divisions were in position VII Corps had helped by extending its flank south to within twenty-five miles of their line of departure.

On 15 January the III Panzer Corps' tanks jumped off to the east, making good if not spectacular progress. That same day First Panzer Army took command of XXXXVI Panzer Corps and began shifting some of its strength east for the second phase of the counterattack. On the 17th III Panzer Corps came within a mile or two of making contact with the VII Corps flank and began turning north for an attack into the First Tank Army flank.

Unseasonably high temperatures, in the daytime well above freezing, had persisted since the latter half of December. Rain and snow turned the roads into mud and when the temperature sank the roads became icy. On the 18th First Panzer Army complained that poor visibility and difficulties in reconnaissance had made it lose track of the Russians' movements just as the army was getting ready to deal First Tank Army a decisive blow.

During the next six days III Panzer Corps jockeyed itself into position while the army brought up the Adolf Hitler Division and the 18th Artillery Division to restore the striking power XXXXVI Panzer Corps had lost in extending its line. Early on 24 January XXXXVI Panzer Corps, the Adolf Hitler Division in the lead, attacked out of the corps front west of Vinnitsa. The breakthrough was speedily accomplished, but before noon the operation was wavering on the edge of disaster. At a small stream an engineer sergeant had pulled out a bridging platoon when it came under fire. It was nearly nightfall before the platoon, which had subsequently gotten itself thoroughly lost, returned and laid bridges to get the tanks across. The next day III Panzer Corps attacked from the east and met strong resistance almost at once. Clearly the moment for catching First Tank Army by surprise and throwing it off balance was lost.

XI AND XXXXVI CORPS ENCIRCLED

On 26 January the Stavka played its trump. A mechanized corps and a guards tank corps penetrated the First Panzer Army right flank at the VII Corps-XXXII Corps boundary. Fourth Guards Army had plunged into the Eighth Army front southwest of Cherkassy the day before, and a classic double envelopment was in the making. First Panzer Army was helpless. To stop the counterattack on the left flank while First Tank Army stayed intact would have restored the initiative there to the Russians and so would not have freed any units for transfer to the right.

While the XXXXVI and the III Panzer Panzer Corps ground their way into the flanks of First Tank Army, the Soviet armor on the First Panzer Army right flank took advantage of its free rein, pushed south at top speed, and on 28 January closed the ring around XXXXVI Corps and XI Corps. Almost simultaneously the points of the XXXXVI and the III Panzer Corps made contact, trapping several Soviet divisions

Wreckage-strewn path of German breakout near Cherkassy.

to the south. The army ordered the 17th Panzer Division to begin pulling out and the two panzer corps to finish mopping up behind their new front, fast. By 31 January all of III Panzer Corps was out and heading east.

The operation against First Tank Army was a moderate success: it netted an estimated 701 tanks and assault guns destroyed and 8,000 Russians killed and 5,436 captured. The responsibility for the catastrophe on its right flank, First Panzer Army justifiably believed, lay elsewhere. It had twice been forbidden to take the flank back. In the army war diary Hube remarked, "One can only obey, even in the deepest anxiety."

THE CHERKASSY POCKET
(KORSUN' SHEVCHENKOVSKIY)[18]

At the turn of the year Eighth Army held a 100-mile sector from Kanev to twenty miles due east of Kirovograd. South of Kanev the army still

---

18. Although Cherkassy was not in the pocket, the Germans used the designation "Cherkassy pocket" or, more specifically, "the pocket near Cherkassy." The Russian designation, "The Battle of Korsun' Shevchenkovskiy," is perhaps more accurate since that locality remained inside the pocket throughout.

held twenty miles of the original Dnepr front. From the river the front angled away to the southwest, its configuration determined by successive Soviet thrusts and by Hitler's insistence on defending every yard of ground that could possibly be held. In effect it was nothing more than the line where Hitler's will temporarily counterbalanced the Russians' pressure against the army.

KIROVOGRAD

On 5 January, three days after Eighth Army had cleaned up a breakthrough fifteen miles north of Kirovograd, Second Ukrainian Front threw a powerful blow directly at the Eighth Army-Sixth Army boundary. Expanding the attack northward rapidly, the Russians penetrated nearly to Kirovograd in a matter of hours and the next day swept north and south around the city, encircling XXXXVII Panzer Corps, which was attempting to make a stand beyond the eastern suburbs. The speed and strength of the attack indicated that Konev and Vatutin—actually, Zhukov, since he was co-ordinating the two fronts' offensives—might be trying for an encirclement of the First Panzer and Eighth Armies east of the Bug. Acting quickly, Manstein gave Eighth Army two panzer divisions and the left flank corps of Sixth Army. On 8 January XXXXVII Panzer Corps had to pull out to the west, giving up Kirovograd. Once that was accomplished, the army recovered its equilibrium and in a few days threw a screening line in a semicircle behind the city.

If Zhukov and Konev had originally meant to go farther, they were probably dissuaded by the fast German reaction and by the weather, which was the worst imaginable. Rain and wet snow turned the ground into thin, watery mud. Temperatures hovering around the freezing mark coated guns and tanks with ice, which had to be knocked off before they could go into action. Clothes, soaked in the daytime, froze stiff at night.

On 10 January the Commanding General, Eighth Army, Woehler, told the army group chief of staff that the bulge on the inner flanks of the First Panzer and Eighth Armies was becoming a source of deepest concern to the army. His combat strength, he said, was very low, and he cited one infantry regiment which was reduced to two officers and fifty enlisted men. That same day First Panzer Army, which held the most exposed part of the bulge, urged that the line be taken back. The army group concurred, but Hitler, as Manstein had predicted four days earlier, would not hear of it.

Although Zhukov and Konev kept several armies concentrated near Kirovograd, they did not try to get the offensive there rolling again; even under the best conditions the Soviet commanders generally shied away from too extensive enveloping maneuvers. When the weather continued warm and rainy and First Panzer Army began to brake the southward advance past Vinnitsa, Zhukov waited at first and then shifted to other objectives, more modest but also more certain of attainment. An obvious one was to cut off the bulge in the German line, not at its base but farther east where the distances were shorter and the tactical problems fewer. By mid-January something of the sort had, in fact, become necessary in order to shorten the front. First Ukrainian Front had extended from a little more than 100 miles to over 250 miles and could not keep on advancing west much longer without closing up from the east. Moreover, even though it is difficult to discover any basis for such fears, the Stavka apparently had become worried about the flanks of the First and Second Ukrainian Fronts. Tactically the Russians had not had such an opportunity for a set piece double envelopment since Stalingrad. First Panzer Army and Eighth Army had their main forces committed and tied down on their outer flanks, and their inner flanks, projecting eastward, were depleted and exposed.

THE ENVELOPMENT

On 24 January a Second Ukrainian Front reconnaissance in force against Eighth Army about midway between Cherkassy and Kirovograd hit a 12-mile stretch on which the army had no more than one infantryman for every fifteen yards of front. By the end of the day the probing attacks had penetrated deep in a number of places. The next morning Fourth Guards Army opened a full-scale attack and by the end of the day had poured twelve rifle divisions into the breakthrough. Eighth Army again asked to eliminate the bulge, but the army group could not get an answer from Hitler.

On 26 January two armored corps of Sixth Tank Army ripped through the First Panzer Army front between the flanks of VII Corps and XXXXII Corps. With a show of daring they had until then not often displayed, Soviet armored commands headed south at full tilt. While the two German armies pleaded vainly for a decision from higher headquarters, the Soviet thrusts gained speed on the 27th. On the afternoon of the 28th air reconnaissance showed that the spearheads had met at Shpola. The XI Corps and XXXXII Corps—56,000 troops, including several thousand Russian auxiliaries—were encircled. When Hitler refused even then to let the corps move, Manstein took the first steps toward restoring contact. Transferring XXXXII Corps to Eighth Army, he promised the army the 24th Panzer Division from Sixth Army and ordered First Panzer Army to close out its counteroffensive against First Tank Army and start shifting units east.

As Zhukov no doubt knew before he started, the German reaction could not be swift. Even if the First Panzer and Eighth Armies could release forces from their outer flanks, the regrouping would be delayed by the roads and weather. The Russians had another advantage: their tracked vehicles—tanks and assault guns—had broader treads than those of the Germans and therefore performed better on soft ground and in mud.

On the other hand, and fortunately for the Germans, the latter advantage was a relative one. The quick advance to Shpola from the east and north had obviously placed a great strain on Soviet equipment, and Zhukov was not able to maintain the pace in establishing the outer screening line around the encirclement. He could not, as he had at Stalingrad, take advantage of the initial shock to throw the main front back so far as to make a relief exceedingly difficult or impossible.

THE RELIEF

On 1 February Manstein ordered the relief. He told First Panzer Army to shift III Panzer Corps to its extreme right flank and Eighth Army to put XXXXVII Panzer Corps on its extreme left. (Map 20) On the 3d, the 4th at the latest, the two corps were to strike toward the pocket, converging on its eastern rim. The objective, ostensibly, was only to regain contact with the encircled corps; Hitler was as far as ever from consenting to a withdrawal. The armies thought at first that they would be able to start on 3 February, but they had to ask for a 24-hour postponement on the 2d, when warm weather and heavy fog set in.

On the 3d the Chief of Staff, Army Group South, advised Manstein that after the operation began the troops of the XXXXII and XI Corps would have to stand "with their packs on their backs" ready to break out at the first opportunity. To think of leaving the corps where they were and merely restoring contact, he declared, was "Utopian." That information was passed on to the Chief of Staff, Eighth Army, who agreed heartily. But later in the day, talking to Woehler, Manstein indicated that he

still proposed to reach the pocket and turn the tables on Zhukov by trapping a good part of his forces between the two relief columns and the southwest front of the pocket. He also relayed without comment an intention of "the highest leadership" (Hitler) to carry the thrust north toward Kiev.

The attack began on 4 February in bright sunshine and a temperature well above freezing. At the last minute Hitler released to III Panzer Corps a panzer division which he had detained at Vinnitsa; how much time the division would waste moving through the mud was a question. In spite of a somewhat ragged start the attack in the First Panzer Army zone gained several miles before the end of the day. The army reported that ordinarily it would be certain of success, but the warm weather and mud were multiplying the difficulties.

During the night fog closed in again, and the next day neither side could move. In the meantime the tanks had burned up phenomenal quantities of fuel churning through the mud, and rations and ammunition were running low at the front. Since trucks were useless, the army directed III Panzer Corps and VII Corps to mobilize the civilians in their areas as porters and to requisition all the horses and sledges that could be found.

The Eighth Army effort was, if anything, less promising. At the last minute Hitler ordered 24th Panzer Division returned to Sixth Army. He had transferred Sixth Army to Army Group A on 1 February, partly to reduce Manstein's span of control but mostly to prevent his taking troops away from the south flank. The 24th Panzer Division

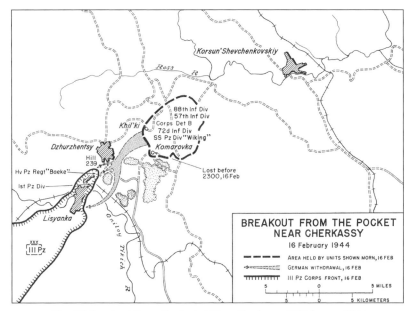

Map 20: Breakout From the Pocket Near Cherkassy, 16 February 1944

had plowed its way through the mud to Eighth Army, when it received orders to turn around and head south again. The division was thus of no use to either Sixth Army or Eighth Army. Realizing this and not wanting to deny Army Group South the division which might make all the difference in getting through to the pocket, Kleist offered to take an infantry division instead; but Hitler refused to change his order.

Inside the pocket XI and XXXXII Corps had a combined strength of six divisions, two of them very weak. The strongest was the SS Wiking Division, which had two armored infantry regiments, a tank regiment, and the Belgian Volunteer Brigade Wallonien. The safety of the Belgian Rexist leader, Léon Degrelle, serving in the latter, was a source of some concern to Hitler. The first orders to the two corps instructed them to hold where they were, but that was clearly impossible since both were already vastly overextended and now would have also to form a front on the south.

On 29 January Eighth Army authorized the first withdrawals on the north and east, and thereafter the corps fell back gradually to a perimeter centering at and west of Korsun'. The movements benefited somewhat from planning and some preparations made for the withdrawal to the Ross River proposed in the first week of January. The corps were favored in that they had collected all the food stocks in the hands of the German agricultural administrators and transported them south of the Ross River to the vicinity of Korsun'. Consequently, the troops could be kept on better than normal rations, and the air supply could be limited exclusively to ammunition and motor fuel.

Air supply began on 29 January. Fog and snow kept the planes grounded much of the time, and rising temperatures in the first week of February softened the landing strips. In the first five days forty-four planes were lost in accidents or shot down by Soviet fighters and antiaircraft fire. On 5 February mud barred use of the two airstrips in the pocket, but by the 9th a new strip had been laid out on drier ground. During the next five days the planes were able to bring in between 100 and 185 tons of ammunition daily, about enough to meet day-to-day requirements.

By 6 February Manstein and both of the army commanders were convinced that neither of the relief forces would be able to punch through all the way to the pocket. XXXXVII Panzer Corps, itself under heavy attack on its flanks, was getting nowhere at all. III Panzer Corps, with a shorter distance (about twenty miles) to go, was pushing ahead slowly but was having trouble bringing up gasoline and ammunition. The tank crews were carrying gasoline to the front in buckets, and many of the infantrymen were slogging through the knee-deep mud barefooted, finding this less exhausting than having to stop and retrieve their boots every few steps. At the same time, air supply to the pocket had again stopped completely, which meant that the pocket might run out of ammunition in three to four days. On 5 February Eighth Army sent an officer courier to alert the two corps to the possibility that they might have to come part way to meet the relief forces. When the army, on the same day, proposed awarding both commanding generals the Knight's Cross of the Iron Cross "to boost morale," Manstein replied that it would be better to wait until an actual order for the breakout had been given "to avoid comparisons with January 1943."

As always, Hitler's approval was slow in coming. He delayed authorizing a preparatory order for the breakout until late on the night of 6 February; the execution was still to depend on further developments. Actually, once the preparations began, complete execution could not be delayed more than a few days, since to mount an attack to the southwest the perimeter of the pocket would have to be drawn in so tightly that every part of the pocket would be exposed to enemy fire. Eighth Army transmitted the order as soon as it came in and directed General der Artillerie Wilhelm Stemmermann, the senior corps commander, to head both corps in the pocket.

During the next four days, while Stemmermann positioned his units, III Panzer Corps inched forward through snow, mud, and fog in local attacks and attempted to bring up enough tanks for a final push on the 11th. On the night of 8 February planes dropped 100 tons of ammunition into the pocket, and on the 10th they began to land again, taking in another hundred tons of ammunition, several thousand gallons of gas, and evacuating 400 wounded. On the 10th rain softened the ground even more than before; but Manstein and Woehler decided the attempt would have to be made the next day because XI Corps, which had started with only one good division out of three, appeared on the verge of collapse. First Panzer Army ordered III Panzer Corps to begin its final drive on the 11th "no matter what," and without the tanks, if necessary.

Spurred by a mood of near desperation, III Panzer Corps attacked early on the 11th and pushed its advance elements, hindered more by the mud than by the Russians, into the southern quarter of Lisyanka, nearly to the narrow but fairly deep Gniloy Tikich River. The army headquarters ordered the corps to cross the river and keep going north, taking advantage of the slight momentum it had. But before the end of the day the corps reported that this was impossible. It would have to stop for supplies; because of the weather the tanks were burning gasoline at three times the normal rate.

The attack out of the pocket, started shortly before midnight on the 11th, surprised the Russians and carried a mile or so to the villages of Khil'ki and Komarovka, off the southwestern rim. But the next day Stemmermann's troops had all they could do to hold the Khil'ki-Komarovka line against furious counterattacks. Despite a "now or never" warning from army headquarters, III Panzer Corps remained stalled south of the Gniloy Tikich throughout the day as rain and rising temperature slowed the efforts to bring up ammunition and refuel the tanks.

On 13 February part of III Panzer Corps crossed the Gniloy Tikich and pushed to the northern outskirts of Lisyanka. Between Khil'ki and Komarovka the Germans and Russians were locked in an all-day battle in which neither side made any worthwhile gains. Yard by yard, III Panzer Corps gained ground the next day but was stopped before nightfall by counterattacks, heavy snow, and mud. The 1st Panzer Division and Heavy Panzer Regiment Baeke were all that the corps could support north of the river. The heavy panzer regiment's Tiger tanks had run up a phenomenal score of 400 Russian tanks destroyed in three weeks, but was itself down to its last half dozen tanks. That night, after deciding that the day's events had shown that III Panzer Corps would not get through to the pocket in time, Woehler authorized Stemmerman to take his northeastern front behind the Ross River and instructed him to mass all the troops he could for a thrust out of the line Khil'ki-Komarovka to Dzhurzhentsy, halfway between the pocket and Lisyanka.

The 1st Panzer Division, with the heavy tank regiment in the lead, gained a little on 15 February but failed to reach either Dzhurzhentsy or Hill 239.0, which commanded a ridge line south of the town and was the highest elevation on the approach to the pocket. First Panzer Army reported that III Panzer Corps definitely did not have enough strength to get through to the pocket. Manstein had already reached the same conclusion. Until then he had thought a relief could be effected by the orthodox method of extending the two fronts toward each other until they met, but that had clearly become impossible. He told Woehler that Stemmermann would have to be given a directive to mass his forces for an all-or-nothing attempt.

Woehler's order to Stemmermann stated that he would have to reach Dzhurzhentsy or Hill 239.0 on his own power. It instructed him to assemble all the artillery he could to open a breach and to place Generalleutnant Theobald Lieb, Commanding General, XXXXII Corps, in command of the assault force. Stemmermann replied that he would attack as ordered at 2300 on 16 February.

BREAKOUT

The 16th was a day to test everyone's nerves. During the past several days wet snow blanketing the familiar mud had piled to depths of three feet in gullies and low spots. To the troops in the pocket the snow at least brought some respite from air attacks and afforded concealment that otherwise was hard to find in the pocket, which had shrunk to a width of about six miles. Lieb noted in his diary that when the snow stopped he could see almost the whole pocket from his command post.

In the morning Manstein ordered the breakout to begin without artillery and the artillery to be positioned so that it could go into action when the first strong resistance was met. In the afternoon the Russians retook Komarovka, the southern anchor of the breakout front. Stemmermann had to revise his plan to incorporate the changes. The loss of Komarovka endangered the south flank, particularly of the units which would follow the first assault waves.

During the day the 1st Panzer Division, with Heavy Panzer Regiment Baeke still in the lead, tried again to reach Dzhurzhentsy, but it could not push its front beyond the northern tip of Lisyanka. The heavy panzer regiment, ranging ahead, managed once to get three tanks atop Hill 239.0, but heavy fire from the flanks forced them back 400 yards behind the hill. By nightfall nothing more could be done. First Panzer Army had brought hospital trains up to the closest station behind the front and had JU-52's standing by to take on wounded at the Uman airfield. Manstein waited out the night aboard his command train in Uman, where First Panzer Army had its headquarters.

On the line of departure in the pocket Stemmermann stationed Corps Detachment B (the 112th Infantry Division and remnants of two other divisions) on the north in Khil'ki, the 72d Infantry Division in the center, and the SS Wiking Division in the south.[19] After Komarovka was lost, the latter two divisions had to occupy the sector originally intended for one, which occasioned some last-minute confusion and scrambling. Each division placed a regiment with

---

19. The "corps detachments" were composed of several divisions greatly reduced in strength operating under a divisional staff. In size they were approximately equal to a standard infantry division.

Soviet rocket fire near Dzhurzhentsy.

artillery in the vanguard and echeloned two approximately regiment-sized units behind it. Stemmermann took personal command of the rear guard, the 57th and 88th Divisions, which was to withdraw to three successive phase lines: the first was to be reached shortly before 2300 on the 16th; the last was approximately the line of departure of the assault divisions. The sixth division, the 389th Infantry Division, had gone out of existence a week earlier when its last 200 men were attached to the 57th Infantry Division. The total strength of the pocket, including Russian auxiliaries, stood at about 45,000 men, including 1,500 wounded who were to be left behind.

The attack began on time an hour before midnight on 16 February. Jumping off in silence and using only knives and bayonets, the three assault regiments cut through the outpost line and main screening line before the Russians knew what had happened. The regiment of Corps Detachment B met no more Russians until it arrived at the Russian line between Dzhurzhentsy and Hill 239.0, which it pushed through easily. Thereafter it guided on white signal flares fired by the 1st Panzer Division and reached the northern tip of Lisyanka at 0500.

The regiment of the 72d Infantry Division had even better luck. On reaching the road running into Dzhurzhentsy from the southeast it encountered four Soviet tanks and a column of trucks moving toward the town. When someone yelled, "Stoi!" (Halt!) the tanks stopped and let the Germans cross the road. The Russians did not realize their mistake until the cannon company went across, and then it was too late. The regiment moved off into the darkness quickly, not paying any further attention to the tanks which had by then become embroiled with other German units coming up behind, and made its way to the 1st Panzer Division front north of Lisyanka shortly after.

The SS regiment was not so fortunate. Passing east of Dzhurzhentsy, it encountered heavy machine gun, antitank, and tank fire from the edge of the settlement. It diverted one battalion to throw the Russians back while the main force turned due south, apparently to avoid heavy tank fire from the direction of Hill 239.0. By turning south, the regiment extended the distance it had to go and placed itself east of the Gniloy Tikich. To reach Lisyanka, it had to cross the river. The only way to do that was to swim. All of the heavy equipment which had come that far stayed on the east bank, and most of the SS men had to discard their rifles in the water. Even so, many of them drowned, the first of hundreds, perhaps thousands, who shared the same fate in the icy water that day.

The second wave followed the first after a 10-minute interval. Then, at a slower pace the heavy equipment began to move out. Stemmermann had ordered all vehicles destroyed except tanks, self-propelled assault guns, tracked prime movers, and enough horse-drawn wagons to carry men wounded during the breakout. That still left enough vehicles to create traffic jams behind the line of departure, particularly since some units disregarded the order and tried to take along ordinary trucks and heavily loaded wagons that promptly got stuck. The attempt to save the vehicles, tanks, and heavy equipment was almost exclusively a battle against the terrain. Many of the vehicles that left Khil'ki had to be abandoned in the bottom of a gully a mile and a half to the south. Those that found a way across or started farther south were all, excepting a few horse-drawn wagons, eventually trapped in the snow and mud. Many piled up against the ridges flanking Hill 239.0. Others turned south, and a few reached the Gniloy Tikich only to be lost in the swampy bottomland or in the river itself.

During the night Stemmermann kept his command post in Khil'ki, most of the time out of touch with his subordinate commands. Tanks, troops, and Russian artillery fire had severed most of the telephone lines, and last-minute transfers of radio sets from trucks to horse-drawn panje wagons had put nearly all the sets out of order. At 0300, having deduced from the receding sound of the fighting that the breakout was succeeding, Stemmermann dispatched orders by radio and by runner to the two rearguard divisions, instructing them to fall back to the second and third phase lines in the next three hours and then strike southwestward toward Lisyanka. An hour later he and his staff followed the last wave of Corps Detachment B out of Khil'ki, intending to set up a new command post about half way to Dzhurzhentsy. South of Khil'ki, in the confused mass of troops and vehicles, he became separated from the staff. Later a soldier reported he had taken the general aboard his wagon shortly before it was blown to pieces by a Russian antitank shell.

Lieb and the officers of his staff, all on horseback, moved out behind the last echelon of the 72d Infantry Division at 0330. Half an hour later they crossed the gully south of Khil'ki, by then filled with smashed, half-buried vehicles which were being ground into unrecognizable junk by Russian tank and antitank gun fire from Komarovka. Dawn found them due west of Dzhurzhentsy. They could hear the noise of heavy fighting coming from the town, Hill 239.0, and the woods to the south, but their own troops were still moving ahead rapidly toward Hill 239.0. By the time they and the troops drew up to the hill the Russians were pouring in artillery and rocket fire from the flanks and had tanks ranged along the woods. All that was left was to turn south.

When Lieb's chief of staff reached the Gniloy Tikich in the midmorning he found several thousand troops there trying to swim across. Some left their weapons on the bank, others tried to throw them across the 50-foot wide river and in most cases failed. While he watched many drowned, and many more collapsed on the opposite shore. Late in the afternoon, after doing what they could to establish some order at the crossing, he and Lieb swam the river and joined the long lines of unarmed, often nearly naked, men trudging up the snowy slope away from the Gniloy Tikich toward Lisyanka.

Stemmermann's chief of staff, who came out with the divisions of the rear guard, observed that all semblance of order disappeared shortly after daylight. By then the Russians had a clear idea of what was going on, and brought the Germans under heavy machine gun, mortar, and artillery fire as soon as they passed west of Komarovka. To escape they took cover in ravines and gullies. Units became completely mixed, and no one thought of anything except to keep under cover and reach safety. Since the fire from the direction of Dzhurzhentsy and Hill 239.0 was the heaviest, except for occasional groups which broke through to northern Lisyanka during the day, almost the entire movement veered south to the bend of the Gniloy Tikich.

In all, 30,000 troops escaped from the pocket. Manstein and the two army commanders were pleased and relieved to have gotten that many out. Even Hitler did no more than grumble briefly about the lost matériel. On the other hand, the psychological state of the men who came out shocked the army group and army commands. The troops of the heavy tank regiment, in constant combat and without a full meal in weeks, were astonished at the good physical condition of the first units from the pocket to reach their line. They were more astonished when both officers and men refused to stay and help their lagging comrades. On 17 February Manstein decided he would have to send all the survivors back into Poland to rest and recuperate. First Panzer Army reported, "It must… be recognized that these troops were encircled since 28 January and, consciously or subconsciously, had the fate of Stalingrad before their eyes." It observed that the "inner substance" was still there, but added, "One must not fail to recognize that only the few soldiers who possess inborn toughness (as opposed to that which might be instilled by military discipline) would be able to withstand such strain more than once."

NIKOPOL AND KRIVOI ROG

When Headquarters, Sixth Army, took control of the former First Panzer Army zone in the lower half of the Great Bend of the Dnepr, it assumed the mission of holding an indefensible front to protect an untenable position—that of Seventeenth Army in the Crimea—and to keep in German hands economic assets which had by then become military liabilities—the iron and manganese mines at Krivoi Rog and Nikopol. (Map 21)

SCHOERNER IN COMMAND ON THE BRIDGEHEAD

To make certain that the most crucial sector of the Sixth Army front would be held no matter what, Hitler had called in General der Gebirgstruppe Ferdinand Schoerner at the end of October 1943 and given him command of the three corps in the loop inside the Dnepr Bend and on the bridgehead. Schoerner was one of the "new" generals, a convinced Nazi whose military reputation thus far was founded on two qualities—energy and determination. He had a knack for cultivating comraderie with the troops, which to some extent concealed a strong tendency toward ruthlessness and severity in his treatment of subordinates. His last command had been XIX Mountain Corps in northern Finland, where he had coined the slogan "The Arctic does not exist" (Arktis ist nicht).

By the turn of the year the chances of Schoerner's talents being brought into play in the manner Hitler had desired were small. North of Sixth Army the Russians had cut in so deeply west of the Dnepr that the army's front was bent in the middle to a right angle. Approximately half the front—that held by Schoerner's three corps—faced southeast. All that was left of the original Dnepr line, it possessed good field fortifications, but behind lay the broad flood plain of the Dnepr, marshy and criss-crossed by watercourses which during that winter hardly ever froze. The exits from the bridgehead were a temporary bridge at the north end east of Nikopol and two single-lane ponton bridges at the extreme south end near Bol'shaya Lepatikha. The other half of the Sixth Army Front, facing north and slightly east, was a tenuous line across the open steppe cut at right angles by numerous gullies and the watercourses of five large rivers. It passed 18 miles north of Krivoi Rog and 30 miles north of Apostolovo Station, the railroad junction where the one railroad still serving the army branched northward and toward Nikopol.

The only all-weather road in the army area was the so-called Through Road IV, which by then lay too close to the front to be of use except locally around Krivoi Rog. The complete absence of any

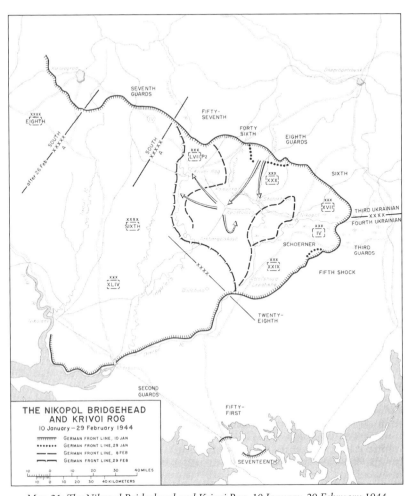

Map 21: The Nikopol Bridgehead and Krivoi Rog, 10 January–29 February 1944.

sort of gravel or suitable stone had prevented even an attempt to lay down hard surfaced roads over the deep, soft clay of the region. In wet weather, when the ground was not frozen—which was most of the time during the winter of 1943-44—the railroad and tracked vehicles were the only dependable means of transportation. The Russians thus merely had to advance the 30 miles to Apostolovo Station to effectively cut off Schoerner and his three corps.

VASILEVSKIY STAGES A TWO-FRONT BATTLE
On the Soviet side the projecting Sixth Army front imposed a drag

on the deep right flank of Third Ukrainian Front and kept Fourth Ukrainian Front from arranging a final reckoning with Seventeenth Army in the Crimea. On the other hand, it offered a first-class opportunity for a double envelopment, and Vasilevskiy was there to exploit it for the Stavka.

When a cold wave in the first week of January firmed up the ground enough for the tanks to get moving, Third Ukrainian Front started the attack on 10 January. Behind a barrage laid down by 220 artillery pieces and as many rocket launchers, 80 tanks pushed south on a four and one-half mile front west of the Buzuluk River. Nine rifle divisions in two waves moved in behind the tanks to exploit the breakthrough, but in one of those tactical fumbles which the Soviet commands still periodically perpetrated, the infantry failed to keep up with the tanks. Three miles behind the front two panzer divisions stopped the tanks and in a few hours destroyed two-thirds of them. Before the end of the day, in spite of efforts by the artillery to blast an opening for the infantry, the Germans closed the front and regained all but a mile or so of the ground they had lost.

During the next three days Malinovskiy committed such masses of infantry that their weight alone pushed the front back five miles. These were five miles Sixth Army could not afford to lose, and the commanding general, Hollidt, decided to take the 24th Panzer Division from the bridgehead for a counterattack; but, before the division could be moved, Fourth Ukrainian Front attacked south of Nikopol at the narrowest point of the bridgehead. Hollidt found himself faced with a choice of sacrificing the five miles in the north or, possibly, losing ground on the bridgehead where a mile or two might be fatal. He decided to do the former, taking, as the army later put it, "the consequences of this two-front battle in which neither front can support the other." On the 16th, having failed to do more than dent the bridgehead, the Russians stopped both there and on the north.

During the next week and a half Sixth Army's chances of withstanding another attack fell sharply. Warm weather turned the ground to soft, soupy mud, and Vasilevskiy took advantage of several days of heavy fog that began on 19 January to move a guards mechanized corps and two guards rifle corps from opposite the bridgehead to the Sixth Army north front, more than doubling the strength there. To disguise the movements Fourth Ukrainian Front feigned heavy traffic toward the Crimea and put dummy tanks in the assembly areas of the units that had pulled out.

Hollidt, astonished that the Russians had not placed more weight there in the first place, was fully aware that next time the fate of the bridgehead would be decided on the north front. To give himself a strong mobile reserve, he decided to take his four panzer divisions out of the line and hold them as a panzer corps behind the north front. On 24 January that still seemed possible, but in the next four days he had to give up, first, an infantry division for the Crimea, then approximately two infantry divisions to Eighth Army, and finally, the 24th Panzer Division, his strongest division, to Eighth Army. In the end, all he could spare for the reserve was the 9th Panzer Division, which was weak in infantry and artillery and down to thirteen tanks, about one-third of its normal complement. After losing the four divisions, Sixth Army had left 20 divisions with average front-line strengths of 2,500 men. Against this force the Third and Fourth Ukrainian Fronts could throw 51 rifle divisions, half of them in full fighting trim, 2 mechanized corps, 2 tank corps, and half a dozen tank brigades.

On the morning of 30 January, after laying down 30,000 artillery rounds on the German front in an hour, Third Ukrainian Front launched a massive infantry assault against a 4-mile stretch of the XXX Corps front west of the Buzuluk River. This time the tanks stayed behind, waiting for the infantry to open a gap, but the German artillery laid down a barrage of its own that hit the infantry before they could jump off and threw them so completely off balance that the attack dissolved into a series of uncoordinated skirmishes.

The next day, leading off with heavier artillery fire than the day before, Malinovskiy tried again, giving the infantry 130 tanks plus an estimated 300 aircraft in support. The thrust carried south two and one half miles on a 7-mile front, still without breaching the XXX Corps line. Hollidt took the 23d Panzer Division out of the front farther west. With it, the 9th Panzer Division, and an infantry division from the bridgehead, he intended to counterattack; meanwhile, Fourth Ukrainian Front had pushed a deep wedge into the south end of the bridgehead toward Bol'shaya Lepatikha. Once again, except for the two weak panzer divisions, all of his strength on both fronts was tied down. At the end of the day he informed Army Group South that if the Russians broke through in the north Sixth Army would be helpless. He applied for permission to evacuate the bridgehead and go back to the line of the Kamenka River.

It was already almost too late. On 1 February Soviet tanks carrying infantry penetrated the XXX Corps line in several places where the defending German tanks and assault guns had fired their last ammunition. By nightfall the Russians had opened a 6-mile gap in the front west of the Buzuluk. In the mud, which was by then knee-deep, they had superior mobility. Wide tracks gave their tanks some buoyancy, and their powerful American-built trucks and half-tracks, though slowed down, could negotiate all but the worst stretches. On the other end of the technological spectrum, they had the small, high-riding, horse-drawn panje wagons. The Germans were handicapped in particular by their trucks, two-wheel drive commercial types that could not cope with the mud. Their prime movers were good but too few. Most of the time their tanks kept moving, though just barely. The self-propelled assault guns performed better.

On 2 February, while the 23d and 9th Panzer Divisions plowed through the mud in a futile attempt at a flank attack, Eighth Guards Army took Sholokhovo and a mechanized corps veered west and crossed the Kamenka. At day's end the Russians stood five miles north of the vital railroad to Nikopol, ten miles north of the Dnepr, and had a solid foothold in the proposed Kamenka line. At 1845 Zeitzler called Kleist at Army Group A and told him to take over Sixth Army immediately. Hitler had approved the army's going back to the Kamenka. He wanted a small bridgehead held around Bol'shaya Lepatikha, and he expected that by shortening its line the army would be able to spare two divisions. One was to go to the Crimea and the other to the lower Dnepr. To make sure these divisions would go where he wanted them was the reason he had taken Sixth Army out of Manstein's command.

RETREAT FROM THE BRIDGEHEAD

Sixth Army ordered Schoerner to begin drawing in the bridgehead front on 4 February. Fortunately two divisions were already standing by east of Nikopol. On the 3d the army managed to get through a trainload of ammunition on the railroad. For two more days the rolling stock could be shuttled to pick up the troops coming across the Dnepr and carry them out to the Buzuluk River, where they threw up a screening line facing west. Schoerner made the painful but unavoidable decision to destroy the heavy equipment, except horse-drawn artillery and tracked vehicles, where it stood. As a result, the troops were gotten out more quickly and in better condition than if they had wasted energy on an almost certainly futile effort to manhandle trucks and guns through the mud.

West of the Dnepr XXX Corps had lost all of its trucks and had broken up into small groups, some platoon size, most smaller. Nobody from the commanding general down had anything he could not wear or carry, and many of the soldiers had lost their boots in the mud. Off the corps' right flank, 9th Panzer Division made its way into Kamenka, which it held long enough to slow somewhat the Soviet thrust toward Apostolovo.

On his side Malinovskiy, as his supply lines lengthened, was having trouble with the mud too, trouble he compounded by tactical extravagance. On the 4th the forward units of Eighth Guards Army reached Apostolovo. During the next few days Forty-sixth Army moved in and began to attempt a sweep west of Apostolovo to envelop Krivoi Rog from the south. At the same time, Eighth Guards Army, instead of going the ten miles from Sholokhovo to the Dnepr, which would have cut off at least one of Schoerner's corps completely, struck out from the vicinity of Apostolovo toward the lower tip of the bridgehead twenty-five miles to the south.

By 4 February Schoerner had two divisions across the Dnepr and ready to block the Russians south of Sholokhovo. Hollidt then faced the choice of merely funneling the troops from the inside of the Dnepr Bend and the northern half of the bridgehead through the corridor below Sholokhovo or attempting to push northwestward from the foothold on the lower Kamenka River toward XXX Corps right flank, which was still on the Kamenka north of Apostolovo. The first, he concluded, would mean using up a considerable part of the strength of two panzer divisions, the 9th and 24th (ordered back to the army on the 4th), to open an escape route in the south for Schoerner's units. Tactically it would accomplish nothing more. The second would get Schoerner's divisions out and offer a chance to regain the Kamenka River line. The plan became more attractive during the next few days as Schoerner's movements went ahead smoothly and the Russian effort dispersed.

By 5 February the 9th Panzer Division, after three days' heavy fighting at Kamenka and Apostolovo, was just about burned out. Hollidt reported that Schoerner could not make the breakout alone and proposed giving up the small bridgehead east of Bol'shaya Lepatikha to get three divisions for an attack from the south. Kleist forwarded the proposal to the OKH and was told that Hitler still wanted the small bridgehead held but gave the army group authority to decide whether or not the divisions should be taken out. The next morning Kleist told Hollidt to evacuate the Bol'shaya Lepatikha bridgehead.

On 7 February the last German troops east of Nikopol crossed the Dnepr, blowing up the bridge behind them. The next day one of Schoerner's corps, IV Corps, attacked west while XXVII Corps, withdrawing out of the Dnepr Bend, screened its rear. For three days IV Corps gained ground. On the 10th the 9th Panzer Division and part of the 24th Panzer Division pushed into the open space south of Apostolovo where they smashed a guards rifle corps. Meanwhile, two of the divisions from the Bol'shaya Lepatikha bridgehead had fanned out along the west bank of the Dnepr and the other was moving north into the area south of Apostolovo.

But the mud and the Russians were too much. After IV Corps made no progress at all on the 11th, the army called a halt, ordering the 9th and 24th Panzer Divisions to turn east and Schoerner to turn south, skirt the southern edge of the Russian advance, and so establish contact with each other. On the night of the 12th Kleist informed the OKH that Sixth Army could patch together a front for the time being but could not hold it. The Russians could strike south to the lower Dnepr and north past Krivoi Rog any time they chose. He proposed taking Army Group A and the right flank of Army Group South back to the line of the Ingul and lower Bug Rivers as, he implied, a first step toward getting both southern army groups back to the next defensible line, that of the Bug.

KRIVOI ROG—THE INGULETS

In the second half of February a peculiar sort of semiparalysis settled on the entire German southern flank. On the 18th Kleist, turning again to the OKH, advised letting Army Group A and most of Army Group South withdraw to the Bug River. To make the prospect "more appetizing" for Hitler, he suggested holding several large bridgeheads from which offensives could be launched later to retake some of the lost ground. The withdrawal to the Bug was not new; Manstein had suggested it before and so had Kleist. Both Manstein and Zeitzler seconded the proposal. Zeitzler seemed to think the withdrawal was inevitable—but nothing happened.

On the 19th, Sixth Army closed the last gap in its front southwest of Apostolovo. The day before, Schoerner had departed to take up a new assignment as Chief of the National Socialist Leadership Corps, the organization for political indoctrination in the Army. Two days later, on the 21st, the Russians broke into the outer defenses of Krivoi Rog. As at Nikopol, the mines had been destroyed, the able-bodied population evacuated, and the movable goods, except for 100,000 tons of mined iron ore, hauled away. To avoid a costly house-to-house battle, Kleist made Sixth Army withdraw behind the city. After that, reluctant as always, Hitler agreed to let Sixth Army go behind the Ingulets River as far south as Arkhangelskoye, but he insisted that the army stay on the Dnepr below Dudchino. The Dnepr afforded a better natural defense line than the meandering Ingulets; on the other hand, by keeping the army there, Hitler again created a large bulge to the east.

In the meantime new trouble loomed on the left flank, where the Sixth Army's left corps and Eighth Army's right corps held a shallow bulge between Kirovograd and Krivoi Rog. Konev had deployed strong forces off the Eighth Army right flank and appeared ready to strike to the southwest at any moment. Fully occupied on his left flank, Manstein transferred the Eighth Army's right flank corps to Army Group A.

At the end of the month the attack had not started, Sixth Army was going back to the Ingulets by stages, and in the south the front was still on the Dnepr, where drifting ice kept the Russians from ferrying troops across and gave the Germans time to catch their breath. In Berchtesgaden Hitler conferred with Antonescu, and although the Rumanian leader argued that in spite of the political disadvantages the Crimea ought to be evacuated for military reasons, Hitler remained more than ever convinced the peninsula had to be held.

DUBNO-LUTSK-KOVEL'

Manstein's 6 January order to the First Panzer and Fourth Panzer Armies was concerned with two enemy thrusts, one to the south, toward Zhmerinka, between the flanks of the two armies and the other against the Fourth Panzer Army north flank toward Rovno and Shepetovka. (Map 22) Since the first had made greater progress and was the more dangerous, he had told the armies to concentrate against it. On the north, he had instructed LIX Corps to continue covering the Fourth Panzer Army flank, using its main force to hold the Russians away from Shepetovka and a smaller one to screen Rovno.

LIX Corps, in the retreat from Korosten, had lost Novograd Volynskiy, giving the Russians access to two main roads, one running due west to Rovno, the other southwest to Shepetovka. In the heavily wooded, swampy terrain on the edge of the Pripyat Marshes roads were important. Since the distance to Shepetovka was shorter and the weight of the Soviet attack was being directed southwest rather than west, Fourth Panzer Army had already ordered the corps to shift its headquarters there and concentrate on holding open the railroad. This left only Corps Detachment C (about the strength of an infantry division) and the 454th Security Division between the Russians and Rovno, where the road and railroad forked northwestward to Kovel' and Lublin and southwestward to Dubno, Brody, and L'vov. The LIX Corps main force, two infantry divisions, was isolated too, but in falling back to Shepetovka it drew closer to the center of the Fourth Panzer Army front. Against LIX Corps, Sixtieth Army was advancing

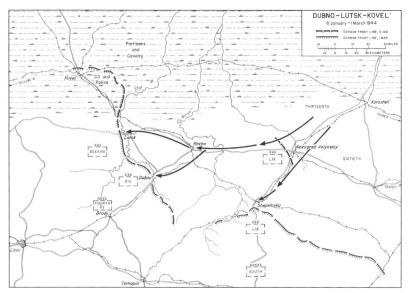

Map 22: Dubno-Lutsk-Kovel', 6 January-1 March 1944.

toward Shepetovka and Thirteenth Army was turning west toward Rovno.

Shepetovka and Rovno were the last German handholds on the main railroad running west of Kiev. If they were lost, the enemy would have complete control of a railroad into the exposed flank of Army Group South. Rovno could be used as a staging area for operations north toward Lublin or, more profitably, southwest toward L'vov. From Rovno to L'vov and the main supply artery of Army Group South the distance was 110 miles, from Shepetovka to Ternopol it was 80 miles. Another 30 to 50 miles would take the Russians across the Dnestr and to the foothills of the Carpathians.

Manstein, as sensitive as ever to the danger on his left flank, could do nothing as long as Hitler insisted on keeping Army Group A and the right flank of Army Group South echeloned east and exposed to simultaneous attacks in half a dozen places. On 14 January Manstein instructed Fourth Panzer Army to shift the Headquarters, XIII Corps, north to take command of Corps Detachment C and of the 454th Security Division, which were still trying to hold a front on the Goryn River twenty miles east of Rovno. Farther north Soviet cavalry supported by partisan bands was already penetrating the outlying forests and swamps of the Pripyat Marshes in the direction of Kovel' and Lutsk. In the woods the Germans had found lukewarm allies in the Ukrainian nationalist partisans, who hated Russians more than they did Germans but whose value from the German point of view was greatly reduced by the lack of a unified command and a deplorable inclination to kill all Poles and Russians, including those in the German service.

XIII Corps was given the missions of holding Rovno and keeping the Russians away from the roads and railroads west of the city, even though no one really believed that the corps could do either. On 21 January the commanding general reported that he could not prevent the Russians' infiltrating through the forests north of Rovno, and for his troops to push them back out was entirely out of the question. At the end of the month he predicted that Rovno would be lost in a matter of days. Two Soviet cavalry corps, which could only be tracked by air, were moving through the woods behind the city and would soon be in position to threaten Lutsk and Kovel'. On 2 February the Russians took Rovno, and on the same day their cavalry drove the German garrison out of Lutsk forty miles to the west.

During the next two weeks the Army Group South left flank came close to dissolving completely. To escape encirclement and protect L'vov, the main body of XIII Corps had to fall back to Dubno. In the north Soviet cavalry ranged at will west of Lutsk and almost to the outskirts of Kovel'. Dubno was half encircled while XIII Corps was still going back toward it, and Hitler demanded that the name of the officer entrusted with the defense of the city be reported directly to him. The officer who had been in command in Rovno he called to Fuehrer headquarters and ordered to face a court-martial.

The army, the army group, and the OKH had recognized before the end of January that to evade a complete disaster they would have to commit several more divisions on the flank, but these divisions were at first nowhere to be found. In the first week of February all the army could supply was the 7th Panzer Division, a kampfgruppe. By 9 February a Soviet guards cavalry corps had pushed west of Dubno and appeared to be getting ready to attack the city from the rear. The next day Manstein, who had hoped to wait until the fighting around the Cherkassy pocket ended, decided he dared wait no longer and began shifting reinforcements to the flank. He gave XIII Corps the 340th Infantry Division (three infantry battalions and two of artillery) and began assembling under the Headquarters, XXXXVIII Panzer Corps, the 7th and 8th Panzer Divisions and two reinforced territorial regiments from Poland for an attack north and east toward the Styr River and Kovel'.

XXXXVIII Panzer Corps was ready west of Dubno shortly after the middle of the month, but heavy, drifting snow kept it from going into action until 22 February. The attack went well, reaching Lutsk and the Styr River on both sides of the city by the 27th. From there the corps turned north, and by the end of the month it had established a line of strongpoints from Kovel' to the XIII Corps left flank west of Dubno.

For the first time in months the gap on the extreme left flank of Army Group South was closed. The effort, however, had left Fourth Panzer Army without the strength to patch a 30-mile gap between the XIII and LIX Corps flanks. Since midmonth the Russians had been building up their strength in the vicinity of Shepetovka, on LIX Corps' left, and on the 26th they began moving fresh troops into the trenches. On 2 March Manstein concluded that they would strike toward Ternopol before the spring thaw set in.

CHAPTER XII

Offensives on Both Flanks—
the North Flank

OPERATION BLAU

During the two years after the first Soviet winter offensive, Army Group North had by comparison with the other army groups occupied an almost stationary front. On the right Sixteenth Army had given up some ground but had kept its line anchored firmly on Lake Ilmen in the north. Below the lake the old Russian towns, Staraya Russa and Kholm, had lain directly in the front since the summer of 1941. Even the breakthrough at Nevel in October 1943 was more significant as a portent of a possible drive to outflank the army group in the south than for the loss of ground it involved. On the left Eighteenth Army had fought three battles south of Lake Ladoga to keep Leningrad under siege and had held the Russians to a token gain of a few miles along the lake shore. From the Volkhov River to the Gulf of Finland the front was reminiscent of World War I—a lacework of trenches and shell holes, the result of two and a half years' fighting in which the gains and losses on both sides could be measured in yards. Ranged along the coast west of the city, the heavy siege artillery transferred north in the summer of 1942 after Sevastopol could still bring all of Leningrad except the northeastern suburbs under fire.

For more than a year, however, the relative stability of the front had not reflected the actual state of the army group. In September and October 1943 Kuechler had had to give up three infantry divisions and the 250th Spanish "Blue" Division, at the same time taking over some sixty miles of inadequately manned front from Army Group Center. As replacements he had received three recently formed SS divisions with mostly non-German personnel and the Spanish Legion, the 1,000 men Franco had substituted for the Blue Division, many of them Loyalists who were looking for a chance to desert to the Russians.

By December the line around the Oranienbaum pocket was being held by two Air Force field divisions and two of the SS divisions, and, except for the critical sectors close to Leningrad and north of Nevel, the rest of the front was liberally sprinkled with Air Force field divisions and SS units newly recruited in the Baltic States. After the Nevel breakthrough the army group had weakened its left flank and center to strengthen the right. Tactically the army group's position had become very similar to that of Army Group South: it was forced to split its effort between the two extreme flanks, holding the one (Oranienbaum-Leningrad) mostly for political and prestige reasons and the other to stave off what could become a military disaster.

In the second week of September 1943 Army Group North had begun work on the PANTHER position, its share of the East Wall. The north half of the PANTHER position was laid behind natural obstacles, the Narva River, Lake Peipus, and Lake Pskov. The south half was not so favorably situated. It had to be stretched east somewhat to cover two major road and rail centers, Pskov and Ostrov, and the tie-in to Army Group Center had to be moved west after the Nevel breakthrough. Nevertheless, when it was occupied it would reduce the army group frontage by 25 percent, and, unlike most of the East Wall, it had by late 1943 actually begun to take on the appearance of a fortified line. A 50,000-man construction force had improved the communications lines back to Riga and Dvinsk and had built 6,000 bunkers, 800 of them concrete, laid 125 miles of barbed wire entanglements, and dug 25 miles each of trenches and tank traps. During November and December building material rolled in at a rate of over 100 carloads a day.

In September the army group staff had begun detailed planning for Operation BLAU, the withdrawal to the PANTHER position. The staff estimated that the million tons of grain and potatoes, half a million cattle and sheep, and military supplies and other material, including telephone wire and railroad track to be moved behind the PANTHER line, would amount to 4,000 trainloads. The withdrawal itself would be facilitated by the network of alternate positions that in the preceding two years had been built as far back as the Luga River. The 900,000 civilians living in the evacuation zone, particularly the men who could, if they were left behind, be drafted into the Soviet Army, raised problems. The first attempts, in early October, to march the civilians out in the customary treks produced so much confusion, misery, and hostility that Kuechler ordered the rear area commands to adopt less onerous methods. Thereafter they singled out the adults who would be useful to the Soviet Union as workers or soldiers and evacuated most of them by train. During the last three months of the year the shipments of goods and people went ahead while the armies worked at getting their artillery and heavy equipment, much of which was sited in permanent emplacements, ready to be moved. At the end of the year, having transported 250,000 civilians into Latvia and Lithuania, the army group could not find quarters for any more and called a halt to that part of the evacuation.

STANDING BY

The army group staff believed that logically BLAU should begin in mid-January and be completed shortly before the spring thaw, in about the same fashion as Army Group Center had executed BUEFFEL the year before, but on 22 December the chief of staff told the armies that Hitler would probably not order BLAU unless another

Soviet offensive forced him to. At the moment, Hitler's opinion was that the Russians had lost so many men in the fighting in the Ukraine that they might not try another big offensive anywhere before the spring of 1944.

Toward the end of the month it appeared, in fact, that Hitler might be right. The bulge on the Army Group North right flank was worrisome, but the Stavka had shifted the weight of the offensive to Vitebsk, for the time being at least. In the Oranienbaum pocket and around Leningrad the Leningrad and Volkhov Fronts had been ready to attack since November, but with the trouble at Nevel out of the way the army group was less concerned than it had been. Intelligence reports from Eighteenth Army indicated that the units in the Oranienbaum pocket, in particular, had been strengthened; and boat traffic between Leningrad and Oranienbaum had been usually heavy during the fall, continuing until some boats were trapped in ice. On the other hand, almost no new units had appeared, and Leningrad Front seemed to be depending for its reinforcements on the Leningrad population. While an offensive sometime in January appeared a near certainty, the longer Eighteenth Army's intelligence officers looked the closer they came to convincing themselves it would be cut in the modest pattern of the three earlier offensives around Leningrad.

On 29 December the OKH ordered Kuechler to transfer to Army Group South one of his best divisions, the 1st Infantry Division which Eighteenth Army was depending on to backstop some of its less reliable units in the Oranienbaum-Leningrad sector. When Kuechler called to protest, Zeitzler told him he would not need the division; Hitler intended to execute Operation BLAU after all and would tell him so personally the next day. During the noon conference in the Fuehrer headquarters on 30 December, Kuechler, expecting to receive his orders, reported on the state of the PANTHER position and the time he would need to complete BLAU. In passing, he remarked that he had talked to Generaloberst Georg Lindemann, Commanding General, Eighteenth Army, who "naturally" had asked for his army to stay where it was even though he lost 1st Infantry Division. To a question from Hitler, Kuechler replied that the Eighteenth Army front was well fortified, almost too well, in fact, since the army did not have enough troops to man it completely. Hitler then terminated the conference without mentioning Operation BLAU.

Kuechler did not fully realize what had happened until the next day, after an order had come in to transfer another good division to Army Group South. Zeitzler told the army group chief of staff that Hitler had begun to falter in his decision as soon as Kuechler made the remark about Lindemann's wanting to keep his army where it was. He thought it would take at least a week to talk Hitler around again. By day's end the chief of staff had a memorandum marshaling the arguments for BLAU ready for Kuechler to sign, but that was scarcely enough. Lindemann would have to be persuaded to reverse himself, since in such instances if in almost no others Hitler always took the word of the man on the spot.

On 4 January—by then a third division was on its way to Army

Group South—Kuechler went to Eighteenth Army headquarters and, citing the necessity to husband the army group's forces, almost pleaded with Lindemann to reconsider. Lindemann replied that his corps, division, and troop commanders in the most threatened sectors were confident they could weather the attack. After that, none of the army group's arguments counted for much. Hitler told Zeitzler he was only doing what Kuechler wanted. Nor could Kuechler and his staff draw any comfort from the knowledge that Lindemann was probably motivated mainly by a desire to draw attention to himself—as a senior army commander he had never had so good an opportunity to show what he could do directly under the eyes of the Fuehrer. No less disquieting for the army group was the knowledge that it was committed to repeating an error which had already been made too often in the Ukraine. To the operations chief at OKH the chief of staff said the army group was marching to disaster with its eyes open, putting forces into positions which in the long run could not be held.

LENINGRAD LIBERATED

On 14 January 1944 the operation began. (Map 23) Leningrad Front, General Polkovnik L. A. Govorov commanding, mounted the main effort. Second Shock Army drove east out of the Oranienbaum pocket while Forty-second Army attempted to push west on the front below Leningrad. Against Forty-second Army, the stronger of the two, the corps artillery of L Corps reacted fast, laying down a well-placed barrage that stopped the attack before it got started. Second Shock Army did better; the 10th Air Force Field Division began to crumble the moment it was hit.

Not a real surprise but, still, only half expected, were the strong thrusts that General Polkovnik Kirill A. Meretskov's Volkhov Front launched the same day north and south of Novgorod on Eighteenth Army's right flank. Novgorod had been considered a danger point, but the army had not been convinced that the Leningrad and Volkhov Fronts would have the strength to attempt simultaneous offensives on a major scale. Lindemann, on 10 January, had rated the build-ups—in the Oranienbaum pocket, southwest of Leningrad, and east of

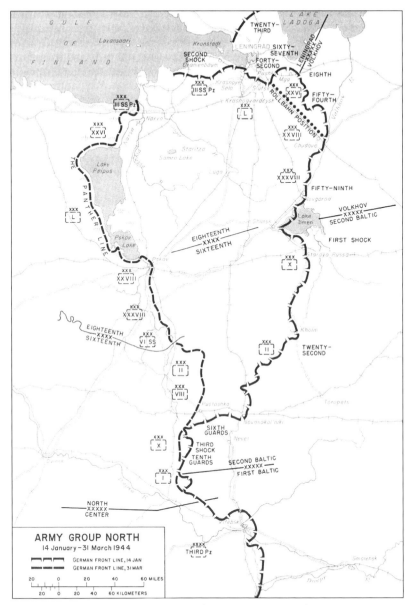

Map 23: Army Group North, 14 January-31 March 1944

Novgorod—as relatively modest, particularly in terms of reserves. He had predicted that without more reserves the thrusts could not go very deep and that the attacks in the Oranienbaum-Leningrad sector and at Novgorod would "very likely" be staggered. In fact, the Leningrad and Volkhov Fronts had Eighteenth Army outnumbered by at least 3:1 in divisions (55 rifle divisions, 9 rifle brigades, and 8 tank brigades to 20 German divisions), 3:1 in artillery, and 6:1 in tanks, self-propelled artillery, and aircraft.

The Soviet commands had chosen exactly the two places in which Eighteenth Army had the least room to maneuver. The loop of the front separating the Oranienbaum pocket from Leningrad was only twenty miles wide at its base. On the Eighteenth Army right flank an envelopment five to ten miles deep was enough to chop out Novgorod and break the tie-in to Lake Ilmen. The danger was, as Zeitzler warned at the end of the day, that minor slip-ups could have consequences similar to the Nevel debacle.

During the second and third days the battle seemed to be going about as the Germans hoped it would. Neither Govorov nor Meretskov put in any new units, which seemed to indicate that they were operating without much in the way of reserves, and it appeared that Leningrad Front did not intend to do more than open the Oranienbaum pocket. On 16 January Kuechler told his army commanders that the Russians had committed all their forces, and Army Group North could win the battle by taking some risks in the quiet sectors.

The next day his optimism started to fade. Lindemann had put in his entire reserve, the 61st Infantry Division, to stiffen the 10th Air Force Field Division, but it was barely managing to stave off a complete rupture. Before noon the army group informed the OKH that the fighting around Leningrad was taking a turn for the worse. Eighteenth Army would have to begin dismantling the siege artillery during the night, and if the army group wanted to see the battle through it would have to withdraw below Lake Ladoga to the ROLLBAHN position along the Leningrad-Chudovo road to shorten the front and gain two divisions. The army group had originally built the ROLLBAHN to provide just such insurance. In the afternoon the answer came from Hitler: he neither approved nor disapproved but thought it would be better to give up the hold on the Gulf of Finland and take back the front between Leningrad and Oranienbaum. Kuechler protested that to do that would give the Russians the victory and an opportunity to turn south with their strength intact.

On the morning of the 18th Lindemann reported that the fronts east of Oranienbaum and west of Leningrad were collapsing. The same was happening at Novgorod where the encirclement was nearly complete, and the few extra battalions the army had been able to throw in would not even be enough to hold open an escape route much longer. After seeing for himself how near complete exhaustion the troops at the front were, Kuechler asked and was denied permission to withdraw to the ROLLBAHN. In the afternoon Forty-second Army's spearhead drove into Krasnoye Selo, the former summer residence of the Czars, and cut the two main roads to the north. After that, Kuechler decided he had no choice but to take back the two divisions on the coast before they were completely cut off. He informed the OKH that he intended to give the order at the end of the day whether he had received permission by then or not. At the midnight situation conference Hitler approved, after Zeitzler told him the order had already been given.

WITHDRAWAL TO THE ROLLBAHN

On 19 January the first stage, which plainly was only the prelude to the battle, ended. The difficult task was to get Hitler to accept the consequences. Kuechler's order had come too late to save the divisions on the coast; some elements escaped, others were trapped and destroyed as the Russians swept in from the east and west. Second Shock and Forty-second Armies then joined forces, and the appearance of several fresh divisions demonstrated that they had more than adequate reserves. At Novgorod eight Soviet divisions encircled five German battalions. Their one hope for escape was to elude the Russians in the swamps west of the city.

Shortly after nightfall, after Zeitzler had argued unsuccessfully for half an hour, Kuechler called Hitler and begged him to give the troops at Novgorod what would certainly be their last chance. Suddenly dropping the argument he had clung to stubbornly throughout the day, that Novgorod could not be given up because of its "extraordinary symbolic significance," Hitler agreed. On the subject of the ROLLBAHN, however, he merely read Kuechler a short lecture on the demoralizing effects of voluntary withdrawals. Fifteen minutes later he called back to give permission for that too. At midnight he changed

Searching for mines outside damaged Tsarskoye Selo Palace, Pushkin.

his mind about the ROLLBAHN, but Zeitzler told him the orders had gone out to the divisions and could not be recalled.

Hitler had also tried to extract from Zeitzler and Kuechler guarantees that the ROLLBAHN position would be held. On the 10th Kuechler, appraising the situation, declared that the two recent tactical setbacks, at Novgorod and southwest of Leningrad, had resulted from lack of reserves and an overtaut front. The same conditions still existed. The withdrawal to the ROLLBAHN would free three divisions, two to go into the front below Leningrad, the other west of Novgorod. With that, the army group would have exhausted its resources for creating reserves. The three divisions would be used up in a short time, and an operational breakthrough could then be expected. He recommended that the pullback to the ROLLBAHN be made the first step in a continuous withdrawal to the PANTHER position, pointing out that the army group was already so weakened that it would have just enough troops to man the front when it reached there.

Less than a day passed before Kuechler's forecast began to come true. On 21 January Forty-second Army attacked toward Krasnogvardeysk, the junction of the main rail lines and roads coming from the south and west. L Corps had not had time to sort out its battered units and start setting up a front.

That night Kuechler flew to Fuehrer headquarters where the next morning, shortly before his interview with Hitler, word reached him that Eighteenth Army could not hold Krasnogvardeysk unless it gave up Pushkin and Slutsk, also important junctions but farther north. Hitler was deaf to all his proposals. The Fuehrer brushed off everything said concerning Pushkin and Slutsk, the PANTHER position, and possible new threats on the army group right flank with a statement that Army Group North was spoiled; it had not had a crisis for more than a year and, consequently, did not know what one was. "I am against all withdrawals," he went on. "We will have crises wherever we are. There is no guarantee we will not be broken through on the PANTHER. If we go back voluntarily he [the Russians] will not get there with only half his forces. He must bleed himself white on the way. The battle must be fought as far as possible from the German border." When Kuechler objected that the PANTHER position could not be held if the army group was too weak to fight when it got there, Hitler blamed all the gaps in the front on the egoism of the army groups and insisted that every square yard of ground be sold at the highest possible price in Russian blood. Finally, demanding that the ROLLBAHN be held, he dismissed the field marshal. Later Zeitzler said the time had been bad and Kuechler should try again in a few days; Hitler was worried about the landing that day by Allied troops at Anzio south of Rome and had not listened to what was said.

Meanwhile, Eighteenth Army was beginning to disintegrate. Fighting in mud and water, the troops were exhausted. Govorov and Meretskov, on the other hand, had managed, since the warm weather set in at midmonth, to give their divisions a day out of every three or four to rest and dry out. On the morning of 23 January, Lindemann gave the order to evacuate Pushkin and Slutsk and reported to the OKH that it could either accept his decision or send a general to replace him. During the day the army completed the withdrawal to the ROLLBAHN, which the Russians had already penetrated in several places.

KUECHLER'S DILEMMA

On the 24th at Eighteenth Army headquarters Kuechler accused Lindemann of having submitted false estimates of Soviet reserves at the end of December. Lindemann admitted "mistakes" had been made. The belated revision of the army's past intelligence estimates was swiftly buried, however, under waves of bad news from the front. In the morning the Russians entered the outskirts of Krasnogvardeysk and rammed through to the bend of the Luga River southeast of Luga. The divisions in the ROLLBAHN position tried to patch the front by throwing in their rear echelon troops. At the end of the day Lindemann reported that his right flank had lost contact with Sixteenth Army and Krasnogvardeysk would fall within twenty-four hours.

Because losing Krasnogvardeysk would badly weaken the supply lines of the corps farther east, the army group asked to go back at least to the Luga River. In the evening Zeitzler replied that Hitler's orders were to hold the corner posts and make the troops fight to the last. Since there was nothing else to do for the time being, he advised the army group command to be "a little ruthless" for a while.

On 27 January, Kuechler and the other army group and army commanders on the Eastern Front attended a National Socialist Leadership Conference at Koenigsberg. Hitler addressed the generals on the subject of faith as a guarantee of victory. He called for a strengthening of faith in himself, in the National Socialist philosophy, and in the ultimate victory and suggested that the generals' faith needed strengthening as much as anyone else's. During one of the interludes, in a private talk with Hitler, Kuechler repeated a situation estimate he had sent in the day before: the Leningrad and Volkhov Fronts were employing four strong attack forces to cut Eighteenth Army to pieces; they were going toward Narva from the east and toward Luga from the north and east; if the attack from the east carried through Luga it would cut the communications lines of six of Lindemann's eight corps. Hitler responded by prohibiting all voluntary withdrawals and reserving all decisions to withdraw to himself. When Kuechler remarked, probably with the subject of the day's meeting in mind, that Eighteenth Army had suffered 40,000 casualties and the troops had fought as hard as could be expected, Hitler replied that the latter statement was "not quite" true. He had heard the army group was not fighting everywhere with as much determination as it might.

That interview destroyed Kuechler as an effective army group commander. When he returned to his headquarters he still seemed, as his chief of staff later put it, to realize that all he could do was retreat, but all he could talk about was showing more determination and attacking—with what, nobody knew. On the 28th the chief of staff, Generalleutnant Eberhard Kinzel, took matters into his own hands and told the Chief of Staff, Eighteenth Army, that the time had come. An order to retreat must be issued, but the army group was forbidden to do that. The army would, therefore, have to act as if it had been given, issuing its own implementing orders orally rather than in writing. He would see to it that the army was covered "in the General Staff channel." The next day Kinzel prevailed on Kuechler at least to submit a report pointing out to Hitler that Eighteenth Army was split into three parts and could not hold any kind of a front forward of the Luga River.

On the 30th Kuechler went to Fuehrer headquarters where Hitler finally approved a retreat to the Luga River but directed that the front then be held, contact with Sixteenth Army regained, and all gaps in the front closed. When Kuechler passed this along to his operations officer the latter protested to the Operations Branch, OKH, that it was impossible to execute; one of the gaps was thirty miles wide, and at Staritza northwest of Luga the Russians were already across the Luga River. Later Zeitzler agreed to tell Hitler that the Luga line could not be held. In the meantime Kuechler had been told to report back to the Fuehrer headquarters on 31 January.

MODEL TAKES COMMAND

At the noon conference the next day Hitler informed Kuechler he was relieved of his command. Model, who had been waiting to replace Manstein, was given temporary command of the army group. Reacting quickly as always, Model telegraphed ahead, "Not a single step backward will be taken without my express permission. I am flying to Eighteenth Army this afternoon. Tell General Lindemann that I beg his old trust in me. We have worked together before."

During the last days of January the Eighteenth Army's attrition rate had spiraled steeply. On 27 January the army north front had lain about ten miles north of the line Narva-Chudovo over most of its length and forty miles northeast of Narva in its western quarter. By the 31st it had been pushed back nearly to the Narva River in the west and slightly below the Narva-Chudovo line in the east, by itself not a surprising loss of ground; but in the interval the front had virtually dissolved. On the situation maps of the 27th it had still appeared as a distinguishable, continuous line, albeit with several large gaps. By the 31st all that was left was a random scattering of dots where battalions and companies still held a mile or two of front. The only two divisions still worthy of the name were the 12th Panzer Division, which had come in during the last week in the month, and the 58th Infantry Division, moving in from the south by train. On 29 January the army group reported that as of the 10th Eighteenth Army had had an infantry combat strength of 57,936 men; it had lost since then 35,000 wounded and 14,000 killed and now had, including new arrivals, an infantry strength of 17,000.

Model had never had a greater opportunity to display his talent as an improvisor, and he took it with a flamboyant zest which, though it did not change the tactical situation, quickly dispelled the sense of hopelessness and frustration that had been hanging over the army group. He also had the advantage of Hitler's tendency to give new appointees, particularly when they were also his favorites, greater latitude, at least temporarily, than he had allowed their predecessors.

Model's first moves were as much psychological as military. To dissipate what he called the PANTHER psychosis he forbade all references to the PANTHER position and abolished the designation. Past experience had shown that in times of adversity, named lines, particularly when the names suggested strength, had a powerful attraction for both troops and commands. On the other hand, the state of Eighteenth Army being what it was, Model could not attempt to enforce his original "no step backward" order. Instead, he introduced something new, the Schild und Schwert (shield and sword) theory, the central idea of which was that withdrawals were tolerable if one intended later to strike back in the same or a different direction in a

Civilians in Leningrad after the siege.

kind of parry and thrust sequence. The theory was apparently Hitler's latest brain child, a remedy for—as he viewed it—the disease of falling back to gain troops to build a new defense line which in a short time would itself prove too weak to be held. That Model placed overly much faith in the theory may be doubted. He was enough of a realist to know that while the withdrawal was usually possible the counter-thrust was not. On the other hand, he was also well enough acquainted with Hitler to know that it was always advantageous to make a retreat look like the first stage of an advance.

SCHILD UND SCHWERT

Model applied the Schild und Schwert theory in his first directive to Eighteenth Army issued on 1 February. He ordered Lindemann to take his main force back to a short line north and east of Luga. After that was accomplished and the 12th Panzer Division had finished closing the gap to Sixteenth Army, as had been directed before the change in command, the 12th Panzer and the 58th Infantry Divisions plus as many more divisions as could be spared from the short line would be shifted west of Luga for a thrust along the Luga River to establish contact with the two corps on the Narva. The first part of the directive gave the army a chance to reduce its frontage by almost two-thirds, which was necessary, the second envisaged a gain of enough strength—which was highly doubtful—to open a counteroffensive and extend the front fifty miles to the west.

To apply the Schild und Schwert theory on the Eighteenth Army left flank was impossible. LIV Corps and III SS Panzer Corps, both under the command of General der Infanterie Otto Sponheimer, the Commanding General, LIV Corps, had fallen back along the Baltic coast from the Oranienbaum pocket. After 28 January they had been thrown back to the Luga River and then to the Narva River, the northern terminus of the PANTHER position. They could go no farther without endangering the entire PANTHER line and the important shale oil refineries near the coast about twenty miles west of the river.

On 2 February, when Model inspected Sponheimer's front, his divisions were crossing to the west bank of the river and pulling back into a small bridgehead around the city of Narva. South of Narva the Russians were probing across the river and before the end of the day had a small bridgehead of their own. Elements of the Panzer Grenadier Division Feldherrnhalle, coming from Army Group Center, and a regiment of the 58th Infantry Division were arriving to strengthen the front below Narva.

Everywhere Model heard the same complaint: the troops were worn out; and everywhere he gave the same order: they would have to see the battle through. The help the army group could give was small enough: an infantry adviser for III SS Panzer Corps; an artillery expert to match the skilled artillerists the Russians were using; requests to Himmler for some experienced SS replacements, to Doenitz for reinforcements for the coastal batteries, and to Goering for air force personnel to be used against the partisans.

Nevertheless, the near collapse of Eighteenth Army at the end of January had had the effect of a temporary disentanglement, at least in places, as on the Narva River. Model's decision to close up the front around Luga gave the army a chance to maneuver and to catch its breath. The next move was still the Russians', but it would be met on a coherent front. For a few days at the beginning of February the points of greatest pressure were in the Sixteenth Army area where the

Second Baltic Front pushed into the front south of Staraya Russa and west of Novosokol'niki, tying down German troops which might be shifted north and, as a bonus, creating entering wedges which might be exploited for deep thrusts later.

By 4 February the Leningrad and Volkhov Fronts had regrouped and were beginning to close in on Eighteenth Army again. Army Group North informed the OKH that Meretskov had massed one strong force and 200 tanks southwest of Novgorod, and Govorov was assembling another east of Samro Lake thirty miles off the Eighteenth Army left flank. They obviously could try for an encirclement around Luga.

Model still intended to attack to the northwest, and he proposed a "large" and a "small" solution. The first would carry the front out to the length of the Luga River; the second would extend it diagonally to the northern tip of Lake Peipus. Kinzel, the Chief of staff, remarked later to the Chief Staff, Eighteenth Army, that it was gratifying just to be able to think about such bold strokes. Whether either would be carried out would depend on how the battle developed. In any event, nothing would be lost because the preliminary movements would be useful no matter what the army did next.

Hitler, usually delighted by talk of an offensive, displayed no enthusiasm. In a rare personal directive to Model he cited the Narva area as most vulnerable and ordered it reinforced without delay. In the sector between Lake Peipus and Lake Ilmen he saw a danger of Eighteenth Army's being pushed east away from Lake Peipus and a threat of an encirclement, and he instructed Model to submit a request for a withdrawal to the PANTHER position as soon as either of those became imminent.

Having appointed the kind of daring, iron-nerved general he wanted, Hitler himself became the advocate of caution. The change probably also resulted in part from Hitler's tendency to associate men with events. Most likely, before dismissing Kuechler he had decided that a retreat to the PANTHER position was necessary, but he had not acted then because he could not bring himself to appear to mitigate what he considered to be Kuechler's responsibility for the defeat.

On 6 February the 12th Panzer Division finished closing the gap to Sixteenth Army. Its next mission was to assemble in Pskov and attack east of Pskov Lake and Lake Peipus. The 58th Infantry Division was standing by farther east, and Eighteenth Army had called for a withdrawal on the front around Luga which would free three divisions in two days. In the pause, short as it was, the Army's strength had begun to rise as stragglers, men recalled from leave, and those released from the hospitals were returned to their divisions. In addition, Model had ordered 5 percent of the rear echelon troops transferred to line duty.

At Headquarters, Eighteenth Army, Model on the 7th issued instructions for the first stage of the projected counteroffensive. By shifting divisions from the north and east the army would create a solid front between the southern tip of Lake Peipus and Luga. Having accomplished that, the army would apply the Schild und Schwert theory by employing two corps on the east defensively to stop the Russian advance from Samro Lake and one corps in the west in a thrust northward along the Lake Peipus shore.

During the next two days Eighteenth Army tried to jockey its divisions into position. Roadblocks laid by the partisans delayed 12th Panzer Division's advance toward Pskov. The 58th Infantry Division established a short front on the Plyussa River at about the center of the proposed new line, but the Russians filtered past on both sides, and the other divisions would have to attack to close up the front. That would not be easy since the divisions only had four understrength battalions each and the enemy strength was growing hourly as units moved in from the northwest. The swampy terrain also raised problems, but, on the other hand, it was probably the main reason why Leningrad Front could not bring its full force to bear more quickly.

By 10 February the 58th Infantry Division was split in two and one of its regiments was encircled. The 24th Infantry Division, trying to close the gap on the right of the 58th Division, got nowhere and for most of the day had trouble holding open the Luga-Pskov railroad. Although Eighteenth Army would try again the next day to regain contact with the 58th Division and close the gap the prospects were worsening rapidly. Air reconnaissance had spotted convoys of 800 to 900 trucks moving southeast from Samro Lake.

The next afternoon Eighteenth Army reported that the battle had taken a dangerous turn. The 24th Infantry Division was stopped. Soviet tanks had appeared. Both regiments of the 58th Infantry Division were surrounded and would have to fight their way back. That they could save their heavy weapons was doubtful. After nightfall Lindemann told Model that the only way he could get enough troops to close the gaps on the left flank was to take the entire front back to the shortest line between the southern tip of Lake Peipus and Lake Ilmen. Govorov had spread the right arm of the pincers out to the Peipus shore and was pushing south toward Pskov. He already had some units far enough south "to pinch the 12th Panzer Division in the backside." Reluctantly, Model agreed to let the army go back.

The next day brought more bad news. At Narva the Russians expanded their bridgehead and created another north of the city. Between Lakes Peipus and Pskov, Govorov poured in enough troops to threaten a crossing into the PANTHER position. If Model were to establish a front between Lake Peipus and Lake Ilmen he would have to fight for it. On the evening of the 12th Model informed the OKH that he still planned to take and hold that line and wanted to know whether Hitler approved. The OKH response indicated that nobody there, including Hitler, liked the idea. The opinion was— for once—unanimous that it was too late to set up a front between the lakes and that, in any event, it was more important to free one division for Narva and another for the Peipus-Pskov narrows. The operations chief in the OKH added that Hitler was repeating every day that he did not want to risk any encirclements forward of the PANTHER position. An hour before midnight Sponheimer reported breakthroughs north and south of Narva. On the north III SS Panzer Corps had managed to close the front and even gain a little, but south of Narva the Feldherrnhalle Division did not have the strength even to offer effective resistance.

THE PANTHER POSITION

In the morning on the 13th Model sent a situation report to Hitler. He said he would fight the battle around Narva to its end. If worst came to worst he would shorten the front by giving up the bend of the Narva

Narva. Two medieval fortresses, Hermannsburg (left) and Ivangorod (right), flank the Narva River.

River. He still believed it would be best to hold between Lake Peipus and Lake Ilmen until more work had been done on the PANTHER position. Hitler's answer would be strengthened with greatest speed. The army group would submit a plan and timetable for a prompt withdrawal to the PANTHER position.

For the moment it appeared that the decision to go back to the PANTHER position might have come too late to save the Narva front, for which, as a last resort, the army group that day released an Estonian brigade. The brigade was the product of a draft the SS, which was responsible for foreign recruitment, had been conducting in Estonia, Latvia, and Lithuania since early January. Because Hitler refused to offer the Baltic States even a promise of eventual autonomy, the draftees were dispirited and their only motivation was fear—of the Russians and the Germans. On the night of 13 February, Sponheimer reported that the Estonians had arrived in complete disorder verging on panic. Some had tried to desert on the way. That left Model no choice but to take troops from Eighteenth Army. He ordered the 58th Infantry Division transferred north after a three-day rest. The division had lost a third of its personnel and all of its heavy equipment in the encirclements.

On the morning of the 14th, after Sponheimer reported that he had no room to maneuver and no troops to close the gaps and was therefore helpless, Model asked to evacuate the small bridgehead still being held east of Narva, to gain three battalions. Zeitzler approved and offered in addition an infantry division from Norway. Then, shortly after daylight news came in that the Russians had staged a landing on the coast northwest of Narva. Later reports revealed that the landing force was not large, about 500 naval troops, supported only by several gun boats from Lavansaari Island in the Gulf of Finland. In the report sent to the OKH Model stated that, nevertheless, the scene around Narva was "not pretty" and he had ordered the bridgehead given up immediately. During the day the landing parties were wiped out without much damage having been done except by the German Stukas that bombed a German division headquarters and knocked out several Tiger tanks.

More troublesome was the appearance of Soviet ski troops on the west shore of Lake Peipus north of the narrows. The security division responsible for the area reported that its Estonian troops were "going home." After that, Model told the OKH that he would begin the withdrawal to the PANTHER position on 17 February and complete it early on 1 March. He would mop up the west shore of Lake Peipus in the next few days and use the first two divisions freed to cover the lake shore. He expected that as soon as Eighteenth Army began to move Govorov and Meretskov would try for an encirclement around the army's "shoulders." They had strong forces in position north of Pskov and on the west shore of Lake Ilmen.

In the two days before the withdrawal began, the Russians did not try again to cross the lakes, and on 17 February Model gave a corps headquarters command of the lake sector and began shifting the 12th Panzer Division into the area. On the Narva the battle began to degenerate into a vicious stalemate in which the two sides stood toe to toe, neither giving nor gaining an inch. Sponheimer could not close the gaps in his front, but that Govorov was less than satisfied with his own progress was confirmed in repeated radio messages offering the decoration Hero of the Soviet Union to the first commander whose troops reached the road running west out of Narva. As the Sixteenth and Eighteenth Armies began to move, the Soviet armies followed close. Through their networks of agents and partisans they knew exactly what was taking place.

On 19 February Army Group North became suddenly and acutely aware of an old danger that had been lurking in the background throughout the last month of crises. On that day, for the first time in two months, the attacks on the Third Panzer Army perimeter around Vitebsk stopped; and air reconnaissance detected truck convoys of 2,000 or 3,000 trucks moving out, most of them heading north and northwest. Army Group North intelligence estimated that two armies could be shifted to the Sixteenth Army right flank in a few days. Model foresaw two possibilities. The first, and most likely, was that after adding to its already strong concentration in the Nevel-Pustoshka area, Second Baltic Front would attempt to break into the PANTHER position below Pustoshka and roll it up to the north before the Sixteenth and Eighteenth Armies could establish themselves there. The second, the "big solution" as the Germans had come to call it, was a thrust straight through to Dvinsk and on to Riga to cut off Army Group North in the Baltic States.

Model also speculated that the activity on the Sixteenth Army right flank might be a sign that the Stavka was becoming discouraged with the attempts to encircle Eighteenth Army. If that was so, it did not result in any lessening of pressure on Eighteenth Army. As predicted, the Volkhov and Leningrad Fronts bore down heavily on the army's shoulders.

Meretskov tried for a breakthrough at Shimsk west of Lake Ilmen on 17 February. For three days, while the flank of Sixteenth Army came back from Staraya Russa, the battle to keep contact between the two armies swayed in the balance. On the 10th, when both began pulling away from Lake Ilmen, that crisis was passed.

Govorov reacted more slowly but more dangerously. Pskov, throughout the war the main communications center of Army Group North, was also the hinge on which the whole withdrawal to the PANTHER position turned. The army group could not afford to lose Pskov but scarcely had room around the city in which to maneuver. In the swamps and forests east of Pskov Lake, Leningrad Front had trouble bringing its forces to bear, but on 24 February it began laying on heavy pressure north of the city and launched probing attacks across the lake. According to intelligence reports, Stalin had called in Govorov and personally ordered him to take Pskov. By 26 February the threats at Pskov and on the Sixteenth Army right flank had made Hitler so nervous that he asked Model to try to speed up the withdrawal.

In the north, on the Narva front, the Germans toward the end of the month had gained only enough strength to tip the scales slightly in their favor. On 24 February General der Infanterie Johannes Friessner, who had proved himself in the fighting on the Sixteenth Army-Eighteenth Army boundary, took over Sponheimer's command which was then redesignated Armeeabteilung Narva. By then troops of the 214th Infantry Division were beginning to arrive. They still needed seasoning, but they could be used to relieve experienced troops from the quiet parts of the line. Going over to what he called "mosaic work," Friessner cut into the extreme tip of the bridgehead south of Narva and pushed the enemy there into two small pockets. Although the Russians ignored the punishing artillery and small arms fire and kept pouring in troops through the open ends of the pockets, the danger of their reaching the coast was averted.

On 1 March Army Group North took the last step back into the PANTHER position, and the Russians demonstrated that they were not going to let it come to rest there. North of Pustoshka two armies hit the VIII Corps front. South of the town two armies threw their weight against X Corps. Leningrad Front massed two armies south of Pskov and poured more troops across the Narva River, attacking out of the bridgehead to the north, northwest, and west. For a week the battle rippled up and down the whole army group front. Except for small local losses, the German line held. On 9 March Second Baltic Front stepped up its pressure against the Sixteenth Army right flank and began straining heavily for a breakthrough.

On the 10th the army group was confronted with a politically unpleasant and militarily insignificant consequence of the disastrous winter. The commanding officer of the Spanish Legion and the Spanish military attaché visited Model to tell him the legion was being called home. Franco, they said, was not turning away from Germany; he wanted to gather all his "matadors" about him to resist an Anglo-American invasion. Since the legion had proved as troublesome in the rear areas as it had been ineffectual at the front, the loss to the army group was not a painful one.

At midmonth Second Baltic Front was still battering the Sixteenth Army flank while Leningrad Front probed for openings around Pskov and Narva. But the weather had turned against the Russians. After a warm winter—for Russia—the spring thaw had set in early. A foot of water covered the ice on the lakes. Sixteenth Army reported that the Soviet tanks were sometimes sinking up to their turrets in mud. Against a weak front the Russians might have continued to advance, as they were doing in the Ukraine, but the PANTHER position, all that remained of the East Wall, was living up to German expectations.

MODEL DEPARTS

On 28 March Hitler's chief adjutant, Schmundt, called on Model to tell him that in a few days Hitler would name him to replace Manstein as Commanding General, Army Group South. For Model the news came at an inconvenient moment. He had just completed a situation estimate in which he said that the army group "might" be able to give two divisions to Army Group South after the front settled down. Hastily he reworked the estimate and in the altered draft reached the conclusion that Army Group North could give up five divisions and a corps staff immediately, and the 12th Panzer Division as soon as two self-propelled assault gun brigades and a battalion of tanks could be sent to replace it.

On the 29th he went to the Fuehrer headquarters. Still officially the Commanding General, Army Group North, he attempted to use his authority to raid the army group for the benefit of his new command. In what Zeitzler later described as "unimaginable goings on" Model first told Hitler that the army group could give up five divisions and then raised the number to six. In a telegram to Army Group North headquarters he stated that the Fuehrer had ordered the six divisions transferred. By telephone he gave the chief of staff half an hour in which to report that the order was being carried out. Finally, Zeitzler

Soviet ski troops on the Northern Front.

was forced to intervene and instruct the army group not to act on any of Model's orders.

On 31 March, with Model safely installed as Commanding General, Army Group South, Zeitzler persuaded Hitler to reduce the proposed transfers to one division and that only in the near future. The next day, after the air had a chance to clear, Hitler agreed. In the meantime, Lindemann, the senior army commander, had been appointed acting commanding general of the army group.

AN "ECHO" IN FINLAND

At the end of January 1944 the OKW took up the painful task of discussing the developments south of Leningrad with the Finns. Keitel wrote Mannerheim that Army Group North would hold the Luga River line and asked the Marshal to suggest how Germany might help strengthen the Finnish front to compensate for the increased Soviet threat. In reply, Mannerheim proposed that Twentieth Mountain Army extend its right flank south to take in the Ukhta sector, which would release one Finnish division. The Commanding General, Twentieth Mountain Army, Dietl, objected. He insisted that it was a waste of manpower to tie down more German troops on a secondary front in Finland and that Finland, "through greater efforts in the sense of total war," was capable of creating a reserve division out of its own resources "without laying claims on the German Army which is already carrying the entire burden." Irritated also by recent Finnish protests against even the smallest withdrawals of German troops from Finland, Dietl wanted to urge Mannerheim not to raise objections if Twentieth Mountain Army were to offer all the troops it could spare to Army Group North, "which is also fighting for Finland."29 But the OKW, remembering the warnings that had come from Finland in the fall of 1943, considered Mannerheim's response comparatively moderate and ordered Dietl to take over the Ukhta sector.

At the Tehran Conference (27 November-2 December 1943), Roosevelt and Churchill had told Stalin that they wished to see Finland out of the war before the invasion of Western Europe planned for the spring of 1944 and that they desired a peace which would leave Finland its independence. Roosevelt, representing the only one of the three countries not at war with Finland, had offered to help persuade Finland to ask for an armistice. Stalin had stated that, in the course of the current Finnish peace feelers, the Soviet Union had declared it had no designs on Finland's independence. He had added, however, that the Soviet Union would demand restoration of the 1940 border plus Pechenga and heavy reparations.

During the night of 6 February 200 Soviet planes bombed Helsinki. The next day the United States Department of State dispatched a note warning the Finnish Government that the longer Finland stayed in the war the more unfavorable the terms of peace would become. On the 8th, in a long editorial, Izvestia took up the subject of a Soviet drive to Helsinki, pointing out that the Soviet Union had more than enough forces to spare for it. On the 10th the text of the United States note was released to the Finnish newspapers where it brought an almost unanimous editorial response in favor of investigating the possibilities of peace. That night 150 Russian bombers raided the Finnish port of Kotka. On the 12th the Finnish Government sent the former Prime Minister and last Ambassador to the Soviet Union, Dr. Juho K. Paasikivi, to Stockholm to receive the Russian terms from the Soviet Minister to Sweden, Madame Alexandra M. Kollontay.

TANNE AND BIRKE

The negotiations going on in Stockholm and the continuing desperate condition of Army Group North prompted the Germans to consider how to preserve their control of the Baltic Sea. The retreat to Narva had already loosened their blockade of the Soviet Baltic Fleet somewhat. A Finnish-Soviet armistice threatened to knock all of the remaining props out from under the German strategy in the Baltic. In neutral Finnish or Soviet hands Suursaari Island and Hanko would no longer serve as corks to keep the Soviet naval forces bottled up in the eastern end of the Gulf of Finland, and the Åland Islands could be used to block the iron ore traffic from Luleå. Once Soviet naval units were able to roam the Baltic at will, submarine training would have to cease and the fate of the submarine fleet would be sealed.

On 16 February Hitler ordered that in the event of a Finnish change of course the Åland Islands and Suursaari were to be occupied. Under the code names TANNE WEST (Åland Islands) and TANNE OST (Suursaari) the OKW took over the planning. (See Map 1.) The 416th Infantry Division, in Denmark, and a parachute regiment were earmarked for TANNE WEST, and the provision of troops for Suursaari was made a responsibility of Army Group North. Finnish resistance was not expected. Control of the TANNE operations remained in the hands of the OKW, which assigned the tactical direction to the OKM and OKL.

Meanwhile, Twentieth Mountain Army had resurrected Fuehrer Directive 50 and worked out an implementing plan under the code name BIRKE. In executing the BIRKE plan, the army proposed to swing its right flank back to a line running roughly from Karesuando near the Swedish border to the Arctic Ocean Highway south of Ivalo. The maneuver was to be completed in two phases. In the first phase XXXVI Mountain Corps and XVIII Mountain Corps would pull out of the Kandalaksha, Loukhi, and Ukhta sectors and fall back to Rovaniemi, establishing a screening front east of Rovaniemi on the line Kemiyärvi-Autinkylä, which was to be held until the main force had safely passed northward through Rovaniemi. In the second phase XXXVI Mountain Corps would go north along the Arctic Ocean Highway to its new sector south of Ivalo and tie in with the

Soviet cavalry in action on the Northern Front.

right flank of XIX Mountain Corps holding the front east and south of Pechenga. XVIII Mountain Corps would withdraw northwestward over the Rovaniemi-Skibotten route and stop on a line northeast of the Swedish border in the vicinity of Karesuando. (See Map 34.)

A definitive plan for the second phase could not be made in advance because how it would be executed depended on the season. In summer it could be carried out as described, but in winter the Finnish end of the Rovaniemi-Skibotten route was impassable. In winter, therefore, both XXXVI Mountain Corps and XVIII Mountain Corps would have to go north over the Arctic Ocean Highway, XVIII Mountain Corps continuing on into northern Norway and XXXVI Mountain Corps providing troops to man the Karesuando positions.

To Twentieth Mountain Army the possibility of its having to carry out the terms of Fuehrer Directive 50 was a source of nagging concern. The army had pointed out when the Fuehrer directive was first issued that to try to hold northern Finland would almost certainly prove futile in the long run since the sea route around Norway could easily be cut, putting an end to both ore and supply shipments. The planning for BIRKE brought to light other dangers. Twentieth Mountain Army did not have enough manpower to construct suitable positions at

Ivalo and Karesuando in advance and, in any event, could not start work at those places without revealing its intentions to the Finns. The withdrawal would be confined to a few roads, difficult to keep open in winter and exposed to round-the-clock air attack in summer; and in northern Finland the army would have to set up a front under the most unfavorable conditions of climate and terrain.

THE SOVIET TERMS REJECTED

For two weeks the Finnish-Soviet talks in Stockholm were conducted in secret. The Russians, meanwhile, continued their bombing raids on Finnish cities, hitting Helsinki on 27 February with a particularly heavy 300-plane raid. The Soviet terms had begun to leak out on the 26th, and on the 28th the Soviet Government published its demands in full: (1) internment of Twentieth Mountain Army, either by the Finns alone or with Soviet help; (2) restoration of the 1940 boundary; (3) return to the Soviet Union of all military and civilian prisoners; (4) demobilization of the Finnish Army—whether partial or complete to be determined by negotiation; (5) reparations to be determined later; (6) the ownership of Pechenga to be negotiated. Points 2 and 3, concerning the boundary and the prisoner exchange, the Soviet Government insisted, were to be met before the armistice. On 8 March, in a softly worded announcement, the Finnish Government declared that those two points were unacceptable as preconditions of the armistice. It also objected to the demand for internment of Twentieth Mountain Army, claiming it was a technical impossibility. When the Soviet Union set 18 March as the deadline for a final reply, the Finns, on the 17th, rejected the terms but expressed a strong desire to explore the matter further.

The Soviet stipulations were in fact more stringent than those Stalin had outlined to Roosevelt and Churchill at Tehran. Coincident with the Finnish rejection, the Soviet Government began adopting a slightly milder tone, indicating that it had not yet made its best offer, and a few days later declared itself willing to clarify the terms. On 26 March Paasikivi and the former Foreign Minister, Carl Enckell, flew to Moscow where Foreign Minister Molotov restated the terms and brought them into approximate consonance with Stalin's commitment at the Tehran Conference. The Soviet Union dropped its demand that some of the terms be executed even before the armistice. It also no longer insisted on internment but gave the Finns the alternative of expelling all the German troops from Finland by the end of April 1944—without the threat of "assistance" from Soviet troops. On two points the Soviet stand had hardened: it demanded $600 million in reparations and full ownership of Pechenga, for which it offered to exchange the leased base at Hanko, one of the spoils of the 1939-40 war.

The Finns rejected the terms a second time on 18 April, giving as the reason the burden of reparations that would be laid upon the country. Still holding large stretches of Soviet territory and having an undefeated army in the field, they had obviously hoped to make a better bargain. Furthermore, the alarm and near panic which had motivated Paasikivi's trip to Stockholm in February had gradually subsided after Army Group North settled into the PANTHER position.

In the early stages of the negotiations the German Government adopted an attitude of restraint, on the assumption that Finland was not yet ready for peace at any price and, consequently, a look at the Soviet demands might be the best remedy for the peace fever. As the Army Group North situation improved and Finnish dismay at the terms grew, Hitler began to apply pressure. In March he reduced the flow of weapons to Finland, and in the first week of April he let Mannerheim be told that German weapons could not be given as long as a danger of their falling into enemy hands existed. On 13 April he halted all grain shipments to Finland, and on the 18th he stopped shipment of war matériel. That the embargo existed was not officially communicated to the Finns. Its effects, of course, were quickly felt.

At the end of the month the OKW invited Mannerheim's chief of staff to Fuehrer headquarters. There, after Keitel had taken him to task over recent Finnish policy, Jodl adopted a friendly tone and told him that an authoritative declaration was needed to the effect that German military equipment supplied to Finland would not one day be surrendered to the Soviet Union. Mannerheim attempted to meet the requirement by a personal letter to Hitler. But Hitler, who claimed the Mannerheim letter was too cautious and diplomatic, refused to relax the embargo beyond letting Finland have enough weapons and ammunition to prevent an outright decline in the army's combat capability.

Throughout the winter, as for the past two years, the Finnish Army front was quiet; but in February Karelian Front began strengthening its forces opposite Twentieth Mountain Army. By early March the number of Soviet troops facing Twentieth Mountain Army had risen from about 100,000 to 163,000, and all the signs pointed to a full-scale offensive before the end of the month. The heaviest build-up was in the XXXVI Mountain Corps sector astride the route across the waist of Finland to the head of the Gulf of Bothnia. There the Russians brought up two new divisions and four brigades plus rocket launchers and artillery, and extended their right flank northwestward until they had a springboard behind the German forward line of fortifications. On 22 March Twentieth Mountain Army concluded that the build-up was completed and the offensive might begin any time.

As March drew to a close and the spring thaw approached, the danger of a Soviet offensive subsided. Dietl concluded that the Russians would have attacked if Finland had accepted an armistice. In April Dietl proposed an operation to eliminate the threat to the XXXVI Mountain Corps flank and asked Mannerheim's help. The marshal refused to employ Finnish troops offensively, and Twentieth Mountain Army, lacking the forces to go ahead alone, was forced to leave the Russians their tactical advantage. The winter thus ended with the barest visible changes but with a deep subsurface weakening of the German-Finnish relationship.

CHAPTER XIII

Paying the Piper

MUD AND STRATEGY

While Soviet offensives were grinding into the north and south flanks of the Eastern Front during January and February 1944 the OKW, which was responsible for all the other theaters, was committed to a strategy of defending with forces in being the entire periphery of Fortress Europe. The Operations Staff, OKW, had advocated that line with increasing insistence since late 1942 after the Dieppe raid, the battle of El 'Alamein, and the North African invasion showed that the Allies actually meant to create a second front. Fuehrer Directive 51 of 3 November 1943 raised the OKW concept to the level of strategic policy. Subsequent events, starting at the end of the month with the Tehran Conference at which Roosevelt and Churchill promised Stalin a second front in the spring of 1944, convinced the OKW it had set the correct course.

In December the Operations Staff worked out a plan for stripping the other OKW theaters to the minimum should the Allies tie themselves down in one big invasion. The Germans would thus not have to keep all of the threatened points in a high state of readiness; but the plan was shelved after the Anzio landing in January 1943 seemed to indicate that the Allies were planning a number of simultaneous or successive landings along the European coasts anywhere from Greece to northern Norway.

The Operations Staff, buttressing a report Keitel gave to Hitler on 13 February 1944, concluded that Germany was conducting a strategic defensive on internal lines without being able to benefit fully therefrom because strong enemy forces in the Mediterranean, the Near and Middle East, Africa, North America, England, and Iceland were free to attack the European coasts at any time and so tied down a large part of the German reserves. The staff affirmed that the German mission was to defend stubbornly every foot of ground in Russia until the initiative could be regained by beating off the expected big Anglo-American landing plus any subsidiary landings. The forces thus freed could then be used to bring about a decision against the Soviet Union.

Even as the paper was being written, the Operations Staff doubted whether the future deployment of German forces could be governed solely by the need to hold in the USSR and to meet and defeat Allied invasions in the other theaters. The Soviet thrust toward the Balkans presaged stepped-up partisan activity and political repercussions in Hungary, Rumania, and Bulgaria which, if military intervention were required, would impose an added strain on the German resources, those of the OKW in particular.

On the other hand, through February 1944 and as laid down in Fuehrer Directive 51, the policy of restricting the Eastern Front to its own resources had been, from the OKW point of view, remarkably successful. Despite the heavy fighting on both the north and south flanks, the OKW theaters had had to relinquish only one division, the 214th Infantry Division from Norway, and three regiments of recruits. After the second week in February it appeared to the OKW that the army groups in Russia had seen another winter through. Model had Army Group North firmly in hand and, anyway, was going back to a well fortified line. Army Groups A and South were less well provided for, but after the breakout from the Cherkassy pocket the Russians were not on the march anywhere. Although the whole south flank was hanging loose between the Dnepr and the next natural line to the west, the Bug River, the spring thaw was approaching and anyone who wanted to overlook the fact that the Russians had kept on the move through an abnormally warm winter could assume that in a matter of days, a few weeks at most, the mud would immobilize the front for a month or so. By the end of February the OKW was convinced the Russians would not try anything big before the thaw. On the 27th Hitler ordered the Adolf Hitler Division to pull out of the front northeast of Uman and get ready for a transfer either to Belgium or the Netherlands.

A SOVIET SPRING OFFENSIVE

At the beginning of March 1944 the Eastern Front south of the Pripyat

Marshes formed a very narrow, elongated S, which could be bisected vertically by a straight line drawn from Kovel' to the Dnepr slightly southwest of Krivoi Rog. (Map 24) Army Groups A and South still held about half the ground between the Bug and the Dnepr. They had lost the easternmost lateral railroad behind the Dnepr and all of the major Dnepr crossings except Kherson, but they still held the L'vov-Odessa railroad. For the first time in more than two months, the front—with one notable exception—did not show any sizable gaps. On the debit side, it followed no natural defense line except for two short stretches on the lower Dnepr and the Ingulets. The appearance of continuity on the situation maps was achieved by resorting to half a dozen different kinds of broken lines indicating various stages of weakness, in some sectors ranging down to uncertainty whether the positions delineated existed at all.

On the Army Group South left flank Fourth Panzer Army, under persistent Russian pressure, failed to close forty miles of its front west of Shepetovka and lost Yampol' on 2 March. Manstein believed the Russians would try at least to push south and cut the L'vov-Odessa railroad between Ternopol and Proskurov before the spring mud stopped them. He was convinced more than ever that the point of greatest danger was on this flank, where a 35-mile advance would take the Russians to the railroad, another 65 miles would take them across the Dnestr, and 30 or so miles more would carry them across the Prut and into the Carpathians. In all, a 130-mile advance would unhinge three potential German defense lines, on the Bug, the Dnestr, and the Prut. In the south Sixth Army was still 100 miles east of the Bug, 200 miles east of the Dnestr, and nearly 300 miles east of the Prut.

THE REGROUPMENT

After the breakout from the Cherkassy pocket was completed Manstein began redistributing the units bunched around the First Panzer-Eighth Army boundary. He moved the Headquarters, III Panzer Corps, four panzer divisions, and the artillery division north behind Proskurov. To Fourth Panzer Army he assigned two panzer divisions and three newly formed infantry divisions being sent from

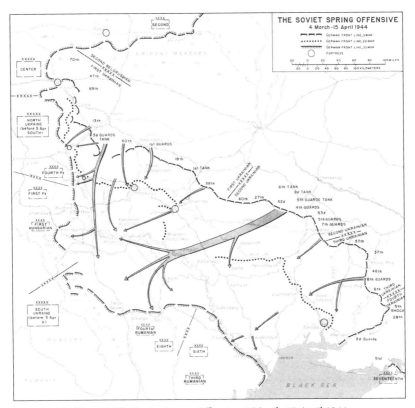

Map 24: The Soviet Spring Offensive, 4 March-15 April 1944

Germany. In the first days of March he shifted his three armies north by giving the threatened right flank corps of Eighth Army to Sixth Army, First Panzer Army's right flank corps to Eighth Army, and the right flank corps of Fourth Panzer Army to First Panzer Army. This gave First Panzer Army responsibility for Shepetovka and Proskurov and gave Fourth Panzer Army the gap west of Ternopol-Shepetovka and the front north to Kovel'. In executing his backfield shift Manstein had to take two serious risks: in the first place, the weather, the mud, and the condition of the troops and equipment made it impossible to get all of the divisions relocated before the end of the second week in March, and secondly, transferring the panzer divisions took all the stiffening out of the right half of the Eighth Army front, which was doubly weakened because that was where the two corps smashed in the Cherkassy pocket should have been.

Even though the Russians had, by 1 March, slowed down or stopped everywhere except west of Shepetovka and the pattern of the previous years could be expected to repeat itself after the full onset of the thaw, the signs were plentiful that they could resume the offensive at will. During the fighting in January and February the four Ukrainian fronts had at no time brought all of their strength to bear, and their reserves, instead of dwindling, had grown enormously. By mid-February the Stavka had five of its six tank armies in the area opposite Army Group South. Three of them stayed in reserve. At the end of the month the sixth also had moved in. Several tank and mechanized corps stood opposite each of the German armies. During the winter the Russians had proved their ability to attack and maneuver in mud. American-built trucks had kept the mobile units going long after the comparable German equipment was completely mired. The Soviet infantry had fallen back on the old-fashioned panje wagon, the light, one-horse, high-riding rig that could negotiate all but the deepest mud. By March every Soviet mortar and machine gun crew and nearly every infantry squad had a panje wagon to carry weapons, ammunition, and rations. The wagons spared the men the exertion of plodding through mud under heavy loads and freed the units from day-to-day concern for their supply lines.

Manstein was right in contending that the Russians would concentrate on his north flank. First Ukrainian Front, the most powerful of the Ukrainian fronts, after it turned over the zone fringing the Pripyat Marshes to the newly created Second Belorussian Front, occupied the sector opposite the First and Fourth Panzer Armies. When Vatutin was seriously wounded on 29 February on an inspection tour Zhukov took command. Konev's Second Ukrainian Front, strong in armor, stood opposite the badly weakened Eighth Army. Malinovskiy's Third Ukrainian Front, facing Sixth Army in the Dnepr Bend, had less armor than the other two but had drawn divisions from Fourth Ukrainian Front, which in its zone south of the Dnepr was concerned primarily with the Crimea. The plan was for First Ukrainian Front to crash through between First Panzer Army and Fourth Panzer Army, and strike across the successive river lines to the Carpathians. In keeping with Soviet doctrine of the time, the main effort was to be supported by only slightly less powerful thrusts to the west by Second Ukrainian Front left of the Eighth Army's center and by Third Ukrainian Front through the center of Sixth Army.

FIRST UKRAINIAN FRONT ATTACKS

On 4 March First Ukrainian Front attacked. In the gap between the flanks of First and Fourth Panzer Armies, Third Guards Tank Army headed south. East of Shepetovka and due north of Proskurov First Guards Army pushed through First Panzer Army. The next day Thirteenth Army attacked west between Lutsk and Dubno.

Caught between the two Soviet armies, LIX Corps on the First Panzer Army left flank fell back to the south away from Shepetovka. North of the railroad between Ternopol and Proskurov all Fourth Panzer Army could muster for the moment were some corps troops belonging to XXXXVIII Panzer Corps. Manstein ordered the First and Fourth Panzer Armies to stop the Russians north of the railroad and to attack into their flanks from Ternopol and Proskurov. First Panzer Army was to assemble III Panzer Corps with four panzer divisions around Proskurov—the divisions were still at Eighth Army, loading on trains or waiting to load. Fourth Panzer Army had two infantry divisions coming toward Ternopol by rail, but they were brand new divisions composed mostly of eighteen-year-olds.

By 6 March the front between the First and Fourth Panzer Armies was torn open along a 90-mile stretch. On the east LIX Corps was isolated at Staro Constantinov. Midway between Ternopol and Proskurov XXXXVIII Panzer Corps had thrown up a short line using elements of the Adolf Hitler Division and the 7th Panzer Division. The latter did not have a single tank and expected, at most, ten back from repairs in several days. The trains bringing the first of the infantry divisions for Fourth Panzer Army had started unloading west of Ternopol; to unload in the city was already too dangerous.

During the next four days the German defense stiffened. The two panzer armies' efforts to strengthen their flanks began to take effect— rather rapidly at that. Fourth Panzer Army used one of its new infantry divisions to establish a line north of Ternopol and sluiced the other into the city by rail. A third infantry division was on its way through

Poland, and Manstein had promised a fourth to be transferred from Denmark. First Panzer Army pulled LIX Corps away from Staro Constantinov toward Proskurov and at the same time committed parts of three panzer divisions to close the gap between the corps and the army main force. Around Proskurov, III Panzer Corps drew its divisions together in a compact block that grew in strength daily as elements arrived from the Eighth Army zone and the units of LIX Corps drew closer.

Simultaneously, Zhukov made his initial bid for full operational freedom. Several times Soviet onslaughts carried nearly to the center of Ternopol, but all were beaten back. Along the railroad east to Proskurov, Zhukov's tanks and infantry spread out on a broad front, but badly shaken though they were, XXXXVIII Panzer Corps' two divisions held their front.

FUEHRER ORDER 11

On 8 March 1944, in Fuehrer Order 11, Hitler introduced a new major tactical concept to the Eastern Front. Although its full impact was not felt until later, the order did affect the battle then beginning on the southern flank. It was motivated both by Hitler's annoyance at losing Nevel and Rovno and by his growing willingness to adopt any measures, no matter how desperate, which might slow Soviet offensives. He had toyed with the idea of "fortresses" before: Stalingrad was an example. Fuehrer Order 11 created the "fortified place," a town or city astride communications lines and suitably manned and fortified, which in Hitler's words, "Was to perform the same functions as forts did in times past."

Each "fortified place" was to have at its head a general or senior field grade officer who was directly responsible to the army group commander and could only be relieved of his mission by him and then only with Hitler's consent. The "fortified places" had one mission: to hold to the last man. They were literally Himmelfahrtskommandos (missions to Heaven). The commandants received the authority of a corps commander, which meant that they could impose the death penalty. Hitler designated twenty-six cities and larger towns on still-occupied Soviet territory as "fortified places," among them Ternopol,

Proskurov, Kovel', Brody, Vinnitsa, and Pervomaysk in the Army Group South zone.

SECOND AND THIRD UKRAINIAN FRONTS ATTACK

Konev and Malinovskiy began their offensives against Eighth Army and Sixth Army on 4 March. Fourth Guards Army backed by Fifth Guards Tank Army and Sixth Tank Army hit the Eighth Army front northeast of Uman. The two German divisions there could not stand up to the massed Soviet infantry and tanks. On the fourth day Fifth Guards Tank Army pushed to within twenty-five miles of Uman, and Konev opened a secondary attack west of Kirovograd on the Eighth Army-Sixth Army boundary.

Two days later, on 9 March, Uman fell; the report reached Eighth Army only minutes ahead of an order from Hitler demanding that the city be held. During the next two days the whole left half of Eighth Army disintegrated; the flank lost contact with First Panzer Army; and the remnants of four divisions were shoved away south and west toward the Bug. The Chief of Staff, Eighth Army, on a reconnaissance flight along the Bug on 11 March, saw German troops drifting back toward the river singly and in small groups. They had no heavy weapons, and vehicles were jammed up and mired along all the approaches to bridges.

Against the Sixth Army center Malinovskiy threw a guards mechanized corps and Eighth Guards Army's three guards rifle corps. Hollidt had to stop the attack in the front if he was to stop it at all. He had moved his two reserve divisions in close, but at one point the Russians hit an artillery battalion employed as infantry and secured a foothold. In two more days they shouldered their way in to a depth of five miles. On 7 March IV Guards Mechanized Corps and IV Guards Cavalry Corps broke loose and, straight as a shot, thrust through twenty-five miles to Novy Bug. That night the Sixth Army staff barely had time to load its communications equipment aboard the command train. The train was under mortar and machine gun fire as it left the city. At the end of the day the army found itself in a by then familiar and thoroughly uncomfortable situation—split in two with strong enemy forces maneuvering at will twenty-five miles behind its front.

On the 8th the army began taking its bulging north flank back "through cold channels," that is, without putting any orders in writing. The night before, Hitler had forbidden a withdrawal on the grounds that the mud made it impossible and the Russians in the breakthrough were not as strong as reported. During the day Hitler changed his mind to the extent of offering the army permission to go back to the line from the mouth of the Ingulets to Novy Bug. By then the Soviet cavalry and tanks were turning south behind the Ingulets and reaching out to the Ingul, the next river to the west. Kleist told Zeitzler Sixth Army could not fight forward of the Bug. If it did, it would be destroyed. It was time, he complained, for higher headquarters to stop rejecting everything the army group proposed.

During the night on 11 March Hitler ordered Sixth Army and Eighth Army to end their retreat "at the latest" on the Bug. On the north, Eighth Army was already losing a deadly race to get divisions off its right flank and behind the Bug before the Russians could cross the river.

THE HAMMER AND THE ANVIL

First Ukrainian Front's offensive was, by the second week in March, falling short of its intended effect. Manstein's determined effort to hold the north flank kept the attack hemmed in from both sides between Ternopol and Proskurov. On 12 March the third new infantry division unloaded behind Ternopol and began deploying on a line south of the city. In the next three days First and Fourth Panzer Armies rejoined their flanks, and on the 16th Fourth Panzer Army estimated that it would be able to clear the railroad in three more days. Manstein cautioned the army not to expend too much effort getting back on the railroad because it was already cut farther south, between the First Panzer-Eighth Army flanks.

Meanwhile, Zhukov had slacked off somewhat in the center and set his right flank armies in motion. On the north Thirteenth Army increased its pressure against Lutsk and Dubno and pushed the Germans out of both on 16 March. Farther north, the SS general commanding the "fortified place" Kovel' on the same day reported that he was surrounded and wanted to get out while he still could.

From his chief, Himmler, he received a telegram, "You were sent to Kovel' to hold it. Do that." In a more realistic vein, Manstein ordered the Headquarters, XXXII Corps, the 131st Infantry Division, and the SS Wiking Division out of their rest areas in Poland and dispatched them east to relieve Kovel'. Both divisions had been in the Cherkassy pocket; neither had any heavy weapons; and the Wiking Division did not have enough rifles to arm all its men. In a singular piece of bad luck, a direct hit on an ammunition car blew up the armored train detailed to give them artillery support.

In the southeast, Konev's offensive against Eighth Army had by 11 March torn away First Panzer Army's anchor on its right, and the infantry divisions of Thirty-eighth Army had plunged through, splitting off First Panzer Army's right flank corps. Assisted by the massive pressure of Second Ukrainian Front's tank armies going west between the Bug and the Dnepr, Thirty-eighth Army rolled up the First Panzer Army flank toward Vinnitsa. The Russian infantry were about 40 percent so-called "booty Ukrainians," recruits the armies scooped up as they advanced across the occupied territory; even so, the weight of their numbers was too much for the overstrained German divisions.

Off the flank XXXXVI Panzer Corps slipped away laterally to the south trying to cover the Dnestr crossings at Yampol' and Mogilev-Podol'skiy. It angled into the path of Soviet Sixth Tank Army, was pushed away to the west north of the river, and could not bring itself to a stop. On 17 March elements of the 75th Infantry Division which had crossed the Dnestr opposite Yampol' blew the bridges there after Soviet tanks carrying infantry broke into the town. Two days later the bridges at Mogilev Podol'skiy were blown. The 75th Infantry Division reported that the Russians were crossing the river at several places, but it could not conduct a reconnaissance because its horses were worn out and the only vehicle it had was a Volkswagen. On 20 March, when Thirty-eighth Army took Vinnitsa, its point was already jabbing southwest past Zhmerinka toward Kamenets-Podol'skiy into the gap between the First Panzer Army flank and XXXXVI Panzer Corps.

By 21 March Zhukov had massed enough strength—three tank armies, the First, Third Guards, and Fourth, plus First Guards Army—

to smash the front between Ternopol and Proskurov with one blow. On that day 200 tanks of First and Fourth Tank Armies rammed through the front along the railroad and headed due south, carrying along with them like drifting islands the last remnants of the German line—the 68th Infantry, Adolf Hitler, and 7th Panzer Divisions.

On the 23d a First Tank Army force wheeled west against the infantry divisions on both sides of Ternopol and threw them back ten miles. The garrison in the city stayed, in accordance with Fuehrer Order 11 and because no one had time to get the "fortified place" designation lifted. On the east Third Guards Tank Army and First Guards Army reached Proskurov. During the day the lead elements of Fourth Tank Army, two tank and one mechanized corps, passed Chortkov, twenty miles north of the Dnestr. They were obviously heading across the river to meet Second Ukrainian Front's armor, which had crossed downstream, below Mogilev-Podol'skiy, and was going west.

When the Soviet tanks passed Chortkov, they cut First Panzer Army's lifeline, one single-track railroad. With the river at its back, the army was as good as encircled. On 23 March, Manstein gave First Panzer Army command of the 7th Panzer, Adolf Hitler, and 68th Infantry Divisions, which were drifting into the army's sector anyway. He ordered the army to take back its front on the north, anchor its right flank on the Dnestr, and attack west to reopen the railroad. Hitler, however, still insisted on holding Proskurov and reserved the decision concerning it to himself. Neither Manstein nor Hube, the army commander, believed that Proskurov could be held. Later the same day Hube directed all the troop commands to begin destroying nonessential vehicles and equipment and to requisition every panje wagon they could lay hands on to make themselves mobile.

FIRST PANZER ARMY BREAKS OUT

On 25 March, Manstein flew to Berchtesgaden where, in a stormy afternoon interview with Hitler, he insisted that First Panzer Army had to break out, the order had to be given that day, and the army group had to be given at least one fresh corps to open a path from the west. Angrily, Hitler refused, claiming Manstein had "dribbled away" all the divisions he had given him and always wanted to go back but never held anywhere. At a second conference, after midnight, Hitler changed his mind, authorized the breakout, and gave Manstein the II SS Panzer Corps with the 9th and 10th SS Panzer Divisions (Hohenstaufen and Frundsberg), and the 100th Jaeger and the 367th Infantry Divisions.

On the 26th, while Manstein was flying back to his headquarters at L'vov, Fourth Tank Army turned a force east and took Kamenets-Podol'skiy behind First Panzer Army. By then Zhukov's and Konev's armor was fanning out behind the Dnestr to throw another ring around the panzer army.

The decision to give Manstein more divisions was painful for Hitler and the OKW. It jeopardized the strategy laid down in Fuehrer Directive 51—and carefully nurtured through the winter—just when the Anglo-American invasion seemed most likely to come. The four infantry divisions sent east earlier in the month and the two Hitler gave on 26 March came out of OKW reserves and the Southeastern Theater, which was bad enough. Losing II SS Panzer Corps and its two spanking new panzer divisions cut directly into the anti-invasion forces, and divisions that went to the Eastern Front, experience taught, were a long time coming back.

For the breakout First Panzer Army had two choices, neither very promising: it could go west and northwest toward Fourth Panzer Army or south across the Dnestr. Hube wanted to go south. On the west he faced two tank armies and would have to cross two sizable rivers, several smaller streams, and numerous gullies. South of the Dnestr he held a small bridgehead around Khotin, and the enemy forces appeared to be more scattered. Manstein was concerned above all with keeping First Panzer Army on the north flank and preventing its being pushed into the Carpathians or slipping south behind Eighth Army; he also doubted that the army could get across the Dnestr, which at Khotin was about a mile wide and approaching flood stage. On 26 March Manstein ordered Hube to go west toward Fourth Panzer Army across the rear lines of the Fourth and First Tank Armies.

The tactical problem confronting Hube was an unusual one, namely, to hold the army together, pull back his front on the north and east, and attack to the rear. The effect would be to create an ambulatory pocket which would move west along the Dnestr like a giant amoeba. Hube divided the army into a north and a south group, each of which would both hold and withdraw with its infantry and attack with its armor. He concluded that getting across the Zbruch River would be crucial. Everything depended on whether the army could get over in the first place and, secondly, once it had done so, whether it would have enough strength left to go any farther. He gave the north group the mission of securing the first bridgehead on the Zbruch. That would cut the rearward lines of the Fourth Tank Army elements around Mogilev-Podol'skiy and enable the south group to break through and close up to the Zbruch. To take advantage of the "booty Ukrainians'" nervousness, the groups were to attack at night and in half-light of dusk or dawn. During night marches the troops were to close up in columns on either side of their panje wagons and use peasants as guides from village to village.

On the opposing side, mud had prevented the Russians' from bringing up artillery to stiffen their grip on the pocket. On 29 March the First Panzer Army north group secured two bridgeheads across the Zbruch. During the next two days, while the north group struck out toward the Seret, the next large river to the west, the south group closed to the Zbruch, and the north and east fronts dropped back. That the whole army would get across the Zbruch was then assured, but Zhukov was moving armor from the north to throw up another line west of the Seret.

Hube estimated that he would need six days to take the army across the Seret at infantry speed, and that with the supplies it had and was receiving by air the army could not fight its way out of another envelopment. On the 31st he considered letting the tanks hammer through to Fourth Panzer Army alone. The infantry would then have to split up into groups of a hundred men or so and, following the example of the Soviet partisans, try to pick their way through the Soviet lines.

At the turn of the month a 3-day blizzard slowed both sides but, on the whole, benefited First Panzer Army. The Air Force transports kept flying through the worst of the storm, and II SS Panzer Corps completed the last leg of its train trip through Poland.

Balkans—typical terrain along the Dnepr in the Ukraine.

On 2 April Zhukov called on the army to surrender before the end of the day. If it did not, he threatened, it would be destroyed and all captured officers would be shot before their troops as punishment for having senselessly spilled the blood of soldiers entrusted to them. That day the north group attacked across the Seret near Chortkov.

When the weather began to clear, on the 3d, Zhukov rushed in tanks and vehicles from the north and south to waylay the army on the Seret. But the next day the north group threw back two tank corps, pushed through Chortkhov, and carried its advance west. Hube concluded that the greatest danger had passed and the breakout would succeed.

During the night of 4 April, 60 Ju-52's loaded with ammunition and gasoline landed in the pocket, and next morning II SS Panzer Corps attacked from the Fourth Panzer Army flank. On the 6th the points of II SS Panzer Corps and the First Panzer Army north group met at Buchach on the Strypa River. By the 10th the army had its front behind the Seret, II SS Panzer Corps had brought in 600 tons of supplies, and the breakout was assured.

SIXTH ARMY RETREATS TO THE BUG

In the second week of March Malinovskiy had enough strength

around Novy Bug to strike due south to the Bug Liman at Nikolaev and encircle the southern half of Sixth Army or to carry the offensive west and get across the Bug behind the army. That he did neither, or rather that he attempted both, was Sixth Army's salvation.

On 11 and 12 March, using several divisions taken out of the front on the east, Hollidt tried to pinch off the Soviet spearhead by closing in on Novy Bug. The counterattack could not gain any ground on the north; in the south it made fair progress until XXXIII Tank Corps hooked south and stopped it completely. After that Hollidt had no choice but to get the army behind the Bug fast.

In the meantime, Malinovskiy had repeated the mistake he had made a month earlier at Apostolovo. He had turned the Eighth Guards Army's armor and cavalry south toward Nikolaev and had sent Forty-sixth Army, all infantry, west toward the Bug above Novo Odessa. Although Sixth Army could stop neither thrust, the splitting of the Soviet forces gave the army its chance to escape. The army's south group, in particular, did not have to confront both Soviet armies at the same time but could meet the greater threat, Eighth Guards Army, first and then fight its way through Forty-sixth Army two days later.

The battle took another unexpectedly favorable turn after 12 March, when Eighth Guards Army began having supply troubles. The tank units suddenly started operating cautiously, and the army command shied away from making the final leap down to Nikolaev and the Bug Liman. Consequently, only three Sixth Army divisions had to break out of complete encirclements.

Nevertheless, the retreat from the Ingulets to the Bug was a punishing experience. The entire country between the two rivers is cut by 30- to 100-foot-deep balkas (gullies), many of which that year were partly filled with water. Sometimes whole divisions were forced to detour for miles before they found crossings and then, often, guns and vehicles became hopelessly stuck in the bottom. When it rained, the ground everywhere dissolved into soupy mud which as it dried clung in heavy, viscous globs to shoes, tires, and tracks.

By 15 March Sixth Army's south group had punched through Eighth Guards Army to the Ingul River. Six days later Hollidt had established a solid front on the Bug. He was himself, in a sense, to become the last casualty of the retreat. His health was broken, and at Fuehrer headquarters the speed with which Sixth Army had caved in the Dnepr Bend and on the Ingulets had left a lingering suspicion, which the army group commander, Kleist, insisted was unfounded, that the army could have been "more tightly" led. On 21 March, Hitler announced that a new commanding general would take over in a few days.

EIGHTH ARMY COVERS THE FLANK

When Hitler, on 11 March, agreed to let the Eighth and Sixth Armies go back to the Bug, Konev's armored spearheads were already reaching out to the river. The next day VII Corps, which was trying to defend Gayvoron and the crossings north and south of there, in the words of the army's journal entry for that day, "hit bottom." The remnants of its divisions practically evaporated, and the Russians swept across the river.

Both Manstein and the Eighth Army commander, Woehler, thought Second Ukrainian Front would most likely turn south between the Bug and the Dnestr to collaborate with the Third Ukrainian Front's armies going toward Voznesensk and encircle the Eighth and Sixth Armies. Eighth Army had the SS Totenkopf Division coming out of the front west of Kirovograd; it loaded parts of the division aboard Giganten, boxcar-size aircraft that were a cross between a glider and a transport, and flew them to Balta to start building a front between the two rivers. Next, Woehler took XXXXVII Panzer Corps off his right flank and shifted it across the river. At first he and Manstein intended to have the corps attack into the Soviet flank, and close up to First Panzer Army, but the mud and the speed with which the First Panzer Army flank was shoved away to the north prevented that.

Eighth Army and Army Group A were both experiencing new kinds of trouble. Their rear echelons were being compressed into a narrow space east of Bessarabia. Because of promises he had made to Antonescu, Hitler was extremely chary of granting permission for German troops to move onto Rumanian soil. Kleist at last declared that Army Group A would move into Bessarabia "in spite of the Fuehrer and in spite of Antonescu." More serious in the long run, the army and the army group were reduced to depending on the Rumanian railroads which, as the front drew closer, were falling into complete chaos. In Transnistria, the Rumanian occupation zone east of the Dnestr, the Rumanian railroad men shunted German troop trains onto sidings to make way for their own evacuation trains. When Eighth Army moved its headquarters from Pervomaysk to Kotovsk by rail, a distance of sixty-five miles, the trip took twenty-seven hours.

In the third week of March Second Ukrainian Front turned two armies and two tank armies west toward Yampol' and Mogilev-Podol'skiy into the First Panzer Army flank and rear. That took pressure off Eighth Army and for the time being reduced the danger of a thrust south between the Bug and Dnestr; but on 18 March Woehler reported that even though Konev had diverted four armies, he still had four armies and a tank army he could use against the south flank. Woehler believed Konev would push across the Dnestr and turn south to cut off the Eighth and Sixth Armies. Eighth Army—all told, four infantry divisions, four kampfgruppen, and four and a half panzer divisions—could not stretch its line any farther. Woehler thought it was high time to go behind the Dnestr; even if the army did, it would lose many of its heavy weapons to the mud and the Russians and would have to be re-equipped behind the Dnestr. The army group did not agree. Manstein's chief of staff told Woehler the next day that Konev was making a mistake in crossing the Dnestr; he would not have enough strength to envelop the Eighth and Sixth Armies behind the river. Probably both estimates were partly right. Konev at that stage was clearly more interested in exploiting his complete operational freedom to the west than in taking on the more difficult task of engaging the two German armies on his left. On the other hand, Eighth Army in fact did not have the strength to continue extending its flank west.

On 20 March Manstein informed Woehler that Sixth Army would take over part of his line on the east to enable him to stretch his front west. The plan was to get XXXXVII Panzer Corps and all the army's tanks across the Dnestr for a jab into Konev's flank. Two days later Woehler reported that Second Ukrainian Front had three armies and three tank armies drawing up to the Dnestr on a 60-mile front between Kamenka and Mogilev-Podol'skiy. Armored reconnaissance units had crossed the river and were in Balti halfway to the Prut River. The Russians were building eight bridges on the Dnestr and soon would be across in strength. They could then turn south or continue on across the Prut to the Carpathians and squeeze Eighth Army and Army Group A between the mountains and the Black Sea. Eighth Army, Woehler insisted, could not hold 100 miles of front east of the Dnestr and build another 60-mile front west of the river; its mission would have to be changed; the order to go behind the Dnestr would have to be given.

Privately, the Eighth Army and Army Group A chiefs of staff had discussed getting Eighth Army transferred to Army Group A. They believed all Eighth Army could do was to hold a front on the north long enough for Sixth Army to make good its escape from the Bug; and they apparently suspected that Manstein, thinking in terms of keeping his north flank strong and talking of an Eighth Army attack into Konev's flank, was only secondarily concerned for the welfare of the two southern armies. On 24 March Woehler and Hollidt met at Woehler's headquarters and agreed that the time had come to take both armies away from the Bug. They decided that if the army group commands did nothing and the decision became imperative, they would act in concert without orders.

The day before, Kleist had asked Manstein whether he thought Eighth Army could protect the Army Group A flank on the west. Manstein had said no; at most, the army could cover it between the Dnestr and the Bug but there, too, the Russians could get through if they really tried. On the 25th the Russians thrust their way into Balta, situated five miles north of the lateral railroad behind Eighth Army and astride a ridge line running deep behind Army Group A east of the Dnestr.

That night Woehler and Kleist met at Kleist's headquarters in Tiraspol. The next morning Kleist called Zeitzler and told him he had taken command of Eighth Army. He had ready the orders for a withdrawal to the Dnestr and proposed to issue them that afternoon. (He had given Woehler a copy the night before.) "Someone," he said, "must lay his head on the block." When Zeitzler advised him to see Hitler first, Kleist agreed he would the next day, after he had made certain the withdrawal was all set for an immediate start. On the 27th Hitler consented to let the two armies go back, provided they held a bridgehead from Tiraspol to Odessa. He refused to consider giving up Odessa, the main supply base for the Crimea.

MODEL AND SCHOERNER TAKE COMMAND

On 30 March Hitler sent his personal Condor to pick up Kleist at his headquarters in Tiraspol and Manstein at L'vov. That night, at the midnight situation conference, he awarded both field marshals the swords to the Knight's Cross of the Iron Cross and relieved them of their commands. He told them he approved of everything they had done in the past months, but had concluded that on the Eastern Front the day of the master tacticians was past and that what he needed were generals who would drive their troops to the utmost and extract from them last ounce of capacity for resistance. When Manstein and Kleist departed, Model, promoted to generalfeldmarschall, and Schoerner, newly promoted to generaloberst, were waiting in the anteroom.

Hitler had for long put off getting rid of Manstein. According to Goering, he had already "drawn the necessary conclusions" in early 1943. Manstein, meanwhile, had persisted in showing flashes of military genius that made him indispensable in individual crises. In the aggregate, however, his displays of talented generalship had only made it harder for Hitler to avoid the realization that Germany was not merely passing through a period of adversity but entering one of hopelessness. Since December 1943 Manstein's successor, Model, had been standing by. The actual low point in Manstein's relations with Hitler had been reached on 27 January 1944, when Manstein, while the Fuehrer was addressing the army and army group commanders, had interrupted (an unheard of occurrence when the Fuehrer was speaking) and objected to a remark that generals "ought to be the last to desert the flag." If Model had not been needed at Army Group North four days later, Manstein would probably not have lasted the two more months in his command.

Kleist had not engaged in any such dramatic encounter with Hitler, but he had consistently opposed him on the question of holding the Crimea and at the end had threatened to take matters into his own hands to get Sixth Army away from the Bug. In November 1943 he had proposed that Hitler devote himself mainly to internal and foreign policy and, in the style of World War I, create a First Quartermaster General of the Wehrmacht who would run the war on the Eastern Front and have strong advisory powers in the other theaters.

It must have cost Hitler a tremendous effort to part amicably with Manstein and Kleist. That he did so evinced their stature in the Army.

Even though it could probably be assumed that the end of the Soviet offensive was in sight, the state of Army Groups South and A, which Hitler on 5 April in a classic empty gesture renamed Army Group North Ukraine and Army Group South Ukraine, was still precarious at the time Model and Schoerner were appointed. In the Fourth Panzer Army's sector Ternopol was encircled, and Brody was nearly encircled. First Panzer Army was at the critical point in its breakout. Sixth Army was beginning its retreat from the Bug.

The Crimea was isolated. In the gap between the army groups' flanks Soviet spearheads had reached the Carpathians west of Chernovtsy and Kolomyya.

MARGARETHE

Behind the front the last act of an impromptu drama that could have added to the army groups' troubles was working out slightly to their benefit. Toward the end of February Hitler had decided a showdown with Hungary was due. He had instructed the Operations Staff, OKW, to refurbish its plan for Operation MARGARETHE, which the Commanding General, Southeast, would execute, probably sometime in the first half of March. Tactically, the operation was to be a variant of the Trojan Horse concept: German troops allegedly in transit through Hungary would suddenly stop, intern the Hungarian Army, and occupy the major centers. Rumania, he decided, did not need to be included; it would not defect because as long as Antonescu stayed in power it had nowhere else to go. On 15 March, after the Soviet offensive had forced diversion of several MARGARETHE divisions to the East, Hitler decided to try an easier way and meet with the Hungarian Regent, Admiral Horthy, first.

On the 18th at Schloss Klessheim, Horthy at first refused and then, finally, accepted Hitler's demands for a government oriented toward Germany and the right to station German troops on Hungarian territory; but he boarded his train and departed for Budapest without signing the protocol. The next morning German troops crossed the border; and when Horthy's train reached Budapest shortly before noon, a German honor guard was at the station to greet him. When Horthy's attitude stiffened after he reached the capital, Hitler concluded it would be necessary to strengthen the occupation forces and disarm the Hungarian Army. Horthy apparently saw what was coming, and on 23 March, just a step ahead of a 6-hour ultimatum the German Foreign Ministry had ready, he appointed Field Marshal Doeme Sztojay, the Hungarian Minister in Berlin, Minister President of Hungary. Sztojay was acceptable to Germany, although Hitler would have preferred Bela Imredy, who, himself allegedly of Jewish descent, had headed an anti-Semitic government in the late 1930's. On the same day, Antonescu entered the picture with a demand that Hungary return the Rumanian territory Germany and Italy had given it in the Vienna Award of August 1940. To evade that complication, the Germans declared all of Hungary east of the Tisza River part of the Eastern Front zone of operations, which by that time, it, in fact, nearly was.

On 24 March, when Zhukov's spearhead approaching the Prut above Chernovtsy came within sixty miles of the Hungarian border, the Operations Staff, OKW, and the Southeastern Theater Command changed their minds about demobilizing the Hungarian Army. They wanted to get Hungarian units into the Carpathians to close the passes, and on the 25th prevailed upon the Hungarian Army General Staff, which had, under the circumstances, proved surprisingly co-operative, to begin calling up men to fill out the home forces. Of the Hungarian occupation forces in Russia, VII Corps was already forming a front on the upper Prut. VIII Corps was still stationed behind Army Group Center.

On the 27th Hungarian troops moving into the mountains reported meeting German stragglers from Army Group South. The OKW, which so far had avoided stationing its German units where they could be drawn into the Eastern Front, faced a dilemma: the

Bridge on the Dnestr after the retreat.

border had to be defended and it could not put Hungarian troops in the Rumanian territory south of Chernovtsy. On the 29th it assembled two reinforced German regiments under a provisional corps headquarters. The next day they moved into the mountains as the Blocking Force (Sperrverband) Bucovina. That still left the most threatened point, the Tatar Pass south of Stanislav, inadequately covered. On the night of 30 March Zeitzler told Army Group South to take command of the First Mountain Division, one of the OKW divisions in Hungary, and move it into the pass. Jodl, Chief of the Operations Staff, OKW, protested to Hitler that the OKW was losing the last division in its central reserve; Zeitzler countered by calling into question the whole OKW strategy and the division of forces it had tried to enforce through the winter. Hitler agreed with Jodl but, unwilling to have another internal upheaval on his hands just when he was getting rid of Manstein and Kleist, ordered the division to move close behind the pass and stay there as the OKW reserve pending a final decision.

FIRST PANZER ARMY SAVED—A FORTRESS SACRIFICED
By the time Model took over at L'vov on 3 April the worst was over

for Army Group South. Brody had held, and II SS Panzer Corps was giving XIII Corps a short boost which would enable it to straighten its line. First Panzer Army's breakout was succeeding.

All that was left was one last, small, and, under the circumstances, rather minor tragedy. In the "fortified place" Ternopol over 4,000 men, most of them eighteen-year-olds, had been encircled since 21 March. On the 25th a tank force had nearly fought its way through with a supply column, but permission to evacuate the city had not been given, and the armor was not strong enough both to guard the trucks and to carry the attack over the last five or so miles. The next attempt was delayed until 11 April, when the 9th SS Panzer Division could be spared from the relief of First Panzer Army. The SS-men set out in rain and deep mud. On the second day, Model asked permission to have the garrison break out. Hitler first refused, declaring the army group was "honor bound" to relieve Ternopol, but later changed his mind and agreed to let the order be given when the relief force had drawn somewhat closer to the city. The 9th SS Panzer Division, as almost always the case with new SS divisions, was a splendidly outfitted aggregation of raw troops and inexperienced officers. On the morning of the 14th Model took the tanks away from the SS division's staff and put them under an Army officer. The attack then carried several miles before being stopped again at the end of the day. By that time the Ternopol garrison was pushed into a small area on the western edge of the city and under incessant air and ground attack. On the 15th the commanding general was killed. That night the senior officer in the pocket gave the order to break out. Fifty-three men reached the Fourth Panzer Army line.

First Panzer Army came out of its encirclement in better shape than anyone had expected. No large number of its troops suffered the complete collapse of morale that had been observed in the survivors from the Cherkassy pocket. The army stayed at the front, and on 16 April III Panzer Corps attacked south across the Dnestr. In Germany the army's feat was celebrated as a victory, clouded somewhat when Hube lost his life in a plane crash in the Austrian Alps the day he went to Berchtesgaden to receive the diamonds to the Knight's Cross of the Iron Cross.

Off the army's right flank, in the second half of the month, Hungarian First Army (VII Corps and VI Corps, the latter formed out of divisions from the home forces) established a front arcing around Chernovtsy and following the line of the Carpathians south to the Rumanian border. Late in the month the Hungarians successfully withstood several rather heavy local Soviet attacks, rearousing the Germans' old suspicion that in Hungarian Second Army, which performed so poorly after Stalingrad, the Hungarians had foisted on the Wehrmacht their worst troops.

TO THE DNESTR

The Sixth and Eighth Armies pulled away from the Bug on 28 March. At Nikolaev, where the only way across the Bug was a ponton bridge built by Austrian Army engineers in World War I, five Sixth Army divisions that had been holding a bridgehead rejoined the main force just in time. Around Novo Odessa the Eighth Guards and Forty-sixth Armies, having reassembled, followed close behind the Germans and began maneuvering for another chance to slice through Sixth Army's center.

By 2 April the Sixth Army left flank was on the bridgehead line it had been ordered to hold around Odessa, but the Russians had drawn in tight and clearly planned to cut the bridgehead in two midway between Odessa and Tiraspol. On that day a sleet storm blew down from the Carpathians. The temperature dropped far below freezing; ice tore down telephone and power lines and clogged artillery pieces and machine guns.

The next night, at the height of the storm, Soviet tanks and cavalry broke through to Razdelnaya and turned south, splitting the bridgehead in half. In three more days the Russian force lunged deep behind Odessa to the Dnestr, capturing the city's water intake station near the village of Belyaekva. Sixth Army then began a hasty retreat behind the river amid scenes of wildest confusion. At the railroad bridge and road bridge west of Tiraspol traffic had been jammed up for weeks. The army had built five smaller bridges at various points, and on the muddy approaches to each miles-long columns of trucks, people, and cattle stood four and five abreast waiting to cross. Hundreds of trains jammed into Odessa, but only a few could be routed through to the west.

The last Germans crossed the Dnestr on 14 April. The army group reported that the scene behind the river was reminiscent of Stalingrad. The Rumanian railroads had failed completely. The troops had no clothing and no supplies. The wounded were lying in the open at the sidings. The daily ration was 200 grams of bread.

Probably as much because Malinovskiy had gone as far as he wanted to as for any other reason, Sixth Army did manage to get a front on the Dnestr from Dubossary south to the Dnestr Liman, but not before the Russians, as was their custom, had gained a number of bridgeheads, the largest of them south of Tiraspol at the center of the front.

West of the Dnestr, Army Group South Ukraine was forced to make all the use it could of the Rumanian Third and Fourth Armies. To keep the Rumanians in hand, the army group command devised an involved chain of command, which, while preserving appearances, actually subordinated Rumanian Fourth Army to Eighth Army and Rumanian Third Army to Sixth Army. Marshal Antonescu, the existence of his regime at stake, gave the alliance his desperate loyalty, but his soldiers at all levels were interested only in personal survival.

Many officers had stopped wearing their German decorations. After talking with the Commanding General, Rumanian Fourth Army, on 27 March, Woehler came away with the impression that the Rumanians "had no discernible desire to fight."

During the first week in April, Eighth Army again raced to keep pace with the westward moving Russians. The Rumanians, after refusing to make a stand on the Prut, had promised to hold the so-called Strunga line between Iasi and Targu Neamt, but they were talking of falling back to the narrows between the Danube and the Carpathians. In the second week of the month German panzer divisions counterattacking across the Prut stopped the Russian spearheads west of Iasi. After that Eighth Army, Rumanian Fourth Army, and Blocking Force Bucovina built a continuous east-west line from Dubosarry-Iasi-Targu Neamt north along the mountains to the Army Group North Ukraine flank.

THE CRIMEA

Seventeenth Army sat out the winter in the Crimea. (Map 25) After the last hope that Manstein might come to its relief had faded in November 1943 and the Russians in the same month had taken beachheads on the south shore of the Sivash and on the Kerch' Peninsula, Zeitzler, Kleist, and Jaenecke had agreed the army should get off the Crimea. They reasoned that the peninsula could not be held in the long run, that the troops were needed on the main front, and that any further diversion of troops there would be an outright waste. But Hitler had insisted the army stay put, and, during the winter, at the expense of Army Groups South and A, had increased its strength in German troops from one infantry division to five, plus two self-propelled assault gun brigades. Marshal Antonescu, who would much rather have taken them out, had left the seven Rumanian divisions with Seventeenth Army.

The army, keeping its main defense line on the Perekop Isthmus, had managed during the winter to reduce the Soviet beachheads to two very small areas, one at the southeastern end of the isthmus and one on the easternmost tip of the Kerch' Peninsula. If the Perekop Isthmus was lost, the only other place the army could make a stand was at Sevastopol. It had built the GNEISENAU line in a rough arc around Simferopol but had troops enough only to fight a rear-guard action there until the main force moved into Sevastopol.

On 7 April 1944 Schoerner inspected the Crimea defenses, pronounced them in excellent shape, and in reporting that the peninsula could be held "for a long time" made one of the least accurate predictions of the war. The next morning Fourth Ukrainian Front attacked. The isthmus line held, but the Rumanian 10th Division holding half of the Sivash bridgehead line was badly shaken the first day and collapsed the next.

That night Jaenecke took the line back to the base of the isthmus. Schoerner told Zeitzler the retreat to Sevastopol might have to begin any minute and therefore Jaenecke should be authorized to make the decision. He was confident, he said, that neither Jaenecke nor his chief of staff would jump to any hasty conclusions. Hitler of course refused. Instead, he dispatched Zeitzler to the army group headquarters where the latter arrived on 10 April just in time to be told the Russians had

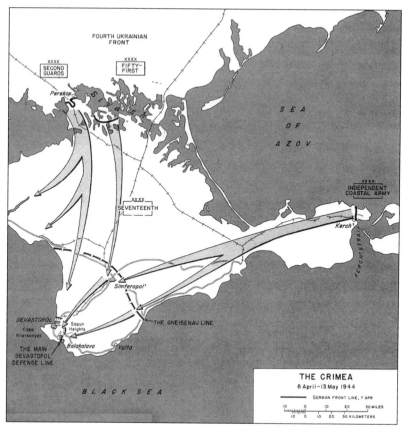

Map 25: The Crimea, 8 April-13 May 1944

pushed into the interior and the first stage of the retreat had started.
Since the first stage, as planned, chiefly involved removing the troops
from the Kerch' Peninsula, Hitler approved, but then, when he
learned the next day that the order for all units to withdraw to the
GNEISENAU line had also been given, fell into a rage and accused
Jaenecke of having lost his nerve. As the German and Russian units
retreated west of Kerch', the Independent Coastal Army (the former
North Caucasus Front) began applying pressure from the east.

When Schoerner and the Army Group South Ukraine chief of staff,
who was on the Crimea at the time, agreed that Jaenecke's decision had
been necessary, Hitler authorized a withdrawal to the GNEISENAU
line and, if necessary, to Sevastopol, but directed that Sevastopol was
to be held indefinitely. Everyone, including Hitler, had previously

believed that when the retreat began it would have to proceed continuously to the last stage, the evacuation. Schoerner reported that the GNEISENAU line and Sevastopol could not be held more than three or four weeks. He had already instructed the Navy to send a convoy from Constanta, Rumania, to take off the service troops.

On the 12th, Soviet tanks broke into the GNEISENAU line in several places; the next day Simferopol was lost. On 16 April, the Russians close behind them, the Seventeenth Army rear guard went into the main Sevastopol line. A day later Hitler told Army Group South Ukraine to take out all troops and equipment not needed for the defense but again insisted that Sevastopol be held.

Casualties in the first ten days numbered 13,131 Germans and 17,652 Rumanians. The ration strength of Seventeenth Army stood at 75,546 Germans and 45,887 Rumanians. The army estimated its combat strength at one-third of the German troops. The Rumanians, it reported, were not fit for combat and ought to be evacuated. It had, therefore, all together, five kampfgruppen of approximately regimental strength facing three Soviet armies with a combined total of 27 divisions and 200 tanks.

In a midnight interview with Hitler at Fuehrer headquarters on 21 April, Schoerner argued that Sevastopol could not be held because

Sevastopol Harbor.

Seventeenth Army lacked the strength, and the Navy could not keep it supplied because the convoys were already having to fight their way in. In an atmosphere reminiscent of Stalingrad, Hitler marshaled his counterarguments: a statement from General der Infanterie Karl Allmendinger, one of the Seventeenth Army corps commanders, that the army could hold Sevastopol if it were given some reinforcements, and a report from the OKM that the Navy could keep Sevastopol supplied as long as might be needed. He did not want to hold Sevastopol very long, Hitler insisted, only the six or eight weeks needed to keep Turkey quiet until he had beaten off the coming Anglo-American invasion.

Four days later, when the Commanding Admiral, Black Sea, at Schoerner's urging, went to Fuehrer headquarters, Hitler asked whether he had enough shipping tonnage. When he answered that he had, Hitler abruptly dismissed him without letting him explain that having the tonnage and getting the ships through to the Crimea were different things. The OKM, seconded by the Air Force, had, according to Zeitzler, given Hitler "a rosy picture" of conditions at Sevastopol.

On the 28th Hitler called Jaenecke to Berchtesgaden and promised him "generous" reinforcements. On learning that the reinforcements amounted to four battalions of half-trained recruits, Jaenecke, in an attempt to place the responsibility for what was about to happen at Sevastopol where it belonged, submitted a letter requesting that Seventeenth Army be made directly subordinate to the OKH (Hitler). Hitler thereupon declared that Jaenecke had demonstrated he was no longer able to conduct the defense of Sevastopol as directed, gave Allmendinger command of Seventeenth Army, and ordered that Jaenecke not be allowed to return to the Crimea. In the meantime, Antonescu had submitted a letter in which he bluntly labeled as nonsense the attempt to hold a distant beachhead when the homeland was in danger. Zeitzler did not give the letter to Hitler because, he said, "It would create an explosion."

On 5 May the Russians hit the front north of Sevastopol. The attack was a feint. The main assault came on the 7th in the south behind Balaklava. By the end of the day the Russians had smashed through to the Sapun Heights, which gave them a clear field of observation

Soviet troops on Sapun Heights.

over the whole beachhead to the tip of Cape Khersonyes. The next day the army regained its original north front but failed to retake the heights in the south. By then the losses were so great that it had become impossible to hold anywhere. That night Hitler agreed to let the army be evacuated.

During the next four nights convoys with enough ships to take aboard all the troops stood off the cape, but some turned back to Constanta empty and others took aboard only a fraction of the men they could have carried. The Navy claimed that the whole cape was shrouded in smoke and the ships could not go inshore. The Chief of Staff, Seventeenth Army, insisted visibility was always adequate for ships to have found their way into the inlets, but several whole convoys failed even to try. The result was a tragic fiasco. Of 64,700 men still at Sevastopol in the first week of May, 26,700 were left on the beach to fall into Soviet hands. In the aftermath the Commanding Admiral, Black Sea, and the Naval Commander, Crimea, were awarded the Knight's Cross of the Iron Cross; and Hitler ordered that neither Jaenecke nor Allmendinger was to be given another command until a court-martial had resolved "the suspicion that all was not done that might have been done to hold the Crimea."

CHAPTER XIV

Prelude to Disaster

KARELIA

THE SOVIET OFFENSIVE BEGINS

The "black day" of the Finnish Army was 10 June 1944. After a massive artillery and air preparation on 9 June, accompanied by probing attacks, the Soviet Twenty-first Army on the morning of the 10th centered its attack on the left flank division of Finnish IV Corps holding the western side of the front on the Isthmus of Karelia. In a massive assault three Soviet divisions annihilated one regiment of the Finnish division and before noon had penetrated to a depth of six miles. (Map 26)

At that stage of the war an offensive against the Finnish Army was hardly a military necessity. Its rationale, as far as the Russians have explained it, was that it diverted enemy attention from the offensive build-up in progress opposite Army Group Center in Belorussia and that it fulfilled a sacred obligation to liberate all occupied Soviet territory. The offensive appears also to have been motivated by a compulsion to establish Soviet claims as victor or liberator in non-Soviet areas of eastern Europe by actual military operations in some form, and it may have been designed to open the way for a more radical settling of the score with Finland than had been envisioned at Tehran.

Operationally, the campaign against Finland must have appeared a thoroughly routine exercise. The Finns had not in any wise been able to keep abreast of the past three years' advances in the technology of warfare. Relatively modest reinforcement, mostly in infantry and artillery, gave the Leningrad and Karelian Fronts crushing superiority. According to Soviet figures the two fronts had 450,000 troops, 10,000 artillery pieces and heavy mortars, 800 tanks, and 1,547 aircraft

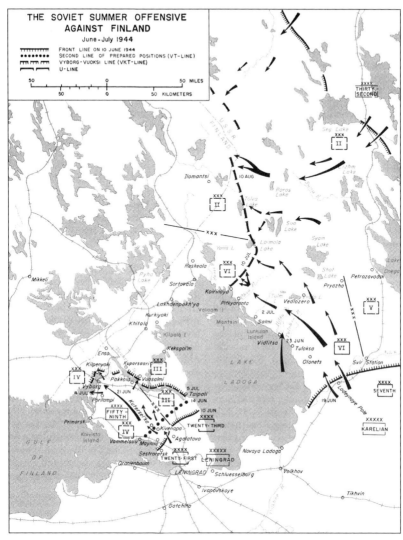

Map 26: The Soviet Summer Offensive Against Finland, June-July 1944

against the Finnish Army's 268,000 men, 1,930 artillery pieces, 110 tanks, and 248 aircraft.

The Finnish High Command was taken by surprise even though it had had warnings of an attack in the making as early as May, and on 1 June Finnish Army Intelligence had predicted that an offensive was to be expected within ten days. Four or five days before the attack the Russians had imposed radio silence—an almost infallible sign. But the

Army operations chief was not convinced, and his judgment carried the greatest weight with Mannerheim.

When the attack began, the two Finnish corps defending the isthmus, III Corps on the left and IV Corps on the right, had three divisions and a brigade in the front, three more divisions and a brigade in the second line, and the Armored Division stationed east of Vyborg. On the isthmus the Finns had three defense lines. The first—in the van—roughly followed the old Finnish-Soviet border. The second, immediately to the rear, laid out on terrain militarily more advantageous than the first, crossed the isthmus in an almost straight line from Vammelsuu on the Gulf of Finland to Taipali on Lake Ladoga. The third ran from Vyborg to Kuparsaari and along the north bank of the Vuoksi River to Taipali. This line had strong natural advantages but with work not started until November 1943 it was far from completed. Between the last isthmus line and the heart of Finland, the so-called Moscow Line followed the 1940 border. It had some concrete emplacements and others were being built, but it had no natural advantages and could only be used for a last-ditch stand.

The Germans had long doubted the Finns' capacity for resistance. In June 1943 Dietl had repeated a prediction he had made in February of that year that the Finnish Army would not be able to withstand a strong Soviet attack. The Finns, he had stated, were superior to the Germans as forest fighters and in dealing with adversities of terrain and climate, but they preferred to avoid pitched battles. In July 1944, after the Soviet offensive had passed its peak, an OKW observer concluded that the Finnish setbacks could be blamed, at least in part, on lack of training and neglect of fortifications. He also believed that in June 1944 the Finns no longer expected a Soviet attack and that, until the shock of the Russian breakthrough on 10 June produced a more realistic judgment, they had a tendency, induced by their experiences in the Winter War and in 1941, to underestimate the enemy. From the latter criticism, the Germans extracted a degree of wry satisfaction, since they had long felt that the Finns failed to appreciate fully the nature of Germany's problems on the Eastern Front.

To achieve and exploit the breakthrough Govorov's Leningrad

Front had deployed two army headquarters (Twenty-first and Twenty-third), ten rifle divisions, and the approximate equivalent of three tank divisions. In the main assault area the Soviet artillery reportedly numbered 300 to 400 guns per kilometer of front. For striking power Govorov relied on his tremendous superiority in tanks, artillery, and aircraft. His rifle divisions' will to fight declined rapidly after the first few days' combat. The tactics—a tremendous commitment of troops and matériel on a narrow front and, following the penetration, exploitation by several corps abreast—followed the standard pattern of the Eastern Front.

Immediately after the breakthrough on 10 June, that IV Corps most likely could not hold in front of the second line became clear. Mannerheim gave the corps a division from the reserve and a regiment from III Corps, ordered the Armored Division to move up from Vyborg, began transferring a division from East Karelia, and recalled the 3d Brigade from Twentieth Mountain Army. By the 12th, IV Corps was in the second line. III Corps, which had not yet been attacked, also fell back. On the same day, Mannerheim ordered a division and a brigade out of East Karelia to the isthmus and asked the OKW to release the weapons and grain that had been meant for Finland but were being held in Germany under Hitler's embargo. The next day Hitler agreed.

The Finnish High Command was forced to consider radical measures. On 13 June Mannerheim's chief of staff told Dietl that if the second line was lost, the Finns would give up the Svir and Maaselkä Fronts and pull back in East Karelia to a short line northeast of Lake Ladoga, thereby freeing two to three more divisions for the isthmus. Since November 1943, work had been in progress on the so-called U-line, the line of the Uksu River-Loimola Lake-Tolva Lake.

Dietl urged the Finns to carry out the planned withdrawal but feared that out of reluctance to give up East Karelia they would hesitate too long. Later, he recommended to Hitler that the German policy be to tie the Finns to Germany by giving them as much support as possible and, at the same time, by requiring them to make the necessary tactical sacrifices, not allow them to dissipate their strength in an attempt to hang on in East Karelia. On the shorter line, he thought, the Finns might hold out indefinitely; they would then save their country and at the same time spare the Twentieth Mountain Army the necessity of executing Operation BIRKE.

While Dietl was at Mikkeli the second line on the isthmus was already under attack. It held for a day but on 14 June the Russians brought up their heavy weapons and, since—as a captured map later revealed—they had reconnoitered the second line in detail before the offensive began, were able to attack in force immediately. Overwhelming the Finns again with artillery and tanks, they cracked the second line at the village of Kutersel'ka and by 15 June had smashed the Finnish front on an 8-mile stretch from there to the coast.

By then it was apparent that the Soviet main effort was being directed along the railroad line to Vyborg. The Finns had virtually no hope of stopping the Russians short of the city and were worried that they might reach and close the 17-mile-wide corridor between Vyborg and the Vuoksi River before III Corps and IV Corps could escape. Such a maneuver would in all probability be decisive, for it would end all Finnish chances of holding the Vyborg-Vukosi line, force III Corps and IV Corps to go north across the Vuoksi, and because there was only one bridge across the river, compel them to abandon much of their heavy equipment on the way.

On 16 June, Mannerheim ordered the retreat to the Vyborg-Vuoksi line. On the 10th, after four more days of heavy fighting, IV Corps, the Russians close behind, moved into the line between Vyborg and the river. III Corps established itself on the north bank of the Vuoksi and held a bridgehead on the south bank across from Vuosalmi. Again the Finnish Army stood in the line where it had stopped the Russians in 1940.

The withdrawal had gone better than might have been expected, chiefly because Govorov, rigidly intent on Vyborg, failed to strike toward the Vyborg-Vuoksi narrows. But the Finns still had no cause for optimism. The Soviet forces on the isthmus had been gradually increased to 20 rifle divisions, 4 tank brigades, 5 to 6 tank regiments, and 4 self-propelled assault gun regiments. Against these Mannerheim, drawing on the last units that could be spared from East Karelia, could assemble no more than 10 divisions and 4 brigades.

GERMAN AID

The military crisis resulting from loss of the second Isthmus of Karelia line brought a political crisis in its trail. After a secret Cabinet meeting on 18 June, the Finns reestablished contact with the Soviet Government. As another upshot of that meeting, Heinrichs asked the German military representative at Finnish headquarters whether Germany would be willing to provide aid other than weapons, specifically six divisions, to take over the front in East Karelia and release Finnish troops for the isthmus.

In Germany the necessity for extending help to Finland had already been recognized and accepted even though the Germans themselves were by then in trouble in Normandy and expected a new Soviet offensive to erupt any day. On 19 June, six days after Hitler lifted the embargo, German torpedo boats delivered 9,000 Panzerfaust (44-mm. recoilless antitank grenade launchers). Three days later 5,000 Panzerschreck (88-mm antitank rocket launchers) were airlifted to Finland. Germany could not give the six divisions the Finns wanted, but on the 10th the OKW informed Mannerheim that it was ready to give every kind of help if the Finnish Army was genuinely determined to hold the Vyborg-Vuoksi line. Aside from weapons and supplies, the Germans offered the 122d Infantry Division, a self-propelled assault gun brigade (the 303d), and air units (a fighter group and a ground attack close support group [Stukas] plus one squadron). The ground troops were drawn from Army Group North and the planes from Fifth Air Force in northern Finland and First Air Force, attached to Army Group North. The aircraft were transferred immediately and on 21 June flew 940 support missions for a Finnish Army.

Although the German aid was offered and, in part, delivered without a prior commitment on Finland's part, its price was known to both parties. On 21 June, Mannerheim informed Hitler that Finland was prepared to establish closer bonds with Germany. The next day Ribbentrop flew to Helsinki to conduct the negotiations in person. The Finns, trying to avoid formally tying themselves to Germany, argued that in view of the strong popular sentiment for peace, which had already produced a movement to bring to power a govenment oriented toward the Soviet Union, they could not enter into any sort of agreement that would have to be ratified by Parliament. Ribbentrop offered to compromise and accept a declaration signed by the President. On 23 June the German hand was strengthened when the Soviet Government informed the Finns that it would not discuss an armistice until the President, Ryti, and the Foreign Minister, Ramsay, declared in writing that Finland was ready to capitulate and appealed to the Soviet Union for peace.

On the 24th Ryti and Ramsay conferred with Mannerheim at Mikkeli. The next day Hitler added pressure. He stated categorically that a public clarification of Finland's attitude was to be secured. If not, support for Finland would stop. Late on the night of 26 June, Ryti called in Ribbentrop and handed him a letter in which he stated that he, as President of Finland, would not make peace with the Soviet Union without the consent of the German Government and would not permit any government appointed by him or any other persons to conduct armistice or peace talks without German consent.

The Germans got what they demanded, but in the form of an unenforceable contract, which the Finnish Government, the life of the nation at stake, had issued not altogether in good faith. The end result of Ribbentrop's mission was to obscure the obvious generosity of German aid extended at a time when it could scarcely be spared and to arouse, instead, in the minds of the Finns a feeling that they had been blackmailed in their hour of greatest need.

For the Finns the June negotiations had one purpose—to get help in stopping the Soviet offensive. The Ryti letter achieved that purpose, but the aid that came was less than the Finns expected. It was, in fact, less than the Germans had meant to give, because, in the meantime, the Soviet offensive against Army Group Center, which began on 22 June, had imposed a nearly overwhelming drain on German resources.

The 303d Self-propelled Assault Gun Brigade reached Finland on 23 June, and the 122d Infantry Division arrived five days later. But a second assault gun brigade for Finland had to be diverted to Army Group Center at the last minute, and a corps headquarters to command the German units in Finland, although withdrawn from Army Group North, was never sent. German weapons and supplies, including some tanks and heavy equipment, continued to flow to

Finland. The Panzerfaust and Panzerschreck greatly increased the Finns' ability to withstand tank attacks and played a major role in restoring the confidence of the Finnish Army.

THE LAST PHASE

On 21 June the Russians occupied Vyborg. The Finns had evacuated it the day before. Although the Army had not planned to defend the old city, its loss was a blow to Finnish morale. Between Vyborg and the Vuoksi, the Russians deployed for another breakthrough; and on 25 June Twenty-first Army attacked the front near Repola with ten divisions reinforced by assault artillery, penetrating the line to a depth of some two and a half miles. In four days' heavy fighting the Finns succeeded in sealing off the breakthrough but could not regain their former front. The Russians kept the salient, which was the more dangerous in that it brought them close to good tank terrain.

On 16 June Mannerheim had issued orders to give up East Karelia. He intended to withdraw gradually from the Svir and Maaselkä Fronts to the general line Uksu River-Suo Lake-Poros Lake. At the last minute, as the withdrawal was starting, the OKW tried in vain to persuade him not to sacrifice East Karelia. In thus going directly against the advice Dietl had given a few days earlier, the OKW was probably influenced by several considerations. The first, most likely, was Hitler's well-known aversion to giving ground voluntarily. More pertinent was the knowledge that in giving up East Karelia the Finns would lose their principal war gain, their last lever for bargaining with the Soviet Union and, consequently, their last tangible motive for staying in the war. The OKW reasoning had much to recommend it from the German point of view, but the Finns had no taste for desperate gambles—nor, for that matter, although they seemed to be acting in agreement with Dietl's advice, did they have any enthusiasm for last stands in the Goetterdaemmerung vein.

In the Maaselkä and Aunus (Svir) Fronts, the Finns had 4 divisions and 2 brigades. Opposite them stood 11 divisions and 6 brigades of Meretskov's Karelian Front. By evacuating the large bridgehead south of the Svir on 18 June the Finns escaped an attack that began the following day, but thereafter the withdrawal went less smoothly than they had expected. Seventh Army kept up an aggressive pursuit and, by crossing the Svir on either side of Lodeynoye Pole and staging a landing on the Ladoga shore between Tuloksa and Vidlitsa, threatened to push the Finnish divisions into the wilderness on the eastern side of the Isthmus of Olonets. The Finns evacuated Petrozavodsk on 30 June and two days later, Salmi.

By 10 July the Finnish divisions were in the U-line. The Finns were by no means certain they could hold the U-line and began work on another between Yanis Lake and Lake Ladoga. They also considered going back to the Moscow Line.

In the first days of July the Finns were given a short respite, at least on the Isthmus of Karelia. On the 4th Fifty-ninth Army, after taking over the extreme western sector of the isthmus in late June, occupied the islands in Vyborg Bay and attempted a landing on the north shore. There it was repulsed by the 122d Infantry Division, which had just arrived. At the same time, Twenty-third Army struck at the Finnish bridgehead south of Vuosalmi, but otherwise Leningrad Front confined itself to local assaults and regrouping, giving the Finns time to strengthen their defenses.

In the Finnish High Command concern for the future was growing, particularly with respect to manpower. At the end of June casualties had reached 18,000, of which no more than 12,000 had been replaced. On 1 July Mannerheim asked for a second German division and more self-propelled assault gun brigades. When Hitler responded with nothing but a promise to build up the assault gun battalion of the 122d Infantry Division to brigade strength, Mannerheim protested that in advising his government to accept the German terms he had assumed a heavy responsibility—if the units were not forthcoming, not only would the military situation deteriorate, but his personal prestige and influence in the country would be destroyed. Hitler replied with an offer of one self-propelled assault gun brigade before 10 July, another to be sent later, and tanks, assault guns, antitank guns, and artillery.

In the second week of July the Finns relinquished the right bank of the Vuoksi south of Vousalmi. The Russians followed up by taking a bridgehead on the north bank. Too weak to eliminate the bridgehead, the Finns tried to contain it. Despite this dangerous development and the continued heavy fighting, which brought the number of Finnish casualties to 32,000 by the 11th, the fronts on both sides of Lake Ladoga were beginning to stabilize. By 15 July the Finns had detected signs— confirmed several days later—that, although the Soviet strength on the isthmus had risen to 26 rifle divisions and 12 to 14 tank brigades, the better units were being relieved and replaced with garrison troops. The tempo of the offensive could be expected to diminish.

PARTISAN WARFARE AT ITS HEIGHT

In 1943 and 1944 the Soviet partisan movement was firmly established. Its strength had leveled off at about 250,000 men, but its influence on the lives and attitudes of millions in the occupied territory, from the Pripyat Marshes north, grew as the German prospects of victory dimmed. The movement, mainly through efforts from the Soviet side of the front, had become a tightly organized, closely controlled, and centrally directed military and political instrument.

ORGANIZATION

By early 1943, the partisans had been put on a thoroughgoing military footing. The Chief of Staff of the Central Staff of the Partisan Movement, General Leytenant Pantileimon K. Ponomarenko, was attached to the Soviet Army General Staff. The partisan units operating close to the front were directly under the staffs of the Soviet Army commands opposite them, those deeper in German territory being controlled from the headquarters in Moscow. Regular officers and enlisted men were detailed to the partisan units as training cadres and specialists. Partisan staffs, often manned by officers who had held Party or government posts in the occupied territory, were attached to the front and army headquarters; they maintained contact with the partisan units, controlled supplies for the units, represented the central partisan headquarters in organizational matters, and transmitted tactical directives from the military commands.

In late 1942 or early 1943, after the military reorganization was in full effect, a certain amount of Party control had been reimposed, probably to save appearances, since partisan activity was in theory preeminently a Party function. The principal result of the change

A partisan in action.

was that subsequently many of the existing partisan staffs were also assigned territorial (political) designations. At the top, Ponomarenko, who was a political general and the prewar First Secretary of the Belorussian Communist Party, became chief of the partisan movement in the Belorussian S.S.R. As chief of the whole partisan movement he also headed the movement in the Russian Soviet Federated Socialist Republic, which did not have a separate territorial command.

The signal feature of the partisan movement in the occupied territory during the years 1943 and 1944 was the emergence of the so-called complexes, aggregations of brigades concentrated in specific areas under unified commands. The process attained its fullest development in Belorussia, where a dozen or more complexes appeared, one otalling 15,000 men in Rossono Rayon north of Polotsk; another of 14,000-18,000 men along the Ushach River between Borisov and Lepel; one almost as large in the swamps along the Beresina River between Borisov and Lepel; more, of 8,000, 9,000, and 14,000 men, near Minsk, Senno, and Vitebsk. By mid-1943 at least three-fourths of the partisan strength was concentrated in such centers. The number of partisans in Belorussia as of June 1944, according to Soviet figures, was 150,000 in 150 brigades and 49 detachments.

The dominant trend in the partisan movement since 1941 had been toward concentration, first into brigades, then into complexes— frequently also called divisions or corps (under the Party terminology, operative groups and operative centers). The immense forests and swamps of Belorussia and northwestern Great Russia fostered the tendency, and the Soviet Command promoted it partly because it simplified logistics, control, and surveillance, partly because it afforded the means for keeping in hand sizable stretches of territory and large numbers of people, and partly in the mistaken belief that strong partisan units could successfully undertake tactical missions against regular forces.

Militarily, the partisan complexes rarely justified the manpower, effort, and equipment expended to support them. Ostensibly, they denied the Germans access to vast areas; actually, most of them were established in areas the Germans had bypassed in 1941 and never brought fully under their military control. The centers served as fixed bases from which small detachments could be dispatched for attacks on the German lines of communications, but for such missions the number of men available probably exceeded by ten times the number who could be effectively employed within a complex's operating radius. The centers superficially formed nodes of strength; they were, however, islands. (A comparison could be drawn with the Japanese on the Pacific islands.) Lacking mobility, they did not constitute striking forces in the tactical sense, nor could one center deploy its forces to aid another under attack. No complex successfully withstood an attack by regular troops.

From the standpoint of military effectiveness, the trend toward consolidation was, moreover, a dubious psychological and sociological phenomenon. Unlike a regular army, a partisan force is not ordinarily expected to win a war, only to contribute to the victory. What constitutes an adequate contribution is difficult to resolve even in a tightly controlled movement such as that in the Soviet Union. The average partisan did not engage in a single-minded pursuit of a heroic demise; he was more inclined to be preoccupied with staying alive. Finding himself in a service that was by definition dangerous, he engaged in a constant effort to reduce his personal risks. The same was true of the whole partisan movement; it was dedicated to its own preservation—not to self-destruction. Those attitudes were persistent and, in the long run perhaps, irresistible. The complexes offered security. Once they reached strengths of 5,000, 10,000, or more men, they became immune to small police actions, and since the Germans could rarely spare enough troops for large-scale counteroperations, they could exist relatively undisturbed for months, even years. The complexes also promoted morale, discipline, and—always important from the Soviet viewpoint—political orthodoxy, but at a considerable cost in efficiency and effectiveness.

PERSONNEL

The partisan movement drew its manpower predominantly from the peasantry and the Soviet Army men left after the 1941 battles. In the years 1943 and 1944 those two groups in about equal numbers accounted for 80 percent of the total partisan strength.

The peasants, for the most part, were drafted. As partisans they were characterized by a fatalistic indifference to the war. Their class interests led them to regard partisan operations primarily as contributing to economic disruption, which reduced the profits from agriculture. At longer range, they viewed the Soviet and German systems as nearly identical evils, the chief difference being that the Soviet Union seemed more likely to win the war. To a minor degree, since the German system offered no compensatory attractions, they were also influenced by a sense of obligation to the Soviet regime as the legal and indigenous political authority.

The stragglers were somewhat more positively motivated. The "business as usual" desires of the peasantry meant nothing to the soldiers, and their espousal of the Soviet cause represented a choice of the lesser of two evils. As soldiers they had clear obligations to the Soviet state, and as stragglers they were already, in the Soviet view, deserters. Partisan activity offered them the opportunity to honor their obligations and, possibly, restore themselves to the good graces of the regime. German policy enhanced the advantages of partisan activity as far as the stragglers were concerned. Outside the partisan nnovement they had three choices: to live illegally, subject to arrest at any time and cut off from legitimate employment; to surrender and endure the hardships of the German prison camps; or to add treason to the counts already against them by joining collaborator police and military units. Even so, the majority of the stragglers dissociated themselves from the war as long as possible, not joining the partisan movement until after 1941, and then mostly out of the fear of punishment aroused by the approach of the Soviet Army.

After 1941 the percentage of Communist Party members in the partisan movement had gone down rapidly. In 1941 Party members comprised as much as 80 percent of some individual units, and units in which Party members averaged from 25 to 40 percent were not unusual. In the later years the Party contingent rarely accounted for more than 10 percent of the unit strengths. The shift was important because it reflected a basic change in the Soviet concept of partisan warfare—from the idea of a relatively limited, elite movement that would rely on Party men, to a mass movement utilizing all available sources of manpower and substituting for political loyalty as the motivating force, the ability of the regime to extend its authority and coercive power into the occupied territory. From 1942 on the Party contingent in the partisan movement was important chiefly as one of the elements of Soviet control. The Party and Soviet state interests in the partisan movement were further upheld by rigid adherence to the commissar system and by the NKVD O.O. (Osobyi Otdel, after 1943 Smersh), special countersubversion and counterintelligence sections that kept the partisan units under surveillance.

OPERATIONS

In 1943 and 1944 the partisan units were well, even elegantly, equipped by guerrilla warfare standards. The Germans could do little to interfere with the low-altitude night supply flights across the front, and the complexes usually controlled enough territory to provide landing strips capable of accommodating planes as large as C-47's. In some places ground traffic back and forth through the front was possible, at times even for columns of men with horses and wagons.

Nevertheless, achieving reasonable combat worthiness in the partisan units remained a problem to the end. The large contingent of inexperienced officers and high percentage of low-caliber recruits posed a constant danger of the movement's sinking into various kinds of erratic activity, losing its military usefulness, and, possibly, becoming a political liability. The rigorous external controls acted as a check on the tendency toward internal disintegration, and the infusion into the partisan detachments of regular Army officers and Soviet-trained personnel raised combat effectiveness. By early 1943 every brigade had some partisan warfare specialists or Army officers to oversee training and discipline.

The missions of the partisan movement were military, economic, and political-psychological. The military objectives were: (1) to reduce German mobility and interdict German logistical support; (2) to gather intelligence; and (3) to destroy and tie down German military manpower. The first, in Soviet parlance "the war of the rails," was the one on which the partisans expended the greatest amount of effort. Ordinarily, in 1943 and the first half of 1944, the daily rate of demolitions on roads and railroads in the occupied territory ran into the hundreds, and occasionally, before Soviet offensives, it mounted into the thousands. Always a nuisance, the partisan attacks could and sometimes did badly snarl German communications at awkward moments. As sources of intelligence the partisan units were effective, though probably less so than the thousands of agents the Army and NKVD intelligence organs employed directly. In actually engaging and tying down or destroying German military forces the partisans were least successful. The Germans rarely diverted first-class troops to fight partisans for whom even the second- and third-rate German security and police units were always more than a match.

The partisan movement, though a big inconvenience, remained on the whole a limited instrument of economic warfare, mostly because it was confined to the poor, relatively unproductive areas of northern Russia. In the south, which lacked the forest cover needed for concealment, partisan activity did not interfere seriously with German economic exploitation. But even in the north, in one of the least productive agricultural areas of the Soviet Union, Army Group North managed to live entirely off the land through 1943. Ultimately, the most severe economic effects fell on the peasants, who frequently found themselves in an intolerable squeeze between the partisans and the Germans.

In the political and psychological spheres, of course, the existence of a partisan movement was by itself a considerable accomplishment. The movement was, if nothing else, a means for sequestering a large segment of the manpower of the occupied territory. It could, further, intimidate or inspire to various forms of resistance other elements of the population. For the German soldier, the partisan movement injected into the war added uncertainty and terror.

ANTIPARTISAN WARFARE

In the spring of 1944 the Germans conducted three large-scale antipartisan operations—the last of the war, as it turned out—against partisan complexes that in the Soviet view had reached the highest stage in their evolution: the stage at which they could engage regular forces on something like equal terms. The Army Group Center left flank behind the Third Panzer and Fourth Army sectors had been the area on the Eastern Front most heavily infested with partisans since the winter battles of 1941-42. There, in 1944, First Baltic Front wanted to employ the partisan complexes as a second front against which it would one day smash the two German armies. The strongest complex, the so-called Ushachi Partisan Republic, controlled a 40-mile stretch of territory between Lepel and Polotsk. It was under the command of Col. Vladimir Lobanok, a former commissar and experienced brigade commander. Other complexes nearly as strong held territory east of Lepel to Senno and to the south between Lepel and Borisov. The 18,000 Ushachi partisans had been given lavish air supply and intensive training. In the spring of 1944 they received orders to fortify their area and hold it against any German attempts to take it.

Beginning on 11 April, 20,000 Third Panzer Army troops aimed two related operations, REGENSCHAUER and FRUEHLINGSFEST, against the Ushachi complex. The partisans offered dogged but uneven resistance. Although they had air support, extensive mine fields, and field fortifications in depth, they could not prevent the Germans' pressing relentlessly in on them. Many of the partisans, sometimes

Russian peasant family with cart.

whole brigades, were green troops who had not been under fire before. Captured orders signed by Lobanok revealed the partisans' shortcomings: some brigades gave way under the first attack; others, staffs and all, panicked. Because of wide variations in performance, the brigades were frequently unable to conduct a co-ordinated defense or an organized retreat. Some of the partisans plundered the civilians. Advancing at a deliberately slow pace to keep a tight line and prevent the partisans from slipping through, the Third Panzer Army troops by mid-May completely smashed the Ushachi complex. Partisan losses amounted to an estimated 7,000 dead and over 7,000 captured.

On 22 May Third Panzer Army began a large operation, KORMORAN, against several complexes in the area bounded by Lepel, Senno, Borisov, Minsk, and Molodechno. Again the defense was loose and unco-ordinated. Driving in from all sides, the Germans forced the partisans into an ever-narrowing pocket and set about systematically cutting them to pieces. KORMORAN had to be called off when the Soviet summer offensive started, but by then it had inflicted a reported 13,000 casualties on the partisans.

During July and August 1944, as the German armies retreated from Soviet territory, the partisan movement went out of existence. For most individual partisans the sequel was a profound disappointment. During the period of the great Soviet advance, German agents reported that partisan units overtaken by the Soviet Army, instead of receiving the preferential treatment they expected, were granted short leaves and thrown into front-line units. Given the intensely suspicious nature of the Soviet regime and the heterogeneous partisan make-up, it is likely that even the dedicated partisans, after their return to Soviet control, counted themselves lucky if they avoided being remanded to Army punishment battalions. The trusted Party men in command no doubt benefited from their service. Those fortunate rank-and-file partisans who survived the political screenings probably managed at best to bask modestly in the glory of the continued favorable publicity given the movement as a whole in Soviet newspapers and magazines and in the published memoirs of the prominent commanders.

THE WEST AND THE EAST

In the spring of 1944, German strategy faced its supreme challenge, that of a full-fledged two-front war. This grim test had become as inevitable as the passage of time itself. Like the approach of death, it had cast a long shadow and since Stalingrad had clouded every major German decision. For the Germans the second front existed before it was a reality. It divided their armed forces and split their command, the latter perhaps more deeply than if there had actually been a second front.

Zeitzler's attempt on 30 March 1944 to seize the OKW's 1st Mountain Division had brought to a head the long-standing conflict between the OKW and the OKH over the deployment of the German ground forces. Hitler, shortly thereafter, directed Jodl to work out a strategic survey, to be distributed to the Chief of Staff, OKH, and the army group commands, showing clearly that the deployment was justified by the total German situation. By 13 April Jodl had completed the survey. He opened with the familiar argument that certain persons in the higher command echelons on the Eastern Front had out of ignorance of the total situation drawn false and even "dangerously critical" conclusions. They had, he said, contributed to the spread of such subversive witticisms as: "Fifty-three percent of the Army is fighting in Russia for the existence of the German people, and the other forty-seven percent is sitting in western Europe waiting for an invasion that doesn't come," or, "Germany lost World War I because of the Navy in being and will lose this one because of the Army in being." What those critics did not realize, he went on, giving history a severe wrench, was that Germany had been forced to take advanced footholds in Finland, Norway, Denmark, France, the Low Countries, Italy, and the Balkans to create the military and economic prerequisites for a long war against Great Britain, the United States, and the Soviet Union. Anyway, he added, to give up any of those places would bring Allied air bases closer to Germany and would lengthen rather than shorten the front. Therefore, he concluded, the only point in doubt was whether divisions could still be spared for the Eastern Front.

There he was on firmer ground. Of 131 divisions in the OKW theaters, 41 had the arms and equipment to make them suitable for employment on the Eastern Front, but of these 32 were already engaged, as in Italy and Finland, or defending the coasts. The remaining 9 represented about one-third of the reserves needed in the OKW theaters.

In April 1944 few would still have contended that the OKW theaters could be stripped for the benefit of the Eastern Front. On the other hand, Jodl's survey no doubt rang hollow to those who had argued since Stalingrad that Germany could not fight a war with two sets of armed forces, one committed in the East, the other for the most part tied down in a sterile so-called strategic defensive.

In its tone the Jodl survey was symptomatic of a psychological attitude that chronically afflicted Hitler and his personal entourage, namely, that Hitler made no mistakes; if things were going wrong the blame belonged elsewhere. By the same reasoning, those who thought differently were subversives and the defeats in Russia were there to prove it. The source of all current troubles seemed to be lack of faith, and at Fuehrer headquarters faith meant not only telling Hitler what he wanted to hear but believing it oneself.

The ultimate result was that the inner circle at Fuehrer headquarters had become dedicated to preserving its own—and above all

Hitler's—illusions. In March Hitler's chief adjutant, Schmundt, observed that letters from Seydlitz, the ranking member of the Soviet-sponsored League of German Officers, to the generals in the Cherkassy pocket had aroused Hitler's mistrust of all generals. To soothe the Fuehrer, Schmundt persuaded the field marshals to sign a declaration denouncing Seydlitz. On 19 March, in the presence of the other marshals, Rundstedt, the senior officer of the Army, read the document aloud to Hitler and then formally presented it to him. In April Hitler addressed the generals and told them every officer had to identify himself with the "ideas" of national socialism; there could be no such thing as an apolitical officer. In May, Guderian, who had convinced himself that his tanks, used the way he thought they should be used, could still win the war, wrote a letter intended for Hitler's eyes in which he characterized the Army General Staff as a body of weak kneed defeatists. When Zeitzler demanded that Hitler either reject the charge or accept his resignation as Chief of Staff, OKH, Hitler said only that in view of the situation at the moment he would not make a decision. Toward the end of the month Schmundt toured the Eastern Front and returned with the impression that the changes in command of the two southern army groups "had produced especially favorable results."

In April and May 1944 it seemed, in fact, that destiny might yet bow to the Fuehrer's will. If the invasion could be defeated, Germany could turn its full strength east. The prospects of a victory in the West appeared good. By the end of April new panzer divisions had filled the gap in the western defenses created when II SS Panzer Corps was transferred east. The southern half of the Eastern Front was a jerrybuilt nightmare, but in the center, 290 miles west of Moscow, between Vitebsk and Orsha, the gateway to the Soviet capital was still in German hands. At the closest point, the Russians were still 550 miles from Berlin. In May the Russians occupied themselves with extensive troop movements, but gave no sign that they would do anything to make the Allies' landing easier. The Soviet May Day proclamation, which could, of course, be variously interpreted, set the liberation of all Soviet territory, "including the entire boundary from the Barents Sea to the Black Sea," as the first Soviet objective and appeared to put the drive toward Germany distinctly into second place. Had they known, the Germans could probably also have drawn encouragement from the Stavka's directives issued to all the fronts in the first week of May ordering them to set up training programs, maintain general reconnaissance against the enemy, and clear a 25-km. strip behind their own lines to preserve security; in other words, to establish the routines that went with a long or at least indefinite period of inactivity.

Although in the spring German Army strength on the Eastern Front reached a new low (2,242,649 men) and that of the Soviet Army another high (6,077,000 men), in other respects German strength was actually in an upswing.[20] Industrial output was rising. The Air Force total complement stood at 5,585 planes in January 1944 as against 3,955 the year before. Synthetic oil production reached its peak in April 1944, and stocks of aviation fuel were larger than at any time since 1941. The Jaeger Stab (Fighter Staff), organized in early 1944 to rationalize the aircraft industry, performed so effectively that fighter plane production rose every month between March and September 1944 even though the British and American Air Forces resumed daylight bombing in March. Enough tanks and weapons to equip new divisions for the Western Front and replace some of the losses in Russia were coming off the assembly lines. The best equipped, if militarily not always the most effective, segment of the Wehrmacht, the Waffen SS, reached a strength of 400,000 men in late March. All in all, it appeared that Germany could await the next roll of the dice with confidence.

By mid-June the dice had been rolled and Germany had lost. Beginning in April and continuing through May and into June the United States and British Air Forces staged raids that knocked out, if in part only temporarily, more than 40 percent of the Rumanian oil production and 90 percent of the German synthetic oil capacity. On 6 June United States and British troops landed in Normandy, and in the next several days the strategy, carefully nurtured since

---

20. The army group strengths were as follows: Army Group North, 540,965; Army Group Center, 792,196; Army Group North Ukraine, 400,542; and Army Group South Ukraine, 508,946.

Fuehrer Directive 51 was issued in November 1943, collapsed. The "powerful counterattack" Hitler had envisioned did not materialize. Because he expected a second landing north of the Seine, Hitler failed to take enough troops from Fifteenth Army, which was closest to the beachhead, and decided instead to call in reinforcements from more remote areas. The German armies in Normandy were forced to the defensive. In the East the Russians were ready to march.

CHAPTER XV

The Collapse of the Center

DECEPTION AND DELUSION

In the first week of May 1944, looking beyond the lull then settling in along the Eastern Front, the Eastern Intelligence Branch, OKH, forecast two possible Soviet offensives: one across the line Kovel'-Lutsk cutting deep behind Army Groups North and Center via Warsaw to the Baltic coast; the other through Rumania, Hungary, and Slovakia into the Balkans. Believing the former would require so high a level of tactical proficiency that the Stavka would probably not attempt it, the Eastern Intelligence Branch concluded that the Soviet main effort would continue in the south toward the Balkans, where it could take advantage of the already shaky state of Germany's allies and finally establish the long-coveted Soviet hegemony in southeastern Europe. North of the Pripyat Marshes, the Eastern Intelligence Branch predicted, the front would stay quiet.

The intelligence estimate jibed almost exactly with the thinking of the OKH and the army group staffs. The one difference was that Army Groups Center and North Ukraine were concerned over very heavy railroad traffic and other signs of a buildup in the Kovel'-Ternopol area. Zeitzler agreed that the activity off the inner flanks of the two army groups was not to be taken lightly, and he proposed taking units from Army Group Center and Army Group North to create a reserve army so that "then one would be able to do something if a big attack were to come." In early May, Army Group Center began reinforcing its right flank corps, LVI Panzer Corps, with tanks, self-propelled assault guns, and artillery. On 12 May the Eastern Intelligence Branch revised its estimate: the main effort would still be in the south, between the Carpathians and the Black Sea, toward the Balkans, but a large offensive force was also being assembled between the Carpathians and the Pripyat Marshes to attack toward L'vov, Lublin, and Brest.

The prospect of a secondary offensive between the Carpathians and the Pripyat Marshes had one almost attractive aspect: if the rest of the Army Group Center front stayed quiet as predicted, the attack would come at a place where the Germans for once could bring considerable strength to bear. On 10 May Zeitzler suggested using the projected reserve army of which LVI Panzer Corps would form the nucleus, to strike first. The Army Group Center and North Ukraine staffs, apprehensive of another fiasco like Operation ZITADELLE, were cold to the idea, but Model saw in it a chance to employ his Schild und Schwert theory of active defense and, presumably, an opportunity to euchre his less alert colleague, Busch, out of the very substantial array of strength then being assembled under Headquarters, LVI Panzer Corps.

On the 15th, Model asked Hitler to let him have LVI Panzer Corps to try "an offensive solution." That the thought would appeal to Hitler was obvious. During the next several days reports from Model's headquarters prompted a change in the intelligence picture: it suddenly became clear that the offensive north of the Carpathians would miss Army Group Center completely. On 20 May Hitler transferred LVI Panzer Corps to Army Group North Ukraine. Army Group Center thereby gave up 6 percent of its front and lost 15 percent of its divisions, 88 percent of its tanks, 23 percent of its self-propelled assault guns, 50 percent of its tank destroyers, and 33 percent of its heavy artillery.

Busch, who had ignored a warning from Weiss, the Commanding General, Second Army, that Model was trying to get his hands on LVI Panzer Corps, surrendered the corps without a protest. As if that did not fully reveal his passive philosophy of leadership, Busch called in the army commanders on 24 May and told them the main, in fact the only, point of the meeting was to impress on them the Fuehrer's unshakable determination to hold the line in the East under all circumstances. He ordered the armies to curtail drastically all work behind the front and concentrate everything on the main line of resistance. As it was, the army group had only one major switch position, the BIBER plan on the Beresina River, designated neither "line" nor "position" out of regard for Hitler's easily aroused suspicion that the armies were "looking backward" and because it actually did not amount to much.

The Germans played exactly into the Russians' hands. The Soviet Command had a completely free strategic choice; it had the enemy hopelessly on the defensive and the forces and matériel to deploy in overwhelming strength anywhere on the front. In the third week of April, allegedly on the basis of a State Defense Committee decision that it was "necessary" to eliminate the residual threat posed by the German occupation of Belorussia, the Stavka initiated a covert build-up opposite Army Group Center and an elaborate deception that would mislead the Germans into assuming the summer offensive would again be in the south. The opportunity for such a deception was there. During the winter the offensive deployment, including the tank armies, had been away from the center. The desired impression was already convincingly established; all that was needed was to build up the center without too much disturbing it.

Around the first of May, at the same time the German attention was beginning to linger south of the Pripyat Marshes, the build-up began opposite Army Group Center from the Third Panzer Army left flank east of Polotsk to the Ninth Army right between the Dnepr and the Beresina south of Zhlobin. During May and the first three weeks in June the First Baltic and the First, Second, and Third Belorussian Fronts received increases of 60 percent in troop strength, 300 percent in tanks and self-propelled guns, 85 percent in artillery and mortars, and 62 percent in supporting air strength. Between 1 and 22 June more than 75,000 railroad carloads of troops, supplies, and ammunition were dispatched to the four fronts.

When the build-up was completed the number of Soviet combat troops in the offensive zone, from west of Vitebsk to south of Bobruysk, was 1.2 million—against an Army Group Center total strength of slightly over 700,000. All told, the number of Soviet troops readied to participate in the offensive, including reserves held back by the Stavka until the operation was in progress, was 2.5 million. Four thousand tanks, 24,400 cannon and mortars, and 5,300 aircraft gave the Soviet forces armored, artillery, and air superiorities ranging upward from 10:1 at the initial assault points.

The Russians concealed their movements skillfully, and the Germans did not begin to detect the activity opposite Army Group Center until 30 May, when Ninth Army reported a build-up north of Rogatchev.

Thereafter the signs multiplied rapidly as the deployment went into high gear, but they were not enough to divert the OKH's attention from Army Group North Ukraine, where Model was readying his "offensive solution" under the appropriate cover name SCHILD UND SCHWERT. The Eastern Intelligence Branch dismissed the activity opposite Army Group Center as "apparently a deception."9 The Army Group Center command noted the changes on the Soviet side in the Third Panzer, Fourth, and Ninth Army sectors but scarcely reacted to them at all. Busch was more worried about Second Army's deep right flank and the chances of getting back LVI Panzer Corps after Model had finished with it.

On 14 June, Zeitzler called the army group and army chiefs of staff to a conference. In advance he stated that what was to be said "would not particularly concern Army Group Center." The expected offensive against Army Group North Ukraine continued to preoccupy the OKH; even the predicted Balkan operation had receded into the background. At the meeting the chief of the Eastern Intelligence Branch warned that simultaneous attacks on Army Groups Center and South Ukraine could be expected as preliminaries to the big offensive against Army Group North Ukraine.

During the next week the portents of trouble on the Army Group Center east front multiplied. The armies reported new Soviet units in their sectors. A downed Russian pilot confirmed rumors picked up by agents that Zhukov was in command. Prisoners stated that in the political indoctrination the emphasis was on retaking all the Soviet land as the first objective. On the night of 19 June partisans planted over 5,000 mines on the roads and railroads behind the Second and Fourth Armies. At Army Group Center headquarters the reports aroused no excitement and only routine interest. A brief entry in the army group war diary under the date 20 June states that the stepped-up partisan activity "makes it appear that an early start of the offensive cannot be ruled out." On the afternoon of that day Busch flew to Germany where he intended to see Hitler at the Berghof on the 22d about administrative matters.

As the often-repeated slogan "nur keine Schema" implied, a cardinal principle of German general staff doctrine was the avoidance of rigid or schematic tactical and operating conceptions. In June 1944 on the Eastern Front that rule was forgotten. To a Soviet deception, the German commands added an almost hypnotic self-induced delusion: the main offensive would come against Army Group North Ukraine because that was where they were ready to meet it.

Under Busch, Headquarters, Army Group Center, had become a mindless instrument for transmitting the Fuehrer's will. Busch did not intend to exercise any leadership outside the very narrow bounds of Hitler's order to hold the front exactly where it was. The state into which the army group had fallen was described by General der Infanterie Hans Jordan, in a 22 June 1944 entry in his Ninth Army war diary:

Ninth Army stands on the eve of another great battle, unpredictable in extent and duration. One thing is certain: in the last few weeks the enemy has completed an assembly on the very greatest scale opposite the army, and the army is convinced that that assembly overshadows the concentration of forces off the north flank of Army Group North Ukraine... The army has felt bound to point out repeatedly that it considers the massing of strength on its front to constitute the preparation for this year's main Soviet offensive, which will have as its object the reconquest of Belorussia.

The army believes that, even under the present conditions, it would be possible to stop the enemy offensive, but not under the present directives which require an absolutely rigid defense... there can be no doubt... if a Soviet offensive breaks out the army will either have to go over to a mobile defense or see its front smashed...

The army considers the orders establishing the "fortified places" particularly dangerous.

The army, therefore, looks ahead to the coming battle with bitterness, knowing that it is bound by orders to tactical measures which it cannot in good conscience accept as correct and which in our own earlier victorious campaigns were the causes of the enemy defeats—one recalls the great breakthrough and encirclement battles in Poland and France.

The Commanding General and Chief of Staff presented these thoughts to the army group in numerous conferences, but there, apparently, the courage was lacking to carry them higher up, for no counterarguments other than references to OKH orders were given. And that is the fundamental source of the anxiety with which the army views the future.

THE BATTLE FOR BELORUSSIA

PLANS AND FORCES

The final directives for the offensive against Army Group Center went to the front commands on 31 May. (Map 27) The strategic objectives the Stavka set were to liberate Belorussia and advance to the Vistula and the border of East Prussia.[21] Marshals Zhukov and Vasilevskiy were made responsible for planning the operation and were each to co-ordinate two fronts in its execution; Vasilevskiy, the First Baltic and Third Belorussian Fronts and Zhukov, the Second and First Belorussian Fronts. The offensive was to be sprung on a wide, 300-mile expanse from south of Polotsk to south of Bobruysk. The first phase objective was to chop out the German strongpoints and communications hubs, Vitebsk, Orsha, Mogilev, and Bobruysk. After that, the forces on the flanks would close in upon Minsk from the northeast and southeast, following the Orsha-Minsk and Bobruysk-Minsk roads, to envelop Fourth Army. Strong columns would go north past Minsk to Molodechno and from Bobruysk via Slutsk' to Baranovichi to block the escape routes from Minsk and to get control of passages through the chain of swamps and forests formed by the Pripyat Marshes, the Nalibocka Forest west of Minsk, and the swampy lowland north of Molodechno between the Viliya and Dvina Rivers.

Their lines of thrust converging on Minsk, the fronts were deployed in a sweeping arc. First Baltic Front, about half of its sector facing Army

---

21. The objectives are those given in Soviet sources, which almost always set the end objectives exactly on the line on which a given operation ended.

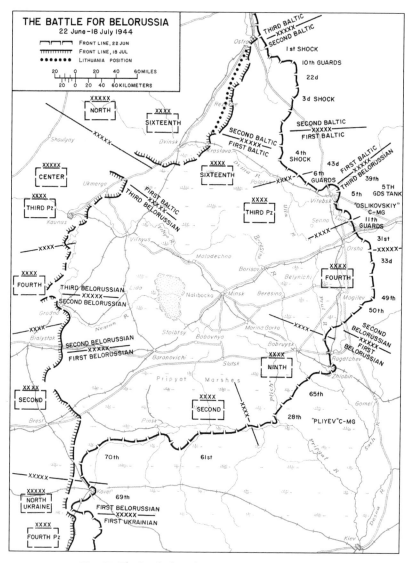

Map 27: The Battle for Belorussia, 22 June-18 July 1944

Group North, from north of Polotsk to Vitebsk; Third Belorussian Front from Vitebsk to south of Orsha; Second Belorussian Front on both sides of Mogilev from south of Orsha to north of Rogatchev; First Belorussian Front from north of Rogatchev to south of Kovel'. First Belorussian Front's sector was broader than those of the other three together, but only its right flank would be engaged.

First Baltic Front, under General Armii Ivan K. Bagramyan, was to attack northwest of Vitebsk with the Sixth Guards and Forty-third Armies, cross the Dvina, and envelop Vitebsk from the west; as the offensive proceeded it would provide flank cover on the north. Third Belorussian Front, commanded by General Polkovnik I. D. Chernyakovskiy, was split into two assault groups. On the north the Thirty-ninth and Fifth Armies were to break through south of Vitebsk, complete the envelopment, and advance southwestward to Senno. On the south the Eleventh Guards and Thirty-first Armies would attack on both sides of the road toward Orsha. After the armies had broken across the Luchesa River, the Cavalry-Mechanized Group Oslikovskiy would begin a fast drive due west past Senno.[22] Third Belorussian Front held Fifth Guards Tank Army in reserve to be committed later behind either the north or south group, depending on how the battle developed.

Subsequently, Chernyakovskiy, his main effort north of the Minsk-Orsha road, would advance via Borisov to Minsk and north of Minsk to Molodechno. Second Belorussian Front, composed of the Thirty-third, Forty-ninth, and Fiftieth Armies, under the command of General Armii Matvei V. Zakharov, was to break open the center of the Fourth Army bridgehead east of the Dnepr, take Mogilev, and wall in the pocket around Minsk from the east. Rokossovskiy's First Belorussian Front (formerly Belorussian Front) would employ the Third and Forty-eighth Armies east of the Beresina and Sixty-fifth Army, Twenty-eighth Army, and the Cavalry-Mechanized Group Pliyev west of the river to encircle Bobruysk. Having accomplished that, it would send one force northwest toward Minsk and another west via Slutsk' to Baranovichi.

The build-up for the offensive was accomplished with a minimum of unit shuffling. Toward the end of May the Germans became aware that West Front had been supplanted by the Second and Third

---

22. The cavalry-mechanized groups first appeared as independent commands in the summer of 1944. Each had one tank or mechanized corps and one cavalry corps. They took their designations from the names of their commanding generals, in this instance General Leytenant N. S. Oslikovskiy. Substantially smaller than the tank armies, they were primarily intended for the rapid exploitation of breakthroughs.

Belorussian Fronts—which should have alerted them but did not. Three new armies—Sixth Guards, Fifth Guards Tank, and Twenty-eighth—were put into the front. Up to 22 June German intelligence had not identified any of these. Apparently the manpower build-up was actually not as massive as in the previous offensives, and it was accomplished mainly by reinforcing units already in the front. By then the Soviet commands at all levels were capable of handling larger numbers of troops, and reintroduction of the rifle corps helped by extending the army's span of control.

Except for the lengthening of its right flank along the Pripyat River, the Army Group Center front had not undergone important changes after late 1943. On the left Third Panzer Army held a sector on both sides of Vitebsk tying to Army Group North near Polotsk. Fourth Army tied in with Third Panzer Army north of Orsha and with the Ninth Army north of Rogatchev and held a bulging, 25- by 80-mile bridgehead east of the Dnepr. On its left Ninth Army covered around Bobruysk and to the southwest on a line that followed the Prut and Dnepr to south of Zhlobin and then veered southwest across the Beresina to the lower Ptich' and the Pripyat. The Second Army front followed the Pripyat upstream and joined the Army Group North Ukraine left flank north of Kovel'.

Army Group Center had 38 divisions, one of them Hungarian, in the front, 3 panzer or panzer grenadier divisions and 2 infantry divisions in reserve, and 3 Hungarian and 5 security divisions stationed in the rear. Though still numerically the strongest army group, it also held by far the longest front, 488 miles. Army Group North Ukraine, by comparison, had 35 German and 10 Hungarian divisions, including 8 panzer divisions, and held a 219-mile front. Army Groups North Ukraine and South Ukraine together had 18 panzer or panzer grenadier divisions (including 1 Hungarian and 1 Rumanian armored division) as against Army Group Center's 3. The distribution of air support was similarly unbalanced. Of 2,085 combat aircraft on the Eastern Front, Sixth Air Force, supporting Army Group Center, had 775 and Fourth Air Force, supporting Army Groups North Ukraine and South Ukraine, had 845, but the Sixth Air Force strength included 405 long-range bombers and reconnaissance planes intended for

Soviet motorcycle troops dash forward.

strategic missions. Fourth Air Force, on the other hand, had 670 fighters and ground support bombers while Sixth Air Force had 275.

BREAKTHROUGH

On the morning of 22 June, the third anniversary of the invasion, the offensive against Army Group Center began. The First Baltic and Third Belorussian Fronts attacked northwest and southeast of Vitebsk. Northwest of the city, Sixth Guards Army, which had moved in undetected, took Third Panzer Army completely by surprise. From the outset Third Panzer Army was in desperate trouble; the army group had to commit one of its reserve infantry divisions, and the OKH released a reserve division standing by in the Army Group North zone near Polotsk. Busch, who received the news at the Berghof, headed back to his headquarters at Minsk without waiting for his interview with Hitler.

The next day the Russians tore through Third Panzer Army and closed in behind Vitebsk. Extending the offensive south against Fourth Army, the Third and Second Belorussian Fronts drove toward Orsha end Mogilev, and by day's end Fourth Army's front was near breaking. During the day Busch reported that he could see no way of closing the

Third Panzer Army front without giving up Vitebsk or getting new units from somewhere else. The OKH was not willing to take divisions from Army Group North Ukraine, and Busch did not want to take any from Second Army because he was still worried about an attack toward Brest.

On the 24th First Belorussian Front hit Ninth Army and penetrated along its north boundary and south of the Beresina. Fourth Army's left flank corps was beginning to fall apart. In the Third Panzer Army sector, the Russians reached Senno and east of there had tanks turning south behind the Fourth Army flank. Busch secured Hitler's permission to let four of the five divisions encircled at Vitebsk break out—too late.

Everywhere else Busch held to his and Hitler's original idea of a rigid defense. He refused two requests to take back the Fourth Army bridgehead front, and the next day, when the Commanding General, Fourth Army, General der Infanterie Kurt von Tippelskirch, took matters into his own hands and ordered the withdrawal, Busch attempted to reverse the order and to force the units to retake their old front. When Ninth Army, on 25 June, wanted to take its main force out of the trap forming between the Dnepr and the Beresina, Busch answered that the army's mission was to hold every foot of ground and not give up anything on its own initiative. In the army war diary, the Commanding General, Ninth Army, Jordan, noted, "Having made a responsible report, one must accept the orders of his superiors even when he is convinced of the opposite. What is worse is to know that the completely inadequate directive from the army group is not a product of purposeful leadership trying to do its utmost but merely an attempt to carry out orders long overtaken by events."23

By the end of the fourth day Army Group Center had committed all its reserves without stopping or delaying the Russians anywhere. Five divisions were encircled and as good as lost at Vitebsk. Third Panzer Army was trying to hold on the Dvina and Ulla Rivers fifty miles west of Vitebsk. Fourth Army had taken command of Third Panzer Army's right flank corps, remnants of five divisions that were rapidly being pushed south out of a widening gap west and south of Senno. The

Fourth Army front on the bridgehead could hold together only as long as it kept withdrawing. In the Ninth Army sector, Rokossovskiy's armies were heading toward Bobruysk from the east and the south.

In executing the breakthroughs, the Russians showed elegance in their tactical conceptions, economy of force, and control that did not fall short of the Germans' own performance in the early war years. They used tightly concentrated infantry and artillery to breach the front on, by their previous standards, narrow sectors. The tanks stayed out of sight until an opening was ready, then went straight through without bothering about their flanks.

The Soviet air support was concentrated against the German artillery, which, because the danger from the air had not been great in the past, was stationed close to the front in open emplacements that gave wide fields for direct antitank fire but no protection against air strikes. The Russians had overwhelming air superiority. By contrast, German Sixth Air Force, nearly paralyzed by shortages of planes and gasoline, had, according to one account, only 40 fighters in working order on 22 June and not enough gas to keep them flying.

THE BOBRUYSK POCKET

Ninth Army was the first to succumb. On 26 June the Russians were three miles southwest of Bobruysk and across the Mogilev road twelve miles north of the city. The injunction to hold every foot of ground stayed in force throughout the day. Early the next morning the army received permission to retreat to Bobruysk and the Beresina, which was what the army had wanted to do two days earlier and which could at least have been used as an excuse to maneuver for an escape northward toward Fourth Army. Before the army could act, however, an order arrived forbidding any sort of withdrawal.

In the afternoon the OKH authorized a breakout to the north, but followed it with several sharply worded admonishments through the army group to hold the "fortified place" Bobruysk under all circumstances. By then it was too late. Ten Soviet divisions had closed the pocket. Two corps, a total of 70,000 German troops, were trapped in and east of Bobruysk. In the city thousands of leaderless troops milled about, panicky and confused. Headquarters, Ninth Army,

A Russian woman attacks a German prisoner.

outside the pocket, transferred its one intact corps to Second Army and, with no troops except half of the 12th Panzer Division coming in through Minsk, moved back to Marina Gorka, thirty miles southeast of Minsk, to try to hold open an escape route for Fourth Army. Rokossovskiy, just beginning to hit his stride, lost no time in striking out for Minsk and behind Second Army toward Slutsk'.

THE MINSK POCKET

In the Fourth Army sector Zakharov's lead elements crossed the Dnepr north of Mogilev on 26 June. By then the neighboring fronts were deep into the army's flanks. Tippelskirch on his own responsibility ordered his army to go behind the Dnepr. To the west, behind the army, lay a 40-mile wide band of swamp and forest between the Prut and the Beresina traversed only by the Mogilev-Beresino-Minsk road. If it retreated any farther, the whole army would have to go on that road and across one 8-ton bridge at Beresino. Radio monitors already had picked up messages to Soviet tank spearheads off the north flank ordering them to take the Beresina crossing.

On the morning of the 27th Fourth Army radioed to army group, "Army requests directive whether to fight its way west or let large elements be encircled." At noon the army group intelligence officer arrived at Fourth Army headquarters in a light plane with an order to hold the Dnepr line and the "fortified places" Orsha and Mogilev. If it was forced back, the army was to set up another line on the Prut. Tippelskirch was certain he would have to withdraw, and in the afternoon, after receiving a report that the Russians were coming around the south flank, so directed. At the last minute Busch interposed an order that Mogilev was to remain a "fortified place." By then the Russians were in Orsha.

On 28 June the Fourth Army staff moved from Belynichi to Beresino over the road the army would have to take. The 30-mile trip lasted nine hours. Columns of barely moving trucks choked the road, and between daylight and dark Soviet planes attacked the Beresino bridge twenty-five times. During the day two corps commanders were killed. To move at all the army staff had to organize details to clear burning trucks and dead horses off the road.

At Beresino, Tippelskirch found waiting for him an injunction from Busch to get Fourth Army behind the Beresina fast. In his personal diary he noted, "This order has come too late!" Toward midnight another message from Busch relayed Hitler's decision to let Mogilev be given up. Nothing had been heard from that "fortified place" for twenty-four hours.

On the morning of the 28th Busch gave Zeitzler a situation report. Ninth Army was smashed; Fourth Army was retreating; and Third Panzer Army, one corps left out of its original three, was pierced in numerous places. Nevertheless, Busch intended to execute Operations Order 8, which had come in during the night, to the letter. In that order Hitler, apparently using a ruler, had laid out a line due north and south of Beresino on which he demanded that all three armies stop.

Busch was satisfied to have another line to try to hold. He told Reinhardt, whose divisions were already west of the line, to attack because the army group was "iron" bound to the operations order. He instructed Ninth Army, also west of the line, to commit its half a panzer division "offensively."

During the day the army group and the Operations Branch, OKH, concluded that the offensive against Army Group Center was more ambitious than they had previously assumed and probably was aimed at retaking Minsk, but the OKH believed a more powerful blow might yet be expected against Army Group North Ukraine. To resolve the dilemma, Hitler announced in the afternoon that Model would take command of Army Group Center the next day and at the same time retain command of Army Group North Ukraine to facilitate exchanges of forces between the two. Giving Model command of Army Group Center was for Hitler also a handy way to sidetrack an OKH proposal to take Army Group North back to the line Dvinsk-Riga and so gain divisions for the battle in the center.

The change in command pleased the armies for other reasons. Ninth Army, in which General der Panzertruppen Nikolaus von Vormann had replaced Jordan as commanding general, received the news with "satisfaction and renewed confidence."29 Tippelskirch, in his last conversation with Busch, "could not resist expressing his bitterness over the developments which had resulted from the way the army group had been led."30 The irony of Model's being called on to rescue Army Group Center from a disaster in which he was substantially, if indirectly, implicated was overshadowed by the fact that he was obviously the man for the job. In the first place, the reinforcements from Army Group North Ukraine would otherwise have come slowly if at all; in the second, he was, next to Rundstedt, who was busy enough in France, the best tactical mind the Germans still had in active command.

During the day of the 29th a Soviet plane scored a hit that blew away thirty feet of the Beresino bridge. After that was repaired, another hit knocked down forty-five feet of the span. Truck columns two and three abreast lined the road for thirty miles to the east. Behind Fourth Army, Headquarters, Ninth Army, had a thin screening line set up southeast of Marina Gorka, but deeper in the rear, off Fourth Army's north and south flanks, spearheads of the Third and First Belorussian Fronts that day they reached Borisov and Slutsk.

Fourth Army's fate was sealed on 30 June. The Russians had tanks and self-propelled artillery within range of the Beresino bridge. Even to get the troops across the river without their equipment appeared nearly hopeless. Elsewhere the army group gained a day's respite when the Russians stopped before Borisov and Slutsk'. Model told Hitler he might be able to hold both places if he could get divisions from Army Group North, which could spare two or three divisions if it pulled back its right flank, then still east of Polotsk. He also wanted Army Group North to extend its flank south and restore contact with Third Panzer Army, which had broken away two days before. Hitler ignored the proposals but instructed Model to start swinging Second Army back to cover Slutsk' and Baranovichi.

When the morning air reconnaissance on 1 July showed a column estimated at 35,000 German troops moving north out of Bobruysk along the west bank of the Beresina, Ninth Army sent a panzer regiment that opened a corridor from the west. The German luck did not hold. While the hoops from the pocket funneled through on foot to the railroad at Marina Gorka, Rokossovskiy's tank and motorized spearheads pushed past Slutsk' and Borisov toward Baranovichi and Molodechno. When word came that the Russians were at Bobovnya, thirty miles northwest of Slutsk', the Ninth Army staff pulled out of Marina Gorka toward Stolbtsy, on the railroad half way between Baranovichi and Minsk, where it hoped to hold the Neman River crossing, the last escape route south of Minsk. On the way it was stopped for several hours by troops streaming east and claiming the Russians were behind them. Around Minsk the roads were crammed with service troops and vehicles. Panic gripped the city.

To open the road south of Minsk Ninth Army on 2 July directed the panzer division at Marina Gorka to strike toward Stolbtsy. The army staff had tried but failed to organize a scratch force of stragglers to defend the town. The stragglers, officers and men alike, disappeared as fast as they could be assembled. On the north Fifth Guards Tank Army was approaching Minsk. In the pocket some of the troops who had escaped from Bobruysk were aboard trains trying to get out through Minsk and Molodechno; the majority, on foot, plodded in heat and dust toward Stolbtsy. Exccpt for a rear guard all of Fourth Army was across the Beresina, but its forward elements were stopped east of Minsk. During the day Headquarters, Fourth Army, went to Molodechno to try to hold open the railroad there. Ninth Army's panzer division did not get to Stolbtsy, which the Russians had entered in the morning, but some of the troops from the pocket found a crossing farther downstream on the Neman.

The next day Rokossovskiy's and Chernyakovskiy's troops took Minsk. Ninth Army tried and again failed to open the bridge at Stolbtsy. On 4 July the Russians going toward Baranovichi forced Ninth Army to center its effort there, and after that the only troops to get out of the pocket were individuals and small groups who made their way through the Nalibocka Forest, sometimes helped by the Polish peasants.

In twelve days Army Group Center had lost 25 divisions. Of its original 165,000-man strength, Fourth Army lost 130,000. Third Panzer Army lost 10 divisions. Ninth Army had held the pocket open long enough for some thousands, possibly as many as 10,000-15,000, of its troops to escape. By the time it reached Baranovichi Headquarters, Ninth Army, did not have enough of its staff and communications equipment left to command the divisions being sent north from Second Army. After a few days of trying to operate through Second Army's communications net, it was taken out and sent to the rear to reorganize.

RETREAT

By 1 July Model was certain the most easterly line he could try to hold was between Baranovichi and Molodechno. He expected some advantage from earthworks and trenches left there from World War I, but told Hitler he would need several divisions from Army Group North to defend Molodechno. He was worried most about his left flank. Between the Army Group North flank, "nailed down" at Polotsk by Hitler's orders, and the Third Panzer Army left flank northeast of Minsk, a 50-mile gap had opened. A gap nearly as wide separated the panzer army's right flank and the Fourth Army short line around Molodechno. Third Panzer Army could be encircled or simply swept away any time the Russians wanted to make the effort, and thereafter the road to Riga and the Baltic coast would be open.

Although Model branded it "a futile experiment," Hitler insisted that Army Group North hold Polotsk and strike to the southwest from there to regain contact with Third Panzer Army. The Commanding

Soviet machine gun crew in Vil'nyus.

General, Army Group North, Lindemann, reported that with two divisions, all he could spare if his flank had to stay at Polotsk, he could not attack. When on 3 July, after receiving permission to go back a short distance from Polotsk, Lindemann continued to insist he could not attack, Hitler dismissed him and appointed Friessner in his place.

When the Russians reached Minsk, Army Group Center, judging by past experience, assumed that they had attained their first major objective and, having gone 125 miles, more than their usual limit on one issue of supplies, would pause at least several days to regroup and resupply. The army group was mistaken. The first objective, indeed, had been reached, but the Stavka had ordered the offensive carried west on a broad front without stopping. First Baltic Front was to go toward Dvinsk, Third Belorussian Front to Molodechno and then via Vil'nyus and Lida to the Neman, and First Belorussian Front to Baranovichi and west toward Brest. Second Belorussian Front stayed behind to mop up around Minsk.

The Russians moved faster than Army Group Center could deploy its meager forces even to attempt a stand. Russian troops were through the narrows south and east of Molodechno by 6 July, and the army group reported that they had full freedom of movement toward Vil'nyus. Second Army committed enough troops around Baranovichi to brake the advance a few days, but one panzer division and a Hungarian cavalry division could not stop four Soviet tank corps backed by infantry. Baranovichi fell on 8 July as did Lida, the road and rail junction west of the Nalibocka Forest.

By stretching its front west, Army Group North narrowed the gap to Third Panzer Army to about twenty miles. Friessner was going to attack south with three divisions, but First Baltic Front's Fourth Shock and Sixth Guards Armies began pressing toward Dvinsk and thus tied down everything on the army group's flank. Friessner then proposed as a "small solution" to let Sixteenth Army withdraw to the LITHUANIA position, a line being constructed from Kraslava east of Dvinsk to Ostrov; Hitler refused to consider going more than half that distance.

On the 8th Model reported that he could not hold the line Vil'nyus-Lida-Baranovichi—in fact, the attempt had already failed completely. The first town was surrounded and the latter two were lost. Since he did not expect any reinforcements within the next eight days, he could not attempt to stop the Russians anywhere. He asked for an audience with Hitler the next day.

At Fuehrer headquarters, Hitler proposed giving him a panzer division from Germany and two divisions from Army Group North right away, two more later. With these Third Panzer Army was to attack north and close the gap. On the question of the "big solution," taking Army Group North back to the Riga-Dvinsk-Dvina River line, which was what Model wanted most, Hitler was adamant. Admiral Doenitz, he said, had submitted a report proving such a withdrawal ruinous for the Navy.

For the next several days the Army Group Center front drifted west toward Kaunas, the Neman River, and Bialystok. The help from Army Group North did not come. Friessner could neither release the divisions promised Army Group Center no attack south himself. Between the Dvina and the Velikaya, Second Baltic Front and the right flank army of Third Baltic Front were engaging Sixteenth Army in a series of vicious and costly battles. South of the Dvina, around Dvinsk, First Baltic Front troops cracked the line in two places.

On 12 July Friessner reported to Hitler that he still proposed to attack south toward Third Panzer Army, but even if the attack succeeded it would have no lasting effect. Bagramyan's armies would keep on going west. Moreover, he could no longer maintain a stable defense anywhere on his own front south of Ostrov. He urged—"if one wants to save the armies of Army Group North"—taking Armeeabteilung Narva back to Reval and from there by sea to Riga, Liepaja, or Memel and withdrawing the Sixteenth and Eighteenth Armies to the line Riga-Kaunas. "I cannot," Friessner wrote, "reconcile with my conscience not having made every effort in this fateful hour to spare these loyal troops the worst that could befall them and not having found for them an employment that would make it possible to hold the enemy away from the eastern border of our Homeland." If Hitler could not give him freedom of action he asked to be relieved of his command.

Hitler, who rejected Friessner's proposal emphatically, had another plan. He intended to give Model five panzer divisions, including the big Hermann Goering Parachute Panzer Division, and have them assembled behind Kaunas to attack and close the gap between the army groups. The OKH operations chief pointed out that the battle was moving too fast; in the time it would take to assemble the divisions, the front would undoubtedly change so greatly that the attack would be impossible.

On 13 July Model reported that he would try to stop the Russians forward of the Kaunas-Neman River-Grodno-Brest line, but he would have to use the fresh panzer divisions to do it. Counting new arrivals expected through 21 July, he would then only have 16 fully combat-worthy divisions against 160 Russian divisions and brigades. In a conference at Fuehrer headquarters in Rastenburg on the 14th, Hitler changed his mind to the extent of giving Model the dual mission of first halting the offensive and then creating an attack force on the north flank.

During the third week of the month the Third Panzer and Fourth Armies managed to come to stop on a line from Ukmerge south past Kaunas and along the Neman to south of Grodno. Second Army, echeloned east, was consolidating as it drew back toward Bialystok.

German POW's being paraded through Moscow, 17 July 1944.

The Ninth Army staff supervised work on a line protecting the East Prussian border and organized blocking detachments to catch stragglers. The army group was beginning to regain its balance.

The Russians, having covered better than 200 miles without a pause, had for the time being outrun their supplies. They were now deep in territory ravaged by recent fighting, and bridges had to be rebuilt and rails relaid. Where there had been time to use it, the Germans' Schienenwolf (rail wolf), a massive steel plow towed by a locomotive had, as on other similar occasions, turned long stretches of railroad into tangles of twisted rails and broken ties.

A THREAT TO ARMY GROUP NORTH

On the 17th, the day the Russians marched 57,000 German prisoners through the main streets of Moscow to mark the victory in Belorussia, Army Group Center radio monitors intercepted messages to Soviet tank units north of Vil'nyus telling them to attack into the gap between Army Groups Center and North. Another, possibly greater, German disaster seemed to be at hand. Model advised the OKH he could not assemble the projected attack force in time to stop the Soviet armor; Army Group North would have to do it or suffer the consequences.

Army Group North was fully occupied trying to get into the LITHUANIA position, which was beginning to crack at the points where it had been reached. On 16 July Friessner informed Hitler that it was "a marvel" that the Russians had not already sent a force toward Riga to envelop the army group flank. He had nothing to use against them. He was taking one division out of the front at Narva; but it would be fully committed by the 10th; after that he would have no more reserves. "From then on," he concluded, "that the front will fall apart must be taken into account."

In a conference with Model and Friessner on 18 July, Hitler ordered the fighting in the gap conducted with mobile forces. He would have two self-propelled assault gun brigades there in four days, and by that time Goering would have strong air units ready to help. The army groups would each supply some infantry and a half dozen or so panzer and self-propelled artillery battalions. Goering, who was present, for once screwed up his courage and remarked that one had to speak out, the only way to get forces was to go back to the Dvina line. Hitler agreed that would be the simplest. But, he contended, it would lose him the Latvian oil, Swedish iron ore, and Finnish nickel; therefore, Army Group North's mission would be to hold the front where it was "by every means and employing every imaginable improvisation."42 Trying for the last time to talk Hitler around, Zeitzler carried his argument to the point of offering his resignation and, finally, reporting himself sick. Hitler countered with an order forbidding officers to relinquish their posts voluntarily.

THE BATTLE EXPANDS TO THE FLANKS

By mid-July, when the frontal advance against Army Group Center began to lose momentum, the Stavka was ready to apply pressure against the flanks. In the north the gap between the Third Panzer and Sixteenth Armies, the "Baltic Gap," offered a ready-made opportunity. First Baltic Front, given the Second Guards and Fifty-first Armies, which had been moved up from the Crimea, deployed them for a strike west toward Shaulyay and from there north toward Riga.

On the south, Army Group North Ukraine was still strong, by current German standards, but it was not the massive "block" that had been created in May and June. It had lost three panzer and two infantry divisions outright and in exchanges had received several divisions that were not battle tested. In the southern three-quarters of the North Ukraine zone, Konev's First Ukrainian Front had ten armies, three of them tank armies. In the northern quarter First Belorussian Front had three armies, reinforced during the second week of July by a guards army and a tank army transferred from the two southern fronts and the Polish First Army, a token force of four divisions. Apparently using the operation against Army Group Center as a model, Rokossovskiy and Konev had positioned their armies for thrusts in the north toward Brest and Lublin, in the center toward Rava Russkaya and L'vov, and in the south toward Stanislav.

ARMY GROUP NORTH UKRAINE BROKEN THROUGH

The Army Group Center disaster mitigated the Army Group North Ukraine command problem somewhat in that it produced a slightly more flexible attitude in the highest headquarters. At the end of June Hitler lifted the "fortified place" designations on Kovel' and Brody and a week later allowed Fourth Panzer Army to give up Kovel' and go into a shorter line fifteen miles west of the city. In the second week of July he also allowed the army to straighten a bulge on its right flank around Torchin.

When Fourth Panzer Army started back from Torchin, Konev, hoping to catch the Germans off balance, opened his attack toward Rava Russkaya on 13 July, a day earlier than planned. (Map 28) That move disconcerted both sides. Third Guards Army made a ragged start. The German divisions in motion stopped where they were supposed to, but a division a few miles farther south crumbled and a panzer division ordered to backstop it was slowed by air attacks. Next day Thirteenth Army found the weak spot and worked in deeper.

On 14 July two armies hit the First Panzer Army left flank due east of L'vov. The army had two reserve panzer divisions close behind the front. On the 15th they counterattacked from the south, stopped Thirty-eighth Army, and even drove it back a mile or two. But farther north Sixtieth Army opened a small breach in the German line.

Without waiting for the gaps to be widened, Konev on 16 July

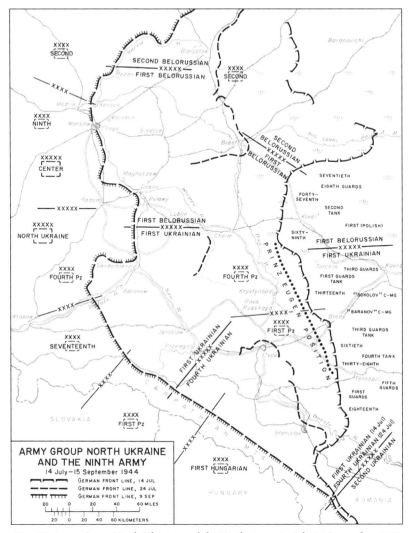

Map 28: Army Group North Ukraine and the Ninth Army, 14 July-15 September 1944.

committed First Guards Tank Army to the fighting on the Fourth Panzer Army right flank and a day later did the same with Third Guards Tank Army on the First Panzer Army left flank. The two German armies took their flanks back fifteen miles to a switch position named the PRINZ EUGEN, but before that was done the Russians penetrated the new front at the two crucial points. Elsewhere the withdrawal did not shorten the line enough to release troops either to close the gaps or to stop the westward rolling tank columns.

On the 18th Soviet armored spearheads from the north and south met on the Bug River thirty miles west of L'vov. Behind them XIII Corps (five German divisions and the SS Division Galicia), was encircled. During the same day First Guards Tank Army, going toward Rava Russkaya, crossed the Bug near Krystynopol. That night Fourth Panzer Army began taking its whole front back to the Bug. The withdrawal was necessary both because of the breakthrough in the south and because Second Army, its neighbor on the north, was being forced back toward Brest. Fourth Panzer Army reported that it had 20 tanks and 154 self-propelled assault guns in working order; the Russians had between 500 and 600 tanks. The army's 12 divisions faced 34 Soviet rifle divisions, 2 mechanized corps, and 2 tank corps. The Russians had 10 rifle divisions, 2 cavalry corps, and 4 independent tank regiments in reserve.

After 18 July the whole Army Group North Ukraine front from Stanislav north was in motion. Having waited for Fourth Panzer Army to start toward the Bug, First Belorussian Front began its thrust to Lublin. On the 10th Eighth Guards Army forced its way across the river nearly to Chelm.

That day, First Guards Tank Army, striking between the Fourth and First Panzer Armies, reached Rava Russkaya, and Third Guards Tank Army passed north of L'vov, while the newly committed Fourth Tank Army closed up to the city from the east. XIII Corps, encircled forty miles east of L'vov, was drawing its divisions together for an attempt to escape to the south before the right half of the First Panzer Army front was pushed too far west.

On 22 July the Second Army right flank went into the Brest defense ring. Against Fourth Panzer Army Soviet tanks rammed through at Chelm in the morning, covered the forty miles to Lublin by afternoon, and after nightfall 70 enemy tanks and 300 to 400 trucks were reported going northwest past Lublin. Hitler refused to lift the "fortified place" designation, and the 900-man garrison stayed in the city. In the gap between the Fourth and First Panzer Armies, by then thirty miles wide, First Guards Tank Army had an open road to the San River. Fourth Panzer Army told the army group that the only way it could save itself was to withdraw behind the Vistula and San Rivers without delay. During the day XIII Corps staged its breakout attempt, but it had too far to go. Of 30,000 men in the pocket no more than 5,000 escaped. Around L'vov First Panzer Army resisted more strongly than the Russians expected, which probably explains why Konev did not launch his planned thrust toward Stanislav.

THE BALTIC GAP

By 18 July the increased weight against the adjacent flanks of Army Groups Center and North was also being felt. (Map 29) A captured Soviet officer said that he had seen Second Guards Army moving west toward the Third Panzer Army north flank. Fifth Guards Tank Army, with Thirty-third Army close behind, had closed up to the Third Panzer Army front east of Kaunas and along the Neman River south of the city. Reinhardt, who had a weak panzer division and 4 infantry divisions facing 18 rifle divisions, 3 tank corps, a mechanized corps, and 3 independent tank brigades, reported that he saw no chance of restoring contact with Army Group North and proposed that he be allowed to take back his flank on the north enough at least to get a strong front around Kaunas. Model, having returned from the day's conference with Hitler, told him the army would have to stay where it was. Stretching the facts slightly, he said Army Group North would take care of closing the gap. He promised Reinhardt the Herman Goering Division.

During the next three days, while Fifth Tank Army increased its threat to Kaunas by working its way into several bridgeheads on the Neman, Second Guards Army moved west into the Baltic Gap and began pushing the Third Panzer Army flank south. By 22 July the flank division, trying to hold off six guards rifle divisions, was beginning to fall apart, and the gap had opened to a width of thirty-six miles. During the day Second Guards Army's advance elements reached Panevezhis, forty miles behind the Third Panzer Army front. The army was down to a combat effective strength of 13,850 men, but Model again refused a request to go back. As far as reinforcements were concerned, he told Reinhardt, the army would have to withstand the "drought" for two or three more days.

Sixteenth Army, meanwhile, had completed its withdrawal into the

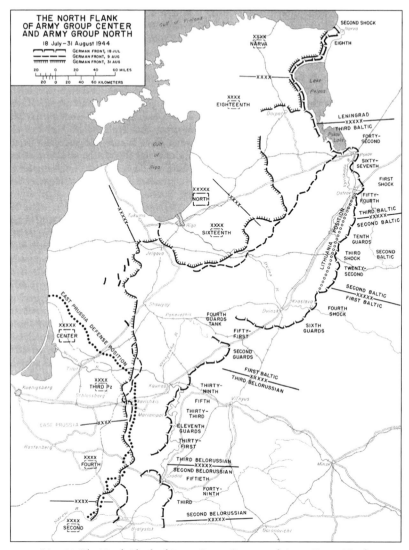

*Map 29, The North Flank of Army Group Center and Army Group North,
18 July-31 August 1944.*

LITHUANIA position on 19 July but had not been able to stop the
Russians there. On the 22d Friessner ordered the army back another
five to ten miles, which meant giving up its northern anchor at Pskov.
To Hitler he sent word there was no other way of holding the army
together; the new line also would not hold, and then he would have
to go back again. Soon, he added, the front would lose its Pskov Lake-

Lake Peipus tie-in, and getting behind the Dvina would then become a "question of life or death" for the whole army group.

ATTENTAT!—GUDERIAN—SCHOERNER

In the Fuehrer headquarters on 20 July the Attentat (attempted assassination) against Hitler had taken place. A time-bomb had injured all nineteen of the officers at the afternoon situation conference, three of them fatally, and had demolished the building in which the meeting was being held; but Hitler had escaped with minor burns, bruises, and an ear injury.[23] In the first few hours after the explosion, a widespread anti-Hitler conspiracy centered in the Army and reaching into the highest command echelons, especially the Army General Staff, came to light. It was quickly smashed, and before the day was out Hitler had placed new men in a number of key posts. The most significant change as far as the Eastern Front was concerned was Guderian's appointment as Acting Chief of Staff, OKH.

Guderian got the appointment by default. In fact, Hitler's first choice was General der Infanterie Walter Buhle, who was among those wounded in the assassination attempt, and now could not assume the post until he had recovered. Hitler never completely forgave a general who had once failed him, but on 20 July 1944 Guderian was perhaps the only general in the OKH not under direct suspicion. Although his motives were not entirely clear, Guderian had been the officer who, in Berlin on the afternoon of the assassination attempt, had turned back the tank battalion drawn up to take the SS headquarters on the Fehrbelliner Platz. He had, moreover, lately been full of ideas for winning the war, and he had not attempted to dissemble his low opinion of the field generalship on the Eastern Front since the time he had been relieved of command there. His recent charges of defeatism in the General Staff made it appear unlikely that he had been a member of the conspiracy.

On his appointment, Guderian moved swiftly to give fresh evidence of loyalty to the Fuehrer and to dissociate himself from his

---

23. Hitler later said that after the explosion the tremors in his left leg, which had long bothered him, almost disappeared, but, he added, the treatment was not one he would recommend.

predecessors. In an order to all General Staff officers, he demanded of them an "exemplary [Nazi] attitude" on political questions and that publicly. Those who could not comply were to request to be removed from the General Staff. "In order to ease the transition to, for them, possibly new lines of thought," he directed further, that all General Staff officers were to be given opportunities to hear political lectures and were to be detailed to National Socialist leadership discussions.

On his first day in his new post Guderian demonstrated how he proposed to conduct the war on the Eastern Front. When the Army Group North chief of staff told him Friessner was convinced the course Hitler was following would lose him the Baltic States and the Sixteenth and Eighteenth Armies to boot, Guderian dismissed the statement with a sneer, saying he expected "General Friessner will be man enough to give the necessary orders [to surrender] in the event of a catastrophe."53

After Friessner sent in his 22 July report his hours in command of Army Group North were numbered. The next day, at Guderian's behest, Friessner and Schoerner traded commands. Guderian told Model he was confident Schoerner would "put things in order" at Army Group North. It was time, he added, also to stiffen the Army Group North Ukraine command's backbone.

Schoerner went to Army Group North with a special patent from Hitler giving him command authority over all combat forces of the three Wehrmacht branches, the Waffen-SS, and the party and civil offices in the Baltic States. Unusual as such sweeping power was, substantively it did not amount to much. It placed at Schoerner's disposal a few thousand men who could be committed in the gap on the army group's south flank; otherwise, its main effect was to underscore Hitler's determination to hold what was left of the Baltic States.

"THE THRUST IS THE BEST PARRY"

Worried by the threatening developments the day before on his front and flanks, Model, early on 23 July, predicted that the Russians would strike via L'vov to the San River, thrust past Lublin to Warsaw, encircle Second Army at Brest, advance on East Prussia across the Bialystok-

Grodno line and by way of Kaunas, and attack past the army group left flank via Shaulyay to Memel or Riga. During the day Model's concern, particularly for his south flank, grew to alarm as the Russians moved north rapidly between the Vistula and the Bug toward Siedlce, the main road junction between Warsaw and Brest. In the late afternoon, after several of his reports had gone unanswered, Model called to tell the Operations Branch, OKH, it was "no use sitting on one's hands, there could be only one decision and that was to retreat to the Vistula-San line." The branch chief replied that he agreed, but Guderian wanted to set a different objective. Later the army group chief of staff talked to Guderian, who quickly took up a proposal to create a strong tank force around Siedlce but would not hear of giving up any of the most threatened points. "We must take the offensive everywhere!" he demanded, "To retreat any farther is absolutely not tolerable."

Before daylight the next morning Guderian had completed a directive which was issued over Hitler's signature. Army Groups North and North Ukraine were to halt where they were and start attacking to close the gaps. Army Group Center was to create a solid front on the line Kaunas-Bialystok-Brest and assemble strong forces on both its flanks. These would strike north and south to restore contact with the neighboring army groups. All three army groups were promised reinforcements. The directive ended with the aphorism "The thrust is the best parry" (der Hieb ist die beste Parade). After reading the directive Model's chief of staff told the OKH operations chief it would be seven days before the army groups would get any sizable reinforcements—in that time much could happen.

During the last week in the month the Soviet armies rolled west through the shattered German front. On 24 July First Panzer Army still held L'vov and its front to the south, but behind the panzer army's flank, 50 miles west of L'vov, First Tank Army, Third Guards Tank Army, and the Cavalry-Mechanized Group Baranov had four tank and mechanized corps closing to the San River on the stretch between Jaroslaw and Przemysl. That day Fourth Panzer Army fell back 25 miles to a 40-mile front on the Wieprz River southeast of Lublin; off both its flanks the Russians tore open the front for a distance of 65 miles in the south and 55 miles in the north. Second Army had drawn its three right flank corps back to form a horizontal V with the point at Brest. Behind the army a Second Tank Army spearhead reached the outskirts of Siedlce at nightfall on the 24th, and during the day Forty-seventh and Seventieth Armies had turned in against the south flank.

To defend Siedlce, Warsaw, and the Vistula south to Pulawy, Model, on the 24th, returned Headquarters, Ninth Army, to the front and gave it the Hermann Goering Division, the SS Totenkopf Division, and two infantry divisions, the latter three divisions still in transit. From the long columns coming west across the Vistula, the army began screening out what troops it could. In Warsaw it expected an uprising any day.

The next day Fourth Tank Army crossed the San between Jaroslaw and Przemysl. To try to stop that thrust, Army Group North Ukraine, on orders from the OKH, took two divisions from Fourth Panzer Army and gave the army permission to withdraw to the Vistula. In the Ninth Army sector Rokossovskiy's armor pierced a thin screening line around the Vistula crossings at Deblin and Pulawy and reached the east bank of the river.

Morning air reconnaissance on the 26th reported 1,400 Soviet trucks and tanks heading north past Deblin on the Warsaw road. At the same time, on the Army Group Center north flank reconnaissance planes located "endless" motorized columns moving west out of Panevezhis behind Third Panzer Army. During the day Second Army declared it could not hold Brest any longer, but Hitler and Guderian refused a decision until after midnight, by which time the corps in and around the city were virtually encircled.

In two more days First Panzer Army lost L'vov and fell back to the southwest toward the Carpathians. Fourth Panzer Army went behind the Vistula and beat off several attempts to carry the pursuit across the river. Ninth Army threw all the forces it could muster east of Warsaw to defend the city, hold Siedlce, and keep open a route to the west for the divisions coming out of Brest. South of Pulawy two Soviet platoons crossed the Vistula and created a bridgehead; Ninth Army noted that the Russians were expert at building on such small beginnings.

In the gap between Army Groups Center and North, Bagramyan's motorized columns passed through Shaulyay, turned north, covered the fifty miles to Jelgava, and cut the last rail line to Army Group North. In a desperate attempt to slow that advance, Third Panzer Army dispatched one panzer division on a thrust toward Panevezhis. Hitler wanted two more divisions put in, but they could only have come from the front on the Neman, where the army was already losing its struggle to hold Kaunas.

The 29th brought Army Group Center fresh troubles. Nine rifle divisions and two guards tank corps hit the Third Panzer Army right flank on the Neman front south of Kaunas. Rokossovskiy's armor drove north past Warsaw, cutting the road and rail connections between the Ninth and Second Armies and setting the stage for converging attacks on Warsaw from the southeast, east, and north.

On the 30th the Third Panzer Army flank collapsed, the Russians advanced to Mariampol, twenty miles from the East Prussian border, and could have gone even farther had they so desired. Between Mariampol and Kaunas the front was shattered. In Kaunas and in the World War I fortifications east of the city two divisions were in danger of being ground to pieces as the enemy swung in behind them from the south. Model told Reinhardt that the army group could not grant permission to give up the city and it was useless to ask the OKH. Reinhardt replied, "Very well, if that is how things stand, I will save my troops"; at ten minutes after midnight he ordered the corps holding Kaunas to retreat to the Nevayazha River ten miles to the west.

On the Warsaw approaches during the day Second Tank Army came within seven miles of the city on the southeast and took Wolomin eight miles to the northeast. In the city shooting erupted in numerous places. In the San-Vistula triangle First Tank Army stabbed past Fourth Army and headed northwest toward an open stretch of the Vistula on both sides of Baranow. Off the tank army's south flank the OKH gave the Headquarters, Seventeenth Army, command of two and a half divisions to try to plug the gap between Fourth Army and First Panzer Army.

On the last day of the month elements of a guards mechanized corps reached the Gulf of Riga west of Riga. Forty miles south of Warsaw Eighth Guards Army took a small bridgehead near Magnuszew.

Between the Fourth and Seventeenth Armies, First Tank Army began taking its armor across the Vistula at Baranow. That day, too, for the first time, the offensive faltered: Bagramyan did not move to expand his handhold on the Baltic; apparently short of gasoline, the tanks attacking toward Warsaw suddenly slowed almost to a stop; a German counterattack west from Siedlce began to make progress; and Chernyakovskiy did not take advantage of the opening between Mariampol and Kaunas.

At midnight on 31 July Hitler reviewed the total German situation in a long, erratic, monologue delivered to Jodl and a handful of other officers. The news from the West was also grim: there the Allies were breaking out of the Cotentin Peninsula, and on the 31st U.S. First Army had passed Avranches. Nevertheless, the most immediate danger, Hitler said, was in the East, because if the fighting reached into Upper Silesia or East Prussia, the psychological effects in Germany would be severe. As it was, the retreat was arousing apprehension in Finland and the Balkan countries, and Turkey was on the verge of abandoning its neutrality. What was needed was to stabilize the front and, possibly, win a battle or two to restore German prestige.[24]

The deeper problem, as Hitler saw it, was "this human, this moral crisis," in other words, the recently revealed officers' conspiracy against him; he went on:

In the final analysis, what can we expect of a front… if one now sees that in the rear the most important posts were occupied by downright destructionists, not defeatists but destructionists. One does not even know how long they have been conspiring with the enemy or with those people over there [Seydliz's League of German Officers]. In a year or two the Russians have not become that much better; we have become worse because we have that outfit over there constantly spreading poison by means of the General Staff, the Quartermaster General, the Chief of Communications, and so on. If we overcome this moral crisis… in my opinion we will be able to set things right in the East.

Fifteen new grenadier divisions and ten panzer brigades being set

---

24. That afternoon Guderian had told the Army Group Center chief of staff that an attack on both flanks absolutely had to be made in order to influence the current negotiations with Turkey.

up, he predicted, would be enough to stabilize the Eastern Front.[25] Being pushed into a relatively narrow space, he thought, was not entirely bad; it reduced the Army's need for manpower-consuming service and support organizations.

THE RECOVERY

In predicting that the front could be stabilized, Hitler came close to the mark. In fact, even his expressed wish for a victory or two was about to be partially gratified. Model was keeping his forces in hand, and he was gradually gaining strength. Having advanced, in some instances more than 150 miles, the Soviet armies were again getting ahead of their supplies. The flood had reached its crest. It would do more damage; but in places it could also be dammed and diverted.

CROSSCURRENTS

On 1 August Third Panzer Army, not yet recovered from the beating it had taken between Kaunas and Mariampol, shifted the right half of its front into the East Prussia defense position. Third Belorussian Front, following close, cut through this last line forward of German territory in three places and took Vilkavishkis, ten miles east of the border. The general commanding the corps in the weakened sector warned that the Russians could be in East Prussia in another day.

The panzer army staff, set up in Schlossberg on the west side of the border, found being in an "orderly little German city almost incomprehensible after three years on Soviet soil." But Reinhardt was shaken, almost horrified, when he discovered that the Gauleiter of East Prussia, Erich Koch, who was also civil defense commissioner for East Prussia, had not so much as established a plan for evacuating women and children from the areas closest to the front. The army group chief of staff said that he had been protesting daily and had been ignored; apparently Koch was carrying out a Fuehrer directive.

---

25. On 7 July Hitler had ordered the new divisions created. Most of the grenadier divisions were built around the staffs and supply and service elements of divisions that had lost all or nearly all their combat troops in the early weeks of the Soviet offensive. To get the personnel for the grenadier divisions and the panzer brigades, the Army had to use all the replacements scheduled for the Eastern Front in July and August and 45,000 men released from hospitals.

In Warsaw on 1 August the Polish Armia Krajowa (Home Army), under General Tadeusz Bor-Komorowski, staged an insurrection. The Poles were trained and well armed. They moved quickly to take over the heart of the city and the through streets, but the key points the insurgents needed to establish contact with the Russians, the four Vistula bridges and Praga, the suburb on the east bank, stayed in German hands. Worse yet for the insurgents, south of Wolomin the Hermann Goering Division, 19th Panzer Division, and SS Wiking Division closed in behind the III Tank Corps, which after sweeping north past Warsaw had slowed to a near stop on 31 July. In the next two or three days, while the German divisions set about destroying III Tank Corps, Second Tank Army shifted its effort away from Warsaw and began to concentrate on enlarging the bridgehead at Magnuszew, thirty-five miles to the south.

Stalin was obviously not interested in helping the insurgents achieve their objectives: a share in liberating the Polish capital and, based on that, a claim to a stronger voice in the postwar settlement for Premier Stanislaw Mikolajczyk's British-and-American-supported exile government. On 22 July the Soviet Union had established in Lublin the hand-picked Polish Committee of National Liberation, which as one of its first official acts came out wholeheartedly in favor of the Soviet-proposed border on the old Curzon Line, the main point of contention between the Soviet Union and the Mikolajczyk government. That Mikolajczyk was then in Moscow (he had arrived on 30 July) negotiating for a free and independent Poland added urgency to the revolt but at the same time reduced the insurgents in Soviet eyes to the status of inconvenient political pawns.

Army Group North Ukraine on 1 August was in the second day of a counterattack, which had originally aimed at clearing the entire San-Vistula triangle, but which had been reduced before it started to an attempt to cut off the First Tank Army elements that had crossed the Vistula at Baranow. Although Seventeenth Army and Fourth Panzer Army both gained ground, they did not slow or, for that matter, much disturb Konev's thrust across the Vistula. A dozen large ponton ferries, capable of floating up to sixty tons, were transporting troops, tanks, equipment, and supplies of Third Guards Tank and Thirteenth Armies

Immobilized German tank near Warsaw.

across the river. By the end of the day Fourth Panzer Army had gone as far as it could. The next afternoon the army group had to call a halt altogether. The divisions were needed west of the river where First Tank Army, backed by Third Guards Tank Army and Thirteenth Army, had forces strong enough to strike, if it chose, north toward Radom or southwest toward Krakow.

On the night of 3 August Model sent Hitler a cautiously optimistic report. Army Group Center, he said, had set up a continuous front from south of Shaulyay to the right boundary on the Vistula near Pulawy. It was thin—on the 420 miles of front thirty-nine German divisions and brigades faced an estimated third of the total Soviet strength—but it seemed that the time had come when the army group could hold its own, react deliberately, and start planning to take the initiative itself. Model proposed to take the 19th Panzer Division and the Hermann Goering Division behind the Vistula to seal off the Magnuszew bridgehead, to move a panzer division into the Tilsit area to support the Army Group North flank, and to use the Grossdeutschland Division, coming from Army Group South Ukraine, to counterattack at Vilkavishkis. He planned to free two panzer divisions by letting Second Army and the right flank of Fourth

Army withdraw toward the Narew River. With luck, he thought, these missions could be completed by 15 August. After that, he could assemble six panzer divisions on the north flank and attack to regain contact with Army Group North.

For a change, fortune half-favored the Germans. The Hermann Goering Division and the 15th Panzer Division boxed in the Magnuszew bridgehead. Against the promise of a replacement in a week or so, Model gave up the panzer division he had expected to station near Tilsit. The division went to Army Group North Ukraine where Konev, after relinquishing the left half of his front to the reconstituted Headquarters, Fourth Ukrainian Front, under General Polkovnik Ivan Y. Petrov, was now also pushing Fourth Tank Army into the Baranow bridgehead. The bridgehead continued to expand like a growing boil but not as rapidly as might have been expected considering the inequality of the opposing forces.

In the second week of the month three grenadier divisions and two panzer brigades arrived at Army Group Center. On 9 August the Grossdeutschland Division attacked south of Vilkavishkis. Through their agents the Russians were forewarned. They were ready with heavy air support and two fresh divisions. This opposition blunted the German attack somewhat, but the Grossdeutschland Division took Vilkavishkis, even though it could not completely eliminate the salient north of the town before it was taken out and sent north on 10 August.

A CORRIDOR TO ARMY GROUP NORTH

In the first week of August the most urgent question was whether help could be brought to Army Group North before it collapsed completely. On 6 August Schoerner told Hitler that his front would hold until Army Group Center had restored contact, provided "not too much time elapsed" in the interval; his troops were exhausted, and the Russians were relentlessly driving them back by pouring in troops, often 14-year-old boys and old men, at every weak point on the long, thickly forested front. To Guderian he said that if Army Group Center could not attack soon, all that was left was to retreat south and go back to a line Riga-Shaulyay-Kaunas, and even that was becoming more difficult every day.

On 10 August Third Baltic and Second Baltic Fronts launched massive air and artillery-supported assaults against Eighteenth Army below Pskov Lake and north of the Dvina. They broke through in both places on the first day. Having no reserves worth mentioning, Schoerner applied his talent for wringing the last drop of effort out of the troops. To one of the division commanders he sent the message: "Generalleutnant Chales de Beaulieu is to be told that he is to restore his own and his division's honor by a courageous deed or I will chase him out in disgrace. Furthermore, he is to report by 2100 which commanders he has had shot or is having shot for cowardice." From the Commanding General, Eighteenth Army, he demanded "Draconian intervention" and "ruthlessness to the point of brutality."

To boost morale in Schoerner's command, the Air Force sent the Stuka squadron commanded by Major Hans Rudel, the famous Panzerknacker (tank cracker), who a few days before had chalked up his 300th Soviet tank destroyed by dive bombing. Hitler sent word on the 12th that Army Group Center would attack two days earlier than planned. From Koenigsberg the OKH had a grenadier division airlifted to Eighteenth Army.

Army Group Center began the relief operation on 16 August. Two panzer corps, neither fully assembled, jumped off west and north of Shaulyay. Simultaneously, Third Belorussian Front threw the Fifth, Thirty-third, and Eleventh Guards Armies against Third Panzer Army's right flank and retook Vilkavishkis. During the day Model received an order appointing him to command the Western Theater. Reinhardt, the senior army commander, took command of the army group, and Generaloberst Erhard Raus replaced him as Commanding General, Third Panzer Army.

The next day, while the offensive on the north flank rolled ahead, Chernyakovskiy's thrust reached the East Prussian border northwest of Vilkavishkis. One platoon, wiped out before the day's end, crossed the border and for the first time carried the war to German soil. In the next two days the Russians came perilously close to breaking into East Prussia.

On the extreme north flank of Third Panzer Army two panzer brigades, with artillery support from the cruiser Prinz Eugen standing offshore in the Gulf of Riga, on the 10th took Tukums and made contact with Army Group North. On orders from the OKH, the brigades were immediately put aboard trains in Riga and dispatched to the front below Lake Peipus. The next day Third Panzer Army took a firmer foothold along the coast from Tukums east and dispatched a truck column with supplies for Army Group North. On the East Prussian border the army's front was weak and beginning to waver, but the Russians were by then concentrating entirely on the north and did not make the bid to enter German territory. Reinhardt told Guderian during the day that to expand the corridor and get control of the railroad to Army Group North through Jelgava would take too long. He recommended evacuating Army Group North. Guderian replied that he himself agreed but that Hitler refused on political grounds. The offensive continued through 27 August, when Hitler ordered a panzer division transferred to Army Group North.

At the end, the contact with Army Group North was still restricted to an 18-mile-wide coastal corridor. For the time being that was enough. On the last day of the month the Second and Third Baltic Fronts suddenly went over to the defensive.

THE BATTLE SUBSIDES

Throughout the zones of Army Groups Center and North Ukraine, the Soviet offensive, as the month ended, trailed off into random swirls and eddies. After taking Sandomierz on 18 August First Ukrainian Front gradually shifted to the defensive even though it had four full armies, three of them tank armies, jammed into its Vistula bridgehead. North of Warsaw First Belorussian Front had harried Second Army mercilessly as it withdrew toward the Narew, and in the first week of September, when the army went behind the river, took sizable bridgeheads at Serock and Rozan. But for more than two weeks Rokossovskiy evinced no interest in the bridgehead around Warsaw, which Ninth Army was left holding after Second Army withdrew.

In Warsaw at the turn of the month the uprising seemed to be nearing its end. One reason why the insurgents had held out as long as they did was that the Germans had been unable and unwilling to employ regular troops in the house-to-house fighting. They had brought up various remote-controlled demolition vehicles, rocket projectors, and artillery—including a 24-inch howitzer—and had turned the operations against the insurgents over to General von dem Bach-Zelewski and SS-Gruppenfuehrer Heinz Reinefarth. The units engaged were mostly SS and police and included such oddments as the Kaminski Brigade and the Dirlewanger Brigade.[26] As a consequence, the fighting was carried on at an unprecedented level of viciousness without commensurate tactical results.[27]

On 2 September Polish resistance in the city center collapsed and 50,000 civilians passed through the German lines. On the 9th Bor-Komorowski sent out two officer parliamentaries, and the Germans offered prisoner of war treatment for the members of the Armia Krajowa. The next day, in a lukewarm effort to keep the uprising alive, the Soviet Forty-seventh Army attacked the Warsaw bridgehead, and the Poles did not reply to the German offer. Under the attack, the 73d Infantry Division, a hastily rebuilt Crimea division, collapsed and in another two days Ninth Army had to give up the bridgehead, evacuate Praga, and destroy the Vistula bridges. The success apparently was bigger than the Stavka had wanted; on the 14th, even though 100 U.S. 4-motored bombers flew a support mission for the insurgents, the fighting subsided. Until 10 September the Soviet Government

---

26. The Kaminski Brigade, under Mieczyslaw Kaminski, a Pole who claimed Russian nationality and had attempted to create a Russian Nazi Party with himself as its Fuehrer, was composed of Cossacks and other Russians including Soviet Army deserters. Until the fall of 1943 it had held the so-called Self-Government Area Lokot in the heavily partisan-infested Bryansk Forest. After Lokot was lost, the 7,000-man brigade, with over 20,000 camp followers and dependents, had gradually drifted westward with the retreating Germans, marauding as they went. Undisciplined and haphazardly armed and uniformed, the brigade resembled a 16th or 17th century band of mercenaries more than a modern military unit. In the fourth week of the uprising the Germans had Kaminski shot because he refused to accept any kind of authority.

The Dirlewanger Brigade, under SS-Standartenfuehrer (Col.) Oscar Dirlewanger, was composed, except for the officers and a few others, of men from the concentration camps, some of them communists and other political prisoners, most of them common criminals. Dirlewanger was a drunkard who had once been expelled from the SS after being convicted of a serious moral offense. He had shaped the brigade in his own brutal image. Had it not been for Himmler's protection, he would more than once have been court-martialed for atrocities committed in and out of combat.

27. The greatest atrocities, the massacres of men, women, and children in the Wola and Ochota Quarters on 5 and 6 August 1944, were committed before the operations against the insurgents actually began. Hitler and Himmler at first welcomed the uprising as an opportunity to destroy the capital of an ancient enemy and to create an object lesson for other conquered countries.

had refused to open its airfields to American planes flying supplies to the insurgents. On 18 September American planes flew a shuttle mission, but the areas under insurgent control were by then too small for accurate drops and a second planned mission had to be canceled.

During the night of 16-17 September Polish First Army, its Soviet support limited to artillery fire from the east bank, staged crossings into Warsaw. The Soviet account claims that half a dozen battalions of a planned three-division force were put across. The German estimates put the strength at no more than a few companies, and Ninth Army observed that the whole operation became dormant on the second day. The Poles who had crossed were evacuated on 23 September. On the 26th Bor-Komorowski sent parliamentaries a second time, and on 2 October his representatives signed the capitulation.

The psychological reverberations of the summer's disasters continued after the battles died down. In September Reinhardt wrote Guderian that rumors in Germany concerning Busch's alleged disgrace, demotion, suicide, and even desertion were undermining the nation's confidence in Army Group Center. He asked that Busch be given some sort of public token of the Fuehrer's continuing esteem. In the first week of October, Busch was permitted to give an address at the funeral of Hitler's chief adjutant, Schmundt, who had died of wounds he received on 20 July. If that restored public confidence, it was certainly no mark of Hitler's renewed faith either in Busch or in the generals as a class. He had already placed Busch on the select list of generals who were not to be considered for future assignments as army or army group commanders. After most of the eighteen generals captured by the Russians during the retreat joined the Soviet-sponsored League of German Officers, Hitler also decreed that henceforth none of the higher decorations were to be awarded to Army Group Center officers.

Where Hitler saw treason in high places, others saw more widespread, more virulent, more disabling maladies: the fear of being encircled and captured and the fear of being wounded and abandoned. The German soldier was being pursued by the specters of Stalingrad, Cherkassy, and the Crimea. Once, he could not even imagine the ultimate disaster—now he expected it.

CHAPTER XVI

The South Flank

ESCAPE TO THE CARPATHIANS

The summer offensive against Army Groups Center and North Ukraine drove an enormous blunt wedge into the center of the Eastern Front. The flanks, reaching out to the Arctic Ocean and the Black Sea, still held up, but they were stretched taut and ready to snap under the slightest pressure. Though much of the strain was beneath the surface, it was not on that account any the less acute.

ARMY GROUP SOUTH UKRAINE

By 23 July, when Schoerner was called in the early morning hours to take command of Army Group North, Army Group South Ukraine had experienced more than two months of deepening quiet ruffled only by Schoerner's strenuous training and fitness programs. The Russians had taken so many divisions off the front that the OKH directed the army group to do something about tying down those that were left.

The front had not changed since the Soviet spring offensive had stopped. On the left, in a very rough arc from Kuty to east of Iasi, Armeegruppe Woehler, Eighth Army with Rumanian Fourth Army sandwiched in its middle, held a sector—about half in the eastern Carpathians and half east-west across Moldavia north of Targul Frumos and Iasi. Sixth Army reached from east of Iasi to the Dnestr River below Dubossary and then followed the river to about the center of the Soviet bridgehead below Tiraspol, where it tied in with the left of Rumanian Third Army on the lower river line. Sixth Army and Rumanian Third Army formed the Armeegruppe Dumitrescu under the Commanding General, Rumanian Third Army, Col. Gen. Petre Dumitrescu. (Map 30)

Two large rivers, the Prut and the Siret, cut the army group zone

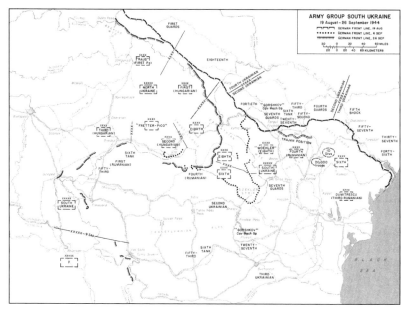

Map 30: Army Group South Ukraine, 19 August-26 September 1944

from north to south, and the Russians were across the upper reaches of both. Rugged, wooded terrain in the Targul Frumos-Iasi area partly compensated for that disadvantage, at least as long as the army group retained enough German divisions to backstop the Rumanians. The biggest tactical change during the early summer was Army Group North Ukraine's retreat deep into Poland, which left Army Group South Ukraine virtually stranded east of the Carpathians. Malinovskiy's *Second Ukrainian Front* opposed Armeegruppe Woehler and Tolbukhin's *Third Ukrainian Front,* Armeegruppe Dumitrescu.

At the time of the change in command, the Army Group South Ukraine staff's foremost concern was to determine how dangerous were the strains beneath the thin veneer of the quiet front and what could be done before they reached the breaking point. Two days before he was transferred, Schoerner wrote Hitler that leading personalities in Rumania were wavering and trying to establish contacts with the Allies, and that Antonescu was losing his hold on the country. Schoerner thought a personal interview with Hitler might strengthen Antonescu's position. On 25 July the army group staff drafted a report stating that after being forced to transfer 6 panzer divisions, 2 infantry divisions, and 2 self-propelled assault gun brigades in the past month, the army group could no longer hold its front against a full-fledged attack. The staff recommended that the army group be authorized in advance to pull back as soon as such an attack developed. That report was not sent, apparently because the estimate of the new commanding general, Friessner, was more optimistic.

RUMANIA

The most pressing worry for the moment was the internal condition of Rumania. Army Group South Ukraine, although entirely dependent on the Rumanian railroads and forced in large part to subsist off the local economy, had no executive authority in Rumania. Everything had to be decided between Bucharest and Berlin; and the army group staff by late July was convinced that on the most important question, Rumanian loyalty to the alliance, something was seriously out of tune. That Antonescu, on whose personal authority alone the alliance was based, no longer possessed that authority, seemed to be no secret to anyone in Rumania except three persons: the Marshal himself, Manfred Freiherr von Killinger, the German Minister to Rumania, and General der Kavallerie Erik Hansen, the chief of the German military mission. The latter two were the responsible German representatives in Rumania. Both von Killinger, a World War I U-boat commander and long-time Nazi turned diplomat, and Hansen, an energetic but inflexible officer, were blinded by their own faith in Antonescu. Consequently, they reinforced the already strong tendency in Hitler's circle to confuse Antonescu's personal loyalty with that of the Rumanian Army and people. The Army Group South Ukraine staff was certain that Antonescu was being kept in power only by his opponents' rapidly diminishing unwillingness to take the risks of an attempt to remove him, and that the country, Antonescu included, was staying in the war solely because its fear of the Russians still slightly exceeded its desire for peace.

On 1 August, anticipating repercussions throughout southeastern Europe when Turkey broke diplomatic relations with Germany, which it did the next day, Friessner ordered each of his two armies to set up a mobile regiment that could be used to counter "possible surprises in Rumanian territory." Strangely and, as it later proved, fatefully, the army group concentrated its attention almost exclusively on the dangers which would arise if Rumania defected. It did not pursue the, for it, equally vital question, What, if anything, remained of the Rumanian Army's never very strong will to fight? And the Rumanians held 160 miles of the army group's 392-mile-long front.

In the first week of August, Antonescu went to Rastenburg to talk to Hitler. The two met under a darkening cloud of German reverses in France and the East and in an atmosphere of mutual complaints and suspicions; yet, in the last analysis, neither had any real choice but to tell the other what he wanted to hear. In May, after more or less open negotiations in Cairo with the Americans, British, and Russians, Antonescu had rejected one set of armistice terms. When secret negotiations conducted at the same time in Sweden with the Soviet Union alone had brought a somewhat more lenient offer, he had again not been able to steel himself to take the plunge. The report on the conference at Fuehrer headquarters which reached Army Group South Ukraine described the results as "very positive." Hitler had told the Marshal what was being done to restore the German situation, and both parties had promised each other "everything possible." In the transmission, someone had added, "It now remains to be seen how far the promises will be carried out."

Because many of the individual points to be discussed arose out of its presence on Rumanian territory and because the time appeared ripe for raising fundamental questions, the army group had sent its operations officer to Fuehrer headquarters while Antonescu was there. Friessner had sent along a letter for Hitler in which he stated that the army group could hold its front if it did not lose any more divisions but had to be prepared for all eventualities. He recommended giving the army group control of all German military activities in Rumania and the appointment of a single, responsible political agency with which the army group could collaborate. The operations officer, on Friessner's instructions, told Guderian that the OKH would have to reconcile itself to permitting the army group to go back to a line on the Carpathians and lower Danube if the army group had to give up more divisions or if the Rumanians became unreliable. After talking to Hitler, Guderian replied that he "hoped" if events took such a turn to be able "to give the necessary order in time." The prospect that such an order would be given, however, faded after the talks with Antonescu revealed that, even though he had argued in the spring for going back to the Carpathians-Danube line, he had in the meantime convinced himself that for Rumania to sacrifice any more territory would be fatal.[28]

To Keitel the army group operations officer broached the question of having Friessner named Armed Forces commander in Rumania and proposed replacing Hansen with an officer "who would represent the German interest more emphatically." Keitel appeared impressed at first but, after the talks with Antonescu, said he saw no need for any changes because Rumania would stand by Germany "through thick and thin." In sum, the tottering alliance was patched together for a last time at Army Group South Ukraine's expense.

THE OFFENSIVE BEGINS

On 8 August air reconnaissance for the first time detected Soviet troop movements east of the Prut. Heavy traffic toward and light traffic away from the front confirmed that the troops were coming in, not going out. On the 13th the OKH took another division from the army group, bringing the total transfers since June to eleven divisions and the overall strength reduction to nearly one-third—much more, almost three-fourths, in terms of panzer divisions. On that day, too, a rumor that Antonescu had been overthrown touched off a spell of confusion and near panic in the army group rear area.

Armeegruppe Woehler reported on the 16th that the Russians would be ready to attack in a day or two, probably west of Iasi, to drive a wedge between Iasi and Targul Frumos. The Rumanians, the Armeegruppe declared, were "completely confident." (See Map 30.) By the afternoon of the 19th, after Second Ukrainian Front, Malinovskiy commanding, had launched artillery-supported probing attacks along the Armeegruppe Woehler front, the army group expected to be hit

---

28. Guderian in his memoirs states that Antonescu offered to let the front be taken back, but Antonescu's statement to Friessner later makes it appear unlikely that he would have done so.

heavily the next day west of Iasi and predicted a secondary attack south of Tiraspol.

The day dawned hot and sunny on 20 August 1944. The Soviet artillery laid down heavy barrages on two fairly narrow sectors, one northwest of Iasi, the other south of Tiraspol. By the time the infantry of *Second* and *Third Ukrainian Fronts* jumped off, several Rumanian divisions were about to collapse.

Two of Armeegruppe Woehler's Rumanian divisions protecting Iasi abandoned their positions without a fight. On the west side of the gap left by the Rumanians, German reserves threw up a screening line, but on the east the Russians continued south, turning into Iasi in the afternoon. South of Tiraspol the attack struck the Sixth Army-Rumanian Third Army boundary. Sixth Army's right flank corps, the hardest hit, held its ground, but the Rumanian division tying in on the boundary collapsed, carrying with it its neighbor on the south. By day's end Friessner realized that the Rumanian's performance would fall below even their customary low standard. How far below he had yet to learn.

The two Ukrainian *fronts*—Marshal Timoshenko co-ordinating for the *Stavka*—had, according to the Soviet figures, superiorities of slightly less than 2:1 in troops, better than 2:1 in artillery and aircraft, and better than 3:1 in tanks and self-propelled artillery. All together Malinovskiy and Tolbukhin had 90 divisions and 6 tank and mechanized corps, 929,000 men.

The main effort, by *Sixth Tank Army* and *Twenty-seventh, Fifty-second,* and *Fifty-third Armies,* was in Malinovskiy's sector northwest of Iasi. There *Sixth Tank Army* went in on the first afternoon, and by nightfall it and *Twenty-seventh Army* were driving for an operational breakthrough. On the right, north of Targul Frumos, *Seventh Guards Army* and the *Cavalry-Mechanized Group Gorshkov* were poised for a thrust south along the Siret. Tolbukhin had the *Thirty-seventh* and *Fifty-seventh Armies* and two mechanized corps charging out of the Tiraspol bridgehead. On their left *Forty-sixth Army* had split its forces to envelop Rumanian III Corps on the lower Dnestr.

On the morning of the second day Friessner still thought the battle would develop about as had been expected. Although he did not have a clear picture of enemy strength, the army group's intelligence seemed to confirm that the build-up had not been up to the previous Soviet level for an all-out offensive. Furthermore, the main effort was against Armeegruppe Woehler and there the second line, the TRAJAN position on the heights behind Iasi, was considered exceptionally good.

When Antonescu arrived at the army group headquarters in midmorning, Friessner told him that he would close the front below Tiraspol and, taking everything he could from Armeegruppe Dumitrescu, strengthen the north front enough to prevent a sweep behind the Prut. The Russians, he thought, could not bring as much strength to bear against Dumitrescu as they could against Woehler and, having gone deeper the day before than expected, would probably have to pause to regroup. Antonescu, formerly always the advocate of a flexible defense, insisted that the front, including Iasi, absolutely had to be held. He declared that he was personally answerable for every piece of ground lost and it was not the fate of Bessarabia that was being decided but the fate of the whole Rumanian people "forever."

During the day every report from the front brought more alarming news than the last. In the north Iasi was lost and the offensive expanded west to Targul Frumos. Tanks of *Cavalry-Mechanized Group Gorshkov* drove through the TRAJAN position at a point near Targul Frumos, and tank-supported infantry drew up to it along most of the stretch west of the Prut. Armeegruppe Woehler reported that five of its Rumanian divisions had fallen apart completely. South of Tiraspol a 20-mile gap opened between Sixth Army and Rumanian Third Army.

In the afternoon Friessner decided to take Armeegruppe Dumitrescu behind the Prut and try to free enough German troops to reinforce Armeegruppe Woehler. The army group and the Operations Branch, OKH, agreed that would be only a first step in a withdrawal which could not end forward of the Carpathians-Danube line. Hitler, after being assured that Antonescu was now "letting himself be guided solely by military considerations" and therefore had no objections, gave his approval during the night. By then an order was out to Sixth

Army to get everything it could behind the Prut immediately. The Sixth Army staff was among the first elements to go, because Russian tanks were already closing in on its headquarters at Komrat.

For the next two days the battle continued as it had begun. The Rumanians, even the supposedly elite Rumanian Armored Division, refused to fight. The Russians moved south fast behind the Prut and through the torn-open center of Armeegruppe Dumitrescu without the Germans being able to commit anything against them. Behind the Prut the Soviet tank points reached Barlad and Husi on the 23d. *Third Ukrainian Front's* advance west carried past Komrat nearly to the Prut, and *Forty-sixth Army* turned its left flank southeast and on its right attacked across the Dnestr Liman to encircle Rumanian III Corps and one German division. The main body of German troops, the whole front from the Prut east of Iasi to Tiraspol, was falling back to the southwest fast but not fast enough to outrace the Soviet pincers closing behind it.

RUMANIA SURRENDERS

In the early evening on 23 August army group headquarters heard that Antonescu had been called to an audience with the King in the afternoon; the government had been dissolved, and Antonescu and its members arrested. Later the chief of staff talked to von Killinger, who had returned from the palace where the King had informed him that a new government had been formed and it intended to sign an armistice. One condition that would not be accepted, the King had assured him, was that Rumania should take up arms against the Germans. But the King's broadcast that night was less reassuring. In it he stated that Rumania would join the United Nations against the common enemy—Germany—and, in what practically amounted to a declaration of war against Hungary, that Rumania denounced the Treaty of Vienna of 30 August 1940 which had awarded the Szekler Strip in Transylvania to Hungary.

The contradiction in the King's statements apparently arose from the existence of two sets of armistice terms. Although the Rumanian Government in the public statement accepted the more stringent terms which had been offered by the three powers—the United States, Britain

Soviet submachine gunner attacking.

and the Soviet Union—at the negotiations which began that night in Cairo, the Rumanian delegation was instructed to secure amendments which would include the concessions the Soviet Union had offered in secret. The latter would have allowed Rumania to declare itself neutral in the conflict with Germany and, of much greater moment to the Rumanians, proposed arrangements which would assure the continued existence of an independent Rumanian state.[29]

Shortly before midnight on the 23d, Friessner telephoned Hitler an account of the Rumanian coup and told him he had taken command of all Wehrmacht elements in Rumania and was going to take the front back to the Carpathians-Danube line. At midnight the Operations Branch, OKH, relayed an order from Hitler to smash the "Putsch," arrest the King and "the court camarilla," and turn the government over either to Antonescu or, if he were "no longer available," to a pro-German general. On learning that von Killinger, Hansen, and the

---

29. With a crushing victory in the making, the Russians were not inclined to compromise and the negotiations dragged out until 12 September when, probably as much because they were trapped by their own double dealing as for any other reason, they agreed to reduced reparations, the return of the ceded territory in Transylvania to Rumania, and Rumanian civil administration of the areas outside the combat zone in compensation for placing the Rumanian armed forces under Soviet command in the war against Germany.

commanding general of the German air units in Rumania, General der Flieger Alfred Gerstenberg, were being held under guard in the legation, Friessner turned Hitler's assignment over to an SS general whom he located in one of the installations outside Bucharest. The SS general reported at 0300 that troops would arrive from Ploeşti in an hour and a half and would then move into the city.

Before dawn Hansen called to tell Friessner that the Rumanian War Minister had declared that if the German measures against the new government were not stopped within air hour the Rumanian Army would turn its weapons against the German Army. Hansen added that he and the others with him were convinced the German forces were not strong enough to take Bucharest. When Friessner asked whether he was under restraint, Hansen replied that he was.

Friessner transmitted a résumé of the conversation to the Fuehrer headquarters along with a reminder that the King had allegedly promised not to fight the Germans. A few minutes later Jodl called to say that Hansen was not making a free decision, anyway the whole affair was bound to go awry sooner or later, so it was best to make a clean sweep right away. Almost simultaneously, a call came in from Gerstenberg, whom the Rumanians had released thinking he would attempt to stop the impending German action. He described the new Rumanian Government as a small, frightened clique, protected only by a thin screen of troops around the capital. Friessner thereupon gave him command in the Bucharest area.

At 0730 6,000 German troops began to march on the capital. Ten minutes later they met sharp resistance and were stopped. Shortly before noon, Gerstenberg admitted that so far he had not been able to get past the outlying suburbs. He had taken the radio station but nothing else worth mentioning. In the meantime, Friessner had learned that not a single Rumanian general was willing to go along with the Germans.

In the afternoon, on Hitler's orders, Fourth Air Force bombed the royal palace and government buildings in Bucharest. The bombing not only gave the government an excuse for a complete, open breach with Germany, which it would probably have effected anyway, but also united national sentiment against the Germans. As the day ended, the deadlock around the capital continued while Gerstenberg waited for reinforcements from the Southeastern Theater. Friessner had asked for troops from Hungary as well, but the OKW had replied that it was also "getting strange reports" from that country.

SIXTH ARMY DESTROYED

The 24th and 25th were days of unmitigated disaster for Army Group South Ukraine. On the 24th the armored spearheads of *Second Ukrainian Front* took Bacau on the Siret River and crossed the Barladul downstream from Barlad. Sixth Army, all of it except service troops, was drawing together south and east of Husi. Parts of two corps were west of the Prut, but the main body was still east of the river. The army headquarters, which from its location in Focsani only had intermittent radio contact with its corps, wanted to command the whole force to turn south and try to escape across the lower Prut or the Danube. Friessner, assuming that the Russians would close the crossings before Sixth Army could reach them, ordered a breakthrough west past Bacau to the Carpathians.

On the 25th, when Rumania declared war, the destruction of the army group was nearly complete. It did not know what was happening to Sixth Army or what would happen to the numerous German units and installations in Rumania. Friessner told the OKH that what was left would have to retreat into Hungary and close the passes through the Carpathians and the Transylvanian Alps.

On the 26th Tolbukhin's troops took Kagul, completing the ring around Sixth Army, and Malinovskiy's forces began turning southwest across the lower Siret. From the right flank of the 3d Mountain Division in the mountains west of Targu Neamt to the mouth of the Danube 250 miles to the southeast, Army Group South Ukraine had no semblance of a front anywhere. In that fantastic situation Hitler intervened with an order to hold the line of the Carpathians, Focsani, Galatz, and the lower Danube.

The next day Malinovskiy's spearhead across the Siret took Focsani. Headquarters, Sixth Army, after trying briefly to hold a line between Focsani and Galatz with rear echelon troops, fell back toward Buzau. Fragmentary radio reports from the army's encircled divisions indicated that two pockets had formed, one, the larger (10 divisions), stationary on the east bank of the Prut east of Husi, the other (8 divisions) moving west slowly south of Husi. North of Bucharest the Rumanians had the German attack force surrounded. At Ploești the 5th Flak Division had lost the oil refineries and half of the city. Eighth Army, going back from the Siret, had barely enough troops to organize blocking detachments in the Oitoz Pass and the passes to the north. The mountains offered cover, but the deep flank, 190 miles in the Transylvanian Alps from the southeastern tip of Hungary to the Iron Gate, was entirely unprotected. The planes of Fourth Air Force were using their last gas to fly into eastern Hungary. On the south the Bulgarians, not officially at war with the Soviet Union and looking desperately for a way to keep the Soviet Army off their territory, were disarming and interning all Army Group South Ukraine troops who crossed the border.

RETREAT TO THE CARPATHIANS

During the night of 29 August OKH ordered Army Group South Ukraine to establish a solid front along the spine of the Transylvanian Alps and the Carpathians tying in with the Southeastern Theater at the Iron Gate and Army Group North Ukraine on the Polish border. Hungarian Second Army, forming in eastern Hungary, was placed under Friessner's command.

The mountains, in fact, afforded the best defense line, provided that Friessner could muster enough strength to take and hold the passes on Rumanian territory in the Transylvanian Alps. How difficult that would be became clear the next day when he reported that of Sixth Army not a single complete division had escaped. What was left, the headquarters and service troops with some 5,000 vehicles, was jammed into the Buzaul Valley and was as yet by no means out of the Russians' reach.

The army group had, all told, four full divisions; three had been on the left flank and not hit by the offensive and one had been on its way out of the army group zone and was returned after the offensive began. All the army group actually held was an intermittent front in the Carpathians. If the Russians decided to make a fast thrust north through the Predeal and Turnu Rosu Passes, the army group chief of staff added, "The jig will be up out here."

On 30 August, Malinovskiy's troops took Ploeşti and the next day marched to Bucharest. In carrying out *Stavka's* orders, Malinovskiy, on 29 August, had split his forces. He had sent the *Sixth Tank, Twenty-seventh,* and *Fifty-third Armies* between the Danube and the Carpathians to clear southern Rumania to Turnu Severin. With the smaller half he undertook to force the Germans out of the eastern Carpathians. *Fortieth Army* moved against the relatively intact Eighth Army left flank. *Seventh Guards Army* and the *Cavalry-Mechanized Group Gorshkov* were to force the Oitoz Pass and push across the mountains toward Sibiu and Cluj.

When the Russians began to move west south of the mountains, Friessner decided he might yet have a chance to close at least the Predeal and Turnu Rosu Passes. (The Southeastern Theater Command had assumed responsibility for the Iron Gate.) The remaining pass, the Vulcan, was at the moment out of reach of both the Southeastern Theater and Army Group South Ukraine. At the same time, considering the chances of getting the passes slight, Friessner ordered the armies to reconnoiter a line on the Muresul River across the western end of the Szekler Strip.

On 5 September Hungarian Second Army attacked south from the vicinity of Cluj to close the Turnu Rosu Pass. The day before, air reconnaissance had picked up signs that Second Ukrainian Front was beginning to turn north, and Friessner had alerted the armies to get ready, if ordered, to act fast and get behind the Muresul in one leap. For the moment the order did not have to be given. Hungarian Second Army gained ground rapidly against feeble resistance by the hastily reconstituted *Rumanian Fourth Army.* (*Rumanian First* and *Fourth Armies* went under Malinovskiy's command on 6 September.)

During the day Sixth Army brought its last troops out of the Buzaul Valley. But that and the Hungarians' success were only minor bright spots on a predominantly dismal scene. After hearing nothing for several days, the army group was forced to write off as lost the five corps staffs and eighteen divisions in the two pockets. The Russians going west reached Turnu Severin, ten miles southeast of the Iron

Soviet tanks entering a Rumanian town.

Gate, during the day. By evening Friessner had concluded he would have to take Sixth Army and Eighth Army behind the Muresul but decided to wait a day or two—long enough to mitigate the unfortunate contrast of German troops retreating while their Hungarian allies were advancing.

THE FRONT REBUILT

RETREAT TO THE MURESUL—CRISIS IN HUNGARY

Hungarian Second Army advanced again on 6 September, but not as fast as it had the day before. Sixth Army, which had taken command of Eighth Army's right flank corps, reported that the Russians were in the Oitoz Pass and, off the army's south front, were already through the Predeal Pass and assembling at Brasov. Friessner authorized the army to start back during the night if the pressure became too great. He told Guderian that the Hungarians could not be expected to reach the Turnu Rosu Pass; the Rumanians had asked for Russian help. He had talked to the Hungarians and they were agreed on going back to a shorter line.

The next day the Hungarian offensive came to a standstill. The effect of its first two days' success could be observed farther south. Soviet *Sixth Tank Army,* which had been going toward the Iron Gate, had stopped and turned north. One of its mobile corps was crossing the Turnu Rosu Pass, another was heading into the Vulcan Pass. By noon the lead elements were through the Turnu Rosu and in Sibiu, forty miles from the Hungarian front Friessner then decided to stop Hungarian Second Army, take it into a defensive line, and back it up with all the German antitank weapons that could be scraped together. Orders went out to Eighth and Sixth Armies to start withdrawing that night. During the night the Operations Branch, OKH, tried to interpose an order from Hitler forbidding the withdrawal. When the army group answered that it had already begun, the Operations Branch replied that Hitler "had taken notice" of the withdrawal to the first phase line but reserved all subsequent decisions to himself.

Five days earlier Hitler had personally instructed Friessner to get ready to fall back some forty miles farther west than the proposed line on the Muresul River. In the meantime he had changed his mind, because he was determined to hold onto his last legitimate ally, Hungary, and because he was arriving at a new and novel estimate of Soviet strategy.

The first reason was the more immediate. Hungary, never a pillar of strength in the German coalition, had since Rumania capitulated been in a state of acute internal political tension. Horthy had dissolved all political parties and had declared his loyalty to Germany. His first impulse had seemed to be to seize the opportunity to annex the Rumanian parts of Transylvania, to which Hitler was only too happy to agree after Rumania declared war. But by 24 August the internal condition of Hungary appeared so uncertain that the OKW moved two SS divisions in close to the capital to be ready to put down an anti-German coup.

The events of the next few days, however, were at least superficially reassuring. The military in particular, appearing to be loyal to the alliance, set about mobilizing their forces for the war against their ancient enemy Rumania with, under the circumstances, surprising energy. The appointment on 30 August of Col. Gen. Geza Lakatos as Minister President to replace Sztojay, who was sick, and the appointments to his Cabinet preserved the hold inside the Hungarian Government which the Germans had established in the spring.

On the other hand Horthy kept out representatives of the radical rightist, fanatically pro-German Arrow-Cross Party.

The first overt alarm was raised on 7 September when, in a flash of panic touched off by a false report that the Russians were in Arad on the undefended south border 140 miles from Budapest, the Hungarian Crown Council met in secret and later, through the Chief of Staff, presented an ultimatum to the OKH: if Germany did not send five panzer divisions within twenty-four hours Hungary would reserve the right to act as its interests might require. Guderian called it extortion but gave his word to defend Hungary as if it were part of Germany and announced that he would send a panzer corps headquarters and one panzer division. Later he added two panzer brigades and two SS divisions, bringing the total to roughly the five divisions demanded. Because Hungary was in so shaky a condition Hitler refused to sacrifice the Szekler Strip even though Friessner and the German Military Plenipotentiary in Budapest assured him that the Hungarians were reconciled to losing the territory.

On 9 September Friessner went to Budapest where he persuaded Horthy to put his agreement to the withdrawal in writing. The impressions he received from talking to Horthy, Lakatos, and the military leaders were so disturbing that he decided to report on them to Hitler in person the next day. At Fuehrer headquarters Friessner learned the second reason why Hitler did not want to give up the Szekler Strip. He had concluded that having broken into the Balkans (*Third Ukrainian Front* had crossed into Bulgaria on 8 September), the Soviet Union would put its old ambitions—political hegemony in southeastern Europe and control of the Dardenelles—ahead of the drive toward Germany. In doing so, it would infringe on British interests and the war would turn in Germany's favor because the British would realize they needed Germany as a buffer against the Soviet Union.[30] Since the withdrawal had started, he agreed by the

---

30. At a time when a split between the Soviet Union and the Western Powers, remote as the

end of the interview to let the army group go to the Muresul on the conditions that the line be adjusted to take in the manganese mines at Vatra Dornei and that it be the winter line. He also decided, after hearing Friessner's report, to "invite" the Hungarian Chief of Staff for a talk the next day.

In Budapest on the 10th Horthy conferred with a select group of prominent politicians, and a day later informed the Cabinet that he was about to ask for an armistice and desired to know which of its members were willing to share the responsibility for that step. The vote went heavily against him—according to the account the Germans received at the time all but one against and, according to his own later statement, three for him. The Cabinet then demanded his resignation. He refused; or, as he put it in his *Memoirs,* he decided not to dismiss the Cabinet.

Either way, when the Hungarian Chief of Staff went to Fuehrer headquarters on the 12th he went as an ally. The day's delay had mightily aroused Hitler's suspicion, and he told the Hungarian military attaché that he had no further confidence in the Hungarian Government. The Chief of Staff's visit went off, as Antonescu's had in August, in mutual complaints and recriminations that were finally obscured by a thick fog of more or less empty promises. On his departure Guderian gave him a new Mercedes limousine, which came in handy a few weeks later when he went over to the Russians.

HITLER PLANS A COUNTEROFFENSIVE

Army Group South Ukraine completed the withdrawal to the Muresul on 15 September. Tolbukhin's armies were temporarily out of the way in Bulgaria, and Malinovskiy's advance from the south was developing more slowly than had been expected. His tanks and trucks had taken a mechanical beating on the trip through the passes. On the other hand, a new threat was emerging on the north where *Fourth Ukrainian Front* on 9 September had begun an attempt to break through First Panzer Army and into the Dukla Pass in the Beskides of eastern

---

possibility might be, was the brightest of Germany's remaining prospects, such reasoning was not easy to refute. Friessner stated after the war that he assumed that Hitler was talking from knowledge, not merely spinning empty theories.

Czechoslovakia and toward Uzhgorod. Behind that sector of the front the Germans were at the same time having trouble with an uprising in Slovakia in which the Minister of War and the one-division Slovakian Army had gone over to the partisans.

While Friessner was at Fuehrer headquarters Hitler had instructed him to use offensively the new divisions being sent. He wanted them assembled around Cluj for an attack to the south to smash *Sixth Tank* and *Twenty-seventh Armies* and retake the Predeal and Turnu Rosu Passes. Friessner issued the directive on 15 September, but the prospects of an early start were not good. Hitler had some of the reinforcements stop at Budapest, in readiness for a political crisis there.

At the front, the Hungarians, who had not done badly against the Rumanians, were disinclined toward becoming earnestly embroiled with the Russians. To give them some stiffening, the Army group merged Hungarian Second Army with Sixth Army to form the Armeegruppe Fretter-Pico under the Commanding General, Sixth Army, Fretter-Pico. On the 17th Fretter-Pico reported that Second Army was in a "catastrophic" state and that one mountain brigade had run away.

TANK BATTLE AT DEBRECEN

At mid-month the *Stavka* also gave new orders. It directed Tolbukhin, still occupied in Bulgaria, to give *Forty-sixth Army* to Malinovskiy, and it transferred the *Cavalry-Mechanized Group Pliyev* from *First Ukrainian Front.* It instructed Malinovskiy to send his main thrust northwest from Cluj toward Debrecen, the Tisza River, and Miskolc, expecting him thereby both to benefit from and assist *Fourth Ukrainian Front's* advance toward Uzhgorod. For a week, beginning on 16 September, *Sixth Tank* and *Twenty-seventh Armies* tried unsuccessfully to take Cluj, which, because of Hitler's plan, was exactly the place Army Group South Ukraine was most determined to hold.

Friessner was far short of the strength both to fight the battle at Cluj and establish a front west of there. On 20 September a minor Russian onslaught threw back to Arad the Hungarians covering his flank on the west, and the following day they gave up the city without a fight.

Thereafter the Hungarian General Staff activated a new army, the Third, composed mostly of recruits and recently recalled reservists, to hold a front on both sides of Arad. Reluctantly, it agreed to put the army under Army Group South Ukraine.

Losing Arad sent another wave of panic through Budapest even though the army group (redesignated Army Group South at midnight on 23 September) was certain that Malinovskiy did not yet have enough strength at Arad to attempt to strike out for Budapest. The German Military Plenipotentiary in Budapest reported on the 23d that the Hungarian command had completely lost nerve. It had pulled First Army back to the border, it intended to move two divisions of Second Army west, and it wanted to withdraw Third Army to the Tisza River. The OKH promptly whipped the Hungarians into line and had their orders rescinded. "In view of the Hungarian attitude," Guderian then sent several strong panzer units to "rest and refit" just outside Budapest.

The Hungarians' nervousness was premature, but not by much. Malinovskiv was shifting his main force west to the Arad-Oradea area, and Army Group South had too few German troops to keep pace. On the 24th, when Friessner called for reinforcements, the Operations Branch, OKH, replied that it recognized the need the reason the army group had not been given any so far was that Hitler was still convinced the Soviet Union would first attempt to settle affairs in the Balkans on its own terms.

On the 25th elements of *Sixth Tank Army,* shifted west from Cluj, began closing in on Oradea. Friessner informed Hitler that the next attack would come across the line Szeged-Oradea, either northwest toward Budapest or north along the Tisza to meet *Fourth Ukrainian Front's* thrust through the Beskides. He could not stop it without more armor and infantry. Operations Branch, OKH, replied that Hitler intended to assemble a striking force of four panzer divisions around Debrecen for an attack south, but that could not be done before 10 October. Until then Friessner would have to deploy the forces he had in trying to check the Russians in the Szeged-Oradea area.

By the end of the month Hitler had fleshed out his plan for the proposed striking force. The attack would go south past Oradea and then wheel west along the rim of the Transylvanian Alps to trap the Russians north of the mountains. After mopping up, Army Group South could establish an easily defensible winter line in the mountains. For a while it appeared that he might have time enough to put the striking force together. After taking Oradea on 26 September and losing it two days later when the Germans counterattacked, *Second Ukrainian Front* reverted to aimless skirmishing.

The Stavka was also looking for a quick and sweeping solution. (Map 31) On its orders, Malinovskiy deployed Forty-sixth Army, Fifty-third Army, and the Cavalry-Mechanized Group Pliyev on a broad front north and south of Arad for a thrust across the Tisza to Budapest. To their right Sixth Tank Army, now a guards tank army, was to strike past Oradea toward Debrecen, the Tisza, and Miskolc, there to meet a Fourth Ukrainian Front spearhead that would come through the Dukla Pass and by way of Uzhgorod. The pincers, when they closed, would trap Army Group South and First Panzer and Hungarian First Armies. Twenty-seventh Army, Rumanian First Army, and Cavalry-Mechanized Group Gorshkov were to attack toward Debrecen from the vicinity of Cluj. Timoshenko co-ordinated for the Stavka.

The plan was ambitious, too ambitious. Men and matériel for an extensive build-up were not to be had at this late stage of the general summer offensive; both *fronts* were feeling the effects of combat and long marches; and their supply lines were overextended. Because of the difference in gauges, the Rumanian railroads, if anything, were serving the Russians less well than they had the Germans, and *Second Ukrainian Front* had to rely mainly on motor transport west of the Dnestr. Malinovskiy's broad-front deployment gave him only about half the ratio of troops to frontage usual for a Soviet offensive. As a prerequisite for the larger operation *Fourth Ukrainian Front's* progress through the Dukla Pass was not encouraging; it had been slow from the start and at the end of the month the offensive was almost at a standstill.

After the turn of the month the Soviet attack into the Dukla Pass began to make headway, partly because Hitler had taken out a panzer division there for his striking force, and on 6 October the Russians took the pass. That morning Malinovskiy's armies attacked. Hungarian

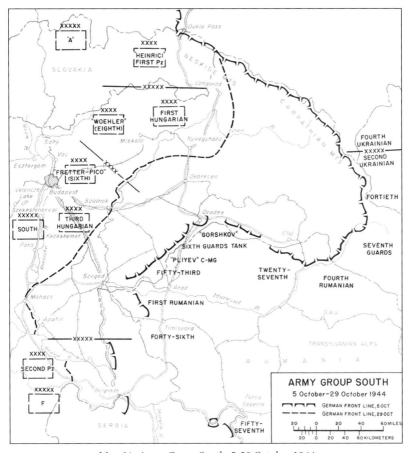

Map 31: Army Group South, 5-29 October 1944

Third Army melted away fast. At Oradea, however, *Sixth Guards Tank Army* met Germans and was stopped.

On the 8th, as his left flank was closing to the Tisza, Malinovskiy turned *Cavalry-Mechanized Group Pliyev* around and had it strike southeast behind Oradea. That broke the German hold. By nightfall a tank corps and a cavalry corps stood west of Debrecen, and Friessner, over Hitler's protests, ordered the Armeegruppe Woehler to start back from the Muresul line.

The army group still had one panzer division stationed near Budapest and another, the first of the proposed striking force, at Debrecen. On 10 October the divisions attacked east and west below Debrecen into the flanks of the Soviet spearhead. Late that night their points met. They had cut off three Soviet corps. The army group envisioned "another Cannae," and Hitler ordered Armeegruppe Woehler to stop on the next phase line.

The next day, when *Sixth Guards Tank Army* put up a violent fight to get the corps out, who had trapped whom began to become unclear. The flat Hungarian plain became the scene of one of the wildest tank battles of the war. Malinovskiy reined in on his other armies. By the 12th the Russians in the pocket were shaking themselves loose, and Friessner ordered Armeegruppe Woehler to start back again. On the 14th the Russians were clearing the pocket, and Army Group South began concentrating on getting a front strong enough to keep them from going north once more. In the Beskides *Fourth Ukrainian Front* was moving slowly again south of the Dukla Pass and trying to get through some of the smaller passes farther east.

HORTHY ASKS FOR AN ARMISTICE

During the battle at Debrecen the Germans were aware that they were, as someone in OKH put it, "dancing on a volcano." They sensed that in Budapest a break might come any day, almost any hour. Their suspicion was well founded. In late September Horthy had sent representatives to Moscow to negotiate an armistice, and on 11 October they had a draft agreement completed and initialed without a fixed date. To be ready for any sudden moves, Hitler had sent in two "specialists," SS General von dem Bach-Zelewski and SS Col. Otto Skorzeny. Von dem Bach had long experience in handling uprisings, most recently at Warsaw. Skorzeny commanded the daredevil outfit that had rescued Mussolini.

The crisis in Hungary resolved itself less violently than the Germans expected. As Hungarian head of state for a generation, Horthy had accumulated tremendous personal prestige, but his authority had declined, and his political position was badly undermined. In the Parliament during the first week of October the parties of the right formed a prowar, pro-German majority coalition against him. The Army was split; some of the generals and many of the senior staff officers wanted to keep on fighting. On 8 October the Gestapo arrested the Budapest garrison commander, one of Horthy's most faithful and potentially most effective supporters, and, on the 15th, it arrested Horthy's son, who had played a leading role in the attempt to get an armistice.

The Soviet Union demanded that Hungary accept the armistice terms by 16 October. In the afternoon of the 15th Radio Budapest broadcast Horthy's announcement that he had accepted. By then he was acting alone. The Lakatos Cabinet had resigned on the grounds that it could not approve an armistice and Parliament had not been consulted on the negotiations.

The next morning, to the accompaniment of scattered shooting, the Germans took the royal palace and persuaded Horthy to "request" asylum in Germany. In his last official act, under German "protection," Horthy appointed Ferenc Szalasi, the leader of the Arrow-Cross Party, as his successor. Szalasi, whose chief claim to distinction until then had been his incoherence both in speech and in writing, subsequently had himself named *"Nador"* (leader), with all the rights and duties of the Prince Regent.

On 17 October Guderian, in an order declaring the political battle in Hungary won, announced that the next step would be to bring all of the German and Hungarian strength to bear at the front. How that was to be accomplished he did not say. In terms of the military situation the victory was one only by comparison with the immediate, total dissolution that would have come if Horthy's attempt to get an armistice had succeeded. Morale in the Hungarian Army hit bottom. Some officers, including the Chief of Staff, some whole units, and many individuals deserted to the Russians, who encouraged others to do the same by letting the men return home if they lived in the areas under Soviet control.

TO THE TISZA

On the night of 16 October Hitler ordered Army Group South to see the battle through at Debrecen but also to start taking Armeegruppe Woehler back toward the Tisza. Meanwhile, Malinovskiy had reassembled his armor, the two cavalry-mechanized groups and *Sixth Guards Tank Army,* south of Debrecen. On the 10th the *Cavalry-*

Mechanized Group Pliyev broke through past Debrecen, and two days later it took Nyiregyhaza, astride Armeegruppe Woehler's main line of communications.

The Armeegruppe, which had also taken command of Hungarian First Army, its neighbor on the left, held a bow-shaped line that at its center was eighty miles east of Nyiregyhaza. Friessner's first thought was to pull the Armeegruppe north and west to skirt Nyiregyhaza. His chief of staff persuaded him to try a more daring maneuver, namely, to have Woehler's right flank do an about-face and push due west between Debrecen and Nyiregyhaza while Sixth Army's panzer divisions, in the corner between Nyiregyhaza and the Tisza, struck eastward into the Russian flank.

The maneuver worked with the flair and precision of the blitzkrieg days. On the 23rd the two forces met and cut off three Soviet corps at Nyiregyhaza. Before Russians could break loose, almost the whole Armeegruppe Woehler bore down on them from the east. In three days the Germans retook Nyiregyhaza. On the 29th the survivors in the pocket abandoned their tanks, vehicles, and heavy weapons and fled to the south.

On that day, too, for the first time in two months, Army Group South had a continuous front. On the north it bent east of the Tisza around Nyiregyhaza and then followed the middle Tisza to below Szolnok, where it angled away from the river past Kecskemet to the Danube near Mohacs and tied in with Army Group F at the mouth of the Drava. But it was not a front that could stand long. The Tisza, flowing through flat country, afforded no defensive advantages—the Russians had easily driven Hungarian Third Army out of better positions than those it held on the open plain between the Tisza and the Danube.

CHAPTER XVII

Retreat and Encirclement

THE BALKAN PENINSULA

THE SOUTHEASTERN THEATER

The German Southeastern Theater was a haphazard structure in the true Balkan tradition. (Map 32) It had inherited many of that area's ancient troubles and had acquired new ones arising out of the Axis invasion: tripartite (German, Italian, and Bulgarian) occupation, Hitler's ruthless dismemberment of Yugoslavia, the tangle of interests and rivalries—German, Italian, Bulgarian, legitimate nationalist, separatist nationalist, and communist—not to mention Western and Soviet efforts to build up the anti-German resistance with an eye at the same time on the postwar future. By the spring of 1943 an Allied seaborne invasion of the Southeastern Theater had been a possibility, and a year later the Russians were poised to break in from the east.

Until August 1943 Italy had held the most territory, the western third of Croatia, Montenegro, an enlarged Albania, and two-thirds of Greece. Germany had held northern Slovenia, Serbia, Macedonia around Salonika, a strip of Greek territory on the Turkish border, the Piraeus, the islands in the Aegean, and Crete. Bulgaria had occupied western Thrace and Yugoslavian Macedonia. Hungary and Rumania had each taken a slice out of Yugoslavia north of the Danube. Croatia, including Bosnia and Hercegovina, was a semiautonomous state under Dr. Ante Pavelic and his Ustaši Movement. After Italy surrendered, Germany had taken over the Italian zone; the Bulgarian area had been enlarged somewhat; and puppet governments had been established in Albania and Montenegro to match those in Serbia and Greece.

The Italian surrender had vastly increased the German military and administrative responsibilities. Troop requirements could

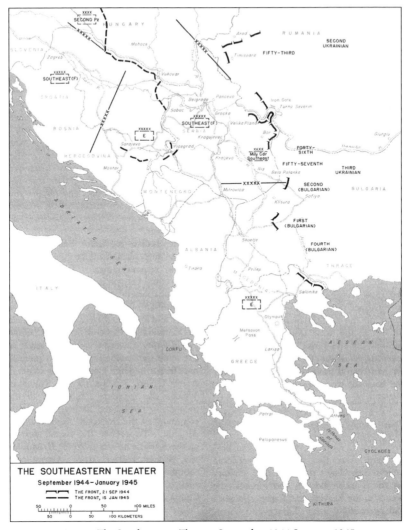

Map 32: The Southeastern Theater, September 1944-January 1945

only be partly met, and mainly with collaborator units at that. The theater command was dealt with more lavishly. Hitler had appointed Field Marshal Weichs as Commanding General, Southeast *(Oberbefehlshaber Suedost),* and, in a sense, at the same time made him his own subordinate by naming him Commanding General, Army Group F. In his first function Weichs was supreme commander in the theater; in the second he had operational command of the troops in Yugoslavia and Albania. To oversee the coastal defense on the Adriatic he was given the Headquarters, Second Panzer Army. Operational command in Greece and on the islands went to Generaloberst Alexander Loehr as Commanding General, Army Group E. Below the theater command but not directly subordinate to it the OKW had installed a Military Commander Southeast with territorial responsibility for military government and relations with the governments of the puppet states.

The Southeastern Theater Command had two military missions: to defend the coasts of the Balkan Peninsula; and to combat the guerrilla movements in the interior. Because of the mountainous terrain and because Germany could not afford to keep the equipment and vehicles required for mobile forces in an inactive theater, the coast defense was static, which forced Weichs to spread his strength thinly over a vast area. Some of his best units were on Crete and the islands in the Aegean, where by the spring of 1944 they were completely immobile and could be reached only by air or by small island-hopping boats. The troops that could be spared for the war against the guerrillas were always less than enough to conduct a thoroughgoing campaign. On the other hand, the Germans benefited from conflicts between the guerrilla movements.

The first Balkan guerrilla movement, Col. Draza Mihailović's Četniks, had been organized before the 1941 campaign against Yugoslavia had ended; but after Tito's (Josip Broz') Partisans became active, the Četniks had devoted the greater part of their effort to fighting them. Mihailović, until May 1944 Minister of War in the Yugoslav government-in-exile, was concerned above all with ensuring the postwar return of the monarchy and Serbian predominance in the restored Yugoslavia.

Tito's Partisans were the strongest and most effective of the Balkan guerrilla forces. They had received a great boost in strength when they succeeded in taking over large stocks of weapons, including some artillery and tanks, from the withdrawing Italians, and another after the Tehran Conference of November-December 1943, which had elevated the Partisans to the status of a national force and pledged them full Allied and Soviet support. Nevertheless the Germans, aided by the Četniks and other nationalist groups, had managed until the fall of 1944 to keep Tito bottled up in the mountains of western Yugoslavia, the former Italian occupation zone which had all along been his stronghold.

In Greece the guerrilla movements, communist and nationalist, had been slower getting started and were not nearly as strong as those in Yugoslavia. Despite British efforts to get them to work together, most of the time they preferred fighting each other to fighting the Germans. When the Communists began making headway against the nationalists, the latter negotiated a truce with the Germans which they kept until August 1944.

In the German strategy the Southeastern Theater had at first threatened the British sea lanes in the eastern Mediterranean and had acted as a counterweight to Allied pressure on neutral Turkey. By mid-1944 it had completely lost its effectiveness in both those respects. Militarily, as far as the war on the active fronts was concerned, the theater had become a liability; but a withdrawal anywhere would have given the Western Powers new bases or another foothold on the Continent, would possibly have led to Turkey's dropping its neutrality, and would, at the very least, have greatly increased the apprehensions of the Bulgarian, Rumanian, and Hungarian Governments.

The forces in the Southeastern Theater were therefore tied down without being engaged, and they were looking seaward when the deadliest threat was at their backs. An about-face would, perhaps, have carried with it severe military and political consequences; but that it would in any event, one day have to be made seems not to have been given adequate consideration. The reason appears to have been that the theater's role, to the extent that it still had one, was regarded as strategic and therefore Hitler's and the OKW's concern. Weichs might be aware that he could suddenly find himself embroiled in the next tactical mess on the Eastern Front, but until that happened or was obviously about to happen the relationship between his theater and the Eastern Front was a matter of grand strategy that could be evaluated only at the highest command level. Moreover, as commander of an OKW theater, he was in a completely separate command channel from the Eastern Front and almost in a different war.

WEICHS AND HITLER WAIT AND SEE

The first overt change in the situation of the Southeastern Theater came in early August 1944. Turkey's break with Germany on the 2d raised a possibility of landings on the islands in the Aegean and gave the Bulgarian Government the nudge it needed to set a course out of the war. During the next two weeks Bulgaria re-established consular relations with the Soviet Union and restricted German movements through its territory. A coup was out of the question because all the Germans had in that country was a small military mission, Weichs could not spare any troops, and the Bulgarian Army, considering the small part it had played in the war, was rather well outfitted with German tanks and planes.

On 17 August the Bulgarian Premier told the Parliament the government was "determined to remove all obstacles to peace." Weichs thereupon concluded that when Bulgaria defected he would have to take his troops in Greece back to the Yugoslav border because the flank on the east and the sea frontier in Thrace would become hopelessly exposed. He did not know that his colleague on the east, Friessner, was having strong doubts about Rumania, and Friessner, on his side, did not learn until later about what was going on in Bulgaria. Each general took for granted that the other was keeping his own house in order and both apparently assumed that Hitler had the political affairs in hand.

Weichs was at Fuehrer headquarters on 23 August when the report came in that Rumania was quitting the war. Because of Rumania and Bulgaria, Hitler then decided that the front in Greece, particularly on the Peloponnesus, was henceforth to be considered an outpost line to be evacuated if the Americans and British attacked. The weight of the defense would be moved north into Yugoslavia, and the "tendency" would be to draw Army Group E north and concentrate its strength around the Athens-Salonika-Belgrade railroad.

On the 25th Hitler ordered all civilians and noncombatant military out of areas that might suddenly become combat zones. The panic and confusion in Rumania, where the German personnel were trying to get out at the last minute, had inspired the order. Coming when it did, it gave Weichs a chance to pare down excess baggage and reduce the administrative overhead, which was especially high in Greece, where women, academicians, and others who preferred to contribute their bit toward the "final victory" in sunshine and surrounded by the monuments of antiquity, had found assignments particularly congenial.

After Rumania surrendered, Hitler, the OKW, and Weichs were still inclined to wait and see, even though prudence, the condition of the theater forces, and the course of the battle in Rumania all would seem to have demanded an early decision.

The Southeastern Theater forces were neither very flexible nor very reliable tactical instruments. The theater had a ration strength of 900,000 men, including naval and air contingents and what the Germans called *"Wehrmachtsgefolge,"* the technicians, bureaucrats, police, and mere hangers-on who followed the armed forces into occupied countries. The ground combat strength was, roughly, 600,000 men in 38 divisions and brigades of which 7 were Bulgarian divisions and 9 foreign collaborator divisions which included in their ranks Russians, Italians, Arabs, and all of the Balkan nationalities. The 15 German divisions and 7 German fortress brigades were, in the main, not first-class units, and most of them were not fully combat-trained or equipped. The divisions were in part, and the fortress battalions almost entirely, made up of over-age and limited service men. Of the total strength, Army Group E in Greece had 300,000 men, some 90,000 of them on the islands. Its ratio of German to foreign troops was somewhat higher than in the theater as a whole; it had half of the German divisions and all but one of the fortress battalions. The mobility of the units in the theater ranged from low to non-existent. The lines of communication were sparse and primitive. Army Group E had one railroad, the Athens-Salonika-Belgrade line; it and the one or two reasonably good roads into Greece ran through Bulgarian-occupied Macedonia.

On 26 August, Weichs instructed a mountain division to move out of Greece and into southern Serbia just north of the Bulgarian occupation zone. On the 30th, certain by then that Bulgaria would be out of the war in a matter of days, he told the mountain division to stop at Nis and an SS division and an Air Force field division to

Tito (right) with partisan leaders.

move into the Bulgarian zone from Greece and hold the road and rail junction at Skoplje.

The OKW, in no greater hurry than Weichs was, had issued an "Order for the Defense of the Southeast" the day before. It directed Weichs to deploy his reserves in the Belgrade-Nis-Salonika area and begin getting ready for a withdrawal in Greece to the line Corfu-Mount Olympus. To start getting the troops off the islands the furlough quotas were raised. But the object for the time being was "above all" to avoid giving the impression that an evacuation was under way.

BULGARIA SURRENDERS

The Bulgarians, since they were not at war with the Soviet Union, hoped to get terms that would let them revert to complete neutrality and keep Soviet troops out of the country. To give their case what substance they could they offered to assist Turkey in repelling any—by then, to say the least, hypothetical—German invasion attempt; they demanded that Germany withdraw its military mission; and they disarmed and interned the Germans who fled across the border from Rumania. But their negotiations with Soviet representatives in Turkey failed to make headway.

On 2 September, the day Russian troops reached the border at Giurgiu on the Danube, a new Cabinet was formed; two days later Bulgaria unilaterally declared an end to the state of war with the Allies and a return to full neutrality. For the Russians that was not enough. Claiming a neutral Bulgaria would become a refuge for the retreating Germans, the Soviet Union declared war on 5 September.

On the night of the 8th, after *Third Ukrainian Front* had crossed the border during the day, Bulgaria declared war on Germany. By then the realignment was in full progress. The German military mission had left Bulgaria. In Macedonia the Germans were disarming and interning the Bulgarian occupation corps without much trouble. At Skoplje three Bulgarian divisions abandoned their weapons and equipment and fled into the mountains. At Prilep several regiments put up a fight that lasted into the fourth week of the month.

A FRONT ON THE EAST

The Rumanian surrender and Bulgaria's defection opened a 425-mile front on the east from the Hungarian border to the Aegean Sea—one that Southeastern Theater Command had somehow to defend. For the moment the danger was greatest in the south, where a front had to be created east of the line Salonika-Skoplje-Nis if Army Group E was to have a chance to escape out of Greece. On 9 September Weichs shifted the Army Group E boundary north to Klisura and added Albania to the army group zone. That made Loehr responsible for the most vulnerable stretch of his own retreat route. Some Army Group E troops were already in Macedonia; others were coming to Salonika from the islands. At midmonth the army group was succeeding in closing the crossings on the prewar Bulgarian border and had a line on the Strimon River. It was troubled most by lack of means to transport the troops to the front and by the necessity for completely re-equipping those who came from the islands.

In the Army Group F zone between Klisura and the Iron Gate, on 5 September, when the *Sixth Guards Tank Army* spearhead reached Turnu Severin, a motorized brigade going east to hold the Iron Gate was delayed in Belgrade where air attacks had destroyed the bridges. After the tank army turned north on the 6th, the Military

Commander Southeast set up a thinly manned front that followed the Yugoslav border and straddled the Danube just west of the Iron Gate. At midmonth Weichs sent part of a division and two police battalions into the Army Group South Ukraine zone to try to take and hold Timisoara, the southern gateway to the Hungarian plain and the Banat. Second Panzer Army had to stay where it was for the time being to hold Croatia in case Hungary surrendered and Croatia tried to follow.

That Army Group E could not stay in Greece and that getting it out would, in time, become more difficult, maybe impossible, were accepted facts at all German command levels, but Weichs was not letting himself be rushed, which apparently suited Hitler and the OKW. On 10 September Weichs indicated he was not ready to make a decision. He told Loehr the decision would depend on how things went in Macedonia; the theater command would give the order when the time came.

Meanwhile, to the Germans' surprise, the troops were coming off the islands by air, some even by sea, with no interference. It appeared to Weichs that the Allies were "trying to build golden bridges" for him. He and the rest of the German Command, including Hitler especially, wondered why the British and Americans, while smashing the retreat routes out of Greece through Yugoslavia, were at the same time letting the Germans get off the islands.

The Allied Balkan Air Force had started RATWEEK on 1 September; it was intended to cut the exit routes from Greece and southern Yugoslavia and to help Tito's Partisans push east into Serbia to meet the Russians advancing through Rumania. Heavy strikes on the 3d cut all the transportation arteries running through Nis and badly damaged all the Danube and Sava bridges at Belgrade. These and other attacks on the roads and railroads did not give the Partisans as much of a leg-up as had, perhaps, been expected; but, until the damage was repaired, they snarled German troop movements in eastern Yugoslavia, sometimes critically, as in the case of the motorized brigade going toward the Iron Gate, and they stalled all traffic except by air to and from Greece.

The inexplicable tactics, from the German point of view, of the

Allies led Hitler and the OKW to speculate that the British wanted to get the Germans off the islands but wanted to keep them in Greece as a kind of police force and as a counterweight to the Russians. On 15 September Hitler authorized full evacuation of the islands and at the same time directed Weichs to "play off against each other the crosscurrents" between the Soviet Union and the Allies in order to exploit the apparently passive attitude of the latter toward the German withdrawal.

His scheme got no further. On that same day, in a surprise raid, British and American bombers hit the airfields around Athens, badly damaging them and destroying a large number of JU-52 transports. During the next few days British ships, including aircraft carriers with night fighters, moved into the Aegean, and German losses on the flights to and from the islands mounted.

Nevertheless, Hitler continued to see in the absence of an attempt to invade the Greek mainland an impending falling out among his enemies and was, therefore, inclined to go on trying to keep his own hand in the game. That the British and Americans could be fully occupied in their other theaters, as in fact they were by then, and that neither the Western Powers nor the Soviet Union would have been willing at that stage of the war to risk a conflict over the Balkans, as was demonstrated by the Balkan arrangement Churchill and Stalin made in Moscow in October, seems not to have occurred to Hitler.

In the third week of September Southeastern Theater Command detected the beginnings of a Soviet build-up on its eastern front. In Rumania, north of the Transylvanian Alps, *Second Ukrainian Front* moved *Fifty-third Army* into the Arad-Timisoara area. South of the mountains, lead elements of *Forty-sixth Army,* coming north across the Danube from Bulgaria, reached Turnu Severin. Another of *Third Ukrainian Front's* armies, the *Fifty-seventh,* was observed, south of the Danube, moving west toward the Yugoslav-Bulgarian border. Most ominous was a sudden increase in the numbers of Soviet planes on the airfields in western Bulgaria and Rumania. Aerial photographs taken on 19 September showed 372 aircraft on two fields near Sofiya.

The Bulgarians were deploying their home forces along the border. On 22 September Bulgaria proclaimed general mobilization. Even though the actual Bulgarian capabilities were still in question, that they could contemplate going into action at all was an unpleasant surprise; the Germans had expected the Bulgarian Army to disintegrate in the aftermath of the surrender.

On 18 September Weichs secured permission from the OKW to evacuate Corfu and start taking the front back from the coast in western Greece. Two days later he submitted, "as background for the Fuehrer's decision," a situation report calling attention to the Soviet and Bulgarian movements and the possibility that as a consequence Hitler would "soon and suddenly" be faced with "fundamental decisions regarding Greece." His diary reveals that on 21 September he still had not made up his own mind. An offensive in the crucial Skoplje-Nis sector, he believed, could come soon and with it the danger of Army Group E's being cut off; therefore, the time was approaching when he would have to stop the flights from the islands and use the planes to fly Army Group E troops north to reinforce the Macedonian front. When should the decision be made? Loehr wanted it right away; but, Weichs reasoned, aside from the increased air strength, there were no "positive" signs that the Russians were about to do anything. If they wanted to, they could move fast, maybe so fast that any decision would then come too late to save Loehr's troops. Nevertheless, he still believed everything "humanly possible," including taking risks on the Macedonian border, ought to be done to get the men off the islands. He was apparently not yet thinking at all of forcing to an issue the bigger question, when to evacuate Greece altogether.

In resolving his quandary, Weichs was not getting any help from his opponents. The Russians were moving, but neither as fast nor as purposefully as they might have. The flights to the islands, in spite of losses, were more than double the forty-four per day averaged early in the month. Even though Loehr had pulled his troops on the Peloponnesus back to two bridgeheads in the north, one at Patrai and the other on the Isthmus of Corinth, the only sign that the Allies had so much as taken notice was a British landing on 21 September on Kithira off the southern tip of the peninsula.

While the Russians appeared to be giving it time, Southeastern Theater Command desperately needed all it could get. The front in

Yugoslav partisans on the move.

the east was pitifully thin. Communications to the front and laterally behind it were in a constant snarl from air and Partisan activity. The theater command was trying to go to war with, even by the then prevailing German standards, a motley assortment of units; and at its back stood Tito eyeing what were for him the ultimate prizes, Serbia and the capital, Belgrade. In Greece, Army Group E had several divisions either moving or ready to move north, but some of the units, those from the islands, were unarmed and completely immobile, and all overland traffic was slow.

Without waiting to complete an orderly build-up, a *Third Ukrainian Front* force, on 22 September, crossed the Danube into the bend west of Turnu Severin. At first, the Russians were just strong enough to make modest headway against the German outposts there, but by the 25th Weichs began to become concerned. He decided to put in the 1st Mountain Division to clean out the bend. Tolbukhin by then had one division across the river and four standing by on the other side.

Early on the morning of the 27th a report reached Weich's headquarters in Belgrade that *Second Ukrainian Front's* left flank was advancing west between Timisoara and the Danube. He had parts of two SS divisions at Timisoara and a motorized brigade north of the Iron Gate but nothing in between; the assumption had been that the Russians were more likely to go north west past Timisoara into Hungary. Weichs right away suspected what was coming—two thrusts from the east on either side of the Danube toward Belgrade, to be reinforced, perhaps later, by Tito's forces from the west—but he did nothing. Although the motorized brigade north of the Danube was in trouble and on the 28th was nearly encircled, the counterattack south of the river was going well.

On the 29th the opinion in Weich's staff was that "gradually" it was beginning to appear, at least "the thought could no longer be discounted," that the Soviet *LXXVII Corps* and *Forty-sixth Army,* both in the sector between Timisoara and the Danube, had Belgrade as their "general objective." During the day Weichs decided to bring up from Greece, in addition to a *Jaeger* division on the way, two regiments, one by rail and one by air.

BELGRADE—DECISION TO EVACUATE GREECE

On the 30th Weichs and his staff for the first time became genuinely alarmed. North of the Danube the Russians had 3 corps in action against 7½ understrength German battalions; south of the river the 1st Mountain Division was engaging 4, possibly 5, Soviet divisions; in both places the Russians had at least again as much strength in reserve. Weichs once more mulled over in private the question what to do about Army Group E and concluded that a decision would have to be made soon.

By 2 October the theater command was painfully aware that it was almost helpless. Bad weather kept the regiment scheduled to come by air grounded in Greece. No one could tell when the other regiment would arrive; the first trains bringing the *Jaeger* division were just coming into Belgrade—they had been on the way fourteen days.

On the 2d the Operations Staff, OKW, giving Weichs a nudge, asked him to set the time for evacuating Greece. He promised an answer in twenty-four hours. The next day he and Loehr agreed that everything could be ready to move on 10 October, and the theater command ordered Army Group E to evacuate Albania, southern Macedonia, and Greece. The flights to the islands were to continue as long as the gasoline stores in Greece lasted and the airfields stayed in German hands. Hitler approved.

In Serbia, half the battle for Belgrade was lost before it had properly begun. On 4 October the Russians reached Pancevo on the north bank of the Danube ten miles downstream from Belgrade. In two more days they took Pancevo and pushed the Germans back into a small bridgehead across the river from Belgrade. To get his communications equipment out of danger, Weichs, on 5 October, moved his headquarters from Belgrade to Vukovar. On that day he also changed the designation of the Military Command Southeast to Armeeabteilung Serbia and proposed to the OKW that Second Panzer Army be taken away from the coast to a line in the mountains. In doing so, he relieved the former Military Command Southeast of its territorial functions and made a start toward converting Second Panzer Army from an amorphous collection of coast defense detachments into something like a tactical organization. In two respects the Germans' luck seemed to have improved. On 3 October the railroad bridges at Kraljevo and Mitrovica, out since early September, were repaired and the troop trains from Greece could run straight through to Belgrade; and Soviet *Forty-Sixth Army,* by the time its left flank closed up to Belgrade, had turned its main force northwest to join the offensive across the Tisza into Hungary.

But Weichs still had more troubles than he could handle, and time was working against him. To make the attempt to clean out the Danube bend west of Turnu Severin, the 1st Mountain Divison had been forced to strip its original front on the Bulgarian border. Just after the first of the month the Russians crossed the border past the division's south flank, and Partisans moved in behind it, cutting the division's supply lines. An SS division tried to restore contact from the south; but *Fifty-seventh Army* kept coming across the border and poured through wherever it found an opening on the front from Bela Palanka north to the Danube.

One mechanized corps slipped past Bor unnoticed and on 8 October appeared in the Morava River valley fifty miles behind the front. There, by nightfall, it had crossed the river and cut the railroad running into Belgrade from the south. In the meantime, the Partisans had pushed into Serbia southwest of Belgrade and west of Nis. On the 9th Bulgarian *First Army* began attacking past Bela Palanka toward Nis.

Weichs told the troops coming by rail from the south to unload at Kragujevac and attack north to clear the Morava Valley. He gave Headquarters, Second Panzer Army, command on the Tisza and on the Danube south to Belgrade. The army, its withdrawal from the coast nearly completed, could bring two divisions east, but that would take several weeks. For the moment all it could do was free Headquarters, Armeeabteilung Serbia, to concentrate on defending Belgrade. The Armeeabteilung decided to take all the troops it could get by paring down the Belgrade defenses—about the equivalent of one division—and strike east to the mouth of the Morava, link up there with the 1st Mountain Division, and then advance upstream along the Morava to meet the assault coming from the south.

The attack out of Belgrade reached the Morava and, on the 12th, carried upstream to Velika Plana where the Russians had first crossed the river, but it was too late. *Fifty-seventh Army* had a whole mechanized corps across. By noon on the 13th the Soviet armor was deploying six miles south of Belgrade for the advance into the city. Meanwhile, the 1st Mountain Division had withdrawn west to the Morava and joined the force in the river valley, but, with the Russians at Belgrade, both were cut off. Weichs put all the troops in the Morava Valley under the Commanding General, 1st Mountain Division, Generalleutnant Walter Stettner Ritter von Grabenhofen; ordered Armeeabteilung Serbia to hold Belgrade until Stettner could break out and get across the Sava; and instructed Second Panzer Army to station some troops south of the upper Sava in case Stettner had to go farther west.

On the night of the 14th the Russians and Partisans entered Belgrade. By the next afternoon they had taken the center of the city; Armeeabteilung Serbia put all the strength it could spare, including a motorized artillery battalion from Second Panzer Army, into a bridgehead around the Sava bridge. During the day on the 15th Stettner started going west and his point reached Grocka fifteen miles southeast of Belgrade. The next day he gained another ten miles but failed in an attempt to reach the city on the 17th. After getting word that he intended to try again on the 18th, Armeeabteilung Serbia suddenly lost radio contact, and thereafter nothing more was heard from Stettner. An officer who came across the Sava two days later stated that Stettner had enjoined destruction of the heavy equipment and an escape to the west toward the Sava.

On the 19th Armeeabteilung Serbia evacuated the Belgrade bridgehead. On the 21st some thousands of Stettner's troops crossed the Sava at Sabac; 12,000 was the number recorded in the Army Group F journal, but a later entry states that the actual number "was substantially smaller."

ARMY GROUP E'S WITHDRAWAL

After also losing Nis on 15 October, Weichs had no front at all in the 120 miles between Nis and Belgrade and no prospect of doing anything about it. He gave Second Panzer Army command from Belgrade north and told it to bring the Russians to a stop on the line of the Tisza, Danube, Sava, and Drina Rivers. He gave Army Group E command north to Kraljevo and the responsibility for keeping open its retreat route Skoplje-Kraljevo-Visegrad. Second Panzer Army was to hold the road open from Sarajevo to Visegrad. Army Group E had decided to stop on the line Scutari-Skoplje-Klisura; now it would have to go farther north and west to the Sarajevo-Mostar area.

Even after Belgrade and Nis were lost, and with them the most direct route out of Greece, Weichs' lengthy irresolution regarding Army Group E was more and more looking like masterful deliberation. The more than a month's delay had given Loehr time to ship out the noncombatants and superfluous equipment, and to commandeer enough civilian trucks and automobiles to give himself some mobility. By the time the move began on 10 October every unit was poised and ready. The timetable was perfected, and the British, who were cautiously moving onto the Peloponnesus, did nothing to disrupt it. Just when Army Group E began to move, Balkan Air Force shifted the greater part of its effort from Yugoslavia to support of the British in Greece, thereby giving the army group some relief in the north and not adding any noticeable pressure from the south.

The German rear guard left Athens on the 13th, stopped briefly on the line Metsovon Pass-Larisa on the 21st, and then resumed the march north. On the 31st Salonika was evacuated, and on the night of 1 November the rear guard crossed the Greek border. On the islands 45,000 men, a third of them Italians, were left behind. Someone had invented the euphemism *Kernfestung* (core fortress) to make it appear that they still had a mission.

In the last week of October the Russians and Bulgarians made strong bids to take Kraljevo and Skoplje. Having the troops to spare and the railroad, Loehr could meet the challenge, if in both places none too soon. On 2 November Army Group E stopped the Russians at Kraljevo and in the next several days halted the Bulgarians east of Skoplje. The success of the withdrawal through Macedonia was then assured. North of Skoplje the army group would have to veer west onto poorer roads, but it would be spared the almost certain disaster of a winter march through the coastal mountains.

A FRONT ON THE DRINA

In the last two weeks of October Second Panzer Army had to retreat. Its best units were smashed, and the rest were in a complete tangle. It was so short of troops that it put the physically and psychologically battered survivors of Stettner's force back into the front without a rest, securing the equipment for them by disarming the SS Handschar Division, a beautifully outfitted but unreliable division of Balkan Moslems. Off the army's north flank the Russians were across the Tisza and going west to the Danube.

Weichs, as Commanding General, Army Group F, had tried to create a front on the east; but, as Commanding General, Southeast, he had failed to make the decision that would have enabled him to do so; he had therefore fought the battle for Belgrade piecemeal, always several steps behind the enemy. Nevertheless, after he had lost Belgrade and as the month wore on, it began to look, in the north as well as in the south, as if he had displayed a genuine feeling for timing and a talent for sure-footed retrograde maneuver. Tolbukhin left the pursuit west of Belgrade and the Tisza mostly to the Partisans. Toward the end of the month *Fifty-seventh Army* shifted its corps north of the Danube. This gave Second Panzer Army a chance to make a phased withdrawal between the Danube and the Sava, where it had no river line to fall back on. On 2 November the army stopped; its front followed the Danube from the Hungarian border to Vukovar, and from there it bridged the river gap to the mouth of the Drina and then followed the Drina south. The next day Army Group F confirmed that *Fifty-seventh Army's* main force had gone north into Hungary to join the offensive toward Budapest.

BUDAPEST

THE FIRST THRUST

In the Army Group South sector, on 29 October Forty-sixth Army, reinforced by a guards mechanized corps, attacked west of Kecskemet, about halfway between the Danube and the Tisza. (Map 33) Malinovskiy was trying to push the offensive to Budapest without pausing for a build-up. Fourth Ukrainian Front's thrust from the north had bogged down, and his armies, the armored forces in particular, were in far from prime condition. The Cavalry-Mechanized Group Gorshkov had disappeared.

Probably it was merged with the remnants of the *Pliyev Group*. Malinovskiy expected that as *Forty-sixth Army* advanced, it would ease the way for *Seventh Guards Army* to cross the Tisza. He had another two mechanized corps standing by to make the final push to Budapest.

Forty-sixth Army began to roll on the second day and took Kecskemet on the 31st. Headquarters, Sixth Army, as Armeegruppe Fretter-Pico, then took command of all German and Hungarian units between the rivers. It was bringing German divisions down from the Tisza front, but on the 31st all it had was one panzer division. On 2 November the Soviet point was seven miles south of Budapest. Hungarian Third Army had virtually evaporated. The next day the leading Soviet tank column broke into the Budapest bridgehead, a semicircular ring of defenses the Germans had laid out east of the Danube skirting the suburbs, but by then Armeegruppe Fretter-Pico had two SS divisions and a panzer division in the bridgehead. Off *Forty-sixth Army's* east flank five panzer divisions were moving in on the line of the Budapest-

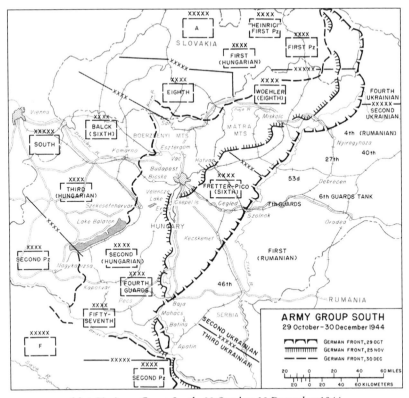

Map 33: Army Group South, 29 October-30 December 1944.

Cegled-Szolnok road. On 4 November Hitler ordered Army Group South to concentrate all the strength it could in the Cegled-Szolnok area for an attack west toward Kecskemet to cut the Russians off, but *Seventh Guards Army* had already crossed the Tisza, taken both Cegled and Szolnok, and was ready to attack north.

While German and Soviet tanks battled in the Budapest suburbs on 4 and 5 November, the city, according to the Army Group South war diary, "completely lost its head." The panic was inspired as much by a minor incident inside the city as it was by the approaching Russians. German engineers, fusing demolition charges beneath the Danube bridges, accidently set one off and blew several spans out of the Margaret Bridge. The accident brought to the surface the population's most deep-seated fear: the Germans when they left would unloose a crippling wave of destruction. The city was anything but in a mood to sacrifice itself at the last minute. The populace wanted to believe reassurances by the Russians that they were not as bad as the Germans painted them.

On the 5th Soviet radio traffic revealed that the units assailing Budapest were running short of ammunition. Malinovskiy, eager for the capture of Budapest to coincide with the 7 November anniversary of the Bolshevik Revolution, urged them on. To the commanders he wrote: "Comrades, exert yourselves so that we can lay the Hungarian capital at the great Stalin's feet. Fame and rewards await you; if you fail I fear for your health." But on the 6th *Forty-sixth Army* took its troops and tanks out of the bridgehead and back to a line several miles to the south. The ammunition shortage and a small assault Armeegruppe Fretter-Pico had staged against its right flank, a much watered-down version of the counterthrust Hitler had called for, made the army command cautious. It also, probably, was keeping the experiences at Debrecen and Nyiregyhaza in mind.

In Budapest, desperately ignoring the future, the residents eagerly, it seemed to the Germans frivolously, grasped the chance to return to their everyday routines. Combing the city, the Germans and the Hungarian Gendarmerie rounded up the soldiers of Hungarian Third Army—those they could find—and returned them to the front. The trip was not a long one; it could be made by streetcar. Many of the Hungarian officers took to spending their nights at home.

MALINOVSKIY MANEUVERS

By the time *Forty-sixth Army* gave up the attempt, Malinovskiy apparently had concluded that Budapest could not be taken head-on. The *Stavka*, agreeing, directed him to put the *Seventh Guards, Fifty-third, Twenty-seventh,* and *Fortieth Armies* into a broad-front attack west from the Tisza. In the succeeding weeks he committed these armies in a series of enveloping maneuvers that very likely could not have been more elaborate had they been specifically designed to make the job look hard.

At the same time, Friessner was trying to talk Hitler and Guderian out of trying to defend Budapest in a house-to-house battle. He resolved, if he could not hold the enemy on the edge of the city, to go behind the Danube and blow the bridges. The army group did not have the strength, he said, to fight the Russians and simultaneously suppress the "big-city mob." Hitler was unconvinced; still, he did not issue a definite order for a house-to-house defense until 26 November; as of that date the army group had not constructed any positions inside the city—for fear of inciting the people.

Malinovskiy began the roundabout approach to Budapest on 11 November. His armies attacking away from the Tisza headed northwest, their extreme left flank skirting the northeastern corner of the Budapest bridgehead. On the fifth day they reached Hatvan and Miskolc. Hatvan, on the southern fringe of the Matra Mountains, controlled a low-lying corridor leading northwest to the Danube bend above Budapest. Miskolc, in the Sajo River valley twenty-five miles southeast of the Czechoslovakian border, was an iron, steel, and arms-producing center situated astride a fairly easy route into Slovakia. The advance stopped on, roughly, the line Budapest bridgehead-Hatvan-Miskolc. The German front wavered and buckled but did not break. At Miskolc Armeegruppe Woehler also had to deal with an uprising; the factory workers had barricaded themselves in the plants to prevent the Germans from destroying them.

On 22 November *Forty-sixth Army* sent several divisions across the Danube to Csepel Island, the elongated island south of Budapest. Friessner thought the stage was being set for the push into the city, but the Russians stopped after they had taken the southern half of the island. On the 25th they started taking units out of the Hatvan concentration and shifting them south to the Danube. Severe as the bloodletting at Hatvan and Miskolc had been, Army Group South considered itself fortunate. If *Second Ukrainian Front* had put all its weight behind a thrust straight through to Budapest, the consequences would have been much more serious.

TOLBUKHIN JOINS IN

In the second half of November *Third Ukrainian Front* took its turn. After his main forces went north, Tolbukhin had moved his headquarters from Belgrade to Baja on the Danube in southern Hungary. On 7 November he had taken a small bridgehead on the

Danube across from Apatin ten miles north of the Army Group F-Army Group South boundary.

On the 10th the OKW had extended the Army Group F zone north to Baja to give Weichs responsibility for defending his own flank, since Army Group South was too heavily engaged northeast of Budapest to maintain more than a token defense by Hungarian Second Army on the Danube. That night the Russians had established a second bridgehead at Batina fifteen miles north of Apatin. It, too, was small, but the Russians soon began unloading bridging equipment there, a sign that they had something big in mind. Second Panzer Army was getting a division from Italy, and Weichs had directed Army Group E to send several divisions as soon as they could be brought through from the south; when they would arrive, however, was hard to tell. For the moment, Second Panzer Army, struggling to keep the Partisans off its supply lines, barely had enough troops to screen the bridgeheads.

On 22 November *Fourth Guards* and *Fifty-seventh Armies* broke out of the two bridgeheads. During the next several days they cleared the southern tip of the Drava-Danube triangle, and on the 26th took Mohacs. A major offensive west of the Danube was clearly in the making. *Fifty-seventh Army* struck west toward Pecs and Kaposvar. *Fourth Guards Army* turned northwest toward the northeastern tip of Lake Balaton.

Again Weichs' chief handicap was his own earlier indecision; he had potential reserves but no prospect of bringing them to bear in time. Army Group E's withdrawal had gone without a hitch through mid-November. Then, on the 18th, Bulgarian *Second Army* had opened a strong attack north of Skoplje. The next day Balkan Air Force bombers had destroyed the Drina bridge at Visegrad, backing up truck and troop columns eighty five miles east to Kraljevo. In Albania strong partisan units hemmed XXI Mountain Corps in on all sides as it tried to join the retreat. Army Group E had to put back into its own front some of the troops it had intended to release, and the rest were stalled in central Yugoslavia 200 miles and more from where they could do any good.

Aided by a miners' uprising, the Russians took Pecs on 29 November. They were nearly out of the short range of hills between the Drava and the Danube and thereafter could be expected to gain speed. The Germans had so far not determined where to put the weight of the defense. Friessner was certain Tolbukhin would make a two-pronged thrust northwest, his left going toward the southern tip of Lake Balaton to take the oil fields and refineries near Nagykanizsa and his right going past the lake to envelop Budapest from the south and west. Weichs tended to agree but, when it came to deciding where to commit Second Panzer Army, was inclined to assume the offensive would go due west toward Zagreb to cut his main communications lines out of the Balkans. Friessner wanted Second Panzer Army to put its main effort north of the Drava and keep it there; Weichs would have allowed the army to withdraw behind the river, leaving Army Group South to find the means to defend the area between the river and Lake Balaton.

On 1 December Tolbukhin definitely showed his hand; *Fifty-seventh Army* made a quick thrust northwest from Pecs to Kaposvar, and *Fourth Guards Army* swept north along the Danube. That night Hitler gave Army Group South command of Second Panzer Army. The next day Friessner ordered the army to break contact with Army Group F and concentrate on getting and holding a front between the southern tip of Lake Balaton and the Drava southwest of Nagykanizsa.

Tolbukhin's northward thrust forced Army Group South into a round of unit shuffling that was nearly as wearing on troops and equipment as combat and that could quickly have proved fatal had the Russians themselves not been far below top form. Hungarian Second Army had practically vanished. To close the ensuing gap between Lake Balaton and the Danube, Fretter-Pico was having to put in German divisions from the Budapest-Hatvan area. The transfer of a panzer division from the Miskolc front led to the loss of that city by 4 December.

BUDAPEST ENCIRCLED

On 5 December, when *Fourth Guards Army* approached the northern end of Lake Balaton, the *Second* and *Third Ukrainian Fronts* resumed the drive to envelop Budapest. *Forty-sixth Army,* back under *Third Ukrainian Front,* attacked from Csepel Island across the west channel of the Danube to Ercsi. The *Seventh Guards* and *Sixth Guards Tank Armies* ripped through beyond Hatvan. On the 8th Malinovskiy's advance reached Vac on the Danube bend north of Budapest, and Tolbukhin's closed to the line Lake Balaton-Velencze Lake southwest of the city.

The OKH decided to give Friessner two panzer divisions and three 60-tank Tiger battalions for a counterattack. The question was, Attack in the north or the south? Friessner saw the greater danger in the south, between the lakes; Guderian believed it was in the north. In the end, Hitler decided to deploy the reinforcements as Friessner proposed, partly for tactical reasons, partly because he was worried about losing the bauxite mines situated between the lakes near Szekesfehervar.

The decision made, Friessner waited for the panzer units to arrive and for a change in the weather. Rain and above-freezing temperatures had turned the plain southwest of Budapest into a morass; in places the roads and entrenchments were under water. The weather, the need to rest their troops, and, apparently, another fit of caution like those they had several times recently displayed also held back the Russians in the Balaton-Velencze Lake-Budapest sector. If they moved before the German armor arrived and before the ground froze, Friessner would clearly be in trouble; they had the strength to keep going, if need be, with infantry alone. Armeegruppe Fretter-Pico was manning the 19-mile front between Velencze Lake and the Budapest bridgehead with one volksgrenadier division (900 infantry), 800 police—mostly non-Germans—and some Hungarian hussars, altogether about 2,500 men.

North of Budapest, after taking Vac, *Sixth Guards Tank Army* and *Seventh Guards Army* did not try to cross the Danube; instead, they went northwest into the Boerzsenyi Mountains toward Sahy (Ipolysag), the northern gateway to the western Hungarian plain. To defend Sahy, Friessner had to take a panzer division from the Budapest bridgehead and bring in the Dirlewanger Brigade from Slovakia where, since the end of the Warsaw uprising, it had been fighting partisans. The Dirlewanger Brigade had six full-strength battalions—the concentration camps gave it a more than ample replacement pool—but committing it at the front was risky. Part of its troops were German Communists, and all were considerably less than dedicated soldiers of the Reich. The officers were roughnecks and sadists, impromptu executioners rather than tacticians. On 14 December, after one of Dirlewanger's battalion commanders put up a thin outpost line where he should have committed his whole battalion, the Russians took Sahy. The commander may have had a reason for keeping his men back: the next day a company of Communists deserted; and in the succeeding days the brigade slid into a state that by normal standards would have been considered mutiny—some troops shot their officers, some deserted, some did both.

After it took Sahy *Sixth Guards Tank Army* did not make a major bid for a breakthrough into the plain deep behind Budapest, but Guderian thought it would. South of Budapest, meanwhile, the panzer divisions for the counterattack had arrived, but the rain continued. The weather, though colder, was not cold enough to freeze the ground solid, only enough to thicken the mud. Guderian, getting more nervous by the day, on 17 December urged Friessner to get going. The Army, he insisted, could not afford to have strong panzer forces standing around idle. Friessner answered that he had to wait for a heavy freeze; otherwise, if anything went wrong, he would lose all the tanks, and even if the attack succeeded, most of them would be disabled by the second day. After arguing it out with Friessner face to face on the 18th, Guderian agreed to wait, provided the staffs and the infantry of the two panzer divisions were sent north in the interim to help hold the front west of Sahy.

On 20 December Malinovskiy attacked out of the Boerzseny Mountains south of Sahy, and Tolbukhin struck on either side of Velencze Lake. During the day a tank column going northwest from Sahy reached the Hron River, but south of Sahy the Germans had enough new strength coming in—the infantry of Friessner's panzer divisions—to prevent a penetration along the Danube. The next day the German armor, two of the panzer divisions without their staffs and infantry, counterattacked west of Velencze Lake, but they had to try to cover the whole front. While the German tanks roared back and forth burning up their gasoline, Tolbukhin's infantry, avoiding the roads, pressed along through the woods and still unfrozen swamps, keeping out of reach. Many of the tank commanders did not even realize what was happening until, seeking to refuel, found they had to fight their way to the gasoline dumps and, as often as not, discovered the Russians had been there before them. Guderian insisted that with what he described as "a tank armada larger than any ever seen before on the Eastern Front" the army group ought to be able to stop the Russians. Friessner replied that without infantry the tanks were helpless.

By 22 December it was certain the Russians were trying for what the Germans called the "small solution," the close-in encirclement of Budapest. Except for a secondary strike to the northwest to take Szekesfehervar, Tolbukhin's thrust was due north from Velencze Lake toward Esztergom. When Friessner suggested taking the front on the Budapest bridgehead back to the inner ring to gain a division for the battle west of the city, the OKH replied that Hitler had "political scruples" about endangering the capital. Friessner answered that then Budapest would be encircled. On the night of the 22d the Operations Branch, OKH, telephoned that Friessner and Fretter-Pico had been relieved; Woehler would take the army group and General der Panzertruppen Hermann Balck would replace Fretter-Pico.

Guderian then told the new commanding generals they should have only one battle cry, "Attack!"—by patrols, locally or on a big scale. Germany, he said, could not afford a setback in Hungary that would force it to divert forces from the successful offensive in the west; the fate of the Reich was at stake.

In the illusionary strategy being pursued in the German High Command Budapest had become linked with the Ardennes offensive. Hitler had said that losing Budapest would reduce the effect of the victory in the west by 50 percent. Moreover, and of greater significance for the future, to Hitler Budapest had become a symbol, as Stalingrad once had been: there could be no question of giving up the city even if it meant, as Guderian indicated, diverting strength from the offensive in the Ardennes.

Tactically, as he promptly demonstrated, Woehler agreed entirely with Friessner. In his first telephone conversation as army group commander with Guderian, Woehler asked leave to take a division out of the Budapest bridgehead. Guderian answered that the decision given Friessner, not to take out troops or reduce the bridgehead, was irrevocable. Army Group South, he continued, had more armor "than any other place," enough to retake the Lake Balaton-Velencze Lake-Budapest line; and he was going to send an officer from the OKH to investigate why that armor had not been properly used.

In Budapest substantial military readiness for a siege had been achieved. The bridgehead line of defenses had been extended around the city on the west, barricades and tank traps had been constructed, and buildings had been altered to house firing positions. Headquarters, IX SS Mountain Corps, under SS-Obergruppenfuehrer (Lt. Gen.) Karl Pfeffer-Wildenbruch, had taken command of the four German and two Hungarian divisions and assorted smaller units in the bridgehead that were to form the garrison. In contrast, next to nothing had been done about the civilian population. Szalasi, who had originally not wanted to defend Budapest, had lately, after talking to Hitler, changed his mind; however, clinging to his supernumerary role, he disclaimed any direct responsibility for the city. The people, unwilling to abandon their homes and possessions, had ignored his halfhearted evacuation orders, and the Germans had been reluctant to enforce an evacuation because the small corner of Hungary they still held was already crammed with refugees and any more would have had to be taken into Austria or Germany proper. Budapest wore a holiday appearance; Christmas shoppers filled the streets; but deaths from malnutrition were beginning to be reported. The army group chief of staff had told Guderian that the army group opposed putting troops into a siege in which they would also have to stand off over a million starving people. Guderian had replied that the question was "immaterial."

During the day on 23 December, *Fourth Guards Army* took Bicske and cut the road and railroad running west out of Budapest. That left only a mountain road into the city from the northwest, through Esztergom. On the afternoon of the 24th Woehler called Guderian again to argue that historically Budapest had always been defended only on the west bank of the Danube. Guderian's mood had changed; he said he saw several possibilities, including giving up Budapest, but he would have to talk to Hitler first because the matter affected grand strategy. Three hours later he gave Woehler Hitler's decision: Budapest, including the bridgehead, was to be held; the army group could take up to two divisions out of the bridgehead; the OKH would send the Headquarters, IV SS Panzer Corps, and transfer the SS Divisions Totenkopf and Wiking from Army Group Center; in the three or four days before the reinforcements could arrive "everyone who can carry a rifle" was to be put into the front around Budapest.

By the 24th, it was too late to take divisions out of Budapest. The first divisions Woehler ordered to move had to be put into the line around the western suburbs. Army Group South no longer had any chance of stopping Tolbukhin's spearhead going north. On 26 December it reached Esztergom and completed the encirclement. The next day the Russians pushed the garrison back to the inner defense ring. On the same day, a surprise thrust west almost carried to Komarno, the best staging area for a relief operation. On the 28th, the Russians suddenly stopped. By then Hitler had several more divisions en route to Army Group South, and the plan for the relief was taking form.

CHAPTER XVIII

Defeat in the North

THE FINNISH ARMISTICE

In the last two weeks of July 1944 the Finnish Army began to regain its equilibrium. On orders from the Stavka, Leningrad Front shifted to the defensive on the Isthmus of Karelia. In East Karelia only Thirty-second Army, on Seventh Army's right east of Ilomantsi, continued to advance, and it was not headed toward any strategic objective. The Stavka had apparently decided that to clinch the victory in Finland would take more troops and matériel than it was willing to spare from the offensives against Army Groups Center and North.

COBELLIGERENCY DISSOLVED

To the Finns the fate of Army Group North was almost as momentous as that of their own army. Once the Baltic coast was in Russian hands the sea routes to Germany, on which the Finns depended for foodstuffs and almost all of their military equipment and supplies, could be cut. The loss of Pskov on 23 July and of Narva four days later were staggering blows for them. The shock was intensified when, two days after Narva had fallen, Hitler ordered the 122d Infantry Division back to Army Group North. Mannerheim asked that the division depart through Hanko rather than Helsinki to avoid alarming the public. The OKW insisted that the decision to recall the division had only been made because the Finnish front was relatively quiet and assured Mannerheim that help would be sent if another crisis developed, but, under the circumstances, these explanations rang hollow.

In a secret meeting on 28 July at Mannerheim's country house in Sairala the Finnish leaders decided that Ryti should resign as President of Finland. On 4 August the Finnish Parliament elevated Mannerheim to the presidency without the formality of an election. The stage was set for a repudiation of the Ryti-Ribbentrop agreement and a new approach to the Soviet Union.

The Germans suspected that the change was not to their advantage. That Mannerheim intended to rally the national resistance appeared far less likely than that he would assume the mantle of peacemaker. Powerless to exercise any substantial influence over Finnish policy, they nervously hastened to reassure Mannerheim. On 3 August, in response to a Finnish inquiry concerning the military situation in the Baltic States, the OKW sent Schoerner to report to Mannerheim in person and announced that Keitel would follow in a few days.

To draw encouraging conclusions from the Army Group North situation required a man of Schoerner's zeal and determination. Fifth Guards Tank Army was just then standing on his army group's rearward communications lines west of Riga. The repercussions were being felt in Finland: the Lufthansa had suspended commercial air traffic between Germany and Finland and the direct telephone connections had been broken. Undaunted, Schoerner promised the Baltic littoral would be held, Army Group North would be supplied by air and sea, and armored forces from East Prussia would reopen the land lines. Ironically, his promises were kept—at least, long enough for the Finnish to get out of the war before they were completely isolated.

In August the Finnish military position was, if only temporarily, as favorable as even a confirmed optimist would have dared predict a month or so earlier. Third Panzer Army opened a corridor to Army Group North. Between mid-July and mid-August the Russians reduced their forces on the Isthmus of Karelia by ten rifle divisions and five tank brigades; on 9 August, in East Karelia, the Finnish Army ended its last major operation in World War II with a victory when the 14th Division, 21st Brigade, and Cavalry Brigade trapped and all but wiped out two of Thirty-second Army's divisions in a pocket east of Ilomantsi. It appeared that as in the Winter War of 1939-40, although the Soviet Union could claim a victory, its offensive fell short of the success it ought to have had, largely for the same reasons—underestimation of the Finnish capacity to resist and rigid, unimaginative Soviet tactical leadership.

Keitel went to Helsinki on 17 August, carrying an oak leaf cluster for

Mannerheim and a Knight's Cross of the Iron Cross for Mannerheim's chief of staff. To present an encouraging picture of the German total situation at that time was enough to strain even Keitel's indomitable optimism. The Allied breakout in Normandy had succeeded, and the liberation of Paris was only days away. In southern France a secondary offensive was developing rapidly. In Italy the Germans were driven back to the Gothic Line, and on the Eastern Front the Russians stood on the outskirts of Warsaw. The end for Germany suddenly seemed very close, much closer than it was.

Mannerheim took the Keitel visit as an opportunity to clear the air, possibly not so much for the Germans' benefit as to pave the way for an approach to Moscow. The 60,000 casualties incurred during the summer, he said, had been replaced, but Finland could not endure a second blood-letting on that scale. Turning to what was probably also uppermost in Keitel's mind, the status of the Ryti-Ribbentrop agreement, he stated that Ryti, in a desperate hour, had made a contract which had proved highly unpopular. Finland regarded that contract as nullifed by Ryti's resignation. Keitel's response, a lame refusal to accept the statement on the ground that he was not empowered to receive political communications, betrayed the Germans' impotence.

DECISION

In Finland, after the middle of the month, peace sentiment increased daily, and rumors of all sorts gained currency. The report that Rumania had sued for an armistice injected a sense of urgency. On 25 August, through its legation in Stockholm, Finland asked whether the Soviet Government would accept a Finnish armistice delegation. An accompanying note stated that Mannerheim had told Keitel he did not consider himself bound by the Ryti-Ribbentrop agreement. A formal note repudiating the agreement was sent to Germany the following day.

In its reply on 29 August the Soviet Government made its willingness to receive a delegation contingent on prior fulfillment of two conditions: Finland had to break off relations with Germany immediately and must order all German troops to leave Finnish territory within two weeks, at the latest by 15 September, and in case

German outpost in Finland.

the Germans failed to comply the Finns would take measures to intern them. The Parliament accepted the Soviet conditions on 2 September and on the same day approved a government motion to break relations with Germany.

The decision took the Germans by surprise. Although the German Minister in Helsinki had been informed on 31 August that the negotiations had been opened, the Germans more than half expected the terms would prove unacceptable. In the past a glance at the Soviet terms had been the best means of inhibiting Finnish peace sentiment. On 2 September, in a last-minute attempt to inspire a repetition of that pattern, Generaloberst Lothar Rendulic, who had replaced Dietl in command of Twentieth Mountain Army after the latter was killed in a plane crash on 23 June, had called on Mannerheim and emphasized that the Soviet demands might provoke a conflict between German and Finnish troops which, he maintained, would result in 90 percent losses on both sides since the best soldiers in Europe would be opposing each other.

The Finnish leaders were already fully aware of the risks they ran in severing the ties with Germany. One of these, the danger of an economic collapse after German assistance stopped, they had temporarily averted in August when Sweden agreed to cover the

Finnish requirements in grain and some other foodstuffs for six months. Another was the possibility that some elements, particularly in the Army, would refuse to acknowledge the surrender and create internal dissension or join the Germans. It raised alongside Rendulic's specter of a German-Finnish conflict that of a civil war.

During the summer the Germans had, in fact, toyed with various ideas for keeping Finnish resistance alive by extra-legal means. In June, when Ribbentrop went to Helsinki, he had proposed, somewhat wildly, that the German Minister find "a thousand reliable men to take over the Government." Hitler, shortly before Dietl was killed, had instructed him to draw Finnish troops into Twentieth Mountain Army in the event of a separate peace. Later Rendulic envisioned the 122nd Infantry Division in southern Finland as a nucleus around which a Finnish resistance could be built and proposed one of the Finnish generals as a man who might be persuaded to take the lead. None of these projects got beyond the talking stage; and one which was tried after the armistice, reactivation of the traditional Finnish 27th Jaeger Battalion (a World War I German unit which had given the Finnish Army almost the whole of its officer corps), attracted only a scattering of volunteers. The overwhelming majority of the Finnish population was willing to follow its government; moreover, the Finnish Government had been careful throughout the war to prevent the emergence of potential Quislings.

After announcing their intention to meet the Soviet conditions, the Finns formed an armistice delegation—which, as it developed, would also have to negotiate the peace terms as well—under the leadership of Minister President Andi Hackzell. Mannerheim undertook to clarify the Finnish action in a personal letter to Hitler and explained that although Germany could never be completely destroyed, Finland, a small nation, could be, both as a people and a nation; therefore, Finland had to make peace to preserve its existence. In a second letter, to Stalin, he proposed a cease-fire to prevent further bloodshed while the negotiations were in progress. Both sides accepted 0700 on 4 September as the time; although the Finns stopped their operations as agreed, the Russians, either by mistake or to underscore their victory, let theirs run another twenty-four hours.

The Finnish delegation arrived in Moscow on 7 September, but the Soviet Government delayed a week before presenting its terms. Restoration of the 1940 border was a foregone conclusion. In addition, the Soviet Union demanded the entire Pechenga region and a 50-year lease on Porkala, which would give it a base astride the main rail and road routes in southwestern Finland and within artillery range of the Finnish capital. The reparations were set at $300,000,000, to be paid in goods over a 5-year period.[31] The Finnish Army was to withdraw to the 1940 border within five days and be reduced to peacetime strength within two and a half months. The Soviet Union was to be granted the right to use Finnish ports, airfields, and merchant shipping for the duration of the war against Germany; and a Soviet commission would supervise the armistice, which was to become effective the day it was signed.

On 18 September the Cabinet formally considered the terms but could not reach an agreement. The Soviet Union demanded that the signing be completed by the following afternoon. Early on the morning of the 19th Parliament gave its approval after being informed that, under the most favorable circumstances, Finland could not continue the war more than another three months. In Moscow the armistice was signed shortly before noon.

RETREAT FROM NORTHERN FINLAND

Finland's appeal for an armistice left the Germans in a state of painful indecision regarding Twentieth Mountain Army, mainly because none of the possible courses of action gave more than a hope of avoiding a disaster. Although the army remained committed to the execution

---

31. The reduction from the earlier demand for $600,000,000 was probably in part brought about in spring of 1944 by a Finnish propaganda effort that had used the opinions of Swedish economists to demonstrate to world opinion that the first demand could not be met and in part by a concession to American and British objections in principle to reparations. The Finns later maintained that the Soviet Union had only given the appearance of relenting. By insisting on using the year 1938 as the price base and restricting the quantity of wood products it would accept, it nearly doubled the actual value of the reparations. The Soviet "take" was further increased at the 1945 Potsdam Conference by $600,000,000 as compensation for German property in Finland and property removed from the territory ceded to the Soviet Union. Later the reparations burden was eased somewhat, partly through British intercession, by extension of the payment period, first to six years and then to eight.

of Operation BIRKE, the withdrawal to a front in the extreme north of Finland, for the sake of the nickel mines, there was no assurance it would succeed in establishing a tenable front in the north, not to mention the near certainty that sooner or later its sea routes would be cut, making its downfall inevitable. On the other hand, the risks of a continuous withdrawal through the Finnish Arctic into Norway, with winter only weeks away, appeared equally great.

The TANNE operations, the occupation of the Åland Islands and Suursaari, also presented several formidable disadvantages. TANNE WEST had been in doubt since its inception because of Sweden's interest in the Åland Islands and the necessity for avoiding any provocation that might result in loss of the Swedish iron ore and ballbearings. On 3 September Hitler decided to abandon TANNE WEST because the division from Denmark assigned to the operation could not be spared. On the same day, the Navy, which was responsible for TANNE OST, reported that it could not be executed because no trained troops were available.

BIRKE

On 6 September BIRKE began. (Map 34) The decision to hold Pechenga and the region surrounding it in northern Finland had not been revealed to the Finns. The operation was to be conducted at a deliberate pace that would allow enough time to transfer the army's supplies and keep the two southern corps, XXXVI Mountain Corps and XVIII Mountain Corps, in position to deal effectively with a Soviet or Finnish pursuit.

A serious concern for the army's open right flank was allayed when the Finnish 14th Division offered to keep contact on the right until XVIII Mountain Corps had withdrawn behind the border. What would happen thereafter was a question on which German and Finnish opinion differed sharply. The Finns maintained that the Russians would not go beyond the 1940 border. They contended that, therefore, once the Germans were behind the border the withdrawal would become purely a routine troop and supply movement. Rendulic claimed the Finns had either lost touch with reality or were being deliberately dishonest. He thought it extremely unlikely that the

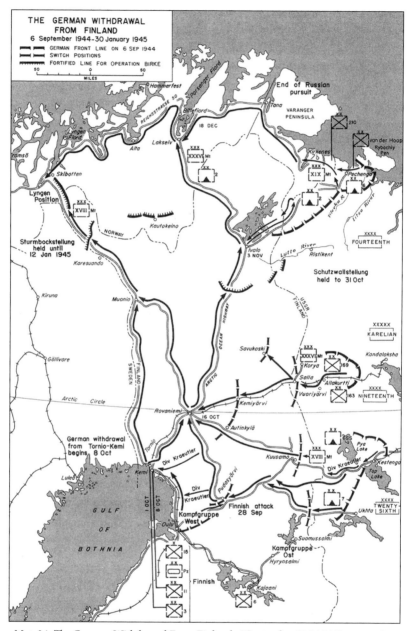

Map 34: The German Withdrawal From Finland, 6 September 1944-30 January 1945

Russians would respect the border and much more probable that they intended to find or create an excuse for occupying all of Finland north of the line Tornio-Suomussalmi, essentially the Twentieth Mountain

Army zone. He was wrong, but as a prudent commander he could not well have assumed otherwise.

XVIII Mountain Corps accomplished its march back into Finland without a hitch. Elements of Twenty-sixth Army followed to the border and stopped. XXXVI Mountain Corps received two shocks: one, when the Nineteenth Army took advantage of the north flank extension it had made in the spring and cut the corps' main retreat route; the other, when T-34 tanks the Russians had somehow moved through the forests and swamps went into action deep in the corps' flank. But the corps had long ago built an alternate road south of the one that was cut, and the tanks' performance did not equal their initial psychological impact.

As 15 September approached, the last day of grace allowed under the armistice for a voluntary German evacuation, relations between Twentieth Mountain Army and the Finnish Army remained cordial.

Rendulic admonished his troops to behave "loyally" toward the Finns, and the Finnish liaison officer at army headquarters disclosed that his command was willing to "make compromises" but wanted to create the impression "outside" that it had broken with the Germans completely. On 13 September the Finns informed Twentieth Mountain Army that they would order all railroad rolling stock between Rovaniemi and Salla moved west of Rovaniemi on the 14th but would do nothing if the Germans took possession of the equipment. Twentieth Mountain Army, in return, agreed to turn the port of Oulu over to Finnish troops on the 15th.

The first break in the spirit of mutual accommodation came from the German side. In the second week of September the Navy, after the naval liaison officer on Suursaari reported that the Finnish commandant on the island had said he would never fire on German troops, suddenly changed its estimate of the prospects for TANNE OST. Encouraged, Doenitz declared that so important a strategic point ought not be abandoned to the Soviet Union without a fight. When successive reports from the liaison officer indicated that the Finns might evacuate the island by the 12th, Hitler, on 11 September, ordered a landing to be executed within the week.

A naval task force embarked a regiment at Reval and began the landing on the morning of the 15th. After the first wave, 1,400 men, was ashore the Finnish garrison opened fire, and shortly after daylight the Russians joined in with heavy air strikes. The second wave could not be landed, and part of the first wave was left stranded on the beach. The Finns claimed 700 prisoners.

Mannerheim retaliated with a demand that Twentieth Mountain Army immediately evacuate the area south of the line Oulu-Suomussalmi and give up the Baltic coast from Oulu to the Swedish border. Rendulic refused but offered to negotiate for a gradual withdrawal. That suited Mannerheim who, having given the Soviet Union a demonstration of good faith at Suursaari, apparently had no desire to become further embroiled with the Germans. By the 17th Rendulic's and Mannerheim's representatives had agreed on what the Finnish operations chief described as "fall maneuvers," a phased withdrawal that would let the Germans set their own pace, keep the two forces out of each other's way, and at the same time let the Finns report progress "of the advance" to the Russians. The one question that most bothered the Germans was how long the Finns could keep their side of the bargain. Rendulic observed that, although they did not want to fight the Germans, they were determined to have peace at any price and would therefore accept all Soviet demands.

For ten days the "fall maneuvers" went exactly as planned. On 26 September Twentieth Mountain Army reported that the Finns were following from phase line to phase line according to the agreement and leaving so much no-man's-land between the forces that exchanges of fire were scarcely possible. The Finnish panzer division was committed along the Oulu-Kemi road, the worst route that could have been chosen for an armored division because of the many river crossings, and the German troops were destroying the bridges and ferries as they passed, sometimes while the Finns stood by and watched.

The picture changed suddenly on the morning of 28 September. A Finnish battalion opened fire at Pudasyärvi and during the day rejected several German offers to restore the truce. At midnight Rendulic sent Finnish Lapland Command an ultimatum demanding that it reaffirm the agreement or take the consequences of full hostilities. On 1 October fighting broke out in the ports of Kemi

German twentieth mountain army troops with reindeer and sleds.

and Tornio, where Finnish troops who had been guarding industrial plants took possession of several road and railroad bridges. During the day the Finnish 3d Division, coming by sea from Oulu, began disembarking at Tornio. The incident of the bridges brought several excited messages from the OKW—Hitler apparently saw a tactical parallel with the Allied attack two weeks earlier on the Rhine bridges at Arnhem in Holland. Rendulic did not feel the bridges at Kemi and Tornio were that important, but to placate Hitler and because it might be worthwhile to keep the Finns from using the ports a while longer, he ordered counterattacks.

On 2 October the Finns rejected Rendulic's ultimatum, on the grounds that an agreement contrary to the Soviet-Finnish armistice terms could not have been made and that any exchanges of information which might have taken place between individuals were not binding on the Finnish command. The next day Rendulic declared that Twentieth Mountain Army would henceforth operate against the Finns "without restraint." Abandoning the policy, thus far scrupulously observed, of restricting property destruction to roads, railroads, and bridges, he ordered, "As of now, all cover, installations, and objects that can be used by an enemy are to be destroyed."

The fighting in Kemi and Tornio lasted until 8 October. The one understrength division Rendulic was able to commit had only a small chance of success from the first and none at all after 6 October, when the Finnish 11th Division landed at Kemi. The last two days of the battle were taken up entirely with extricating part of the division from a Finnish encirclement. On the 8th the Germans retreated north, and by then the main forces of the XXXVI and XVIII Mountain Corps had passed through Rovaniemi. The Finns, satisfied with their successes at Tornio and Kemi (they had brought in foreign journalists to witness the fighting), followed close behind the Germans but did not attack again.

NORDLICHT

In the meantime, the Operations Staff, OKW, had taken under review the whole German strategic position in Scandinavia and Finland. The review, concerned principally with the question of leaving Twentieth Mountain Army in northern Finland, was tied also to the growing hostility of Sweden and to the increased strategic importance of the Norwegian submarine bases, owing to the recent loss of the French bases and the projected resumption of full-scale submarine warfare with improved U-boat types. The Operations Staff concluded that the British naval and air forces formerly committed against the French bases would be lured north by the Norwegian bases, Twentieth Mountain Army's vulnerable sea supply lines, and the desire to prevent the Soviet Union's getting a foothold in northern Scandinavia. It also found that to hold northern Finland was no longer worth the risk since the war production chief, Speer, had recently stated that the stockpiles of nickel in Germany were adequate. On the other hand, taking Twentieth Mountain Army into Norway offered a chance to strengthen the Norwegian defenses against the Allies and against Sweden. On 3 October, after seeing the Operations Staff's conclusions, Hitler approved a withdrawal into Norway to the Lyngen position, a potentially almost impregnable short line across northern Norway from the Lyngen Fiord to the northernmost tip of Sweden. In the next two days the preliminary orders were sent to Twentieth Mountain Army and the code name NORDLICHT was assigned.

Tactically, NORDLICHT was an extension of BIRKE with the added problems of setting XIX Mountain Corps, east of Pechenga, in motion and evacuating the army's eight months' stockpile of supplies. As an expedition by a 200,000-man army with all its equipment and supplies across the Arctic in winter it had no parallel in military history. The season was already far advanced. Reichsstrasse 50, the German-built coastal road in northern Norway, was normally considered impassable between Kirkenes and Lakselv from early October to the first of June because of snow; therefore, even though the fall of 1944 was unusually mild, XIX Mountain Corps would need luck and would have to be west of Lakselv by 15 November at the latest. XXXVI Mountain Corps could use an all-weather road from Ivalo to Lakselv. The road XVIII Mountain Corps would use was about half completed between Skibotten and Muonio and unimproved between Muonio and Rovaniemi; its low-carrying capacity was at least in part compensated for by its being the most southerly and direct route to the Lyngen Fiord.

While the roads and weather posed unprecedented technical problems, the tactical situation was certain to be dangerous and could at any moment become catastrophic. The Finnish Army could, potentially, stage offensives with superior forces against both the XXXVI and XVIII Mountain Corps. The Russians could be trusted not to let XIX Mountain Corps escape without a fight and beyond that had a variety of choices. They could try to waylay XXXVI Mountain Corps at Ivalo; strike across the head of the Gulf of Bothnia and through northern Sweden to cut the army off at Narvik, demanding from Sweden, use of the Luleå-Narvik railroad as a quid pro quo for the Germans' use of the Swedish railroads in 1941; or they could carry the pursuit through northern Finland into Norway.

From all appearances British and American intervention was only slightly less certain than trouble with the Russians. Reichsstrasse 50, broken by numerous ferry crossings and, lying close to the coast for long stretches, was temptingly vulnerable to naval and air strikes. Not to be taken lightly either was the danger from Sweden, which having abrogated its trade agreements with Germany appeared to be veering toward a complete break. Twentieth Mountain Army was already under standing orders to avoid any incident that could be construed as a provocation, a difficult task since XVIII Mountain Corps' route of march took it directly along the Swedish border for several hundred miles.

THE BATTLE IN THE ARCTIC

How the first phase of NORDLICHT would be executed was determined by the Russians who, after a build-up the Germans had watched apprehensively since mid-September, opened an offensive against XIX Mountain Corps on 7 October. (Map 35) XIX Mountain Corps stood in the line it had held since late summer 1941. On the left the 6th Mountain Division held the fortified front on the Litsa River, and on the right the 2d Mountain Division manned the strongpoint line stretching southwest toward Ivalo. The Divisionsgruppe van der Hoop held a front across the neck of the Rybatchiy Peninsula, and the 210th Infantry Division manned the coastal defenses between Pechenga Bay and Kirkenes. Opposite XIX Mountain Corps, Fourteenth Army had been brought up to a strength of five rifle corps, 97,000 men against the mountain corps' 53,000. On the Rybatchiy Peninsula the Northern Defense Area had two naval brigades. XIX Mountain Corps, nevertheless, had to make a stand to protect the corps retreating from the south and to safeguard the tremendous stockpiles of supplies and equipment which were beginning to be evacuated.[32]

On the morning of 7 October CXXXI Rifle Corps hit the 2d Mountain Division strongpoint line at the division boundary south of Chapr Lake. XCIX Rifle Corps joined in on the right. The two corps, supported by artillery, aircraft, and—to the Germans' surprise— tanks, swept over several of the German strongpoints and by noon had almost reached the Titovka River on the Finnish-Soviet border. The 2d Mountain Division, badly shaken, retreated toward Luostari along the Lan road. At Luostari the army's main artery, the Arctic

---

32. Anticipating that Twentieth Mountain Army might be isolated, Hitler in 1942 had ordered the army's supply reserves built up. By the time NORDLICHT was executed many of the items in the army depots had become, as one officer put it, "rare commodities" in Germany, and the chances of the army's being resupplied when it reached Norway were not good.

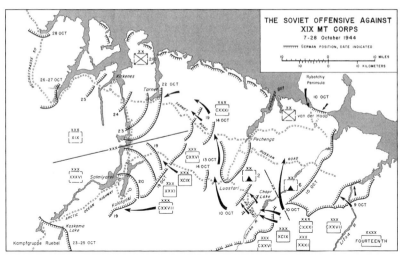

Map 35: The Soviet Offensive Against XIX Mountain Corps, 7-28 October 1944.

Ocean Highway, was threatened. Rendulic ordered the 6th Mountain Division to evacuate the Litsa front and release troops to protect the highway.

On 9 November CXXVI Light Rifle Corps attacked around the 2d Mountain Division south flank toward the Arctic Ocean Highway. On the Lan road the division's north flank was driven back, and a gap opened between it and the flank of the 6th Mountain Division. Rendulic dispatched as reinforcements a regiment and two battalions from XXXVI Mountain Corps.

The 10th was a day of crises. At midnight the 12th Naval Brigade staged a landing on the mainland west of the Rybatchiy Peninsula and during the day turned the flank of Divisionsgruppe van der Hoop, forcing it back from the neck of the peninsula. Between the 2d and 6th Mountain Divisions CXXXI Rifle Corps sent two regiments due north through the gap to cut the Russian road, the 6th Mountain Division's main route west. Off the 2d Mountain Division's right flank CXXVI Light Rifle Corps made good its threat of the day before and cut the Arctic Ocean Highway five miles west of Luostari. Rendulic ordered the 6th Mountain Division to clear the Russian road and then withdraw to the line Pechenga-Luostari. He also dispatched the 163d Infantry Division north from Rovaniemi by forced marches and ordered the Kolosyoki Nickel Works destroyed. The latter was a demolitions job of major proportions.[33]

In the next two days the 6th Mountain Division reopened the Russian road and, together with Divisionsgruppe van der Hoop, withdrew toward Pechenga. The 2d Mountain Division managed to hold the road junction at Luostari. The Russians by then held about five miles of the Arctic Ocean Highway. To prevent their expanding their hold west, Kampfgruppe Ruebel (two regiments of the 163d Infantry Division under the commanding general, Generalleutnant Karl Ruebel) set up a screening line straddling the highway.

On 13 October, while Kampfgruppe Ruebel and the 2d Mountain Division attacked north and south in an unsuccessful attempt to clear the highway, CXXVI Light Rifle Corps sent a force north between them and cut the Tarnet road, thereby effectively isolating the 2d and 6th Mountain Divisions and the Divisionsgruppe van der Hoop, since in the rocky tundra large units could not move off the roads. In one week Fourteenth Army had destroyed a front on which the Germans had lavished three years' labor. Rendulic ordered the divisions to give up Pechenga and Luostari and withdraw to the Norwegian border.

Even the Soviet troops, most of them specially trained, could not maintain a fast pace across the tundra for long. On the 14th they stopped to regroup. The three German divisions fought their way through on the Tarnet road during the next several days, but by the time they were out the 2d Mountain Division was in such poor condition that it had to be sent south to rest and refit behind Kampfgruppe Ruebel.

On the 18th, expecting the Russians to start moving again in a day or so, Rendulic ordered Kampfgruppe Ruebel to withdraw to Salmyärvi in three days and, since that would give the Russians access to the road that had been used to transport the nickel ore between Kolosyoki and Kirkenes, told the 6th Mountain Division to defend the southern approaches to Kirkenes. When these movements were

---

33. The Kolosyoki works had been completely bombproofed. Some of the installations were buried in bunkers deep underground; others, left on the surface, were protected by massive concrete "bells." Reputedly the works had stronger antiaircraft defenses than any other spot on the Eastern Front.

completed XIX Mountain Corps and Kampfgruppe Ruebel would be separated and facing opposite directions.

On 18 October Fourteenth Army resumed the offensive, putting four of its corps into an attack on the Kampfgruppe Ruebel. The kampfgruppe escaped the full force of the frontal attack by drawing back along the Arctic Ocean Highway, but its position became precarious the next day when CXXVII Light Rifle Corps attacked around the flank and threatened to cut the highway behind it. To keep its line of retreat open it had to fall back to the Kaskama Lake narrows. Soviet pressure then slackened as the kampfgruppe continued its withdrawal to Ivalo.

CXXXI Corps attacked the 6th Mountain Division front screening Kirkenes, aiming its thrust at Tarnet, where the hydroelectric plant that supplied power to Kirkenes was located. By 22 October the plant was under fire, and Rendulic, informing the OKW that without electricity to operate dock facilities ships could not come into Kirkenes, requested permission to stop evacuating supplies and operate according to the tactical situation. After several hours' delay the permission was granted, and subsequently the troops east of Kirkenes fell back rapidly, the last passing west onto Reichsstrasse 50 on the 24th. After rearguard actions on the 27th and 28th the Soviet pursuit slowed down. Of the corps' supplies one-third (45,000 tons) had been saved.

On 26 October the withdrawal from the Varanger Peninsula began. The Russians followed as far as Tana Fiord. Ahead of XIX Mountain Corps two Army of Norway divisions had moved in between Skibotten and Lakselv to defend the vulnerable points on Reichsstrasse 50 until Twentieth Mountain Army had passed. On orders from Hitler, intended to prevent either the Soviet Union or the free Norwegian Government from taking a foothold north of Lyngen Fiord, Rendulic instituted a scorched-earth policy. The civilian population (some 43,000 persons) was evacuated, mostly by small boats to avoid jamming the Reichsstrasse.

NORDLICHT COMPLETED

In the XXXVI Mountain Corps zone, in mid-October, the 169th

Infantry Division occupied the SCHUTZWALL position, which had been constructed south of Ivalo for BIRKE. On the east, in the direction of Lutto and Ristikent, it established a screening line. There on 21 October the corps experienced a brief alarm when radio monitors identified the Soviet Nineteenth Army headquarters and three divisions in the Lutto Valley. However, ground reconnaissance established that the radio traffic was a deception.

After the units of the former Kampfgruppe Ruebel passed through Ivalo toward Lakselv, the Lutto front was abandoned on 30 October, and the withdrawal from the SCHUTZWALL position began the next day. On 2 November the 2d Mountain Division entered Reichsstrasse 50 at Lakselv to begin the final stage of the XIX and XXXVI Mountain Corps retreat. The next day the rear guard of the 169th Infantry Division left Ivalo.

On 29 October, after holding Muonio until the large ammunition dump there had been evacuated, XVIII Mountain Corps began falling back to the STURMBOCK position west of Karesuando. There, in the fortifications constructed for BIRKE, the 7th Mountain Division stayed behind to hold the narrow strip of Finnish territory projecting northwestward between Sweden and Noway as a temporary flank protection for the Lyngen position and the units coming west on Reichsstrasse 50. On 18 December the rear guard on Reichsstrasse 50 passed Billefiord. The 7th Mountain Division stayed in the STURMBOCK position until 12 January 1945 when it began a leisurely march back to the Lyngen position, which in the meantime had been manned by the 6th Mountain Division.

At the end of January NORDLICHT was terminated. At the extreme northwestern tip of Finland a small slice of Finnish territory that had been included in the Lyngen position stayed in German hands until the last week of April 1945. East of Lyngen Fiord to the Varanger Peninsula, Norwegian Finnmark was empty except for small German detachments at Hammerfest and Alta that continued evacuating supplies until February 1945. In January the Norwegian Government sent a token police force from England and Sweden; and thereafter the Soviet forces gradually withdrew, leaving only a detachment at Kirkenes.

Although Operation NORDLICHT constituted an outstanding display of skill and endurance, good fortune was possibly equally significant in its success. Of the most serious dangers and threats which had been anticipated none materialized. The weather was as favorable as could have been expected in the Arctic, and winter set in much later than usual. Most fortunately of all for Twentieth Mountain Army, NORDLICHT was executed exactly at the time when the resources of both the Soviet Union and the Allies were stretched to the limit on the main fronts, so that the Soviet effort was modest and the Allies put in no appearance at all.

ARMY GROUP NORTH'S RETREAT TO COURLAND

The Finnish armistice, Twentieth Mountain Army's withdrawal, and the failure to take Suursaari almost completely invalidated Hitler's long-standing rationale for holding the northward extension of the Eastern Front; and tactically Army Group North was, by mid-September 1944, in a most dangerous position. (Map 36) The front, from the latitude of Koenigsberg north, had been reduced to a serpentine coastal strip averaging 70 to 80 miles in width and somewhat over 400 miles long. It was pinched near the center, in the Tukums-Riga area, where Fifth Guards Tank Army had broken through to the coast at the end of July, to a width of less than 20 miles. Essentially, Army Group North and Third Panzer Army were committed in an elongated, meandering beachhead, vulnerable everywhere and dangerously shallow.

VASILEVSKIY'S SEPTEMBER OFFENSIVE

In August, Vasilevskiy took in hand the planning and co-ordination for the three Baltic fronts. Govorov's Leningrad Front stayed under the direct control of the Stavka, and its left boundary was shifted south to give it the sector flanking Tartu between Lake Peipus and the Vortsjaerv. In September Govorov transferred Second Shock Army from the vicinity of Narva to south of Tartu for a thrust north behind Armeeabteilung Narva. The Baltic fronts deployed for converging thrusts toward Riga, each initially putting two armies into its main effort. That of General Armii I. I. Maslennikov's Third Baltic Front was to go southwest via Valga and Valmiera. Second Baltic Front, under

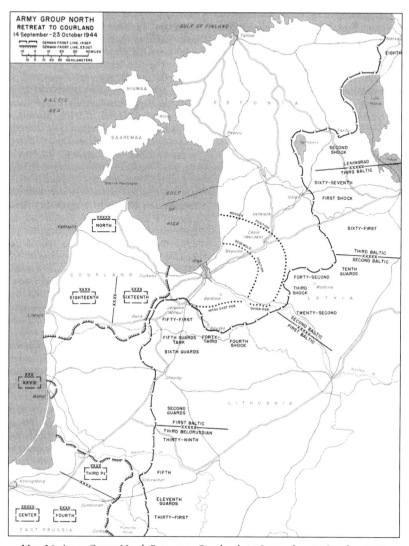

Map 36: Army Group North Retreat to Courland, 14 September-23 October 1944.

Yeremenko, was to strike due west from Madona. Bagramyan's First
Baltic Front had the shortest distance to go, thirty-five miles from
Bauska to Riga.

That Bagramyan had a possibility for a second, most crucial
thrust—to the Baltic coast across the Tukums-Riga corridor—has been
omitted from Soviet accounts of the planning. However, contemporary
German intelligence reports show that in addition to the Fourth Shock

and Forty-third Armies at Bauska, Bagramyan had a stronger force, the Fifth Guards Tank, Sixth Guards, and Fifty-first Armies, deployed in the vicinity of Jelgava. If he and Vasilevskiy had not in fact planned to use those armies to cut the Tukums-Riga corridor, they committed, to say the least, a remarkable tactical oversight.

The Soviet build-up proceeded slowly enough for the Germans to be able to follow it in detail. Army Group North's problem was dismayingly simple. The prudent and obvious decision would have been to take the army group out of the Baltic States while the Tukums-Riga corridor was still open. Since, as was also obvious, there was almost no likelihood of that decision being made, the army group had constructed a network of rearward positions. The most important—as the only ones with a chance of being held—were the Wenden position, a quarter circle on a 60-mile radius from Riga; the Segewold position, ten miles inside the Wenden position; and the Mitau-East and Dvina positions, on an almost straight line beginning twenty miles south of Riga and connecting with the Segewold and Wenden positions on the east.

Even Schoerner could not bring himself seriously to contemplate holding Estonia and northern Latvia against a determined Soviet attack; the Russians were 35 miles from Riga on the south and 50 miles from the coast below the Vortsjaerv, while in Estonia Armeeabteilung Narva's left flank was 120 and its right flank 220 miles from Riga. The army group had prepared Map Exercise ASTER, which was called that because of Hitler's antipathy to planning for retreats, but was actually an advance directive to Armeeabteilung Narva and Eighteenth Army for a withdrawal to the Wenden position.

The OKH, however, intent on holding the Tukums-Riga corridor, on 12 September instructed Third Panzer Army to reinforce its left flank corps for an attack from Auce into the rear of First Baltic Front's concentration around and west of Bauska. The chances of the army's being able to accomplish that feat vanished on the morning of 14 September when First, Second, and Third Baltic Fronts attacked and First Baltic Front made a dent four miles deep in the German line. The other two fronts did not do as well either that day or the next, but on the 15th Bagramyan's force, taking advantage of the foothold in the German line it had gained on the first day, drove a spearhead through to the Mitau-East position, twenty-five miles south of Riga. Schoerner asked for permission to evacuate Estonia, stating that it was "the last minute to get away from there at all."39 The next day he flew to Fuehrer headquarters to report in person.

As always, Hitler was reluctant to approve a retreat. With inverse logic, he argued that III SS Panzer Corps on the outer flank between Lake Peipus and the Gulf of Finland would not be able to get away in any event. He also claimed that the Soviet Union had peace feelers out, and he needed the Baltic territory to bargain with. He bemoaned, as in every previous discussion of the subject, the Navy's loss of its Baltic training area. In the end he gave a conditional "yes," after being assured that under Exercise ASTER the withdrawal would not begin for another two days and could be canceled in the meantime.

During the day on the 16th, Third Panzer Army started its attack. None of the three divisions committed found a soft spot in the Soviet front, and by day's end they were pushed out of the few places they had managed to penetrate. That night Guderian told Reinhardt that because "great things" were in progress in foreign policy (the alleged Soviet peace feelers?) Hitler "absolutely had to have a success either at Third Panzer Army or at Army Group North." The "instant" he could see that his attack was not going to succeed, Reinhardt was to report it to Hitler and get ready to transfer the divisions to Army Group North.

On the 17th Second Shock Army struck north past Tartu, breaking Armeeabteilung Narva's hold between the Vortsjaerv and Lake Peipus. That night Schoerner drastically revised ASTER. He ordered III SS Panzer Corps to make the 120-mile march from the Narva River to Paernu on the Gulf of Riga by the 10th. Its baggage and supply trains were to be evacuated through Tallinn or shipped across the straits to the Baltic islands. The withdrawal therewith became a more or less controlled flight with very slender prospects of success. The corps might run away from one encirclement only to be caught in another; Eighteenth Army had reported that it could not hold on to the southern tip of the Vortsjaerv any longer.

For several crisis-ridden days the fate of Army Group North hung by a thread that miraculously never quite broke. Schoerner gave Eighteenth Army a clutch of antiaircraft guns, antitank guns, and small motorized detachments from Armeeabteilung Narva and ordered it to keep its grip on the Vortsjaerv. Subsequently the army's line buckled but did not break.

On 17 and 18 September Third Panzer Army's attack picked up momentum and drove a 10-mile-deep wedge into Bagramyan's flank; but by the 18th the army was in the uncomfortable position of not being able to keep going, because Army Group North needed reinforcements, and of not being able to stop completely, because that would free too many Soviet troops. Reinhardt believed that he had, nevertheless, at a critical moment prevented Bagramyan from putting his reserves into the attack north of Bauska and from developing a second thrust across the Tukums-Riga corridor.

On the 19th a spearhead from Bagramyan's First Baltic Front went past Baldone nearly to the Dvina ten miles south of Riga, but it did not have enough force to press farther. On the 10th III SS Panzer Corps reached Paernu, having disengaged on the Narva front with astounding ease. Meanwhile the other Armeeabteilung Narva corps, II Corps, had executed a 180-degree turn pivoting on the northern end of the Vortsjaerv.

Hitler was still angling for a victory of some sort. On the 10th he transferred Third Panzer Army to Army Group North and authorized Schoerner to continue the ASTER withdrawal past the Wenden position to the Segewold position. The infantry divisions freed by taking Eighteenth Army and Armeeabteilung Narva into the shorter line were to be used to relieve several panzer divisions in the Third Panzer Army front on the Tukums-Riga corridor. Schoerner was to plan a counteroffensive using the panzer divisions to attack from west of Shaulyay and infantry divisions in a converging thrust from north of Bauska. The objective was to destroy Bagramyan's forces in the salient below Riga and push the front out to a straight line between the Segewold position and Shaulyay.

Between 20 and 24 September Vasilevskiy tried again to achieve his original objective of cutting up and destroying Army Group North. Using half a dozen divisions that no longer had to be held back after

Third Panzer Army's offensive subsided on the 19th, Forty-third Army pushed closer to Riga. On the 22d Second Baltic Front, with massed tanks and infantry, smashed X Corps west of Madona, and Third Baltic Front broke through past Valga.

South of Riga the SS Panzer Grenadier Division Nordland, after forced marches that in four days brought it 250 miles from the outermost flank on the Gulf of Finland, arrived just in time on the 22d to prevent a catastrophe. Against X Corps Yeremenko failed to commit his mobile reserves in time to exploit the advantage. Third Baltic Front's thrust carried to Valmiera, but that was not deep enough to do more than complicate the German withdrawal somewhat. On the 25th Sixteenth Army reported that First Baltic Front had given up the attempt to reach Riga and had "sacrificed" the most advanced spearheads, which were then being cut off and destroyed. By the morning of 27 September the Germans were in the Segewold position, and the Second and Third Baltic Fronts also went over to the defensive.

BAGRAMYAN'S THRUST TO THE BALTIC

Tactically, the September offensive against Army Group North had had the opposite of its intended effect. Instead of splitting the army group, it had reduced the German front north of Riga-Madona by better than two-thirds, from 240 miles to about 70 miles. Armeeabteilung Narva and the Eighteenth and Sixteenth Armies, their strength eroded but organizationally intact, had been compressed into a tight knot around Riga. For the Soviet forces, the breakthrough to Riga had, consequently, become both more difficult and less profitable. On 27 September Sixteenth Army reported heavy enemy truck traffic going southwest away from its front.

The Stavka had decided on the 24th to make a fresh start. In the last week of the month Bagramyan dispersed his concentration south and southeast of Riga and moved the Fourth Shock, Forty-third, Fifty-first, and Fifth Guards Tank Armies to the Shaulyay area for a thrust west to Memel (Klypeda). The Second and Third Baltic Fronts retained their missions to attack on a broad front toward Riga and were, as the operation progressed, to pursue Army Group North into

Soviet troops crossing East Prussian border in American-built trucks.

Courland.[34] Leningrad Front was ordered to occupy the Baltic islands, Muhu, Saaremaa, and Hiiuma. On Bagramyan's left Third Belorussian Front prepared to commit an army in an attack toward Tilsit.

At the end of the month Hitler was more than ever determined to have Army Group North attack. During a conference with Schoerner on the 28th he moved the jump-off point for Third Panzer Army to south of Shaulyay and that of Sixteenth Army to west of Riga. Two days later Schoerner told Hitler that the army group would first have to take its front east of Riga back, close to the city, start evacuating Riga as a precaution, absorb some 30,000 replacements (yet to be sent), and execute an extensive regroupment. He believed 3 November would be the earliest date on which the attack could start.

On the 30th the Army Group North chief of staff told the operations officer, Third Panzer Army, that most likely there would be no offensive because the Russians would strike first, but the mission was "not unwelcome" because it gave the army group a chance to make some useful dispositions. Third Panzer Army had reported earlier in the

---

34. Courland, the westernmost province of Latvia and the historic Grand Duchy of Courland, is bounded on the west by the Baltic, on the northeast by the Gulf of Riga, and on the south by the Lithuanian border.

day that the Headquarters, Fourth Shock Army, had been identified northwest of Shaulyay and the Soviet radio traffic in that whole area had suddenly stopped.

Although the signs were clear, the Army Group North staff as late as the morning of 5 October did not believe First Baltic Front could finish redeploying its armies in less than ten days. It was therefore inclined to tailor its regroupment to the schedule for its own projected attack on the assumption that this would also bring enough forces into the right place in time to stop the Russians. Several panzer divisions had moved into the Shaulyay-Raseynyay area by the 5th, but Third Panzer Army was still woefully weak in infantry. The 551st Grenadier Division west of Shaulyay was holding a 24-mile line that it could man only at strongpoints. The first infantry reinforcement for the army was not expected until 16 October.

On 5 October First Baltic Front attacked west of Shaulyay toward Memel. The next day Bagramyan put in Fifth Guards Tank Army to make a run for the coast, and Thirty-ninth Army on Third Belorussian Front's right flank began attacking toward Tilsit. During the day Leningrad Front, having occupied lightly defended Hiiumaa and Muhu several days earlier, staged a landing on Saaremaa.

In a day and a half the Russians took all of Saaremaa except the Soerve Peninsula at the southwestern tip. Far more serious, the Third Panzer Army front broke open on the 7th. Fifth Guards Tank Army and Forty-third Army went through and two days later reached the coast north and south of Memel. The Third Panzer Army command post was overrun and the staff had to fight its way out to Memel, where XXVIII Corps, caught between the two Soviet armies, was being forced into a beachhead around the port.

Knowing what the Fuehrer would expect, Schoerner declared he would attack toward Memel. To get enough divisions and to defend the northern tip of Courland, where Leningrad Front would have less than twenty miles of water to cross after it took the Soerve Peninsula, he proposed giving up Riga. Soviet submarines were in the Gulf of Riga; the port was under artillery fire; the last convoy sailed on 10 October; the city was hardly worth holding. Still, Hitler protested and delayed a day before giving his approval.

Army Group North had the strength to hold its own in Courland and could probably have spared enough forces to mount a powerful counterattack, but the issue was to be decided elsewhere. On 10 October the OKH returned Third Panzer Army to Army Group Center. With a single corps—one corps was at Memel and one had been cut off with Army Group North—the army had to defend the Army Group Center flank against the strong thrust Thirty-ninth Army was making toward Tilsit. What was happening to Army Group North was another military disaster of which there had been many. The threat to Army Group Center was something else, since a Russian advance onto German territory in East Prussia threatened the whole German outlook on the war. The Stavka had set its traps well, and the last was about to be sprung.

On 16 October two, later three, Soviet armies charged across the East Prussian border between Schirwindt and the Romintener Heide toward Gumbinnen. On the third day of the battle Hitler had to transfer armor from Third Panzer Army and let the army go behind the Neman. On the 21st, under the influence of two shocks—the loss of the first German city, Aachen, to the Allies and a report from Fourth Army that in another day Gumbinnen might be lost—he ordered Army Group North to go over to the defensive in Courland.

The Soviet bid for a deep breakthrough into East Prussia failed two days later, and, although Third Panzer Army's retreat behind the Neman had substantially reduced its chances of success, Army Group North again proposed to attack south to restore contact. At the end of the month Hitler rejected this proposal as unfeasible and began withdrawing divisions from Courland.

CHAPTER XIX

The January Offensive

TWO FRONTS,
THE FUEHRER'S WILL, AND GERMAN RESOURCES

On Christmas Eve, 1944, Guderian dined at the Adlerhorst, the Fuehrer headquarters in the Taunus Mountains ten miles northwest of Bad Nauheim. Hitler had left Rastenburg early in the month and after a short stay in Berlin had, before the Ardennes offensive began, moved to the headquarters from which he had directed the victorious 1940 campaign against France. Guderian had arrived that morning after an overnight trip in his command train from the OKH headquarters at the Maybachlager in Zossen, south of Berlin. He was there to ask Hitler to call off the offensive in the West and send the surplus strength east. During the past forty-eight hours it had become certain that the Ardennes operation would not achieve its planned objective, and on the Eastern Front north of the Carpathians the Russians had completed the heaviest buildup of the war.

Hitler refused to surrender the initiative in the West and scoffed at the OKH's figures on the Soviet forces deployed against Army Groups A and Center. He called the build-up "the greatest bluff since Genghis Kahn." He refused to consider creating reserves for the East either by taking units from the West, from Norway, or from Courland; the Eastern Front would have to shift for itself. At dinner that night, Himmler, who had lately embarked on a military career as an army group commander in the West, advised Guderian not to worry so much; the Russians, he insisted, would not attack; they were trying "a gigantic bluff." All Guderian's visit accomplished was that Hitler waited until the next day, when the Chief of Staff was on the way back to Zossen and out of touch for several hours, to order Headquarters, IV SS Panzer Corps, and two panzer grenadier divisions transferred to Army Group South to relieve Budapest.

THE DOWNTURN

For Germany in the last days of 1944 the end did in fact not seem as near as it had in midsummer. The vise the Allies and the Soviet Union had talked about was not closing. The Ardennes offensive was not going to be a strategic blow that would give Germany a free hand against the Soviet Union; but the Germans had the initiative, and it would be a while before the Allies could take up their march into the heart of the Reich. North of the Carpathians the Russians had made no substantial advance in two and a half months, and, after being almost completely destroyed in August, Army Group South was so close to holding its own in Hungary that a relief of Budapest did not appear impossible. Army Group E was in the last stage of its withdrawal from Greece, Albania, and southern Yugoslavia. In Italy, Army Group C had stopped the British and Americans at the Gothic Line.

Nevertheless, Hitler's strategy was bankrupt. He was rigidly committed to holding everything he still had. He had put his last block of liquid military assets into the attempt to bail himself out in the West and failed. He could only fight for time, and he knew it. In late December he told one of the generals, "The war will not last as long again as it has lasted. That is absolutely certain. Nobody can endure it; we cannot and the others cannot. The only question is, who will endure longer? It must be he who has everything at stake. We have everything at stake." But even so, he did not have nearly as much time as he apparently imagined; the German capacity to hold out, to endure, was heading into an irreversible downward spiral.

Both on the east and the west, Germany's enemies had unmatchable matériel superiority. German industrial output had withstood the ravages of the bombing surprisingly well, but it was on a seesaw that progressively dipped lower, stayed down longer, and rose more slowly. The aircraft plants had turned out 3,000 fighters in September 1944, a wartime high. In October jet fighters had begun to come off the lines. In December fighter production was still higher than in any month before May 1944. Armored vehicle production, including tanks, assault guns, and self-propelled assault guns, reached its wartime peak of 1,854 units in December 1944, but mainly because the heavy components had long lead times and therefore had been put into the production pipeline months earlier. On the other hand, the base of the industrial pyramid was crumbling. Heavy bombing of the Ruhr in December reduced pig iron, crude steel, and rolling mill production for that month to about half of the September 1944 level and one-third that of January 1944. The bombing had also by late 1944, according to the U.S. Strategic Bombing Survey, so severely damaged the German railroad system that the country "could not hope to sustain, over any period of time, a high level of war production."5

Industries with short lead times were already feeling the pinch. The motor vehicle industry was hard hit both by bomb damage to its plants and by the breakdown of the railroads. In October and November 1944 the assembly plants turned out 12,000 trucks by rebuilding all the disabled Army trucks that could be found in Germany. In December only 3,300 of the 6,000 new trucks needed were produced, and Hitler earmarked 70 percent for the offensive in the West. In January the truck strengths authorized for panzer and panzer grenadier divisions would have to be reduced 25 percent, and the Army would have to begin mounting the panzer grenadiers on bicycles. Hitler tried to console himself with thoughts that the armored divisions had too many vehicles anyway, that the time of the sweeping maneuver was past, and that, if it came down to cases, the infantry divisions could move faster than the so-called mobile divisions, which he said only created traffic jams.

Militarily, what hurt most was the catastrophic decline in oil production that had begun in May 1944. In spite of the top-priority Geilenberg program to disperse, repair, and build synthetic oil plants, output had fallen during the summer. In September, because of the bombings, no synthetic plants had operated. The Rumanian oil had been lost at the end of August. In October and November synthetic oil production had resumed at a low rate, but by the end of December, renewed heavy bombing had knocked out all but one of the large plants, and 20 percent of the small ones. Army Group South held the Hungarian fields at Nagykanizsa, but, owing to loss of the refineries at Budapest and resistance by the workers, the gasoline output was not enough to meet the army group's own requirements. In June 1944 the German Air Force had consumed 180,000 metric tons of aviation gasoline; its total supply for the rest of the war amounted to no more than 197,000 metric tons. Although aircraft production stayed high through the end of the year, the Air Force lacked enough gasoline to give the pilots adequate training and to employ the planes effectively. The shortage of motor fuel was almost as stringent, and the Army had similar troubles with its armored vehicles.

Although the downturn in military manpower had begun earlier than the decline in production, it had to a degree been amenable to various palliative measures; by late 1944 most of these that showed any promise, and some that did not, had been or were being tried, and they were not bringing in enough men to prevent the German Army's burning out at the core. Between June and November 1944 the total German irrecoverable losses on all fronts were 1,457,000, and of these 903,000 were lost on the Eastern Front.[35] On 1 October 1944 the Eastern Front strength stood at 1,790,138, about 150,000 of these Hiwis (Russian auxiliaries).[36] This was some 400,000 men less than in June and nearly 700,000 less than in January 1944, when the Western Theater could still be regarded as a semireserve.

The manpower shortage was affecting most the old and experienced divisions. In the period 1 September to 31 December 1944 one-third of the replacements for all fronts, 500,000 men, went into new or completely rebuilt divisions. At the end of the same period the old divisions had over 800,000 unfilled authorized spaces—after a 700,000-space reduction in the 1944 tables of organization.

In August 1944 Hitler had called on Goebbels, as Reichs Plenipotentiary for Total War, to procure a million men through party channels. They were to be used to create new divisions and were to be called up without regard for previous draft status. At the year's end Goebbels had secured 300,000 new recruits and about 200,000 interservice transfers. In October Hitler had activated the Volkssturm—a home guard—under party leadership, composed of

35. The breakdown was as follows: Western Theater 440,000, Southwestern Theater (Italy), 97,000; Southeastern Theater (the Balkans), 17,000; Army Group North, 94,000; Army Group Center, 435,000; Army Group A, 117,000; Army Group South, 243,000; Twentieth Mountain Army, 14,000.

36. The army group strengths on 1 October 1944 were as follows: Army Group North, 420,844; Army Group Center, 694,812; Army Group A, 457,679; and Army Group South, 216,803.

men aged 16 to 60 otherwise draft-exempt. The members were to be put into Army uniforms, if available; if not, they were to wear the party uniform or civilian clothes. He had also authorized the "Gneisenau" and "Bluecher" programs whereby some 200,000 men were to be organized into territorial divisions in the eastern military districts. In November, for the first time, he had agreed to allow Russian collaborator troops to fight on the front in the East and actually to constitute the long-talked-about Russian Army of Liberation with Vlasov as its commanding general.[37] In the attempt to sustain the Army's combat strength, Hitler was not above permitting some organizational and arithmetical sleight of hand. He authorized artillery corps with brigade strengths, panzer brigades of two battalions, and panzer Jaeger brigades with one battalion. For the months August through December, the number of men called up (1,569,000) slightly exceeded the total decline in field strength for the same period, but a closer look revealed that 956,000 of the recruits would not reach the field until well after 1 January 1945.

In October and November 1944, the Organization Branch, OKH, had called for combat-condition reports from the armies and army groups. As was to be expected, they all agreed that what they needed most were more replacements. They reported that troop morale was "affected" by the recent losses of prewar German territory in the West and in East Prussia and by the "terror bombing." The general attitude of the troops was still confident, but for the "great majority" the confidence was grounded "exclusively" on the hope that soon new weapons would appear which could stop the air raids and break the enemy ground superiority.

How deeply in trouble Germany was Hitler knew better than the poor Landsers and grenadiers who still believed in secret weapons. He also knew exactly what he was going to do—in fact, had known all along. He had, in the past, wavered, even lost his nerve completely, when his fortune was at a crest but never when it was in a trough. On 28 December 1944 in the Adlerhorst, addressing the commanding

---

37. On 10 February 1945, when the first division created was turned over to Vlasov, it lacked 55 percent of its clothing and equipment and 85 percent of its motor vehicles.

generals of the divisions that were to open an offensive on New Year's Day in northern Alsace, he admitted that the Ardennes offensive had failed and that Germany would henceforth be fighting for its naked existence. Then he went on:

I would like to interpose immediately, gentlemen, when I say that, you should not infer that I am thinking of losing the war even in the slightest. I have never in my life learned the meaning of the word capitulation, and I am one of those men who has worked his way up from nothing. For me, therefore, the circumstances in which we find ourselves today are nothing new. The situation for me was once altogether different and much worse. I say that only so you can judge why I pursue my goal with such fanaticism and why nothing can break me down. I could be yet so tortured by worries and, as far as I am concerned, my health could be destroyed by worry without its in the slightest changing my decison to fight until in the end the balance tips to our side.

The refrain was an old one, but formerly, even in a similar speech to the generals on the eve of the Ardennes offensive, it had a strong political and strategic counterpoint. Hitler then still spoke as a statesman and strategist bringing his will into play to accomplish purportedly rational objectives. Now his will alone was all that counted; armies and battles were secondary; what was important and all that was important was that he not weaken. He went on to tell the generals that history refuted the argument that one had to look at impending defeat from the sober military point of view; in the last analysis, it was the strength and determination of the leadership that decided whether wars were won or lost. He cited Cannae and "the miracle of the House of Brandenburg" when Frederick the Great, defeated in the Seven Years' War, regained by the Peace of Hubertusburg all the territory he had lost and some to boot after the coalition against him fell apart. Hundreds of thousands were to die while Hitler awaited the second such miracle.

GUDERIAN GOES TO THE EASTERN FRONT
On 5 January 1945 Guderian visited the Army Group South headquarters in Eszterhaza. During the following night his train took

him north across Czechoslovakia to the Army Group A headquarters, in Krakow. It was no ordinary inspection tour. He was deeply troubled. The Budapest relief operation was taking more time than could prudently be spared for it, and Army Groups A and Center were expecting an offensive, more powerful than any they had experienced, to start in the middle of the month.

North of the Carpathians the Eastern Front had not changed significantly since the end of summer. (Map 37) Between Christmas and New Year's Army Group North in Courland had beaten off the third Soviet attempt in three months to break open its front. Elsewhere the front had been calm since the first week in November, when a Fourth Army counterattack drove the Soviet armies in the sector east of Gumbinnen off all but a fifteen-mile by fifty-mile strip of East Prussian territory.

The outstanding features of the Army Group A and Center fronts were the five Soviet bridgeheads: Rozan and Serock on the Narew; Magnuszew, Pulawy, and Baranow on the Vistula. They were the wedges that could splinter all the rest. In November Army Group A had taken command of Ninth Army; thereafter its zone reached from Modlin to the northern border of Hungary. Its armies—Ninth, Fourth Panzer, Seventeenth, and Armeegruppe Heinrici (First Panzer Army and Hungarian First Army)—straddled the direct routes of attack into Germany proper. Army Group Center, with the Third Panzer, Fourth, and Second Armies, covered the East Prussia-Danzig area. The months of quiet had given the army groups time to build a close-meshed network of field fortifications extending back from the Vistula and Narew to the Oder. The major road junctions were ringed with defenses and designated as fortresses.

The Eastern Intelligence Branch, OKH, at first had thought that the next Soviet offensives would be aimed at taking East Prussia and clearing the lower Vistula and at taking Upper Silesia and Vienna in a wide pincers movement that would also engulf Czechoslovakia. In December the estimate changed: the main effort, the intelligence branch predicted, would be by the First Belorussian and First Ukrainian Fronts against Army Group A, and the attack would go west and northwest. A simultaneous thrust against Army Group

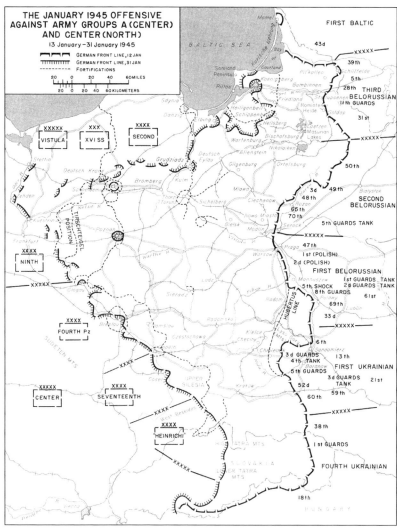

*Map 37: The January 1945 Offensive Against Army Groups A (Center)
and Center (North)*

Center was to be expected, possibly with a more limited objective than
the full conquest of East Prussia, because the efforts to smash Army
Group North had so far not succeeded. By early January it appeared
that the Russians would also go for the "big solution" against Army
Group Center, the thrust to the lower Vistula, and that against Army
Group A they intended to go deep, possibly as far as Berlin.

Strength comparisons showed that opposite 160 German units

of roughly division or brigade size on the whole Eastern Front the Russians had 414 units in the front, 261 in front reserves, and 219 in reserves in depth.[38] Even with allowances for a Soviet unit size 30 percent smaller than the German and an over-all 40 percent under authorized strengths (with no similar understrength allowance for the German units), the Soviet superiority worked out at over 2.3:1. The actual ratio was in fact higher, and at the crucial points it was overwhelming. Against Army Group Center the Second and Third Belorussian Fronts had 1,670,000 men, over 28,000 artillery pieces and mortars, and 3,300 tanks and self-propelled artillery, which gave them over-all superiorities of 2.8:1 in troops, 3.4:1 in artillery, and 4.7:1 in armor. In their sectors opposite Army Group A, the First Belorussian and First Ukrainian Fronts had a total of 2,200,000 troops, 6,400 tanks and self-propelled artillery, and 46,000 artillery pieces (including heavy mortars and rocket launchers). Against these the German Ninth, Fourth Panzer, and Seventeenth Armies could field about 400,000 troops, 4,100 artillery pieces, and 1,150 tanks. At their points of attack, the bridgeheads, the First Belorussian and First Ukrainian Fronts had the Germans outnumbered on the average by 9:1 in troops, 9-10:1 in artillery, and 10:1 in tanks and self-propelled artillery. In the Magnuszew bridgehead alone First Belorussian Front had 400,000 troops, 8,700 artillery pieces and mortars, and 1,700 tanks.

In the air on 1 January 1945, the Germans could put up 1,900 planes on the Western Front, and 1,875 on the Eastern Front. The main effort was still in the West. North of the Carpathians the First and Sixth Air Forces had some 1,300 planes. The Russians had over 10,000.

The Army Group A staff had a plan ready to present to Guderian when he arrived in Krakow. The outlook, no matter what the army group did, was not good. In December, prompted by the loss of two reserve divisions to Army Group South, the army group chief of staff

---

38. The breakdown of Soviet forces was as follows:

Units in the Front		Front Reserves		Reserves in Depth	
Total	**414**	**Total**	**261**	**Total**	**219**
Rifle divisions	253	Rifle divisions	119	Rifle divisions	67
Rifle brigades	30	Rifle brigades	14	Rifle brigades	13
Cavalry divisions	13	Cavalry divisions	3	Cavalry divisions	6
Tank brigades	29	Tank brigades	44	Tank brigades	42
Tank regiments	46	Tank regiments	31	Tank regiments	47
Assault gun regiments	43	Assault gun regiments	50	Assault gun regiments	44

had conducted a war game which showed that the Russians could break through and reach the Silesian border in six days and that they could be stopped on the Oder was by no means certain. A subsequent study showed that the most the army group could do was to give itself what might be a fighting chance. The first major switch position, the so-called HUBERTUS line, paralleled the western face of the Baranow bridgehead about five miles to its rear and then ran in an almost straight line north to the western tip of the Magnuszew bridgehead. The army group proposed to pull back to the HUBERTUS line in the two nights before the offensive began—to get the inner flanks of the Fourth Panzer and Ninth Armies out of probable encirclement, get Fourth Panzer Army's right flank out of the front on the Baranow bridgehead before the Soviet artillery preparation started, shorten the front, and give the army group some reserves. Guderian reviewed the plan and approved it on 8 January, but that Hitler would do likewise was scarcely to be expected.

On the 9th, after having also received an Army Group Center proposal to go back from the Narew to the line on the East Prussian border, Guderian reported to Hitler in the Adlerhorst. According to Guderian's account, Hitler refused to believe the intelligence estimates of Soviet strength and told him whoever had concocted them ought to be placed in an asylum. He also rejected both army groups' proposals. The surviving fragment of the stenographic record contains rambling remarks by Hitler on the folly of having given ground in Russia in the first place and an admonishment that those who were "beginning to whine" ought to look at the example of what the Russians had gone through at Leningrad.

That night, after Guderian had gone, Hitler was still thinking of arguments to refute the intelligence figures. The enemy needed 3:1 numerical superiority in tanks, he said, just to stay even; the Russians could not have as many guns as Guderian claimed; they were not "made of artillery"; and, even if they did have the guns, How many rounds could they fire? Ten or a dozen per piece. Referring, apparently, to the Army Group A plan, he grumbled, "This operational idea—to go back here [pointing], create two groups, and attack with them—is downright dangerous."

Whether Hitler wanted to believe it or not, the respite was over. On 3 January he had officialy abandoned the objectives of the Ardennes offensive; on the 8th he had issued an order to let the spearhead army, the Sixth SS Panzer Army, fall back and become a reserve to meet Allied counterattacks. The offensive in northern Alsace was still on, but it had, at most, nuisance value. On 7 January Army Group A detected fresh Soviet units moving into the front on the west face of the Baranow bridgehead. In the Pulawy and Magnuszew bridgeheads the Russians were reinforcing their artillery. The final deployment was obviously under way.

THE STAVKA'S PLANS

The Stavka had prepared two offensives, related but separated geographically by the course of the Vistula west of Warsaw. The stronger of the two was to be opened between Warsaw and the Carpathians by the First Belorussian and First Ukrainian Fronts with an assist on the left from Fourth Ukrainian Front. First Belorussian Front, Zhukov commanding, was to strike out of the Pulawy bridgehead toward Lodz, out of the Magnuszew bridgehead toward Kutno, and on its right flank encircle Warsaw. Konev's First Ukrainian Front was to break out of the Baranow bridgehead westward toward Radomsko, turning one force northwest to collaborate with the First Belorussian Front left flank in destroying the Germans in the Kielce-Radom area and another southwest toward Krakow and the Upper Silesian industrial area. Subsequently, both fronts were to advance abreast west and northwest toward the Oder. North of the Vistula bend Second Belorussian Front, Rokossovskiy in command, was to break out of the Serock and Rozan bridgeheads, strike northwest to the Baltic coast, cut off East Prussia, and clear the line of the lower Vistula. On Rokossovskiy's right, Chernyakovskiy's Third Belorussian Front was to attack due west south of the Pregel River toward Koenigsberg, split Third Panzer Army off from the Army Group Center main force, and envelop Fourth Army among and west of the Masurian Lakes.

Strategically, the Stavka intended nothing less than to end the war—in about a 45-day operation, according to its estimates. Following standard general staff practice, the detailed plan covered only the initial phase. Its success was considered certain, and no more than 15 days were allotted to it. The second phase would require somewhat more daring and time, but not much more of either. The Stavka knew that the German center, the Army Group A zone, was dangerously weak. The forces on the flanks, particularly Army Group Center in East Prussia, appeared relatively stronger, but in the least favorable situation they could be immobilized. Therefore, in the second phase, for which 30 days were allowed and which would follow the first without a full stop, the Stavka intended to run the First Belorussian and First Ukrainian Fronts straight through to Berlin and the Elbe River.

During the four months, September to January, the Soviet Command provided massive logistical support for the coming offensive. The railroads in eastern Poland were converted to the Russian gauge and, at the Vistula bridgeheads, were extended across the river. First Belorussian Front received over 68,000 carloads of supplies, only 10 percent less than had been sent to all four fronts before the June 1944 offensive against Army Group Center. Over 64,000 carloads went to First Ukrainian Front. At the Magnuszew bridgehead, First Belorussian Front stockpiled 2.5 million artillery and mortar shells and at the Pulawy bridgehead 1.3 million. By comparison, in the whole Stalingrad operation Don Front had fired less than a million artillery and mortar rounds. Together, First Belorussian and First Ukrainian Front's gasoline and diesel oil stocks amounted to more than 30 million gallons. Second and Third Belorussian Fronts, located off the main road and railroad nets and having less crucial missions, would have to economize somewhat on motor fuel and rations but not on ammunition. Together the two fronts had as initial issues 9 million artillery and mortar rounds, of which two-fifths were earmarked for the opening barrage.

In preparing for the offensive, the Soviet Command had recast its troop indoctrination program. For a year or more, the central theme had been the liberation of Soviet territory, but henceforth the Soviet armies everywhere would be fighting on foreign soil. The new theme, in a word, was Vengeance! It was disseminated in meetings, by slogans, on signs posted along the roads, and in articles and leaflets authored by prominent Soviet literary figures. Political officers recounted stories of crimes the Germans had committed against Russian women and children and of German looting and destruction in the Soviet Union. Soldiers and officers told what had happened to their own families. The objective was to give each man the feeling that he had a personal score to settle.

The starting date for the offensives, according to Soviet accounts, had originally been 20 January. After Churchill, on the 6th, asked Stalin what he could do on the east to take some of the pressure off the Allies, it was moved ahead eight days to the 12th. In December, except for the sideshow going on around Budapest, the Eastern Front, from the Allies' point of view, had been dismayingly quiet. At midmonth Stalin had told U.S. Ambassador W. Averell Harriman that a winter offensive would be launched, but he did not offer more precise information. On 15 January Stalin talked to Air Chief Marshal Sir Arthur W. Tedder, who headed a SHAEF (Supreme Headquarters Allied Expeditionary Force) party sent to learn the Soviet intentions. Stalin explained that the offensive had been delayed by the weather but had been started earlier than intended because of the Allies' difficulties in the west; his objective was to reach the line of the Oder.

German intelligence reports confirm that after mid-December the Stavka had probably been waiting for a change in the weather. The winter was colder than the one before, but snow, fog, and clouds interfered with air activity and artillery observation.

Starting early undoubtedly cost the Russians something; on the other hand, with the Yalta Conference in the offing, it was no disadvantage to Stalin to have his armies on the move, Poland in his pocket, the Soviet-supported Lublin government safely established in Warsaw, and the Allies in his debt for a favor rendered a shade late.

FROM THE VISTULA TO THE ODER

BREAKOUT

On the west face of the Baranow bridgehead, between the Vistula and the Lysogory, XXXXVIII Panzer Corps had three divisions, one man for each fifteen yards of front. The divisions had a dozen self-propelled assault guns apiece, and each corps held about 100 in reserve. The front was no more than a chain of strongpoints. Fifteen miles back, the reserve corps, XXIV Panzer Corps, had deployed two panzer divisions, and it had stationed two more panzer divisions off the north face of the bridgehead. To make the breakout, First Ukrainian Front had five armies, two tank armies, and better than a thousand tanks.

In the early hours of 12 January the temperature stood a few degrees above freezing. The roads were icy. Low-hanging clouds and fog would, as they had for several days past, keep the aircraft grounded. Before dawn the massed Soviet artillery, estimated at 420 pieces per mile, laid a barrage on the northern two-thirds (approximately twenty miles) of XXXXVIII Panzer Corps' front. After three hours the fire shifted to a strip pattern and the infantry moved out into the openings. The Germans were caught forward of the main battle line; they had expected the Russians to wait for better weather. During the morning the Russian infantry drove in deep; by noon it had opened gaps wide enough for the armor to come through. XXXXVIII Panzer Corps' three divisions were cut up and destroyed. XXIV Panzer Corps had orders to counterattack, but its two divisions west of the bridgehead were overrun in their assembly areas.

On the 13th Fourth Tank Army wheeled northwest toward Checiny, and Fifty-second Army and Third Guards Tank Army pushed due west past Chmielnik. During the night some of the tank spearheads had reached the Nida River. Across the Nida a 40-mile-wide path to Upper Silesia and the Oder was open. On the north flank XXIV Panzer Corps, what was left of it, dug in around Kielce.

Ninth Army expected the attacks out of the Magnuszew and Pulawy bridgeheads when they came on 14 January, but it fared only slightly better. The Russians broke into the German artillery positions, and both defending corps lost half their strengths on the first day.

On the 15th Forty-seventh Army on the First Belorussian Front right flank broke through north of Warsaw to Modlin, and Thirty-eighth Army, the right flank army of Fourth Ukrainian Front, began pushing west toward Krakow. During the day Thirteenth, Fourth Tank, and Third Guards Armies pushed XXIV Panzer Corps out of Kielce, thereby removing that not very significant threat to First Ukrainian Front's flank.

On the 13th Hitler had ordered two infantry divisions transferred from the West. The next day, in a move that was to hurt Army Group Center, which was also under attack, more than it benefited Army Group A, he ordered Center to give up Panzer Corps Grossdeutschland and its two divisions to Army Group A. On the 15th he ordered Army Group South to send two panzer divisions to Army Group A.

From Zossen, on the second and third days of the battle, Guderian sent two situation estimates to the Adlerhorst. The tenor of both was the same: the Eastern Front could not survive without reinforcements from the West; at the very least the Army Group South offensive would have to be stopped and the armored divisions sent to Army Group A. The intelligence estimate of 15 January stated flatly that the offensive against Army Group A could not be stopped with the forces then on the Eastern Front. Hitler refused either to stop Army Group South or to send more divisions from the West.

On the night of the 15th Hitler moved his headquarters from the Adlerhorst to the Reichs Chancellory in Berlin. Minutes before the departure, Guderian called and, as Jodl recorded it, "Requested urgently that everything be thrown east." The next day, when Guderian talked to him in Berlin, Hitler said that he was going to send Sixth SS Panzer Army's two corps, the most readily available reserves in the West, to the Eastern Front, but to Army Group South in Hungary, not to Army Group A. He had decided that the outcome of the war hinged on holding the Hungarian oil fields.

Back in Berlin, Hitler took the Eastern Front directly in hand. On 16 January he relieved Generaloberst Joseph Harpe and gave Schoerner command of Army Group A, calling Rendulic in from Norway to take over Army Group North. During the day, apparently before Hitler had arrived in Berlin, the OKH had issued a directive giving Army Group A freedom of decision in the great bend of the Vistula, including authority to evacuate Warsaw. When Hitler saw the directive he ordered a new one written to supersede it. Fighting from the map, as was his habit, he demanded "as a minimum" that

Army Group A stop on, or regain, a line from east of Krakow to west of Radomsko and thence along the Pilica River to the vicinity of Warsaw; Warsaw and the Vistula to Modlin were to be held. The army group was to be told that the two panzer divisions from Army Group South would be the last it would get for two weeks; by way of a concession, it could let Seventeenth Army and Armeegruppe Heinrici go far enough back in the Carpathians to release a division or two.

PURSUIT

On 17 January the Russians completed the breakout phase of the offensive. First Belorussian and First Ukrainian Fronts had cleared the entire line of the Vistula from east of Krakow to west of Modlin. On that day XXIV Panzer Corps, the last island of resistance between the two fronts, broke loose northwest of Kielce and began to drift erratically as it fought its way west to the Pilica. Konev's spearheads were across the Pilica and up to Czestochowa and Radomsko. First Belorussian Front took Warsaw. The Stavka ordered Zhukov and Konev to accelerate the thrusts toward the Oder and instructed Konev to use his second echelon, mostly infantry which had not yet been in action, and his left flank units to take Krakow and the Upper Silesian industrial area.

The failure to hold Warsaw set off an explosion in Berlin. Army Group A reported that the revised directive had come too late; the Warsaw garrison had destroyed its supplies and was leaving the city by the time it arrived. Hitler suspected sabotage—not without reason, by his lights: the original OKH directive was hardly one which any officer acquainted with Hitler could have expected him to approve. On 18 January he had the three senior officers in the Operations Branch, OKH, arrested. The next day he signed an order that took away the last shreds of discretion left to the field commanders. Henceforth every army group, army, corps, or division commander was to be personally responsible for seeing to it that every decision for an operational movement, whether attack or withdrawal, was reported in time for a counterorder to be given. The first principle in combat would be to keep open the communication channels, and all attempts to gloss over the facts would be met with Draconian punishment.[39]

Schoerner, as always, made his presence felt from the moment he took command. One of his first acts was to dismiss the Commanding General, Ninth Army, General der Panzertruppen Smilo Freiherr von Luettwitz, on the charge that on the day Warsaw was lost his conduct of operations had been insufficiently "clear and rigorous."[49] General der Infanterie Theodor Busse took command of the army. Schoerner had given the army group the first taste of his by then well enough known ruthlessness; others in all ranks were to feel it before the battle ended.

Also in the Schoerner style, the reports and orders coming out of army group headquarters began to exude confidence. The daily report of 18 January stated that the mission of defending the Upper Silesian industrial area could be "successfully" accomplished if the two panzer divisions coming from Army Group South arrived soon. The Soviet thrust toward Posen, going into a gap between Fourth Panzer Army and Ninth Army, would require "a speedy development of new forces," but it, too, could then be stopped and counterattacks could be begun on its flanks. The report did not indicate where the army group proposed to get the new forces.

The next day Schoerner gave Seventeenth Army the mission of defending Upper Silesia, ordered Fourth Panzer Army to stop the Russians west of Czestochowa and on the line of advance toward Breslau, and ordered Ninth Army to hold between Lodz and the Vistula and at the same time counterattack south off its right flank. If the assignments to Seventeenth Army and Ninth Army had at least theoretical substance, the mission given to Fourth Panzer Army bore slight relationship to hard reality. The army had nothing left but parts of two divisions and one or two brigades; XXIV Panzer Corps and the remnants of the army's left flank divisions were still encircled and fighting their way northwest into the Ninth Army sector.

---

39. On 23 January the OKH issued an implementing directive which stated that special radio teams would be stationed with selected army and corps headquarters. Through them the commanders were to report all important events immediately and report at least four times a day "all the facts that may be necessary for decision making by the highest leadership."

By 19 January the offensives against Army Groups A and Center were both running full tilt. The army groups had lost contact with each other, and in the Army Group A zone broad gaps had opened between the Ninth and Fourth Panzer and between the Fourth Panzer and Seventeenth Armies. South of Lodz Ninth Army's XXXX Panzer Corps and Panzer Corps Grossdeutschland were trying to hold a short line until XXIV Panzer Corps (Gruppe Nehring) could cross the Pilica. East of Breslau Fourth Panzer Army was being thrown back to the German border; at Namslau and east of Oppeln the Russians were across the border.[40] Seventeenth Army had a nearly continuous 40-mile front on the eastern border of the Upper Silesian industrial area; but it lost Krakow on the 19th.

The Soviet armies moved in columns on the roads, the tank armies averaging 25-30 miles a day and the infantry armies 18 miles. First Belorussian Front's main force struck past Lodz toward Poznan, First Ukrainian Front's toward Breslau while its infantry turned off the flank toward Upper Silesia. The weather had cleared and the overwhelming Soviet air superiority added to the Germans' troubles. The Luftwaffe had begun shifting fighter and ground support aircraft east after 14 January, but the losses, mostly in planes captured on the ground when their landing fields were overrun, outnumbered the new arrivals. Aircraft repair and assembly plants dispersed in Poland to escape the Allied bombing were falling into the Russians' hands.

Behind the front vehicles of all descriptions jammed the roads leading into Germany. In the mass of humanity fleeing westward were civilian refugees, party and administrative personnel, and not a few stragglers from combat units; Army Group A did not have enough military police even to begin screening out the latter. The refugee treks, a long-familiar sight on the Eastern Front, for the first time were composed of Germans. For the first time, too, the treks did not need to be urged onward; they were propelled by sheer terror. The Russian vengeance on German civilians was swift, personal, merciless and,

---

40. In the former German territory east of the Oder and Neisse Rivers and in East Prussia, Polish, in some instances Russian, names have been substituted for all the German place names. Between 1939 and 1945 the Germans changed the place names in the Polish territory absorbed into the Reich. In this narrative the pre-1939 place names are used.

Soviet planes on a mission.

more often than not, brutal. To debate here whether the misery and destruction the Germans visited on half of European Russia in the execution of Nazi occupation policy exceeded the rape, arson, pillage, and wanton murder that accompanied the Russian march into Eastern Germany would be profitless. Certainly thousands on thousands of Germans and Russians suffered horribly and most of them innocently. The sheer, massive inhumanity of the war on the Eastern Front in World War II has no equal in modern history.

The cluster of industrial cities in Upper Silesia had succeeded the bombed-out Ruhr as Germany's number one coal- and basic-metals-producing center. At the end of the third week in January the factories and mines were still going full blast. To the east Seventeenth Army's left flank stood like a windbreak, but it was open on the north where Fourth Panzer Army was being shoved west toward the Oder. On 21 January Konev turned Third Guards Tank Army at Namslau and sent it doubling back to the southeast along the Oder behind Seventeenth Army's flank.

On 22 January XXIV Panzer Corps made contact with Panzer Corps Grossdeutschland on the Warthe River near Sieradz. Caught in the Russian tide, both corps continued to drift west. On the same day the First Ukrainian Front left flank reached the Oder. During the next three days Konev's armies closed up to the river on a 140-mile stretch between Cosel and Glogau. At Breslau Fourth Panzer Army held a bridgehead; upstream and downstream from the city the Russians crossed the river in half a dozen places. Schoerner ordered counterattacks; the armies could not execute them.

ARMY GROUP VISTULA

On the 25th First Belorussian Front's main force passed Poznan heading due west toward Kuestrin on the Oder. Its advance was now taking it away at a right angle from Second Belorussian Front, which had turned north along the east bank of the Vistula. On that lengthening front between the Vistula and the Oder Hitler had put in the newly created Army Group Vistula and given Himmler command.

Guderian had wanted to bring Weichs and his headquarters up from Yugoslavia to command Army Group Vistula, but Hitler professed to see signs of authentic if late-blooming military talent in Himmler's recent handling of Army Group Oberrhein. Hitler gave Himmler the mission of closing the gap between Army Groups Center and A, preventing breakthroughs to Danzig and Poznan, and holding open a corridor to East Prussia. He gave Himmler the further responsibility of organizing the national defense behind the whole Eastern Front.

When Himmler arrived on the scene on 23 January, one of the missions was already obsolete; Second Army had broken away from the Army Group Center flank and the Russians were closing up to the Baltic coast at the mouth of the Vistula; Army Group Center was cut off. Second Army had a front along the lower Vistula, but west of the river all the way to the Oder, as Himmler reported, there was "nothing but a big hole."56 By 25 January another of the missions was beyond executing; on that day the Russians passed Poznan.

Himmler had come east in the Steiermark, his tremendously long and elegantly outfitted special train. It was parked at first in the station at Deutsch-Krone. In it he had a mobile command post from which he controlled his vast personal empire. He carried along with him skeleton staffs for his functions as Reichsfuehrer-SS, Minister of the Interior, Chief of the German Police, and Commanding General of the Replacement Army, to mention only the most important. Each of the staffs had its own clerks and files. The train was outfitted with radio and teletype, but the sets, fully occupied with administrative traffic, could not also carry that of an army group command. Himmler, moreover, would not have neglected his political interests for the sake of the army group. As an army group commander he had nothing— no communications with his front line units, no staff, virtually no troops, and no vehicles. For several days on his island of luxury, which contrasted grotesquely with the columns of refugees wandering through the snow and cold outside, he had no more contact with the war than he could get from occasional, mostly outdated, situation reports. The first of his military staff to arrive was the operations officer, an Army colonel, who made the trip from Berlin by car. Several days later the chief of staff, an SS general with no staff experience, arrived.

On 26 January, for no discernible purpose, unless it was to confuse students of the war, Army Group North was renamed Army Group Courland, Army Group Center became Army Group North, and Army Group A became Army Group Center. The next day Army Group Vistula took command of Ninth Army, thereby extending its zone south to Glogau on the Oder. The army group front, if it could be called a front at all, followed the Vistula from its mouth south to Kulm, then veered west north of the Netze River until it turned south again on the Tirschtiegel switch position, which, following a chain of lakes, was about fifty miles east of Kuestrin on the north, and at its south end tied in on the Oder above Glogau.

The rivers and lakes, though plentiful in the army group zone, afforded no defensive advantages. Nearly all were frozen solid enough to carry heavy tanks. To defend the 160-mile line north of the Netze and the Tirschtiegel switch position Himmler had, on 27 January, two improvised SS corps headquarters, one provisional corps headquarters, three divisions (one of them a newly formed Latvian SS division), and assorted odds and ends, Ninth Army remnants, Volkssturm, and whatever else could be scraped up locally or behind the Oder. Off the front, two divisions were encircled in the fortress Thorn (Torun) and an equally strong force was encircled in Poznan. Headquarters, Ninth Army, brought with it one corps headquarters and little more than the staffs of three divisions. XXIV Panzer Corps and Panzer Corps Grossdeutschland, still fighting their way out, had gone under Army Group Center.

THE THAW

Reinforcements were starting to flow east: Gneisenau battle groups set up by the Replacement Army and battalions composed of the personnel of training centers, NCO, and weapons schools. Hitler had refused Guderian's repeated requests to evacuate Army Group North (Courland), but on 17 January he had ordered out of Courland a panzer division and 2 infantry divisions and, five days later, an SS Corps headquarters and 2 SS divisions. The corps headquarters and the 5 divisions were to go to Army Group Vistula. By 25 January one of the divisions had reached Gdynia. On the 22d Hitler had ordered the Western Theater to give up Sixth SS Panzer Army and an additional panzer corps: all together 6 panzer divisions, a volks-grenadier division, 2 brigades, and several volks artillery corps. He still intended, however, to send the stronger part of those forces, the I and II SS Panzer Corps, to Army Group South.

By 27 January four of Fourth Ukrainian Front's armies had closed in on and almost encircled the Upper Silesian industrial area. Third Guards Tank Army, bearing down from the northwest, deliberately left the southern end of the pocket open to let the Germans escape and thus avoid a last-ditch battle that would have destroyed the mines and factories. Between the 28th and the 30th Seventeenth Army retreated out of the pocket. Because of his known ruthlessness, Schoerner could sometimes order retreats that Hitler would have forbidden to any other general. In the meantime, Ameegruppe Heinrici had begun withdrawing in Czechoslovakia to behind the High Tatra.

On 27 and 28 January a blizzard blew across central Europe piling deep snowdrifts on the roads in the Army Groups Vistula and Center zones. Then, at the turn of the month, the temperature rose rapidly; the snow melted; and the ground, a few days before frozen rock hard, began to thaw. On 1 February Himmler wrote to Guderian, "In the present stage of the war the thawing weather is for us a gift of fate. God has not forgotten the courageous German people." The

Germans, he went on, were fighting in their own country (he added, "unfortunately") where they had good road and railroad networks; the Russians were having to bring their supplies forward long distances either by truck, over much poorer roads, or by air. The warm weather, he thought, would give the Germans a chance to bring in and deploy their reinforcements, would slow the Soviet tanks, make them more vulnerable, and might even afford opportunities to "retake pieces of precious German ground."

The thaw, coming when it did, was in fact something of a gift of fate. Zhukov was beginning to worry about his lengthening north flank (the old Soviet flank sensitivity); his troops had, moreover, covered more than 250 miles without a pause. Konev's right flank had gone nearly as far. On the Oder Schoerner was hammering together something like a front. The thrust toward Berlin between the Oder and the Army Group Vistula front in Pomerania was becoming too narrow for the Soviet taste. On 4 February, in a teletype message to Hitler, Schoerner wrote, "My Fuehrer: I can report that the first onslaught of the great Russian offensive against Army Group Center has been substantially intercepted. The front is still under pressure in many places, but in others we are making local counterattacks."61 By then a semicoherent front was also beginning to take shape in the Army Group Vistula zone.

After putting in most of its second echelon and reserves on the north flank, First Belorussian Front had reached the Oder north of Kuestrin on 31 January. By 3 February it had closed to the Oder from Zehden south to its left boundary, but then it stopped. At Kuestrin and Frankfurt the Russians were forty miles from Berlin. The Germans held bridgeheads at both places, and the Russians had bridgeheads north of Kuestrin and south of Frankfurt.

EAST PRUSSIA

At the beginning of December 1944 Army Group Center had 33 infantry divisions and 12 panzer or panzer grenadier divisions. Of the latter 3 were in the front, 9 in reserve. The army group held a 360-mile front, roughly ten miles of frontage per division, about as good a ratio as the Germans were accustomed to at that stage of the war. To the rear, in East Prussia, it had an extensive system of field fortifications and on the border of East Prussia and around Koenigsberg some concrete emplacements; the latter had been built before the war and would have been more valuable if in the meantime the guns and barbed wire had not been removed and installed elsewhere, in the Atlantic Wall, for instance.

In early December Army Group Center could have faced an attack with confidence; by the turn of the year it no longer could; in the interval it had lost 5 panzer divisions and 2 cavalry brigades by transfers. On 4 January Reinhardt estimated that the Russians had 5 armies on the Narew and an equally strong group of 50-60 divisions south of the Neman in the Goldap-Schillfelde area. Since he was on notice to give up another panzer division (ordered a few days later), he concluded, with obvious irony, that the OKH considered East Prussia less important than other areas and was willing to risk a large loss of territory there. He asked for a directive telling him what part of East Prussia had to be held so that he could deploy the reserves he still had. He did not get an answer.

ARMY GROUP CENTER ISOLATED

On 12 January, in an attempt to mislead the Germans and tie down their reserves, the Russians attacked Fourth Army north and south of the Romintener Heide. The next day, opening the offensive in earnest, Third Belorussian Front hit Third Panzer Army at Stallupoenen and Pil'kallen. On the 14th Second Belorussian Front attacked Second Army out of the Serock and Rozan bridgeheads. Both armies held up well in the first two days, went into the main battle line, and patched the holes. Fog prevented the Russians from bringing their air power and armor into play. Unfortunately for the army group, this momentary success—especially by comparison with what Army Group A was experiencing, looked almost like a defensive victory. On the 14th, when Guderian reported to Hitler that apparently Army Group Center could prevent an operational breakthrough on the Narew and into East Prussia, Hitler ordered Panzer Corps Grossdeutschland and its two panzer divisions transferred to Army Group A.

On 15 January Second Army was pushed back to the first switch position. In the north the weather was clearing, and during the day heavy air and tank attacks forced Third Panzer Army to start drawing in the front south of Pil'kallen to prevent its breaking apart. The next day the weather cleared in the Second Army sector, and a tank spearhead broke through past Nowo Miasto. Second Belorussian Front's main force, five armies, one of them a tank army, plus a tank corps, a mechanized corps, and a cavalry corps, was beginning to move out of the Rozan bridgehead. From Nowo Miasto it aimed northeastward toward the mouth of the Vistula. The two armies and a tank corps, pushing out of the Serock bridgehead to provide cover on the left in the direction of Bielsk and Bromberg, would have no trouble; the Army Group A flank south of the Vistula had broken away. Third Belorussian Front, having failed to break through on a broad front, began shifting its weight north to the Pil'kallen area. For Army Group Center the obvious next move was to start pulling back the still untouched Fourth Army so as to get divisions to close the breakthrough against Second Army and prevent, if it could, the envelopment of its right flank. Reinhardt proposed this on the 16th.

By the 17th Second Army was clearly strained to the limit. After Guderian told him that afternoon that Hitler refused to let Fourth Army withdraw, Reinhardt called Hitler and was treated to the Fuehrer's standard lecture on the futility of voluntary withdrawals. The most Hitler would agree to was taking two divisions from Fourth Army by thinning its front.

On 18 January Second Army's front snapped, opening a gap on both sides of Mlawa. Reinhardt put in a panzer corps headquarters and the entire army group reserve, seven divisions, but knew they were not likely to be enough. The next day the leading Soviet tanks stood south of Gilgenburg; Fifth Guards Tank Army was ready for the dash to the coast. On that day, too, Third Panzer Army's front broke open north of the Pregel River.

The 20th was a relatively quiet day; Rokossovskiy and Chernyakovskiy were getting ready to shift into high gear. Hitler again refused to let Fourth Army move. He promised a panzer division from Army Group North and twenty naval replacement battalions from Denmark.

The offensive picked up speed on 21 January. Against Second Army, Second Belorussian Front went as far as Deutsch Eylau and turned a force north toward Allenstein. Third Belorussian Front took Gumbinnen, removing that obstacle on the route to Koenigsberg along the Pregel. The thrust to the coast to cut off the army group was developing; Second Army reported that it might delay but could not prevent it. More alarming, the attacks south of the Pregel and toward Allenstein seemed to presage an attempt to force the whole army group away from the coast and into an encirclement in the interior of East Prussia. Fourth Army was already lying in the bottom of a lopsided sack 130 miles from the coast.

After Reinhardt reported that all the lower commands were pressing for relief and that a complete loss of confidence in the higher leadership was impending, Hitler finally agreed to let Fourth Army withdraw to the eastern edge of the Masurian Lakes. This was something, but far from enough. Reinhardt noted in his diary that in the long run the army group would have to take everything back to the Heilsberg triangle, the line of fortifications built in the 1920's when all the 100,000-man Reichswehr expected to be able to defend in the event of war was Koenigsberg and a foothold in East Prussia. For ten years no one had imagined that relic of German weakness would ever again figure in a military plan.

By nightfall on 23 January Second Belorussian Front had cut all the roads and railroads crossing the Vistula except the coast road through Elbing. After dark, Fifth Guards Army's lead tank detachment approached the city. Finding that it had not been alerted—the streetcars were running and on one street German soldiers from a local armored school were marching in formation—the Russian crews turned on the headlights of their tanks and rolled through the main streets firing as they went. By daylight, when the next wave of Soviet tanks arrived, the Germans in Elbing had recovered enough to fight them off and force them to detour east around the city. In the meantime, however, the Russian lead detachment reached the coast, and Army Group Center was isolated.

Reinhardt reported that he would put all the troops he could muster into counterattacks from east and west to restore contact. Hitler, anticipating withdrawals elsewhere to get the troops, countered with an order forbidding Reinhardt to take Fourth Army farther west than Loetzen and Ortelsburg. As reinforcements, he offered instead the two divisions at Memel, which he had insisted until then on holding as "a springboard to Army Group North." The divisions would have to be brought south by small boats or over the Kurische Nehrung, the narrow, 60-mile-long tongue of sand hills spanning the Bay of Courland.

For nine days Third Panzer Army had managed to preserve a front of sorts by retreating gradually toward Koenigsberg; but on 24 January the Russians broke through south of the Pregel and threatened to cut off Koenigsberg on the south. The army group command was trapped between reality and Hitler's illusions. Reinhardt knew he could not hold Koenigsberg and the Samland Peninsula, let the Fourth Army front continue to bulge eastward to the Masurian Lakes, and still counterattack to the west. But he could not bring himself to confront Hitler with those issues and he went so far as to transfer to Third Panzer Army two divisions Fourth Army had taken out for the counterattack. When Fourth Army evacuated the outer defenses of Loetzen without permission during the day on the 24th, Reinhardt said nothing; he knew the army would have to go back farther, much farther; but he also accepted without protest Hitler's angry demand for a full-scale investigation.

TREASON?

On the afternoon of the 24th the Commanding General, Fourth Army, General der Infanterie Friedrich Hossbach, acting independently, called in three of his corps commanders. He told them that the army's land communications with Germany were cut and no relief could be expected, therefore, he had decided to break out to the west. The breakout and retreat would begin on the night of the 26th, or on the next day. He intended to put the whole army into it and to give up East Prussia. The civilians would have to stay behind. That sounded horrible, he said, but it could not be changed; the paramount objective had to be to get the army back to Germany proper with its combat potential intact. He did not mention Third Panzer Army. Probably he assumed that this army would have to make its own choice whether to go or to stay when the time came. On the necessity for an attack to the west he and Reinhardt agreed in general terms, and the withdrawal east of Loetzen had showed that Reinhardt was not determined to hold on the east. Hossbach apparently concluded that it was not worthwhile to tell him more.

On the 25th Chernyakovskiy's troops got to within twelve miles of Koenigsberg on the southeast. They seemed again to be intent on pinching off the neck of the sack. Fourth Army's east front was ninety miles from the coast; on the coast the Fourth and Third Panzer Armies' fronts, back to back, were less than forty miles apart. That night Reinhardt, who had been wounded in an air raid during the day, tried to persuade Guderian that the time had come to reduce the bulge. Guderian insisted that the front stay where it was; he refused to hear of any further withdrawals. During the day the army group had been renamed Army Group North and Second Army had been transferred to Army Group Vistula.

Fifth Guards Tank Army had a solid hold on Baltic coast northeast of Elbing by 26 January. On its right Fourth Army deployed divisions for the breakout. The movement west weakened the army's southeast and northeast fronts; Loetzen was lost, and the Russians, crossing the frozen lakes, punched numerous holes in the front. Before noon the army group reported that it was about to order Fourth Army to withdraw thirty miles to the line Wartenburg-Bischofsburg-Schippenbeil-Friedland. Talking to Hitler, Reinhardt added that he intended, further, to break out to the west and take the front into the Heilsberg triangle. Hitler replied that he would give a decision later and hung up.

Realizing that he was being presented with a fait accompli, Hitler fell into a rage. He told Guderian what Reinhardt projected, diametrically opposed his, Hitler's, basic plan and was treason. He demanded that Reinhardt and Hossbach be relieved immediately. To the army group he sent an order forbidding any withdrawal beyond the line Wartenburg-Nikolaiken—which would only have cut a narrow slice off the southeastern tip of the bulge. Thereafter communications with the OKH suddenly ceased; no one with any authority would talk to the army group. Finally, at 1915, Reinhardt decided on his own responsibility to let Fourth Army withdraw to the line he had originally proposed. He tried to sweeten the dose by reporting that the army group would try to get a solid front "at the latest" in the line Wartenburg-Bischofsburg-Schippenbeil-Friedland. Two hours later a telegram came through relieving him and his chief of staff.

Before noon the next day Rendulic was in command. He had orders from Hitler to hold Koenigsberg and what was left of East Prussia. The counterattack to the west had begun during the night, although by then it was wasted effort. Only the breakout and retreat that Hossbach had planned could have succeeded, and with Rendulic in command and Hitler alerted that was impossible.

At the end of the month, General der Infanterie Friedrich Mueller, who had made a reputation as an improvisor during the retreat from Greece, replaced Hossbach. The withdrawal Reinhardt had ordered before he was dismissed took some of the pressure off Fourth Army's east front, but on the north Bagramyan's First Baltic Front had added its weight to the advance on Koenigsberg and had pushed Third Panzer Army onto the Samland Peninsula. On the south Fourth Army held open a narrow corridor into Koenigsberg. The greatest danger was that the Russians in Samland might go the remaining fifteen or so miles to Pillau on the Frische Nehrung and cut the army group's sea supply line. (From Pillau trucks could cross the frozen bay to Heiligenbeil.)

On 1 February Fourth Army made a last attempt to break through to Elbing. It ran into a strong counterattack and was stopped dead.

During the succeeding days the flood of civilian refugees out of East Prussia reached its peak. Some were taken out by boat, most walked to Danzig across the Frische Nehrung and the Vistula delta. By mid-February 1,300,000 of the 2,300,000 total population were evacuated; of those who stayed about half were Volkssturm and others absorbed into the Wehrmacht.

Rendulic, in the few months left in the war, was setting out to carve for himself a niche in history next to Schoerner. One characteristic remarked on by all of his former superiors had been his absolute nervelessness. For him, keeping the army group in East Prussia raised no questions other than how it could best be accomplished. In one order he made the battalion and regimental commanders responsible for every "foot of ground" voluntarily given up and appended the example of a captain he had ordered shot the day before for taking his battalion back a mile after it had been broken through. In another, he ordered "flying courts-martial" created to scour the rear areas. Every soldier not wounded, picked up outside his unit area, was to be tried and shot on the spot.

THE BUDAPEST RELIEF

While Soviet armies marched on Germany north of the Carpathians, a tragic drama played to a gruesome finish on the Danube at Budapest. In sheer horror nothing since Stalingrad compared with the Budapest siege. Almost the entire population, normally over a million, was trapped in the city without the barest provision for subsistence or health, driven to the cellars by air and artillery bombardments. In most quarters, the electricity, gas, and water services failed in the first days. The garrison had less than the fragmentary supply and medical services that had remained with Sixth Army at Stalingrad. Faulty staff work in the IX SS Mountain Corps headquarters had lost most of its supply stockpile, including 450 tons of ammunition and 300,000 rations, to the Russians the day the pocket closed. On 31 December Army Group South sent a river boat loaded with 400 tons of supplies down the Danube; it ran aground upstream from the city. The air supply was an old story: winter weather, gasoline shortages, and lack of airstrips in the pocket reduced the flow to a mere trickle.

Consequently, the foreseeable margin of time for the relief operation was very narrow, so narrow that the army group immediately began to consider a breakout and evacuation. The apparent pressure of time also strongly influenced the army group's choice of its approach route. (Map 38) From the front southeast of Komarno the distance to Budapest was about thirty miles, about half of it through the Vertes Mountains. Northeast of Szekesfehervar, though the distance was ten miles greater, the terrain was good for tanks; but the assembly would have taken five days longer and would have required more gasoline. Against strong doubts, the savings in time and gasoline prevailed, and

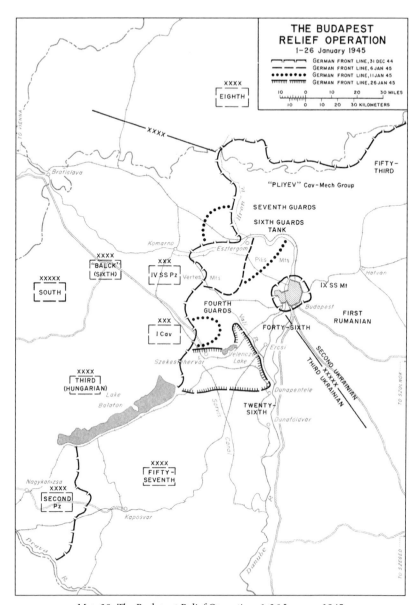

Map 38: *The Budapest Relief Operation, 1-26 January 1945*

at the end of December the army group and the OKH agreed on the approach from Komarno. The OKH directive contemplated a breakout "in the most extreme case" but reserved the decision to Hitler.

The operation began on New Year's Day. During the night an infantry division crossed the ice-choked Danube five miles west of

Esztergom and, striking behind the Russians south of the river, gave IV SS Panzer Corps a quick start along the Komarno-Budapest road. In the mountains a start was not enough. On the second day, the prospects several times appeared good, but the Russians always had just enough infantry and antitank guns to keep IV SS Panzer Corps from shaking itself loose. In another twenty-four hours the Russians had the defense tightly in hand, and by the time Guderian arrived at the Army Group South headquarters, on 5 January, Sixth Guards Tank Army was ready to counter north of the Danube with an advance across the Hron River toward Komarno.

Guderian, nevertheless, brought with him a set of objectives that raised the relief operation, so far not glowingly successful, to the status of a major offensive, The army group was first to retake Budapest and the line Lake Balaton-Velencze Lake-Ercsi and then turn south to destroy the enemy west of the Danube. On 6 January, the day Guderian left, IV SS Panzer Corps came up against a solid front; the offensive had run tight. During the day, too, the Sixth Guards Tank and Seventh Guards Armies attacked, gaining better than eight miles, and threatened the IV Panzer Corps rear from north of the Danube.

On 7 January, in an attempt to catch the Russians off guard, I Cavalry Corps broke into their line northwest of Szekesfehervar. The momentary surprise was not enough; Fourth Guards Army reacted fast and before nightfall was contesting every yard of ground. The day was a dark one for the army group. Both of its attacks were stalled.

In the meantime, at Budapest in the week since New Year's, the Russians had smashed the old bridgehead front around Pest, the half of the city east of the Danube. In the ensuing house-to-house battle, the wounded could not be cared for, the fires put out, or the dead buried. Describing the scene, a German war correspondent wrote, "A nauseating stench of decaying corpses is carried with a rain of sparks over the ruins."79 In numerous places where they had driven deep into the city, the Russians mounted loudspeakers that they used, whenever the noise of battle subsided, to announce where the next artillery salvos or aerial bombs would fall or to call on the Germans and Hungarians to surrender while they still could.

On the 7th, the Budapest garrison appeared to be rapidly approaching the end of its strength. Driving snow and low-hanging clouds kept the supply planes grounded; artillery and small arms ammunition were running short; the city population was hostile; and the Hungarians were deserting. Balck believed the order to break out would have to be given within twenty-four hours. Woehler decided to take his chances north of the Danube, let the IV SS Panzer Corps and I Cavalry Corps operations go on for another day, and try a quick infantry thrust through the Pilis Mountains, off the IV SS Panzer Corps north flank, that might at least give the breakout a better prospect of success.

The next day Hitler refused to approve a breakout. This left the army group no choice but to keep on trying to punch through the front. Woehler then began to prepare what he called "a hussars' ride," a fast thrust through to Budapest by a motorized battalion. It might, for a few hours, open a corridor through which supplies could be sent into the city or through which the garrison could escape if Hitler changed his mind.

For the army group, getting a relief column through to Budapest was the first objective; Hitler's primary, perhaps only, concern was to get the front out to the Danube. On the 9th he talked about shifting IV SS Panzer Corps south for a try between Lake Balaton and Velencze Lake. The next day, a counterattack north of the river eliminated the threat to Komarno, but the "hussars' ride" failed. On the 11th Hitler awarded SS-Oberstgruppenfuehrer Pfeffer-Wildenbruch the Knight's Cross of the Iron Cross and renewed the order to hold Budapest. The next morning he ordered the army group to shift IV SS Panzer Corps south.

In five days, over mountain roads and through snowdrifts, IV SS Panzer Corps marched seventy miles to the northern tip of Lake Balaton. On 18 January it jumped off east, and by nightfall the next day it had covered the forty miles to the Danube at Dunapentele. The Germans appeared to have recovered their touch, and the IV SS Panzer Corps staff predicted a fast push to Budapest even though Third Ukrainian Front had put in a tank corps and had two guards mechanized corps still uncommitted.

Elsewhere, the day's developments were less encouraging. North of the Danube the last elements of two panzer divisions being transferred to Army Group A departed, leaving the front east of Komarno to be held by one infantry division. In the Budapest pocket, during the night and early morning hours, Pfeffer-Wildenbruch had evacuated Pest, a move that was long overdue but for which he had received Hitler's permission only the day before. In crossing the bridges, which were raked the whole time by Soviet fire, the troops from Pest took heavy losses. Nevertheless, the bridges stayed jammed with humanity—men, women, and children, young and old, wounded who could barely walk, and vehicles of all descriptions from trucks to baby carriages— until, shortly before daylight, the charges were set off that destroyed the elegant spans that had been the pride of Budapest.

For the next three days the Russians fought hard to hold a front flanking Velencze Lake on both sides. The German panzer divisions chewed their way through, taking Szekesfehervar and reaching the Vali River on 22 January, but by then they had lost most of their initial momentum. In the meantime Woehler and Balck had become uncomfortably aware that the Headquarters, IV SS Panzer Corps, in spite of its good showing on the 18th, was not competent to command a large-scale offensive. The commanding general, Obergruppenfuehrer (Lt. Gen.) Herbert Gille, was a well-meaning bumbler who spent most of his time at the front. The chief of staff took a lighthearted attitude toward paper work, so lighthearted that on the 22d Balck had to go out himself to find out where the front was. Woehler decided to keep Gille, who was at least something of a morale builder, and get rid of the chief of staff.

On 22 January Guderian urged Woehler to consider whether he could clean out the whole west side of the Danube with his own forces and some help from the Southeastern Theater. The success so far had whetted Hitler's appetite for a victory, and Guderian was obviously worried about having to divert more forces to the south. The question was a very serious one, he said, "a matter of conscience." He did not reveal what he knew by then, namely, that Hitler intended to send Sixth SS Panzer Army's two SS corps into Austria behind Army Group South.

IV SS Panzer Corps wasted the day of the 23d sorting out its units east of Szekesfehervar. The next day it closed to the Vali on a broad front but failed to get across. Woehler proposed that Second Panzer

Army attack toward Kaposvar from south of Lake Balaton to siphon some of the Soviet strength away from IV SS Panzer Corps. The OKH told him not to; Hitler was nervous about the oil fields and was afraid Second Panzer Army would get into trouble.

After a probing attack upstream along the Vali on 25 January failed to create an opening, Woehler reported the next day that a fast breakthrough to Budapest was impossible; the Russians had reinforced every likely point of attack. Guderian then proposed turning IV SS Panzer Corps south to join Second Panzer Army in an offensive between Lake Balaton and the Danube. The army group asked whether, since in that case the advance toward Budapest would be stopped, the order to break out should not be given.

The answer came on the 27th when Hitler in an order of the day again called on IX SS Mountain Corps to hold out until it was relieved. The pocket was then about three miles wide and four miles long. Into it were jammed 34,000 German and Hungarian troops, 10,000 wounded, and 300,000 Hungarian civilians.

On their side, for several days past, the Second and Third Ukrainian Fronts had ominously reshuffled units. Malinovskiy had taken Sixth Guards Tank Army out of the Hron River bridgehead. Its neighbor on the north, the Cavalry-Mechanized Group Pliyev, had been relieved by Bulgarian divisions. German Intelligence had lost track of both the tank army and the cavalry-mechanized group. Northeast of Szekesfehervar and northwest of Dunafoldvar, Tolbukhin had pushed through heavy armored build-ups.

On 27 January a dozen rifle divisions with strong armor behind them hit the southeastern face of the IV SS Panzer Corps salient between Dunapentele and the Sarviz Canal. When Guderian brought in the first reports that afternoon, Hitler ordered the Budapest relief stopped. It no longer made sense, he said. Ignoring Guderian's remarks about the garrison, he asked whether Sixth SS Panzer Army's two corps were moving—snow and gasoline shortages had delayed their getting out of the Ardennes and back to the railheads. Jodl said one corps would reach Vienna in fourteen days, the other four or five days later. Relieved, Hitler remarked, "They will arrive just in time; the next crisis will be down there."

CHAPTER XX

The Defense of the Reich

MISSIONS

GERMAN

For the German people, the first week of February was the darkest of the war. The coming months would bring despair and destruction but not another shock equal to the sudden appearance of the Russians on the Oder River. Three weeks earlier, the front had still been deep in Poland and nowhere on German soil. Now Upper Silesia was lost; in East Prussia a German army group was being cut to pieces; West Prussia and Pomerania were being defended by a skeleton army group under a novice commander; and the defense of the Oder would have to be entrusted to armies that had already been defeated on the Vistula and chased across Poland. If the Russians maintained their rate of advance, and there seemed to be no reason why they could not, they would be on the Rhine in another three weeks.

In the depths of a crisis, Hitler had always found relief and refuge in the untrammeled power of decision and the illusion of being able to determine the outcome. He did so again that first week of February. To Himmler's Army Group Vistula he gave four missions: to establish a solid front on the Oder upstream from Schwedt; to stop the Russians south and west of Stargard and hold a staging area there for an attack into the flank of Second Guards Tank Army, which was leading the advance to the Oder; to keep his front anchored on the Vistula in the east; and, lastly, to prevent the Russians from pushing north into Pomerania and West Prussia. As a postscript Hitler added that after the Elbing road had been cleared Second Army was to "resume" the advance toward Army Group North. In his orders to that army group he did not mention restoring contact with Second Army. He told Rendulic to place his main effort in the north, in the Koenigsberg area, and on the southwest to hold the line Braunsberg-Wormditt and prevent Fourth Army's being pushed away from the coast.

The directive to Army Group Courland, which on 3 February had successfully seen through what was called the Fourth Battle of Courland, instructed it to finish transferring two infantry divisions to Army Group Vistula and one to North (ordered on 1 February) and prepare to take out a fourth division. Generaloberst Heinrich-Gottfried von Vietinghoff genannt Scheel, Rendulic's successor, answered that losing another division gave him "a fright," his front was becoming so thin. On the other hand, he observed, the army group was not tying down an equal proportion of Soviet strength, and he, therefore, did not believe holding Courland served a militarily useful purpose. He hinted that the whole army group ought to be evacuated before, with the advent of spring, the days began to lengthen.

On the southern half of the front, Army Group Center's mission, to try to get a front on the Oder, was obvious without a directive. In the Army Group South zone, even though Hitler ranked the Nagykanizsa oil fields as the strategically most vital area on the whole Eastern Front, it appeared that for the near future, at least, the initiative would have to be surrendered to the Russians. The Budapest relief had failed, and Hitler had no further interest in the garrison except to have it hold out as long as possible. On the night of 5 February he again refused to permit a breakout, claiming that it could not succeed anyway.

The I and II SS Panzer Corps were on the way to Austria, but troop movements by rail across Germany were taking more time than had once been required to reach central U.S.S.R. The Western Theater Command reported that frequently the stations were bombed out before the troops reached them; the trains had to be made up and loaded at night without any lights; the rolling stock was in poor condition; sometimes tanks and trucks broke through the car beds; up to one-third of the cars were unusable. The days when a main line could be cleared for troop trains were past; even the existence of a continuous line of any kind to the destination could not be guaranteed from hour to hour.

On 6 February, Hitler ordered Woehler to station four of the SS divisions near Györ and the fifth behind Nagykanizsa. Their presence was to be kept secret, and they would stay under the control of the OKH., The Russians, Hitler predicted, were ready to strike toward Vienna. The mission of the army group was to hold Nagykanizsa, Szekesfehervar, and Komarno and prevent the breakthrough to Vienna.

SOVIET

In three weeks the Soviet Army had accomplished its most spectacular victory of the war. Stalin could go to Yalta with Poland in his pocket. While his armies stood scarcely more than a day's march away from the German capital, the Allied armies on the west were still fighting to retake ground they had lost during the Ardennes offensive. On 26 January, Zhukov reported that, if he were allowed four days to bring up fresh troops, supplies, and some new equipment, he could be ready by 1 or 2 February to attack toward Berlin. Konev stated that he could be ready two or three days later to carry the offensive across the Oder in his sector.

The offensive had run thus far without a hitch. The Soviet armor and other mechanical equipment, no doubt, needed to be replenished and repaired. The infantry, on the other hand, particularly that of Zhukov's and Konev's fronts, had engaged in comparatively little heavy fighting. Soviet casualties in January, the Germans calculated, were close to 20 percent less than the average monthly losses during the four months' 1944 summer offensive. Because of the relatively light Soviet casualties and the splitting off of additional German forces, the offensive, German Intelligence concluded, "Has imposed an enormously greater strain on our own strength than it has on that of the enemy."10 The January thaw, which a former Soviet correspondent remembers as "Bringing out the snowdrops and purple crocuses in neglected gardens," was the most untoward occurrence of the offensive thus far. The ice breaking up in the Oder made the river more of an obstacle than it might otherwise have been, and the mud slowed the Soviet tanks and possibly increased the effectiveness of Hitler's bicycle-mounted Panzerjaeger against them, but those were petty annoyances.

In response to Zhukov's proposal to strike toward Berlin in the first days of February, Stalin raised only one objection. He told Zhukov that he was worried about the thinly held 90-mile sector between the First Belorussian and Second Belorussian Fronts' flanks and instructed him to wait until Rokossovskiy had come farther west. He thought that would take ten days or two weeks. The Stavka then ordered Zhukov to shift his front's weight west as Rokossovkiy advanced and to concentrate on expanding the bridgeheads flanking Kuestrin.

Meanwhile, the other fronts were to keep moving. The Stavka transferred Rokossovskiy's three right flank armies to Third Belorussian Front, thereby relieving him of any concern with the cleaning out of East Prussia, and directed him to use his remaining armies plus an army from the reserve to occupy West Prussia and Pomerania from Danzig to Stettin. Konev, under orders to push toward Dresden, in seven days shifted three armies, including Third Guards Tank Army, from Upper Silesia to the Steinau bridgehead north of Breslau.

THE SOVIET OFFENSIVE FALTERS

KONEV STOPS ON THE NEISSE

On 8 February First Ukrainian Front attacked out of the Steinau bridgehead between Glogau and Breslau with five armies, two of them tank armies. (Map 39) German Intelligence had detected the shift from Upper Silesia early, and the OKH had put three divisions, two of them still rebuilding, at Schoerner's disposal. Schoerner also had to worry about the Brieg-Ohlau bridgehead south of Breslau, where two armies and two tank corps had for several days been threatening to break away and cut the army group's lateral communications lines forward of the Sudeten. He had relocated the Fourth Panzer-Seventeenth Army boundary to give the former responsibility for the Steinau bridgehead and the latter for the Brieg-Ohlau bridgehead.

On the first day, the 8th, Third Guards Tank Army battered its way out of the southern end of the Steinau bridgehead and the adjoining small Leubus bridgehead. By nightfall it reached the outskirts of Liegnitz and began turning elements southwest behind Breslau. On the 10th the army went past Liegnitz to the Bober River below Bunzlau. To the north Fourth Tank Army overran Panzer Corps Grossdeutschland

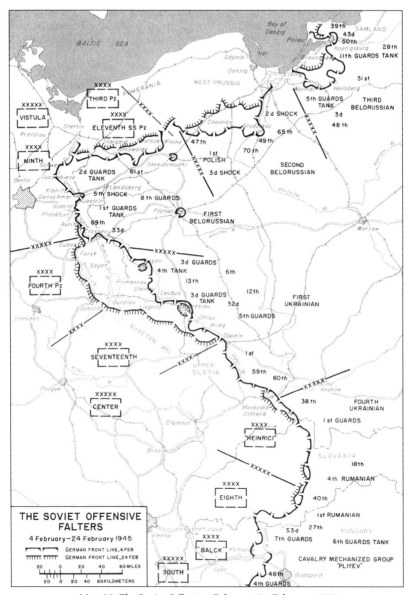

Map 39: The Soviet Offensive Falters, 4-24 February 1945

and took Primkenau, seven miles east of the Bober. To frustrate Fourth Panzer and Seventeenth Armies' attempts to prevent the thrusts out of the bridgeheads from meeting behind Breslau, Konev then resorted to the maneuver he had employed east of the Oder in January. He turned Third Guards Tank Army south and in three days' heavy fighting encircled Breslau; 35,000 troops and 116,000 civilians stayed in the city. The main thrust continued west to and across the Queiss River and northwest across the lower Bober north of Sagan. The fortress Glogau (4,100 soldiers and 7,800 civilians) was encircled.

Relieved temporarily by Third Guards Tank Army's turning south, Fourth Panzer Army, on 14 and 15 February, counterattacked along the Bober north of Sagan, cutting behind Fourth Tank Army, which was driving toward the Neisse. By the 16th Third Guards Tank Army had turned west again and was ready to strike across the Queiss toward Goerlitz. Schoerner threw one panzer division into a flank attack from the south, but that could not even slow the tank army. By the 18th Fourth Tank Army had cleared its lines to the rear, and in the next three days five Soviet armies closed to the Neisse from its confluence with the Oder to five miles north of Goerlitz; from there the front angled east and slightly south in an almost straight line to the Oder at Oppeln.

On 21 February the OKH advised Army Groups Vistula and Center that the Soviet main effort would be on the Oder-Neisse line between Schwedt (on the right flank of Army Group Vistula's Oder front) and Goerlitz; the expected thrusts toward Berlin and Dresden would probably be accompanied by secondary offensives into Pomerania and toward Moravska Ostrava. Five days earlier the Eastern Intelligence Branch, OKH, had concluded that because of the progress of operations in Lower Silesia and Pomerania the Stavka had decided it did not need to worry about the flanks any longer and could go ahead with the offensive into central Germany.

Agent reports on 15 February indicated that First Belorussian Front was drawing infantry off the front in Pomerania to relieve the First and Second Guards Tank Armies along the Oder. By the 17th the two tank armies were out of the Oder front and appeared to be regrouping in the rear for an attack west. Along the river, agents and air reconnaissance were picking up numerous other clues to an offensive in the making: heavy artillery and antiaircraft batteries were moving up, mine fields were being cleared, changes were being made in radio traffic patterns, and new tanks and trucks were being brought in.

In the Army Group Center zone Third Guards Tank Army's fast about-face west of Breslau showed it was obviously in a hurry to get to the Neisse. Air reconnaissance disclosed that the Polish railroads had been relaid to east of Poznan (the Poznan fortress held out until 23 February) and east of Breslau. In Lower Silesia the Soviet engineers were rushing to build bridges on the recently crossed rivers, an indication that the First Ukrainian Front planned to keep the offensive rolling. From one of the Soviet tank corps the Germans captured maps covering the area between the Elbe and the Neisse.

Crossing the Neisse against the six divisions Fourth Panzer Army had on the river should not have been difficult; nevertheless, on 21 February Konev called a halt. Perhaps the offensive had not gone as well as he had expected. The Germans two or three times had created at least inconvenient situations, and the tank armies had not achieved a full-scale operational breakthrough.

Most likely, however, the decision to stop First Ukrainian Front on the Neisse was part of a fundamental revision of Soviet strategy brought on by developments of which the operation in Lower Silesia was only a part.

THE ODER, WEST PRUSSIA, AND EAST PRUSSIA

While the First Ukrainian Front was engaged between the Oder and the Neisse, the First and Second Belorussian Fronts had been grappling for elbow room against Army Group Vistula. Zhukov had used the infantry armies on his right flank to clean out the pockets at Arnswalde, Schneidemuehl, and Deutsch-Krone and had ordered his first echelon to enlarge the Oder bridgeheads.[41] With four untested, incomplete divisions—Doeberitz, Kurmark, Gross-Berlin, and 30 Januar—and two panzer divisions from the Western Theater, Ninth Army had put up a stiff fight on the river.

In the first week of the month the Russians had joined the three small bridgeheads at Guestebiese, Kienitz, and Genschmar north of Kuestrin, expanded the Aurith bridgehead south of Frankfurt, and

---

41. Himmler, not always so perceptive in military matters, had quickly appreciated the disadvantages in establishing his headquarters at Deutsch-Krone and had moved behind the Oder to an alternate SS command post in the woods south of Prenzlau. There, with the river between him and the Russians and with a full retinue, including masseur and private physician, he could hold court in the style befitting the Reichsfuehrer-SS, keep in touch with affairs in Berlin, forty-five miles away by autobahn, and still be at least a part-time army group commander.

taken a new one at Goeritz in which they pushed far enough north and west to cut off the Kuestrin fortress. But on 9 February a Ninth Army counterattack had reopened a corridor to Kuestrin. Even though the army was nowhere near strong enough to execute the order Hitler had issued the next day, to "smash" all the Oder bridgeheads within forty-eight hours, it had held its ground, in places gained a little, and might have done better had it not had to transfer a panzer division to Army Group Center.

On 10 February Second Belorussian Front had attacked west of Grudziadz. In the West Prussian woods and swamps the thaw had made the going rough, and Second Army had fought hard to stave off the fate that had befallen its neighbors to the east. Advancing slowly, the Russians had reached Choinice on the 14th. A breakthrough there would have cut off Second Army in West Prussia; the army's center now dipped southeast of Grudziadz. When Weiss asked permission to evacuate Grudziadz, contending that he could either keep the contact on his right or defend West Prussia and the ports, Danzig and Gdynia, but not do both, Himmler had answered that Second Army had three missions: keep a secure contact on its right, protect the ports, and hold Grudziaz. In the latter instance it was to follow the "great example" of Courbière. Examples from the Seven Years' War and the Napoleonic Wars had recently become popular in Hitler's circle, and, unfortunately for many a German soldier, it seemed that nearly every old Prussian city had successfully withstood a siege in one war or the other. On the 15th Second Belorussian Front had pushed north and east between Choinice and Grudziadz; but after gaining another five or so miles on the west and twenty on the east without achieving a breakthrough, Rokossovskiy had stopped the offensive on 19 February.

In East Prussia, by 13 February, Third Belorussian Front had pushed Fourth Army out of the Heilsberg triangle. First Baltic Front had forced the remnants of Third Panzer Army, renamed Armeeabteilung Samland, back to the tip of the Samland Peninsula. Together, the two fronts had isolated Koenigsberg. In another week, Third Belorussian Front had confined Fourth Army to a 35- by 15-mile beachhead around Heiligenbeil. In the fighting the front commander, Chernyakovskiy, was killed and Vasilevskiy took command. Though the German position was hopeless, that of the Russians was at least frustrating. Heavy snowfalls early in the month followed by a sudden thaw had snarled Soviet supply movements and interfered with air operations. First Baltic Front, short on equipment and ammunition from the start, did not have first class troops or leadership. The presence of two major commands operating against three separate groups in a small area induced on the Soviet side something like a musclebound condition.

Toward the end of the third week in the month, the Stavka, after some urging, got Bagramyan to disregard Koenigsberg for the time being and concentrate his forces against the Germans on Samland while Vasilevskiy did the same against the Heiligenbeil pocket. But on the 20th, two days before Bagramyan's push was to begin, Armeeabteilung Samland launched a spoiling attack that caught the Russians off guard and carried all the way to Koenigsberg. The end of the battle for East Prussia, to the Russians the "cradle of German militarism," was not yet in sight. The Stavka abolished First Baltic Front, joined its units to Third Belorussian Front as the Samland Group, and gave Vasilevskiy a month to reorganize and clean out the German pockets.

By the end of the third week in February the great Soviet 1945 winter offensive had come to a dead halt. Caution was in the air. Obviously, the Stavka had decided that the time to deliver the death blow was not yet. The Stavka's decision coincided exactly with two incidents: one took place at Stargard in Pomerania, the other on the Hron River in Hungary.

OPERATION SONNENWENDE

The Stargard offensive ranks as one of the war's closest approaches to a planned fiasco. The idea of a two-pronged counterattack east of the Oder to pinch off the tip of the Soviet spearhead aimed at Berlin was Guderian's. It was an attractive variant of Hitler's pet formula for stopping breakthroughs—hold the corner posts and counterattack on the flanks. But, to evade the compelling logic of Guderian's argument that Sixth SS Panzer Army should be one of the attack groups, Hitler opted for a single-pronged offensive out of the Stargard area.[42]

42. In the first week of February part of Headquarters, Sixth SS Panzer Army, moved in briefly behind Ninth Army; and the commanding general, Oberstgruppenfuehrer (General) Josef (Sepp) Dietrich, submitted a rough plan for an attack from the Guben-Crossen area to meet the

Having lost the southern half of his offensive, Guderian became all the more determined to see through the half that was left. He demanded breadth (three attack groups on a 30-mile front), depth, and speed. Above all, speed. The offensive, he insisted, had to be readied and executed "like lightning" before the Russians could get a firm hold on the Oder. Himmler, at first, when all he saw was the chance for a brilliant victory, was enthusiastic.

In what, for the time, was itself a remarkable feat, the OKH scraped together two corps headquarters and ten divisions, seven of them panzer divisions, for the Stargard offensive. To bring together quickly a force that size over railroads operating, when they ran at all, at about 40 percent of normal efficiency because the engines were burning lignite, and to outfit and supply it in the face of catastrophic equipment, ammunition, and gasoline shortages was all but impossible. By 10 February, the eighth day of the assembly, of the trains loaded less than half had arrived.

Headquarters, Third Panzer Army, was ordered out of Samland to take command, but because it arrived late the command stayed in the hands of the newly created Headquarters, Eleventh SS Panzer Army. Under a strict injunction not to commit any of the forces allocated for the offensive prematurely, the army group was hard put to hold the assembly area and finally had to put several of the new divisions into the front anyway. The upshot was that the army group staff and the OKH soon diverged in their thinking as to when the offensive could start.

Talking to Himmler on 9 February, Guderian, in an offhand manner he sometimes affected, remarked, by way of soliciting the actual decision, that he expected the offensive would be in progress by the 16th. Himmler replied that he was not ready to commit himself to a specific date and wanted to await the next several days' developments before making a decision. Unfortunately for Himmler, his patent lack of qualifications as an army group commander left his judgment open to question even when it appeared sound. In Guderian

Stargard force on the Warthe at Landsberg east of Kuestrin. By then his panzer divisions were headed toward Hungary, and an announced "separate order" assigning him divisions from the West was never issued.

Soviet infantrymen approach a disabled German tank.

he met an antagonist whose own judgment was less than impeccable. Guderian apparently convinced himself that Himmler was stalling to conceal his incompetence. The idea was not difficult to come by since Himmler, in moving his headquarters behind the Oder and refusing to show himself anywhere near the front, had revealed a deficiency of combative spirit that contrasted sharply with the martial tone he cultivated in speaking and writing.

On 13 February Guderian arranged a showdown and, in Hitler's presence, demanded that his deputy, General der Panzertruppen Walter Wenck, be given a special mandate to command the Army Group Vistula offensive.[43] At the end Hitler told Wenck that he was to go to Army Group Vistula with a "special mandate," but he did not say what Wenck's authority was. The effect was to take the power of final decision away from Himmler without specifically giving it to Wenck, which probably suited Guderian exactly, since he seems to have been

---

43. Wenck, long-time Sixth Army chief of staff and one of the top-rated General Staff officers, was officially chief of the Command Group *(Fuehrungsgruppe)*, OKH, a post Guderian created after his own appointment as Chief of Staff, OKH.

intent mainly on using Wenck to force his own concepts on the army group.

Wenck, on his arrival at Army Group Vistula, and after paying his respects to Himmler, went across the Oder to Eleventh SS Panzer Army to inspect the preparations in person—a worthwhile undertaking since Himmler had thus far not taken the trouble to do it and the Eleventh SS Panzer Army staff, an upgraded corps staff under SS-Oberstgruppenfuehrer (General) Felix Steiner, fell short of being the ideal instrument for conducting a major offensive. After satisfying himself that the units for the offensive were in fact not fully assembled or equipped, Wenck resorted to the unpromising alternative of starting piecemeal, mostly, it would appear, to satisfy Guderian. On the night of 14 February Eleventh SS Panzer Army reported that on the basis of the total Eastern Front situation, as Wenck described it, the army realized that even a small attack was urgently needed; it intended, therefore, to make a thrust toward Arnswalde (seven miles off the front with a small encircled German garrison) the next morning.

The one-division Arnswalde attack caught the Russians unawares; the division's point reached the town in the early afternoon. It would have taken more self-control than Army Group Vistula and the OKH shared between them to throw away so tempting a start. The army group ordered the whole operation, hopefully code-named SONNENWENDE (Solstice), to begin the next day.

Unready and inexperienced, Eleventh SS Panzer Army wasted the 16th trying to feel out the enemy. It was not until the afternoon of the 16th that the army command was prepared to decide tentatively where to concentrate its effort; by then, even though Steiner insisted he could get rolling within another two days, the offensive was stuck. That night, on the way back from a conference with Hitler, Wenck was severely injured in an automobile accident. That he could have salvaged SONNENWENDE, as Guderian later claimed, is doubtful.

Rain and mud confined the tanks to the roads. Himmler ordered the attack to continue through the night of the 17th, but that did not help. The next day mine fields and strong antitank defenses brought SONNENWENDE to its inglorious conclusion. Eleventh SS Panzer

Army had gained at the most two to three miles by the night of the 18th, when by a "directive for regroupment," Himmler stopped the offensive.

As far as the Germans could tell, the offensive had hardly evoked a ripple behind the Soviet front. Ninth army reported on the 19th that the Oder sector was "conspicuously" quiet; all the signs indicated that First Belorussian Front would attack toward Berlin within the next few days. Ninth Army predicted that, off its right flank, First Ukrainian Front would be crossing the Neisse in a day. On the 21st, in conjunction with the directive issued to Army Groups Vistula and Center on that day, Hitler officially ended SONNENWENDE and ordered Himmler to transfer a corps headquarters and three of the divisions to Army Group Center. Headquarters, Third Panzer Army, took command of the divisions that were left, and Steiner and his staff, currently not in favor with Himmler, moved across the Oder to act as a central collecting agency for stragglers.

Unknown to the Germans SONNENWENDE had achieved an impact on the Soviet side altogether out of proportion to the befuddlement that had surrounded the operation since its inception. A complete failure on the ground, it, nevertheless, hit exactly the most fragile feaure of the Soviet plan, the requirement for a certain amount of daring in the second phase of the offensive. At mid-February, unless the Germans were deliberately deceived, which is unlikely because it would have been pointless, the First Belorussian and First Ukrainian Fronts were fully deployed for the attack toward Berlin. SONNENWENDE, as the Germans observed, did not disturb the deployment; but on 17 February the Stavka suddenly scrapped the whole original plan and ordered Zhukov to turn north and join Rokossovskiy against Army Group Vistula. Four days later Konev stopped on the Neisse.

THE HRON BRIDGEHEAD

Before SONNENWENDE had run its brief and ragged course, Army Group South had begun laying the last small roadblock on the Soviet road to victory. On 10 February Woehler had returned from Berlin with Hitler's permission to use I SS Panzer Corps in a drive against the Hron River bridgehead to deny the Russians that platform for an attack toward Bratislava and Vienna. The chance looked too good to miss; nearly all of the Soviet armor was out of the front, refitting.

Hitler in the meantime had all but forgotten Budapest. The pocket in Buda, encompassing the government buildings and the royal castle and protected on the east by the river, had proved a strong fortress. The populace had become apathetic, and what internal disturbance there was came almost entirely from the armed bands of Arrow-Cross Party members, who shunned combat and devoted themselves to murder and plundering. Troop morale had stayed relatively high as long as the relief appeared to have even the barest chance of succeeding. Rations for the fighting troops had had to be reduced to horse-meat soup and a third of a pound of bread per day. The wounded in the cavernous cellars of the royal castle received only thin soup. On 29 January, the German national holiday celebrating Hitler's accession to power, Himmler had sent what was announced as a special added ration. When the airdrop containers were opened they were found to contain canned horse meat, cookies, and cigarettes.

On 10 February Hitler had conferred the oak leaf cluster to the Knight's Cross of the Iron Cross upon Pfeffer-Wildenbruch. That last-minute gesture to stiffen the morale of the commanding general was, if at all, only relatively more effective than the similar attempt had been in the case of Paulus at Stalingrad. The garrison was down to its last ammunition and rations and split into two pockets, both too small for airdrops. On the morning of the 11th Pfeffer-Wildenbruch had issued orders for a breakout to the west. That night the defenders had attempted to force their way out along the Italian Boulevard (subsequently renamed Malinovskiy Boulevard). The staffs took a roughly parallel route through a subterranean drainage canal. Many were killed coming out of the castle gates, and few had gotten as far as the suburbs. Of close to 30,000 Germans and Hungarians—10,600 wounded were left behind—less than 700 reached the German lines.

The Hron bridgehead offensive began on 17 February and achieved a complete surprise. In a week the Germans pushed the front east to the river. The success was dimmed slightly by a suspicion that the Russians, after being caught off guard initially, had deliberately sacrificed the bridgehead rather than disrupt their armor's refitting. Encouraged, nevertheless, Woehler, on 21 February, revived the planning for a major offensive in the Balaton-Drava-Danube triangle.

Under its original concept of taking some mild risks on the flanks, the Stavka had intended to dispatch Second Ukrainian Front toward Brno and Vienna in the wake of Zhukov's and Konev's main thrusts. On 17 February, the day the Berlin operation was canceled and the day the Germans hit the Hron bridgehead, a new order went out to Timoshenko instructing him to plan and co-ordinate an independent offensive by both of his fronts against the German south flank. For the time being, the Germans having shown some bite, the Russians decided to wait.

THE GERMAN CONDITION

For Germany the blunting of the Soviet winter offensive could be no more than a reprieve. By mid-February the Replacement Army no longer had enough small arms to equip the new divisions. The manufacture of powder had fallen below the level required to maintain ammunition production. Against a monthly demand of 1,500,000 tank and antitank artillery rounds, January output was 367,000. For lack of aviation gasoline, the OKW was forced to order a radical reduction in the combat employment of aircraft; the planes were to be used only at decisive points and then only when nothing else was practicable. On the west the defense of the Rhineland was beginning to crumble.

PARRY AND THRUST—VIENNA

On 22 February Woehler submitted to Hitler four outline plans for an offensive to be executed under the wistful cover name FRUEHLINGSERWACHEN (Awakening of Spring). (Map 40) The objective, ostensibly, was to put a more substantial buffer between the Russians and the Nagykanizsa oil fields. This required a main thrust to the southeast out of the area between Lake Balaton and Velencze Lake, but the Russians were strongest west of Budapest, in the flank and rear of such a thrust. For lack of time and forces, Woehler had to reject at the outset the tactically soundest approach: to clear out the Budapest-Velencze Lake-Vertes Mountains area before striking between Lake

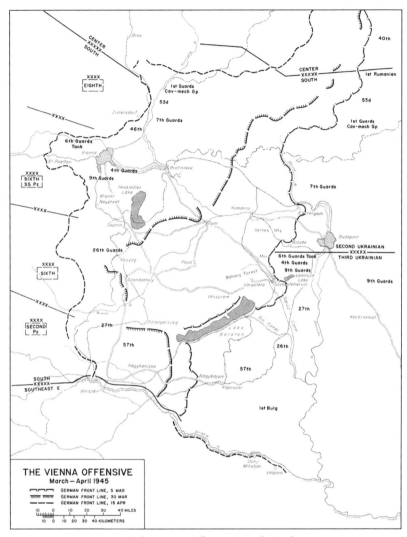

Map 40: The Vienna Offensive, March-April 1945

Balaton and the Danube. He recommended a compromise, a short initial phase that would get a solid front facing north between Velencze Lake and the Danube to be followed by a turn and thrust south. At a conference in Berlin on 25 February Hitler decided to place the main effort from the start into an attack southeast between the Sarviz Canal and the Danube because it promised the best opportunity for a big gain fast.

"THE AWAKENING OF SPRING"

No one—except, possibly, those diligent students of past experience, the Russians—noticed that the stage was set for a second ZITADELLE. Again at the end of a disastrous winter the enemy pressure had suddenly relaxed and Hitler found himself holding an uncommitted reserve. Again Hitler decided to try for a prestige victory. Again the Stavka let him have the next move.

The Germans played out their part with near somnambulistic unconcern. Woehler dutifully called attention to the danger on the north flank and to Sixth SS Panzer Army's weakness in infantry, but no one protested the pointlessness of conducting a major offensive merely to gain ground that most likely could not be defended. The Operations Staff, OKW, questioned whether in view of all the other threats and dangers Sixth SS Panzer Army could justifiably be tied down in Hungary until mid-April or beyond, but followed up with an imprecise proposal for a truncated offensive that would have gained nothing except, perhaps, a slight savings in time; the suggestion was consigned directly to the files.

FRUEHLINGSERWACHEN began at midnight on 5 March when Army Group F troops took bridgeheads on the Drava opposite Donji Miholjac and Valpovo. The next morning Second Panzer Army attacked out of its center toward Kaposvar. Sixth SS Panzer Army, deploying in mud and driving wet snow, had reported it would be ready to start that morning, but as often the case with estimates by SS commands, when morning came only I SS Panzer Corps on the west side of the Sarviz Canal was ready. II SS Panzer Corps, in the crucial sector east of the canal, did not start until the following morning.

The weather was warm; the snow had melted; off the roads the mud was deep; and the roads themselves were mined and swept by Soviet antitank fire. Elaborate security precautions had failed to keep secret the build-up that had taken more than a month.

Except for aircraft, the Stavka had left its own offensive build-up in the Second Ukrainian Front zone intact. Third Ukrainian Front, which it had heavily reinforced with aircraft, artillery, and antitank guns, had built a broad belt of mine and artillery-protected defenses between Lake Balaton and the Danube. In December, when drifting ice endangered boat traffic on the river, Third Ukrainian Front's engineers, using the supports of a destroyed bridge at Baja, had erected a cableway capable of carrying 600 tons every twenty-four hours. After the river froze solid, the engineers had also laid a road and gasoline pipeline over the ice.

On 7 and 8 March I SS Panzer Corps cut through successive defense lines on the west side of the Sarviz Canal and gained nearly twenty miles. By then Tolbukhin had committed his second echelon, Twenty-seventh Army and almost all his reserves—three rifle corps, a tank corps, a mechanized corps, and a guards cavalry corps. Because he had spread his armor thin he still could not mount a bid for the initiative anywhere. On the fourth day he asked for the strategic reserve, Ninth Guards Army, which had recently been moved into the Kecskemet area as a precaution, but the Stavka decided it was essential to save the army for its own projected offensive.

On the 10th, in snow and rain, I SS Panzer Corps closed to the Sio Canal and the next night took two small bridgeheads. The advance revealed how well dug in the Russians were, which augered ill for II SS Panzer Corps. On the east side of the Sarviz Canal the corps had gained no more than five miles by 12 February.

On the 13th, having pulled together his armor, Tolbukhin counterattacked on both sides of the Sarviz Canal. To keep the initiative, Woehler proposed taking out II SS Panzer Corps, which was attracting the heaviest counterattacks, and putting the weight of both SS corps east of the canal, where the sandy ground would make the going somewhat easier for the tanks. Hitler withheld approval until late on the night of the 15th; he suspected, correctly as it turned out, that II SS Panzer Corps would be diverted to meet the coming Soviet offensive.

THE SOVIET COUNTEROFFENSIVE BEGINS

On the afternoon of 16 March the Soviet offensive began in snow and fog—and therefore without substantial armor or air support—against IV SS Panzer Corps and the south flank of Hungarian Third Army on the front between Velencze Lake and Bicske. The original plan had been to dispatch Second Ukrainian Front toward Vienna in an advance straddling the Danube, but to exploit the chance to trap Sixth SS Panzer Army east of Lake Balaton, the main effort had been shifted south to Third Ukrainian Front's right flank.

The thrust was aimed west and northwest along the line Szekesfehervar-Varpalota-Papa-Sopron-Vienna. Inside it Second Ukrainian Front would attack along the Danube toward Györ.

On the second day, Hungarian Third Army's flank collapsed and the Russians pushed through the Vertes Moutains north of Mor. Neither of the large mobile forces, Sixth Guards Tank Army or First Guards Cavalry-Mechanized Group (formerly Cavalry-Mechanized Group Pliyev), had appeared yet to exploit the breakthrough. Army Group South decided to cancel the attack east of the Sarviz Canal "for the time being," and send I SS Panzer Corps into the area southwest of Szekesfehervar for a counterattack. By day's end it was also getting II SS Panzer Corps ready to turn around and move north.

Malinovskiy began turning his left flank army north toward Komarno behind Hungarian Third Army on the 18th. On the same day Tolbukhin's Ninth and Fourth Guards Armies broke through IV SS Panzer Corps between Mor and Velencze Lake. Tolbukhin was slow in taking advantage of the latter breakthrough: Sixth Guards Tank Army was not ready because it had had to regroup south after the change in plans. During the day Woehler decided to attempt a castling maneuver: he ordered 6th SS Panzer Army and its two corps to shift north into the sector between Velencze Lake and the Danube and gave Sixth Army command between Velencze Lake and Lake Balaton. Sixth SS Panzer Army successfully made its way out between the lakes, but I SS Panzer Corps failed to get a firm front in its new sector on the edge of the Bakony Forest west of Varpalota.

On 20 February Sixth Guards Tank Army attacked between Varpalota and Szekesfehervar toward the tip of Lake Balaton. Hitler demanded that Szekesfehervar be held, which meant in effect that Sixth Army had to stay east of Lake Balaton. On the 21st, except for a tenuous corridor along the lake shore, Sixth Army was encircled. Hitler refused to let go of Szekesfehervar. The OKH explained he was afraid that if he did, the whole front would start to "slip," which was what was happening in any event. Woehler replied that he did not dare risk another encirclement; the memory of Budapest was too recent; the armies were already infected with the Kessel (pocket) psychosis. Varpalota fell in the afternoon, and that night, Hitler's protests notwithstanding, Szekesfehervar fell.

For the next twenty-four hours Sixth Army ran a gantlet between the Russians and the lake. No one could tell from hour to hour how much longer the pocket might stay open. The army command lost track of IV SS Panzer Corps completely—of deserters rounded up 75 percent were SS-men. That the army survived at all probably has to be charged mostly to Sixth Guards Tank Army's late and uncertain start.

By 23 February Sixth Army was west of the lake, but still in trouble. During the day Tolbukhin's troops took Veszprem, the key point and main road junction in the Bakony Forest. Malinovskiy's forces on that day split the bridgehead Hungarian Third Army was holding west of Esztergom and forced the army to retreat across the river. On the south Army Group F evacuated its two bridgeheads on the Drava. Second Panzer Army, still attacking, gained some five miles south of Lake Balaton—an exercise in futility. At day's end Hitler gave Woehler permission to take a division, no more, from Second Panzer Army. During the day the Stavka had issued orders for the next phase of the offensive. The Ninth Guards and Sixth Guards Tank Armies were to strike toward Köszeg, Twenty-sixth Army toward Szombathely, and Twenty-seventh Army toward Zalaegerszeg.

From the Commanding General, Sixth Army, Balck, came an ominous report. He said the troops were not fighting the way they should. Some were saying the war was lost anyway, and they did not want to be the last to die. All were afraid of being encircled. The loss of confidence was spreading into the higher commands.

On 25 February the Russians completed the breakthrough phase of the offensive. Sixth Guards Tank Army came out of the Bakony Forest east of Papa. Sixth SS Panzer Army held a front from Papa north to the Danube at Komarno, but the army, although numerically relatively strong, was showing astonishing shortcomings. The SS-men from top to bottom appeared unable to adjust to conditions in which they did not have ample equipment and supplies and plenty of time to plot every move. Sixth Army had the impossible mission of holding its right flank on Lake Balaton to protect Second Panzer Army and maintaining contact with Sixth SS Panzer Army on its left. South of Papa the gap between the armies' flanks was ten miles wide, and Woehler told Guderian he could think of no way to close it. Replying to a demand from Guderian that Sixth Army "finally come to a stop," Balck insisted that the tactical crisis by itself could be mastered were it not for an acute loss of faith in the leadership, rooted, he said, in Stalingrad and Budapest: the troops simply would not hold. To add to the Germans' troubles, Second Ukrainian Front began attacking across the Hron that day.

TO VIENNA

The next day the Second and Third Ukrainian Fronts began what Soviet accounts later described as the pursuit, an adequate enough term except that it implies on the enemy side either a planned retreat or a rout. Hitler would not have permitted the former, and the Russians never quite achieved the latter. A more precise description would be an attempted active defense with wholly inadequate means and inappropriate objectives.

On 27 March the Sixth Guards Tank, Fourth Guards, and Ninth Guards Armies crossed to the Raab River on a broad front west of Köszeg. The meager reinforcements coming to Army Group South were destined—because of Hitler's concern for the oil—for the flanks, two divisions to Second Panzer Army and one to Eighth Army. After hearing that Hitler continued to insist on holding Komarno for the oil refineries, the army group chief of staff told the OKH to have him look at an aerial photograph. There was nothing there anymore but bomb craters. Second Panzer Army, which had so far been spared, reported that it expected an attack soon. Its Hungarians were deserting "in droves," and it asked to go back to the main defense line between the Drava and Lake Balaton. When the army group forwarded the request with its endorsement, Guderian answered that to lay the matter before Hitler was a waste of time, for him the words "oil fields" were "spelled in capitals."

In another two days Sixth Guards Tank Army had crossed the Raab between the Sixth and Sixth SS Panzer Armies' flanks and drawn up to the Austrian border in the Köszeg-Szombathely area. Hitler let the two armies withdraw to the Austrian border defenses but made the armies on their flanks stay put. At nightfall on the 29th Eighth Army still had a tenous hold on Komarno. Second Panzer Army, attacked for the first time during the day, had lost Nagybajom in the center of its front south of Lake Balaton and had taken command of Sixth Army's right flank corps at the southern tip of the lake to protect its deep flank and rear.

On 30 March, Sixth Guards Tank Army crossed the border and turned north toward the corridor between the mountains west of Wiener Neustadt and the Neusiedler Lake. On its right Ninth Guards Army and Fourth Guards Army began to wheel northwest toward Vienna. Hitler demanded a counterattack to close the gap behind the tank army; Woehler replied that neither Sixth Army nor Sixth SS Panzer Army had the slightest prospect of even starting a counterattack. The army group would consider itself lucky if Sixth SS Panzer Army could create, ahead of the Russians, some kind of a front between Wiener Neustadt and the lake. He had sent officers of his staff out to the troops; they had all reported that the men were exhausted and morale was low; to expect them to stage a counterattack was futile. Sixth Army, moreover, was in almost as much trouble on its right as on its left. It had broken away from Second Panzer Army's flank, and Twenty-seventh Army was pushing south.

At the end of the month Tolbukhin and Malinovskiy closed in on Vienna. Second Ukrainian Front north of the Danube went to Bratislava. The Third Ukrainian Front right flank pushed into the narrows between the Danube at Bratislava and Neusiedler Lake. On 2 April Sixth Guards Tank Army thrust past Wiener Neustadt toward Vienna. Second Panzer Army had retreated west of Nagykanizsa to a line in the heights that barely contained the oil fields.

To defend Vienna, Hitler sent the 25th Panzer Division and the Fuehrer Grenadier Division. On the 3d he ordered Woehler "finally" to attack the flanks of the breakthrough and to give up trying to oppose the Soviet armored spearheads frontally. After Woehler replied that the army group was in no condition to counterattack and had to put something in front of the Russians to keep them from breaking away "into the infinite," Hitler called Rendulic in from Courland and gave him command of Army Group South.

When Rendulic arrived at the army group headquarters in the Alps southwest of St. Poelten at midnight on 7 April—even army group commanders did not travel fast in Germany any more—the Russians were in Vienna to the Guertelstrasse and on the Danube west of the city. Third Ukrainian Front had brought Forty-sixth Army across the Danube to the north bank and was advancing beyond the Morava to envelop Vienna on the north.

In those last days Skorzeny, on a special mission from Hitler, appeared in Vienna, hanged three officers on the Floridsdorf Bridge, and claimed that the situation in the city was "dismal," no orders were being given, and despondency and other "signs of disintegration" were widespread. Rendulic, who, whatever else he was, did not associate himself with the nihilistic bitter-enders of the SS, protested that Vienna was no different from any other large city with street fighting and a disaffected population and threw Skorzeny out. The battle went on in the city until the afternoon of 13 April but without any attempt to create another Budapest.

At the end of the second week in April, Sixth SS Panzer, Sixth, and Second Panzer Armies had an almost continuous front in the outlying Alps from west of St. Poelten to the Drava east of Varazdin. The loss of the Hungarian oil fields had gone almost unnoticed in the greater excitement over Vienna. After they crossed the Hungarian border the Russians relaxed their pressure against the two southern armies.

In the second half of the month, the weight of the offensive shifted north of the Danube. The First Guards Cavalry-Mechanized Group attacked across the Morava toward Brno, and Fourth Ukrainian Front bore in toward Olomouc against the bulging Army Group Center right flank. Hitler ordered Army Group South to retake the small Austrian oil field at Zistersdorf twenty-five miles north of Vienna. The attempt was not made.

CLOSING IN?

The abortive Stargard operation brought the Germans a substantial, unexpected, and unearned dividend of time that, while it appeared to do no more than prolong the agony, may have profoundly affected Germany's future. In the fit of caution that took hold in mid-February, the Stavka dismantled its preparations for an advance to Berlin and beyond into central Germany and committed its main forces in marginal, wholly unspectacular clearing operations on the flanks in Pomerania and Silesia. For nearly a month and a half, Berlin and the German territory west of the Oder appear to have dropped out of the sight even of the Stavka. No doubt, observing that the Allies were still west of the Rhine, which they did not cross anywhere until the end of the first week in March, the Soviet command concluded it had time enough. This could have provided a rationale for cleaning out the flanks in anticipation of a deeper thrust into Germany than originally intended and, meanwhile, letting the Allies bleed themselves out; but the sequence of events in March indicates that caution and a consequent inability to decide upon a clean-cut, direct solution to the final strategic problem also weighed heavily.

ZHUKOV AND ROKOSSOVSKIY AGAINST ARMY GROUP VISTULA

In a major intelligence estimate submitted to Hitler on 26 February, the Eastern Intelligence Branch, OKH, predicted that the Soviet main effort would be "concentrated exclusively in the decisive direction— toward the west." It seemed obvious that the Soviet Command would concentrate exclusively on perpetuating the crisis on the German side in order to effect a decision in the war. The intelligence analysts found it difficult to imagine that the Stavka would let itself be deflected from the supreme objective by illusory threats to its flanks, especially after the Stargard failure. Moreover, with better than six million men against the Germans' two million, it appeared the Russians could handily cope with any diversions the Germans might attempt and at the same time carry the advance forward in the main direction.[44] In

---

44. At 2 million the German strength was slightly higher than on 1 January 1943. The increase was in the form of new divisions and divisions transferred from other theaters. Of 660,000 German casualties in January and February less than half had been replaced, which meant a further "burning out" of the old Eastern Front divisions. A fourth of the total German strength in the east (556,000 men) was bottled up in Courland and East Prussia.

terms of combat readiness the Soviet armies were in good shape; the estimated 680,000 casualties in January had been less than the Soviet forces had sustained in any of their other recent major offensives. The prediction was wrong, but the logic of the situation on which it was based was ultimately compelling for both sides, and for the Germans, as long as the war lasted, it was inescapable.

On 25 February the deployment of the First Belorussian and First Ukrainian Fronts' four tank armies indicated that both fronts were oriented west. (Map 41) The First and Second Guards Tank Armies of First Belorussian Front were out of the line, and, although both were north of the Warthe, neither had intervened in the Stargard battle. Fourth Tank Army was on the Neisse between Guben and Forst, and Third Guards Tank Army was west of Goerlitz.

Between 24 and 26 February the Germans picked up the first signs of a change in the Soviet intentions. On the 24th Second Belorussian Front launched heavy probing attacks along its whole front west of the Vistula. On the extreme left flank, at the Third Panzer Army-Second Army boundary, Nineteenth Army, newly arrived from Finland, struck a weak spot, broke in on the first day, and by the 26th, when it took Bublitz, had covered about half the distance to the Baltic coast. On the 26th agent reports from the First Ukrainian Front zone confirmed that Fourth Tank Army had left the Guben-Forst area and moved south to Liegnitz. The Germans concluded that as a brief prelude to the main offensive the Stavka had decided to eliminate all semblances of threats to the flanks. In Pomerania the OKH expected the Russians would be content with splitting apart the Third Panzer and Second Armies and breaking the land communications to Danzig and Gdynia. In Silesia it expected them to attempt to force the Seventeenth Army and the Armeegruppe Heinrici back to the Sudeten Mountains and as a dividend, if it could be done fast, take the Moravska Ostrava industrial complex.

A map captured on February revealed that Second Belorussian Front was in fact aiming for the coast east of Koeslin to split the Third Panzer and Second Armies. Army Group Vistula ordered a counterattack into the Russian flanks east and west of Bublitz, but Second Army was dangerously short of artillery ammunition and

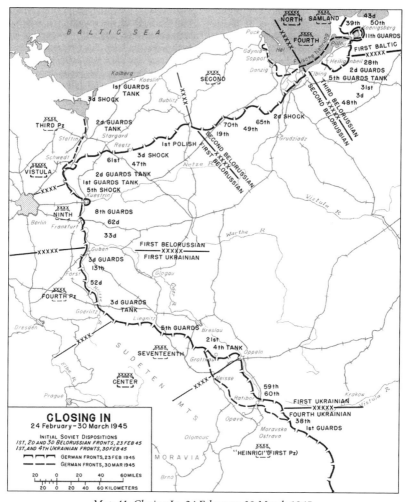

Map 41: Closing In, 24 February-30 March 1945

gasoline, and the army group had trouble finding gas for the armor it was bringing in on the west. During the last two days of the month, Rokossovskiy reined in on his armor and set his infantry to opening the flanks. On 1 March, while the German counterattack made minor progress east of Bublitz, III Guards Tank Corps crossed the road and railroad east of Koeslin, cutting the communications to Second Army and to Danzig and Gdynia, the main bases of supply for Army Groups North and Courland.

On 1 March, after apparently waiting to see whether the Germans would repeat the Stargard attempt, First Belorussian Front attacked Third Panzer Army's center at Reetz. Third Shock Army made the breakthrough, and the First and Second Guards Tank Armies followed, the former going north toward Kolberg and the latter northwest toward the lower Oder. Only weeks before, the Goebbels propagandists had released the movie Kolberg, a color epic—the most lavish ever made in Germany—depicting Gneisenau's successful defense of the city against the French in 1807.

On 4 March First Guards Tank Army reached the coast, isolated Kolberg, and made contact with the left flank of Second Belorussian Front, which took Koeslin on that day. Third Panzer Army's left flank was trapped and was breaking up into small pockets. Hitler ordered the army to counterattack to close the "gap." General Kinzel, the one-time Army Group North chief of staff recently called in as Himmler's "second chief" to replace Wenck, told Guderian's deputy to tell the Fuehrer he was fighting the war "on paper" and not in accordance with reality; the situation was hopeless; and the only thing left to do was to save what could be saved of the army for the battle on the Oder.

The following day First Guards Tank Army joined Second Belorussian Front to give it an assist against Second Army, and Zhukov turned his flank west toward the Oder. During the next few days, while Hitler went on talking about a counterattack, Third Panzer Army was pushed into a bridgehead east of Stettin. After a quiet day on the 12th, Hitler instructed Army Group Vistula to consider how it could expand the bridgehead enough to open the port of Stettin for contact by sea with Danzig and Gdynia.

When the Russians resumed the assault against the bridgehead on the 15th, Hitler ordered Third Panzer Army to stay on the defensive and release several divisions as reinforcements for Ninth Army. Late on the afternoon of the 19th General der Panzertruppen Hasso-Eccard von Manteuffel, whom Hitler had put in command of Third Panzer Army several days earlier after taking a sudden dislike to Raus, reported that the battle in the bridgehead was at an end one way or the other: Hitler could either give up the bridgehead before the day's end "or lose everything tomorrow." Hitler gave his approval an hour later.

Goebbels' propaganda epic about Kolberg barely escaped being also engulfed in the Third Panzer Army's disaster. The old city on the Baltic, which had surrendered only one of the three times the Russians besieged it in the Seven Years' War and had stood off Napoleon's troops, though lost at least did not capitulate. The garrison held out until the 18th. By then 80,000 inhabitants and refugees had been evacuated by sea, and the last few hundred soldiers escaped on board a destroyer.

Rokossovskiy's operation against Second Army took longer and could not be brought to as clean-cut a conclusion. By 11 March Second Belorussian Front had reached a line skirting the west half of the Bay of Danzig about ten miles in from the coast. A day later First Guards Tank Army broke through to the coast at Puck and cut off the northernmost German corps, which subsequently withdrew to the Hel Peninsula.

On the 13th, in a command shuffle occasioned by command changes in the West and in Italy, von Vietinghoff returned to Italy, Rendulic returned to Army Group Courland, and Weiss was appointed Commanding General, Army Group North. At the same time, Second Army, General der Panzertruppen Dietrich von Saucken commanding, was transferred to Army Group North. Hitler told Weiss to hold the Hel Peninsula, Gdynia, Danzig, Pillau, the Frische Nehrung, and enough ground on the mainland in East Prussia to keep contact with Koenigsberg. Hitler and Doenitz still considered the Baltic ports essential for the Navy.

For ten more days Second Army held its own against the full weight of Rokossovskiy's front. On 13 March the Russians finally reached the coast at Sopot, splitting Gdynia off from the German main force at and east of Danzig. From that entering wedge, they took Gdynia on the 28th and Danzig two days later. The Second Army survivors retreated east into the Vistula delta.

After 13 March Third Belorussian Front had pushed Fourth Army into a ten by two mile beachhead west of Heiligenbeil before Hitler on the 29th finally allowed the army to retreat across the Frisches Haff to the Nehrung. By then the army had left 60,000 able-bodied men and 70,000 wounded. Hitler ordered the army to keep all but the most seriously wounded for use as replacements as they recovered. At the end of the month, Army Group North precariously straddled the Bay of Danzig from Samland and Koenigsberg to the mouth of the Vistula; the remnants of two corps held small beachheads north of Gdynia on the Hel Peninsula.

FORTRESS BERLIN

The Soviet advance from the Vistula to the Oder had astonishingly little visible effect in Berlin. Life in the capital and its close environs, which housed the entire central government and the highest Wehrmacht commands with their main communications centers, continued in its accustomed routine that by then had long included the frequent American and British bombing raids. The exodus of governmental officers, siege preparations, and panic that had marked the German approach to Moscow in October 1941 were completely absent. Russian tanks might be on the Oder, scarcely a day's running time away, but what was to be done in Berlin still depended entirely upon the Fuehrer. Even the questions when and how the city would be evacuated or defended could not safely be raised without a cue from Hitler, and he was thinking of retaking Budapest, not of defending Berlin. At the end of January, in fact, very little had been done to prepare defenses anywhere west of the Oder. For political and psychological reasons, Hitler had insisted that military operational control not be imposed on German territory until the very latest possible time. Therefore, the OKW had waited until 14 January before giving the OKH authority to issue directives concerning fortification and defensive preparations to Wehrkreis III, the military district which included Berlin and a broad band of territory on either side of the city east to the Oder.

On 2 February Keitel issued the first written order concerning Berlin. In it he made the Commanding General, Wehrkreis III, responsible for defending the city. The Wehrkreis was a housekeeping and administrative command without permanently assigned tactical troops. The Keitel order merely increased the Wehrkreis commander's authority over troops that might be stationed in his area and gave him command "for ground combat" of the 1st Flak Division, the Berlin antiaircraft artillery. For his tactical orders the Wehrkreis commander would report directly to Hitler at the daily situation conferences.

At the end of the third week in February, Hitler still had not expressed a decision on Berlin. An OKW inquiry to the Reichs Chancellory regarding the "intentions of the highest governmental agencies in the event of a battle for Berlin" brought the reply that the only instructions issued so far were to stay in Berlin. That the city might become involved in the fighting "or even encircled" had not been discussed. Women and children were being allowed to leave, but no public announcement would be made.

Early in March, beginning with the transfer of Wehrkreis III's responsibility to Generalleutnant Hellmuth Reymann as Commander, Berlin Defense Area, the planning for Berlin assumed a somewhat more concrete aspect. Reymann's title indicated how little had been accomplished until then: the term "defense area" was applied to "exceptional cases of fortresses not yet completed."

On the 9th Reymann signed the Basic Order for the Preparations to Defend the Capital. In parts of it Hitler's rhetoric stands out unmistakably. The mission was to be to defend the capital "to the last man and the last shot." The battle was to be fought "with fanaticism, imagination; every means of deception, cunning, and deceit; and with improvisations of all kinds... on, above, and under the ground." "Every block, every house, every story, every hedge, every shell hole" was to be defended "to the utmost." That each defender was trained in the fine points of the use of weapons was less important than that "each... be filled with a fanatical desire to fight, that he knows the world is holding its breath as it watches this battle and that the battle for Berlin can decide the war."

Berlin was to be another fortress, the last in a chain that had stretched east to Stalingrad. The outer defense perimeter was plotted about twenty miles from the center of the city. Inside it were two more rings, one about ten miles from the city's center, the other following the S-Bahn, the suburban belt railway. In each of eight pie-slice-shaped sectors a commandant was appointed. A small inner ring around the government quarter was designated Sector Z (ZITADELLE, or citadel). The troop dispositions, however, indicate that Hitler really considered the fortress as a marginal affair. Aside from the 1st Flak Division, which would remain in the antiaircraft defense until ground fighting began, Reymann had as reserves six battalions, two of them Volkssturm, one a guard battalion, and the rest SS and police. The sector commandants would not actually command any troops until the code word CLAUSEWITZ, the enemy approach warning, was given. They would then assume command of the Volkssturm and any troop units that happened to be in their sectors and of whatever troops came in or were driven in from the outside.

Hitler was, no doubt, fully aware that the capital and the German heartland could be defended, if at all, only on the Oder-Neisse line, not on the Berlin S-Bahn. As long as he imagined that he still had strategic choices—as recently as the competition between the Stargard and Budapest operations, for instance—he had neglected the Berlin sector. As a consequence, the front on the Oder and Neisse was only little less of a sham than the Berlin fortress.

By early March Hitler and the rest of the German Command were agreed that a Soviet breakthrough toward Berlin was the greatest danger they faced, partly because the Russians had lately been moving much faster than the Americans and British but equally because they could conceive no greater horror than having the Russians march into the center of Germany. On the other hand, Hitler claimed knowledge that the Russians were not completely settled on Berlin and central Germany as the next objectives. That was Zhukov's intention, he maintained, but Stalin wanted a two-pronged offensive into western Czechoslovakia via Moravska Ostrava and the Moravian Gate on the north and Bratislava-Brno from the south, to be executed either before or simultaneously with the Berlin offensive.

Late as it was, the Oder-Neisse defense would have been neglected longer had not Hitler decided on 15 March in a flash of "intuition" that the Russians would choose the Berlin operation, which presumably, since every threat to their right flank was eliminated, they could begin almost any day. That night he conferred with Himmler, Guderian, and Busse. If he had time before the Russians moved, he wanted Ninth Army to strike north out of its own bridgehead at Frankfurt and "smash" the Soviet concentration south of Kuestrin. The next day he told Himmler to get ready for battle on the lower Oder and particularly to strengthen the Kuestrin-Frankfurt-Guben sector.

The apparent imminence of the crucial battle agitated the German command. Guderian and Speer, in an attempt to avoid adding to the approaching final defeat a complete internal dislocation in Germany, ordered that henceforth during withdrawals roads, bridges, and railroads were to be rendered temporarily unusable but not destroyed—allegedly to facilitate their restoration when the lost territory was retaken. Hitler, on 19 March, branding as an "error" the idea that temporary disruption of communications would be enough, ordered a full-scale scorched-earth policy and canceled "all directives to the contrary."87 Four days later, however, when Goebbels in his capacity as Gauleiter of Berlin proposed to convert the Charlottenburger Chausee into a landing strip, Hitler, displaying another of his characteristic vagaries, forbade him to cut down the trees flanking the boulevard in the Tiergarten.

When Guderian secured lukewarm backing from Doenitz in an attempt to persuade Hitler to evacuate Courland and bring the troops back to Germany, Hitler refused on the ground that besides causing heavy German losses, it would release a large number of enemy divisions. Rendulic's return to Courland underscored Hitler's determination to hold out there. On 13 March the so-called Fifth Battle of Courland, begun on 27 February, had ended. Von Vietinghoff had reported that the army group probably could not withstand another really determined onslaught.

In a different direction, an effort to remove Himmler from the Army Group Vistula command, Guderian had more success. At the middle of the month Himmler almost gladly accepted Guderian's offer to propose his retirement. After the Stargard fiasco and the consequent loss of favor with Hitler, he had evaded direct responsibility for the army group and had finally withdrawn under his physician's care to his estate at Hohenlychen, claiming to be suffering from angina pectoris. On 20 March Generaloberst Heinrici took command of Army Group Vistula, and two days later Hitler agreed to let Guderian bring in the Army Group F staff to replace most of Himmler's staff.

Guderian's own tenure was nearing an end. Hitler had resolved to give him "a long leave for his health" and was waiting impatiently for Wenck to recover sufficiently to assume the duties of Chief of Staff,

OKH. Lately, Hitler had indicated that he would have preferred to dispense with conventional military organizations and leadership altogether. What he needed, he said, were men like those who had created the Freikorps (freebooting detachments) after World War I, men who could hammer together units on their own. The best such officers he had at the moment, he thought, were the SS-men von dem Bach, Skorzeny, and Reinefarth. The two Army generals he rated highest were unavailable, both having recently been jailed for illegally appropriating captured property.

Before Ninth Army could organize its spoiling attack out of the Frankfurt bridgehead, First Belorussian Front, on 22 March, irrupted from its bridgeheads flanking Kuestrin and encircled the garrison in the Kuestrin Alt Stadt (the Kuestrin Neu Stadt, east of the Oder, had fallen earlier in the month). A counterattack by two panzer divisions that had been earmarked for the Frankfurt operation failed on the 24th. After that, Heinrici and Busse concluded it would be better to forego a second attempt and conserve their strength, but Hitler read Heinrici a lecture on "the futility of always being a move behind the enemy" and demanded the attack, to "smash" the Soviet build-up before it was completed.

On 27 March the second attempt to relieve Kuestrin failed. After an angry interview with Busse and Guderian the next day, Hitler gave Guderian six weeks' "sick leave" and made General der Infanterie Hans Krebs, Wenck's substitute, acting Chief of Staff, OKH. Krebs, who had been Busch's and more recently Model's chief of staff, was known for his unquenchable optimism and his chameleonlike ability to adapt to the views of his superiors. On 30 March the commandant in Kuestrin, Reinefarth, decided against a heroic demise and ordered the breakout from the Alt Stadt.

KONEV IN UPPER SILESIA

The Soviet Upper Silesian offensive, as it developed in late March, appeared to confirm Hitler's assumption that the Russians planned a large operation in Czechoslovakia as a prelude or a companion piece to the thrust to Berlin and into central Germany. Indeed, the Upper Silesian offensive remains difficult to explain in any other terms. The

Soviet authorities maintain that nothing more was intended than was accomplished, namely, to force Army Group Center away from the Oder above Oppeln and back to the edge of the Sudeten. Although the operation did remove a possible, though remote, danger to Konev's deep right flank and shortened his front somewhat, it fell far short of improving the situation in the south as radically as was being done in Pomerania and West Prussia. Such an improvement could only have been accomplished by a deep thrust into Czechoslovakia to Olomouc, Brno, and in the Prague direction behind Army Group Center.

First Ukrainian Front had been slow getting the offensive ready to move. Apparently its armor had needed refitting; on 14 March all of the larger armored units were out of the front. But by then Fourth Tank Army, out of action for nearly three weeks, was rested, refitted, and, together with Twenty-first Army, was deployed and ready for the offensive in the Grottkau area west of Oppeln. The Fifty-ninth and Sixtieth Armies were likewise ready in the Oder bridgehead north of Ratibor. East of Moravska Ostrava the reinforced right flank of Fourth Ukrainian Front had run a preliminary attack for three days beginning on 10 March. The Germans, watching the build-up, had trouble deciding what to make of it, particularly after the rapid success against Army Group Vistula east of the Oder made it appear that the offensive across the Oder and Neisse could come soon.

On 15 March First Ukrainian Front attacked south of Grottkau and west out of the bridgehead north of Ratibor. Fourth Ukrainian Front resumed its thrust toward Moravska Ostrava. In a day or two, Fourth Ukrainian Front's attack stalled.

Konev's armies, because of their overwhelming matériel superiority, had the upper hand from the start but did not make, from the Army Group Center point of view, alarming progress until the afternoon of the 17th, when Fourth Tank Army sluiced a tank corps through a small gap east of Neisse, and linking up with the force coming west out of the Ratibor bridgehead, encircled LVI Panzer Corps southwest of Oppeln. That the Commanding General, Seventeenth Army, General der Infanterie Friedrich Wilhelm Schultz, was caught in the breakthrough and chivied across the Silesian landscape until almost nightfall by Soviet tanks did not enhance the speed of the German reaction. On the 20th LVI Panzer Corps escaped from the pocket with heavy losses.

On 22 March Konev turned his attack south toward Opava, and Fourth Ukrainian Front began striking west toward Ratibor. To the Germans it appeared that the main phase of the offensive was just beginning. The thrusts in both directions were being gradually reinforced, and by the 26th Konev had brought Fourth Tank Army down from the Neisse area.

On the 30th Schoerner had to give up Ratibor to prevent a breakthrough to Moravska Ostrava. He reported that the Russians appeared as intent as ever on forcing their way past Opava and Moravska Ostrava into the Moravian basin. In the Army Group South zone the First Guards Cavalry-Mechanized Group was heading northwest through Slovakia toward Moravia. Then a day later, without having reached any of their apparent objectives, the First and Fourth Ukrainian Fronts stopped the offensive.

CHAPTER XXI

Berlin

THE EVE OF THE BATTLE

While the Russians conducted their sideshows in Pomerania, West Prussia, and Silesia, the Allies took charge in the center ring in a style that by the end of March had completely changed the strategic picture in Germany. They had closed to the Rhine along its whole length, had deep bridgeheads across the river, and were rapidly completing an encirclement of the Ruhr that would chop Army Group B out of the German front, opening for them a broad boulevard east to the Elbe. In Switzerland they had entered into secret negotiations looking toward the surrender of the German forces in Italy. From these the Russians, though informed, were excluded.

THE SOVIET DECISION TO TAKE BERLIN

In Moscow on the night of 31 March the Allied representatives presented to Stalin a message from General of the Army Dwight D. Eisenhower outlining the Allied Supreme Commander's plans for his operations in central Germany. Eisenhower stated that his next objective, after he had encircled and destroyed the Germans in the Ruhr, would be to split the enemy forces by making a junction with the Soviet armies. He believed that could best be accomplished by a thrust along the line Erfurt-Leipzig-Dresden. As soon as he could, he would make a secondary advance to meet the Russians in the Regensburg-Linz area and so prevent the Germans from establishing a redoubt in southern Germany.

Replying—with altogether unusual alacrity—the next day, Stalin agreed that the Allied and Soviet forces should meet as Eisenhower proposed in the Erfurt-Leipzig-Dresden and Regensburg-Linz areas. Berlin, he added, had lost its former strategic significance, and the Soviet Supreme Command planned only to allot secondary forces in that direction. The Soviet main offensive, he stated, would probably be resumed in the second half of May.

Even as Stalin wrote, the Soviet armies from north of Opava to the mouth of the Vistula were beginning, in almost frantic haste, the redeployment for an operation that had Berlin as its primary objective. In Upper Silesia, where First Ukrainian Front's offensive ended on 31 March with the abruptness already noted, Fourth Tank Army, redesignated "Guards," was pulling its units out of the front, getting ready for the move north to the Neisse. The air units that had flown support missions on the First Ukrainian Front left flank were moving north as was Fifth Guards Army from the area west of Breslau. Second Belorussian Front, which with First Guards Tank Army still attached was fully committed against the remnants of German Second Army on the Bay of Danzig on 30 March, was starting a fast about-face and a march to the lower Oder.

The true mood of the Soviet Command, disguised in the deliberate tone of Stalin's reply to Eisenhower, was revealed on 3 April when Stalin, protesting the negotiations in Switzerland, wrote to President Franklin D. Roosevelt, "As regards my military colleagues, they, on the basis of information in their possession, are sure that negotiations did take place and that they ended in an agreement with the Germans, whereby the German Commander on the Western Front, Marshal Kesselring [Generalfeldmarschall Albert Kesselring] is to open the front to the Anglo-American troops and let them move east, while the British and Americans have promised, in exchange, to ease the armistice terms for the Germans." Sounding very much like a man who had just discovered that he had for some time been looking in the wrong direction—and drawing false conclusions from his original faulty assumption—Stalin added almost plaintively, "I realize that there are certain advantages resulting to the Anglo-American troops… seeing that the Anglo-American troops are enabled to advance into the heart of Germany almost without resistance; but why conceal this from the Russians, and why were the Russians, their allies, not forewarned?"

HITLER WORRIES ABOUT THE FLANKS

On 30 March, Hitler had warned Army Group Vistula that the

developments on the Western Front could induce the Russians to attack across the Oder without waiting to redeploy their forces from East and West Prussia. (Map 42) He directed the army group to construct a main battle line two to four miles behind its front and emplace the artillery so that it could lay down barrages between the two lines. But he apparently still was not convinced that the decisive battle would be at Berlin. He had ordered the 10th SS Panzer Division transferred from Army Group Vistula to Army Group Center and stationed southeast of Goerlitz, where it appeared that Third Guards Tank Army might attempt a breakthrough south toward Prague. On 2 and 3 April he transferred the Fuehrer Grenadier Division and the 25th Panzer Division to Army Group South for the defense of Vienna. The transfers cost Army Group Vistula half of its armored and mobile forces.

In orders to Army Groups North and Courland, Hitler re-emphasized their missions of tying down enemy forces away from the main front and denying the Russians access to the Baltic ports. Too late to save the garrison, much less the civilians, he authorized a breakout from the Glogau fortress on 30 March. He demanded that Breslau hold out as "an example for the whole German people" and "the surety for a change in the East."

On 2 April Headquarters, Army Group North, was recalled, and the Second and Fourth Armies went under the direct command of the OKH. After Second Belorussian Front turned west, the Soviet strength opposing Second Army sank rapidly, leveling off in the second week of the month at about nine divisions against the Germans' six.

On 3 April the sixth and last Courland battle ended (begun 17 March). Although Army Group Courland was badly weakened, Hitler instructed it to stay in the front it then held in order to draw the maximum enemy forces against itself and, presumably, away from the front in Germany.

Koenigsberg had become a prestige objective for Hitler and for the Russians. On 6 April Vasilevskiy threw four armies into a converging attack, and on the 9th the city surrendered. Hitler had the fortress commandant, General der Infanterie Otto Lasch, condemned in absentia to death by hanging. After Koenigsberg fell, Hitler, partly as

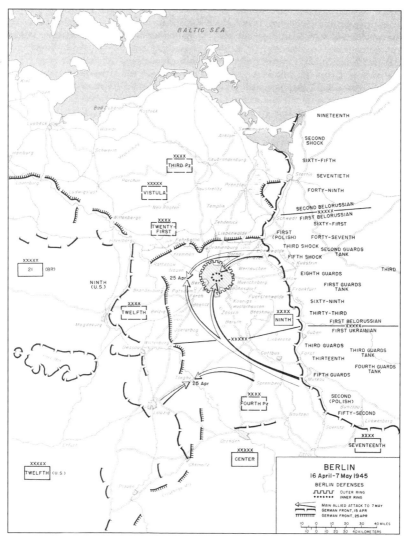

Map 42: Berlin, 16 April–7 May 1945.

an expression of his displeasure and partly because there was no longer any need for two army commands in the area, sent Headquarters, Fourth Army, out of East Prussia and combined what was left of the army with Second Army to form the Army of East Prussia.

SOVIET REDEPLOYMENT AND PLANS
In the first two weeks of April the Russians executed, apparently under

Zhukov's direction, their fastest major redeployment of the war. First Belorussian Front pulled its boundary down from the Baltic coast to the level of Schwedt as Second Belorussian Front moved in on its right; First Ukrainian Front shifted its main weight from its left and center to its right. The three Soviet fronts had all together 2.5 million men, 6,250 tanks, 7,500 aircraft, 41,600 artillery pieces and mortars, 3,255 multiple rocket projectors, and 95,383 motor vehicles.

In view of the dark suspicions aroused by the recent Allied successes, the redeployment and the coming offensive had one overriding objective: to take possession at top speed of at least the German territory east of the Elbe, the projected Soviet occupation zone. To do that, even disregarding—though the Russians undoubtedly did not—the likelihood that if the Allies had made a deal their occupying Berlin was part of it, the main effort had to be against Berlin because, strategic objective or not, the battle for possession of the Soviet zone could not be won, above all not won quickly, until and unless the city was taken.

The plan for the offensive was a three-way compromise: it centered the main weight of the attack on Berlin but provided for simultaneous maximum breadth and depth of penetration. To achieve an early start, it accepted the handicap of Second Belorussian Front's starting several days late. It also left open a chance for a quick turn south into Czechoslovakia off the left flank.

First Belorussian Front positioned its main force, five armies including the First and Second Guards Tank Armies, for a frontal attack toward Berlin out of the Kuestrin bridgehead. At the eastern edge of the city the armor was to veer north and south, forming the northern arm of a close-in encirclement and supporting the encirclement on the south. Second Belorussian Front was to cross the Oder north of Schwedt and strike toward Neustrelitz. This thrust was to force Third Panzer Army back against the coast and cover the advance toward Berlin on the north; but because Rokossovskiy needed more time for his deployment and would start at least four days late, First Belorussian Front ordered two of its armies to provide flank cover on the north by a thrust south of the Finow Canal to Fehrbellin. A second 2-army force was to attack toward Brandenburg out of the bridgehead north of Frankfurt, cover the main force on the south, complete the southern arm of the Berlin encirclement, and, in conjunction with First Ukrainian Front forces, envelop what was left of the Ninth and Fourth Panzer Armies on the Oder and lower Neisse.

First Ukrainian Front planned two thrusts: one, by the Third and Fourth Guards Tank Armies plus three infantry armies, to go across the Neisse between Forst and Muskau and to carry via Spremberg west and northwest, the other, by two armies, from north of Goerlitz to Dresden. Konev's primary mission was to close to the Elbe on the stretch from Dresden to Wittenberg where the junction with the Americans was expected. He intended to carry the advance as far north and west as Belzig and from there furnish elements to support the First Belorussian Front right flank at and south of Berlin. The object apparently was to hold to the minimum the First Ukrainian Front forces that would become tied down in the fighting around Berlin in order to permit an early regroupment south for an advance via Dresden toward Prague; but the tank armies on the north flank were an insurance and a variant of the plan provided for their being turned sharply north toward Berlin. The responsibility for co-ordinating the whole offensive was Zhukov's. In early April he turned command of First Belorussian Front over to Sokolovskiy.

HITLER PREPARES FOR THE BATTLE

The Germans no longer had the manpower, war plant, or transportation to accomplish a true build-up on the Oder-Neisse line. To defend the sector directly east of Berlin, Ninth Army had 14 divisions. Opposite it, First Belorussian Front deployed 18 Soviet armies with a complement of 77 rifle divisions, 7 tank and mechanized corps, 8 artillery divisions, and an extensive assortment of artillery and rocket launcher brigades and regiments. Third Panzer Army, on Ninth Army's left, had 11 divisions; Second Belorussian Front moving in against it had 8 armies totaling 33 rifle divisions, 4 tank and mechanized corps, and 3 artillery divisions plus a mixture of artillery and rocket launcher brigrades and regiments. First Belorussian Front had 3,155 tanks and self-propelled guns; Second Belorussian Front had 951; Ninth Army and Third Panzer Army

The infamous Katyusha was one of the most feared weapons in the Soviet armoury. These lorry-bourn rocket launchers are seen here being deployed in a Berlin suburb during April 1945.

had 512 and 242, respectively. First Belorussian Front had 16,934 artillery pieces to Ninth Army's 344 pieces of regular artillery and 300 to 400 antiaircraft guns. Third Panzer Army had practically no artillery other than 600 to 700 antiaircraft guns. Second Belorussian Front had 6,642 artillery pieces. In spite of strict conservation, motor fuel and ammunition stocks could not be accumulated at anywhere near the rate required for a major operation. On 11 April the artillery ammunition in the Army Group Vistula zone stood at .9 of a basic load. First and Second Belorussian Fronts had 3.2 and 1.9 basic loads as initial issues for their vastly greater arrays of artillery.

Hitler did little to compensate for deficiencies. He ordered the antiaircraft guns, most of which were taken from the Berlin air defense, emplaced so that they could fire on ground targets. The armies added depth to the front by constructing the WOTAN position ten to fifteen miles to the rear. To replace the Panzer divisions transferred to Army Groups South and Center, Hitler promised Heinrici 100,000 troops but only delivered about 35,000 untrained Air Force and Navy men.

The total German situation was too uncertain to permit any coherent planning in the event the defense on the rivers failed. The one overriding objective left was to prolong the war. Hitler had never been more firmly in command, and as long as he lived there was no way out short of total defeat in the field or the miracle he predicted. Anticipating an Allied-Soviet junction that would split Germany in two, Hitler, on 10 and 14 April, issued orders naming Doenitz commander in chief in the north and Kesselring in the south. The appointments were to take effect after the contact between the two areas was broken. Hitler expected to retain the supreme command in one or the other himself.

On the 15th Hitler transferred command of the Berlin city defense to Army Group Vistula; until then it had been directly under him. That night at the army group headquarters the Berlin commander, Reymann, took part in what for him must have been a dismayingly painful conference. Speer, there on a mission of his own—to oppose Hitler's scorched-earth policy—told Reymann that the destruction of the bridges and other facilities in the city would have doubtful military value but was certain to cause starvation, epidemics, and an economic collapse that might take years to overcome. Heinrici agreed and added that, if it came to that, the army group did not propose to fight in the city; Ninth Army would retreat past it on both sides.

At midmonth, aside from the by then obvious First Belorussian Front concentration east of Berlin, the Germans had only a hazy and, in one important respect, completely false picture of the Soviet deployment and intentions. Hitler and Schoerner—who took his cue from the Fuehrer—had become convinced in late March that the Russians would try both the so-called Zhukov (Berlin) and Stalin (Prague) offensive solutions. In April German Intelligence lost track of Third Guards Tank Army, placing it east of Bunzlau where it would have been deployed had it intended to attack south toward Zittau into the gap between the Erzgebirge and the Sudeten and thence toward Prague. On 10 April Schoerner, awarded his marshal's baton five days before, told Hitler, "It is to be assumed that the enemy attack will be centered in the area between Goerlitz and Loewenberg [that is, southwest of Bunzlau]."19 The Eastern Intelligence Branch estimate of 13 April hedged a bit on the question of where the attack would come but reached essentially the same conclusion, namely, that First Ukrainian Front's main offensive concentration was northeast of Goerlitz-Loewenberg. Consequently, when the Soviet offensive began, Schoerner was holding half of his reserves, two panzer divisions, fifty miles southeast of the Soviet main effort.

On 11 April Hitler advised Heinrici to order his army group into its main battle formation that night or the next. The Americans, he explained, had reached the Elbe at Magdeburg that day; the Russians, if they wanted to take their share of central Germany, might be forced to attack before they were ready. (The vanguard of U.S. Ninth Army reached Magdeburg on the 11th, and after crossing the Elbe was fifty-three miles from Berlin at nightfall the next day.)

On the 12th Krebs told the Army Group Vistula operations officer that the Fuehrer was convinced the army group would have a "colossal" victory; nowhere in Germany was a front so strongly held or so well supplied with ammunition. The operations officer replied that the Fuehrer should also consider the enemy's strength, that the ammunition the army group had could hardly last for the expected long fight, and that its motor fuel was already short.

On the 14th five Soviet divisions and 200 tanks tried unsuccessfully to storm the Seelow Heights west of Kuestrin. When the attempt was not repeated the following day, Heinrici concluded that the Russians might have decided to wait a while longer. He considered ordering the troops out of the main battle line and into the original front, but decided not to because the previous day's attack had showed that they were "clinging" to the main battle line and needed every physical support they could be given. Hitler in an order of the day on 14 April ranted about traitorous German officers in Russian pay and German women reduced to barracks whores and pretended to see the hand of a benign power in the "death of the greatest war criminal of all time" (Roosevelt), and boasted that he had done so much since January to strengthen the front "that the Bolsheviks this time too will suffer the old fate of Asia and bleed to death before the German capital." He called for the defense "not of the empty concept of a Fatherland but of your homes, your women, your children, and thereby our future."

Soviet heavy artillery deployed on the streets of Berlin.

THE ENCIRCLEMENT

KONEV BREAKS THROUGH

First Belorussian and First Ukrainian Fronts attacked before dawn on 16 April. First Belorussian Front, the stronger, also had by far the tougher assignment. Its main force, deployed in a 20-mile sector between Wriezen and Seelow, had to cross the marshy bottomland of the Oder and Alte Oder and take the Seelow Heights. The attack, begun in darkness, was intended to achieve surprise, and batteries of powerful searchlights had been positioned to illuminate the German line and blind the defenders. The infantry moved out behind a shattering artillery preparation, but the lights did not have the expected effect. In the mud, smoke, and darkness the waves of infantry piled up on each other. By daylight, the confusion was complete. The Russians were lucky that the Germans, nervous and preoccupied, failed to appreciate what had happened and so left them to work out the problems by themselves.

During the day, apparently on orders from Stalin, Sokolovskiy committed the First and Second Guards Tank Armies, which could

Soviet infantrymen dash forward into action during the final assault on Berlin.

not help tactically, since the German line was not broken anywhere, but which added mightily to the tangle as the armor tried to push forward. At nightfall the divisions that had charged in the morning behind unfurled banners were all still in front of the German main battle line. To make the day complete, neither of First Belorussian Front's two flanking forces had any success.

The performance was comic opera played by five armies on a 20-mile stage. But the Russians could afford their mistakes, and the Germans could not afford theirs. Against Fourth Panzer Army on Schoerner's left flank, Konev's infantry crossed the Neisse between Muskau and Forst and north of Goerlitz, breaking in as deep as six miles.

After the Third and Fifth Shock Armies and Eighth Guards Army again failed to get moving on the morning of the second day, Sokolovskiy threw in a reserve army—the Forty-seventh—and both tank armies and zeroed in on two small areas, southeast of Wriezen and at Seelow. Two reserve panzer divisions, slowed by air attacks, arrived just in time to hold them to minor gains.

On the 18th Sokolovskiy drew his armor together more tightly and broke in ten to twelve miles west of Wriezen and southwest of Seelow. Ninth Army held its front together through the day. Heinrici reported that the battle was approaching its climax and would soon be decided.

The Russians were straining to the utmost, putting service troops into the front and threatening the death penalty for failure to advance on orders. Zhukov—according to the Soviet official history, the Stavka—had changed the plan on the second day and had ordered the Third and Fourth Guards Tank Armies to strike for Berlin as soon as they broke through. He ordered Second Belorussian Front, not yet in action, to direct its advance southwest instead of northwest so as to complete the Berlin encirclement from the north in case First Belorussian Front failed to get through.

At the end of the third day First Ukrainian Front's northern force was on the Spree north and south of Spremberg and across the river south of the city. Its southern force was approaching Bautzen. Schoerner also reported that the battle was reaching its climax in his zone. He thought the Russians' extremely heavy losses might be exhausting their ability to keep up the attack, and he intended to put his last troop and ammunition reserves into counterattacks the next day.

At Fuehrer headquarters 18 April was a day of optimism. During the situation conference held in the small hours of the morning, Hitler expressed the belief that the offensive against Fourth Panzer Army had "substantially" run itself tight. Doenitz's adjutant recorded that the "voices of hope were loud." As far as he could determine, however, much of the optimism seemed to be based on Keitel's dubious rule of thumb that offensives stalled if they had not made the breakthrough by the end of the third day. Hitler told Generaloberst Karl Hilpert, Commanding General, Army Group Courland, that his army group would have to hold out "until the turn that has occurred in every war has taken place."

The next day the south group of First Belorussian Front's main force got as far as Muencheberg. The north group, Second Guards Tank Army in the van, broke through west of Wriezen. It could have gone faster and farther, but the flank covering force was not yet out of the bridgehead. Hitler, "determined" to fight out the battle of Berlin on the Ninth Army front, gave Heinrici permission to take all the combat-worthy troops he could find out of the Berlin defenses.

Meanwhile, First Ukrainian Front was putting its armor across the Spree north and south of Spremberg. South of Spremberg the Fourth Panzer Army still had a vestige of a front; north of the city almost the whole Third Guards Tank Army was across the Spree. Schoerner reported that he had "hopes" of stopping Konev's southern thrust toward Bautzen. He intended to try again to close the front on the north, but, he added, "The laboriously organized defense in depth has only in a few places accomplished what one was forced to promise oneself from it."

On the 20th, Hitler's birthday, the battle for Berlin was lost. The Third and Fourth Guards Tank Armies pulled away from the Army Group Center flank and by day's end had strong armored spearheads thrusting north past Jueterbog, the Army's largest ammunition depot, and closing up to the German screening line ten miles south of Zossen. Second Belorussian Front attacked across the Oder from Schwedt to Stettin under the cover of smoke and created several bridgeheads. North of Berlin Second Guards Tank Army reached Bernau. The south group of First Belorussian Front's main force was still having trouble pushing toward Berlin, but it got a spearhead through to the southwest past Muencheberg to Fuerstenwalde behind Ninth Army.

Busse, the Commanding General, Ninth Army, reported in the morning that the only way he could get a solid line east of Berlin was by taking his front back from the Oder at and south of Frankfurt. No reply came from Fuehrer headquarters until late in the afternoon when Krebs called Heinrici to say that Hitler doubted whether the troops, particularly the heavy antiaircraft guns, could be gotten away from the Oder and wanted to talk to him before making a decision. The army group chief of staff replied that Heinrici was away at the front but had said that he could not be responsible for mastering the situation if the order were not given soon.

By then the Russians were approaching Fuerstenwalde. During the early half of the night, by telephoned commands relayed through Krebs and the Operations Branch, OKH, Hitler tried to juggle divisions to stop the Russians at Bernau and Fuerstenwalde. Half an hour after midnight Heinrici returned, called Krebs, and told him that he now had orders to hold everywhere and at the same time take out troops to support the threatened deep flanks. He was convinced that the mission could not be fulfilled and would "never succeed." He proposed to go to the Fuehrer, tell him so, and ask to be relieved and allowed to "take up a rifle and face the enemy."

HITLER DECIDES TO SEE THE BATTLE THROUGH

The observance of the Fuehrer's birthday before the afternoon situation conference had been subdued. The Chief of Staff, OKL, Generaloberst Karl Koller, had brought word that the last roads south would not stay open many hours longer. Those who were to go south would have to leave shortly by automobile because the Air Force did not have the planes to fly them out.

During the night General der Gebirgstruppe August Winter, Jodl's deputy, who was to be chief of staff of Command Staff B (the southern command post), departed with most of the essential personnel of the Operations Staff, OKW, and the Operations Branch, OKH. Goering left at high speed after midnight, having had to take cover for several hours in the public air raid shelters in Berlin, where he had a last opportunity to wring some laughs out of his old joke stemming from a speech he had made early in the war in which he had told the Germans they could "call me Meyer if the Allies ever bomb Berlin."40 It was expected that Hitler would also leave Berlin, probably for the south, because there was not enough of a staff left in the city and because after the big Army communications center at Zossen was lost, which could happen almost any hour, command from the capital would be impossible. Hitler had that day given Doenitz full power over matériel resources and manpower in the northern area.

The 21st, although the First Russian artillery shells fell in Berlin that day, brought a glimmer of good news; Fourth Panzer Army made some local progress in a counterattack northwest of Goerlitz. Hitler saw in it the makings of a major thrust that would close the 40-mile gap between the Army Group Vistula-Army Group Center flanks, and from that illusion he derived a "basic order" which Krebs transmitted to the army group by phone in the midafternoon. The "successful" attack at Army Group Center would soon close the front at Spremberg; therefore, it was "absolutely necessary" to hold the corner post at

Cottbus. (Ninth Army had taken command the day before of Fourth Panzer Army's left flank corps at and north of Cottbus.) Ninth Army would set up a front facing west between Koenigswusterhausen and Cottbus and attack west into the flank of the Russians going toward Berlin from the south. Steiner would command an operation to close the front north of Berlin on the line of the Berlin-Stettin autobahn. Third Panzer Army would eliminate "every last bridgehead on the Oder" and get ready to attack south. Reymann, relieved as Berlin commandant, would command the front south of Berlin.

Heinrici had given Steiner's III SS Panzer Corps headquarters, which had no troops of its own, the task of scraping together enough to set up a screening line on Third Panzer Army's flank along the Finow Canal. In the order that went out to Steiner in the late afternoon, Hitler elevated Steiner's command to an Armeeabteilung and gave him the 4th SS Police Division, the 5th Jaeger Division, and the 25th Panzer Grenadier Division, all north of the Finow Canal, and LVI Panzer Corps, standing east of Berlin with its north flank just below Werneuchen. With the three divisions Steiner was to attack south from Eberswalde on the canal to the LVI Panzer Corps flank and close the front.

To the tactical directive Hitler added, "Officers who do not accept this order without reservation are to be arrested and shot instantly. You yourself I make responsible with your head for its execution."45

As soon as he received the order Steiner called the army group headquarters to report that it could not be carried out. Of the 7th SS Police Division only two battalions were at hand, and they were not armed for combat. The 5th Jaeger and 25th Panzer Grenadier Divisions were tied down in the front and could not be used until the 3d Naval Division arrived from the coast to relieve them.

When Krebs phoned a résumé of the Steiner order to the army group headquarters, Heinrici asked him to impress on Hitler the necessity for taking back Ninth Army, which was being encircled and even then could no longer withdraw toward Berlin but would have to go around the lake chain south of the capital. If Hitler insisted on keeping his previous orders in force, then Heinrici asked to be relieved because he could not execute them and he could not reconcile them with his

Weary German infantrymen emerge from a Berlin sub-way station and surrender to the victorious Red Army.

conscience and his responsibility to the troops. Krebs answered that the Fuehrer took the responsibility for his own orders.

On 21 April Second Guards Tank Army gained nearly thirty miles north of Berlin, and an attack southwest of Werneuchen carried to the Berlin outer defense ring. North of Mueggel Lake the First Guards

Tank and Eighth Guards Armies also reached the outer defense ring. Between Mueggel Lake and Fuerstenwalde Ninth Army observed a strong build-up in progress, but the Russians did not continue the attack to the southwest to cut the army off from the city. Behind Ninth Army the point of Third Guards Tank Army reached Koenigswusterhausen.

The Soviet command decisions on the 21st were intended, first, to accomplish the encirclement of Berlin and, in the second order of business, to envelop Ninth Army. North of the capital the two armies that had been assigned the flank thrust were finally making enough speed to take over their screening mission, and Sokolovskiy ordered the Second Guards Tank and Forty-seventh Armies to concentrate on completing the encirclement. Approaching Berlin, First Guards Tank and Eighth Guards Armies had slowed down and then come almost to a stop on the outer defense ring, which delayed the encirclement of Ninth Army southwest of the line Mueggel Lake-Fuerstenwalde. First Belorussian Front's 2-army force in the Frankfurt bridgehead had not accomplished anything; its original mission had become superfluous and it was, therefore, assigned to assist in the encirclement of Ninth Army. The Third Guards Tank and Thirteenth Armies' rapid advance had stretched thin the enveloping front behind Ninth Army and had tended to draw the two Soviet armies east. On the 21st Konev put in Twenty-eighth Army from the reserve to take over part of the front against Ninth Army and free the Third Guards Tank and Thirteenth Armies to close in on Berlin from the south while Fourth Guards Tank Army attacked toward Potsdam.

At the afternoon situation conference on the 22d Hitler broke down. When, having waited impatiently through the morning and early afternoon for a report from Steiner, he learned that Steiner had not attacked, he fell into a tearful rage, declared that the war was lost, blamed it all on the generals, and announced that he would stay in Berlin to the end and kill himself before the Russians could take him prisoner. Keitel and Jodl refused an order to fly out to the southern command post and pledged themselves to stand by him.

As had happened many times before, the emotional storm passed quickly. Jodl remembered that they had the newly created Twelfth Army, of which Wenck had assumed command after his recovery,

'Desyanti'- Soviet tank riders on their way into the battle for Berlin.

facing west on a line southeast of Magdeburg but not yet solidly tied down.[45] Hitler first rejected as a waste of time a suggestion that they turn the army around and have it attack east. Then, in a few minutes, be took up the idea and was off on another round of planning.

During his breakdown, Hitler had finally admitted that his regime was utterly bankrupt. For him and his close associates all that was left was the consolation they could draw from keeping the machinery running even though it could accomplish nothing. Keitel was the outstanding example. Filled with purposeless dedication, he took on himself the role of field marshal-messenger and set out to carry the turn-around order to Wenck, a task which could be and, in fact, was accomplished far more quickly by phone.

---

45. Twelfth Army was created in early April 1945. It had seven divisions, including a panzer and a motorized division, all newly formed from the tank and officer training schools in central Germany. Its initial mission had been to assemble in the Harz Mountains and attack west to relieve Army Group B. By 12 April, the day on which the army headquarters assumed effective command, the offensive in the Harz had become all but impossible, and in the succeeding days, while organizing its divisions, the army had assumed the mission of defending the general line of the Elbe and Mulda Rivers from north of Magdeburg to south of Leipzig. The army's single notable asset, for the time a considerable one, was the youth and high morale of its troops.

Festivities after meeting of U.S. and Soviet troops at Torgau.

Before the conference ended, Krebs was on the phone to Heinrici telling him the Fuehrer was making the decision; Schoerner and Wenck would be briefed; Wenck would attack east; Schoerner's attack east of Bautzen was succeeding; Ninth Army would have to hold Cottbus and the Oder line to the south of Frankfurt. In short, Hitler was back at trying to build a front east of Berlin.

The reports coming in from the front revealed how slim the chances were. Steiner called after dark to report that he had not been able to attack because his troops were not assembled. Heinrici ordered him to attack that night, ready or not. Against Third Panzer Army, Second Belorussian Front had, by nightfall, taken a bridgehead ten miles long above Stettin. Ninth Army lost Cottbus and was broken through south of Frankfurt. North of Berlin Russian tank points were on the Havel River, and on the east the Russians had at one point penetrated the inner defense ring.

But when Krebs called Heinrici again at nine o'clock, he was full of optimism. The Wenck attack would bring relief fast, he said; one division would attack that night. Heinrici disagreed. Wenck had a long way to go. Heinrici wanted at least to take Ninth Army back twenty miles or so out of the bulge on the Oder upstream from Frankfurt. "Tell the Fuehrer," he added, "I do not ask this because I am against him but because I am for him."52 Finally, at midnight, Heinrici was authorized to let Ninth Army withdraw to a line from north of Cottbus to Lieberose, Beeskow, and the Spree. In doing so, Busse was to free divisions for an attack west to meet Twelfth Army.

COMPLETING THE CIRCLE

The next day, the 23d, the encirclement of Berlin entered its final stage. First Belorussian Front committed its second echelon, Third Army, to cut the narrow corridor connecting Ninth Army with Berlin. From the south the Third Guards Tank and Thirteenth Armies closed to the outer defense ring, and Fourth Guards Tank Army approached Potsdam. North of Berlin Second Guards Tank Army crossed the Havel below Oranienburg and began turning south. In the city that afternoon Hitler held his last big situation conference. When it broke up, Keitel went out to bring his "personal influence" to bear on Twelfth Army, and Jodl headed north with the OKW staff to Neu Roofen, behind Third Panzer Army.

In the afternoon Hitler ordered General der Artillerie Helmuth Weidling, Commanding General, LVI Panzer Corps, to take over with his troops, which Busse had wanted to use to protect Ninth Army's north flank, the eastern and southeastern defenses of the city. Hitler later also made Weidling, whom he had only the day before intended to have shot, defense commandant of all Berlin. When Krebs announced the appointment, Weidling said he would rather they had shot him.

After the situation conference, Heinrici received a telephoned order to stop the Steiner attack "at once," give up the Eberswalde bridgehead, and shift Steiner's headquarters and all the troops that could be released west of Oranienburg for an attack into the flank of the Russians crossing the Havel. The order added that Twelfth Army was sending XXXXI Panzer Corps to hem the Russians in from the west. Steiner had made some progress south of Eberswalde early in the day but far short of enough to have any effect.

By the end of the day, Hitler, through his order pulling LVI Panzer Corps into Berlin, had made it a certainty that Ninth Army would soon be completely isolated and encircled. When Heinrici talked to Busse that night, after the telephone connections had been out all day, the latter reported that he would have to make the breakout to the west with small arms, since artillery ammunition was exhausted. His north front was disintegrating because it was losing the support it had been getting from Berlin. He summed up his predicament in a sentence, "I was kept forward too long." Heinrici replied, "That was a crime." When they finished, Heinrici called Wenck and told him he must rescue his "old friend," Busse.

On the 24th the Russians worked systematically to complete the great circle of steel and fire around Berlin. The battle was lost; it would have been given up but for one man, who, prematurely aged, palsied, and buried under 20 feet of earth and concrete out of sight and hearing of the destruction rolling in on him, demanded and got absolute obedience. Berlin was no Stalingrad. It might hold out, through fanaticism and terror, for a few days, no more. On the north and east the Russians were approaching the S-Bahn defense ring. During the day the First Belorussian and First Ukrainian Fronts' forces met at Bohnsdorf to close the encirclement on the southeast and isolate Ninth Army. Fourth Guards Tank Army reached the lakes flanking Potsdam, and Second Guards Tank Army, coming from the north, went as far as Nauen and south almost to Spandau. In the city LVI Panzer Corps occupied the southeast sector; the rest was held by Volkssturm, SS, and Hitler Youth formations. The four massive flak towers stood like stranded concrete battleships, powerful yet helpless. Weidling discovered that his predecessors had tried to exercise command through the public telephone system.

Deprived of all but the last remnants of his once elaborate command apparatus, Hitler, nevertheless, ordered, "The OKW... will command in accordance with my directives which I will transmit through the Chief of Staff, OKH, who is with me." He terminated the OKH command functions and undertook to command in the north directly through the Operations Staff, OKW, and in the south more loosely through the Command Staff B and the army groups. For the south he issued a halfhearted directive to create, as far as that could still be accomplished, a redoubt in the Alps. His conception of how that

A Soviet rifleman peers carefully round the corner of a bridge in an attempt to locate a German sniper.

should be done did not go much beyond the general statement that it was to be "envisioned as the final bulwark of fanatical resistance and so prepared." For him the war had narrowed down to Berlin. He established as "the main mission" of the OKW to attack from the northwest, southwest, and south to regain contact with Berlin and "so decide the battle for the capital victoriously."

In Jodl and Keitel, Hitler had ideal collaborators in futility. Neither gave a thought to anything beyond getting through to the Fuehrer, above all not to the question, Why? Before the day was out Jodl had changed the directions of the Ninth and Twelfth Armies; the one was to attack northeast, the other northwest toward Berlin.

On 25 April the Soviet spearheads met northwest of Potsdam. On the Elbe, U.S. First Army and Soviet Fifth Guards Army made contact at Torgau. In an order to Doenitz, Hitler described the fighting in and around Berlin as the "battle for the German fate," all other fronts and missions being secondary. He instructed the Admiral to send reinforcements to Berlin by air and to the fronts around the city "by land and by sea." The OKW had already directed the theater

German troops clogging a road after escaping the Russians.

commanders to regard the conflict with the Soviet forces as paramount and to accept "greater losses of territory to the Anglo-Americans" for the sake of releasing units to be committed against the Russians.

To the extent that the German fate still remained to be decided, the day's most significant development was neither at Berlin nor on the Elbe but on the Oder, where Second Belorussian Front, completing the breakout it had begun the day before from its bridgehead south of Stettin, crossed the Randow Swamp toward Prenzlau.

THE LAST ACT

"A DAY OF HOPES"

Half an hour after midnight on the night of 25 April a directive that Hitler had written the evening before reached the OKW headquarters at Neu Roofen. It called for the "fastest execution of all relief attacks, without regard for flanks and neighbors." Although he must have known that his time was running pitifully short, Hitler still insisted on attempting nothing less than to restore a complete and solid front on the east. Twelfth Army was to attack northwest from Belzig to Ferch at the tip of the twin lakes south of Potsdam while Ninth Army attacked west to meet it. After they had joined, both armies were to advance toward Berlin from the south "on a broad front." Ninth Army, meanwhile, was also to hold its eastern front so that Army Group Center could close up from the south. Steiner was to attack toward Berlin from northwest of Oranienburg with the 25th Panzer Grenadier Division, the 3d Naval Division, and the 7th Panzer Division. Third Panzer Army was to "prevent an expansion of the Oder bridgehead."

Jodl answered that all the relief attacks had begun or were about to begin. He also called attention to the Second Belorussian Front threat east of Prenzlau and a 21 Army Group (British) build-up southeast of Hamburg that indicated a thrust toward Luebeck. To counter those he proposed withdrawing the German forces on the coast west of the Elbe.

Weidling remembered 26 April as "the day of hopes"; Krebs repeatedly phoned him at his command post in the Bendlerstrasse to announce good news. The naval liaison officer's morning report to Doenitz reflected the interpretation that was being put on Jodl's message in the Fuehrer bunker: the Ninth and Twelfth Armies were having "gratifying successes"; Steiner was "making progress"; and Schoerner's attack at Bautzen showed that "when the will is there, the enemy can be defeated even today." Hitler's resurgent confidence found expression in his reply to Jodl. He wanted the Elbe line held and the "bridgehead" east of Prenzlau not only contained but reduced. He did not object to taking forces from west of the Elbe, but it should be done without losing the ports, Emden, Wilhelmshaven, and Wesermuende, or losing the use of the Kaiser Wilhelm (Kiel) Canal.

In the evening the telephone lines to Berlin went dead, and the communications to and from the pocket were shifted to line-of-sight short wave received and transmitted from a balloon run up near the OKW headquarters. In a spirit of self-immolation, Jodl and Keitel intended to fly into the city that night for one more situation conference, but the landing strip in the Tiergarten was closed by smoke, shell holes, and wrecked aircraft. The last to land that night were Generaloberst

Robert Ritter von Greim and Hanna Reitsch, the daredevil woman test pilot. Hitler promoted von Greim to Generalfeldmarschall and appointed him Commander in Chief, OKL.[46]

During the day on the 26th the German commands launched into the pursuit of two incompatible and, considering the state of the German forces, mutually exclusive objectives: Heinrici became intent on holding together what was left of his front and rescuing Ninth Army, while Keitel and Jodl concentrated entirely on the Berlin relief. Heinrici wanted to save what could still be saved. Keitel and Jodl tried to force reality to submit to the Fuehrer's will. To them this was nothing new. They had watched him sacrifice armies in an almost unbroken succession of similar attempts since Stalingrad. It was the essence of the Fuehrer principle; it was Hitler's formula for victory; and it had one fault—it never worked.

Steiner had advanced and taken a small bridgehead on the Havel west of Oranienburg during the night, but after daylight he was stopped. All he had was the 25th Panzer Grenadier Division. The 3d Naval Division was strung out on the railroads between Oranienburg and the coast, and the 7th Panzer Division, brought into Swinemuende by sea from Danzig only days before, had no vehicles with which to move out of its assembly area west of Neubrandenburg. Before noon Heinrici proposed giving up the Steiner attack, because it could not be expected to succeed, and using the divisions against the breakthrough east of Prenzlau. Jodl refused.

By late afternoon Second Belorussian Front had chewed through Third Panzer Army's last reserves and was approaching Prenzlau. Manteuffel started taking back his flanks to get troops to put into the gap opening in his center. Heinrici concluded that a decision had to be made concerning Steiner; his operation could not influence the fate of Berlin and it was tying down the army group's "last and only" motorized division. The question was, where could the decision come

---

46. Hitler had, two days before, dismissed Goering from all his official posts (including, as Bormann put it, that of Reichs Chief Hunter) and had him arrested. Goering, who until then considered himself Hitler's anointed political heir and successor, had been misled, by a remark of Hitler's that he would "leave the negotiating to Goering," into inquiring whether Hitler intended by his decision to stay in Berlin to turn the powers of government over to him.

The Reichstag after the fall of Berlin.

from? By direct interference Jodl and Keitel had practically removed Steiner from Heinrici's command.

Twelfth Army, the mainstay of the relief operation, did not expect to accomplish more than to get a wedge through that would allow the Berlin civilians and garrison to escape. After several changes, its assigned missions were to assist the Steiner operation from the west with XXXXI Panzer Corps, cover the Elbe line and defend Brandenburg—to hold open a corridor between the Russians and the Americans—and advance northeast from Belzig. On the 26th, XX Corps, the relief corps, was engaged in defending the line Brandenburg-Belzig-Wittenberg to protect its staging area.

Ninth Army began its breakout with a thrust west to the Baruth-Zossen road. Its strength was sinking fast. The night before, all the promised air supply had been diverted to Berlin. Jodl, after his last telephone conversation with Hitler, was still determined to "make clear to Ninth Army that it must turn sharply [north] together with Twelfth Army to relieve Berlin."72 Jodl and Heinrici argued over where the air supply, such as it might be, should go. Heinrici maintained that the army deserved the aid because the higher commands were responsible for its being where it was. Jodl insisted that the people of Berlin and

607

A T-34 in the thick of the last battles for Berlin.

the "Head of State" could not be left in the lurch and suggested that any thought to the contrary was treason. Off Ninth Army's south flank, Schoerner's attack, having made about fifteen miles in six days, was close to a standstill with forty miles yet to go.

KEITEL AND JODL IN COMMAND

During the night of the 26th Third Panzer Army withdrew to the Uecker River and the line of the lakes south of Prenzlau. It was the army's last chance to keep from being overrun, and it failed. The next morning Rokossovskiy's tanks broke through past Prenzlau and his infantry streamed into the gap behind them. In the afternoon Heinrici's chief of staff went to Doenitz's headquarters in Ploen to report to the admiral that the army group was defeated, could not stop the Russians, and was retreating west through Mecklenburg.

If Heinrici expected a decision from Doenitz, he was disappointed. At a situation conference several hours before—at which Doenitz and Himmler, to their mutual chagrin, both insisted on receiving Keitel's and Jodl's reports seated as was Hitler's practice—it had been decided that Doenitz would not exercise military command until it became impossible for the OKW to secure its orders from Hitler. In any event, nothing much could have been expected of Doenitz's military judgment; he had lately begun to quibble about holding Stettin and Swinemuende, where Third Panzer Army's north flank was threatened with encirclement, so that the Navy could keep contact with Army Group Courland. Doenitz might have stretched his civil powers to include negotiating a surrender; but he was not the man for that; though less ostentatiously, he counted himself among Hitler's paladins as much as did Jodl and Keitel.

The OKW, marking time on 27 April, issued commands in all directions. To stop the Prenzlau breakthrough, Headquarters, Twenty-first Army (the former Fourth Army Staff), under General Tippelskirch, was to be put in with two regiments, neither of them available for at least another twenty-four hours. Hitler had lost faith in Steiner, and an order went out for XXXXI Panzer Corps to take command of the Oranienburg attack, but the corps headquarters was too far away to assume effective command. Hitler had called on the Ninth and Twelfth Armies to do their duty, to unite and attack toward Berlin, and so attain "the decisive turning point of the war." To the order to the armies Keitel added, "History and the German people will despise everyone who does not do his utmost to save the situation and the Fuehrer." Keitel directed Schoerner, in case contact with the OKW was lost, to keep on attacking north from Bautzen toward the Ninth and Twelfth Armies.

Late in the afternoon Jodl at last concluded, "The enemy clearly has broken through Third Panzer Army at Prenzlau." He decided, "onerous as it is," to stop the Steiner attack; but he could not, even yet, bring himself to give it up completely. The order to Heinrici stated that he could have the 25th Panzer Grenadier Division and the 7th Panzer Division for a counterattack into the Russian flank from the southwest. Presumably, afterwards the divisions were to be turned south toward Berlin again.

An hour and a half before midnight Manteuffel called the army group and reported that half of his divisions and the flak artillery had quit fighting. A hundred thousand men were fleeing west. He had not seen anything like it even in 1918, Manteuffel said; it would take hundreds of officers to stop them. The war was over, he added; the soldiers had "spoken"; some of the officers would stand and let themselves be shot, but that would not accomplish anything. He proposed sending Jodl out to see for himself what a waste of time it was to talk about relieving Berlin; all that was left was to negotiate, preferably with the Allies, and meanwhile retreat west fast enough to hold the remnants of the army together.

The next morning, 28 April, Keitel set out toward the front intending to lend the stimulus of his presence to the preparations for the counterattack on the Third Panzer Army flank. At Zehdenick on the Havel, to his huge astonishment and dismay, he encountered a rear party of the 5th Jaeger Division surveying a defense line on the river. He had thought the front was twenty miles farther east and, complying with his orders, would stay there. Subsequently he also learned that the counterattack from Templin would not be made. Heinrici and Manteuffel had decided the evening before that the 7th Panzer Division and 25th Panzer Grenadier Division could not be assembled there in time and, therefore, should be put in farther north, east of Neubrandenburg and Neustrelitz, to oppose the Russians frontally.

In the afternoon Keitel met with Heinrici and Manteuffel. By then Jodl had been on the phone to Heinrici talking of treason and threatening the "ultimate consequences" if Heinrici did not execute orders as they were given. In what Heinrici described as a "colossal discussion" and an "atrocious development," Keitel ordered the army group to stand and to counterattack southeast of Neustrelitz.

Keitel gave the order to stand in the midst of a front that was disintegrating all around him—Heinrici took three hours covering the twenty or so miles back to his headquarters. The roads were clogged with refugees and retreating troops; Neubrandenburg was completely blocked. The troops, Heinrici observed, were "marching home in columns."

After midnight Heinrici called Keitel and told him that the Russians had reached the Havel on Third Panzer Army's south flank. Keitel replied that that was what happened when "one gives up positions voluntarily." Heinrici protested that he had been deprived of the authority to make decisions within his own command. Keitel answered

This King Tiger was one of the last Panzers to engage in battle. These machines were impervious to many Soviet weapons and were more often destroyed by their crews who ran out of ammunition or fuel.

that it had been necessary because the Fuehrer's orders were not being carried out and therewith relieved Heinrici, ordering him to turn the command over to Manteuffel as the senior army commander.[47]

In and around Berlin on that day, 28 April, the end was approaching rapidly. Keitel kept alive the fiction of an attack from Oranienburg, but the only one of the relief operations that had any prospect of being executed was Wenck's. Ninth Army's breakout failed; the tank point in the lead became separated and was not heard from again. Busse reported that the army was neither in condition to make another concerted attempt nor to hold out much longer. In Berlin eight Soviet armies had begun attacking through the S-Bahn ring on the 26th, after heavy bombings during the previous day and night. By nightfall on the 27th the Russians had cut off Reymann's force in Potsdam and pushed the Berlin defenders into a pocket nine and a half miles long

---

47. Various accounts have been given of the incidents leading up to Heinrici's dismissal. Some maintain that Heinrici had decided to retreat west and surrender to the Americans. Manteuffel had, in effect, proposed doing that on the night of 27 April. Although the ultimate effect would have been the same, it appears from the Army Group Vistula records that Heinrici's decisions on 27 and 28 April were made in the light of the immediate tactical situation and not as part of a farther reaching plan.

from east to west and from one to three miles wide. On the west the pocket still reached nearly to the Havel River, but the Russians had closed the crossings. In the center, the Soviet armies competed for the honor of taking the Reichstag—which to the Russians, even though it had been a charred ruin since 1933, was the symbol of the Third Reich—and had driven in spearheads from the north and the south to the edges of the government quarter.

TOO LATE FOR A MIRACLE

The battle for Berlin was fought outside the city; what went on in the capital was hardly more than a contested mop-up. The fortress had never come into existence. When SS-Brigadefuehrer (Brig. Gen.) Gustav Krukenberg came into Berlin on 24 April to take command of the SS Nordland Division, he found the Havel bridges near Spandau barricaded but not defended. From there he drove through all of west Berlin "without encountering soldiers or defense installations of any kind." In the Fuehrer bunker, Krebs told him that the ninety volunteers from the Charlemagne Division Krukenberg had brought with him were the only ones who had arrived of numerous officers and troop units ordered into Berlin. The Nordland Division, Krukenberg discovered, had the strength of about a battalion. Three days later, when he became a sector commander in the center of the city, his command post was a subway car with neither telephone nor lights. The fighting in Berlin lasted as long as it did because a great metropolis, bombed out though it might be and no matter how amateurishly fortified, cannot be quickly taken even against a lame defense, particularly not by troops who know the war is over and intend to see their homes again.

Berlin did not go down, as Hitler had imagined, in a Wagnerian burst of glory but in a ragged wave of destruction and despair. Corpses hanging in the streets, the work of single-officer flying courts-martial that passed only death sentences, showed soldiers and civilians what they could expect of their own leadership. But that leadership was operating on residual momentum, it could no longer formulate, deliver, or enforce purposeful orders. Individuals might be hanged; whole units could hide out. With rockets and artillery, the Russians evened the scores for Leningrad and Stalingrad as far as they could. But in the cellars in which Berlin life had centered for months (Berlin was heavily bombed 83 times between 1 February and 21 April) Soviet shells had nowhere near the effect that Allied bombs had had, nor did they greatly add to the damage already inflicted on the city.

Scenes of horror were commonplace; but the most famous, the alleged deliberate flooding of subway tunnels filled with wounded and civilians, appears to have been mostly invented. The official who was in charge when the subways were pumped out in October 1945 has stated that the flooding was gradual and none of the bodies found showed evidence of drowning. All apparently had died of wounds before being placed in the tunnels.

In an attempt to stiffen the Berliner's resistance, Goebbels had, since January, saturated the news broadcasts with refugees' accounts of Russian atrocities, among them the pathetic instance of a woman who insisted that she had been raped exactly twenty-four times. What had happened in East Prussia, Pomerania, and Silesia also happened in Berlin, but by then Soviet policy discouraged personal acts of license and vengeance. As indication of an intent, at least, to restore order quickly, General Polkovnik N. Z. Berzarin took control as city commandant on 28 April.

Hitler did not concern himself with the human aspect of the fighting in Berlin any more than he had when the front was deep in Russia. The concrete Fuehrer bunker and the steady roar of the diesel-driven ventilating system provided almost perfect insulation against sight and sound; nevertheless, occasionally, shell explosions close by shook the bunker and the ventilators drew in dust and fumes. The tiny bunker rooms were more crowded than ever, mostly with persons engaged in caring for and protecting Hitler, or in maintaining his contact with the outside. Of the top Nazi hierarchy only Goebbels and Bormann stayed, Goebbels out of loyalty to the Fuehrer and because he had vague faith in the miracle, Bormann to promote his own interests and do what damage he could to his rivals. The parade of generals had ended. Until the 27th Hitler continued to hold the regular situation conferences. Although he attempted still to maintain the tone of a strategist, his span of practical concern had narrowed to

Remains of the German Chancellory.

such decisions as the appointment of a detachment that was to act "in case a Russian tank by some sly trick or other digs me out of here." A recurring theme in his rambling discourses was the correctness of his decision to stay in Berlin—as an object lesson to all the generals who had ordered retreats and as the only means of achieving a "moral" victory that would convince the British and Americans of his value to them in the, in his opinion, forthcoming conflict with the Russians.

During the night of 28 April Weidling brought a breakout plan to Hitler. The Fuehrer listened with some interest but then declared it was better that he stay where he was, otherwise he would only have to await the end "somewhere under the open sky or in a farmhouse." Hitler had made his last military decision. At midnight Doenitz's liaison officer in the bunker radioed, "We will hold out to the end." Greim and Hanna Reitsch flew out that night in an old training plane a Luftwaffe pilot managed somehow to land and get off the ground again. Greim had orders to organize air support for Wenck's attack.

During the evening, news had reached the bunker of Himmler's attempt to negotiate an armistice through Count Folke Bernadotte, and in the early morning Bormann dispatched the following radio message to Doenitz: "The foreign press reports fresh treason. The Fuehrer expects that you will act with lightning speed and iron severity against all traitors in the North German area. Without exception, Schoerner, Wenck, and others must give evidence of their loyalty through the quickest relief of the Fuehrer."

At daylight on the 29th Wenck's XX Corps attacked with the Clausewitz, Scharnhorst, and Theodor Koerner Divisions, all so-called youth divisions made up of men from the officer training schools. To a dismal scene, they added a last flash of the old German élan and by afternoon covered fifteen miles to the tip of Schwielow Lake southwest of Potsdam; but the flanks were open and the Lehnin Forest behind them was filled with Russians who were rapidly recovering from the initial surprise and shock. To continue the advance toward Berlin, still twenty miles away, was clearly out of the question. After dark the Potsdam garrison made contact and began coming out by rowboats across the lakes. Later in the night Keitel authorized Wenck to stop the attack, "If the Commanding General, Twelfth Army, in full knowledge of his present situation at XX Corps and despite the high historical and moral responsibility that he carries considers continuing the attack toward Berlin not executable…"

Through the better part of the day on 29 April Army Group Vistula was without an effective command. Heinrici refused to order any withdrawals, which meant in effect that he gave no orders at all. He learned during the day that Jodl had intervened in the internal workings of the army group to the extent of instructing at least one of the corps on the south flank to report to him immediately any withdrawal orders coming from the army group. In the morning Manteuffel declined to take command, stating in his message to Keitel, "Beg not at this time of crisis in own army to be charged with the mission that the [present] commanding general, who has the full confidence of all commanders, is alleged not to have carried out." The army commanders, Manteuffel and Tippelskirch, whose Headquarters, Twenty-first Army, was then taking over the south front from Steiner, had agreed beforehand not to let the command be taken out of Heinrici's hands.

In the afternoon, Keitel and Jodl, knowing that Tippelskirch also intended to refuse, went to Tippelskirch's command post and in an interview that took place between 1600 and 1700 prevailed on him to take acting command until Generaloberst Kurt Student could arrive from Holland. Keitel "reminded Tippelskirch of his duty most forcefully." Tippelskirch, although he, like most German generals found it virtually impossible to refuse a direct order, was no coward and had shown independence of judgment before, notably as Commanding General, Fourth Army, during the 1944 collapse of Army Group Center. Apparently what convinced him to desert Heinrici was Jodl's argument that the army group had to hold as much territory as it still could, not for the sake of relieving Berlin, but to give the political authorities something with which to bargain.

During the day Second Belorussian Front's offensive carried past Anklam on the north, past Neubrandenburg and Neustrelitz in the center, and across the Havel in the Zehdenick-Liebenwalde sector in the south. Behind Army Group Vistula, Field Marshal Sir Bernard L. Montgomery's 21 Army Group established a bridgehead across the Elbe at Lauenburg upstream from Hamburg. Doenitz, worried by the threat of a thrust from Lauenburg toward Hamburg and Luebeck, asked that the reinforcements for Army Group Vistula and Twelfth Army be committed on the Elbe instead. Shortly after noon, the balloon being used to beam voice transmissions into Berlin was shot down. Since its headquarters by then was practically in the front, the OKW began moving north from Neu Roofen several hours later.

In the Fuehrer bunker the 29th was a day of waiting while, above ground, destruction rained down on all sides. Hitler had married his long-time mistress Eva Braun the night before and in the early morning hours had written his personal and political testaments. In the latter he named Doenitz his successor as Reichs President and the head of state and, dictator to the last, appointed a Cabinet to take office under the admiral with Goebbels as Chancellor and Bormann, Party Minister. He knew almost to the hour how much time he had left. Weidling had reported that the planes had dropped only a few tons of supplies during the night; in the coming night he expected none at all; most likely, the ammunition would run out by nightfall on the 30th.

Before midnight Hitler dispatched his last message. In five short questions addressed to Jodl he reached for the miracle one more time:

The destruction around the Brandenberg gate shortly after the official surrender.

1. Where are Wenck's spearheads?
2. When will they attack again?
3. Where is the Ninth Army?
4. To where is it breaking through?
5. Where are Holste's [XXXXI Panzer Corps] spearheads?99

There would be no miracle; the Fuehrer had to be told; and Keitel, conscious of history, took the responsibility. In the dry, impersonal language of a situation report he put a period to one of the greatest and most disastrous military adventures the world had ever seen:

To 1. Wenck's point is stopped south of Schwielow Lake. Strong Soviet attacks on the whole east flank.

To 2. As a consequence Twelfth Army cannot continue the attack toward Berlin.

To 3 and 4. Ninth Army is encircled. A panzer group has broken out west. Location unknown.

To 5. Corps Holste is forced to the defensive from Brandenburg via Rathenow to Kremmen.

The attack toward Berlin has not progressed at any point since Army Group Vistula was also forced to the defensive on its whole front from north of Oranienburg via [Neu] Brandenburg to Anklam.

On the afternoon of the 30th, between 1500 and 1530, Hitler and his wife committed suicide. The SS guards carried the bodies outside, tried to burn them in gasoline, and when that failed and the gasoline ran out, buried the remains in a nearby shell hole. A quarter mile away the Russians were storming the Reichstag. Bormann sent a radio message to Doenitz telling him that he was appointed Hitler's successor and was "empowered immediately to take all of the measures required by the current situation." Bormann did not, however, include the most vital piece of information, namely, that the Fuehrer was dead. That was a trump he was not ready to let out of his hand.

THE SAND RUNS OUT

At exactly the time the SS-men were disposing of Hitler's body behind the pile of rubble that had been the Reichs Chancellory, Keitel transmitted a directive to Winter at the Command Staff B. The first sentence read: "The attempt to relieve Berlin has failed." In the north, Keitel continued, the intention was to have Twelfth Army fight its way north to Army Group Vistula and thereafter, with the combined forces, to hold a line from the mouth of the Elbe to Havelberg (at the confluence of the Havel and the Elbe) and thence north to Rostock. The mission for the south was to form "a great ring" with the main effort in the east "to preserve as much territory as possible from Bolshevism." "The battle to win political time," the directive concluded, "must be continued. Every attempt at military or political dissolution must be put down with ruthless force."

Those who were left in the Fuehrer bunker that night still held three assets, which they hoped to use to their own advantage: the knowledge that the Fuehrer was dead, the seat of the government (what was left of it), and what could have been the two most powerful offices in the successor government. At 0100 1 May Krebs went through the lines to carry for Stalin's exclusive information the news of Hitler's death and to try to negotiate an armistice that would allow the successor German Government to function in the capital. He was taken to Eighth Guards Army's forward command post, where the Commanding General, Chuikov, heard his proposal. Later, probably with instructions from Moscow, Sokolovskiy arrived to interview Krebs and give him his answer.

At 1000, possibly because it appeared that Krebs had not gotten through, Bormann sent a second radio message to Doenitz. Laconic as the first, it stated only that the testament was in force; Bormann would come to Ploen; and he advised not making the information public until he arrived. At noon Krebs returned. The Russians had agreed to let Doenitz come back to Berlin and assemble the government there, but they demanded capitulation and would not grant an armistice. Goebbels insisted that in accordance with Hitler's wishes there be no capitulation and reiterated his already announced resolve to share the Fuehrer's fate.

In the afternoon, just twenty-four hours after the event, a message signed by Goebbels and Bormann informed Doenitz that the Fuehrer was dead and named the major appointments Hitler had made in addition to Doenitz's own. (Three couriers carrying copies of the testament for Doenitz and for Schoerner—whom Hitler had appointed his successor as Commander in Chief, Army—had left the bunker on the 29th. None of them reached his destination.) Goebbels and his wife committed suicide after killing their children. Bormann probably was killed trying to make his way out of Berlin to claim his post in Doenitz's Cabinet. Krebs and Generaloberst Wilhelm Burgdorf declared that they intended to commit suicide and probably did.

Weidling considered a breakout, but he had neither the room nor the means to organize it. At five o'clock on the morning of 2 May he crossed the lines and surrendered the city. It was another two days before the fighting died completely.

Doenitz, on 1 May before he knew Hitler was dead, had pledged "immutable loyalty" to the Fuehrer and "to conduct this war to its end in the manner the unique, heroic struggle of the German people demands." But Doenitz's loyalty was professional not sentimental. The next day he determined that the German military situation was hopeless, a conclusion which until then he seems successfully to have avoided. In directives issued during the day he established as his policy to continue the war against the Soviet Union in order to keep as many Germans as possible from falling into Soviet hands and to

Jodl arriving at Reims to negotiate an unconditional surrender.

offer resistance to the Americans and British only to the extent that they interfered with the attainment of the first objective. He decided to attempt to evade the unconditional surrender by negotiating piecemeal surrenders "at the army group level." As a first step, he appointed Generaladmiral Hans-Georg von Friedeburg head of a delegation to negotiate an agreement with Montgomery to spare Hamburg and "to discuss farther-reaching questions."

For Army Group Vistula the end came quickly and more mercifully than the Germans could have expected. The 21 Army Group, after breaking out of its Elbe bridgehead the day before, on 2 May reached the Baltic coast at Luebeck and Wismar. Elements of U.S. Ninth Army pushed east to Ludwigslust and Schwerin. In Schwerin the American armored troops captured the Army Group Vistula quartermaster section. Student, who had taken command on the 1st, escaped just ahead of the American tanks. Second Belorussian Front reached Wittenberge, Parchim, and Bad Doberan. Between the two fronts the Third Panzer and Twenty-first Armies were squeezed into a corridor fifteen to twenty miles wide, stretching from the Elbe to the coast. During the night Manteuffel and Tippelskirch surrendered their armies, which by then had almost completely disintegrated, to the Americans. Jodl had drafted an order authorizing such a move, but it went into the files with the notation "Could no longer be transmitted."

Twelfth Army's XX Corps had begun falling back southwest of Potsdam during the night of 1 May. In the morning it had taken through its line 30,000 Ninth Army survivors whom, by means of radio contact established the day before, it had guided away from the strongest Russian concentrations. On the afternoon of the 3d Wenck sent General der Panzertruppen Maximilian Freiherr von Edelsheim across the Elbe to U.S. Ninth Army to negotiate a surrender. The next morning Ninth Army consented to let as many of the German Ninth and Twelfth Armies' troops cross the Elbe as could without (except for the wounded) assistance from the Americans. Between the morning of the 5th and the night of the 7th most of Wenck's force found refuge behind the American line.

Army Groups Center and Courland and Army of East Prussia, those monuments to Hitler's strategy, posed greater problems. Doenitz's first impulse had been to order Army Group Center to start retreating westward at once; but he had been dissuaded by Keitel who, drawing the wrong conclusions to the last, had argued that if the army group left built-up lines, it would not be able to preserve a solid front. To Army Group Courland and Army of East Prussia, Doenitz sent word that he intended to secure British and American toleration of, "under certain circumstances support for," an evacuation that would return to Germany 50,000 men from Army Group Courland and as many as 100,000 from Army of East Prussia "in the first ten days." On 4 May, when von Friedeburg reported that Montgomery had agreed to accept the surrender of all the German forces in Holland, Denmark, and north Germany, Doenitz instructed him to contact Eisenhower for the purpose of negotiating another partial capitulation. He was "above all to explain to Eisenhower why a total capitulation on all fronts appears impossible to the Grand Admiral." On the 6th von Friedeburg reported that Eisenhower insisted on an immediate and simultaneous unconditional surrender.

SURRENDER

On the afternoon of the 6th Jodl arrived at the Supreme Headquarters Allied Expeditionary Forces in Reims. Doenitz had sent him with instructions to lay before Eisenhower again "completely and openly" the reasons why a total capitulation was impossible. Failing of success in that, he was to try to get a phased capitulation with as long an interval as possible between the time the fighting terminated and the time the troops had to surrender their arms and cease all movements. Fifteen minutes after midnight Doenitz received a radio message from Jodl stating that Eisenhower insisted the total capitulation be signed "today" to take effect at midnight on the night of 8 May; otherwise, he would close all the Allied fronts to Germans, including individuals coming from the east. Jodl added, "I see no way out but to sign."

Doenitz concluded that Jodl, who before his departure had been the one who argued most strongly against the total capitulation, must have become convinced that no better terms could be attained. He empowered Jodl to sign, and at 1245 the new Foreign Minister, Graf Lutz Schwerin von Krosigk, announced the surrender over the German radio. At 0130 Doenitz ordered Schoerner, Rendulic, and Loehr to take their fronts west as fast as they could and to "fight their way through the Russians" if they had to; all hostilities against the Allies were to stop at once. At 0141 Jodl placed his signature on the Act of Military Surrender. The time for all German forces to cease active operations and "to remain in the positions occupied at that time" was set at 2301 Central European Time on 8 May. (The formal ratification was completed in Berlin a half hour before midnight on 8 May.)

Having signed the surrender, Doenitz and the OKW were not certain they could enforce it in the east. That uncertainty was undoubtedly in part inspired by their own desire to see the terms concerning surrender to the Russians evaded to the greatest extent possible without incurring severe reprisals. Jodl had taken out some advance insurance by securing a statement from Eisenhower's chief of staff, Lt. Gen. Walter Bedell Smith, that the OKW would not be held responsible if "individual soldiers and some troop units" did not follow orders and refused to surrender to the Russians.

Keitel signing the surrender terms at Soviet Headquarters in Berlin.

The source of most concern was Army Group Center, because it was the largest single force still on the Eastern Front, because it had the farthest to go to reach the Allied lines (of those that had any chance of doing so at all), and because no one knew how Schoerner would react to the surrender. Schoerner had reported on 2 May that he had a tight hold on his troops and was starting to manufacture his own ammunition and motor fuel. The last that had been heard from him was that he intended to fight his army group through to the line of the Elbe and Vltava (Moldau) before surrendering. On the 8th an OKW staff colonel with an American officer escort went to Schoerner's headquarters. The colonel reported that Schoerner had ordered the surrender terms observed but claimed he did not have the means to make certain they were carried out everywhere. The colonel "assured him that the command difficulties would be brought to the attention of the Americans and the OKW." The OKW need neither have worried that Schoerner would attempt a last-ditch battle nor have hoped that he would find a means to extricate his army group.

Schoerner deserted his troops on the 8th and in civilian clothes flew a light plane out of Czechoslovakia. He was arrested in Austria ten days later by First Panzer Army troops and turned over to the Americans.

The OKW calculated the actual strengths (Army, Navy, Waffen-SS, and Air Force) on the Eastern Front at the hour the surrender went into effect as follows:[48]

Southeastern Theater: 180,000
Army Group Ostmark (formerly South): 430,000
Army Group Center: 600,000
Army of East Prussia: 100,000
Army Group Courland: 200,000
Total: 1,510,000

Only Army Group Ostmark succeeded in saving a major part of its force from Soviet (or Yugoslav) captivity. For the approximately one and a quarter million troops who became prisoners of war in the East after the surrender it was to be a long way home.

---

48. The ration strengths, which included various auxiliaries, were in most cases substantially higher.

CHAPTER XXII

Conclusion

The most striking aspect of the German-Soviet conflict in World War II was the vastness of its dimensions. With scarcely an interlude, the fighting lasted for 3 years, 10 months, and 16 days. From autumn 1941 to autumn 1943 the length of the front was never less than 2,400 miles and for a time late in 1942 it reached 3,060 miles. The conflict seesawed across eastern and central Europe between the Elbe and the Volga, the Alps, and the Caucasus. The German armies thrust 1,200 miles into the Soviet Union and Soviet troops countermarched 1,500 miles to Berlin. The total number of troops continuously engaged averaged between 8 and 9 million, and the losses were appalling. The Wehrmacht dead from all causes apparently numbered between 3 and 3.5 million. The military service deaths on the Soviet side reached more than 12 million, about 47 percent of the grand total (26.8 million) of soldiers of all nations killed in World War II.[49] The war and the occupation cost the Soviet Union some 7 million civilians and Germany about 1.5 million. The losses, civilian and military, of Finland, the Baltic States, and eastern and southeastern European countries added millions more.

The great struggle completely unhinged the traditional European balance of power, and the line on which it ended retained all the essential characteristics of a military front. The war consolidated the Soviet regime in Russia, and enabled it to impose the Communist system on its neighbors, Finland excepted, and on the Soviet

---

49. The Bulletin of the Press and Information Office of the German Federal Republic (volume I, Number 7, 25 June 1953) gives 13.6 million as the total Soviet military losses, including 1.75 million permanently disabled. The much larger Soviet losses can be accounted for by the extremely heavy losses of the 1941 and 1942 campaigns, less efficient medical services, and the Soviet tactics, which throughout the war tended to be expensive in terms of human life. The Germans, on the other hand, although they often deliberately sacrificed masses of men, by doctrine expended manpower sparingly.

Captured German soldiers stream through the streets of Berlin.
Note the extreme youth of the foreground figures.

occupation zone in Germany. The victory made the Soviet Union the second-ranking world power.

The Soviet victory was a victory of raw manpower and industrial production by a regime that could exploit both with complete ruthlessness. The Germans contributed in two ways: after their initial blitzkrieg attempts failed, by trying to force a stalemate in the World War I style; and by the extreme and uncompromising nature of their war aims. The one placed a price in blood and matériel on ground; but the price could not be set higher than the Soviet Union could pay and, consequently, the Soviet leadership was guaranteed a virtually unbroken series of victories without which it might not have been able to extract such heavy sacrifices from its people. The other gave the Soviet people no choice except that between an indigenous and a foreign tyranny.

However serious, all the German mistakes counted for less than the genuine, spontaneous heroism, self-sacrifice, and industry of the Soviet people. The Soviet bureaucracy proved itself capable of mobilizing manpower, industry, and agriculture for the war effort even under the tremendous handicap of having lost in the first months nearly two-thirds of its resources, industrial plant capacity, and agricultural production. The principal achievements were the relocation and rebuilding of existing industries, the construction of new mines and plants, the development of new agricultural lands, and, far from least, the unprecedented and unequaled concentration on war production. In actuality, the absolute increase in Soviet productive capacity was less important than the massive concentration on turning out the implements of land warfare, guns, ammunition, tanks, and fighter and ground-support aircraft.

The Soviet Union enjoyed certain important advantages over the other major belligerents. It fought on one front. Except to a minor extent in the Far East, it did not have to contemplate the emergence of other theaters. It fought an exclusively land war. It fought on its own or immediately adjacent territory and hence did not need to establish lengthy new supply lines, particularly over water, or construct and stock remote bases. Its troops and civilian population generated economic demands of a much lower order than did those of most of the other belligerents. Additionally, the Soviet Union received 10.2 billion dollars' worth of lend-lease assistance, mostly from the United States. Although, as the Russians maintain, they fought the war with weapons of their own design and manufacture, that they could do so owed in no small part to the support it received through lend-lease. Between 22 June 1941 and 20 September 1945 the Soviet Union received among other items 409,526 jeeps and trucks, 12,161 armored vehicles, 325,784 tons of explosives, 13,041 locomotives and railroad cars, and 1,798,609 tons of foodstuffs.

Against the Soviet quantitative advantage in manpower and matériel, Germany had a general qualitative advantage, specifically, a higher level of military proficiency. The ratio of the one to the other was not constant, and the shift was in the Soviet favor. The qualitative gap narrowed and, as the war progressed, declined in significance. The quantitative gap widened.

The Germans' advantage was not enough to secure a victory in 1941 and 1942, and by late 1942 the quantitative element predominated. The Germans accepted the terms imposed thereby even though they ran directly counter to the principles under which Germany had fought the war thus far. The German High Command did not attempt again to formulate a strategy founded on their superior generalship and tactics. To have done so would probably have required at the outset a decision to fight for a draw. As the war went on, the qualitative advantage that remained to the Germans was in the middle and lower command echelons where its effect was mitigating but not decisive. Eventually, the higher German commands passed to the hands of generals who tried merely to substitute quality for quantity. By then the Soviet Union had developed commanders—Zhukov, Vasilevskiy, Konev, and possibly others—and formations, the tank armies in particular, that although they were still not the equals of the Germans in their prime, had achieved effective parity in performance. This achievement plus the quantitative advantage more than compensated for the continuing Soviet lag in other respects.

Every assessment of the German decline and defeat must inevitably take into account Hitler, his leadership, and his responsibility. The single national leader was a distinguishing feature of World War II. The tendency toward fusion of the military and political authority in wartime was not new. What was unusual was that popular opinion strongly inclined toward entrusting the powers of military decision to the political rather than military leadership. Franklin D. Roosevelt generally refrained from intervening in military operations. Churchill did intervene when he could and would gladly have done so more often had he not been discouraged by his own and the combined staffs and by the example of his American colleague. Stalin left his mark on Soviet strategy but, after the painful lessons learned early in the war, contented himself for the most part with a largely counterfeit military image. Hitler, however, decided German strategy from the outbreak of the war to its end, and after December 1941 he was in direct command of the German ground forces.

The responsibility for the German mistakes was chiefly Hitler's as was a major share of the credit for the successes. Undoubtedly, the former were greater than the latter and more decidedly his own; therefore, at the highest command level he was responsible for the German defeat. More fundamentally, he also bore the responsibility for the root causes of the defeat: the attempt to pursue unlimited objectives with limited means; and the creation of a political system that made itself intolerable to most of the rest of the world.

But Hitler was no mere incompetent accidentally propelled into a commanding position from which he could sabotage the efforts of the military professionals. His conduct of the war displayed a devastating logic that even at its most destructive found at least as many convinced adherents as it did opponents among the leading military men. He inspired public confidence and represented the will of the nation to a greater degree than any other person or group. He gave Germany the kind of leadership it wanted. Where he failed was in not possessing the ability to produce the results he promised; that failure was appreciated earlier by some than by others but by all too late.

In statistical terms, numbers of troops engaged, length of front, distances covered, and major battles fought, the Eastern Theater dominated the war against Germany. On the basis of those statistics and ignoring the fact that space and distance in the Soviet Union meant less than in the rest of Europe, the Russians claimed the preponderant contribution to the war against Germany.

To determine the true proportions of the Soviet contribution to the victory the theater must be looked at in strategic perspective. Four significant limiting features can be identified immediately: the war in the East was a ground war in a single theater; the Soviet Union contributed nothing to the employment of strategic air power against Germany; the Soviet contribution to the war at sea was small, so small that the Baltic Sea remained a German lake and the German naval training ground until 1945; and the Soviet Union benefited through being relieved of the second front threat in the Far East.

Proper perspective also requires an examination of how the German defeat was accomplished on the ground. Stalingrad and the North African Campaign put an end to the period of the German strategic initiative and demonstrated that both the Allies and the Soviet Union had achieved the capability of bringing superior strength to bear at decisive points. In the aftermath of Operation ZITADELLE the Soviet Union took the strategic initiative on the east. On the west the Allies began exercising their own strategic initiative with the invasion of Sicily. Subsequently, in their deployment, the Germans rated the

Wermacht-Heer prisoners being marched off to face an uncertain future in captivity.
Many would not return, others were held as forced labourers for 10 years or more.

threats from east and west as about equal. In fact, they were inclined to regard that from the west as potentially the more dangerous because of the shorter distances to the German vital centers. Up to the time of the landing in Normandy, even though the Allies were actually engaged only in a secondary theater in Italy and great battles were being fought on the Eastern Front, on balance the Allied and Soviet strategic accomplishments were about equal. The German strength was split about evenly between east and west.

Essentially, until the late spring of 1944 the Soviet Union and the Allies were maneuvering into position to deliver the crucial blows. The environments were different. For the Allies the war had a global aspect in which air and sea activities and logistics operations weighed heavily. Theirs was the problem of staging a gigantic amphibious invasion, a one-shot, do-or-die undertaking that afforded no latitude for preliminary sparring and an appallingly black and white prospect of victory or defeat. The Soviet problem was to reduce the still substantial buffer of Soviet territory the Germans held and get within striking range of the Reich. The Soviet forces had cleared the Ukraine and northern Russia and were deployed in the center on the axis Warsaw-Berlin. They had exacted and had themselves paid heavy prices in blood and matériel. The Allies had completed the less spectacular but technologically and economically more demanding preparations on their side and had in the meantime brought the air and sea operations against Germany nearly to a climax. The invasion succeeded. By the end of summer the Allied armies had plunged to the German border, and the Soviet armies had reached the Vistula and the border of East Prussia. In December Hitler committed his last strategic offensive potential on the west, and the Russians broke through to the Oder. From mid-February 1945 to mid-April the Soviet armies stood on the Oder, and the Allies crossed two-thirds of Germany to the Elbe. By then, fear and hatred and the will of one man were all that kept the war alive.

The Soviet contribution to the victory in Europe was important but not overwhelming. Soviet postwar claims notwithstanding, the war in no sense demonstrated the superiority of Marxist theory. The German-Soviet conflict was euphemistically billed in Germany from the start as a crusade against Bolshevism, but the Soviet Government chose not to submit its system's popularity to a direct test and, instead, nominated itself to lead a war for national survival. The Soviet people opted for the indigenous dictatorship. That was possibly the most enduringly important decision of World War II. The margin of decision was narrow, and even though the Germans failed to offer more than superficial inducements, remained so until the last glimmer of an alternative had vanished. The war was a true test of strength between ideologies only in that the Soviet regime evinced greater adaptability in identifying itself with Russian nationalism.

Likewise, Soviet strategy in World War II was by no means a convincing display of ideological superiority. It was cautious, methodical, and politically oriented. Its most distinguishing feature was the heavy political overburden it carried. At, no doubt, some considerable additional cost in life and matériel, the Soviet armies always fought for ground as much as to defeat the enemy. The Soviet command planned its operations as if under a compulsion to legalize every territorial acquisition by actual military conquest. In the end, when time had run out, it went so far as to insist on staging a sham battle for Czechoslovakia; similarly it had insisted on a token invasion of Bulgaria after that country surrendered. Soviet strategy was grasping rather than sweepingly aggressive as the German strategy had been; it was inhibited, psychologically defensive, and morally ruthless.

Nevertheless, the German defeat was an outstanding victory for Marxism in that it broke the quarantine in Europe which had for a generation confined communism as a system of government within the boundaries of the Soviet Union. That changed the complexion of the war in its final stage and made genuine peace impossible. In the postwar era it has sometimes appeared that any alternative would have been preferable. Probably none could have been devised that would not in some form have given Hitler his miracle.

Appendices

APPENDIX A

TABLE OF EQUIVALENT RANKS

German	Soviet
1. Army Groups	1. *Fronts*
On the Eastern Front 4 to 5 plus the Twentieth Mountain Army and the Finnish Army to September 1944	10 to 12
2. Armies	2. Armies
2 to 4 in an army group	3 to 9 in a *front*. Probable average 5 to 7
3. Corps (including Panzer Corps)	3. Rifle Corps
2 to 7 in an army	An average of 3 in an army
4. Divisions	4. Divisions
2 to 7 in a corps	2 to 3 in a corps

AUTHORIZED STRENGTHS, DIVISIONS		AUTHORIZED STRENGTHS, ARMORED CORPS AND DIVISIONS	
Panzer Division (103 to 125 tanks)	14000 to 17,000	Tank Corps (189 tanks)	10,500
Motorized Division (48 tanks)	14,000	Mechanized Corps (186 tanks)	16,000
Infantry Division, 9 battalions	15,000	Rifle Division	9,375
Infantry Division, 6 battalions	12,700	Guards Rifle Division	10,585
Artillery Division (113 guns)	3,380	Artillery Division (210 guns)	6,550

APPENDIX B

COMPARATIVE SIZES OF MAJOR COMMANDS, NOVEMBER 1942 TO MAY 1945

German	Soviet	U.S. Equivalent
Reichsmarschall*	None	None
Generalfeldmarschall	Marshal Sovetskogo Soyuza	General of the Army
None	Glavnyi Marshal	None
None	Marshal	None
Generaloberst	General Armii	General
General der Infanterie, der Artillerie, der Flieger, and so forth	General Polkovnik	Lieutenant General
Generalleutnant	General Leytenant	Major General
Generalmajor	General Mayor	Brigadier General

Created for Hermann Goering in July 1940 and held only by him.

NOTE ON SOURCES

I

When the Allied armies overran Germany in the spring of 1945, they uncovered tons of German official records. The military collections were brought to the United States and remained in military custody until their transfer to the National Archives in 1958. Shortly after completion of research for this volume, the majority of captured German records were returned to the Federal Republic of Germany. Microfilm copies of these records and guides containing descriptions are available from the National Archives and Records Service, General Services Administration, Washington, D. C. 20408.

In the continuing absence of significant Soviet documentary evidence the German military records remain the best source for the study of German and Soviet operations in World War II. Of the German collections the Armed Forces High Command (OKW), Army High Command (OKH), and field commands (army groups, armies, corps) are the most useful. Of the relatively few pertinent German Air Force records that have survived, the best general summary is Air Ministry (British) Pamphlet 248, The Rise and Fall of the German Air Force (London: His Majesty's Stationery Office, 1948). The German Navy was not involved directly in the main operations on the Eastern Front; however, three items from the naval records are extremely valuable for the light they often shed on the functioning of the German Command at its highest level. They are the OKM, Weisungen OKW (Fuehrer), 1939-45, a unique collection of Fuehrer and other top-level German directives, published as Walter Hubatsch, ed., Hitlers Weisungen fuer die Kriegsfuehrung 1939-1945 (Frankfurt a. M.: Bernard and Graefe, 1962); the War Diary, German Naval Staff, Operations Division (Kriegstagebuch, SKL), a comprehensive chronological account of the war as seen from the Naval High Command; and the Fuehrer Conferences on Matters Dealing With the German Navy, 1939-45 (1947), summaries of Fuehrer conferences attended by the Commander in Chief, Navy, or his personal representatives.

In matters pertaining to the Eastern Front the OKW records have several limitations: the collection is incomplete, the Eastern

Front was not an OKW theater and, particularly during the period covered in this volume, the OKW was deliberately excluded from influence on and often even from direct knowledge of events and decisions relating to the Eastern Front. Nevertheless, the OKW War Diary (OKW, Stellvertretende Chef des Wehrmachtfuehrungsstabes, Kriegstagebuch), published as Kriegstagebuch des Oberkommandos der Wehrmacht (Wehrmachtfuehrungsstab), edited by Percy Ernst Schramm (Frankfurt a. M.: Bernard and Graefe, 1961-1965), is the most comprehensive and complete chronological high-level record of the entire war on the German side. Helmuth Greiner's Aufzeichnungen ueber die Lagevortraege und Besprechungen im Fuehrerhauptquartier vom 12. August bis zum 17. Maerz 1943 (MS # C-065a) affords a valuable supplement to the OKW War Diary, as does Percy E. Schramm's The German Wehrmacht in the Last Days of the War, 1 January-7 May 1945 (MS # C-020). Both Greiner and Schramm worked from notes they had made as keepers of the OKW War Diary. In spite of some questionable details, Joachim Schultz, Die Letzte 30 Tage (Stuttgart: Steingruben-Verlag, 1951), is apparently what it purports to be, a rendering of the OKW War Diary for the last month of the war. The Tagebuch Generaloberst Jodl, Chef des Wehrmachtfuehrungsstabes des Oberkommandos der Wehrmacht (Jodl Diary) sheds random but sometimes crucially important light on decisions and events from the source closest to the top of the German High Command.

The most voluminous and complete of the OKW records pertinent to the German-Soviet conflict are those dealing with the last days of the war and the capitulation. They include German strength and loss estimates for the final period of the war, materials concerning the change in government and the decision to capitulate, and a draft of a projected White Book setting forth the history of the establishment and policies of the Doenitz government. The file Befehle vor der Kapitulation und anlaesslich Kapitulation an die Truppe contains the Armed Forces Operations Staff orders issued after the OKH was dissolved.

The OKH was the central staff for the conduct of the war against the Soviet Union, and after September 1942 the Eastern Front was its exclusive and sole operational responsibility. The OKH records that have survived, though substantial in bulk, are fragmentary. No complete, consecutive account similar to the Halder Diary or the OKW War Diary is available for the later years of the war. The diary of the Operations Branch, OKH, is reasonably continuous only for the months January to April 1945. The most valuable of the OKH documents are the Lage Ost (Situation East) maps, printed daily by the Operations Branch, OKH, at a scale of 1:1,000,000 and showing both the German and Soviet dispositions. The set is virtually complete and is the source, with some corrections and additions to Soviet dispositions, for the maps which appear in this volume.

Of the documents of the Organization Branch, OKH, those that are still in existence give information concerning German strengths, losses, replacements, manpower resources, and changes in the Army organizational structure. The most nearly continuous of the OKH files, though far from complete, are those of the Eastern Intelligence Branch (Fremde Heere Ost). The Eastern Intelligence Branch produced a vast number of intelligence estimates dealing with individual sectors and with the whole Eastern Front. It issued frequent short- and long-range summaries and from time to time made comparisons of German and Soviet strengths. Enough of these have survived to form a complete intelligence picture for the Eastern Front as it appeared to the Germans. The relatively small files of the Inspector General for Armor (Generalinspekteur der Panzertruppen) contain significant documents relating to Guderian's incumbency and his appointment as Acting Chief of Staff, OKH. A particularly valuable document for the light it sheds on Hitler's attitudes towards his generals and the Army General Staff in the period October 1942-October 1944 is the Taetigkeitsbericht des Chefs des Heerespersonalamts, the activity report of the OKH officer personnel section for the time during which it was directly under Hitler and his chief adjutant, Schmundt.

It is fortunate that both the OKW and the OKH records provide their best coverage for the last months of the war, the period for which relatively few field command records remain in existence.

One important set of high-level documents not properly belonging either to the OKH or the OKW collections is Fuehrer Conference Fragments (Fragmenten des Stenographischen Dienstes im F. H. Qu.), translated excerpts of which have been published in Felix Gilbert, ed.,

Hitler Directs His War (New York: Oxford University Press, 1951), and which have been published in full in Helmut Heiber, ed., Hitlers Lagebesprechungen, (Stuttgart: Deutsche Verlags-Anstalt, 1962). The Fuehrer Conference Fragments are the remains (fifty in all for the months December 1942 to March 1945) of the transcripts of situation and other military conferences kept by the stenographic service in the Fuehrer headquarters.

For the history of the war against the Soviet Union the army group records are the prime sources. The army group commands were the direct link between the High Command (Hitler and the OKH) and the front, and were, within the limits imposed by Hitler's method of command, themselves originating agencies for operational decisions. In accordance with German practice the field commands each kept an Ia (Operations) war diary in which were recorded the incoming and outgoing orders, summaries of reports and conferences, situation estimates, the progress of operations, weather, temperature, and other items of operational or historical significance. The orders, reports, and so forth, were filed separately in annexes (Anlagen) to the war diaries. Together, the Ia war diaries and their Anlagen were the central records of the field commands. At the army group level the war diaries were generally kept with a conscious eye to history, sometimes by trained historians; and frequently the commanding generals and chiefs of staff confided matters to the war diary that were not recorded elsewhere or transmitted outside the command. The army group records also provide operational plans, after action reports, transcripts of telephone and other conferences, message files, and files of Chefsachen—top secret documents that were not entered in the war diaries.

Of the army group Ia war diaries the following segments have survived: Army Group A (South Ukraine, South) 1 October 1942-31 March 1945, with Anlagen, October 1944-March 1945; Army Group Don (Anlagen only), 7 December 1942-28 February 1943; Army Group North, 1 October 1942-15 June 1944 with scattered Anlagen; Army Group Center, scattered Anlagen for the years 1943 and 1944 only (a photostat of the Ia war diary 22 August 1943-24 September 1944 was secured from the former keeper of the war diary, Prof. Herman Gackenholz); Army Group Vistula, Anlagen with longhand notes for the war diary 21 January-29 April 1945. Morning and evening reports (portions of the September 1944-May 1945 war diaries of Army Group North and Courland) were available to the author of MS # P-114a, Der Feldzug gegen die Sowjetunion im Nordabschnitt der Ostfront, and are extensively quoted in the text and appendices.

The records of the armies are similar to those of the army groups in organization and content, but the armies usually did not have the top-level contact that the army groups had. In bulk the army records are far more voluminous than the army group records, partly because in most instances the war diaries and Anlagen are nearly complete to July 1944 and partly because the army records contain more after action reports, operational plans, and reports on antipartisan operations.

II

Except for captured records, interrogations, and analyses which have filtered through the German wartime intelligence agencies, virtually no significant Soviet documents relating to military operations in World War II have been made available. During the war the Soviet Army's Directorate of Military History, under the former Chief of Staff, Boris M. Shaposhnikov, from late 1942 until his death in 1945, issued through its department for the Utilization of the War Experience several series of monographs dealing with selected operations. Of those the most thoroughgoing and candid, and therefore the most restricted in distribution (division commanders and above), were the so-called Sborniks (Collections [of Materials for the Study of the War Experience—Materialov po izucheniyu opyta Voyny]). The purpose of the Sborniks was not primarily historical; they were intended to coach the higher commanders in battle-tested tactics; but to do that they had within limits, that is to say, avoiding criticism which struck higher than the front headquarters, to be concrete and objective. For the latter part of the war the Sborniks dealing with Stalingrad and the 1942-43 winter offensive are the most useful.

In the postwar period up to and for several years after Stalin's death, the few Soviet histories of military operations in World War II that appeared read like anthologies of the wartime communiqués from Moscow, which, in fact, they for the most part were. Interpretation was restricted to panegyrics to Stalin and vituperrative blasts against former friends and enemies alike. The most substantial publication to appear was a collection of Stalin's orders of the day interlarded with some of his other public utterances on military subjects.

In the years following the Twentieth Party Congress (1955), at which Soviet Premier Nikita S. Khrushchev gave impetus to a new approach to the study of World War II and announced the forthcoming publication of a Soviet official history of the war, the Soviet writings on World War II rapidly grew to a flood. The volume of information, however, though large by comparison with that released earlier, was not proportionate to the number of new works that found their way into print. Several of these stand out as marking high-water points in the disclosure of concrete information. The first to appear was Vazneishie Operatsii Velikoy Otchestvennoy Voyny (Moscow: Voen. Izdat., 1956), edited by Col. Pavel A. Zhilin.

It was a collaborative work and a collection of battle studies rather than a complete narrative history. It was carefully doctored to present a homogenized impression of military infallibility, but it did deal with the early defeats—as defensive successes. Stalin's name virtually disappeared, and the glory and credit were redistributed to the Party, the Army, and the Soviet people. Scattered mention of mistakes and errors, none big enough or reaching high enough to roil the smooth surface, gave a touch of critical analysis. Nevertheless, the book's great virtue was that it came closer to being a factual narrative than any Soviet work on World War II published up to that time. In 1958 General S. P. Platonov published a complete, one-volume history of World War II, Vtoraya Mirovaya Voyna (Moscow: Voen. Izdat.) The Platonov volume carried somewhat further the trend toward limited objectivity begun in the Zhilin volume and broached aspects of the Soviet conduct of the war that Zhilin's fragmentary approach had side-stepped. Both Zhilin and Platonov were associated with the Soviet Army Directorate of Military History and both were members of the editorial board of the Soviet military historical journal Voyenno-istoricheskiy Zhurnal. After Platonov other comprehensive single-volume histories appeared, some, like K. S. Kolganov's Razvitye Taktiku Sovetskoy Armii v Gody Velikoy Otehestvennoy 1941-45 (Moscow:

Voen. Izdat., 1959), dealing with specific aspects of the war. Platonov's history remains the best of the shorter works. B. S. Tel'pukhovskiy, Velikaya Otchestvennaya Voyna Sovetskogo Soyuza 1941-1945 (Moscow: Voen. Izdat., 1959), an inferior, blatantly theatrical piece of historical writing, deserves mention on two counts: the author named all the important commanders—not a universal practice in Soviet writing of military history—and, apparently because the book is a revision of an earlier work published in 1955, Marshal Zhukov figures more prominently than in other Soviet works.

The absolute high-water mark, at least for the time being, in the Soviet writing on World War II was reached with the publication, beginning in 1960, of the six-volume official Istoriya Velikoy Otchestvennoy Voyny Sovetskogo Soyuze 1941-1945 (Moscow: Voen. Izdat., 1960-63). The official history covers in substantial detail the whole military, political, and economic history of World War II, including its origins and its aftermath. The authorship is collective and includes prominently three of the writers mentioned above, Zhilin, Platonov, and Tel'pukhovskiy among some dozens of others. Certain of the sections dealing with Soviet military operations appear to follow, in places almost word for word, the Platonov history. On the whole, the accounts of military operations carry forward the trends observed in the Zhilin and Platonov works without achieving genuine frankness. Names, dates, units, tactical maneuvers, and operational plans are given more coherent treatment than in the earlier works. Soviet mistakes, defeats, and setbacks, with relatively few known exceptions, though not ignored, are often as not handled so obliquely as to escape all but the closest attention. Strengths, losses, and other statistics are given in detail for the German and other armies but not for the Soviet forces. For the first time a few Soviet strengths are given in concrete figures, but the Soviet casualties and losses continue to be thoroughly ignored. The volumes are heavily documented with sources published outside the Soviet Union but only with meaningless file-number references to Soviet documents. The process of high-level decision making is left nebulous except for frequent citations of uniformly correct, timely, and presumably unanimous decisions and directives from the Stavka.

III

To provide the Army with a comprehensive record of the German military experience in World War II, the Foreign Military Studies Program of the Historical Division, United States Army, Europe, produced by the time it was terminated in 1961 some 2,400 manuscripts. The authors were, for the most part, former high-ranking German officers. At first they wrote mainly from memory about events in which they had personally played key roles. Beginning in 1948 more comprehensive projects were initiated. These were assigned to teams who then made use of records in the custody of the United States Army, records secured through private sources, interviews, and their own experience. The over-all supervision and direction was in the hands of the Control Group, headed throughout its existence by Generaloberst a. D. Franz Halder. In 1954 the Historical Division, United States Army, Europe, published a complete list of the manuscripts then completed or projected in the Guide to Foreign Military Studies 1945-54. A full set of the manuscripts is on deposit in the Office of the Chief of Military History, Department of the Army, Washington, D.C. A second set has been furnished to the historical office of the German Bundeswehr.

In the Foreign Military Studies Series the war against the Soviet Union is covered at the strategic level by MS # T-9, Generaloberst a. D. Gotthard Heinrici, Der Feldzug in Russland ein operativer Ueberblick; and at the army group level by MS # P-114a, Generalleutnant a. D. Friedrich Sixt, Der Feldzug gegen die Sowjetunion im Nordabschnitt der Ost front, by MS # P-114b, General der Infanterie a. D. Rudolf Hofmann, Der Feldzug gegen die Sowjetunion im Mittelabschnitt der Ostfront, and by MS # P-114c, General der Artillerie a. D. Friedrich Wilhelm Hauck, Die Operationen der deutschen Heeresgruppen an der Ostfront 1941 bis 1945 suedliches Gebiet. The events of 1944 and 1945 in the Southeastern Theater are covered in MS # P-114c Supplement, Generalmajor a. D. Erich Schmidt-Richberg and Generalmajor a. D. Curt Ritter von Geitner, Die Kriegsereignisse auf dem Balkan im Rahmen der deutschen Operationen an der Ost front, 1944-1945. Army, corps, and division operations are treated selectively in separate studies.

Particular aspects of the war in the East are dealt with in, among others, MSS # P-060 a-0, Generalmajor a. D. Hellmuth Reinhardt and others, Small Unit Actions (condensed version published as Department of the Army Pamphlet 20-269, July 1953, Small Unit Actions During the German Campaign in Russia) and MS # T-12, Generalmajor a. D. Oldwig von Natzmer and others, Das Zurueckkaempfen eingekesselter Verbaende zur eigenen Front (published as Department of the Army Pamphlet 20-234, January 1952, Operations of Encircled Forces). Incidents and events of particular historical interest are treated in such accounts as MS # B-606, Oberst a. D. Guenther Reichheim, The Last Rally, Battles Fought by the German Twelfth Army in the Heart of Germany, and MS # B 220, General der Panzertruppen a. D. Maximilian Freiherr von Edelsheim, Die Kapitulationsverhandlungen der 12. (deutschen) mit der 9. (amerikanischen) Armee am 4 Mai 1945 in Stendal.

The Foreign Military Studies Program also produced important primary source materials for the study of the war in the Soviet Union. In addition to the Schramm and Greiner works already mentioned, those pertinent to the last years of the war are MS # C-073, General der Infanterie a. D. Waldemar Erfurth, Finnlands Letzte Krieg (published as Der finnische Krieg (Wiesbaden: Limes Verlag, 1950)); MS # D-406, Generaloberst a. D. Kurt Zeitzler, Das Ringen um die grossen Entscheidungen im zweiten Weltkrieg; MS # D-408, Oberst i. G. a. D. Hans Georg Eismann, Aufzeichnungen Oberst i. G. Eismann als Ia der Heeresgruppe Weichsel; MS # C-099 c, d, i, l, m, and o, General der Artillerie a. D. Walter Warlimont, Commentaries on the OKW War Diary (text in German); MS # P-049, Warlimont, Die Strategie der deutschen obersten Fuehrung im Zweiten Vierteljahr 1943; MS # P-215, Warlimont, Interpretation and Commentary on the Jodl Diaries, 1937-1945 (text in German including a transcription of the diaries by General Warlimont); and (no MS number) Generalfeldmarschall Maximilian Freiherr von Weichs, Auszuege aus dem Tagebuch des Feldmarschalls Freiherr von Weichs aus den Jahren 1943 und 1944, aus den Original-Notizen in Gabelsberger Stenographie uebertragen durch Generalmajor a. D. Curt Ritter von Geitner.

IV

The body of general literature dealing with the German-Soviet conflict is large and growing. Very little of it, however, has been written in English or found its way into the language through translation. Comprehensive bibliographies, periodically brought up to date, are to be found in the Revue d'Histoire de la Deuxieme Guerre Mondiale and the Buecherschau der Weltkriegsbuecherei. Both list books and articles in all languages and carry bibliographical articles and reviews of significant works. Hillgruber and Jacobsen's lengthy introduction to Boris S. Tel'puchowski, Die Sowjetische Geschichte des Grossen Vaterlaendischen Krieges, 1941-1945 (Frankfurt a.M.: Bernard und Graefe, 1961) provides a useful analytical bibliography and a study of the Western and Soviet approaches to the history of the war.

The works thus far available in English deal with certain selected aspects of the war. Gerhard L. Weinberg, Germany and the Soviet Union, 1939-1941 (Leiden: E. J. Brill, 1954) covers the period of the Nazi-Soviet pact and Hitler's decision to invade the Soviet Union. Department of the Army Pamphlet 20-261a, The German Campaign in Russia—Planning and Operations (1940-1942) (Washington, 1955), provides the background for the present volume pending publication of the projected first and second volumes in the OCMH series on the Soviet-German war. Alexander Dallin, German Rule in Russia, 1941-1945 (New York: St. Martin's Press, 1957), provides a comprehensive history of the German occupation, and the War Documentation Project, Project "Alexander" Studies (Washington: Air Research and Development Command, 1953-55), condensed in John A. Armstrong, ed., The Soviet Partisans in World War II (Madison: University of Wisconsin Press, 1964), furnish a similarly comprehensive account of the Soviet partisan movement. Alexander Werth, Russia at War (New York: Dutton, 1964) covers the whole war from the Soviet side in considerable detail but not systematically. T. Dodson Stamps and Vincent J. Esposito, eds., A Military History of World War II With Atlas (West Point: United States Military Academy, 1953) contains a summary of military operations 1941-1945 and excellent maps. The best short account of German operations, Kurt von Tippelskirch, Geschichte des Zweiten Weltkrieges (Bonn: Athenaeum, 1956), has not been translated. The author was both a trained historian and a corps and army commander on the Eastern Front. The two most substantial German works translated to date are Heinz Guderian, Panzer Leader (New York: Dutton, 1952) and Erich von Manstein, Lost Victories (Chicago: H. Regnery, 1958). Both are memoirs and to some extent display the deficiencies of that genre. On the Soviet side the memoir literature is increasing, but the individual works are very narrowly focused. The best example available in English is Vasili I. Chuikov, The Battle for Stalingrad (New York: Holt, Rinehart and Winston, 1964)

The Soviet operations were for the most part carried out independently of its role as a member of the World War II coalition against the Axis Powers, the chief reasons being the relative isolation of the front in the Soviet Union, the static Soviet strategic position, and the reservations which the Soviet Union attached to its membership in the Big Three. The Soviet part in the whole war against Germany has been described in, among others, Herbert Feis, Churchill, Roosevelt, Stalin (Princeton, N. J.; Princeton University Press, 1957); Llewellyn Woodward, British Foreign Policy in the Second World War (London: Her Majesty's Stationery Office, 1962); Maurice Matloff and Edward M. Snell, Strategic Planning for Coalition Warfare, 1941-1942 (Washington, 1953); Maurice M. Matloff, Strategic Planning for Coalition Warfare, 1943-1944 (Washington, 1959); and John Ehrman, Grand Strategy (London: Her Majesty's Stationery Office, 1956), Volumes V and VI. The Soviet version of that aspect of the war is given in Istoriya Velikoy Otechestvennoy Voyny Sovetskogo Soyuza, 1941-1945 and in G. A. Deborin, Vtoraya Mirovaya Voyna (Moscow: Voen, Izdat., 1958).

Finally, the massive Allied aid shipments to the Soviet Union through the Arctic ports and the Persian Gulf have been treated in T. H. Vail Motter, The Persian Corridor and Aid to Russia (Washington, 1952); Richard M. Leighton and Robert W. Coakley, Global Logistics and Strategy, 1940-1943 (Washington, 1955); S. W. Roskill, The War at Sea (London: Her Majesty's Stationery Office, 1954-); Samuel Eliot Morison, "History of United States Naval Operations in World War II," The Battle of the Atlantic, September 1939-May 1943 (Boston: Little, Brown, 1951) and Samuel Eliot Morison, "History of United

States Naval Operations in World War II," The Battle of the Atlantic Won, May 1943-May 1945 (Boston Little, Brown, 1956).

GLOSSARY

- Armeeabteilung: A German command intermediate between a corps and an army, usually under an enlarged corps headquarters
- Armeegruppe: A group of armies, a German command arrangement under which one army headquarters was subordinated to another
- Berghof: Hitler's Bavarian retreat
- East Wall: The projected German fortified line across the Soviet Union from Narva on the Baltic Sea to Melitopol on the Black Sea and on which work was begun in August 1943
- Ferdinand: A German tank first produced in early 1943. It mounted an 88-mm. long-barreled antitank gun in a fixed turret on a Tiger tank chassis. The Ferdinand weighed 73 tons, carried 200-mm. front armor, and had a top speed of 12.5 miles per hour.
- front: A Soviet army group
- Fuehrer: Hitler's title as German chief of state
- Gruppe: A German ad hoc military formation, usually composed of more divisions than a normal corps but utilizing a corps command apparatus
- Guards: An honorific designation given to Soviet units which had distinguished themselves in combat
- Hero of the Soviet Union: The highest Soviet military decoration
- Hiwi, Hilfswillige: Russian auxiliaries serving with German units on the Eastern Front in various noncombatant capacities
- Iron Gate: The 2-mile-long gorge and rapids on the Danube River above Turnu Severin
- Jaeger: Term used to designate German light infantry
- JU-52: The German Junkers 52 trimotor transport airplane
- Kampfgruppe: A means of designating German divisions which had been seriously reduced in strength through combat losses
- Knight's Cross of the Iron Cross: The highest class of the Iron

Cross and the most prized of the German World War II military decorations

- Maybachlager: The OKH command and communications center at Zossen south of Berlin
- NKVD: *Narodnyi Komissariat Venutrennikh Del* (Peoples Commissariat for Internal Affairs, the Soviet internal security organization)
- OKH: *Oberkommando des Herres* (The German Army High Command)
- OKL: *Oberkommando der Luftwaffe* (The German Air Force High Command)
- OKM: *Oberkommando der Kriegsmarine* (The German Navy High Command)
- OKW: *Oberkommando der Wehrmacht* (The German Armed Forces High Command)
- *Panje*: German World War I army slang for Poles and Russians. Used in World War II to describe the Soviet peasant wagons.
- Panther: A German tank, originally designated Panzer V, that first went into quantity production in early 1943. It mounted a long-barreled 75-mm. gun, and in its sloping armor and low silhouette it was patterned after the Soviet T34. The Panther weighed 50 tons, carried 110-mm. armor on the turret front, and had a top speed of 35 miles per hour.
- Panzer III: A German prewar-model tank, mounting in its latest version (1942) a long-barreled 50-mm. antitank gun. The Panzer III weighed 24.6 tons, carried 50-mm. front armor, and had a top speed of 35 miles per hour. Although the Panzer III disappeared from combat in the last years of the war, its chassis continued to be used in several models of self-propelled assault guns.
- Panzer IV: The latest of the prewar German tanks, and mounting in its final version (1942) a long-barreled, high-velocity 75-mm. gun, it replaced a short, 75-mm. low-velocity gun. The Panzer IV weighed 26 tons, carried 60-mm. front armor, and had a top speed of 25 miles per hour.
- *Panzergrenadier*: Armored infantry
- *Panzerjaeger*: Literally, tank hunters. Bicycle-mounted German

troops armed with antitank grenades and rockets and organized in early 1945.

- Reichsfuehrer-SS: Himmler's title as chief of the SS
- Reichsstrasse 50: German-built road in northern Norway from Narvik to Kirkenes
- Szekler Strip: A piece of territory in eastern Transylvania which had been in dispute between Hungary and Rumania during the interwar period and was awarded to Hungary through German mediation under the Treaty of Vienna, 30 August 1940
- *Schild und Schwert*: A German theory of active defense
- Self-propelled assault gun: A lightly armored, tracked vehicle mounting a relatively heavy gun and intended to be used as close-support artillery
- SS: *Schutzstaffel* (Elite guard of the Nazi Party)
- *Stavka*: *Stavka Verkhovnovo, Glavnokommandovaniya* (the Soviet Supreme Command)
- *Stuka*: *Sturtzkampffugzeug* (Dive bomber)
- T34: The tank that was the mainstay of the Soviet armored forces throughout World War II. Put into quantity production in early 1941, it mounted a 76.2-mm. gun (after early 1944 an 85-mm. gun), carried 45-mm. front armor, and had a top speed of about 30 miles per hour. Sloping armor on the turret and glacis plate gave it particularly good protection against antitank gun fire.
- Tiger: A German tank, originally designated Panzer IV, that first appeared in action in late 1942. Mounting an adaptation of the German 88-mm. antiaircraft gun, the Tiger weighed 63 tons, carried 100-mm. armor on the turret front, and had a top speed of 25 miles per hour.
- *Trek*: A refugee column
- *Totenkopf*: Death's head
- Volksgrcnadier: Designation given to a number of German divisions hastily formed after July 1944 by filling up burned-out divisions from the Eastern Front with new recruits
- *Volkssturm*: The German home guard composed of overage and draft-deferred men.
- *Waffen-SS*: The combat units of the SS

- Winter War: The Soviet-Finnish War of 1939-40
- Wehrmacht: The German Armed Forces
- *Wiking*: Viking

CODE NAMES

- ASTER (Aster) Map Exercise : Army Group North plan for withdrawal in the Baltic States, September 1944
- BARBAROSSA (Barbarossa): The 1941 German offensive in the Soviet Union
- BIBER (Beaver) Plan: Major switch position in the Army Group Center zone, 1944
- BIRKE (Birch): The Twentieth Mountain Army withdrawal to northern Finland, 1944
- BLAU (Blue): The 1942 German offensive in the Soviet Union. The code name was also used for the planned Army Group North withdrawal to the PANTHER position, fall and winter 1943-44.
- BUEFFEL (Buffalo): Army Group Center's withdrawal in February-March 1943
- FRUEHLINGSERWACHEN (Awakening of Spring): The Army Group South offensive south of Budapest, March 1945
- FRUEHLINGSFEST (Spring Festival): German antipartisan operation in Belorussia, April 1944
- GNEISENAU line: German prepared position on the Crimea flanking Simferopol, 1944
- GOTENKOPF (GOTH's Head): The German bridgehead on the Taman Peninsula, 1943
- HABICHT (Hawk): A proposed German operation across the Donets River in the Chuguyev-Kupyansk area, March 1943
- HAGEN (Hedge) position: German line of field fortifications constructed across the base of the Orel salient, July 1943
- HEINRICH: German antipartisan operation conducted west of Nevel in November 1943
- HUBERTUS line: German switch position behind the Baranow bridgehead, 1944-45

- KORMORAN (Cormorant): German antipartisan operation in Belorussia, April 1944
- KUGELBLITZ (Ball Lightning): A German antipartisan operation in the Surazh Rayon of Belorussia, February 1943
- LITHUANIA position: Switch position behind Army Group North, July 1944
- MARGARETHE: German plan for the military occupation of Hungary, September 1943
- NORDLICHT (Northern Lights): The Twentieth Mountain Army withdrawal into Norway, 1944
- PANTHER position: The northern half of the projected East Wall, 1943-44. Also used for a projected expansion of Operation HABICHT.
- PRINZ EUGEN (Prince Eugene) position: Switch position behind Army Group North Ukraine, July 1944
- REGENSCHAUER (Rain Shower): German operation against the partisans in Belorussia, April 1944
- ROLLBAHN (Highway) position: Line of field fortifications paralleling the Leningrad-Chudovo highway in the Army Group North zone, 1943-44
- SCHILD UND SCHWERT (Sword and Shield): A projected Army Group North Ukraine offensive, June 1944
- SCHUTZWALL (Bastion) position: German line of fortifications south of Ivalo, Finland, 1944
- SILBERSTREIF (Silver Streak): German propaganda campaign, May-July 1943, intended to increase Soviet desertions
- SONNENWENDE (Solstice): The German counteroffensive at Stargard, February 1945
- STURMBOCK (Battering Ram): German line of fortifications west of Karesuando, Norway, 1944
- TANNE OST (Fir East): The German landing on Suursaari Island, October 1944
- TANNE WEST (Fir West): A projected German occupation of the Åland Islands
- TRAJAN position: Rumanian fortified line near Iasi
- WINTERGEWITTER (Winter Storm): The Stalingrad relief operation, December 1942

- WOTAN (Woden) position: The southern half of the projected East Wall, fall 1943. Also used for the German switch position constructed behind the German Oder front, April 1945.
- ZITADELLE (Citadel): The German operation against the Kursk bulge, July 1943